BUSINESS AND ECONOMICS PUBLICATIONS

WILLIAM HOMER SPENCER, *Editor*

Dean of The School of Business

The University of Chicago

THE ECONOMICS OF LABOR

Volume II

LABOR'S RISKS

AND

SOCIAL INSURANCE

THE ECONOMICS OF LABOR

THIS VOLUME

VOLUME II: *Labor's Risks and Social Insurance*

OTHER VOLUMES

LABOR'S RISKS

AND

SOCIAL INSURANCE

BY

HARRY A. MILLIS

*Professor and Chairman of the Department of
Economics, The University of Chicago*

AND

ROYAL E. MONTGOMERY

Professor of Economics, Cornell University

McGRAW-HILL BOOK COMPANY, Inc.

NEW YORK AND LONDON

1938

368.400973
M 655 l

PREFACE

This, the second of the three-volume series on *The Economics of Labor,* is concerned chiefly with the problems of unemployment, industrial injury, sickness and nonindustrial accident, and invalidity and industrial old age. Like the other volumes in the series, it perhaps departs somewhat from the requirements usually observed in the preparation of textbooks. The treatment of the problems is, in general, detailed. Factual material is presented freely, and somewhat more of economic theory has entered into the discussions than is usually found in books on labor problems. Nevertheless, we hope that the volume will be of service to mature students and to other readers interested in the field of social security.

Unusually rapid changes occurred while the several chapters were being prepared, and extensive revision and rewriting were therefore involved. No doubt they have left their marks. An attempt has been made to bring the historical and descriptive material reasonably up to date. In most of the chapters the story for the United States has been brought down to the end of 1937.

There is much controversy on many of the subjects herein discussed. This is particularly true of the stabilization of business and employment, the most desirable system of unemployment compensation, health insurance, and the most suitable provision for the old. In discussing these matters the authors have stated their positions frankly. With many factors involved, with much needed research remaining to be done, with relatively short experience in the operation of many experiments, it is only to be expected that many readers will not share the authors' interpretations, evaluations, and views.

As was said in the Preface to Volume I, the length of this treatise necessitated the assumption by one or the other of the authors of the drafting of, and primary responsibility for, different segments of the work. The chapters constituting the present volume were drafted by Mr. Millis. But, as was stated in the Preface to Volume I, in connection with the reversed situation there of primary and secondary responsibility, all chapters of the treatise have been drafted after numerous consultations between us, and they constitute a joint product for which joint responsibility is assumed.

It is impossible to mention the names of all persons to whom the authors are indebted. We are, however, particularly indebted to Professor E. E. Witte, Professor Paul H. Douglas, Dr. Michael Davis, Dr. Isador Falk, and Dr. Walter F. Dodd for the results of their research,

upon which we have drawn heavily.   Wilbur Cohen of the Social Security
Board has been most helpful in providing data relating to social security
legislation.   To the University of Chicago Press we are under obligation
for permission to reprint, with some revisions, Chapters V, VI, and VII,
published as *Sickness and Insurance* last year.   For helpful suggestions
as well as for gathering data, the authors are indebted to George S.
Wheeler, Robert K. Burns, Dan Goldy, and Lily Mary David.   Without
their assistance these chapters could not well have been completed.
Mrs. Margaret Finnamore and Mrs. Helen Saunders have greatly
lightened the burden of proofreading.   Finally, we wish to acknowledge
our indebtedness to the Social Science Research Committee of the
University of Chicago for grants-in-aid.

HARRY A. MILLIS,
ROYAL E. MONTGOMERY.

May, 1938.

CONTENTS

CONTENTS

CHAPTER IV

CHAPTER V

CHAPTER VI

CHAPTER VII

CHAPTER VIII

LIST OF TABLES

xi

LABOR'S RISKS AND SOCIAL INSURANCE

CHAPTER I

THE PROBLEM OF UNEMPLOYMENT: AMOUNT, CAUSES, AND EFFECTS

It was inevitable that mention of the major risks of labor in a system of capitalistic free enterprise, of the circumstances out of which these risks emerge, and of some of the proposals for their mitigation, should have protruded itself into the chapters of Vol. I of this treatise. For the problems of wages and incomes and of their underlying determinants, of hours of labor, and of attempts at governmental control are inextricably interwoven with those of unemployment, of industrial superannuation, of economic provision for illness and accidents. Although some of the problems already discussed, and some of those before us in the present volume, would obtain in any type of economic organization, both their character and the means to be employed in attacking them are conditioned by the institutional arrangements under which labor power is bought and sold. These institutional arrangements constitute a common basis making separability arbitrary. But the treatment of labor's risks in the preceding volume necessarily was incidental to emphasis upon other, although related, problems. In the present volume we turn to detailed examination of labor's risks and insecurities and of the means to their amelioration.

To those who have lived through the postwar period no argument is necessary to prove that unemployment is outstanding among these risks and presents to working people their biggest single problem. Because of the generality of experience with it and the devastating effects of its recurrent visitations, unemployment is "the curse of American workmen." In this chapter we shall attempt to state the problem in terms of numbers unemployed, and in terms of the causes and effects of unemployment. In the following two chapters we shall discuss the methods of dealing with the problem.

Unemployment is not a new problem, one appearing only in the modern economic order. Before the industrial revolution there were maladjustments due to a variety of causes: labor was neither as mobile

1

nor as adaptable as at present; seasonal influences, as in the building trades, were very great. Nevertheless, in spite of increasing control over nature and of increasing mobility and adaptability of labor, there is reason for thinking that the problem of unemployment for some generations has become a more extensive one than it used to be. With the extension of markets, with a greater degree of interdependence, with industry more speculative, there has been a greater instability than in the old order. Until in very recent years there has certainly been a larger turnover of labor; this, of course, was frequently accompanied by loss of working time. Certainly with urbanization of population and with the sources of income supplementary to wages counting for relatively less and less in working-class families, to be unemployed has become a more serious matter for the worker.

The misfortunes of recent years arouse interest in the question whether or not during the last generation or half century unemployment has become a more or less extensive fact. Does the existing economic order tend, as the decades pass, to produce more and more unemployment? Trade-union statistics, beginning in 1860 and coming down into the present century, indicate worse and better years but no tendency for the volume of unemployment in Great Britain to increase or decrease. Likewise, the American data examined by Professor Douglas in making his index of unemployment, for the period 1890–1926, led to the conclusion that "there has been no observable and pronounced tendency for the volume of unemployment either to diminish or increase."[1] In the postwar period, however, dislocated markets, tariff barriers, and disrupted monetary and credit systems have been accompanied by a volume of unemployment in many countries larger and more persistent than had been experienced before 1914. How long this maladjustment will continue remains to be seen.

Rowntree's definition of unemployment has been widely adopted. "A person," he states, "is unemployed who is seeking work for wages, but is unable to find any suited to his capacities and under conditions which are reasonable, judged by local standards." Implicit in this definition is the necessary distinction between the "work-shy" and those seeking work; between those who are disabled by sickness or accident or old age or who are unemployable for other reasons and those who are able to work; between those who are on vacation or are merely unoccupied and those who are without jobs. The work-shy, the disabled, the unemployable, those on vacation, or on strike, or merely unoccupied are not to be listed as unemployed. On the other hand, Rowntree's definition would include among the unemployed those who might secure work, but only at wages unduly low as compared to the wages they have commonly

---

[1] Quoted, with permission, from Paul H. Douglas and Aaron Director, *The Problem of Unemployment* (The Macmillan Company, 1931), p. 33.

received or are being currently paid, or in occupations commonly regarded as unsuited to their training and experience, or in places too far removed from where they reside, or at tasks left undone by men on strike or locked out. In other words, unemployed men are those who are in involuntary idleness because, though they are able to work and are seeking work, they cannot find suitable employment.

The problem is not wholly in the joblessness of such as these. Finding place in it also is the involuntary short-time work of those who, while in employment, are working part days or weeks, or are "laid off" for periods not long enough and under such circumstances as to be equivalent to discharge. This has been called "unemployment within employment." It involves the involuntary spending of normal working time outside the plant. There is a third element also—time lost in the plant, such, e.g., as the time the pieceworker loses while waiting in the plant for material to be delivered to him. Both "unemployment within employment" and "unemployment on the job," as well as being without a job, find place in the problem of unemployment. Though the last-mentioned of these problems is in all respects the most important element, from the point of view of loss of earnings the other problems are not unimportant.

THE AMOUNT OF UNEMPLOYMENT

For the United States, as for most other countries, there are no inclusive official statistics showing the amount of unemployment at all accurately during a period of years. No country has had or can have such statistics until it has operated an inclusive system of public employment offices for placing workers and a system of unemployment insurance for the payment of benefits to those who, through no incapacity or fault of theirs, lose time. Yet we have a considerable body of data from which, with very large margins of error, estimates of the number of workers without jobs and the amount of time lost in jobs have been made.

The American data have been obtained from censuses, from surveys and family inquiries, from reports made by labor organizations, from payrolls showing the number of wage earners employed from time to time and their earnings, and from special investigations of certain industries.[1] Some of the sources of data will be noted specifically in connection with a few of the better statistics bearing upon our problem. It will be

[1] For a discussion bearing upon the different types of data, see E. S. Bradford, *Publications American Statistical Association*, vol. 17 (1921), pp. 983–994. Much the same ground has been covered and the more important data presented and analyzed in "Industrial Unemployment," U. S. Department of Labor, *Bulletin 310* (1922). This bulletin was prepared by Bradford, who gave expert assistance to the President's Conference on Unemployment, 1921. See also Paul H. Douglas, *Real Wages* (1930), Paul H. Douglas and Aaron Director, *The Problem of Unemployment* (1931), and Social Security Board, *Social Security in America* (1937), pp. 55–72.

helpful first of all, however, to set down briefly what the data available indicate as to the amount of unemployment and its incidence.

Such roughly comparable data as are available indicate that before the Great War unemployment and short-time work were more extensive in the United States than in the European countries generally.[1] The explanation of this fact is found partly in the less stable and more frequently changing conditions in this country, partly in a large immigration which usually gave us a redundant supply of labor, and partly in the smaller effort we had devoted to solving the problem. Whatever the explanation, it would appear that the number of wholly unemployed workers in this country on the average, previous to 1929, was at least 6 per cent of the entire number, while in Great Britain, trade-union statistics for 1904 to 1913 showed an average of 4.7 per cent to be without work. The corresponding figure in Germany was 2.6 per cent. Of course, the postwar situation in Europe as well as the situation in the United States since 1930 has been quite different. In most of the continental countries—Sweden and Germany among them—the number of unemployed workers has generally been greatly in excess of the number recorded before the War. The situation in Britain has been, and still is, bad,[2] though perhaps not so much worse than before the War as the percentages of the unemployed would indicate, for the War had the effect of drawing the unoccupied and those on the fringe of the unemployable into industry and they helped to increase the number registered for work or insurance after the return of peace. Nevertheless, previous to the War, unemployment was a problem of much less importance than that presented by low rates of pay; since 1921 it has been Britain's largest domestic problem. Since the industrial reaction set in, the number of unemployed persons officially reported by the government has seldom fallen as low as a million and at times it has greatly exceeded that figure. Most of the time the percentage of insured workers reporting themselves

[1] For convenient summary statistics on unemployment in different countries, see International Labor Organization, *Series C*, and Paul H. Douglas and Aaron Director, *op. cit.*, Chaps. 2, 3, and 4. The *Ministry of Labour Gazette* (British) gives more recent data. See, *e.g.*, the issue of January, 1936, p. 27. See also, *Monthly Labor Review*, vol. 42 (January, 1936), pp. 228–232.

[2] Percentage of insured people unemployed in Great Britain and Northern Ireland from *Ministry of Labour Gazette* (January, 1936), p. 2.

Year	Per cent	Year	Per cent	Year	Per cent
1921	17.0	1926	12.5	1931	21.3
1922	14.3	1927	9.7	1932	22.1
1923	11.7	1928	10.8	1933	19.9
1924	10.3	1929	10.4	1934	16.7
1925	11.3	1930	16.1	1935	15.6

as out of work has been as high as 10 and at times it has been very much higher, in 1932, for example, averaging 22.1 per cent.

The data available have led some students of the subject, taking a period of years together but not including 1930 to date, to conclude that unemployment has reduced the earnings of American workers considerably more than 10 per cent. The United States Commission on Industrial Relations, reporting on the "extent and character of unemployment," stated that wage earners in the principal manufacturing and mining industries in this country lost on the average from one-fifth to one-fourth of working time during the normal year. About two-thirds of this loss, they explained, was due to lack of work, about a quarter due to disabling sickness, while accidents and strikes would each account for less than 2 per cent.[1] Bradford (in 1921) estimated[2] that in manufacture and mechanical pursuits, mining, transportation, and communication the time lost between jobs had averaged thirty days per worker per year, and that unemployment within employment and unemployment on the job had averaged another thirty days. Thus, he concluded that on the average the amount of unemployment in these branches of industry had been some sixty days per man per year.

These estimates of the amount of unemployment are not conclusive, however, and, with recent years excluded, exaggerate the worker's loss caused by lack of work. The percentages out of work in trade, finance, and other urban pursuits run materially lower than the percentages out of work in manufacture, mining, construction and building, and all branches of employment must be given due weight in arriving at an inclusive estimate. Moreover, it appears to be erroneous to state that the number of days lost because of underemployment has been as large as that lost because of total unemployment. The (average) total loss due to lack of work the authors would estimate at not far from twenty-five days per worker per year for the thirty years ending with 1929. This estimate, more conservative than many have been inclined to make, is indicated by the better data, some of which will be introduced presently.

The evidence shows that while the risk of unemployment is a general one, most workers at some time or other suffer from loss of earnings because of it, and while many are in almost constant fear of losing their jobs because their labor may not be needed, the problem is all the worse because the sacrifice is by no means evenly distributed over the entire working population. Instead, the amount of lost time has varied greatly as between industry and industry and also sometimes between occupation and occupation in a given industry. Moreover, the time lost has been greatest among the unskilled, partly because their numbers have usually been most redundant, partly because the nature of their work has been

[1] U. S. Commission on Industrial Relations, *Final Report* (1915), pp. 161–163.

[2] "Industrial Unemployment," U. S. Bureau of Labor Statistics, *Bulletin 310* (1922).

what it was, and partly because they could be dismissed and taken on as needed without any great risk on the part of the employer. Certainly the policy in labor management has been to discriminate between the skilled and the unskilled. Even in a fairly acute depression, as well as in slack seasons, the more efficient and tractable among the skilled have usually been retained on the payroll, and not infrequently they have then been set at tasks commonly performed by the semiskilled and the unskilled. On the other hand, in the absence of union organization and security of tenure, the unskilled have been rapidly "laid off" or discharged when not needed. No doubt the degree of discrimination and the disproportions differ from one country to another, and as between one time and another in a given country, but Bradford estimated that in the United States the burden of lost time has fallen twice as heavily upon the unskilled as upon the skilled.[1] This appears to be probable in view of the fact that the ratios of quittings and layoffs are twice as large and the ratio of discharges is three times as large for the unskilled as for the skilled. And, finally, where tenure of the job is not secure and equal division of work required, as it is in a number of unionized industries, the burden falls much more frequently and more heavily upon the less than upon the more desirable employees, for it is the business of management when adjusting numbers to labor needs to select for employment those who will constitute the best personnel. While from certain points of view this is very desirable, it has the incidental effect that the old and slow, the less strong, the less efficient, and the less tractable are frequently "culled out." Hence the larger part of the sacrifice, in so far as discharges and long layoffs are concerned—and these present the biggest problem—falls upon a limited number, undermining their character and ambition, and shoving them down toward, if not into, the class of casual laborers, and not infrequently the unemployable. It is the unequal distribution of unemployment in these several respects and its large volume when an industry is "slack" or business generally is depressed that cause the problem of unemployment to be such a serious one.[2]

The unequal distribution of time lost by unemployed persons is generally known, but until 1933 few quantitative studies of the duration of unemployment had been made. One such study of the effects upon workers of displacement during relatively prosperous times was completed in 1929 by Isador Lubin.[3] More than 750 displaced workers in representative industries in different industrial centers were covered. These

---

[1] Technological unemployment, however, falls most heavily upon the skilled workers. See p. 33 for discussion of the subject.

[2] See pp. 35–39 for studies of the incidence of unemployment upon workers displaced by technological improvements.

[3] Isador Lubin, *The Absorption of the Unemployed by American Industry*, Brookings Institution Pamphlet Series (1929), no. 3.

workers had all been discharged within the preceding 12 months. Of the 754 workers, more than 45 per cent (344) were unemployed at the time of the survey. Of those who had found jobs, only 11.5 per cent had been reemployed within one month, 43.7 had found work within 3 months, and 76.1 per cent within 6 months. Of those still unemployed, 12.5 per cent had been out of work less than 1 month, 34.9 per cent less than 3 months, 23.9 per cent from 3 to 6 months, while 40.3 per cent had been unemployed more than 6 months, and 8.4 per cent 12 months or more. Of the workers who found employment, 32.7 per cent remained in the same industry, while 66.6 per cent shifted to another. Of the workers on new jobs, 18.8 per cent had better, 48.8 per cent had the same, and 27.1 per cent had less good wages than they had been paid in their old jobs.[1]

The surveys of unemployment in Buffalo also show the great differences in duration among individuals and in addition reveal the large increase in length of time lost by the unemployed during a depression period. In 1929, 51.3 per cent of the unemployed had lost less than 10 weeks' work; in 1933, only 18.0 per cent had been unemployed less than 10 weeks. Of those unemployed in 1929, nearly 30 per cent had lost a year's time or more; in 1933 the corresponding figure had jumped to 68.2 per cent. In that year 54.1 per cent of the unemployed had been without work for two years or more.

TABLE 1.—DURATION OF UNEMPLOYMENT IN BUFFALO, 1929 TO 1933[1]

Duration in weeks	Per cent (both sexes)				
	1929	1930	1931	1932	1933[a]
Under 2............................	11.2	4.3	2.7	1.5	2.7
2 and under 4......................	17.1	7.7	4.8	2.9	5.2
4 and under 10.....................	23.0	21.7	13.1	6.2	10.1
10 and under 20....................	9.6	18.0	13.9	8.3	5.7
20 and under 30....................	5.5	14.5	11.9	11.1	4.4
30 and under 40....................	2.7	7.8	6.5	5.6	2.3
40 and under 52....................	1.0	5.3	5.2	5.2	1.4
52 weeks and over.................	29.9	20.7	41.9	59.2[b]	68.2[b]

[a] The 1933 percentages are for males only. The inclusion of females would, however, not materially change the total percentages.
[b] 35.4 per cent had been unemployed more than 104 weeks in 1932, and 54.1 in 1933.
[1] "Surveys of Unemployment in Buffalo," New York State Department of Labor, *Bulletin 179* (1934) and *Monthly Labor Review* (March, 1934), p. 526. See also Alvin Hansen and others, *An Analysis of Three Unemployment Surveys in Minneapolis, St. Paul and Duluth,* University of Minnesota Employment Stabilization Research Institute, vol. 1, Bulletin 6 (1932).

One more survey, made by the Bureau of Labor Statistics in cooperation with the Bureau of the Census in the spring of 1934, should be cited. The duration of unemployment for 11,051 unemployed workers

[1] No data on the wages of the others.

in Bridgeport, Conn., is shown in Table 2. Of these workers, 8,002 were men and 3,049 were women.

TABLE 2.—PERCENTAGE DISTRIBUTION OF UNEMPLOYED WORKERS IN BRIDGEPORT, CONN., ACCORDING TO DURATION OF UNEMPLOYMENT[1]

Duration of unemployment	Men	Women	Total
Unemployment of:			
Under 2 weeks	2.1	3.2	2.4
2 and under 5 weeks	5.3	9.5	6.5
5 and under 26 weeks	19.4	30.0	22.3
26 and under 52 weeks	8.0	10.2	8.7
1 and under 2 years	12.3	14.4	12.9
2 and under 3 years	19.9	15.6	18.7
3 and under 4 years	16.1	9.0	14.2
4 years or more	16.7	8.1	14.3
All unemployment	100.0	100.0	100.0

[1] The results for the City of Bridgeport were published in the *Monthly Labor Review* (March, 1935), pp. 626–634. Similar surveys for Springfield and Lancaster may be found in the *Monthly Labor Review* (April, 1935), pp. 878–881, and *ibid.* (May, 1935), pp. 1181–1184, respectively.

The table indicates that an appalling proportion of the workers (60.1 per cent) had been out of work for more than one year, and that 14.3 per cent had been unemployed for four years or more. The percentage of men unemployed two years and longer was 52.7 as compared with 32.7 for the women.

Since we now have in mind the relative extent of unemployment in different countries and the general facts regarding its incidence, it will

TABLE 3.—IDLENESS OF ORGANIZED WAGE EARNERS IN NEW YORK, 1902 TO 1916[1]
(Mean Yearly Percentage)

Year	Mean percentage of idle	Same on account disputes	Same on account disability	Same on account lack of work
1902	14.8			
1903	17.5			
1904	16.9	3.6	1.2	12.1
1905	11.2	1.6	1.2	8.5
1906	9.3	1.4	1.2	6.8
1907	16.2	1.2	1.4	13.6
1908	29.7	0.4	1.4	28.0
1909	18.5	2.2	1.3	14.9
1910	19.1	4.2	1.3	13.6
1911	21.1	1.2	1.2	18.7
1912	17.3	0.9	1.2	15.2
1913	25.2	3.5	1.0	20.9
1914	28.9	0.3	1.1	27.5
1915	28.5			
1916 (6 mo.)	16.8 (about)			

[1] Compiled from "Idleness of Organized Workers in 1914," New York Department of Labor, *Bulletin 69* (1915), and "Course of Employment in New York State from 1904 to 1916," *Bulletin 85* (1917).

be well at this point to summarize briefly some of the better American data bearing upon the amount of unemployment.

New York, Massachusetts, New Jersey, Wisconsin, Illinois, and other states have published statistics of the unemployed or data showing the variations in payrolls, for longer or shorter periods. In New York from 1902 to 1916 and in Massachusetts from 1908 to 1923 the data are for the number of union men reported as idle on given days, the idleness being recorded as due to industrial disputes, disability, or lack of work. The data are perhaps none too reliable and because of the particular industries covered it is fairly certain that the figures exaggerated the amount of unemployment. Nevertheless, the data indicate some facts of importance.

It will be noted that in New York (Table 3) the percentages idle because of disability were fairly stable, varying between 1.0 and 1.4 and averaging approximately 1.2, while the percentages idle because of industrial disputes and lack of work varied greatly. Those reported as really unemployed ("lack of work") varied between 6.8 per cent in 1906 and 28.0 per cent in 1908, following the "bankers' panic," the average for the years 1904–1914 being some 15.8 per cent. The percentages idle, when averaged, varied between a little less than 30 in the building and clothing and textile trades and 9.2 in printing and 7.5 in restaurants, mercantile establishments, etc.

The data for Massachusetts, like those for New York, were obtained from union secretaries but showed considerably less idleness. The difference between the data for Massachusetts and those for New York appears to have been due largely to differences in the relative importance of the industries covered by the reports of the labor organizations.[1] The summary figures for Massachusetts are given in Table 4.

In recent years a number of the states and the Federal Government have been publishing employment indexes based upon payroll data obtained from an increasing number and variety of establishments.[2] Though these show only trends in employment, they have frequently been used to show the trend of unemployment, so that passing reference should be made to them at this point.

Since 1914, the Federal Bureau of Labor Statistics has published index numbers showing the relative number of persons on the payrolls of representative firms in different branches of manufacture. Not all cooper-

[1] In New York, of those reported in September, 1914, 23.6 per cent were in the building trades and 32.5 per cent in the clothing industry, both of which have been very unstable. In Massachusetts the largest group reported on were in the textile and the boot and shoe industries.

[2] The Ohio statistics are the most inclusive of the state employment statistics since all employers are required by law to report. See "Fluctuations in Employment in Ohio, 1914–1929," U. S. Bureau of Labor Statistics, Bulletin 553 (1932), and Monthly Labor Review, vol. 42 (January, 1936), pp. 46–61.

TABLE 4.—IDLENESS OF ORGANIZED WAGE EARNERS IN MASSACHUSETTS, 1908 TO 1922
(Mean Yearly Percentage)

Year	Total	Due to lack of work or material	Due to strikes and lockouts	Due to disability (sickness and accident)
1908	14.2	12.5	0.6	1.1
1909	8.0	6.6	0.2	1.2
1910	7.5	6.1	0.1	1.3
1911	8.1	6.5	0.3	1.3
1912	8.3	5.1	1.9	1.3
1913	8.7	6.5	0.9	1.3
1914	13.0	11.0	0.5	1.5
1915	10.7	7.9	1.1	1.7
1916	5.7	3.3	0.9	1.5
1917	7.2	4.6	1.1	1.5
1918	6.1	3.3	0.4	2.4
1919	7.5	5.3	0.9	1.3
1920	19.7	16.5	2.0	1.2
1921	26.5	21.0		
1922	18.0	10.8		

ating establishments have reported every month, and the number of establishments covered has greatly increased; hence the data have not been for identical establishments from one month or one year to another. Nevertheless, the index numbers undoubtedly show the general trend of employment in manufacture. The "general index of employment," by years, is shown in Table 5.

While these indexes, like several others, show the general trend of employment in manufacture,[1] they should not, as many have assumed, be used as though they provided inverted unemployment indexes. They do show good years (1916–1920) and bad years (1921, 1922, 1931–1934) according to the state of trade, and also reflect the effects of the many technological changes which go far to explain a shrinkage of employment in manufacture between 1920 and 1927. They do not, however, reflect the fact that during these years the number of persons employed in mercantile pursuits increased by approximately 1,400,000, in the professions by about 600,000, in finance and in miscellaneous employments by correspondingly large figures.[2] And if we had the trends in all branches

[1] The index numbers do not, however, show the fluctuations with as much accuracy as the reader might assume. Perhaps the firms reporting have had a larger fluctuation than manufacturing in general; certainly all branches of manufacture have not been adequately represented. The index numbers indicate an 8.2 per cent drop in the number of wage earners from 1923 to 1925, while the Census, covering the mass of manufacturing plants, shows a decrease of only 4.4 per cent. Moreover, the index numbers indicate a 10.4 per cent drop from 1923 to 1929, while the Census shows an increase of 0.7 per cent in the average number of wage earners employed.

[2] Report of the Committee on Recent Economic Changes, of the President's Conference on Unemployment, Recent Economic Changes in the United States, vol. 2 (1929), pp. 472–473.

TABLE 5.—INDEXES OF EMPLOYMENT AND PAYROLLS FOR MANUFACTURING INDUSTRIES IN THE UNITED STATES, 1914 TO 1936[1]

Year	(1923 = 100)		(Average 1923–1925 = 100)	
	Employment	Payrolls	Employment[a]	Payrolls[a]
1914 (7 mo.)	94.9			
1915	97.0	54.9		
1916	110.4	61.9		
1917	115.0	76.3		
1918	114.2	96.7		
1919	108.2	103.6	106.7	98.3
1920	109.9	125.9	107.8	118.2
1921	85.1	80.0	82.2	76.9
1922	88.4	79.9	90.3	81.6
1923	100.0	100.0	104.1	103.3
1924	90.3	90.6	96.4	96.0
1925	91.2	93.1	99.5	100.7
1926	.....	.....	101.3	103.7
1927	.....	.....	98.9	101.7
1928	.....	.....	98.7	102.4
1929	.....	.....	104.7	109.1
1930	.....	.....	91.3	88.5
1931	.....	.....	77.3	67.4
1932	.....	.....	65.5	46.4
1933	.....	.....	72.0	49.4
1934	.....	.....	82.5	62.9
1935	.....	.....	86.0	71.3
1936	.....	.....	91.9	82.4

[a] Adjusted to the 1933 Census of Manufactures.
[1] *Monthly Labor Review*, vol. 21 (1925), p. 576, and vol. 44 (1937), p. 733.

of employment, some of which have not been covered by indexes, we should not be able to estimate the number of unemployed persons without an estimate of the number of the unemployed in the basic year and data for the number of persons in the active labor supply as population grows and changes in age distribution and other respects take place.

The indexes of employment and payrolls in nonmanufacturing industries have also been expanded by the Federal Bureau of Labor Statistics until nearly all important industrial groups are now included. Table 6 shows the changes since 1929 in employment and payrolls in nonmanufacturing groups, the railroads, and 89 manufacturing industries. It will be noted that the decline in employment from 1929 to 1933 was not as great as the decrease in payrolls, and that producers of raw materials, as indicated by metalliferous mining, suffered more drastic declines than utilities, such as the telephone and the telegraph.

A review of American unemployment statistics that is concerned with both methods of measurement and results portrayed should mention the

TABLE 6.—COMPARISON OF EMPLOYMENT AND PAYROLLS IN THE UNITED STATES, 1929 TO 1936[1]

Industrial group	Employment indexes (1929 = 100)							Payroll indexes (1929 = 100)						
	1930	1931	1932	1933	1934	1935	1936	1930	1931	1932	1933	1934	1935	1936
Anthracite mining	93.4	80.5	62.5	51.7	59.6	53.2	51.8	95.3	75.4	53.7	45.8	55.9	47.5	45.7
Bituminous coal mining	93.4	83.2	67.4	67.9	77.2	76.7	79.0	81.3	57.5	35.6	37.8	54.2	58.2	70.8
Metalliferous mining	83.2	59.1	36.5	34.6	41.6	47.3	60.3	78.0	44.8	21.6	20.6	26.7	33.9	48.4
Quarrying, etc	84.3	67.4	49.0	44.9	48.9	46.0	49.5	79.3	53.4	29.1	24.7	29.6	30.7	38.9
Crude petroleum	87.4	65.7	55.3	62.2	77.7	74.9	72.9	85.9	61.7	44.1	44.1	56.9	57.9	58.6
Telephone and telegraph	97.9	86.6	79.1	70.4	70.3	70.1	72.2	102.9	93.7	81.1	68.2	71.5	74.5	78.9
Power and light	103.0	95.6	83.0	78.8	83.8	84.8	90.5	104.3	96.7	79.8	72.0	77.9	81.4	88.8
Electric railroad and bus	93.4	84.7	75.5	70.0	72.1	71.2	72.0	93.5	83.4	68.0	58.9	62.2	63.7	67.2
Wholesale trade	96.0	85.8	76.8	76.1	82.8	84.0	86.7	95.9	81.9	64.2	56.8	63.0	65.6	69.4
Total retail trade	95.9	87.7	76.8	76.1	82.0	82.3	85.7	96.2	83.1	63.2	55.2	60.9	62.1	66.3
Hotels	99.2	91.7	79.0	74.9	84.9	81.0	83.6	98.5	85.4	64.5	54.4	65.1	63.4	67.2
Laundries	.....	93.1	83.5	78.8	81.3	81.5	86.1	.....	88.3	70.1	59.5	64.9	66.9	73.9
Dyeing and cleaning	.....	85.6	75.2	74.3	77.1	77.5	81.2	.....	76.1	57.3	49.5	56.1	57.9	61.7
Manufacturing industries (1923-1925 = 100)	91.3	77.3	65.5	72.0	82.5	86.0	91.9	88.5	67.4	46.4	49.4	62.9	71.3	82.4
Class I railroads (1923-1925 = 100)	83.3	70.6	57.8	54.4	56.5	55.7	59.6							

[1] *Monthly Labor Review*, vol. 36 (January, 1933), pp. 203–219; vol. 40 (March, 1935), pp. 764–789; and vol. 44 (March, 1937), pp. 720–749.

pioneering study of Hornell Hart.[1] Using the data then available for the period 1902–1917, Professor Hart, like students who have made later studies, estimated total labor supply, and from this estimate deducted his estimate of the numbers at work. The estimates arrived at are presented in Table 7.

Of course, there is always the "reserve army of the unemployed." It will be noted that when there was a labor shortage in 1906, the "reserve" is estimated by Hart at 1,000,000, in 1917 at 1,300,000. These were the best years, when the percentages of idle workers in nonrural occupations were estimated at 5.5 and 4.7 for the two years, respectively. In contrast to these are the depression years. In 1908, following the "bankers' panic," the percentage is estimated at 14.8, in 1914 at 15.8, and in 1915 at 16.0. For the sixteen-year period, Hart estimated the average at 9.9.

A more recent careful statistical study of unemployment in the United States has been made by Professor Wolman, along similar lines. The study covered the years 1920–1927. The summary figures arrived at are presented in Table 8.

These estimates call for no special comment, except that they should not be compared too closely with those made by Hart. It will be noted

[1] *Fluctuations in Unemployment in Cities of the United States, 1902 to 1917.* Studies from the Helen S. Trounstine Foundation, vol. 1 (1918).

TABLE 7.—ESTIMATED NUMBER, IN MILLIONS OF UNEMPLOYED WORKERS, IN OCCUPATIONS OTHER THAN AGRICULTURE IN THE UNITED STATES, 1902 TO 1917[1]

Year	Average	Percentage of supply	Number unemployed, by months											
			Jan.	Feb.	Mar.	Apr.	May	June	July	Aug.	Sept.	Oct.	Nov.	Dec.
Average	2.5	9.9	3.4	3.1	2.8	2.5	2.4	2.5	2.6	2.3	2.0	1.9	2.1	2.4
1902	2.7	14.1	3.5	3.3	2.9	2.7	2.9	2.9	2.8	2.6	2.4	1.8	2.0	2.2
1903	1.9	9.3	2.5	2.4	2.0	1.6	1.8	2.0	2.1	1.9	1.8	1.6	1.5	1.5
1904	2.4	11.5	2.9	2.0	2.3	2.2	2.3	2.4	3.0	2.7	2.1	1.9	2.3	2.7
1905	2.0	9.3	2.7	2.8	2.5	2.0	2.1	2.4	2.1	1.8	1.6	1.2	1.3	1.5
1906	1.2	5.5	1.9	1.8	1.2	1.1	1.1	1.3	1.4	1.0a	1.0a	1.0a	1.0a	1.0a
1907	1.4	6.0	1.0a	1.0a	1.0a	1.0a	1.0a	1.0a	1.0a	1.0a	1.0a	1.7	2.6	3.6
1908	3.5	14.8	4.1	3.8	3.8	4.2	3.9	3.6	3.4	2.9	3.3	3.0	3.2	3.2
1909	2.1	8.6	3.5	3.3	2.7	2.3	2.0	2.1	2.3	2.1	1.4	1.0a	1.2	1.5
1910	1.7	6.5	2.5	2.6	2.1	1.7	1.4	1.5	1.7	1.6	1.1	1.1	1.5	2.1
1911	2.8	10.8	3.2	3.5	3.1	2.9	2.7	2.8	3.0	2.9	2.3	2.1	2.4	2.9
1912	2.6	9.6	3.5	3.7	3.2	2.9	2.7	2.8	2.8	2.3	1.7	1.5	1.7	2.1
1913	2.6	9.3	3.2	3.2	2.8	2.5	2.1	2.4	2.6	2.5	2.0	2.0	2.6	3.3
1914	4.5	15.8	4.6	4.6	4.4	4.1	4.0	4.4	4.8	4.8	4.3	4.2	4.8	5.5
1915	4.6	16.0	6.5	6.4	5.8	5.3	4.8	4.8	4.8	4.5	3.5	3.1	3.1	3.2
1916	2.1	7.1	4.2	3.9	3.0	2.2	1.8	1.9	1.7	1.3	1.3a	1.3a	1.3a	1.3a
1917	1.4	4.7	1.8	2.0	1.5	1.3a	1.3a	1.3a	1.3a	1.3a	1.3a	1.3a	1.3a	1.3a

a Items represent months in which the demand for labor exceeded the normal supply, and only the incidental reserve margin of labor was unemployed. It will be noted that with the attraction of large numbers into industry during the War, the labor reserve was increased from 1.0 to 1.3 millions.

[1] See Hornell Hart, *Fluctuations in Unemployment in Cities of the United States, 1902 to 1917*, Studies from the Helen S. Trounstine Foundation, vol. 1 (1918), No. 2, p. 48.

TABLE 8.—NUMBER AND PERCENTAGE OF PERSONS ATTACHED TO NONAGRICULTURAL INDUSTRY, UNEMPLOYED, BY YEAR, 1920 TO 1927[1]

Year	Number attached (000 omitted)	Number unemployed (000 omitted)	Percentage unemployed
1920	27,558	1,401	5.1
1921	27,989	4,270	15.3
1922	28,505	3,441	12.7
1923	29,293	1,532	5.0
1924	30,234	2,315	7.7
1925	30,941	1,775	5.7
1926	31,808	1,669	5.3
1927	32,695	2,055	6.3

[1] See *Recent Economic Changes*, vol. 2 (1929), p. 478.

that while without question unemployment was more prevalent in 1921 than in any other recent year prior to 1930, Wolman's estimate for that year is slightly less than Hart's estimates for 1914 and 1915. This is accounted for, in part at least, by the fact that Dr. Wolman's estimates were very conservatively made to show the minimum amount of unemployment. His estimates should be used accordingly.

A careful estimate of the amount of unemployment in the United States over a long period of time is that made by Professor Douglas. His figures cover manufacture, transportation, the building trades, and mining for the thirty years 1897–1926. They are presented in Table 9.

TABLE 9.—UNEMPLOYMENT IN MANUFACTURING, TRANSPORTATION, BUILDING TRADES, AND MINING, 1897 TO 1926[1]

Year	Total labor supply (000 omitted)	Total unemployed (000 omitted)	Percentage unemployed
1897	7,015	1,266	18.0
1898	7,164	1,214	16.9
1899	7,327	766	10.5
1900	7,527	755	10.0
1901	7,805	584	7.5
1902	8,347	569	6.8
1903	8,702	609	7.0
1904	8,748	883	10.1
1905	9,349	622	6.7
1906	9,817	577	5.9
1907	10,129	695	6.9
1908	10,103	1,654	16.4
1909	10,394	925	8.9
1910	10,726	774	7.2
1911	10,921	1,025	9.4
1912	11,124	775	7.0
1913	11,357	936	8.2
1914	11,570	1,899	16.4
1915	11,725	1,822	15.5
1916	12,189	774	6.3
1917	12,841	774	6.0
1918	13,081	719	5.5
1919	12,841	880	6.9
1920	13,006	938	7.2
1921	12,599	2,913	23.1
1922	12,777	2,338	18.3
1923	12,837	1,010	7.9
1924	12,573	1,506	12.0
1925	12,552	1,120	8.9
1926	12,793	962	7.5

[1] Paul H. Douglas, *Real Wages in the United States* (1930), p. 460.   See also Paul H. Douglas and Aaron Director, *The Problem of Unemployment* (1931), Chap. 2.

It is to be remembered that these figures relate to labor in certain industries only. It should be noted also that they include those disabled by sickness or accident.[1] The average percentage of idle during the

[1] At any given time, between 2 and 3 per cent of those constituting the labor supply will be unavailable because of illness, accidents, and strikes—these standing over against "lack of work."

thirty years was, according to Douglas, 10.68. Unlike Hart's and Wolman's data, Professor Douglas' do not include data for public housekeeping, domestic service, and mercantile and miscellaneous trades. Had these been included, the percentage of the idle would have been somewhat smaller, for while the data for these other trades have been so unsatisfactory that the facts are not really capable of measurement, there is no doubt that the extent of unemployment in them is smaller than in the four branches of industry included.[1] The general correspondence between Hart's and Douglas' indexes will be noted. The great changes between good and bad times require no comment.

Most of the data thus far reviewed cover losses from part-time work as well as from total unemployment. Some of the data now to be presented relate to part-time work only or separate it from other forms of unemployment. They are sufficient to indicate the fact that this partial employment, though it is not accompanied by some of the evils found in total unemployment, is in the aggregate responsible for a large amount of lost time and reduced earnings.

Among the best available data are those obtained from an extensive survey made in 1919 by the Bureau of Labor Statistics. This survey covered more than 300,000 wage earners in a large number of industries. The period was about normal in respect to the volume of employment. The male wage earners employed worked 88.8 per cent, the female 88.7 per cent, of full working time. In other words, they lost 11.2 and 11.3 per cent, respectively, of normal working time. This was due in part to sickness or other personal causes, but was in part due to lack of work. A similar survey of the boot and shoe industry in the spring of 1920 showed that the 21,268 workers covered lost 9 per cent of normal working time. The same figure was found in slaughtering and meat-packing in April, 1921.[2]

During the depression of 1914–1915, the Metropolitan Life Insurance Company cooperated with the Bureau of Labor Statistics to ascertain the number of wage earners out of work or working part time. Its agents secured information in respect to this for all wage earners in families called upon in making their rounds in certain cities. Sixteen eastern and middle-western cities were covered in the spring of 1915. It was found that 9.51 per cent of the wage earners were without jobs because there was "no work to be found," while 16.6 per cent were working part time. In all but five of the sixteen cities the number of part-time workers exceeded the number wholly unemployed.[3] Twelve western cities were

---

[1] One reason for this is that technological unemployment has been more important in industry than in the service trades.

[2] See "Industrial Unemployment," U. S. Bureau of Labor Statistics, *Bulletin 310* (1922), pp. 25–30.

[3] See "Unemployment in the United States," Bureau of Labor Statistics, *Bulletin 195* (1916).

canvassed in June and July of the same year. Of the wage earners, 12.9 per cent were without jobs, chiefly because of lack of work, while 20.2 per cent were working part time. In all but one of these cities those working part time exceeded the number of the wholly unemployed.[1] Unfortunately no distinction was made in either of these investigations between the relatively few for whom short time was a voluntary matter and those for whom it was due to lack of work. More unfortunate still was the failure to ascertain the amount of the loss by the part-time workers, who in some cases, no doubt, were employed less than half time while others may have been working as much as 80 per cent of the normal week.

Among the more thorough local studies made of idleness and part-time work are those made by Dr. Croxton and his associates in Columbus, Ohio, and Buffalo, N. Y. While the periods covered and the cities in which the investigations were made cannot be accepted as entirely representative, the data are more representative than most, for they were drawn from occupations generally rather than from "industry" alone. The investigation in Columbus covered the five years 1921–1925, and about a ninth of the male and about a twelfth of the female workers over 18 years of age as reported by the preceding census. Table 10 has been compiled to show the general results obtained.

TABLE 10.—EMPLOYMENT STATUS IN COLUMBUS, OHIO, 1921 TO 1925[1]

Employment status	1921	1922	1923	1924	1925
Number persons enumerated	11,086	12,121	12,299	10,834	12,151
Percentage employed:					
Full time	76.5	86.2	87.5	79.3	82.4
Part time:					
Two-thirds, but less than full	2.5	2.2	2.6	5.0	4.3
One-half, but less than two-thirds	5.8	3.2	2.9	4.9	3.9
One-third, but less than one-half	1.2	0.7	0.6	1.7	1.0
Less than one-third	0.6	0.5	0.1	0.5	0.5
Total, part time	10.1	6.6	6.2	12.1	9.7
Idle (unemployed, sick, injured, etc.)	13.4	7.1	6.3	8.7	7.9

[1] Compiled from "Unemployment in Columbus, Ohio, 1921 to 1925," U. S. Bureau of Labor Statistics, *Bulletin 409* (1926), pp. 6–7.

The ratio of the part-time to the idle workers varied somewhat from year to year, but for the five years the totals for the two groups were practically the same.[2] The greatest contribution made by the study, however, is found in the analysis made of the part-time workers. Though there were variations from year to year, on the average 37.4 per cent of the part-time workers were found to be working at least two-thirds of normal time; 46.2 per cent, half but less than two-thirds; 11.4 per cent, a third

[1] See *Monthly Labor Review*, vol. 1 (November, 1915), p. 6.
[2] The part-time workers totaled 5,176, the idle 5,022.

but less than half; and 4.9 per cent, less than a third. Roughly estimated, the part-time workers lost something less than two-fifths of normal working time. In Columbus, during these five years the ratio of the loss due to complete unemployment to the loss due to part-time work was about 8 to 3.

Unfortunately the Columbus surveys were not continued after 1925, but beginning in 1929 similar studies were made in Buffalo, N. Y. Table 11 gives the percentage of workers employed full time, part time, and unemployed.

TABLE 11.—EMPLOYMENT STATUS IN BUFFALO, 1929 TO 1933[1]

Employment status	1929	1930	1931	1932	1933
Total number of workers in samples..........	14,476	13,475	15,039	14,909	15,729
Percentage employed (both sexes):					
Full time.................................	87.5	66.0	54.5	46.3	58.2
Part time.................................	6.8	17.3	21.8	22.5	13.6
Two-thirds, but less than full............	2.9	7.2	7.3	6.6	3.8
Half, but less than two-thirds............	2.6	6.7	8.1	8.9	5.4
One-third, but less than half:............	0.7	2.3	3.3	3.8	2.5
Less than one-third......................	0.3	1.0	3.0	3.2	1.9
Not reported.............................	0.3	0.1	0.1	.0	.0
Unemployed...............................	5.7	16.7	23.7	31.2	28.2

[1] "Unemployment in Buffalo," New York State Department of Labor, *Bulletin 179* (1934) and *Monthly Labor Review*, vol. 38 (March, 1934). See *Bulletin 173* (1932) for a similar study of 7,302 persons in Syracuse, N. Y.

Though adversely criticized[1] because of omissions in taking the schedules and because of the nature of the recording and form of reporting, the data provided by the Federal Census of Population, April, 1930, must be regarded as most accurately answering the question as to the number of persons without jobs and the number working part time on a given date. It will be remembered that this Census was taken during the first stages of the depression, when the volume of employment was much fuller than during the dismal months of 1932 and 1933. The total number of persons 10 years of age or over attached to industry was 48,832,589. Approximately 5 per cent of these (2,429,062) were returned in "Class *A*" as out of a job, able to work, and looking for employment. In addition to these and exclusive of those sick or voluntarily idle, there were in "Class *B*" 758,585 or 1.6 per cent on layoff without pay. Had the facts been available, it would have been better to relate the jobless and the laid-off persons to the number of wage earners and salaried persons, for few employers and self-employed persons found place in the count of the unemployed. In other words, in making comparisons, not far from 25 per cent should have been deducted from the more than 48 millions

[1] Mary Van Kleek, "The Federal Unemployment Census," *Journal of American Statistical Association, Proceedings*, vol. 26 (1931), pp. 189–200.

returned as gainful persons. This, of course, would have had the effect of increasing the percentages given above by approximately one-third.

Partly because of persistent factors, partly because of seasonal and other factors affecting the volume of employment on a given day in the year, the percentages of the unemployed were found to vary widely from industry to industry. A summary view is presented in Table 12.

TABLE 12.—PERCENTAGE OF GAINFUL WORKERS UNEMPLOYED, BY INDUSTRY GROUP, IN THE UNITED STATES, 1930[1]

Industry group	Percentages in	
	Class A	Class B
Agriculture (farm laborers only)....................	3.8	1.1
Forestry and fishing..............................	7.3	3.1
Extraction of minerals............................	7.8	8.5
Building...	15.4	3.6
Manufacture and mechanical industries (excluding building)......................................	6.2	2.7
Transportation...................................	4.7	1.7
Trade..	3.3	0.6
Public service...................................	2.2	0.6
Professional service..............................	2.2	0.6
Domestic and personal service.....................	4.4	0.7
Industry not specified............................	23.7	2.2
Average all industries............................	5.0	1.6

[1] The data here used will be found in Fifteenth Census of the United States, 1930, *Unemployment*, vol. 1, pp. 53–57.

While the census of 1930 has given us the most inclusive enumeration of the unemployed and the most detailed analysis of those among the normally occupied who were then idle, there is reason to believe that the results understated the true figures in the depression situation then obtaining. In the first place, failure to secure complete scheduling was of more or less importance. Again, not all part-time employment due to lack of work was recorded. Finally, no account was taken of young persons who had not become attached to industry but who in a more normal situation would have been reckoned among the gainful persons enumerated. How many more would have been added by a more acceptable recording of the unemployed is difficult to estimate,[1] but the figures arrived at were possibly in excess of the average for a period of years.

[1] The National Bureau of Economic Research (*Report on National Income, 1929–1932*, made pursuant to Senate Resolution 220, 72d Congress, first session) estimated that the U. S. Census reports of 1930 underestimated the number of unemployed by approximately 1,000,000. See *Senate Report*, 73d Congress, second session, *Document No. 124* (1934), p. 261.

In January, 1931, a second census of unemployment was taken in nineteen of the largest cities of the country. By that time unemployment had reached the stage in which it presented an emergency. The percentage of the population of these cities recorded as unemployed (Class *A*) was then 9.4 as against 3.8 in the preceding April. The percentage recorded as laid off without pay (Class *B*) had risen from 0.7 to 1.8.[1] In terms of per cent of workers unemployed, the figure had increased to 20.4 in Class *A* and 3.9 in Class *B*.[2]

It is generally agreed that from 1930 until about March, 1933, the total amount of unemployment substantially increased. The estimates of the peak number vary from about 11,000,000 to 16,000,000. The Secretary of Commerce placed the estimate at "over 12,000,000 in 1933,"[3] while the American Federation of Labor estimated that 15,166,000 were unemployed in January, 15,653,000 in March, and 12,374,000 in November, 1933.[4] The normal increase in working population has an important bearing upon the amount of unemployment. On the basis of census returns for 1920 and 1930, Dr. Kuznets estimates the annual addition to the number of gainful workers at 703,000. The addition of these workers to those who had become unemployed raised his estimate to 9,700,000 in 1931 and 14,400,000 in 1932.[5] With this method of estimation, which seems to be as accurate as any available, the number unemployed in March, 1933, would be about 16,000,000. From this peak in 1933 the number unemployed wavered unsteadily downward to 12,364,-000 in 1934 and to 12,208,000 in 1935.[6] By September, 1937, it had fallen

[1] For a summary of the results, see *Monthly Labor Review*, vol. 32 (April, 1931), p. 39, or Fifteenth Census of the United States, 1930, *Unemployment*, vol. 2, p. 366.

[2] A very good picture of the employment situation in the larger cities the first week in December, 1930, is obtained from the results of a canvass made of wage earners in families with industrial policies in the Metropolitan Life Insurance Company. All told, 355,759 wage earners in 213,787 families, residing in 46 of the largest cities, were scheduled. Of the 355,759, 195,309, or 54.9 per cent, were employed full time, 75,823 or 21.3 per cent, were working part time, while 84,627, or 23.8 per cent, were unemployed. "Unemployed" included not only persons who were jobless and looking for work, but also those on temporary furlough or on layoff from their regular jobs, and a few not at work because of sickness or voluntarily idle and not looking for work or on vacation. The cities canvassed, it should be pointed out, had, according to the Census of April, 1930, a percentage of unemployment approximately twice as large as that for the rest of the country. [For the report made by the Metropolitan, see *Monthly Labor Review*, vol. 32 (March, 1931), pp. 48–56.]

[3] *New York Times*, Jan. 1, 1934, p. 38.

[4] *American Federationist*, vol. 43 (April, 1936), p. 426.

[5] Dr. Simon Kuznets, "National Income, 1929–1932," *Bulletin 49* of the National Bureau of Economic Research (June 7, 1934), p. 7. In computing the number of unemployed, the number of those employed on part time was reduced, wherever possible, to an equivalent number of fully unemployed.

[6] The American Federation of Labor estimated that the number of unemployed increased more in January, 1936, than in any other January for five years. Unemployment rose

to some 8,500,000 or 9,500,000, if an unusually large number of unemployables may be included among them. Then, with business recession, the number of unemployed persons again rapidly increased. By the middle of November, 1937, according to the census taken by voluntary registration, there were approximately 10,870,000 persons out of work.[1] These persons included others as well as wage earners.

The foregoing data include the more reliable estimates of the volume of unemployment and of the amount of part-time work. It is difficult to estimate the time and earnings that are lost because of "unemployment on the job." That bad routing of materials, slow orders, "unbalanced sections," and other factors reduce appreciably the time men might be engaged in productive activities is beyond question. This reduction in time actually worked is, however, of perhaps more importance as a form of waste in industry than as an element in the problem of unemployment. Much of the waiting is by time workers, and the rates of the piece workers in many cases reflect—although generally most imperfectly—the amount of waiting to which they are subject. Enough has been said to indicate that underemployment is an important cause of lost time and earnings. Perhaps unemployment, in its different forms, has cost the average American wage earner twenty-five working days per year during the three decades ending with 1929. More recently, the volume of unemployment has, of course, been much larger. Even if the experience of the depression of the 1930's is not taken into account, it is obvious that unemployment has been and remains the greatest of the risks of the American workers.

THE CAUSES OF UNEMPLOYMENT

Inevitably, some of the causes of unemployment have been suggested by the data relative to its extent, but a more detailed examination of the various causes is now in order. For the most part, our attention may be centered upon the causes of total unemployment, with secondary emphasis upon the causes of partial unemployment.

The causes of unemployment are, of course, complex and to a great extent interrelated; and numerous analyses and classifications have been made. For our purposes, very brief mention of the more immediate and

---

from 11,397,000 in December, 1935, to 12,646,000 in January, 1936. Of this number, however, 3,524,000 had work under the WPA program. *American Federationist*, vol. 43, no. 2 (February, 1936), pp. 304 and 307.

Estimates of unemployment, covering the period 1929 to date, made by the American Federation of Labor, The National Industrial Conference Board, and the Alexander Hamilton Institute, and for the period 1929 through 1935 by Robert Nathan (*International Labor Review*), may be conveniently found in *Selected Current Statistics*, vol. 1, no. 10 (June, 1937), pp. 54–56, published by the Social Security Board.

[1] The figure given is an official estimate made. Of the 7,822,912 who registered as being unemployed, 2,001,877 had relief work.

apparent of these causes may be made, and attention may then be centered upon those demanding more detailed analysis.

There are numerous reasons, but of very unequal importance, why men lose or leave their jobs and find themselves among the unemployed. Some leave their jobs on strike or are locked out. The lockout is successful or the strike unsuccessful; idleness then becomes unemployment for the men who must find new jobs.

But strikes and lockouts function as a cause in still another way. Very likely, suspensions in coal mining or in railroad transportation or in the manufacture of autos cause workers to be laid off or placed on short time in dependent industries. Moreover, if large numbers are involved for a considerable period of time, the demand for all sorts of goods and services may be adversely affected with results registered in payrolls. The soft-coal strike of 1919, the shopmen's strike of 1922, and the British coal stoppage of 1926 are good examples.

Workers become disabled by sickness or accident. Not infrequently when they are able to resume work their places have been filled and they must seek employment elsewhere.

Some workers, especially young boys, find employment in blind-alley trades which offer no future. When they become too old to serve as office boys or as messengers, say, they quit to find more suitable employment, or, possibly, they are discharged.

Workers are discharged because they are intractable, or frequently tardy or absent, or are undesirable for other reasons. A much larger number quit their jobs; among separations there are many more quittings than discharges. Perhaps the leaving of employment is due to a harsh, tyrannical, or unfair foreman, or to an unsatisfactory machine, or to too much or too little overtime, or to failure to receive promotion; but it may be, and frequently is, for no more definite reason than a desire on the part of the workers "to make a change."[1] In a large number of these quittings as well as in cases of discharge, the separation takes place before there is any definite plan for other employment. A large turnover of labor caused by such things as those indicated is accompanied by a great deal of lost time. Certainly poor personnel administration and unstable human nature loom large in the turnover of labor and find place in an explanation of unemployment.

Workers lose their places because of the introduction of a new machine or of a new process which displaces labor or renders it economical to employ a different class of labor, and, likely, at a lower wage. The story of the industrial revolution is familiar. But displacive changes in proc-

---

[1] For data on the relative importance of voluntary separations and discharges, cf. P. F. Brissenden and Emil Frankel, *Labor Turnover in American Industry* (1922), S. H. Slichter, *The Turnover of Factory Labor* (1921), and data issued regularly by the U. S. Bureau of Labor Statistics.

esses and equipment are always taking place somewhere in industry and in recent years they have been so numerous that we in the United States have found ourselves in the midst of a new industrial revolution with its so-called technological unemployment.[1]

Some workers lose their jobs because of the failure of, or suspension of business by, the firms employing them. There are thousands of such instances in the United States in a normal year.

Other workers lose their jobs or are laid off and lose time because unfavorable weather conditions cause work to be suspended or greatly curtailed. This is frequently true in construction work, though distinct progress has been made in overcoming the difficulties presented by nature. Some lose their jobs or are laid off for a time as contracts are completed, for other contracts may not have been secured or the work on them developed to the point where the labor in question is needed. Here, again, the building trades afford a good example.[2]

Some lose their jobs or are laid off when the "rush season" is over and the "slack season" sets in. The needle trades furnish the best example of this, though canning, preserving, meat-packing and a large number of other industries might be cited as examples almost as well. The Governor's Advisory Commission, in reporting on employment in the cloak, suit, and skirt industry[3] in New York in 1924, stated that the median inside shop gave 36 weeks, the median submanufacturing shop, 26 weeks, of employment in the year. Consequently the more than 30,000 workers employed in these establishments experienced long layoffs as they divided the work among themselves, but no doubt many quit or were discharged to find difficulty in securing employment elsewhere. The case of seasonality in industry here presented is somewhat extreme, but the needle trades as a whole have been notorious for their long slack seasons.[4]

Not a few workers have no regular jobs in their callings; they get employment "catch-as-catch-can." The stock illustration of this is found in employment at the Liverpool Docks at an earlier time. A good illustration has been found at the New York docks also, where relatively few of the workers secure regular jobs. Most of the men needed in load-

---

[1] See pp. 27–39, for discussion of technological unemployment.

[2] For good data and an excellent analysis, see William Haber, *Industrial Relations in the Building Industry*, Chap. 4, "The Waste of Unemployment" (1930).

The leakage connected with the contract system, weather conditions, and other factors caused a loss of 31 per cent of possible working days in Philadelphia in 1920 (p. 98). In Boston, in 1921, the building tradesmen were idle about 25 per cent of the time (p. 101). The loss in Ohio for the years 1914–1924 was 19 per cent (p. 107).

[3] *Report of an Investigation*, dated March 10, 1925, p. 81.

[4] For good discussions of steps taken to overcome irregularity of employment consequent upon the seasonal character of different trades and industries, cf. Edwin S. Smith, *Stabilizing Seasonal Employment* (1931), Herman Feldman, *The Regularization of Employment* (1925), and L. Edie (ed.), *The Stabilization of Business* (1923).

ing and unloading vessels have been selected as they lined up on the
wharf at which the vessel docked. As many as were needed have been
selected and have worked for the comparatively short time the job
required. They have been paid off, and once more have taken their
places along with those who had been rejected, to await a call.[1]

When depression overtakes an industry, the numbers on the payroll
are reduced by discharges and indefinite layoffs (as well as by quittings),
and part-time operation and unemployment appear. Instances of this
occur even when industry in general is prosperous. For example, the
textile industry was greatly depressed in 1913 following upon the enactment of a new tariff law. Some years ago it was in a depressed condition, though there was much talk of prosperity in the country as a
whole. Then there are instances of industries shifting from old to new
centers, with depression, unemployment, and part-time work as outstanding facts in the old. Again, an industry may run its course and be marked
by extreme depression before the necessary readjustment is made. The
manufacture of buggies and "pleasure carriages" provides an example of
this.

But after all, the outstanding fact is that as a country because of the
adverse swing of the business cycle enters the trough of general depression, millions of workers lose their jobs and other millions are reduced to
the necessity of working part time. The statistical data presented in the
preceding section give sufficient detail relating to the frequency of such
occurrences, indicate some of the worst years, and show the great emphasis which must be given to this cause of unemployment. In the literature
relating to our problem general depression has naturally received the
greatest emphasis in explaining how unemployment develops. With
pardonable exaggeration, general industrial depression has frequently
been called "the cause of causes" of unemployment.[2] It is during general
depression that by far the largest numbers are involved, joblessness
stretches out over the longer periods, and the problem becomes most
acute.

It is for these reasons that men lose or quit their jobs. The number
out of jobs at any time, however, depends as well upon the difficulties
involved in finding new employment. When we ask, at any time, why
these unemployed men have not found suitable or acceptable employment, the answer may be that there are not enough jobs to go around. So
it is in time of general depression, not only because of a decrease in the
volume of production, but also because of the greater effort then made

---

[1] An excellent description of longshore employment conditions is the report by Boris
Stern, "Cargo Handling and Longshore Labor Conditions," U. S. Bureau of Labor
Statistics, *Bulletin 550* (1932).

[2] Paul H. Douglas and Aaron Director attribute to the cycle two-fifths of the
unemployment. See *The Problem of Unemployment*, p. 32.

to reduce costs by mechanization and the elimination of waste and the speeding up of workers who fear for their jobs. Applicants for jobs then greatly exceed the number who are hired. It may well be in concrete cases, and perhaps in England and the United States, say in 1933, that prevailing wages were too high to induce business enterprise unless inflation was resorted to, for unemployed labor will be absorbed in different quantities at different prices.[1] The disparity between the number of applicants and the number of jobs to be filled at prevailing wages may be as several to one.

In normal, and even in prosperous, years there is a large reserve army, owing to a number of facts. For one thing, the kinds of labor in effective demand are changing all the while. There may be a surplus of coal miners and a shortage of labor in the steel industry, a surplus of tailors and a shortage of plasterers, a surplus of common laborers and a shortage of masons, for labor is not readily or quickly adaptable. There is rarely depression so acute that there is not a shortage of some kinds of labor and never business expansion so great that there is not a surplus of workers in some occupations. For years the United States has had 200,000 more bituminous-coal miners than are needed, but what shall be done with them and what methods can be adopted to accomplish the end? The answer finally given to this practical question will be in the form of a program which will take much time to work out. Meanwhile there will be unemployed and underemployed coal miners even when a shortage of labor at good wages occurs in other occupations.

Again, the supply of labor is not readily adaptable with respect to place. Was it not Adam Smith who spoke of man as the luggage most difficult of all to move? The expense involved in moving, the importance of family and other ties are such that we almost as frequently read of a shortage of labor in one place and of unemployed men in another, as of a shortage in certain occupations and an excess in others.

Finally, it is nothing uncommon, in the absence of a good system of labor exchanges and an organized labor market, to find suitable jobs going begging for a time and men seeking just such work in a given city because the jobs are unknown to the unemployed men. The days lost because workers and suitable jobs close at hand are not readily brought together are not an unimportant part of the total loss sustained.

It is obvious that a number of the causes of loss of jobs by some are also causes of involuntary part-time work by others, of what we have called unemployment within employment. Strikes by, or lockouts of, coal miners, as in Great Britain in 1926, may result in much short-time work as well as in an increase in the number wholly unemployed because of lack of fuel and lack of demand for products consumed by miners.

[1] Of course, the same is true of prices of product or service that are kept too high by price maintenance by associations or monopolies.

Lack of orders for any reason, unfavorable weather conditions, depression in an industry, general depression, unbalanced sections in the plant, etc., are accompanied by part-time work by some as well as by total unemployment of others.

The causes of unemployment on the job have been indicated—poor routing of materials, unbalanced sections, and the like.

Such are the more immediate causes of unemployment. No doubt the enumeration is incomplete, but the causes enumerated do show both the complexity of the problem and in some degree the program required to meet it. They may be grouped so as to give these important factors: (a) the instability of business in general, giving rise to a tremendous problem in the trough of the business cycle; (b) depression in special lines due to adverse legislation, changing demand for products with changing styles, etc.; (c) fluctuations due to weather conditions and seasonal purchases; (d) the mortality of individual firms; (e) the turnover of labor, itself due to many things; (f) changing labor needs as affected by changing technology and other things and the lack of adaptability on the part of labor; (g) deficient plant management; and (h) an inadequately organized labor market. Or, for the sake of emphasis, these several immediate causes may be grouped in a more traditional and perhaps more useful way. Though Sir William Beveridge discusses personal and other factors, he concentrates his attention upon seasonal unemployment, cyclical fluctuation, and the labor reserve.[1] Seasonal unemployment is due to the fluctuations during the year caused by weather, the irregular flow of raw materials, etc., affecting production directly and to seasonal purchases (of clothing, automobiles, etc.). Factors in the cyclical fluctuation will be discussed presently. The turnover of labor, an inadequately organized labor market and various other of the immediate causes mentioned above are important in explaining the labor reserve in its swollen dimensions. Or, again, most of the causes may be grouped in discussions of seasonal unemployment, technological unemployment, and cyclical unemployment, as in Douglas' and Director's *Problem of Unemployment*. This is a more acceptable general grouping of causes in such a country as the United States, where changing technology is a very important cause.

The foregoing should have suggested some of the more immediate reasons why men lose their jobs and why they fail to get new ones. Back of these immediate causes, or else impinging upon them, however, lie others—causes emerging from conditions of the labor market, from the technical changes of a dynamic productive system, and from the relationships of different sets of prices. It is especially necessary that we here turn our attention to the "labor reserve," to so-called "technological

---

[1] Sir William Beveridge, *Unemployment, A Problem of Industry* (1930 ed.).

unemployment," to the fluctuations of the business cycle, and to the question of the wage level that will, at any given time, produce maximum employment and maximum labor income.

The Labor Reserve.—A certain "reserve" of labor is, obviously, one of the prerequisites of capitalistic economy. Industries expand or contract in accordance with the dictates of price considerations, and capacity so to expand in the short-run necessitates the immediate presence of workers who can be hired when the business situation dictates greater production. In this sense, if not in the Marxian sense,[1] a certain labor reserve is an inevitable accompaniment of the contemporary mode of producing and distributing economic goods. The causes of the irreducible minimum of labor reserve are to be found in the social arrangements of production, even though social responsibility for maintenance of this reserve has been accepted only in the most laggard fashion.

Yet, even though one grants the inevitability and economic necessity of a labor reserve, its proportions are agreed by all thoughtful students of the problem to be greatly in excess of the necessary minimum. Even during the labor shortage of the War period, as has already been noted, there were—in consequence of the inefficiently organized state of the labor market, the high turnover of employment, the inadaptability of jobless workers to the work available, the relative immobility of labor, and other factors—some 1,300,000 unemployed persons. Some of these causes can be more easily controlled than others, but the unnecessary portion of the labor reserve has always been tremendous.

In the United States, also, immigration prior to the beginning of the restrictive policy two decades ago, contributed to the size of the labor reserve. A correlation between economic conditions and the demand for labor in the United States, on the one hand, and the number of admissions and departures of the foreign-born, on the other, has frequently been noted. When business expanded rapidly, the number immigrating increased; when depression ensued, the number entering this country decreased and the number departing increased. Consequently the immigrant flow tended to equalize the supply of and the demand for labor in this country. Nevertheless, there was a lag in the adaptation of the immigrant stream to changing demand. The large influx was prone to continue for some time after depression set in; and, more important, it continued to flow in considerable dimensions because the migration to this country depended as much upon social, political, and economic conditions abroad and the activities of profit-seeking organizations as upon the opportunity for employment to be found here. In other words, the

---

[1] The Marxian analysis is, of course, based upon the proportions of constant and variable capital and the tendency—à la Karl Marx—for the latter (which is the only capital causing employment of labor) to become relatively less important, in consequence of the surplus value process.

adaptation was halting and only partial. Moreover, there were other phases of the matter of considerable importance.

On the one hand, immigration certainly lay behind a lack of economy of labor on the part of management in American industry. Discharges and indefinite layoffs and conditions giving rise to numerous quittings of jobs received less attention than they would have received at the hands of management had there been a smaller and dearer and less easily recruited labor supply and had its members been of native birth. As a result, the numbers dislocated and finding place in the "reserve" were increased. That this was distinctly true before the War has been shown by the changes introduced by management more recently. On the other hand, our immigration was accompanied by a more or less illogical distribution of labor as between localities and industries, and by numbers in excess of needs—a fact made possible by the ignorance and relatively low standards of living of some elements among the foreign-born. The fact that the immigrant additions to the labor supply did not distribute themselves readily with reference to the needs of industry does not require more than mere mention; it lay behind the programs advanced for a better distribution of the immigrants—programs made effective only to a limited extent. That in many instances low standards of living made it possible for managements to keep present in their communities numbers in excess of production needs was one of the important findings of the Immigration Commission.[1]

Technological Unemployment.—Technological unemployment, or the displacement of workers by improved methods[2] or machinery, has attracted the attention of economists and writers since the beginning of the industrial revolution, when textile workers in England rioted and smashed the new machinery which was throwing them out of work.[3] In postwar years the general interest in technological unemployment was kindled, especially in the United States, where a rapidly changing situation has obtained; and in the more recent years, perhaps because of the simplicity of the idea, many persons came to hold the view that technical improvements were the chief, if not the all-important, cause of unemployment. This idea became the more widespread for a time because of the well-directed publicity of the technocrats. The technocrats were able to point to spectacular examples of "machines doing the work of men," of generating plants with few or no attendants, of teletype, glass

---

[1] U. S. Immigration Commission, *Report* (1911), vol. 1, p. 530.

[2] The importance of nonmechanical improvements, which is commonly overlooked, is shown in the article by W. G. Roylance, "Significance of Non-mechanical Factors in Labor Productivity and Displacement," *Monthly Labor Review*, vol. 37 (November, 1933), pp. 1028–1038.

[3] Those aspects of the problem of technological unemployment most directly relevant to the proposal of a shorter work week are discussed in a preceding chapter. *Cf.* vol. I, Chap. IX.

bottle, and other labor-saving devices. Such examples, together with figures showing the increase in man-hour productivity in the automobile, rubber tire, electric bulb, rayon and textile, and some other industries[1] constituted the bulk of the evidence offered to show that modern methods and machinery had created a permanent army of unemployed men. The technocrats held that with the increasing rapidity of technical improvement and a corresponding increase of unemployment the price system would collapse, to be replaced by an engineer-led technocracy. To quote from the generally recognized leader of the movement, Howard Scott:

"There is a contention that labor which is thrown out of work in one industry is able to find employment in another. But figures covering a long period of years prove beyond contradiction that this is not the case. The high water mark of industrial employment in America was reached in 1918 and ever since that time, through all the great years of the boom, it has been steadily falling. As industry becomes more and more mechanized one door after another is shut to human labor. And all the while the Midas profit is put to producing more goods. In the end one sees the producers, fewer and fewer in number, engulfed in goods which they can neither sell nor use, bowed down with interest and dividend debts which they cannot pay."[2]

While such statements and evidence were convincing to a large part of the uncritical public, there was a strong reaction against them by other groups. The attitude toward technocracy of the trade unionists, particularly those affiliated with the American Federation of Labor, is of special interest. The trade unionists had long argued that machines made possible the shorter work week and eagerly seized upon the examples and evidence offered by the technocrats to bolster up their argument for a shorter week as the solution of the problem of unemployment. A fairly typical example of the reasoning employed appeared in an editorial in the *American Federationist:* "We can never again hope to give work to all who want it with the 48 hour week standard, nor even with the 44 hour week. . . . Even if industry were to resume its 1929 level millions of these unemployed could not find work again. . . . Nor do we expect mechanization to stop today."[3] The 1933 convention of the American

---

[1] For a summary of the productivity trends in the various industries in the United States, see the digest of the studies of the Bureau of Labor Statistics, published in the *Monthly Labor Review*, vol. 35 (November and December, 1932).

[2] Quoted, with permission of the publishers, from *Harper's*, January, 1933, p. 138. See, also, the same author's *Introduction to Technocracy* (1933), and the bibliography included therein.

[3] "The Thirty Hour Week Recovery Standard," *The American Federationist*, February, 1933, pp. 179–181. Of course, the position taken in the editorial quoted is true. David Weintraub and H. L. Posner have estimated that for unemployment in 1937 to drop to the level of 1929, the volume of production would have to be 20 per cent larger than it was in

Federation of Labor adopted by unanimous vote the report of the Committee on the shorter work day which read, in part, "By the same token and with the picture of depressed consuming power and workless millions before us, we insist that the time is here when labor hours must be sharply and promptly revised downward, and wage rates increased as the one and only practical answer to the machine age in which we live."[1]

At the same time the trade unionists were generally unable to accept the idea of the collapse of the capitalist price system, nor did they relish the role which would be assigned to them under technocracy. The result was that while they used similar arguments for their thirty-hour-week program, they ridiculed the technocratic remedies.[2]

It is noteworthy that the American Engineering Council also disclaimed allegiance to the engineers' Utopia and resolved that "The method of presentation has been marked by exaggerated, intolerant and extravagant claims. . . . Contrary to these claims there is nothing in technical improvements which entails social and economic maladjustments."[3]

This position is similar to that usually taken by orthodox economists, which is that, while technical improvements contribute to the volume of labor turnover, these do not necessarily create a permanent body of unemployed workers, and may even result in an expansion of employment. In normal times[4] the effect of introducing a technical improvement may be a temporary decrease in employment, but the long run adjustment may be an offsetting increase in the amount of product taken at the lower price made possible by the improvement, or a shift in consumers' demand and workers to some other product.

The argument of the "orthodox" economists, stated without the numerous minor qualifications, is simplicity itself. They point out, in the first place, that with the introduction of labor-saving devices, some of the displaced workers will be employed in the construction and maintenance of the machines. Obviously, however, this would not absorb all

---

1929 or nearly 55 per cent greater than in 1935. See, "Unemployment and Increasing Productivity," in *Technological Trends and National Policy* (National Resources Committee, 1937), p. 87.

[1] *Report of Proceedings*, p. 364.

[2] H. S. Piquet, "Technocracy: an Epitaph," *The American Federationist*, March, 1933, p. 257.

[3] "Resolution on Technocracy by the American Engineering Council," *Science*, vol. 77 (January, 1933), p. 81.

[4] Bouniation contends that even in times of depression technical improvements do not result in any real unemployment, but, on the contrary, stimulate recovery and employment. Mentor Bouniation, "Technical Progress and Unemployment," *International Labour Review*, vol. 27 (March, 1933), pp. 327–348. *Cf.* Emil Lederer's reply in the July issue of the same periodical. See also J. M. Clark, *Economics of Planning Public Works* (1935).

the displaced workers or there would be little or no incentive to introduce the machine.

Technological improvements, or labor-saving devices, lower the cost of production of a commodity, and in a competitive situation producers are forced to pass these gains on to consumers in the form of lowered prices. If the demand is highly elastic, the number of units of the commodity taken from the market will increase substantially and thus bring about a corresponding expansion of production. In addition, if the number of units of the commodity taken from the market increases, there will be an increased demand for raw materials and an indirect expansion of employment in industries producing them.

Where demand is inelastic and consumers spend a smaller total amount on the commodity at the lower price, the balance or saving in purchasing power will be transferred to other commodities or invested and thus directly or indirectly cause an expansion of employment. In the case of monopoly, the reasoning runs, there will probably be an increase in profits, rather than a reduction in price corresponding to the reduction in costs. This does not upset the argument, however, for the monopolist either spends or invests the increased profits, and in either case employment is created. Since purchasing power is not destroyed by these transfers, the total amount of employment will not be decreased.[1]

The doctrine of the technocrats is not borne out by experience, and this is only less true of the related doctrines to the effect that technological change under the price system leads inevitably to a larger volume of unemployment unless there is a sharp reduction in the hours of work so as to divide up the limited volume of employment. Were the technocratic doctrine a correct one, a large fraction of the population of the United States would have been unemployed for decades, for there has been great technological change, thus greatly decreasing the number of man-hours required to produce a given physical product. As has been noted, however, save for periods of depression, the number of persons gainfully occupied has not only increased tremendously, but has also, with change in age distribution and the increasing percentage of women in employment outside of the home, been an increased proportion of the total population ten years of age or over.[2] Even in manufacture, from which the examples of excessive displacement have generally been drawn, the number of wage earners was practically the same in 1929 as it had been ten years before.[3]

The basic fallacy in the reasoning of those who believe that technological changes must permanently and greatly reduce the volume of

---

[1] For a more detailed analysis of this reasoning, see Paul H. Douglas, "Technological Unemployment," *American Federationist*, vol. 37 (August, 1930), pp. 923–950.

[2] See vol. I, Chap. I, table in footnote, p. 28, and discussion relating thereto. The percentage of the population ten years of age or over, gainfully occupied was 44.3 in 1870, 49.2 in 1890, 50.3 in 1920, and 49.5 in 1930.

[3] See vol. I, Chap. I, Table 1, p. 6.

employment lies in the overemphasis placed upon a limited market. The "1929 level" of production and consumption is frequently regarded as the peak. Any increase in technical efficiency since that year would therefore reduce the number of workers necessary to attain that volume of output, unless hours were reduced, and would also limit purchasing power.[1] Of course, calculations made on such a theory may have merit in estimating the probable trend of employment during a period of a few years, but such reasoning overlooks the obvious expansion which has taken place and which will take place through the growth of old industries and the appearance of new industries and service occupations, provided suitable conditions obtain. The suitable conditions involve proper price and wage relationships, and investment opportunity. There is no inherent reason why improved technology should not release human energy for other useful social activities, new types of consumption, and a rising standard of living.

Technological change does, however, involve readjustments, for it does not affect all branches of production uniformly, and consumers' demands for different products and services change with price as well as with fashion and total individual capacity to spend. As shown in some detail elsewhere,[2] different pursuits have waxed or waned as the years have passed. This may be expected to happen in the future.[3] Shifts in the relative growth of pursuits present problems to investors and workers. And, as will be developed at some length presently, important technological changes may fall heavily upon a given group or groups of workers and involve great sacrifice.

Of course, the entire value of the national product is shared out among the agents involved in producing it. There is a dollar of purchasing power for every dollar of product. This fact is incorporated in the classical doctrine. The problem is, however, to show precisely how, with increased efficiency involving displacement of workers, all displaced workers will be absorbed into the productive process. This is difficult to do with certainty.[4]

Save in the case of monopoly, the orthodox doctrine relies upon competition to lower price to the extent of reductions in costs resulting from

---

[1] An example of this is found in Stuart Chase's article, "What Hope for the Jobless?" *Current History*, November, 1933, pp. 129–136.

[2] Vol. I, Chap. I.

[3] It appears that the United States has reached the point in its development where the capital-goods industries will become of decreasing importance in comparison with the service industries. Technological change has been more marked in the capital-goods industries than elsewhere. Hence, it is likely that, other things equal, changing technology will become a relatively less rather than a relatively greater cause of unemployment. All the while it should be held in mind that as new equipment is displacing workers at the point where used, the manufacture of that equipment is sustaining or adding to employment in the capital-goods industry involved.

[4] For a penetrating discussion of this subject, see Alvin H. Hansen, *Economic Stabilization in an Unbalanced World* (1932), Chap. X.

improvements. It appears to be true, however, that many retail prices of the products of what are regarded as competitive industries are sticky. The element of friction may be large and limit the gain in consumer purchasing power through lowered price of product. It is assumed, however, that any enhanced profit, whether realized in monopoly-controlled industry or from sticky prices, is spent on current consumption, or is saved and invested. If enhanced profit is spent, it will of course be accompanied by some change in the direction demand takes, which will reduce the amount of labor needed at certain points and increase the amount needed at other points. Adjustments will be necessary and these may not be easily or quickly made. However this may be, these shifts and transfers do not prove that additional labor will be needed in the total situation. That might be called for, it would appear, by additional investment in industry or would be induced by cheaper labor because cheaper labor would be used more extensively, the cost of capital remaining the same.

But suppose that larger profits are not spent but saved. Whether savings are invested by being turned back into the industry in which costs have been reduced by technological change, or are invested otherwise, or are not invested at all depends upon how active business enterprise is and upon investment conditions. If they are plowed back into the business, the savings invested will be largely wasted, because of nonexpansion of demand for the product the price of which has not been reduced, at any rate not to the extent of reductions made in costs. If, on the other hand, savings come into the general capital market, the tendency is to enlarge and to ease credit and to reduce the rate of loan interest. Except in time of business uncertainty, this would encourage borrowing for the re-equipment of plants and the expansion of business. In so far as the borrowed funds were used to introduce more or better appliances, this would have the effect of displacement of some workers where those appliances were used while creating additional business and employment in capital-goods industries. Next, it is to be pointed out that in the use of savings there is the possibility that with a lower rate of return to be had in the domestic market, an outflow of capital to other countries may occur. Finally, in connection with what may happen in the money market, the policies of and the control exercised by the government may be important.

Additional investments may assist in absorbing displaced men without any change in wage rates. But, as observed above, lowered wage rates, other things equal, would assist, for lower wages would make it good business to employ more labor and less capital. However, fortunately or unfortunately, wages are among the stickiest of prices, especially where labor is organized. Inasmuch as the relationship of wage rates

to the volume of unemployment will be discussed presently, this phase
of the subject may be temporarily dismissed.[1]

Thus, the process by which workers displaced by technological change
are absorbed is not a simple one or one the outcome of which is certain.
In any event, essential factors take time to work out. The uncertainty
and the length of the run involved in any case do not warrant the optimism which accompanies the orthodox doctrine.

It is to be added, moreover, that the problem of absorbing workers
displaced by technological change, and especially the skilled workers who
are most frequently adversely involved, differs from that of absorbing
workers unemployed due to business recession. The latter have for the
most part to wait for general business recovery and to tide themselves
over somehow. Those displaced by new appliances (or waning of their
industry), on the other hand, all too frequently must make an occupational
shift, involving great sacrifice. Of course, a worker displaced during
boom times may be immediately re-employed, and even at a higher wage.
This is true particularly of unskilled laborers who shift from jobs in
which they have no particular advantage to others. The experience of
skilled men is likely to be different unless the industry affected by
technological change expands so rapidly as to offset the increase in efficiency or unless the hours of work are reduced so as to offset the saving
in labor. A new technique may render useless the special skill of many
workers who over a period of years have enjoyed a high income because
of that skill. They are prone to look long for the kind of employment
to which they are accustomed, and at the wage rate being paid those in
such employment. Perhaps they are union men, and this will cause them
to hold out the longer. Eventually they may be able to make a shift to
another occupation suitable in view of their experience, abilities, and
standard of living, but frequently they are forced to accept what they
can get, and, not infrequently, this is common labor.

Those who do not appreciate the many factors affecting the rate
of absorption of those displaced by technological changes and who con-
ceive of the process as a simple one are of course inclined to impute to the
technological factor relatively small responsibility for the volume of
unemployment at any given time. This raises the question of how
important the technological factor is relative to other causes of unemploy-

---

[1] The trend of prices as well as wage rates have an effect on the number unemployed
because of technological change. If prices are rising and wages do not rise to the same
extent, there is less reason than there would otherwise be to invest in superior appliances
and to employ less labor. On the other hand, profit margins would be larger, these accompanied by optimism, and employers would be more likely to scrap old and to introduce the
new labor-displacing equipment. When prices are falling and wages are sticky, the converse tendencies would operate.

ment. And this question cannot of course be answered without some method of measurement.

Professor W. I. King, after an examination of the 1930 census data, concluded that "an allowance of 3 or 4 per cent (of the total number unemployed) for technological unemployment . . . would seem to be an outside limit, the most probable amount of this type of unemployment being far smaller."[1] But this conclusion is open to question on the ground that the method of obtaining the census data was not reliable. The enumerators asked the worker the cause of his unemployment and it was presumed that his answer was correct. Frequently, however, technological change has been the ultimate cause of displacements, but the displaced victims are not aware of the fact. During periods of prosperity and rising prices, many firms introduce labor-saving machines and hence do not find it necessary to hire as many new workers as they otherwise would in a period of expanding output and sales, but the expansion of demand makes unnecessary the laying off of employees when the technical innovations are instituted. When business falls off, however, more men lose their jobs than would have if machinery making possible a given output with fewer workers had not been introduced. To the workers and to the community the cause of unemployment seems to be "lack of work"—as it of course is in the immediate sense—but the ultimate cause was that technical improvements introduced during a period of prosperity made possible maintenance of the depression volume of production with a smaller work force than would otherwise have been necessary. Or, a plant may have been closed down because of competitive pressure from another company which introduced technological improvements. In this case, again, the imputed cause will not be technological change but "depression." On the other hand, technical change is sometimes erroneously believed to be the responsible factor. After an investigation of unemployment in the printing trades, Elizabeth F. Baker wrote, "Many men who felt themselves victims of technical change were found to be out of work for other reasons, such as the migration or merging of plants."[2] Any particular case of unemployment may be due to a combination of factors, both direct and indirect, which a layman would not be competent to determine.

In addition to the above, it may be observed that in the use of census data care must be exercised lest the size of the problem be underestimated. The use of broad occupational classifications tends to obscure the shifts within the class. For example, in transportation and communication

---

[1] W. I. King, "The Relative Volume of Technological Unemployment," *Journal of the American Statistical Association, Proceedings*, vol. 28 (March, 1933), p. 39. Critical discussion by F. B. Garver is included.

[2] "Unemployment and Technical Progress in Commercial Printing," *American Economic Review*, vol. 20 (September, 1930), pp. 442-466.

the total number of gainfully occupied persons increased by nearly 750,000 between 1920 and 1930. A subdivision of this classification, however, reveals that while the number of chauffeurs and truck drivers was increasing from 285,000 to 972,000, the number of draymen and teamsters was declining from 420,000 to 111,000. Within a decade close to 300,000 workers were forced to find new employment.[1] It might be suggested that the displaced teamsters could find employment as truck drivers, but driving a team does not wholly fit a worker to drive a truck or car. The older men particularly would find it difficult to compete for many of these jobs against younger men with better vision and a general knowledge of mechanics.

Nor does the arduous method of case studies provide a certain method of measuring the extent of technological unemployment. This is obvious from what has been said above. Yet that method leads one to the conviction that the amount of unemployment due to technological change is by no means small.

In completing this statement of the problem of technological unemployment, a few concrete cases and studies may be briefly noted in order to present the matter more realistically and to illustrate some of the observations made above.[2]

The advances in technique in the manufacture of rubber tires have been startling and have frequently been assigned as the explanation of the unemployment in the industry subsequent to 1929. According to a study made by the United States Bureau of Labor Statistics,[3] between 1914 and 1931 the index of man-hour productivity had increased from 100 to 681, while because of a better product, tire renewals for registered cars had decreased from 3.93 to 1.43. Nevertheless the index of man-hours worked rose from 100 in 1914 to 249 in 1929. The explanation is found in the fact that the number of autos purchased increased rapidly, and this fact was, in turn, no doubt, due to improved cars being manufactured and sold at small profit per car. It was not until acute depression developed that man-hours worked and the number of wage earners fell off—the former from the index figure of 249 in 1929 to 150 in 1931, the number of workers from 83,263 to 48,341.

Less comforting, but nevertheless not presenting as great difficulty as many others, was the introduction of the linotype. Typesetting prior to the introduction of the linotype was essentially the same process as in the sixteenth century. After 1887 the linotype machine began to

[1] Fifteenth Census of the United States, 1930, vol. 5, *Population*, Table I.

[2] A wealth of examples may be found in Harry Jerome, *Mechanization in Industry* (1934). See, also, National Resources Committee, *Technological Trends and National Policy* (1937).

[3] See "Labor Productivity in the Tire Industry," in *Monthly Labor Review*, vol. 35 (1932), pp. 1252–1268.

supplant hand composition, each machine having the capacity to set as much type as four hand compositors. There were several factors, however, which tended to reduce the actual amount of displacement below the potential. One of these was that it took some time to attain the skill and speed the operators later acquired. More important was the farsighted policy adopted by the International Typographical Union, which did not oppose the introduction of machinery, but insisted that the operators should be skilled printers. The result was that many of the hand compositors who would otherwise have become unemployed were given an opportunity to learn the machine and became operators. The older hand compositors, however, were subject to a considerable amount of displacement. Generally they were not able to secure employment as machine operators, and there was a surplus of the particular kind of skill which they possessed.[1] During the years 1894, 1895, and 1896 linotype machines were introduced at a very rapid rate and unemployment and distress among printers became acute. Moreover, this was aggravated by the general depression in industry. Competition in the newspaper and job printing industries was strong, however, with the result that much of the economy of machine operation was passed on to the consumers. The demand for printed matter increased so greatly after 1897 that the expansion of the amount sold more than offset the displacing power of machines.[2] The machine was a factor making for a larger printing industry, restoring and then increasing employment for compositors. Other workers in the expanded industry secured great gain.

The introduction of machinery into the glass-bottle industry illustrates the importance of the influence of the type of machinery and the rapidity of its introduction on the volume of employment. The early semi-automatic machines were at first relatively crude affairs, used only in making wide-mouthed bottles and jars, and were only gradually improved and introduced, giving the hand blowers time to adapt themselves to the changed technique, either by shifting to other work not affected by machines or by becoming machine operators. The first of these methods was the more successful, partly because the demand for glass bottles between 1899 and 1906 expanded so rapidly that there was a constant scarcity of hand blowers. The most serious problem for the hand blowers, however, did not appear until after 1905 when the Owens Bottle Machine was introduced. This machine was automatic, did not require skilled operators, and turned out a superior product with tremendous saving of labor time. The machines were therefore introduced rapidly with the result that between 1905 and 1917 the number of hand

---

[1] G. E. Barnett, "Machinery and Labor," *Quarterly Journal of Economics*, vol. 40 (1925), pp. 119–120.

[2] G. E. Barnett, *Chapters on Machinery and Labor* (1926), pp. 4–8.

blowers declined from 9,000 to 2,000. Only a few of the displaced workers were able to get work as machine operators since the hand blowers had no advantage over operators recruited from the unskilled, available at the unskilled wage. Furthermore, despite an increase of 50 per cent in the demand for glass bottles, the number of machine operators between 1905 and 1917 increased only from 1,000 to 2,000 men.[1]

A few studies made of displaced workers may be drawn upon to indicate the loss of time when business is good and the losses other than of wages while unemployed.

In the early summer of 1928, Robert J. Myers made a survey of 370 cutters who had been selected and dismissed[2] from cutting rooms during the years 1921–1926. All of the men had had at least a year and a half in which to find new employment. Some of them had returned to cutting or work similar to cutting, but of the 278 men who had not done so, 42 were not employed and 6 of these had been unable to find any regular job since leaving the table. The time lost by the men before finding other employment varied widely: 28.9 per cent had lost no time, 11.3 per cent had lost one month or less, 23.4 per cent had lost between two and four months, 32.9 per cent had lost six months or more, and 17.9 per cent had lost twelve months or more. The weighted average time lost was five and one-fifth months.[3] The jobs the dismissed cutters had held or were holding at the time interviewed included skilled and unskilled, sales work on commission, self-employment, etc., but most of it far removed in character from the cutting to which they had been apprenticed and in which they had become experienced. Of 276 in jobs supplying data, 84 were earning more than, and 64 were earning approximately the same as, they had earned as cutters, but 128, or 46.4 per cent, were earning less —in some cases very much less. Of 272 who had preferences, 166 wished to return to the cutting table.

The Myers study was made when the volume of employment was relatively high and therefore the amount of time and income the workers lost would average less than in depression periods. Just at the beginning of the last depression another study of the effects of displacement was afforded by the reorganization of the United States Rubber Company and the closing of its Hartford and New Haven plants.[4] These shut-

[1] *Ibid.*, p. 92.

[2] In the clothing industry in Chicago the workers have security of tenure and have a right to share work in slack seasons, including depression periods. Partly because of improved methods introduced during the 1920's the number of cutters became very excessive in some of the shops. Hence the dismissals, in most cases with payment of dismissal wage.

[3] Robert J. Myers, "Occupational Readjustment of Displaced Skilled Workmen," *Journal of Political Economy*, vol. 37 (1929), pp. 473–489.

[4] See Ewan Clague and W. J. Cooper, "Readjustments of Workers Displaced by Plant Shutdowns," *Quarterly Journal of Economics*, vol. 45 (1931), pp. 309–346. Though these

downs involved the permanent layoff of nearly 800 workers in New Haven and more than 1,100 in Hartford. The New Haven plant was closed in April, 1929, and the survey made in March, 1930. The Hartford plant was closed in September, 1929, and the survey was made in July, 1930.

In Hartford, out of 534 men interviewed, 83 had not found any employment and the average time lost for the entire group was 4.33 months. In New Haven 70 per cent of the men and 77 per cent of the women were working at some job at the end of eleven months. For the entire working force in New Haven the average time lost was 4.38 months (out of a possible working period of eleven months). Sex seemed to make little difference in ability to find jobs, but age was an important factor. There was a marked increase in the time lost by both the older men and women. Of all men over forty-five years of age actively seeking work, only 43 per cent had found employment within the specified time, while of those under forty-five, over 71 per cent were in this fortunate class. The corresponding percentages for women were 44 and 67. Of the twenty-eight New Haven men who had never found work, no less than twenty-two were over forty-five years of age. In Hartford the best record in finding employment was made by men twenty-five to thirty-four years of age. The best record made was by women in New Haven fifteen to twenty-four years of age.

The survey indicated that not only was a large amount of working time lost by the displaced workers, but that the newer positions tended to be less remunerative. The typical male worker in the year immediately following the shutdown suffered a loss of 37 per cent in working time and an additional loss of 20 per cent in wage rates, making a total decrease of about 45 per cent in annual earnings; the typical female worker lost 40 per cent of working time, and 24 per cent in wage rates, making a total annual loss of about 50 per cent.

The Hartford plant closed six months after that in New Haven and just before the crash in the stock market in October, 1929, precipitated a general decline in employment opportunities. It would be expected therefore that Hartford workers would, on the average, be unemployed for longer periods than those in New Haven. Actually the figures for average time lost show little difference. This is explained at least in part by the fact that in New Haven the public was generally apathetic to the problems of the workers, while in Hartford the city government, the local manufacturers' association, and social agencies cooperated in a vigorous re-employment drive. The fact that the average time lost for the Hartford group was 4.33 months testifies both as to the worthwhileness of the drive and to the need for some more effective means of meeting the problems of technological unemployment.

---

displacements resulted from plant shutdowns rather than from technological change, the problem presented and the time required for readjustment are the same.

All of these studies indicated that workers past forty-five years of age had more difficulty, on the average, in making readjustments and finding satisfactory employment than had the younger workers. They further indicated that the burden rested very unequally upon different workers and often completely disrupted their accustomed standard of living. This fact explains the strenuous opposition of some unions to the introduction of technical improvements and the widespread fear of such changes. It is indeed of little comfort to such workers that in the long run the industry may expand and employ more workers than ever, or that somewhere in the economic system consumer purchasing power is causing a compensating increase of employment. In the United States there has been no generally used method of spreading the burden of these losses. Instead it has rested largely upon the workers displaced and upon them very unevenly.

There are several ways in which the volume of technological unemployment could be reduced, or the adjustments of displaced workers made easier. Careful planning of the rate of introduction of machinery might permit more time in which to make adjustments. This might be found to be worth while, even if the rate of improvement in technical efficiency were slowed down temporarily. A coordinated system of employment exchanges, with vocational guidance and training, reduces the time lost between jobs, minimizes mistakes in retraining, and facilitates the shifting of workers from declining to expanding occupations. A quitting wage, as a supplement to unemployment insurance, would reduce the hardships of temporary unemployment and increase the mobility of labor as well as discourage too rapid introduction of technical changes.[1]

Cyclical Unemployment.—Most interest attaches to the business cycle as a cause of unsteady employment, for it is during the depression phase of the cycle that the problem of unemployment becomes most acute. As already noted, general depression has frequently been referred to as "the cause of causes of unemployment." From the time of Rodbertus the socialists have made much of it in their indictment of capitalism; for more than twenty years a great amount of thought has been expended by economists in trying to find an explanation for the business cycle and means of bringing it under control.[2]

In explaining depression periods many writers have merely connected them with the effects of war, with undue speculation and bad investments, and similar specific causes which do not emphasize the self-generating

[1] For shorter hours in this connection, see discussions in vol. I, Chap. IX, pp. 497–516, and in this volume, Chap. II, pp. 118–120.

[2] For a more adequate, yet summary, discussion of business-cycle theory, see the article and bibliography by Wesley C. Mitchell on "Business Cycles," *Encyclopaedia of the Social Sciences*, vol. 3, pp. 92–106.

character of the business cycle. One such physical explanation was advanced by Jevons, who thought that regular variations in solar radiations were reflected in periodic crop failures and abundant harvests.[1]

While most economists who have studied the business cycle agree that crop failures, legislative changes, wars, and similar events may play an important role in precipitating or determining the volume of industrial fluctuations, they are emphatically of the opinion that such explanations are not adequate. There is now abundant evidence that there are recurrent, if not periodic, changes in general business activity, and general agreement that during the course of the cycle, from prosperity to crisis, to depression, to revival and to prosperity again, different factors in our economic life change with a fairly regular sequence. It is even fairly generally agreed that changes in some factors usually occur before others, or are greater in magnitude. Wages are thus generally recognized as being more "sticky" than profits, retail prices more sluggish than wholesale.

Beyond this recognition of certain indexes of business conditions there is little agreement as to which factors initiate changes in others, which factors are basic, which can be controlled, and which it would be desirable socially to control. This veritable chaos of opinions and programs persists despite the efforts of such writers as Pigou,[2] Mitchell,[3] and Hansen.[4]

Classification of cycle theories is difficult, not only because of the complex nature of the business cycle itself, but because many of the theories differ chiefly in the emphasis which they place upon the role of one or two factors. One possible classification suggested by Professor Hansen[5] divides the various theories into three schools, with subclasses: (1) The capitalist-economy school, (2) the exchange-economy school, (3) the money-economy school. The socialists, following the lines laid down by Rodbertus[6] and Marx,[7] have long argued that the business cycle is inherent in the capitalist system of production and that periodic crises are the inevitable result of the capitalist's failure to pay the worker the full value of his labor. The only remedy, they hold, is the complete abolition of the profit system and the substitution of a planned, cooperative economy. Hobson[8] also emphasizes the maldistribution of income as the prime cause of crises. Orthodox socialists, as well as some who do

---

[1] W. S. Jevons, "The Periodicity of Commercial Crises and Its Physical Explanation" and "Commercial Crises and Sun-spots," reprinted in his *Investigations in Currency and Finance* (1884), pp. 206–243.

[2] A. C. Pigou, *Industrial Fluctuations* (1929).

[3] W. C. Mitchell, *Business Cycles: The Problem and Its Setting* (1927).

[4] A. H. Hansen, *Business Cycle Theory* (1927).

[5] *Ibid.*, Chap. 1.

[6] J. K. Rodbertus, *Overproduction and Crises* (translated 1898).

[7] Karl Marx, *Capital*.

[8] J. A. Hobson, *The Economics of Unemployment* (1922).

not accept the labor theory of value, the doctrine of surplus value, and the constant and variable capital analysis, have contended that all the factors of the business cycle are traceable to individual entrepreneurship and the profit system. In the sense that the business cycle is a phenomenon of capitalistic organization, this contention is, of course, a mere truism. Ordinarily, however, the socialist indictment is predicated upon the notion that an "undue" proportion of the value product of industry goes to property owners, with consequent "general overproduction." Since the days of Jean Baptiste Say,[1] this thesis has had little standing among "classical" or "orthodox" economists, but among the dissenters and critics it has both had standing and commanded reverence. Another large group of writers has emphasized technological changes, inventions and discoveries, uncertainties due to errors in judgment, changes in consumer demand, excessive optimism or pessimism, and a variety of other contingencies the majority—although not all—of which are peculiar to the capitalistic system of production.[2]

The school explaining the business cycle in terms of money and credit fluctuations usually proposes, as a solution, some form of price control.[3] They differ among themselves, it is true, as to which set of prices should be controlled in order to maintain economic balance. Professor Fisher, for example, would control the general price level by changes in the dollar price of gold; Mr. Keynes seeks variation in the rate of interest; while Professor Pigou suggests that if the supply of labor

[1] *A Treatise on Political Economy* (1798). Say, the French exponent and, to a certain extent, simplifier of the economics of Adam Smith, held that production and demand are merely the obverse and reverse of the same phenomenon, and that therefore a fundamental disparity between them is impossible. The reasoning was based largely upon the conditions of a simple barter society. If all produce more goods, all will have more purchasing power. Exchange ratios between goods may change, owing to differing elasticities of demand, but there can be no such thing as general overproduction. As applied to a system where some persons purchase the labor power of other persons and have legal claim upon the product, and where the complications of money and credit must be taken into account, the classical doctrine implies that purchasing power is transferable but not destructible. The aggregate of demand remains the same, irrespective of whether the proportions going to capital and labor are 50:50 or 60:40, respectively. The implicit assumption of almost instantaneous shifts in purchasing power, underlying this conclusion, should be apparent.

[2] Some of the writers who have stressed, but not exclusively, one or more of these factors are Gustav Cassel (*The Theory of Social Economy*, 1924), D. H. Robertson (*Banking Policy and the Price Level*, 1926), A. Aftalion (*Les Crises Periodiques de Surproduction*, 1913), and A. C. Pigou (*Industrial Fluctuations*, 1929).

[3] Among others, R. G. Hawtrey (*Trade and Credit*, 1928), Irving Fisher (*Booms and Depressions*, 1932, and numerous other writings), J. M. Keynes (*A Treatise on Money*, 1932, *The Means to Prosperity*, 1933, and *The General Theory of Employment, Interest, and Money*, 1936), and F. A. Hayek (*Monetary Theory and the Trade Cycle*, 1933, and *Prices and Production*, 1931). Perhaps needless to say, the fact that these economists have all emphasized the monetary and credit aspects of the business cycle does not mean that their analyses are identical. They are here grouped together merely because of their emphasis upon money and credit factors.

were sufficiently elastic, industrial fluctuations and unemployment could be eliminated. Whether these remedies would be effective is still a subject of debate, and whether it would be "good social policy" to attempt such controls is still more controversial.[1]

Wages and Unemployment.—Such writers as Rodbertus and Karl Marx held that the cause of business depressions lies in the fact that the workers do not receive the full product of industry. The workers cannot, therefore, provide the market necessary for the goods produced; the accumulation of unused goods finally chokes the industrial machine and depression continues until the surplus is cleared away. Historically unrelated, but in substance related nevertheless, to the views of such writers as these is a theory widely proclaimed in the United States, Australia, and elsewhere in recent years by the spokesmen of organized labor to the effect that if high wages do not prevail and if wages do not increase in proportion to the productivity of industry, the market for the product will be limited and impaired, with the result that industry will inevitably be slowed down. The "Reconstruction Program" of the American Federation of Labor stated:[2]

"Unemployment is due to underconsumption. Underconsumption is caused by low or insufficient wages. Just wages will prevent industrial stagnation and lessen periodical unemployment.

"Give the workers just wages and their consuming capacity is correspondingly increased. A man's ability to consume is controlled by the wages received. Just wages will create a market at home which will far surpass any market that may exist elsewhere and will lessen unemployment."

In the report of the Executive Council in 1932 the American Federation of Labor doctrine of wages, consuming power in prosperity and depression was developed at length.[3] "The payment in right proportion of wages, salaries and dividends by each individual operating unit . . . helps to determine whether our economic life as a whole shall go forward with balance in continued growth and prosperity, or be wrecked periodically by business depression."[4] Between 1922 and 1929, wages and salaries, it was said, had increased 45.5 per cent, dividends, 134.1 per cent. Of dividends in 1929, 86.5 per cent were paid to persons who had an investment of at least $100,000. What was the result of this piling

---

[1] The matters here touched upon are dealt with by E. F. M. Durbin in his penetrating volume on *Purchasing Power and Trade Depression: A Critique of Under-Consumption Theories* (1933).

[2] American Federation of Labor Reconstruction Program, conveniently found in David J. Saposs, *Readings in Trade Unionism* (1927), p. 47.

[3] *Report* of the Executive Council of the American Federation of Labor to the Fifty-second Annual Convention (1932), pp. 2–12.

[4] *Ibid.*, p. 5.

up of excess income in the hands of a few? New capital issues between 1922 and 1929 increased 213 per cent; producing capacity expanded beyond the capacity of consumers to buy, for wage and small-salaried workers buy 83 per cent[1] of all goods sold to consumers. Workers' buying power is vital to national welfare; industry depends upon it; the shortage of workers' income was the brake which checked our economic progess in 1929.

This thesis that wages of the workers have been insufficient to absorb the product of industry, with consequent accumulation of stocks and reduction in production, has had its manifestations not only in trade-union wages and hours policies; it was also espoused during the 1920's by no negligible number of business men, and it played an important part in the wages and hours policies of the Federal Government during the depression of the 1930's, and especially during and after 1933.[2] Some of the implications of this doctrine, and of the antithetical theory that maintenance of wage rates during depressions will only postpone recovery and increase unemployment, should be probed at this point.

The trade union position on the matter of wage-rate maintenance during depressions is, of course, one application of the "overproduction"

---

[1] This figure is, of course, much too high, but is the estimate used by the Executive Council in its statement of the case.

[2] In passing, it may be observed that however unsatisfactory our depression experience, both in maintaining or raising wage rates and in slashing them, has been to those who would like verification or refutation in practical experience of the doctrine that maintenance of wage rates will enable a people to ride through a depression quickly, this experience has probably prevented an enlargement of the quantum of vicious *post hoc, propter hoc* reasoning with which discussion of economic problems is cursed. There is even a certain irony in the situation. When the stock-market crash of October, 1929, heralded the beginning of the great depression, the policy of the national administration—a policy to be effectuated by peaceful persuasion—was that of having wage rates maintained, in order that "sustained consumer purchasing power" might prevent any great downswing of business. Had the depression ended, say, during 1930, the American people probably would have been convinced of the ultimate economic validity of the maintenance-of-wage-rates doctrine, and it would have been entrenched in their economic thinking for a generation to come. But the depression did not end in 1930. Then, as the depression continued and deepened, the wage cuts which many believed from the start to be inevitable occurred. Had the depression ended, say, in 1932, the American people probably would have been convinced that when depression appears and commodity prices drop, wage rates must be reduced to stimulate recovery—that in the earlier policy of wage-rate maintenance they had been following an economic friar's lantern. But the depression did not end in 1932. Then, in 1933, the gigantic governmental policy of shortening hours, maintaining or increasing hourly rates of pay, and increasing total labor money income was instituted. (*Cf.* vol. I, pp. 356–370 where the theory and operation of the NRA are discussed in some detail.) Had a more substantial volume of recovery quickly followed institution of this program, popular thinking would probably have accepted the high wage gospel, in spite of earlier experience conducive to skepticism about it. But, as was indicated in vol. I (*cf.* pp. 359–361), the post-1933 experience hardly affords basis for allegation that the purchasing-power theory was demonstrated to be sound.

(or "underconsumption") hypothesis.[1] A convenient mode of procedure will be, first, to set forth the position of "orthodox" economists and orthodox economic theory toward this hypothesis; second, to examine somewhat critically the realism of the assumptions underlying the orthodox treatment of the doctrine; third—and of course not separable from the foregoing tasks—to evaluate the reasoning upon which is based the conclusion that the trade-union position respecting wage maintenance during depressions is a mistaken one; and, finally, to suggest what may be some of the institutional impediments to a realization of the beneficial effects alleged to ensue from reduction of wage rates during depressions.

To no little extent, the position of orthodox economists appears to have been based upon the principle enunciated in 1798 by Jean Baptiste Say—that production and demand are merely the obverse and reverse of the same phenomenon, and that therefore a fundamental disparity between them is impossible. If, in that simple barter economy that seems to be at the base of so much of the reasoning of classical economics, all produce more, all will have more goods with which to purchase the products made and vended by others. Exchange ratios may shift, to be sure, owing to differing elasticities of demand, and a reshifting of capital and labor as among different productive activities may result in consequence of the tendency toward equality of returns in the various lines; but there can be no such thing as general overproduction.[2] Put

---

[1] The other major application of the hypothesis is, of course, that made to periods of increasing production, rising prices, and expanding profits. If wage rates advance sufficiently during such periods, according to the trade-union theory, and labor's share of the value product of industry increases, a situation in which goods are produced that cannot be bought because of insufficient purchasing power in the hands of the consumers, with consequent turning of the period of prosperity into one of depression, will be avoided.

[2] The theory that business cycles and their accompanying unemployment are due to faulty distribution and "oversaving" has been offered with many variations. As is mentioned elsewhere in this chapter, the notion was fundamental in the analyses of Rodbertus and Marx. Among contemporary economists, John A. Hobson and W. T. Foster and Waddill Catchings have been outstanding proponents of different versions of the overproduction theory. (Cf. Hobson's The Economics of Unemployment and Foster and Catchings': Money; Profits; The Dilemma of Thrift; Business Without a Buyer; and The Road to Plenty.) Hobson's explanation is in substance that suggested in the generalized reference to the overproduction doctrine, as given above. The wealthy, unable to consume a large part of their income, reinvest; the output of industry increases in consequence of the resulting increase in capital equipment; consumers are unable to buy the larger output except at lower prices; prices collapse; and business depression ensues. Foster and Catchings also emphasize the alleged failure of consumer demand to keep pace with the production of goods, but they do not regard inequality in the distribution of income as being the sole cause of this failure. According to them, the difficulty arises from two main sources: (1) Industry fails to disburse to consumers—i.e., to wage earners and investors—the equivalent in money of the sales price of its products, since part of its products are used by industry to increase its equipment (and hence its productive capacity); (2) wage earners and owners of corporate securities, in turn, do not spend for consumers' goods as much as they receive from industry in wages and in dividends, but instead save some of their

in money and credit terms, and with allowance for the realistic circumstance that the persons who possess legal title to, and sell, goods are not, for the most part, those whose labor makes the goods, this principle implies that purchasing power is transferable but not destructible. The savings of the wealthy constitute a demand for producers' goods to exactly the extent that they diminish the amount that might have been spent for consumers' goods. In other words, the whole value (in monetary units) of industry's product is disbursed to labor, management, and the owners of property; changes in the relative size of the labor share of value product and of the capital and management share being changes in the direction of the demand for labor, but not a diminution in the aggregate of demand.[1] The very fact that there is a demand for savings by

---

incomes. Part of these savings are invested in securities, either by the individuals themselves or by savings banks—and again business enterprises are enabled to increase their productive capacity. In other words, because of the savings by business enterprises and by consumers, some money is used twice (or thrice, or more) for production before it is used for consumption; and to the extent that money is used more frequently for production than for consumption, the supply of goods outruns the purchasing power of consumers. For good discussions of the thesis that the process of capital creation in one way or another generates business depressions, *cf.* the Brookings Institution studies, *The Formation of Capital* and *The Recovery Problem in the United States;* S. H. Slichter, *Modern Economic Society,* Chap. 26; A. H. Hansen, *Business Cycle Theory,* pp. 11–119; and W. C. Mitchell, *Business Cycles, The Problem and Its Setting,* pp. 23–31.

[1] The sequence of events predicated by the orthodox argument should be traced with a little more particularity. Let us assume that, owing to any one of many possible causes, distribution is altered in a manner adverse to labor and the lower-income classes and favorable to capital and the more wealthy. The capitalists can, of course, do either of two things with the greater number of dollars now coming their way: they can spend them or they can save them. To the extent that they spend, there is no diminution in the aggregate demand for labor. More persons will be needed in the industries producing luxuries and fewer in those producing necessities than if some of the income received by the capitalists had gone to labor instead of as a capital return, and from the social viewpoint this presumably is undesirable; but in point of the aggregate effect upon the demand for labor, and therefore upon the volume of employment and maintenance of economic balance, there is no difference. Suppose, however, that the capitalists save a considerable portion of the greater number of dollars now coming their way (the assumption that is, needless to say, the realistic one in a majority of cases). The major portion of the savings will be devoted to the production of producers' goods rather than consumers' goods. Therefore relatively more labor will be needed in industries turning out producers' goods and relatively less in those turning out consumers' goods, but the aggregate money demand for labor (on the assumption of almost instantaneous shifts in purchasing power and without consideration of the qualifications discussed shortly) will remain the same. Labor's total money wages and the volume of employment may, theoretically, remain the same as before; the change in distribution has not brought "overproduction" and unemployment. It should be noted, however, that since the volume of consumers' goods would decline (or not increase at as rapid a rate as the volume of producers' goods), the prices of consumers' goods would rise, relatively, and the real earnings of the workers would be lower, in spite of the fact that aggregate money earnings remain the same. But there are ultimate correctives of this temporary decline in real earnings: (*a*) the increased profit consequent upon the relatively

business enterprises is evidence that entrepreneurs see (or think they see) opportunities to use capital in such ways as not to diminish profits and therefore employment.

Accepted uncritically and without qualification, the orthodox position with respect to the overproduction doctrine, as just set forth, would lend little support to the thesis here under consideration: that depressions are due in large part to faulty distribution of income, that a distribution more favorable to labor would make for avoidance of depressions, and that maintenance or even horizontal elevation of wage rates during depressions will provide the purchasing power necessary for recovery. But, as always in economic analysis that is not confined entirely to the ivory tower of "pure" theory, realism demands examination of some of the assumptions underlying the abstract reasoning—a search for some of the "disreputable accidents," to use the late Professor Edgeworth's term,[1] which may prevent the tendencies predicated by the orthodox analysis from working themselves out.

It should be apparent, in the first place, that the reasoning underlying the conclusion that general overproduction is impossible presumes almost instantaneous shifts of purchasing power and no diminution in the velocity of money and credit. What would have been spent by wage earners had the wage share been greater and the capital share less will be spent, and as quickly, by those receiving the management and property shares. In practice, however, a negative and destructive force is likely to appear. Workers, who are generally "quick spenders," have less current income than they would have had with a distribution more favorable to them, while the owners of industry may not immediately use the dollars coming their way instead of labor's in such ways as to build up the demand for producers' goods (and therefore for labor employed in the producers' goods industries) in the same proportion and as quickly as the dollars would have been spent had they gone as wages and salaries.[2] In the

higher price of consumers' goods would sooner or later cause more capital and labor to be devoted to their production, and (b) the greater quantity of producers' goods ultimately would begin to turn out more consumers' goods.

[1] In *Mathematical Psychics*, p. 46, Professor Edgeworth has observed, with particular reference to labor questions, that "there is no *determinate* and very *unique* arrangement toward which the system tends under, may we say, a law of Nature, and which would be predictable if we knew beforehand the real requirements of each, or the average, dealer; but there is an indefinite number of arrangements *a priori* possible, towards one of which the system is urged, not by the concurrence of innumerable (as it were) neuter items eliminating change, but (abstraction being made of custom) by what has been called the Art of Bargaining—higgling, dodges, and other incalculable and often disreputable accidents."

[2] For example, if investments do not keep pace with savings, a change in distribution such as is here being assumed may for a time prevent a sustaining of the former volume of production and employment. If the savings should flow into the savings banks and not be immediately invested, then the decline in employment in the consumer-goods industries would not be immediately offset by an increase elsewhere.

second place, the possibility of a shrinkage in values during the processes of fabrication, and therefore of the production of goods that cannot be sold at a price covering cost of production, with consequent beginning of a downward spiral, must be taken into account. This type of ".over-production" is, to be sure, a consequence of the operation of the money and credit system, rather than of the failure of industry to give the workers enough to buy back the goods they have produced; but its practical effects may be much the same.[1] In the third place, it may be observed that a distribution giving large incomes to a minority rather than somewhat smaller incomes for this minority and higher wages for labor is likely to promote injudicious investment—and with injudicious investment an oversupply of some goods in relation to others, disastrous price drops which undermine business confidence in general, and ultimately a minor or major recession of business. Again the logician's distinction must be kept in mind. Injudicious investment is not the same as overinvestment (which is, of course, the circumstance postulated by adherents of the overproduction thesis); the trouble is not with saving or investment *per se*, but with the unwise use—*i.e.*, investment—of savings. From a pragmatic viewpoint, however, the two may sometimes be put in the same category. The comparative sharing of labor and capital is relevant to the extent of injudicious investment; and the extent of injudicious investment is, in turn, relevant to the shattering of business confidence, disproportionate production of some goods as against others, speculation the costs of which must be liquidated, and a general cyclical downswing.

The reasons why orthodox economics has rejected the overproduction notion, as already set forth, suggest the argument that wage rates must be reduced, not increased, during periods of depression in order to promote recovery and fuller employment. The demand for labor is a derived demand, and when prices fall (and output per worker does not increase correspondingly), the maintenance of wage rates makes labor an overpriced factor of production, and can only result in a curtailment of employment. Reduce the price of labor and more of it will be bought; *e.g.*, some of the unemployed will be hired. To retain rigid wage rates when prices

---

[1] To elucidate this matter in a little more detail: If the supply of money and credit does not keep pace with production (assuming their velocity to remain the same), the price level must fall reciprocally. Therefore enterprisers must dispose of raw materials and labor purchased at earlier and higher prices (and now embodied in the goods they make) at the lower price level. But since profits are frequently the residual of price over cost, this shrinkage in prices generally means a far greater proportionate shrinkage in profits. The effects are likely to be cumulative. It should be noted that this difficulty is one emerging from the monetary and banking system rather than from a fundamental error in our economic order; but it is possible to have overproduction in the sense of more goods than can be sold *at the same price level* as that obtaining during the period when the raw materials and labor going into them were purchased.

are falling is, in other words, only to grind business between the upper netherstone of shrinking prices and the lower one of inflexible wage rates, so that profit margins will disappear and production and employment decrease still more.   To bring the component parts of the price structure (the prices that employers pay for the factors of production and the prices they get for their products) into better relationship, a downward readjustment of wages is necessary.   Since given reductions in wage rates will result in more than proportionate increases in employment, labor's gain in fuller employment, consequent upon rate reductions, will be greater than the loss involved in the sacrifice of the higher real hourly earnings that would be received by the smaller number employed at the old wage rate.[1]

The position just set forth with respect to wage reductions during depressions must, according to the conviction underlying these paragraphs, be accepted as being *in general* a correct one, and the trade-union position as being *in general* a mistaken one.   But once more the statement of an obvious cause-and-effect relationship is somewhat simpler than the facts of economic life, and once more attention must be given to the factors that may militate against the predicated readjustment.

Merely a suggestion of some of the factors preventing realization of the desirable consequences of wage cuts during depressions, or making them unnecessary, will be made here.   In the first place, it may be noted that while lowering of wage rates may prevent the laying off of workers that would otherwise result from the excess of the old wage rates over the marginal productivity of the formerly employed number, wage rates are a sluggish price and generally the effective insistence upon their reduction comes after wholesale and retail prices have dropped.   The reduction may enable firms theretofore operating at a loss to make a profit, and hence prevent further declines in employment, but reabsorption of those already thrown out of work necessitates an increase in the volume of business done by business enterprises.   Underlying the assumption of an increase in the volume of business is the expectation that commodity prices will be adjusted to the decrease in costs.   In a period of depression, however, when potential buyers are reluctant to part with purchasing power and hoarding of money may be a factor of importance,

---

[1] For the theoretical proof of this, *cf*. vol. I of this treatise, Chap. IV, pp. 181*ff*.   *Cf*. also P. H. Douglas, *The Theory of Wages*, Chaps. 4 to 10 and *Controlling Depressions*, Chap. 11, and A. C. Pigou, *The Theory of Unemployment*.   Briefly, it may be recalled at this point that the curve of diminishing increments attributable to labor appears to be fairly elastic.   Therefore if wages are pushed above marginal productivity, employed workers will tend to be laid off at considerably more than the rate at which wages are increased. Obviously, the converse of this proposition is that when wages are above the margin of value productivity, in consequence of a depression drop in prices, a reduction in wage rates will increase the total amount paid in wages by causing appreciably larger increases in the number employed.

producers may see no additional market for their commodities even at greatly lowered prices, and therefore—unless competition functions so perfectly as to force them to do so—no reason for attempting to attract more buyers by still further lowering of prices. While the presence of idle equipment and the pressure of overhead costs are conducive to increased output, the substantially lower price at which goods would have to be sold were output increased, in those cases where consumer demand is extremely inelastic, may dictate that firms maintain their old price quotations. In such cases there will be no increase in the volume of business and in employment because labor costs are less. Some firms may take account of the depressing effect of increased output upon price, and engage in the policy of output restriction. To the extent that consumers take each price reduction as a signal that prices will go still lower, and therefore postpone their purchases, the beneficial effects of lower price quotations consequent upon reduction in labor costs are negatived. In the second place, wages during a preceding upswing of business may have failed to keep pace with the value productivity imputable to each worker, and in this case they need not decline as rapidly as this value product on the downward spiral. In the third place, output per worker may have increased during depression years, and in this case hourly wages need not be reduced as much as prices have dropped.[1] In the fourth place, it should be remembered that there are almost always non-labor costs and certain fixed costs that are as susceptible as labor costs to reduction. The costs of raw materials, especially when produced under monopoly conditions, might be lowered; there are, indeed, likely to be many cases where reduction in the prices of electricity, steel, cement, etc., would have a stimulative effect.[2] While the large volume of fixed costs, often consequent upon the financial structure of firms, militates against price reduction, it may frequently be that there is no economic justification for a firm's insisting upon a price sufficient to meet currently during a depression period all its fixed charges. A reorganization may be forced by the failure to meet fixed charges, but this does not prevent the continued operation of the industry.[3] Finally, the effect of wage

[1] In this case, however, piece rates should be reduced more than time rates.

[2] Of course, the statement of this possibility has to be qualified. If the prices of electricity, steel, cement, etc., are reduced, the value productivity of the workers making those things decreases, and therefore the excess of their former wage rates over the marginal productivity of the formerly employed number in these industries is increased. But not all the costs entering into these goods are labor costs; all that is being done here is to suggest some of the possibilities.

[3] Indirectly, however, a forced reorganization may retard recovery in that it may "freeze" temporarily some of the assets of banks and contribute to their failure, thus reducing the volume and velocity of circulating media. It is not intended to imply that fixed charges can be ignored or reduced in all cases, but it is suggested that in many cases a more flexible financial structure could be obtained by the substitution of stocks for bonds, and that in many other cases charges which are now regarded as fixed (*i.e.*, interest paid

cuts upon the quickness of recovery should be taken into account. A general reduction of wages has the effect of establishing a new equilibrium of prices at a lower level; and since wages are a sluggish price, they are likely to regain their former level only in a laggard fashion. Meanwhile, as the following upswing continues, value productivity per worker increases, and the failure of wage rates to keep pace may—for reasons suggested earlier—be a contributing factor in speculation, injudicious investment, and the beginning of another recession. During depressions of short duration, there is much to be said for the maintenance (or most conservative lowering) of wage rates. Of course, prophetic insight would be necessary to know whether a depression was to be of short duration, but the laggardness with which wage rates recover from depression reductions dictates that consideration be given to other cost-reduction possibilities before a stout attack is made upon wages.

Some of the Effects of Unemployment

Unemployment has numerous effects, chiefly, but not altogether, of an evil kind. It is an important cause of industrial and political unrest, of undermined and undeveloped efficiency, of inadequate income, of poverty and dependency, and much else. Some of these effects will be discussed elsewhere. At this point we shall, however, discuss those of a more immediate and tangible character.

As Professor Lescohier has pointed out, unemployment impairs the livelihood and seriously decreases the earning power of more people than any other form of industrial adversity.[1] In its various forms, as we have seen, it has probably averaged in the course of a year (prior to 1930) twenty-five days per worker, which means that about 8 per cent of normal working time has been lost through this form of involuntary idleness. Not only does it reduce earnings in this direct and obvious manner; it causes irregularity of income, means uncertainty of income, and also causes decreases in the efficiency of the unemployed and the under-employed men—decreases that are likely to affect adversely their wage rates when again in regular employment. Moreover, a period of acute unemployment is almost certain to have an adverse effect upon wage rates in general, for wages are then likely to be "deflated." Unemployment, therefore, cuts down both present and future earnings.[2]

---

on bonds which have long since ceased to represent any capital goods used for productive purposes) could be reduced without impairing business initiative. When New Zealand, wishing to improve her position in the world market, reduced fixed charges along with wages determined by compulsory arbitration awards, she did not act without reason.

[1] See D. D. Lescohier, *The Labor Market* (1919), Chap. 3.

[2] See *Business Cycles and Unemployment* (Report and Recommendations of a Committee of the President's Conference on Unemployment), pp. 64–65, for Berridge's study of employment and wage rates.

Payrolls show the great reductions in wages earned when unemployment becomes widespread. W. I. King, in *Employment, Hours, and Earnings in Prosperity and Depression*, has estimated the cyclical declines in the number of employees, the actual hours worked, and wages and salaries earned from the peak in 1920 to the time of the smallest volume of employment, which, with unimportant exceptions, occurred (for that cycle) in the first quarter of 1922. The data were drawn from industries employing approximately 10 per cent of all wage earners in the United States. They should be fairly typical for the purpose here employed. The data were not drawn from all industries, however, and the industries for which data were secured were not represented according to their degrees of importance, so that any figures resulting from averaging "all industries" must have limited value. Table 13 has been compiled to show the general results obtained by King.

TABLE 13.—MAXIMUM CYCLICAL DECLINE IN EMPLOYMENT, HOURS, AND EARNINGS IN
AMERICAN INDUSTRIES BETWEEN 1920 AND 1921 OR 1922[1]
(Decline in Per Cent)

Industry	Employees on payroll	Hours actually worked	Wages and salaries earned
All industries..............................	14.06	16.50	23.16
Agriculture................................	4.17	3.18	19.25
Extraction of minerals......................	26.88	29.66	36.31
Building and construction...................	18.83	18.92	24.54
Other hand trades..........................	0.70	0.00	1.02
Finance....................................	6.75	7.14	5.20
Public and professional service..............	2.00	4.57	4.27 (increase)
Domestic and personal service...............	2.88	4.11	8.15
All transportation..........................	16.23	21.48	28.11
Steam railways.......................	22.27	29.68	36.72
Other transportation..................	5.60	6.77	7.27
Commerce and trade........................	3.08	2.78	5.41
Wholesale.............................	6.27	5.64	17.75
Retail................................	2.78	2.75	4.74
All factories...............................	25.59	29.97	37.60
Food, drink, and tobacco..............	15.94	15.13	30.16
Lumber and its products..............	14.82	18.21	19.66
Metals and metal products............	42.85	50.25	56.85
Paper and printing....................	6.46	10.65	8.82
Mineral products.....................	17.80	18.70	25.97
Textile and leather products...........	14.65	20.09	24.12

[1] Compiled from W. I. King, *Employment, Hours, and Earnings in Prosperity and Depression* (1923), pp. 30, 55, and 104.

It will be noted that employment and earnings in the several industries were adversely affected in very different degrees during the depression. In commerce and trade and in finance, for example, they were not so seriously affected. In mining, transportation, building and construction, and manufacture, where most wage earners find their livelihood and in which most labor problems center, the volume of employment was greatly reduced and earnings still more so. The decline in wages and salaries earned in mining was 36.31 per cent, in steam-railway transportation 36.72 per cent, in building and construction work 24.54 per cent, and in the several branches of manufacture covered, 37.6 per cent.

One of the most conclusive means of demonstrating the economic loss resulting from depressions is to show how greatly they curtail national income. This has been done for the years 1929–1936 by the United States Department of Commerce. As has been indicated in an earlier chapter,[1] the national income produced fell from 81 billion dollars in 1929 to a low of 39.5 billion dollars in 1932, a decline of 41.5 billion dollars, or more than 50 per cent. It was also found that the declines in net rents and royalties and in wages were most severe, while interest payments suffered least. In addition the per-employee decline in wages was much greater than that of salaries or other income payments. This should be borne in mind by those who argue that wages are excessively "sticky" as compared with other costs. Table 14 gives the changes from 1929 to 1936 in the sharing by the different groups of income paid out.

TABLE 14.—NATIONAL INCOME PAID OUT, BY TYPES OF PAYMENT, 1929 TO 1936[1]
(1929 = 100)

Type of payment	1930	1932	1933	1934	1935	1936
Total income paid out	93.2	62.0	57.4	65.2	69.9	79.4
Total labor income	92.2	60.6	57.2	66.1	70.9	80.6
Salaries (selected industries)a	99.0	61.0	54.2	61.3	63.9	72.9
Wages (selected industries)a	82.9	40.3	41.4	52.3	58.3	67.5
Salaries and wages (all other industries)	96.0	70.9	63.7	69.4	74.2	81.5
Other labor income	105.2	117.3	102.9	95.8	107.8	114.4
Total dividends and interestb	100.7	70.7	62.6	65.8	67.7	79.3
Dividends	97.4	46.1	37.1	45.0	51.5	76.6
Interest	103.5	96.9	91.1	90.3	87.8	86.0
Entrepreneurial withdrawals	94.1	65.5	58.8	66.1	72.0	79.3
Net rents and royalties	80.8	42.8	39.1	47.6	54.1	62.3

a Includes mining, manufacturing, construction, steam railroads, Pullman, railway express, and water transportation.
b Includes also net balance of international flow of property incomes.
[1] Robert R. Nathan, in *Survey of Current Business*, vol. 17, no. 6 (June, 1937), p. 15. These data are presented in a different form in vol. I, Chap. III, Table 43, p. 167, "Percentage Distribution of National Income by Type of Payment, 1929–1936."

Attention may be called to tabular data presented on an earlier page (12). Partly because of a decreased number of workers on payrolls and the average number of hours they were employed, partly because of reductions in hourly rates of pay and piece prices, total money earnings in all employments were very much less in 1933 than in 1929. While those employed by telegraph and telephone companies had suffered a

[1] Vol. I, Chap. III.

decrease in payrolls of 31.8 per cent, and those employed by light and power companies a loss of 28.0 per cent, the decline in eighty-nine manufacturing industries was 50.6 per cent, in wholesale trade, 43.2 per cent, in retail trade, 44.8 per cent, in anthracite mining, 54.2 per cent, in bituminous coal mining, 62.2 per cent, in metalliferous mining, 79.4 per cent.

With reference to the effect of unemployment upon the worker, Lescohier has made this graphic summary statement:[1]

"Unsteady employment attacks the worker's efficiency in so many ways that probably no one could enumerate them all. It undermines his physique, deadens his mind, weakens his ambition, destroys his capacity for continuous, sustained endeavor; induces a liking for idleness and self-indulgence; saps self-respect and the sense of responsibility; impairs technical skill; weakens nerve and will power; creates a tendency to blame others for his failures; saps his courage; prevents thrift and hope of family advancement; destroys a workman's feeling that he is taking good care of his family; sends him to work worried and underfed; plunges him into debt."

Unemployment also has important effects upon family life. With reference to this, Professor Gillin has said:[2]

"In addition to the attack on financial resources of the family and the impairment of the efficiency of the workman, unemployment also strikes at every tie which makes for wholesome family life. It forces the mother out of the home to supplement the earnings of the man; it takes children from school at the earliest possible moment and places them in industry. By taking the mother away from home it prevents her giving that care to the children which lies at the foundation of not only good health but of good morals. It forces the family to move into poorer quarters; it compels them to reduce the scale of expenditure not only for those things that contribute to the spiritual development of the family but even those things which are basic necessities for health and vigor. Thus in every way unemployment destroys the very fabric of social life if at all frequent and long-continued."

Most of these statements find substantiation in the excellent study of unemployment and child welfare made by the Children's Bureau during the depression of 1921–1922.[3]

---

[1] Quoted, with permission of The Macmillan Company, from Don D. Lescohier, *The Labor Market* (1919), p. 107. The depressing story of the disintegrating effects of unemployment on workers is well presented by E. Wight Bakke in *The Unemployed Man* (1933).

[2] Quoted, with permission of the D. Appleton-Century Company, Inc., from J. L. Gillin, *Poverty and Dependency* (1921), pp. 468–469.

[3] See "Unemployment and Child Welfare," U. S. Department of Labor, Children's Bureau, *Bureau Publication 125* (1923). See also, Clinch Calkins, *Some Folks Won't Work* (1930), and Paul W. Kellogg, *Case Studies of Unemployment* (University of Pennsylvania, Wharton School, Research Study XII, 1931).

This study shows the problem in somewhat exaggerated form, for the depression was rather acute and most of the normal breadwinners of the families studied had been out of regular jobs for relatively long periods of time. The study covered 231 families in Racine, Wis., and 135 in Springfield, Mass. Of the heads of these families, 5 per cent had been out of regular jobs for less than six months, 32 per cent for six but less than twelve months, 58 per cent for twelve but less than eighteen months, and 5 per cent for eighteen to twenty-five months. The detail must be accepted as typical of cases of long-drawn-out unemployment; though the difference is only one of degree, the losses must be discounted for cases of shorter duration.

Most of the male heads of these families were in the prime of life. Indeed, 49 per cent of them were between thirty and forty years of age. Two-thirds of them were skilled workers. Since the loss of their regular jobs, all but four of the 366 had succeeded in finding some work, usually unskilled and of course temporary, and thus had been able to earn something, though little, toward the support of their families. Only twenty-two of the wives had been gainfully employed previous to the loss of regular jobs by their husbands; now, facing the problem of undermined family incomes, ninety-one others took employment, some of them women with child, others the mothers of young children, and at a time when the volume of employment was greatly reduced and jobs hard to find. In numerous cases children found employment, though the total number of children in jobs in these cities was very much smaller than it had been when there was a shortage of labor. Half of the forty-five children between fourteen and seventeen in these families found to be working regularly became wage earners after their fathers had lost their jobs. Of the twenty-two children who went to work to assist their families, one had completed the sixth grade, four the seventh, nine the eighth, two the first year, and one the second year of high school (the other five not reported). Besides the forty-five working in regular jobs, forty-two children (in thirty-four families) made some contribution toward the family's support by working after school, on Saturday, or during vacations. Because of its effects on schooling, nourishment, housing, and general outlook, unemployment is as great a tax on the efficiency of the next generation of workers as on the efficiency of this. Its effects upon the wife and children are quite as adverse and as important as its effects upon the adult male worker.

Of course, there were among these families instances in which boarders and lodgers were taken in order to piece out income. Frequently families moved to cheaper quarters or sublet a part of the residence in order to save on rent; savings were used; loans were secured and other debts contracted; and in more than half of the cases charity was resorted to.

Table 15 shows the sources of livelihood of these families during the unemployment of the normal breadwinners.

TABLE 15.—SOURCES OF LIVELIHOOD DURING UNEMPLOYMENT, 1921 AND 1922[1]

Sources of livelihood	No. of families reporting	Percentage of cases
Total..	366	100
Father's earnings at temporary work................	362	99
Mother's earnings................................	116	32
Earnings of children.............................	75	20
Income from boarders and lodgers.................	56	15
Income from rent................................	60	16
Savings used....................................	158	43
Loans contracted................................	117	32
Debts for food..................................	240	66
Other debts.....................................	253	69
Aid from relatives...............................	38	10
Charitable aid..................................	191	52
Other sources...................................	15	4

[1] Children's Bureau, *Bureau Publication 125*, p. 29.

The contrast between the average monthly resources during the period of unemployment and during the year preceding gives some conception of the sacrifice involved.   It is shown by Table 16.

TABLE 16.—MONTHLY FAMILY INCOME IN AND OUT OF EMPLOYMENT, 1921 AND 1922[1]

Average monthly income	Percentage of families year preceding loss of regular job	Percentage of families during unemployment
Less than $50..................	0	27
$ 50 to $ 99..................	6	54
$100 to $149..................	42	12
$150 to $199..................	34	3
$200 to $249..................	16	2
$250 and over..................	2	2

[1] Children's Bureau, *Bureau Publication 125*, p. 33.

In the normal situation no family studied had had an income less than $50 per month; during unemployment, with loans, charitable aid, and all sources included, 27 per cent had less than that amount.   In the normal situation only 6 per cent of the families had had less than $100 per month; during the period of unemployment the percentage of such families increased to 81.   In the normal situation, 48 per cent had had less than the $150 which would frequently be required for decent living; during the period of unemployment all but 7 per cent had less than that amount.

This table presents the contrast between the situations. It also indicates that while some of these families, especially those with a number of breadwinners still in regular employment, were well off, a comparatively large number were not adequately provided with the necessities of life. Of course, the needs of the families varied with the number, age, and sex of their members, but it was found that the resources of all but 9 of 186 families studied in detail fell short of a budget acceptable to the Bureau. Indeed, in half of the cases the total resources did not exceed 50 per cent of the budget required for their support.

Public charity is only one, and obviously not the most important, of the costs of unemployment to society in general. Nevertheless, it is not a small cost. It has been noted that 52 per cent of the cases studied in Racine and Springfield had charitable assistance. The United States Immigration Commission in 1909 found from the records of associated charities in large cities from coast to coast that the unemployment of a breadwinner entered into 43.2 per cent of the cases in which application was made for assistance and into 44.3 per cent of the cases in which assistance was granted by these organizations. Only sickness, where the corresponding percentages were 38.4 and 40.4, approached unemployment as a reason for seeking and for granting relief. The percentages for accidents were 3.9 and 4.1; for death of a breadwinner or another member of the family, 6.8 and 7.4; for old age, 6.2 and 2.9.[1]

The depression of the 1930's was much more acute than that of 1908, and unemployment became the great outstanding cause of distress and dependency. As the depression continued, the resources of a larger proportion of the unemployed became exhausted, and more persons were forced to rely on public relief after 1932, even though the trend of employment turned—somewhat unsteadily—upward. In January, 1933, the number of families on relief was estimated at 3,850,000,[2] and by July of that year the number of cases had increased to 3,906,874, or 15,282,000 persons.[3] In May, 1934, a new peak of 4,447,108 cases, or 17,277,487 persons, was reached; and even this appalling figure was soon exceeded, the number of persons dependent on relief during the winter of 1934–1935 hovering around 20,000,000.[4] The real cost to society of a situation in

[1] Philip Klein's *The Burden of Unemployment* (1923) contains the results of a survey made of the problem of unemployment during the depression of 1920–1921. The book is replete with interesting and valuable data.

[2] The number of single persons on relief at that time (January, 1933) is not available. After July, 1933, single persons were counted.

[3] Of course there were variations in the number during this period, in consequence of seasonal activity and shifts in public works and relief policies.

[4] Data from *Monthly Report* of the FERA, Sept. 1 through Sept. 30, 1935, p. 33. Preliminary figures based on a census of eligible workers on relief revealed 6,152,639 such persons in March, 1935, and 6,402,171 workers on Jan. 15, 1936. An occupational census prepared by Philip M. Hauser of the WPA showed 6,152,639 eligible workers on public

which 20,000,000 persons (about 17 per cent of the total population of the United States) were on relief is incalculable.

The costs of unemployment, when considered from the point of view of the workers and of society as a whole, do not tell the whole story. Unemployment as a form of waste is of only less concern to employers and business men generally than to workers and to society as a whole. Employers have an economic interest in the efficiency and earning power of the present generation and of that to follow. They are interested in avoiding discontent and dependency and the heavy tax bills incidental to public relief. Filling places vacated costs employers money and workers earnings. Employers lose money when vacancies are filled only after delay and the workers lose money while waiting for vacancies to become known. Of course, employers frequently say, "Wait until depression comes and labor will be brought to its senses." When depression does come, it is likely that wages are reduced. If they are reduced, any substantial saving may be short-lived, for it is almost certain that labor will attempt to regain the lost ground as soon as business improves. Acute unemployment means unstable wages and unstable industrial relations. Perhaps as a result of culling out the less efficient and the fear of discharge on the part of workers, employers will get more product per man in time of depression than at other times. It may be, however, that the speeding then indulged in will be offset by a slow pace when there is little fear of discharge. Certain it is that if labor dares to do so, it will nurse the job when there is fear of unemployment and will spread work so as to make it last as long as possible when the volume of work to be done is short. The fear of lost time and of lost earnings is the cause of causes of restriction of output by labor. Again, the workers must live somehow. In the seasonal industries especially, wages certainly reflect to some extent the limited opportunity for employment. And where the unemployment is that on the job, the pieceworker is likely to require a rate which will at. least partly offset the loss of time due to unbalanced sections, poor routing, and the like. Unemployment means low, uncertain, and irregular earnings realized by the worker, but as a rule it is not accompanied by low labor cost to the employer.

As we have seen, depression is the greatest cause of unemployment. Earnings are then greatly reduced. Reduced earnings mean reduced consumption and a limited market for products. Moreover, when, because of slack periods or depression, there is unemployed labor, there is unemployed or partially employed capital and management. Labor costs per unit in these circumstances usually increase and overhead costs almost

---

relief rolls in March, 1935. [*Cf. Workers on Relief in the United States, March, 1935*, WPA (January 1937), p. 8.] On Jan. 15, 1936, the number eligible for WPA employment was 6,402,171. [*Usual Occupations of Workers Eligible for Works Program Employment, January 15, 1936*, WPA (January, 1937), p. 6.]

always do. The books of manufacturers in the needle trades tell an interesting story of greatly increased costs per garment in the slack season, and the same is true of the books of business men generally in periods of general depression. Widespread unemployment and bad business go hand in hand. Therefore, all classes of persons are more or less concerned as to methods by which the evils of unemployment may be mitigated.

Chapter II

THE PROBLEM OF UNEMPLOYMENT (*Continued*): METHODS OF DEALING WITH THE PROBLEM

It is evident from an analysis of causes that the problem of unemployment calls for a variety of attacks upon it if the fullest possible, yet necessarily partial, solution is to be found. Students of the subject are in fairly general agreement that the following must find place in the program: (1) first, and indispensable, an efficient system of public employment offices, with controlled private agencies conducted for profit, or better, no such private agencies at all; (2) juvenile placement, guidance, and training, and rehabilitation and transference of adults from overcrowded industries; (3) decasualization of labor in such employments as at the docks; (4) the stabilization of industry and of employment within it; (5) the distribution of public work with due reference to the demand for labor in private employment; (6) sharing of work rather than decreasing the number on the payroll during slack seasons and industrial depression; and (7) unemployment insurance. These will be briefly discussed[1] in the order mentioned. Incidentally, barter schemes and other proposals not discussed in the preceding chapter will be touched upon.

Public Employment Offices

Unless there is an efficient system of public employment offices, the labor market cannot be adequately organized to connect men in need of jobs with jobs in need of men, thus reducing the leakage in man-power and the "labor reserve." In the absence of such a system, workers are recruited by display of window cards, "want ads," and various other devices which are not always effective; workers follow up these ads, walk the streets applying at the door, or congregate at the gates of large establishments, perhaps only to be disappointed day after day. Moreover, private employment agencies conducted for profit develop and bring in their train more or less of evil.

It was estimated that there were, some years ago, between 3,000 and 4,000 profit-making employment agencies in the United States.[2] The fees collected from applicants for work ran into the millions in the course of a year. Investigation shows that frequently the fees collected have

---

[1] This discussion assumes the continued restriction of immigration.

[2] Paul H. Douglas and Aaron Director, *The Problem of Unemployment* (1931), p. 266.

been exorbitant and are highest when there is a shortage of work; sometimes, indeed frequently, fees have been "split" between foreman and agency; not infrequently there have been connections with antisocial institutions; false information as to wages and living and working conditions, and as to the presence of strikes and lockouts, has been given; excessive numbers of workers have frequently been sent to places where labor was needed as a result of various agencies, perhaps operating in different places but in any event acting independently, sending on workers registered with them.

Such have been some of the problems accompanying the development of agencies conducted for profit. To meet them most of the states enacted legislation and perhaps required the agencies to register and to furnish bond to conform to the law relating to their operation. Interesting codes have been developed in such states as Illinois, where a large force of inspectors has been employed to administer the law. In Washington, a law was enacted prohibiting the collection of fees by private agencies, but this was declared unconstitutional on the ground that the statute was arbitrary and oppressive.[1] This was followed by another decision of the Supreme Court in which it was held that fees charged cannot be regulated.[2]

[1] *Adams v. Tanner*, 244 U. S. 590 (1917). An initiated measure (effective 1914) had provided (Sec. 2), "It shall be unlawful for any employment agent, his representative, or any other person to demand or receive, either directly or indirectly, from any person seeking employment, or from any person on his or her behalf, any remuneration or fee whatsoever for furnishing him or her with employment or with information leading thereto." The Act was declared by the Supreme Court of the United States to be in contravention of the Fourteenth Amendment. "The statute is one of prohibition, not regulation. . . . Because abuses may and probably do grow up, in connection with this business, is adequate reason for hedging it about by proper regulations. But this is not enough to justify destruction of one's right to follow a distinctly useful calling in an upright way." Justices Brandeis, Holmes, and Clarke dissented. Justice Brandeis pointed out that there was no prohibition on collecting fees from employers and that in decisions relating to the sale of liquor, oleomargarine, cigarettes, and other commodities, the "court [had] made it clear that a statute enacted to promote health, safety, morals or the public welfare [might] be valid, *although* it [would] compel discontinuance of existing businesses in whole or in part." He entered upon an examination of relevant facts in the situation and made the observation that the Supreme Court of Washington and the Federal District Court, which had upheld the law, were presumably familiar with the local conditions and needs.

[2] *Ribnik v. McBride*, 277 U. S. 350 (1928). An agency had been denied a license on the ground that its fees were too high. The Supreme Court, by majority decision, held that an employment agency is not "affected with a public interest," and that under the Fourteenth Amendment a state may not fix the fees which such an agency may charge for its service. In a brilliant dissenting opinion Justice Stone, with Justices Holmes and Brandeis concurring, pictured the evil practices of profit-making agencies and expressed the view that a state has power to regulate prices in businesses which have become public in their interest. Objective facts should be faced; the legislature of New Jersey may be assumed to have been familiar with the evils of (1) extortionate fees, (2) discriminating fees, (3) fee-splitting, (4) the practice of raising fees in time of acute unemployment.

The regulations which were enforced accomplished something in mitigating the evils that grew up. Moreover, in recent years the agencies themselves have accomplished something by developing a code of ethics through their national organization. Nevertheless, even in those states where the best control has been exercised, there is still much complaint of evils connected with the private agencies. Moreover, and more important, it has been clear all the while that an adequate system for allocating labor could not be secured through private agencies, each operating more or less independently of the others, however free each of them might be from criticisms of the types indicated above. Gaps in the services can be remedied and impartiality and efficiency secured only through a system of public offices in which each office will work in proper coordination with the others.[1]

While most countries of industrial importance developed years ago organic systems of public labor exchanges, the United States is only now actively engaged in doing so. It is interesting to note, however, that interest in the subject developed here in the early days of public-labor-exchange history. As long ago as 1890, Ohio enacted a law for the establishment of some public offices. Similar laws were passed by five other states between 1895 and 1899, and by seventeen others between 1901 and 1915.[2] Moreover, several cities, acting independently, set up municipal offices. Yet when we entered the War, fewer than a hundred public offices were in operation in this country. For each of these there were between thirty and forty private agencies operated for profit. The number of public agencies was adequate in no state; those maintained were efficiently conducted only in Wisconsin, where three were in operation; generally their management was quite deficient; with rare exceptions they had failed to secure or to merit the confidence of either employers or organized labor. In many, if not in most, instances the placements made were largely of domestics and casuals.

Such, briefly, was the situation when the United States entered the War. Then, in order to save man power and to secure workers for war industries, a federal service was established.[3] A beginning was made in January, 1918; by October of that year the number of public offices had increased to 832. Offices had been established in states where there had been none; additional offices had been opened in states which had had one

---

[1] Among the best discussions of the whole matter of private and public agencies are Shelby M. Harrison and others, *Public Employment Offices*, D. D. Lescohier, *The Labor Market*, and Paul H. Douglas and Aaron Director, *The Problem of Unemployment*.

[2] See U. S. Bureau of Labor Statistics, *Bulletin 241* (1918), for an account of public employment offices in the United States.

[3] For an account of this service, and the distribution of immigrants and the placing of harvest labor which had preceded it, see D. H. Smith, *United States Employment Service* (Monograph 28, Institute of Government Research, 1923). See also Ruth Kellogg, *The United States Employment Service* (1933), Chap. 1.

or more in operation; and the whole number had been brought under state-federal management. Between January, 1918, and March, 1919, these offices received 10,164,000 applications for help, registered 5,323,509 applicants for work, and filled 3,776,750 jobs. A good beginning had been made. Yet, largely because of the jealousies between state and federal officials and criticism of the federal director, the system which had been hurriedly built up was quickly curtailed. As against the $4,600,000 requested for the service for the fiscal year 1919–1920, only $400,000 was appropriated by Congress, in spite of the fact that the operating cost of the service had approached half a million per month. Under the circumstances, the activities of the federal service were greatly curtailed in the autumn of 1919; the federal government continued to support only a very limited number of offices, to allocate harvest labor, to collect and publish data on the state of employment, and to interest itself in the guidance and placement of youths in some sixteen cities. From 1919 to 1933 the Federal Employment Service guided thousands of farm laborers each year to employment opportunities, subsidized a part of the state employment offices, and collected and made public data of doubtful quality on the employment situation. Farm-labor placement was done with a fair degree of efficiency; the other operations of the Service had little value. The annual outlay was approximately $200,000.

Meanwhile the states, largely as a result of the development which took place during the period of the War, somewhat extended and, in some instances, improved upon their earlier activities in this field. In 1932 some twenty-four states were operating one or more public offices; eleven others had laws providing for public offices but had none in operation. In Illinois there were twenty-four offices, in Wisconsin ten, in Ohio fourteen; the total number of state and municipal offices, 254 in 1932, was very much larger than before the War. A few of the states were accomplishing much, but in most the employment service was inadequately coordinated, poorly housed, understaffed, and generally ineffective. It is not too much to say that many of the public offices had little more than political significance. In Wisconsin alone, of the larger states, did the public offices place more workers than the private offices conducted for profit within the state. And in Wisconsin much of the placement work was done by private agencies operating in the larger cities of the neighboring states.

Assuming nonpolitical and efficient administration, the students of the subject were in general agreement that the United States had long needed a federal-state system of employment offices in order to establish, or to induce the establishment of, public offices in the laggard states; to extend and improve the work being done by the existing offices in the other states; to coordinate the service as it could be coordinated only from a view of the whole situation and the possibility of using districts not limited by state boundaries; to deal with the transportation problem inevitably involved in adjusting the supply of labor to the demand for it; and to insure needed research work. In short, a federal-state system was needed to function like the system of exchanges in Great Britain, or better, a system similar to the dominion-provincial system which had been developed in Canada, where the political organization is similar to that of the United States.

In Great Britain in December, 1934, there were 1,185 local employment offices of the Ministry of Labour.[1] Most workers reside within convenient reach of one of these. These exchanges are coordinated through nine district organizations, and these, in turn, are coordinated through a national organization for the purpose of making adjustments of supply to demand in different parts of the country, etc. Special rates are made for labor sent from one place to another, as a considerable percentage of the workers placed are; and the cost of transportation is advanced or provided outright to migrating workers when necessary. Though constituting only about one-fourth of the total hirings,[2] most of the placements made through employment offices in Britain are made through these public agencies; with free and fairly efficient service provided by the government, private agencies have come to play a small role except in the placement of specialized kinds of labor. Germany after the War also established a system of labor exchanges, still more thoroughgoing, and forbade the operation of private offices for profit, effective April 1, 1931.

Canada established a dominion-provincial employment service at the close of the War to assist in solving the emergency certain to develop with demobilization and return of industry to the peace-time basis, and then to function when the situation became normal.[3] The number of offices maintained in 1935 was seventy-six, in sixty-six centers. The offices reported 376,651 placements in 1934, and 353,802 in 1935.

[1] Ministry of Labour *Report* for 1934, p. 13.
[2] The percentages placed through public exchanges were:

	1932	1933	1934
Men	18.8	21.0	22.1
Women	37.1	36.0	37.1
Boys	36.0	43.2	38.1
Girls	42.3	46.9	37.9
All departments	21.2	23.6	24.8

(Ministry of Labour *Report* for 1934, p. 13.)

[3] George W. Edwards in *Monthly Labor Review*, vol. 9 (1919), pp. 157–168, gives an excellent account of the system as it had been developed at that time. A more recent summary account may be found in Paul H. Douglas and Aaron Director, *op. cit.*, pp. 305–309. A fuller and later account is found in Industrial Relations Counselors, Inc., *Administration of Public Employment Offices and Unemployment Insurance* (1935). The (Canadian) *Labour Gazette* reports on the operation of the system from time to time.

Save in the Maritime Provinces, the administration and personnel of these agencies was in the hands of the provincial governments.[1] General supervision was, however, in the hands of a Dominion director and the Dominion government granted liberal subsidies on condition that the service was satisfactory. Moreover, the Dominion organization took care of interprovincial clearings of labor, collected valuable data on the state of employment, and standardized the whole service by providing all forms used, etc. It should be added that representative advisory boards were for some years employed by the Dominion, provincial, and local organizations in an effort to secure efficiency and to maintain impartiality in operation.

In the United States, President Harding in the postwar period urged legislation to establish a federal-state employment service; measures designed to do so were presented at each session of Congress, but apathy more than outright opposition prevented enactment until 1931. The Wagner Bill (S. 4157) then passed was vetoed by President Hoover, who favored a federal system, which proposal had been rejected by the Congress. The administration then proceeded to organize employment offices on what came to be known as the "Doak Plan."[2]   In 1931 it was announced that the Farm Labor Service would be expanded and enlarged, the Veterans' Placement Service improved (these branches had been operated), and that a general and efficient placement service would be developed to cooperate with such offices as were being operated by the states. The peak number of federal offices was reached in June, 1932, when there were twenty farm-labor offices, thirty veterans' offices, forty-nine state-directors' offices,[3] and fifty-two branch offices—a total of 151.

The older parts of the service under the Doak reorganization plan operated as before and with a fair degree of efficiency, but the new offices established merited little commendation. They were located in the several states with more reference to the residences of directors and the wishes of Congressmen than to need or to the presence of acceptable state offices already in operation; in the given city they were frequently not located so as to be readily accessible to industry or workers; they were usually housed in federal buildings in order to avoid payment of rent, with inadequate space, equipment, and accommodations; most of the personnel was poor because it was outside of the civil service and usually selected in view of political considerations; comparatively little place-

---

[1] The Employment and Social Insurance Act, effective in 1935, provided for the substitution of a Dominion Service for the Dominion-Provincial Service, in order to administer the Dominion unemployment compensation system provided for.

[2] For a full discussion of this plan, see Ruth Kellogg, *The United States Employment Service* (1933), Chaps. 4, 5, and 6

[3] A director was appointed for each state. The office at which he was located is here called a "director's office," the other general offices, "branch offices."

ment work was done and the placements reported were frequently misrepresented and their number exaggerated; most frequently the records were poorly kept; of cooperation with the state service, when maintained at all, there was little. Viewed from whatever angle, the Doak offices, with exceptions here and there, merited most of the criticism leveled against them. The abolition of the general offices in 1933 and in advance of the creation of a federal-state service was quite justified. With the abolition of the federally operated employment offices on April 1, 1933, there remained in operation 192 state offices, in 120 cities and 23 states.

The Wagner-Peyser Bill passed by Congress and approved by the President June 6, 1933,[1] was a revision of, and improvement upon, the Wagner Bill vetoed in 1931. On July 1, 1933, the new United States Employment Service was inaugurated with the purpose of providing a unified national public employment service. States which wished to receive the subsidies provided in the Wagner-Peyser Act could do so by agreeing to the standards established by the United States Employment Service and by matching the federal grant. Of an annual federal appropriation of $4,000,000, 75 per cent was available for state subsidies. Within two and a half years after passage of the Act, thirty-five states had signed such agreements affiliating with the United States Employment Service, reorganizing, strengthening, and extending their offices. In all but seven states some of the required steps preliminary to affiliation had been taken.[2]

The federal standards include civil-service specifications for personnel (or approval by the United States Employment Service), tenure of office independent of political influence, and standardized methods of account-

---

[1] Public no. 30, 73d Congress (S. 510), "An act to provide for the establishment of a national employment system and for cooperation with the States in the promotion of such system, and for other purposes." Section 3(a) of the bill provides that the Bureau of the U. S. Employment Service is "to assist in establishing and maintaining systems of public employment offices in the several States and the political subdivisions thereof . . . [and] . . . in coordinating the public employment offices throughout the country and in increasing their usefulness by developing and prescribing minimum standards of efficiency, assisting them in meeting problems peculiar to their localities, promoting uniformity in their administrative and statistical procedure, furnishing and publishing information as to opportunities for employment and other information of value in the operation of the system, and maintaining a system for clearing labor between the several States." Section 11(a) provides that the director is "to establish a Federal Advisory Council composed of men and women representing employers and employees in equal numbers and the public for the purpose of formulating policies and discussing problems relating to employment and insuring impartiality, neutrality, and freedom from political influence in the solution of such problems." . . . "The director shall also require the organization of similar state advisory councils."

[2] U. S. Employment Service, *Employment Service News*, February, 1936, p. 3. This monthly publication is a convenient source of information in regard to the U. S. Employment Service. Statistics of placements are also published currently in the *Monthly Labor Review*.

ing and reporting. They also require that the premises of employment offices must meet prescribed specifications and that the employment directors shall carry on educational programs in their communities explaining the services provided by the offices. These provisions were designed to provide an efficient employment service free from the mire of politics, an ideal not easily or fully attained.

The development of the federal-state employment service was greatly influenced during its first years by the necessity of placing workers in government employment, particularly in PWA, CWA, and WPA jobs. To meet the urgent demands of the recovery program, the United States Employment Service created the National Re-employment Service as a temporary emergency division to establish and operate offices in those counties and cities which could not be served by the existing or newly created state offices. The CWA created works projects in every county and with the United States Employment Service responsible for the selection and placement of all persons not already on relief, it was necessary to have at least one employment office in each county. The peak number of National Reemployment Offices was reached on Jan. 1, 1934, when there were 3,271 with a staff of 17,946 persons.[1] With the discontinuance of the CWA, the pressure for emergency placement was relieved and an attempt was made to reorganize the NRS offices as a part of the permanent state-federal system. However, under the WPA it was again necessary to expand the temporary offices. In May, 1936, there were 1,426 National Re-employment Service offices and 288 permanent state-federal offices in 35 states. It was hoped that a decline in volume of relief placements would eventually permit the closing of many of the temporary offices and the absorption of the remainder into the state-federal system under the terms of the Wagner-Peyser Act.

During the first thirty-three months of its existence, the United States Employment Service made 14,500,000 placements. The employment offices had registered and classified nearly 25,000,000 applications and the active files contained the names of more than 9,000,000 persons seeking employment.[2] An indication of the type of placement made is given in the report of the United States Employment Service for the fiscal year ended June 30, 1935. During those twelve months, 2,730,880 placements were made; 1,483,747 on public works, 4,926 on work-relief projects, 175,168 in government employment, 1,067,039 in nonpublic industry, and 8,822 unspecified and miscellaneous. Of the nonpublic

---

[1] W. H. Stead (Associate Director of the Division of Standards and Research, Department of Labor), *Twelve and One-half Million Registered for Work* (1934), p. 6.

[2] *Employment Service News*, May, 1936, p. 2. An excellent analysis of the occupational and employment characteristics of those actively registered with the employment offices in December, 1935, and in July, 1936, may be found in the bulletin of the U. S. Employment Service, *Who Are the Job-Seekers?* (1937).

placements the highest total, 188,894 men, was in agriculture, forestry, fishing, and mining. In manufacturing, 146,911 placements were made; in professional and commercial service and distribution, 95,554; in building and construction (private), 91,476; and in public utilities, 38,981. Among women the largest number of placements was in domestic and personal service.[1]

With the return of the Federal Government to a policy of work relief in the fall of 1935, the United States Employment Service was again faced with the task of filling large scale government requisitions. During the peak of WPA activity, November, 1935, through January, 1936, approximately 2,000,000 placements were made. This volume of governmental work overshadowed the placements in private industry, which during the same period averaged slightly more than 60,000 per month.[2] With the revival of private industry and the diminution of work-relief employment, the proportion of placements in public projects would decrease. It is rather certain, however, that for some time the character of the public employment service in the United States will depend largely upon the federal work-relief program.

After the adoption of the Wagner-Peyser Act, it was decided that more effective service could be rendered to unemployed veterans by providing for special attention to their needs in all employment offices rather than by continuing a limited number of special placement offices for veterans only. That this plan was beneficial to the veterans is shown by the statistics for the first twelve-months period. During that time, 1,029,173 veterans applied for work and 853,852, or 83 per cent, were placed in jobs. In the last seven months of that time placements of veterans exceeded applications in every month except March, when veterans were registering upon discontinuance of CWA.[3] On government projects preference has been given to veterans, and their placements are reported separately.

One of the first important tasks of the United States Employment Service was the development of a uniform system of statistical reporting. Each state with employment offices had developed separate forms and methods of reporting with the result that there was no uniformity in the information with respect to their activities. In order to overcome this difficulty each state was required as a condition of affiliation to adopt the uniform statistical procedure recommended by the United States Employ-

---

[1] *Monthly Labor Review*, April, 1936, pp. 1070–1080. During the year ending June 30, 1936, total placements for all types of employment rose to 5,755,964, of which 2,868,581 were on WPA and relief projects, 1,740,096 in public and governmental employment, and 1,147,287 in private employment. *Ibid.*, August, 1936, p. 478. For an analysis of registrations and placements made by the U. S. Employment Service during the two-year period ending in June, 1936, see its bulletin, *Filling Nine Million Jobs* (1937).

[2] *Employment Service News*, May, 1936, p. 13.

[3] *Ibid.*, pp. 34–36.

ment Service.   In the future this uniform reporting will supply a valuable body of data relating to number of unemployed, length of unemployment, age, sex, past experience, and previous occupations of the registered persons, and other information.   During the first months it was necessary to concentrate upon the task of placing the millions of unemployed in government projects.   Despite the pressure of this work, however, a beginning was made in the collection of statistical data which promise to be increasingly useful in the more efficient allocation of the country's labor supply, in vocational guidance, and in formulating unemployment-insurance policies.[1]

An efficient system of public employment offices protects against the evils accompanying the private profit-making agencies which flourish in its absence.   Its chief function is, of course, to fill vacant places efficiently with jobless men, to prevent leakage of man-power, and to reduce the "labor reserve."   It can do little to create employment when jobs are scarce.   Its chief function then is to protect the unemployed from imposition and needless wandering from place to place; most of the available places will be filled quickly in any event.   In countries with a system of compulsory unemployment insurance, as in Great Britain and Germany for some years and as now being developed in the United States, the employment offices are a necessary part of the administrative machinery.[2] Again, they may be used in developing and carrying out a program of vocational guidance and rehabilitation.   If careful records of all applicants for work and of all applications for help are kept and adequately analyzed and studied by a corps of statisticians, a system of public employment offices provides answers to important questions as to excesses and deficiencies in the labor supply in different trades, as to types of training needed, as to employability, etc.   This, indeed, might be the most important service rendered by a system of public employment offices.

VOCATIONAL GUIDANCE

A second thing needed is to train the young for, and to direct them into, branches of employment with a future rather than permit them to enter blind-alley or decaying trades.   In a considerable number of British localities this is being done.   It has been done in Germany also, and very extensively.   Prior to 1929 the matter had received increasing attention

---

[1] Samples of the kinds of information which may be expected are found in *Monthly Labor Review* (February, 1936), pp. 431–435; W. H. Stead, *op. cit.;* the Philadelphia office of the Pennsylvania State Service, *Thirty Thousand in Search of Work* (1933), and *Employment Trends in Philadelphia* (1933); as well as in current discussions in the *Employment Service News, e.g.,* May, 1936.

[2] To be eligible for benefit, an unemployed person must sign on the employment exchange register on specified days during working hours.   This procedure is described by E. Wight Bakke in *The Unemployed Man* (1933), pp. 78*ff.*

at the hands of school authorities and others in this country. In some cities, Chicago for example, efficient work was done along these lines. With the emergencies created by the depression, however, many municipalities curtailed "unnecessary" expenditures for vocational guidance and related school activities. Fortunately, at approximately the same time, the federal government became concerned with the future of unemployed youths. One of the purposes of the Civilian Conservation Corps has been the training of youths for useful occupations.[1] More directly in point is the apprentice training program undertaken by the Federal Committee on Apprentice Training.[2] The National Youth Administration, created by Executive Order on June 26, 1935, is also concerned with enabling young persons who would otherwise be unable to do so to continue their education. Through the National Youth Administration student-aid program, high school, college, and graduate students have been offered an opportunity to earn a small monthly income from a part-time job. The job-guidance and apprentice-training phases of the National Youth Administration program have been delegated to the Federal Committee on Apprentice Training and affiliated state committees.[3]

Rehabilitation of unemployed adults in overcrowded occupations, so as to fit them into those skilled and semiskilled trades in which labor is relatively scarce, has been greatly neglected. While the rehabilitation of the victims of accident and congenital disease has received a great

[1] *Report* of the Director of Emergency Conservation Work, for the period from April, 1933, to June 30, 1935 (1936).

[2] Discussed in relation to trade-union apprenticeship, vol. III, *Organized Labor*, Chap. IX.

[3] Works Progress Administration, *Report on the Works Program*, March 16, 1936, pp. 40–41.

The Federal Committee on Apprentice Training was appointed by the Secretary of Labor in 1934 to provide sound apprentice training under the NRA codes and at the same time safeguard labor standards. With the unconstitutionality of the NRA, the Committee continued its work under the National Youth Administration and recently has been placed on a permanent basis under the Department of Labor. This fills an obvious need since apprenticeship is a long-run program covering a period of years and must be so geared as to furnish those skilled labor recruits and replacements which are indispensable to our industrial system. Although the number of apprentices may fluctuate with business activity, it is still necessary to maintain adequate labor standards and training facilities for those who are employed as well as to relate the number of apprentices to the employment needs of the trades.

By May, 1937, forty-four states had organized apprenticeship committees, three states —Wisconsin, Oregon, and Arkansas—had enacted apprenticeship laws, while legislation was pending in California, Ohio, and Pennsylvania. Arkansas was the first state to pass a law modeled on the standard bill drafted by the Committee on Apprentice Legislation appointed by the Secretary of Labor at the request of the Third National Conference on Labor Legislation. The act provides for a program of voluntary apprenticeship under approved agreements; labor standards of apprentices are safeguarded and the development of a program of sound apprenticeship in the state is made possible; administration of the act is placed in the state Department of Labor.

deal of attention for some years, the phase of rehabilitation here alluded to has aroused little interest, presumably because the problem does not take the form of individualized cases.[1] It is to be hoped, however, that with millions of workers dislocated and undermined during the great depression and with tens of thousands displaced by technological changes,[2] much needed steps will be taken to rehabilitate a large proportion of them. In connection with rehabilitation of those in need of it, there is a strong case for a quitting wage which would induce as well as enable displaced workers to train for and find suitable employment. A quitting wage is especially needed in the absence of a system of unemployment benefits, and any such system might well arrange for it in order to assist rather than to interfere with the needed adjustment of the supply of labor to the demand for it. Here and there such a wage is being experimented with.[3]

REGULARIZING EMPLOYMENT

The need for regularizing employment in such cases as loading and unloading vessels at the docks has been made familiar by Sir William Beveridge and other writers on unemployment. At Liverpool and elsewhere in England in the old days the system of hiring was as at New York described above. Work was irregular and earnings inadequate; loafing

---

[1] Since 1928, the Transfer Committee in Great Britain has been relocating miners in rather considerable numbers. Provision was made for rehabilitation under the Act of 1927.

[2] *Supra*, pp. 33–38. Those displaced by technological changes call for special consideration. Many of them, even in "good times," are unemployed such long periods that their insurance rights will expire under the legislation being placed in effect. Moreover, a large part of them sooner or later accept employment at wages not supporting the former standard of living. Placement work must be made more effective by a well-devised system of retraining.

[3] For a discussion of the "dismissal wage," see Paul H. Douglas and Aaron Director, *op. cit.*, pp. 155–158. For the use of it in the Chicago men's clothing industry, see R. J. Myers, "Occupational Readjustment of Displaced Skilled Workmen," *Journal of Political Economy*, vol. 37 (1929), pp. 473–489.

Dismissal compensation for railway employees displaced by railroad consolidations has been provided under a five-year agreement signed by representatives of the railway unions and the railroad managements and made effective as of June, 1936. Three provisions for financial allowances to employees affected by railroad coordinations are stipulated: (1) For those employees shifted to lower paid employment, a compensatory allowance is paid during a five-year period sufficient in amount to maintain earnings at their former level. (2) For those deprived of employment, a monthly "coordination allowance" is paid equal in amount to 60 per cent of average monthly compensation during the twelve months prior to the coordination, with duration of payment ranging from six to sixty months for one to fifteen years of service. (3) Those eligible to benefits under the agreement may resign and accept a lump-sum "separation allowance" ranging in amount from three to twelve months' pay for one to fifteen years of service.

Monthly Labor Review, vol. 42 (June, 1936), pp. 1503–1504. For statements issued by the chairmen of the Railway Labor Executives Association and the railroad managements, see *Congressional Record*, May 21, 1936, pp. 7866–7948.

between jobs was accompanied by much that was evil. Central hiring now prevails at one or two British ports, and the workers are hired and paid by the week, have fairly steady work and regular incomes, and lead more nearly normal lives. Unfortunately the old order generally obtains in this country except at the Pacific ports of Seattle, Portland, and Los Angeles. Seattle has the distinction of being the first port in the United States to decasualize, under a system which took effect in 1921.[1] With regular employment of most of the workers, the number required in loading and unloading vessels was reduced to half of its former proportions.[2]

The most important single task is to stabilize industry and employment within it, for prevention is better than alleviation. A systematic handling of the problem of the turnover of labor by those in management would substantially reduce the number of persons unemployed and in the "labor reserve" when business is prosperous or normal and would be helpful in getting a regular flow of work through the shop. Much has been done to apply good business judgment to this problem, but more remains to be done.

Much the same is to be said of the uneven volume of production and employment in most establishments, and especially in those where weather and other conditions may interfere with the productive processes or where the demand for the product is irregular. In this connection the seasonal trades stand out. But here experience shows that constructive efforts can minimize the loss in overhead as well as in man power and earnings.[3] Fortunately science has gone a considerable distance to make the building trades less seasonal; they are, however, still highly seasonal in character. Much can be done to reduce the element of seasonality by campaigns to induce the doing of interior work in "off-seasons" by reducing building costs through lower wage scales and narrower margins of profit and even to induce the doing of exterior construction when the weather conditions are less favorable than they are in what is regarded as the normal season for building operations.[4]

The needle trades, an important group in manufacturing, are, as was indicated in our discussion of the causes of unemployment, for the most

[1] In each of these ports the system of decasualization differed from that employed elsewhere. A brief discussion of the experience in these ports and comparison with nondecasualized ports in the United States may be found in "Cargo Handling and Longshore Labor Conditions," U. S. Bureau of Labor Statistics, *Bulletin 550* (1932), prepared by Boris Stern.

[2] See *Monthly Labor Review*, October, 1924, pp. 134–136.

[3] By the simple expedient of staging the annual automobile show in the fall, and introducing new models then instead of in the spring, the automobile industry has done much to stabilize the production of motor vehicles. Furthermore, this stabilization has enabled suppliers of parts and raw materials, such as sheet steel and rubber tires, to reduce the seasonality of their production and employment.

[4] An excellent discussion of this matter will be found in *Seasonal Operation in the Construction Industries*, President's Conference on Unemployment (1924).

part very seasonal, partly because of the demands for winter, spring, summer, and autumn garments, but also partly because of a demand for style in clothing. Then, too, the contract system enters as both cause and effect of seasonal production. Here it has been found that by a systematic sales policy it is possible to encourage earlier buying which lengthens the busy season. Some firms have combined the manufacture of ready-made suits with the manufacture of "special orders," and in this way have made their business less irregular, for the peak of the busy season occurs in the one branch of manufacture at the time of the greatest slack in the other. In Chicago, workers have been transferred from one branch of the men's clothing industry to the other, which does not materially reduce the manufacturer's overhead, but does reduce the amount of time lost by the workers. In these and in other ways a number of firms in the needle trades have partially stabilized their own businesses, and usually not at the expense of the stability of the businesses of others in the trade.[1]

The busy and slack seasons in the soft-coal trade have been notorious in spite of the fact that only a small part of the product is used for domestic purposes. This was discussed at length by the United States Coal Commission, which recommended concessions in prices to induce consumers to buy early and store coal for winter use, the development of better facilities for storing coal at the mines, and improvements in the system for transporting coal, as desirable in an effort to reduce the existing waste.[2]

Not a few manufacturers have been circumstanced like the Dennison Manufacturing Company, which manufactures certain paper products, the demand for which is most seasonal. However, by introducing new products the demand for which had peaks at different times, by requiring orders to be placed well in advance, by taking orders to be filled part at a time over a long period, and by other devices, this particular firm changed a most unstable business into a fairly stable one.[3]

The problem involved in stabilizing industry in general, of bringing the business cycle under control, presents much more difficulty. In the literature setting out concrete experience during periods of depression, not a few have referred to their gains from price concessions.[4] This method, however, has distinct limitations. While lower prices may have

---

[1] By producing an excellent standardized product and by employing a sound sales policy a well-known shoe company for years operated fifty weeks or more in the year, while the shoe industry in general was employing only half of its capacity.

[2] See U. S. Coal Commission, *Final Report with Recommendations for Legislation* (1925).

[3] The unusual accomplishments of Mr. Dennison can be found in numerous articles and in almost any book on the stabilization of industry. H. Feldman, *The Regularization of Employment* (1925), and John R. Commons (and others), *Can Business Prevent Unemployment?* (1925) are two of the several books treating of this subject.

[4] For example, see some of the chapters in *Business Cycles and Unemployment* (1923).

the effect of increasing the total amount of the product purchased and this in turn of encouraging other business because of the increased buying power made available, the chief effect may be to bring increased business to some at the expense of the business of other firms. Here is an instance in which it is not true that "all can do what one can do" with the same result. All too frequently price cuts, and concessions of other kinds, develop into cutthroat competition, demoralization of the market, and loss to all.

So much, looking at the matter from the point of view of what the individual employer can do. In a competitive economy his control over the problem is rather limited. There are also distinct limitations upon what monopolistic industries and organized groups can be expected to accomplish toward stabilization, for what they naturally do may be precisely the wrong thing from the point of view of a general stabilization. Groups in position to exercise control are prone to maintain prices of their products and to restrict output. This not only affects the consuming public, purchasers of fuels or raw materials, and buyers of capital goods, but all too frequently causes a greater maladjustment between prices than would otherwise obtain. In the swing of the business cycle, price relations get out of balance. Getting them back into balance is a condition of recovery; and keeping them in balance is a condition of maintaining a sound state of trade once a recovery has been made. Indeed, it is in the exercise of control by private groups that the problem is largely to be found. The policies and devices of organized labor, industrial combinations, trade associations, and other control groups have produced increasing rigidity and it has therefore become increasingly difficult to secure proper price relationships.

As has been indicated, unsound tariff, monetary, banking, and other legislation has all too frequently been a cause of instability. On the other hand, governments have long attempted to cope with the problems presented by speculation, booms, and depressions. The attempts to do so have become both comprehensive and widespread with the recurrence of depressions and with the increased interest in, and knowledge of, the business cycle. Measures of many types have been involved: among others with which any general reader is more or less familiar are loans to banks and other private institutions by the Reconstruction Finance Corporation; the NIRA; the AAA with its crop limitations and subsidies; the FCA; control of the sale of securities; a public works program; a devaluation of the dollar; and control of bank credit. Most of these are discussed elsewhere in these volumes.[1] At this point, our discussion will be limited to some current monetary, credit, and fiscal proposals. In spite of the great interest in such proposals, and the undoubted

[1] See particularly, vol. I, Chap. VI (the NIRA); this chapter (Public Works Programs), and, this volume, Chaps. III and VIII (Social Insurance).

importance of monetary and credit controls, the discussion must be summary.[1]

Long since, it has become the practice of the countries of the world to adopt as the monetary standard a certain weight of a fine metal (gold or silver and in most cases the former) as the standard of value. The standard was fixed and the exchange rates between countries were stabilized; prices of the many things exchanged and the general price level fluctuated with technological and other matters affecting costs, the volume of money work to be done, credit facilities, and other factors affecting prices. It has been proposed that instead of requiring the general price level to adjust itself to the monetary standard or volume of currency, prices should be stabilized by from time to time altering the content of the metallic standard or by some other device of a managed currency. In this country the proposal of a managed currency has been most closely identified with the name of Irving Fisher.[2] Beginning many years ago, he has urged that the content of the gold dollar[3] should be increased or decreased as necessary to limit narrowly the fluctuations in the general price level as that level rose or fell. If prices were rising, he would increase the content of the dollar in proportion to the percentage increase; if prices were falling, he would decrease the content of the dollar in proportion to the percentage decrease. Beyond this, in the event a proportionate change in content did not prove to be an adequate corrective, he would make such further changes in the content of the dollar as were found necessary to stabilize the general price level. In more recent years, with almost all countries off the gold standard, proponents of a managed currency have shown an increasing interest in paper money, the amount to be increased or reduced as necessary to effect stabilization.

For the most part the objectives of a managed currency are desirable, but the desirability of a constant price level is questioned. Whatever

---

[1] For those who are informed concerning these matters, this summary statement will leave much to be desired. It will, however, introduce the subject for other readers. For the presentation of diverse points of view see, among others, J. M. Keynes, *Monetary Reform* (1923), pp. 167–222; R. G. Hawtrey, *Trade Depression and the Way Out* (1st ed.), pp. 68–84, and the *Art of Central Banking* (1932), Chaps. 5, 7, and 8; A. D. Gayer, *Monetary Policy and Economic Stabilization* (1935); H. C. Simons, "Rules Versus Authorities in Monetary Policy," *Journal of Political Economy*, vol. 44 (February, 1936), pp. 1–30; Alvin Hansen, *Economic Stabilization in an Unbalanced World* (1932), pp. 277–323; D. H. Robertson, *Banking Policy and the Price Level* (2d ed., 1932); J. M. Clark, *Strategic Factors in Business Cycles* (1934); E. F. M. Durbin, *The Problem of Credit Policy* (1935), pp. 109–241; C. A. Phillips, T. F. McManus and R. W. Nelson, *Banking and the Business Cycle* (1937); A. C. Pigou, *Industrial Fluctuations* (1929); F. A. Hayek, *Monetary Theory and the Trade Cycle* (1933); Gottfried von Haberler, *Prosperity and Depression* (1937).

[2] Of Professor Fisher's numerous books, see, particularly, *Stabilizing the Dollar* (1920), and *Stable Money, A History of the Movement* (1934). For critical comment see A. D. Gayer, *Monetary Policy and Economic Stabilization* (1935), pp. 186–189 and 257–273.

[3] This means, more accurately stated, changing the dollar price of gold.

the correct position on this issue may be, any managed currency is certain to be accompanied by difficult problems. Moreover, the adequacy of currency control to effect a high degree of stabilization remains in doubt.

There is no unanimity of opinion as to the desirability of a constant general price level. Some economists have favored a gently falling price level[1] while others have opposed this and favored a slowly rising one.[2] Still others, such as D. H. Robertson, have held that moderate cyclical movements of prices and output are desirable in the interests of progress.[3] The objective of preserving a stable and just debtor-and-creditor relationship through a stable price level may, over a ten-year period of increasing productivity and output, result in the debtor reaping a disproportionate share of the advantages of productivity and progress. It is questionable, moreover, whether a stable price level would be effective in ironing out industrial fluctuations, since with increasing productivity and sticky wages a stable level of prices would tend to promote an excessive expansion of profits and a boom. Numerous proposals have been advanced for the stabilization of money incomes through adjustment of the money supply to the growth of population or through stabilization of wage incomes.[4] Against these proposals, however, it may be said that a gradual rise in money-wage rates is preferable, since organized labor could not be expected to be reconciled to "frozen" money-wage levels.

Passing over the pressures incidental to the use of a paper currency not based directly on gold or something else of value—the pressure to print more notes, the pressure to prevent retirement of notes, the pressure to finance government otherwise than by taxation—there is the initial question of what prices are to be stabilized. Are they to be wholesale or retail prices? While a wholesale-price index is sensitive and thus makes prompt action possible, such an index would be inflationary since wholesale prices are most affected by improved technology. If, on the other hand, retail prices are stabilized, there is less danger of inflation, but the fact that retail prices are sticky makes it questionable whether such an index would sound the warning soon enough to avoid depression. Perhaps a transaction-value index would be preferable. In any case, a satisfactory price index must be composed of standardized commodities, preferably nonagricultural and largely domestic, enjoying free markets and sensitive to price changes and, so far as possible, removed from monopoly control or sluggish forces of adjustment. Needless to say, it would be

---

[1] F. A. Hayek, *Prices and Production* (2d ed., 1935), pp. 105 *et seq.*

[2] J. M. Keynes, *Treatise on Money* (1930), vol. 1, p. 298; Alvin Hansen, *op. cit.*, pp. 286–291.

[3] D. H. Robertson, *op. cit.*, p. 22.

[4] See discussion by Alvin H. Hansen, *op. cit.*, pp. 294–302, and an excellent summary statement by E. F. M. Durbin, "Money and Prices" in *What Everybody Wants to Know About Money* (1933), pp. 337–345 (edited by G. D. H. Cole).

very difficult to select commodities to conform to these requirements, even assuming that a plan could be set up and permissive controls established. What prices are selected and the weights attached to them are of great concern to pressure groups and therefore to legislators. Administrative and political difficulties are involved in a managed currency.

Next, if a managed currency is national, exchange rates between countries may become unstable. Tariff duties may be indirectly raised or lowered. Trade and capital movements between countries may be disturbed. This would be a source of instability.

Very important, many proponents of a managed currency assume a direct and close relationship between the content of the monetary standard or the volume of currency and the price level. Devaluate the dollar or increase the amount of currency, they say, and prices will tend to rise correspondingly; increase the content of the dollar or decrease the volume of currency and prices will tend to fall correspondingly. Experience, and particularly the experience of the United States with a program of inflation[1] and the devaluation of the dollar made by the President in 1934

[1] Subsequent to the banking crisis in March and the succeeding months of 1933, the following steps served to take the United States off the gold standard and made possible a program of monetary inflation:

1. The Presidential proclamation of March 6, 1933, controlling gold.

2. The monetary sections of the Emergency Banking Act of March 9, 1933. These provided for the control of gold and foreign exchange (sections 1 to 3), and for the issue of emergency currency (Federal Reserve bank notes—sections 401–403) against (a) any U. S. Government securities up to 100 per cent of face value; (b) any notes, drafts, or bills of exchange owned by the Federal Reserve Banks up to 90 per cent of face value. It should be noted that though there is a 5 per cent redemption fund with the Treasury, Federal Reserve bank notes do not require a gold reserve and therefore can be expanded without limit in exchange for government securities. These notes should not be confused with Federal Reserve notes which are secured by eligible business paper, government bonds, and a minimum gold reserve of 40 per cent.

3. Mobilization of gold, under Executive Orders issued March 10 and April 5, 1931.

4. The gold embargo by Executive Order, April 20, 1933.

5. Title III of the Agricultural Adjustment Act of May 12, 1933. This contained five currency measures:

    a. Federal Reserve banks were authorized to purchase government bonds or bonds of corporations of which the government was the majority stockholder (i.e., Home Owners Loan Corporation, etc.,) to the amount of $3,000,000,000, these bonds to be used, as provided in Title IV of the Emergency Banking Act, as collateral for the issue of Federal Reserve bank notes without any specific gold reserve.

    b. Issue of United States notes under the "greenback" law of February, 1862, to the limit of $3,000,000,000. No such notes were issued.

    c. The President was authorized to accept not more than $200,000,000 in silver in payment of intergovernmental war debts.

    d. Reduction of the gold content of the dollar by not more than 50 per cent by the President.

    e. Free coinage of silver at a ratio to gold to be fixed by the President. This was

under authority granted by Congress,[1] casts much doubt upon the closeness of this relation and the directness and immediacy of result. It is by no means a matter of arithmetic; psychological reactions to a given stimulus or sedative may vary widely.[2] In a depression, when the spirit of enterprise is at low ebb, a considerable alteration in the content of the dollar or in the volume of the currency may not have quick or full effect. Most important of all in this connection is the fact that approximately

later supplemented by the passage of the Silver Purchase Act of June 19, 1934, the purpose of which was "to increase the amount of silver in our monetary stocks with the ultimate objective of having and maintaining one-fourth of their monetary value in silver and three-fourths in gold." Under the authority of this act, the President, on August 9, 1934, issued an order nationalizing silver and requiring the delivery to the mints, within 90 days, of all silver situated in the continental United States on August 9, "to be coined into standard silver dollars or otherwise added to the monetary stocks of the United States."

6. Abrogation of gold clauses, June 5, 1933, in all obligations past or future, public or private.

7. The Banking Act of 1933, approved June 16, which provided the Federal Reserve Board with large powers over the extension of speculative credit; created the Federal Deposit Insurance Corporation; separated investment and commercial banking and increased the regulation of holding companies controlling member banks; increased the control over loan and investment policies of national and member banks; and increased the powers of the Federal Reserve Board particularly with reference to centralizing open market operations under a Federal Open Market Committee of the Board.

8. The gold-purchase program and the calling in of small gold holdings.

9. The Gold Reserve Act of 1934 and the revaluation of gold.

Attention should also be called to the administrative changes and legislation affecting agricultural credit during the above period:

1. The agricultural credit agencies of the United States were reorganized on May 27, 1933.

2. The Emergency Farm Mortgage Act of May 12, 1933, which provided for farm mortgage relief through refinancing and reduction of principal of farm mortgages by the Federal Land Bank; the reduction of interest on loans and deferment of principal; and the issuance of Federal Land Bank bonds to a maximum amount of $2,000,000,000 for refinancing farm mortgages.

3. The Farm Credit Act of 1933, approved June 13, 1933, designed to supply short time and seasonal credit for agricultural production and marketing.

[1] The Gold Reserve Act and the revaluation of gold, Jan. 30 and 31, 1934. The Act provided for:

1. The nationalization of all gold, especially that held by the Federal Reserve Banks, for which gold certificates were given in return. The Federal Reserve Act was amended to make gold certificates rather than gold collateral for notes and for reserves.

2. An upper limit of permissible revaluation of the gold dollar at 60 per cent of the existing dollar of 25.8 grains, the lower limit having been fixed at 50 per cent by the Controlled Inflation Act of May 12, 1933.

3. Creation of an exchange stabilization fund of $2,000,000,000 from the "profits" of revaluation, to be under the exclusive control of the Secretary of the Treasury with the Approval of the President.

[2] As R. A. Stevenson and R. S. Vaile have stated in their *Balancing the Economic Controls* (p. 75), "It is not yet possible for economic science to say with any assurance precisely what instruments of control are adequate to regulate the price level or to what degree

90 per cent of the money work done is done with bank deposits, not in cash. Bank deposits as well as the monetary standard or the volume of currency must be controlled if the general price level is to be controlled with any great degree of effectiveness and intelligence. This fact has, of course, come to be generally recognized, and is implicit in the efforts of governments to control the volume of credit.

Two methods of checking booms and lifting depressions, both having to do with credit, have long been advocated and in the more recent years more or less used by leading countries. These are (a) changes in the rediscount rate made by central banks or, in the United States, by the Board of Governors of the Reserve System, and (b) open-market operations by the government or its agency. These may be discussed in the light of the institutional arrangements obtaining in the United States. The discussion, therefore, requires a statement of the essentials of the Reserve System which was introduced in 1914, and which, in American banking, plays a role similar to that performed by central banks in certain foreign countries.

All national banks and approximately a sixth of other banks in the United States have membership in the Reserve System and these possess by far the larger part of our banking resources. These member banks must keep reserves in Reserve Banks against their demand deposits. The minimum reserves permitted are 13 per cent of such deposits in Class *A* cities, such as New York and Chicago, 10 per cent in Class *B* cities, and 7 per cent in the smaller Class *C* cities. A similar reserve of 3 per cent is also required against time deposits. Under the Banking Act of 1935,[1] the Board of Governors of the Reserve System, were, however,

---

they should be applied or at precisely what time. It may be said that control mechanisms undoubtedly work in this or that direction, but the psychological reactions following the introduction of these mechanisms cannot be predicted, and therefore the results flowing from these efforts at control are unpredictable."

[1] This Act, approved Aug. 23, 1935, reflects a broader conception of the functions of the Federal Reserve System in the nation's economic life, and defines more clearly the responsibilities of the Board and the Regional banks.

The main provisions of the Act, other than certain technical sections, are as follows:

1. Responsibility for national credit policy has been concentrated with the Board of Governors of the Federal Reserve by giving them greater authority and control over discount rates and reserve requirements. The power to change member-bank-reserve requirements, formerly changeable only in credit emergencies and with the approval of the President, now rests with the Board.

2. The policy adopted by the Open-market Committee, in which the Board has membership, now becomes obligatory with the individual Reserve Banks.

3. The lending powers of the Federal Reserve Banks to member banks are broadened considerably.

4. The real-estate-loan provisions of member banks have been liberalized.

5. Deposit insurance is continued under a permanent fund. To enjoy its protection, membership in the Federal Reserve System, by state banks (with certain exceptions) whose deposits average $1,000,000 or more in 1941, is made compulsory by 1942.

empowered, within twice the percentages just noted, to require such reserves against deposits as they might deem proper. Only these credits in the Reserve System are counted as legal reserves; the cash in the tills of a bank is not counted for reserve purposes. The credits in Reserve Banks may be obtained by turning over acceptable commercial paper and bankers' acceptances for discount, and by offering government securities as collateral for loans. Member banks can also secure Reserve notes by the same process. In turn the Reserve Banks are required to keep a reserve of 35 per cent in gold or "lawful money" against the member-bank reserves and 40 per cent against Reserve notes. These reserve requirements set the legal limits for the extension of credit by the banks within the Reserve System.

The Federal Reserve Board, now the Board of Governors, has, from the beginning, been empowered to control the rediscount rate on commercial paper, while the Open-market Committee is empowered to make regulations relative to open-market operations by the Reserve Banks.[1] It was expected that if the rediscount rate to the banks were raised, the rate of interest on bank loans would have to be raised also. This would therefore check the demand for credit in a boom situation, halt the rise of prices, and check speculation. On the other hand, were the rediscount rate lowered in a depression situation, it was expected that loan interest rates would be reduced, and the demand for credit to finance business operations enlarged, with a resultant rise in prices, and encouragement to business enterprise. The sale of government obligations, in conjunction with an increased rediscount rate, was expected to reduce reserves and curtail lending power in boom times, the purchase of obligations to enlarge reserves, increase lending capacity, and encourage business in depression.

These powers vested in the Reserve System have at times been haltingly and cautiously used, at other times more vigorously exercised. An example of cautious exercise is found in the 1920's, when because of uncertainty as to what might occur and because of the resistant attitude of the banks and businessmen, action to check the boom was very haltingly taken, and with little effect. It appears that it is difficult and unpopular for a government to interfere with the ways of business in a boom situation. In the depression situation of the thirties, the government, of course, acted more vigorously in the exercise of these powers, but without strong response.

Assuming solvency of the banks in general, experience shows that in depression periods there is no shortage of credit capacity nor are the low interest rates on good collateral then prevailing discouraging to borrowers.

---

[1] For details, see Harold Reed, *Development of Federal Reserve Policy* (1931); C. O. Hardy, *Credit Policies of the Federal Reserve System* (1932); Lauchlin Currie, *The Supply and Control of Money in the United States* (1934); and W. R. Burgess, *The Reserve Banks and the Money Market* (1936).

Any reduction in the rediscount rate has little effect on the bank rate for loans. Soundness of the collateral, whether the principal is secure, is above all else of interest to the bank, and it finds good loans difficult to make. Hence, as in recent years, idle funds are large and an unusual proportion of the resources of the banks find investment in securities yielding exceedingly low returns. On the borrowing side, the demand for loans remains limited whether the rate of interest paid is 4, 5, or 6 per cent, so long as depression is not well on the way to being lifted.

But, after all, it is the control that can be effectively exercised in boom situations that is most important, for depressions result from booms. In boom situations, in addition to the probable tardy and halting exercise of control, there are conditions which limit the effectiveness of increases in the rediscount rate. It appears that only a very considerable increase in interest rates then has any discernible effect upon the demand for loans. This is explained in part by the boom psychology, in part by the prospect of easy profit as labor costs become relatively a smaller item in total costs, in part by the fact that in many situations interest charges are comparatively unimportant items in total costs and a cent or two makes little difference. Moreover, loan rates on ordinary commercial paper are in the United States so much higher than the rediscount rate that any modest increase in the latter may present no particular problem to the banking fraternity.[1]

There is a further aspect of the matter to which attention must be called. Control in a closed economy is one thing, in the actual economy another. In so far as the effective rate to be realized on funds is altered, capital movements between countries are affected. Faced with a low rate of return, capital may move out of a country in search of more profitable investment elsewhere. If there is a fair degree of security, which is not always to be found at the present juncture, investment funds are fairly mobile as between countries.

It appears, therefore, that control of the rediscount rate cannot be expected to be a wholly, if a really important, method of checking booms and of effecting recovery from depressions. But when accompanied by changes in reserve requirements, which the Board of Governors is empowered to make, control of rediscount rates becomes more effective. In recent months, when a measure of recovery had been realized, an undesirable speculation in stocks and evidence of inflation appeared and on two occasions steps were taken to increase the reserves required.[2]

---

[1] A fuller discussion of these matters, with detail, may be found, among other places, in Paul H. Douglas, *Controlling Depressions* (1935), Chaps. 5 and 10.

[2] On Aug. 15, 1936, member-bank requirements were raised 50 per cent and on Jan. 30, 1937, the Board of Governors announced a further increase of 33⅓ per cent, half of the increase to be effective Mar. 1, the remaining half May 1. These orders brought the required reserves up to the maximum under the law. In addition, brokers' loans have been

Though tightened, the reserves appear to have remained in excess of market needs. Though the tangible results of these actions taken are unimpressive, and though reserves in excess of certain percentages cannot be required, it appears that the Board of Governors will find in their power to increase reserve requirements a rather important instrument to use in checking unhealthy inflation and booms.[1]

In this country open-market operations have generally been regarded as a more effective control device than is found in raising or lowering the rediscount rate. The two controls may be used together. An increased rediscount rate might be accompanied by the sale of government securities to banks and the general public. The securities would be paid for by checks on the bank accounts with the Federal Reserve Banks thus lessening their reserves. This would be expected to cause the banks to curtail loans, which would check inflation and a further rise of prices in the boom situation, or to cause the banks to rediscount paper at the Reserve Banks, thus making the higher rate effective and causing an increase in bank rates, with the same result. It would also be expected to lower bond prices, making new flotations more difficult and checking new construction, etc. Conversely, the purchase of government obligations would be expected to have precisely the opposite effects in depression situations. Some economists in the early 1930's maintained that large purchases of federal obligations would break the back of the depression then obtaining.

The Federal Reserve has made extensive, though at times possibly not sufficiently drastic, use of open-market operations. Late in 1929, following the stock-market crash in October, some 300 millions of government securities were bought, and this was followed by the purchase of some 200 millions in 1930. Then in the spring of 1932 further purchases, aggregating almost a billion, were made, with the result that the reserves of the member banks were built up to unprecedented heights. But, as Douglas has said, "the hoped-for expansion of loans and of business did

---

regulated and margin regulations made. Under authority of the Securities Exchange Act of 1934, the Federal Reserve Board announced its first margin regulations in October, 1934. Loans were limited to 55 per cent of the market value of the security offered or to 100 per cent of the lowest price at which the security sold during the preceding thirty-six months, but not to exceed 75 per cent of the current market value. In a bad stock-market situation, new regulations were made, effective Nov. 1, 1937. Cash margins on stock purchases were reduced from 55 to 40 per cent, and, for the first time, a curb was placed on short-selling by requiring 50 per cent in cash on such sales. Moreover, the margin required of brokers when borrowing from banks on stocks as collateral was reduced from 40 to 25 per cent.

[1] This discussion assumes the creation and allocation of credit by private banks. Of course, the possibility of control would be quite different were credit "socialized" or were banks required to keep 100 per cent reserves behind deposits. Though such "reforms" have been advocated, they have received limited acceptance and a discussion of them is not within the scope of these volumes.

not occur. . . . The banks used their new reserves to get out of debt
to the Federal Reserve System and to avoid paying interest to the latter.
They did not increase their loans to industry and the attempt to obtain
revival through open-market operations failed."[1]   The explanation is a
repetition of what has been said in connection with lowering the rediscount rate.   In depression, banks desire security of principal and liquidity
above all else, and the spirit of enterprise is at low ebb.

Perhaps it can be said that such instruments of currency and credit
control as have been commonly employed appear to be of limited effectiveness in depression situations.   Government spending, say on public
works, a subject to be discussed presently, has more direct effect and may
be more helpful in assisting recovery.   On the other hand, the controls
available can be effectively used to check booms.   The question remains,
however, whether the checking of booms in such a manner may not be
accompanied by crashes.

With a banking system in which the creation and control of credit
remains in private hands, a high degree of integrated regulation is necessary in order that the monetary policies of the Federal Reserve System
and the fiscal policies of the Treasury will coincide and not conflict.
In fact, any effective attempts at stabilization necessarily involve complementary action.   In a depression, for example, the failure of the Federal
Reserve System to pursue a sufficiently liberal credit policy may produce
deflationary effects perhaps strong enough seriously to counteract the
inflationary efforts of the Treasury with respect to budgetary policy,
debt management and taxation, and emergency spendings.   Once a
depression is under way, with government revenues falling rapidly while
expenditures, on the other hand, are increasing, deficit financing becomes
both necessary and desirable.[2]   Increased taxation, particularly excise
levies which hamper recovery, finds no place in a program of recovery
from a depression.   Budgetary deficits and borrowing then serve to mop
up idle and hoarded funds and to return them to circulation through the
medium of government spendings and public works expenditures.   With
a resumption of more prosperous economic conditions, taxation should be
increased not only to retire the accumulated debt but also to exercise a
check on any tendencies toward overexpansion.   At the same time public-
works programs can and should be curtailed[3] and with a fall in the volume
of unemployment, economic stabilization will be further promoted by the
automatic decrease in unemployment benefits paid out from the unem-

[1] Paul H. Douglas, op. cit., p. 117.   It should be added that in the autumn of 1931,
when England went off the gold standard, there was for a time a reversal of policy in open-
market operations.

[2] See Chap. II, pp. 111–114, also Balancing the Budget: Federal Fiscal Policy During
Depression, a statement by a University of Chicago Round Table ("Public Policy Pam-
phlets," No. 1, 1933).

[3] See infra, p. 116.

ployment reserve funds.[1] Thus fiscal policy of a central government is important in a stabilization program.

While there is disagreement on, and uncertainty as to, many phases of this matter of stabilization, there should be general agreement on the need for the fullest possible data on production in the main branches of industry, on stocks on hand, and on markets, and also on the trend of costs as related to prices. Such data might be expected to temper the optimism of the overoptimistic and to calm the fears of the overfearful. With accurate knowledge, intelligence and reasoned action could be substituted in a degree for misguided promotion and plunging on the upswing of the cycle.

PUBLIC WORKS, WORK RELIEF

It has been suggested that governments by postponing or accelerating public works according to the state of industry can do much to avoid and to relieve depression situations. The customary definition of public works intended to be included in such a program embraces such diverse government projects as the construction of post offices, school buildings, and hydroelectric plants, street widening, park improvement, land reclamation, river and harbor improvement, and flood control. Usually the result is durable goods or fixed structures, and rarely has the definition embraced services as such. Labor on public works is normally hired, retained and paid, or discharged on the basis of fitness and efficiency, and quite without reference to relief rolls or charitable list. In this respect public works differ from relief work, in which the primary aim is care of the needy unemployed. This distinction becomes less clear when the motives of construction of ordinary public works and aid to the unemployed are combined as they have been in the United States since 1933. Thus, on many of the WPA projects the supervisors, and perhaps a fixed percentage of key workers, have not been drawn from the relief rolls, but the remainder of those employed have been selected in view of their relief needs.[2] As will be indicated shortly, the aims of work relief are not always entirely compatible with those of public works.

The idea of requiring useful work from the indigent in return for aid is not of recent origin. In Elizabethan England, overseers were required to keep stocks of goods on hand on which the able-bodied could be set to work. The Royal Commission of 1834 recommended that agreeable, normal labor should be encouraged and that the work provided "ought to be useful employment."[3] However, the idea that poverty was due to

[1] See Chap. III, pp. 176–178.

[2] Other practical considerations make the distinction difficult. Thus funds intended for public works have been used for relief work and later emergency relief funds have been expended on PWA projects. We will not attempt to trace all these administrative and financial complications.

[3] Sidney and Beatrice Webb, *English Poor Law Policy* (1910), p. 5.

individual shortcomings generally triumphed over these farsighted recommendations and "laborious and undesirable work . . . to discourage applications from all who [were] not really necessitous" was required.[1] In times of acute unemployment, as in the 1890's, in 1914–1915, in 1921–1922 and again since 1930,[2] work on rock piles, in wood yards, and a variety of similar undertakings was frequently resorted to by unimaginative public officials in the United States as well as abroad.

Work relief has been used as a test of worthiness for aid, often with little thought given to the value of the tangible result. The product has generally been of little value as compared to its cost; usually slight attention has been given to efficiency on the job; substandard wages have been paid for part-time work; and the stigma of charity has been present. Such undertakings of charity long since came to be frowned upon by those who were informed and especially by those who had practical experience with them, because of their demoralizing influence and inadequacy.[3] It was with a judgment of this kind that the minority of the British Poor Law Commission in 1905 espoused a program of public works as an intelligent attack upon the problem of unemployment.

In the ordinary course of things, most public-works programs have been undertaken in prosperous times when funds were most readily available. Thus expansion of governmental employment has occurred in boom times, contraction with recession in private employment. One of the first attempts to change this timing and to modify the purpose of public works came in 1902, when the French government officially endorsed a policy of reserving important public works for periods of unemployment.[4] In 1905 the minority of the British Poor Law Commission recommended the scheduling of public works and regular governmental purchases in such a way that a larger amount would be done when private business was less active, thus tending to stabilize the total economic activity of the nation.[5] The theory underlying this proposal was developed and popularized by the Webbs: " . . . even in the blackest period of trade depression something like fifteen-sixteenths of all wage earners still find employment, and something like 95 per cent of the highest aggregate of good years is still being paid in wages. . . . It is calculated by Dr. Bowley . . . that if only 3 or 4 per cent of the Government orders year by year were reserved, to be executed altogether when trade began to fall off, this would counterpoise the cyclical fluctuations, so far

---

[1] *Ibid.*, p. 28.

[2] This was done chiefly by the municipal governments, with the hope that malingerers would automatically be weeded out. During the winter of 1914–1915, ninety-nine cities in this country were furnishing special work for relief purposes. A. D. Gayer, *Public Works in Prosperity and Depression* (1935), p. 5.

[3] See Philip Klein, *The Burden of Unemployment* (1923).

[4] International Labor Office, *Report on Unemployment* (1922), p. 119.

[5] J. M. Clark, *Economics of Planning Public Works* (1935), p. 9.

as all industries are concerned in which cyclical depressions are at present met by dismissal of hands instead of by going on short time."[1] Later (1924) calculations by Bowley and Stuart led to less optimistic conclusions, but nevertheless to an affirmance of the belief that cyclical fluctuations could be much reduced by proper allocation in time of public works.[2] In the United States O. T. Mallery maintained that a different timing of public works could have carried one-third of the burden involved in the acute depression of 1921.[3]

These estimates, particularly the early English ones, were based on business depressions relatively mild in character when compared with the prolonged recessions of business activity in the postwar period, and with the acute unemployment in the United States after 1929. We now realize that a public-works program could not be expected to smooth out such violent fluctuations in private employment and yet operate with reasonable efficiency. This conclusion is amply confirmed by foreign experience. The Commission established in France in 1908 for distributing public work "to balance to a certain extent the depression in the labour market" produced no tangible results.[4] Such proposals as were made in Norway in 1926 for the establishment of a reserve fund for accelerated spending in times of depression were later withdrawn.[5] Great Britain, one of the few countries having laws covering advance planning,

[1] Sidney and Beatrice Webb, *The Prevention of Destitution* (1911), pp. 112–113.

[2] A. L. Bowley and F. D. Stuart in *Is Unemployment Inevitable?* (1924), pp. 366–367. "We reach the conclusion that it is possible to provide funds for regularization of the labour market, if a strong policy is framed and carried out, without otherwise disturbing the demand for labour, that practical difficulties of administering a scheme are serious but not insuperable, and that the transference of expenditure from one year to another could be on such a scale as to make an important reduction in the cyclical oscillation of unemployment; but its effect would be principally on men's unskilled labour, and under the best possible administration would leave a considerable part of the problem unsolved."

[3] The case for the adoption of such a plan is well presented by Otto T. Mallery in *Business Cycles and Unemployment*, Chap. 14, and in *American Labor Legislation Review*, vol. 14, pp. 157–158. See also F. G. Dickinson, "Public Construction and Cyclical Unemployment," in *Annals of the American Academy of Political and Social Science*, vol. 139, no. 228 (September, 1928), and Leo Wolman, *Planning and Control of Public Works*. Professor Dickinson claims entirely too much for advance planning. He presents statistical data designed to show how, with allocations to public works varying between a minimum of $19,000,000 for 1923 and a maximum of $2,527,000,000 for 1921, a large part of the unevenness in factory employment during the period 1919–1926 might have been offset. Of course, much of the work was nonpostponable. Moreover, little of the labor required on public projects would be drawn from manufacture; most of it would be found idle in the nonpublic part of the construction industry. In discussing the role which might be played by public works, one needs to keep in mind that in time of depression private construction is at a low ebb. A very large public construction program would be required to iron out the unevenness in the construction industry itself.

[4] International Labour Office, *Unemployment and Public Works* (Geneva, 1931), p. 34.

[5] *Ibid.*, p. 52. See, also, C. J. Ratzlaff, *The Scandinavian Unemployment Relief Program* (University of Pennsylvania Press, 1934).

has likewise done little of significance in this respect. As early as 1909, the Development and Road Fund Act of that year provided the necessary framework for public works designed to counteract employment fluctuations, but the Act was permissive only with no action definitely assured.[1] During the decade beginning in 1920, a sustained program of public-employment projects was pursued, but owing to poor planning, lack of effective control by the central government over local bodies, delay and bad timing, no sizeable volume of work on public projects was made available during a period of deep depression. In fact, "the great bulk of relief work was performed during the comparatively prosperous years of 1923–29 while no appreciable expenditure for such works was made during the depression years of 1930–1933. The British policy with regard to public works, in short, was primarily directed toward providing immediate relief to the unemployed during the most prosperous postwar years. Neither the size of the program nor its timing was such as to afford it an opportunity markedly to affect the general industrial situation in the British Isles."[2] At the present time, the British Government has turned to less expensive methods of dealing with unemployment and public-works programs are no longer being considered officially except in terms of the normal volume of public construction.[3]

There is, however, a large volume of possible public works, and serious consideration should be given to the problem of planning these undertakings with a view to obtaining the maximum stabilizing effect consistent with efficiency and public need.

The first requisite of such a program is thorough planning of future public works, and a classification of them according to their urgency, the possibility of postponement and acceleration, the types and amounts of labor and material needed, the financial outlays necessary, and necessary plans for financing undertakings. It is only through such comprehensive planning, in both engineering and financial aspects, that a program of public works could conceivably be set in motion in time to be of use in checking a depression. Other and probably more significant advantages of advance planning are that more comprehensive and coordinated projects can be undertaken, that the most useful rather than the most avail-

[1] *Ibid.*, p. 34.

[2] A. C. Hill and Isador Lubin, *The British Attack on Unemployment* (Publication 51, The Brookings Institution, 1934), pp. 239–240.

During the period 1920–1934, the British government expended more than £320,851,000 on unemployment-relief-works programs, and an additional £125,752,000 for trade and export guarantees. It is estimated that £1,000,000 provided direct work for one year for 3,000 men or £333 for one man-year of direct work with an equal amount of indirect work provided in furnishing materials, equipment and transportation. Thus, for the total of £446,000,000 expended, some three million man-years of employment were provided—as contrasted with the 24 million man-years lost by insured persons through unemployment between 1921–1934. (*Ibid.*, pp. 82–83).

[3] League of Nations Publication, *Inquiry on National Public Works* (Geneva, 1934), p. 82.

able work can be done, that wastes can be avoided, and that sound financing can be arranged. Careful planning is the basis of sound public works.

The use of public works as a counterpoise to cyclical fluctuations is, unfortunately, beset with many serious difficulties. Techniques of construction change and may render useless carefully made and costly plans; tastes and requirements of the community are not static and are often unpredictable. Once started, some projects must be completed and hence may carry over from depression into boom times; others cannot be postponed without sacrifice of public advantage. Furthermore, it is easier to finance public construction in good times when public revenues are larger. Political considerations are important; an administration usually wishes to have a record of public improvements made, and incidentally may benefit from the distribution of contracts and jobs among loyal supporters. Once plans for a project are made, contractors and others exert pressure to have them executed without delay.

We shall consider some of these matters more fully presently. Partly because of such difficulties as have been mentioned, no country has consistently developed and carried out through boom and depression such a program of public works. Faced with a stagnant and undermined market and with destitute unemployed persons, what some countries, and most strikingly the United States in recent years, have done has been to hasten public works and to devise relief-work projects in an effort to prime the pump and stimulate recovery and to provide employment on private payrolls by increased spending. This policy has been accompanied by the development of modified theories. In spite of the fact that an enlarged volume of public works prosecuted in depression may be expected, other things equal, to reduce the volume in the boom phase of the next cycle, the emphasis is now generally placed upon ending the deflation which has been in process and effecting recovery while maintaining in a decent way those who through no fault of their own are unemployed. This was the thought behind the public works and the related relief-work plans undertaken in the United States, after September, 1931. A review of these plans, as they have been operated, will be helpful in a more careful examination of the theory of public works and as background for a discussion of unemployment compensation and relief.

Public Works and Relief Work in the United States.—When the depression of the 1930's developed, little had been done in advance planning of public works in the United States, despite the wide discussion of its advantages. A few municipalities had, it is true, developed long-time programs, but these were primarily for making municipal improvements rather than for the stabilization of employment. Between 1915 and 1931 several of the states passed laws intended to stimulate the planning and use of public works as a remedy for unemployment. Except for about $40,000 expended in Pennsylvania during 1921–1922, these laws were inoperative.[1] In 1919 Senator Kenyon introduced a bill in the United States Senate to provide $100,000,000 to create a United States Emergency Public Works Board which would coordinate Federal, state, and municipal efforts to stimulate public works in depression.[2] In nearly every subsequent Congress some effort was made to establish a Federal system of public works in preparation for cyclical depression, yet despite the announced interest of the President-elect in 1928[3] no legislation resulted until 1931.   Thus, largely as a result of procrastination, explained in part by the rather general belief that depressions in the United States were a thing of the past, the national and local governments generally neglected the advance preparation of engineering and financial plans for their public works.

After 1929 the comfortable illusions of security began to dissipate and in February, 1931, Congress passed an act creating the Federal Employment Stabilization Board.[4]   The Board was composed of the Secretaries of Commerce, of Labor, of Agriculture, and of the Treasury, with a permanent staff.   It was instructed " . . . to advise the President from time to time of the trend of employment and business activity and of the existence or approach of periods of business depression in the United States or any substantial portion thereof; to cooperate with the construction agencies in formulating methods of advance planning. . . . "[5]   In event of increased unemployment, the Board was to estimate needed appropriations for public works.   Emergency appropriations were to be limited to highways, river and harbor works, flood control, and public buildings.   It was the Emergency Relief and Conservation Act, however, which represented the first attempt by the Federal Government to plan public works on a large scale to relieve unemployment.

When the Public Works Administration was set up in 1933, one of the first acts of Administrator Ickes was to provide for a National Planning Board,[6] "to advise and assist the Administrator . . . through the preparation, development, and maintenance of comprehensive plans . . . through surveys and research . . . and through the analysis of projects for coordination and sequence . . . and to obtain the maximum amount of cooperation and correlation of effort among the agencies of the Federal, State and local governments."[7]   The National Planning Board with its

[1] A. D. Gayer, op. cit., pp. 7–9.

[2] Ibid., p. 10.

[3] The President-elect announced that a four-billion-dollar fund would be created but no steps were taken to that end.

[4] Federal Employment Stabilization Act, Public no. 616, 71st Congress, 1931 (S. 5776).

[5] Sec. 3(a).

[6] The Board, appointed on July 20, 1933, consisted of Frederic A. Delano, Charles E. Merriam, and Wesley C. Mitchell.

[7] National Resources Committee, Progress Report, June 15, 1936, p. 23.

staff made a number of studies of the social, economic, administrative, and engineering problems involved in planned public works.[1] The recommendations and report of this Board led directly to the establishment by Executive Order of the President on June 30, 1934, of the National Resources Board.[2]   The Board was "to prepare and present to the President a program of procedure dealing with the physical, social, governmental and economic aspects of the use of land, water and other national resources and such related subjects as may from time to time be referred to the Board by the President."[3]   The Board proceeded with its task of compiling lists of proposed public works, showing which should be given priority, and recommended that a central agency be established through which all future projects could be cleared and coordinated.[4]   The work of the National Resources Board was continued by the National Resources Committee, which was established by executive order[5] of the President under powers conferred by the Emergency Relief Appropriation Act.[6]   The essential powers and personnel of the Board and the Committee were the same.   In accordance with the request of the President, two studies for priority lists of public-works projects were undertaken. One was an effort to carry on and revise, with the help of the PWA, the work of the Employment Stabilization Board in assembling the six-year programs of all Federal construction agencies.   The other was a study, in cooperation with state and regional agencies, of the possible ultimate development of some twenty major drainage basins.[7]

[1] Among the most important of these studies are those of J. M. Clark, *Economics of Planning Public Works* (1935), and A. D. Gayer, *Public Works in Prosperity and Depression* (1935).   The work of the Board is reviewed and other studies summarized in its *Final Report*—dated Aug. 1, 1934.   See also Simeon E. Leland and others, "Division of Costs and Responsibility (Public Works)," in *Public Works Planning*, National Resources Committee (1937), pp. 139–208.

[2] In addition to the three former members of the Planning Board, the National Resources Board consisted of the Secretaries of Interior (Chairman), of Agriculture, of War, of Commerce, of Labor, and the Federal Emergency Relief Administrator.

[3] Executive Order 6777, June 30, 1934 (under authority of the NIRA).

[4] In cooperation with state planning boards and other agencies, the Board in January, 1935, began the preparation of a general list of all available public-works projects for use in the then pending work-relief program.   A remarkable feature of this survey was the number of organizations which cooperated in furnishing information.   Returns were received from 21,000 different units, ranging from 81 Federal offices to 7,800 municipal and 468 private organizations.   There were listed 138,300 separate projects, estimated to cost twenty billion dollars.   State authorities who passed judgment on the value of these projects listed about twelve billion dollars' worth as needed.   National Resources Board *Report*, Dec. 1, 1934, p. 4.

[5] Executive Order 7065, dated June 7, 1935.

[6] Approved April 8, 1935, 49 *Stat.* 115.

[7] Consideration was given to pollution control, navigation, reforestation, recreation, soil conservation, water power, flood control—in short, all types of water development. National Resources Committee, *Progress Report*, June 15, 1936.

These studies represent truly remarkable advances in the planning of public works to utilize and conserve our natural resources intelligently.[1] But the work has been almost exclusively advisory or educational; the actual construction of public works depended upon governmental appropriations, which in turn reflected the sentiment of the public and its Congress. In the actual selection of projects for prosecution during the depression crisis, it was often necessary to postpone some useful project given priority in these plans for national development in favor of some less useful project which provided more direct employment per dollar expended.

During the early years of the depression the volume of expenditures for private construction decreased abruptly from a peak estimated at $9,410,000,000 in 1928 to a low point of $1,990,000,000 in 1933, which was less than one-fourth of the prosperity level. In the face of this

TABLE 17.—CONSTRUCTION IN THE UNITED STATES, 1925 TO 1935[1]
(In Millions of Dollars)

Year	Local and state	Federal (incl. fed. aid)	Total public works	Percentage of total construction	Private construction	Percentage of total construction	Total construction
1925	2,470	240	2,710	23.5	8,840	76.5	11,550
1926	2,380	250	2,630	21.8	9,410	78.2	12,040
1927	2,800	240	3,040	25.2	9,010	74.8	12,050
1928	2,750	250	3,000	24.5	9,230	75.5	12,230
1929	2,480	280	2,760	23.7	8,870	76.3	11,630
1930	2,920	310	3,230	31.7	6,950	68.3	10,180
1931	2,410	410	2,820	37.2	4,760	62.8	7,580
1932	1,490	520	2,010	46.2	2,340	53.8	4,350
1933	1,000	590	1,590	44.4	1,990	55.6	3,580
1934	1,030	1,100	2,130	47.9	2,310	52.1	4,440
1935	1,030	1,000	2,030	....	a	....	a

a No final estimate for private construction is as yet available, although the Construction Economics Section of the Department of Commerce has estimated the total to be about $3,370,000,000, bringing the total for all construction to about $5,400,000,000.

[1] Adapted from United States Department of Commerce, The Construction Industry in the United States (April, 1936), p. 13, prepared by H. M. Bookholtz and C. Judkins.

disastrous decline in private construction, the state and local governments at first made an effort to expand their construction work, but after 1931 the loss of tax revenues and the exhaustion of credit forced a contraction of expenditures. In 1929 state and local construction totaled $2,480,000,000; in 1930 this total reached $2,920,000,000, only to drop abruptly to $1,000,000,000 in 1933. In comparison, the volume of Federal expenditures had been small, but in contrast to private and to state and local construction it increased steadily from 1927 to 1933.

[1] Of particular interest are the reports of the National Resources Committee on Regional Planning, e.g., pt. I, Pacific Northwest (May, 1936); pt. II, St. Louis Region (June, 1936); and pt. III, New England (July, 1936).

In 1929 Federal construction (including Federal aid) totaled $280,000,000; by 1933 the total reached $590,000,000 and in the following year jumped to $1,100,000,000 or more than state and local expenditures combined. This great expansion in federally financed construction was, however, not sufficient to offset the decline in state and local public works and was far short of counterbalancing the collapse of private construction. This is clearly shown in Table 17.

During this period the Federal and state public-works policy underwent important changes which reflected the changing political and economic pressures of the crisis. While the mounting relief needs during 1930 and 1931 were to a great extent met by increases in public relief funds, private charity, and aid from existing welfare organizations, such measures were obviously insufficient. Unemployment and destitution continued to mount. Still adhering to the traditional belief in local responsibility for unemployment and eager to dodge their own, several state legislatures swept away some of the restrictions which prevented local governments from obtaining funds; local bond-limitation laws were either annulled or state funds were made available to local governments in the form of loans.[1] Other states sought to finance relief undertakings by new taxes and bond issues.[2] But the emergency demands upon both local and state revenues came at a time when the bond market was inactive, revenues were falling, and legal and financial debt limits in many instances had either been reached[3] or constitutional restrictions prevented necessary borrowing. Thus, with the breakdown of the traditional policy of local responsibility and with the combined efforts

[1] By the middle of 1932 only seven states had made definite provision for state aid. These were New York, New Jersey, Rhode Island, Illinois, Ohio, Wisconsin, and Pennsylvania.

[2] See the following studies by L. Ecker-R published in the *Monthly Reports of the Federal Emergency Relief Administration:* "Sources of State Emergency Relief Funds," July, 1935, pp. 61–73; "State Relief Borrowing," August, 1935, pp. 1–14; and "The Sales Tax as a Source of Relief Revenue," October, 1935, pp. 5–20.

[3] The conditions existing in Alabama in 1931–1932 offer a case in point. Representative George Huddleston of Alabama testified as follows: "The State, county and city authorities say that they are not able to give anything. The county finances will not permit them to give anything. Their credit has been exhausted. The State has a deficit of $30,000,000." *Unemployment in the United States, Hearings before a Subcommittee of the Committee on Labor,* House of Representatives (1932), p. 10.

During the five-year period, July, 1930, to June 30, 1935, expenditures on the part of the forty-two participating states for emergency relief amounted to $532,945,373. Almost two-thirds of this represented expenditures of four states—New York, Pennsylvania, Illinois, and New Jersey. The distribution for the respective years is as follows:

Fiscal year 1931— 4 states contributed a total of $ 546,750
1932—11 states contributed a total of 56,949,948
1933—26 states contributed a total of 90,358,760
1934—39 states contributed a total of 163,507,058
1935—35 states contributed a total of 221,582,857

From Monthly Report of the Federal Emergency Relief Administration, February, 1936, p. 3.

and funds of local and state governments unable to meet the problem of emergency unemployment, the Federal Government was forced to act.

In the Emergency Relief and Construction Act[1] of July, 1932, Congress appropriated $322,224,000 for public works (Title III) and authorized loans to state and local governments through the Reconstruction Finance Corporation up to $1,500,000,000 (Title II). The appropriations under Title III were for traditional types of public works, $120,-000,000 being for Federal highways, $100,000,000 for "emergency building construction," and other large blocks of the fund being earmarked for parks, flood control, and aids to navigation. The RFC loans were restricted to revenue producing or "self-liquidating" projects, and this fact, combined with the relatively high interest rates charged, resulted in few loans being made for public works.[2] The chief purpose of the RFC and the emphasis during the remainder of the Hoover administration was recovery through aid to banks, railways, and other private-profit corporations.

The acute crisis in banking and the continued increase in unemployment made evident the inadequacy of the Hoover recovery program. The Roosevelt administration adopted a much more vigorous policy of expansion of Federal public works and of aid to state and local governments, with funds obtained mainly by borrowing. The demand for a broad public-works program was insistent, even though this necessitated abandonment of traditional monetary policy and further unbalancing of the budget. The outcome is found in provisions of the National Industrial Recovery Act.[3]

The purposes of the National Industrial Recovery Act were twofold: (1) to increase purchasing power and to stimulate recovery and employment by shortening hours and raising wage rates in private industry; and (2) to provide purchasing power and employment through a public-works program of unprecedented scope. The idea that expenditures for public works would release purchasing power to stimulate private business and employment was by no means novel, but the emphasis which it received in the NRA public-works program marks another significant departure from the original purpose of public works. It was hoped that not only would a large amount of direct employment be made available, but also that the expenditures on materials and the expenditures of those provided with jobs, would stimulate other business and employment in an ever-widening circle. "Priming the pump" of private enterprise was to be done on a grand scale.[4]

[1] Public no. 302, 72d Congress, 1st Session, Approved July 21, 1932.

[2] A. D. Gayer, op. cit., pp. 17 and 87.

[3] Public no. 67, 73d Congress. Approved June 16, 1933. It was under the authority of this Act that the National Resources Board was created.

[4] The purposes and underlying theory are discussed in detail in vol. I, Chap. VI.

Title II of the Act created a Federal Emergency Administration of Public Works (PWA) and appropriated $3,300,000,000 to be available for public works. The Act dropped the requirement that the projects must be "self-liquidating" in order to obtain Federal aid. "Any projects of the character heretofore constructed or carried on either directly by public authority or with public aid to serve the interests of the general public"[1] were made eligible. Primary considerations were that a very large part of the cost of construction and materials should represent wages paid to labor and that employment should be made quickly available.

Despite the liberal provisions of the Act, there was considerable delay in using the funds provided and employment on projects lagged behind expectations. This was attributable to a number of factors. There was no adequate staff immediately available to administer the huge fund; state and local governments were slow to submit acceptable and well-planned projects, in some cases because they feared that local rates of wages would be disturbed; in many instances sufficient funds were lacking; frequently local governments encountered legal debt limitations when they undertook to finance their share of the costs. When a project had finally been approved and an allotment made, an interval of at least sixty days elapsed before the first transfer of funds.[2] Some of the delay may have been due also to the Secretary's insistence that the projects must be genuinely useful public works and that political considerations and graft should find no place.[3] Most of the delay was, however, due to rigid economic and legal barriers beyond the control of the PWA, barriers which could have been removed only by planning and preparation before the crisis.

Emergency Conservation Work.—One of the first acts of the Roosevelt administration in adapting its program to the needs of the unemployed was the establishment of the Civilian Conservation Corps, under the Emergency Conservation Work program.[4] From the funds provided by the Emergency Relief Act of 1932[5] an initial allocation of $300,000,000 was made. The "conservation work" has consisted of park development, forest protection and improvement, and soil-conservation projects.[6] From its inception, the CCC program has provided employment for from 250,000 to nearly 600,000 men between the ages of eighteen and twenty-five years.[7] By June 30, 1936, employment had been provided

---

[1] Title II, Sec. 202(c).

[2] A. D. Gayer, op. cit., pp. 113–117.

[3] H. L. Ickes, Back to Work: The Story of P.W.A. (1935).

[4] Public no. 5. Approved Mar. 31, 1933 (48 Stat. 22). Put into operation by Executive Order 6101, Apr. 5, 1933.

[5] 47 Stat. 709.

[6] A detailed description of the work accomplished is given by the Director of Emergency Conservation Work, Summary Report for the Period April, 1933, to June 30, 1935.

[7] War veterans, Indians, and a few other special classes have been exempt from this age limitation.

for 1,686,614 men, of whom 1,515,904 were enrollees and 170,710 were supervisors.[1]

The work is carried on through camps which have been operated in more than 3,000 communities, and up to Jan. 31, 1936, approximately $1,173,400,000 had been obligated, more than half of it for materials, shelter, foodstuffs, clothing, equipment, etc.[2] In many respects the CCC program resembles work relief. Standard wages are not paid, but maintenance is furnished and a cash allowance of $30 per month is made. Men are selected according to need (the work being largely unskilled and suited to inexperienced youths), i.e., they must be unemployed and their familes on relief. Of the $30 cash allowance the men are required to remit to their familes about $25, which serves as an alternative to relief. An important purpose of the program is the rehabilitation of the men employed. In these respects the CCC differs from the standards of public works, yet the projects result in genuinely useful public improvements or public works. The CCC is perhaps the most generally approved part of the entire works program and has been extended for a period of three years by an agreement reached in conference on June 21, 1937.

Relief Work and Work Relief.—In the fall of 1933 it became evident that the Public Works and Emergency Conservation programs would not provide sufficient employment to meet the needs of the increasing number of destitute unemployed persons and that state and local relief funds were approaching the point of exhaustion. Hunger marches and relief riots assumed alarming proportions. The Federal Government was faced with the alternative of providing more funds for direct relief or of modifying the program of public works to provide more immediate employment. The Civil Works Administration (CWA) established[3] in November, 1933, represented a modification of the usual aim of public works, not only in that the primary motive was to provide employment, but also in that such employment was, in part, intended to be a substitute for relief. Significantly the administration of the program was not by Secretary Ickes' Public Works Administration, but by Harry Hopkins' Emergency Relief Administration. It was specified that approximately one-half of the workers employed should be taken from relief rolls, the remainder to be nondependent unemployed. The work was not done by contractors, but directly under government supervision. "Standard" rates of wages for the class and grade of work done were paid, and thirty hours constituted the normal week. A characteristic of the program was "that the maximum of human labor [was] used in lieu of machinery

---

[1] Data supplied by Director of Emergency Conservation Work.

[2] Director of Emergency Conservation Work "Summary of Emergency Conservation Work," Release 114382, Mar. 1, 1936, p. 2.

[3] Under authority of the NIRA.

wherever practicable and consistent with sound economy and public advantage."[1]

The announced purpose of the CWA program was to provide jobs for 4,000,000 unemployed persons, and for this purpose $400,000,000 was allocated from the $3,300,000,000 NIRA public works fund. The Civil Works program achieved its purpose in quickly providing work, and in January, 1934, a peak of 4,100,000 persons were employed.[2] Employment on such a scale and at the wage rates paid quickly exhausted the allotted funds. In February an appropriation of $950,000,000 became necessary to carry the program through the winter.[3]

The Civil Works program unquestionably eased a winter of terrible hardship and the rapid expenditure of funds was a decided fillip to private business.[4] Nevertheless it aroused bitter opposition. Conservative property holders became alarmed at the prospect of increased debt and taxation. Private employers complained that the wage rates paid were too high and that workers preferred government work to private employment.[5] Business men generally were torn between joy at increased business and fear of an increasingly unbalanced budget. Finally, there was much criticism that the hand labor was inefficient, that "make-work" methods were employed, and that projects were not wisely chosen and in many cases not useful.[6] Some of these criticisms were fully warranted, and although the Civil Works program enjoyed an immense popularity with the unemployed, the Administration announced that with the return of "spring employment" the Civil Works program would be rapidly tapered off. By the end of April, 1934, the program was practically terminated.

After the discontinuance of the CWA, the Federal Government did not undertake a similar general works program designed primarily as a substitute for relief until the creation of the Works Progress Administration (WPA) under the Emergency Relief Appropriation Act of 1935.[7] The basic thought of the Act was that aid to the unemployed should be

[1] As provided by Title II, Sec. 206(5) of the National Industrial Recovery Act.
[2] The Works Progress Administration, *Report on the Works Program*, Mar. 16, 1936, p. 8.
[3] Public no. 93, February, 1934 (48 *Stat.* 351).
[4] Some advocates assert that if the CWA expenditures had been continued for even a short time, recovery would have come in 1934.
[5] Minimum wages were the same as those established by the Public Works Administration, the United States being divided into three zones for this purpose. The minimum wage in the northern zone was 50 cts. per hour for unskilled and $1.20 for skilled labor; in the central zone, 45 cts. and $1.10; in the southern zone, 40 cts. and $1.00. A maximum eight-hour day and thirty-hour week were established for manual workers, while clerical workers were restricted to thirty-nine hours a week. Without question, these rates were higher than the prevailing rates paid in industry in many of the smaller places.
[6] A sufficient number of suitable projects, planned in advance to overcome delays of legislation, administration, and financing were needed, but, unfortunately, were lacking.
[7] Public Res. no. 11, 74th Congress, Session 1, April 8, 1935.

given in the form of useful work instead of relief grants. Work provided under the program has taken the place of Federal grants for direct relief to a large part of the destitute unemployed who are able to work. Dependent persons, unable to work, were made the responsibility of state and local governments, assisted through grants-in-aid under the Federal Social Security Act.[1] A sum of $4,000,000,000 was appropriated directly and additional amounts not to exceed $880,000,000 were provided from the unexpended balances of previous appropriations. Forty-four bureaus or divisions of fourteen major administrative agencies participated in the operation of the Works Program and received allocations for work projects,[2] the largest sums going to Emergency Conservation work and the Bureau of Public Roads. Projects operated by such agencies were initiated by the agencies themselves. Others, under the WPA and PWA, were initiated by local governmental units. All project applications were submitted to the WPA for investigation and review, thence to the National Emergency Council, and then to the President's Advisory Committee on Allotments, composed of representatives of Government, business, labor, agriculture, and the United States Conference of Mayors. The recommendations of the Advisory Committee have been presented to the President and with his approval the Treasury has transferred funds for projects. In addition to a wide variety of projects offering employment to skilled and unskilled manual laborers, a special effort has been made to meet the needs of white-collar workers, artists, musicians, architects, and others.[3]

In July, 1935, there were 70,000 employees on WPA projects; by November the number was 2,484,000, this gradually increasing to 3,036,000 at the end of February, 1936, and receding to 2,225,000 persons at the end of June, 1936.[4] The average cost of a man working for the WPA charged to Federal funds was about $65 per month. In addition, the local sponsors contributed about $15 per month. This total of $80 per person included all costs for all purposes.[5] Wage rates and earnings have varied by state and region but were based on a "security wage" varying from $19 to $94 per month, depending upon the classification of the worker, the type of community, and the section of the country in

[1] The Works Progress Administration, *Report on the Works Program*, March 16, 1936. As in the case of the CWA, the WPA was under Harry L. Hopkins.

[2] *Ibid.*, p. 4.

[3] Approximately 76 per cent of the WPA workers were given jobs requiring little or no skill, 8 per cent received skilled manual jobs, 5 per cent clerical and office work, 4 per cent professional and technical, another 4 per cent semiskilled jobs, and the remainder supervisory work. *Ibid.*, p. 27.

[4] *Ibid.*, p. 14.

[5] Statement of Administrator Harry L. Hopkins, *First Deficiency Appropriation Bill for 1936, Hearing before the Subcommittee of House Committee on Appropriations*, 74th Congress, 2d Session, pt. II, p. 9. (Hereafter referred to as "Hearings on First Deficiency Appropriation Bill for 1936.")

which the work was being done. The wages originally paid, unlike those of the CWA, were below prevailing wages and were vigorously opposed by organized labor, with the result that in the appropriation for 1936–1937 (approved, June 1936) the principle of prevailing wage rates was adopted. Weekly wages were not increased, but the hours of work were reduced to bring the hourly wage up to the prevailing rate. The average monthly "security" earnings of persons on WPA projects were $61.62 in Region I, and $30.10 in Region IV, and $53.92 for United States as a whole, in June, 1936.[1] More than 85 per cent of the persons employed had previously been on relief rolls and all but 7 per cent of all persons employed had been assigned at "security-wage" rates.[2]

The Emergency Relief Appropriation Act of 1936[3] appropriated $1,425,000,000 for the continuation of the program of the Works Progress Administration. From these and other funds and balances, it was apparent by May, 1937, that WPA expenditures for the fiscal year ending July 1, 1937, would reach an estimated total of $1,850,000,000. To this must be added expenditures of $175,000,000 by other Federal Agencies on work projects employing 90 to 95 per cent relief labor, making total expenditures on the works-relief program of approximately $2,025,000-000.[4] As against this figure, the appropriation for the fiscal year 1938, under the Emergency Relief Appropriation Act of 1937, provides $1,500,-000,000 for relief, which is a reduction in total available relief funds of approximately 25 per cent.[5] How inadequate this appropriation will be depends upon the length and extent of the present recession.[6] On April 17, 1937, 2,085,000 workers were employed on WPA projects, representing a reduction of about 400,000 from the previous November. Since present costs have averaged $800 per person employed per year under the WPA, it has been estimated that the 1937–1938 appropriation, less certain deductions for the NYA, the United States Employment Service and other items, would give employment to 1,730,000 during the fiscal year. Taking into consideration persons from relief rolls now employed by other Federal agencies and for whom the WPA would be responsible as those projects were finished or funds were depleted, it was

[1] *Report on Progress of the Works Program*, March, 1937, p. 52.

[2] *Ibid.*, p. 50.

[3] Included as Title II of the First Deficiency Appropriation Act of 1936, approved June 22, 1936. The funds were to remain available until June 30, 1937, and, as under the previous act, were to be used at the discretion and under the direction of the President.

[4] Statements of Harry L. Hopkins, *Hearings before the Subcommittee of the Committee on Appropriations*, House of Representatives, 75th Congress, Session I, on the Emergency Relief Appropriation Act of 1937 (May 5, 1937), p. 217.

[5] *Ibid.*

[6] The recurrence of severe drought in more than 956 counties in the Middle West and South during 1936 necessitated large expenditures for relief and relief projects which were not anticipated and which upset budget calculations. Works Progress Administration, *Report on Progress of the Works Program*, Aug. 15, 1936, pp. 1–3.

estimated that private industry must absorb "a total of 525,000 persons now employed on the Works Progress Administration program. This meant, of course, that private employment must increase by a much larger number than this, since there were about 350,000 families with employable members on the local relief rolls who were not on the Works Progress Administration."[1] It was intended, of course, to curtail the works program as rapidly as a revival of private employment permitted since the mounting deficit, in the absence of greatly increased revenues, precluded the indefinite continuance of that program.

A rough summary of the direct employment provided by these various programs is given in Table 18. The most steady employment has been that of the Emergency Conservation Work, in which from less than 250,000 to nearly 600,000 persons have been employed. The PWA employment never reached the proportions commonly expected, the peak number employed being 613,769 in July, 1934.[2] The low point of 176,764 employed in February, 1936, is explained partly by severely adverse weather conditions which retarded construction. In contrast with the PWA and the CCC, the CWA at its peak employed approximately 4,000,000 persons and the WPA more than 3,000,000. It was estimated by Administrator Hopkins in April, 1936, that on the whole Works Program a total of 3,800,000 persons were receiving a "security wage" and that a total of 13,300,000 individuals were thus being supported.[3] In April, 1937, Works Program employment stood at 2,820,000, or about a million below what it was a year before.

Emergency Work Relief.—One of the most striking facts brought out by Table 18 is the manner in which the CWA and WPA employment dovetailed with the employment provided by the work relief programs of the states, in large part financed by the Federal Government. Prior to the CWA, the states and localities had programs of work relief which at their peak in March and April of 1933 provided employment for approximately 2,000,000 persons. Most of the projects were for the construction and maintenance of roads, parks, and public buildings. Employment was mainly of unskilled labor.[4] With the inauguration of the CWA, the number on work relief dropped to negligible proportions,

---

[1] Harry L. Hopkins, *Hearings*, House of Representatives, 75th Congress, Session I, on the Emergency Relief Appropriation Act of 1937, p. 213.

[2] A larger proportion of PWA funds than on other programs was spent for materials and hence the indirect employment was greater. Secretary Ickes has asserted that the total employment thus provided, both directly and indirectly, totaled "nearly 2,000,000 jobs each year." A total of $1,352,000,000, or nearly one-half of the total expended on PWA programs by June 15, 1936, had been spent for materials. *New York Times*, June 15, 1936.

[3] Statements of H. L. Hopkins, Hearings on First Deficiency Appropriation Bill for 1936, p. 158.

[4] *Ibid.*, p. 365.

TABLE 18.—EMPLOYMENT PROVIDED BY PUBLIC WORKS AND WORK RELIEF PROJECTS IN THE UNITED STATES, 1933 TO 1936[1]

	Public works administration[a]	Emergency conservation work[b]	Civil works administration and other programs[c]	Works progress administration	Work relief[d]	Total
1933:			CWA			
July	267	311,677			1,679,256	1,991,200
August	4,719	302,851			1,718,174	2,025,744
September	34,740	241,313			1,439,468	1,715,521
October	139,274	270,421			1,464,269	1,873,964
November	244,839	344,365	814,511		1,552,682	2,956,397
December	282,781	316,047	2,726,167		166,900	3,491,895
1934:						
January	272,243	320,091	4,263,644		93,124	4,949,102
February	281,415	317,978	3,787,943		94,987	4,482,323
March	286,618	249,392	2,452,544		160,002	3,148,556
April	368,693	310,667	104,591		1,088,421	1,872,372
May	491,306	334,477	11,979		1,361,537	2,199,299
June	589,605	280,596	6,845		1,504,579	2,381,625
July	613,769	402,263	4,522		1,725,312	2,745,866
August	600,343	390,856			1,924,453	2,915,652
September	548,078	332,644			1,952,089	2,832,811
October	505,338	405,804			2,000,157	2,911,299
November	478,610	389,679			2,168,009	3,036,298
December	388,370	350,085			2,303,484	3,041,939
1935:						
January	329,883	400,946			2,446,266	3,183,639
February	287,994	388,514			2,434,573	3,111,081
March	302,502	298,205	Other Programs		2,369,605	2,970,312
April	367,575	392,035			2,276,185	3,035,795
May	428,852	388,750			2,196,653	3,014,255
June	454,438	431,595	2,000		2,021,089	2,909,122
July	441,088	486,710	13,605	70,000	1,928,772	2,940,175
August	429,880	528,285	39,994	187,968	1,411,462	2,597,589
September	372,462	572,717	87,537	344,118	889,227	2,266,061
October	334,492	586,890	133,853	594,427	645,009	2,294,671
November	288,706	559,435	243,445	1,623,696	346,155	3,061,437
December	243,654	507,716	256,653	2,660,116	59,428	3,737,567
1936:						
January	197,820	491,694	301,818	2,890,016	28,000	3,909,348
February	176,764	466,900	324,389	3,017,649	22,000	4,007,702
March	202,236	448,770	400,108	2,991,121	24,000	4,066,235
April	264,427	381,675	526,317	2,671,453	22,000	3,865,872
May	315,393	411,900	614,409	2,418,458	20,000	3,780,160
June	349,572	402,000	667,850	2,293,625	19,000	3,731,047
July	336,047	408,240	648,909	2,238,974	20,000	3,652,170
August	330,784	394,640	646,523	2,322,594	17,000	3,711,541
September	311,361	368,800	629,497	2,441,851	16,000	3,767,509
October	284,903	384,135	598,149	2,539,138	15,000	3,821,325
November	269,167	398,990	537,506	2,565,801	13,000	3,784,464
December	242,818	383,520	458,808	2,284,083		3,369,229

[a] PWA data through 1934 are exclusive of national road work and employment on projects financed from the Emergency Relief Appropriation Acts of 1935 and 1936. However, for the years 1935 and 1936, these data are included.

[b] Includes CCC camps, Indian reservations, and conservation work in territories. CCC was not under the Works Program until July, 1935.

[c] CWA was discontinued in July, 1934. A number of other works programs resulted from the legislation of 1935.

[d] These figures include only recipients of relief under FERA.

[1] From Social Security Board, *Selected Current Statistics*, vol. 1, no. 4 (November, 1936), pp. 81–83; vol. 1, no. 6 (January, 1937), pp. 65–70; vol. 1, no. 9 (April, 1937), pp. 40–43. Employment figures are for week ending nearest the middle of the month.

to be shifted again, after CWA, to emergency work relief, until the WPA program was undertaken.

The emergency work relief program differed from the CWA and WPA in several important respects. The emergency work-relief program was administered by state officials, but as the states became more dependent upon the Federal Government for relief funds,[1] the Federal Emergency Relief Administration of necessity imposed certain administrative checks and relief standards. The FERA retained the power to withhold Federal funds if a state did not meet the regulations imposed and also if it did not furnish a fair share of the necessary funds, but the employees and staff were state and local, not Federal, employees.[2]

A basic difference was in the hours and wages policies of the programs.

"Under the Emergency Work Relief program the earnings of a worker are determined by the 'budgetary deficiency' of the worker and his family; the hourly wage rate is determined by the local prevailing wages for the type of work performed; the number of hours worked is the number required, at the given hourly wage rate, to meet the 'budgetary deficiency.' . . . The 'budgetary deficiency' is established by the social case workers of the local relief administrations . . . these earnings will vary with the size and needs of the family. . . . The workers [are] subject to periodic investigation by social case workers."[3]

Under the WPA the workers, once certified for work, have been free from regularly recurring investigation of their economic status. The substitution by WPA of a "security wage" for wages based on case-work examinations marked a significant departure from objectionable relief standards and in the direction of regular public works.[4]

Prior to, and during, the first years of the depression beginning in 1929, destitution was considered to be a local problem, with private charity meeting a large part of the burden. No national system of aid for the unemployed had been developed, and the first attempts to meet the relief problem were through expansion of activities of private welfare agencies together with state and local aid under the existing poor laws. With the deepening of unemployment in 1930, 1931, and 1932, voluntary contributions proved to be inadequate, for relief needs rapidly outgrew

[1] As early as January, 1933, more than 51 per cent of all emergency-relief obligations were met by Federal funds. In November, 1934, the proportion from Federal funds was 77.7 per cent. Federal Emergency Relief Administration Release 8162, *Summary of Emergency Relief Statistics*, November, 1935, p. 5.

[2] Statements of H. L. Hopkins, Hearings on First Deficiency Appropriation Bill for 1936, p. 153.

[3] Federal Emergency Relief Administration, *Monthly Report*, September, 1935, pp. 37, 39.

[4] A detailed explanation of the WPA wage policy may be found in statements of H. L. Hopkins, Hearings on First Deficiency Appropriation Bill for 1936, Appendix C, pp. 310–326.

local resources. Therefore, many states established state emergency-relief administrations and provided funds to supplement local relief. It was only with reluctance that the Federal Government assumed part of this burden which had traditionally been a state problem. By 1932, however, the number requiring relief had unquestionably reached such proportions in many states that Federal assistance was necessary to prevent rioting, bloodshed, and actual starvation. The Emergency Relief and Construction Act of 1932 recognized this situation by appropriating $300,000,000 to be available for loans to states and municipalities for relief purposes.[1]

In March, 1933, the number of persons dependent on relief exceeded 20,000,000 or roughly 17 per cent of the total population.[2] Relief on such a scale involved administrative and financial difficulties with which only the Federal Government could cope, and in May, 1933, Congress passed the Federal Emergency Relief Act which authorized the Reconstruction Finance Corporation to make available $500,000,000 for grants to the states. The Federal Emergency Relief Administration was established to receive applications for funds and to supervise the administration of Federal relief allocations. The Act departed from precedent in two significant respects: for the first time a Federal agency to administer relief was established; and funds were given as grants rather than as loans.

After eligibility of applicants for relief had been determined by local social case workers, they were provided with either direct relief or work relief.[3] In either event the social case worker "determined" the applicant's needs and controlled the amount of cash, food orders, rent, light, gas, fuel, household supplies, medicine, or other supplies which the family or single person could receive.[4] Minimum standards for basic needs were estimated and the relief administration attempted to meet these. The approved method of giving relief was by cash, because it preserved the normal purchasing function of the family and because of the simplicity of administration.[5] Relief in kind was commonly given through store orders on merchants. Huge amounts of clothing and food, much of it

---

[1] Title I, Public no. 302, 72nd Congress, First Session, approved July 21, 1932. The loans were made through the Reconstruction Finance Corporation.

[2] Statements of H. L. Hopkins, Hearings on First Deficiency Appropriation Bill for 1936, p. 361.

[3] Somewhat less than one-half were given work relief during 1933.

[4] Statements of H. L. Hopkins, Hearings on First Deficiency Appropriation Bill for 1936, p. 359.

[5] The amount of these cash payments varied not only with the needs of the family, but also by regions. There was some tendency for the average payment in the United States to increase as the depression continued. Thus, in May, 1933, the average of both direct and work-relief payments per family per month was $15.15; in May, 1934, $24.53; and in May, 1935, $29.33. Ibid., p. 360.

produced by work-relief projects, were distributed directly.   The amount of food distributed was greatly increased as a result of the purchases of farm products by the Federal Surplus Relief Corporation.   With the inauguration of the CWA, the total number of relief cases declined[1] to 2,954,000 in January, 1934.   After the abandonment of CWA, the number of cases on the relief rolls rose precipitously to 4,447,000 in April, 1934, and thereafter moved gradually up to a peak of 5,488,000 cases and 20,676,773 dependent persons in January, 1935.[2]   During the early months of 1935 the Federal obligations for relief increased to more than $140,000,000 monthly.   In some states the Federal Government was furnishing more than 95 per cent of all relief funds.[3]

The administration of relief on a case-work basis to such a large portion of the population required far more qualified social workers than were available.   Complaints of mistakes, of delays in obtaining relief, of autocratic decisions, and of prying into personal affairs, combined with the growing recognition of the evils of forcing able-bodied persons to remain idle or to accept spasmodic relief work, led the Federal Government to withdraw from financing and administering relief.   It was thought that a works program would not only prevent deterioration of skills and morale, but that such a program fell more nearly within the sphere of Federal activity.   The Federal Government therefore announced that it would attempt to furnish work at a "security wage" to all "employables"[4] and regard the care of the indigent who were unable to work as a responsibility of the states.[5]   The abandonment of Federal participation in relief, which was practically completed by the end of 1935,[6] has met with such general approval that it is not likely that the Federal Government will soon again participate in a relief program.

[1] The number of persons receiving *direct* relief actually increased during the period of the CWA.   The number of cases receiving direct relief seldom fell below 2,500,000 but usually remained below 3,000,000 during the entire period.   The large shifts from one type of program to another consisted mainly of those who obtained aid through employment.

[2] These totals include persons assigned to work relief.

[3] It is noteworthy that the average amount of relief funds furnished by state and local governments actually increased from 1933 to 1935.   In 1933 the total amount of state relief funds was $113,262,633, of local funds $198,877,519; in 1935 the states provided $224,243,774 and local governments $242,784,217.   Thus the "collapse" of local relief was due not to a decline in funds provided, but to the enormous increase in amount of funds needed.   The grants made by the FERA totaled $3,045,458,802 in the period from May, 1933, to December, 1935.   See tables *E*-3 to *E*-5 and Chart, Statements of H. L. Hopkins, Hearings on First Deficiency Appropriation Bill for 1936, pp. 363–365.

[4] Just when a person becomes "unemployable" is not clear.   It was found that some WPA workers were so weak from undernourishment that it was a month before they were able to work efficiently.

[5] There has been considerable criticism of the relief standards adopted by the states since the withdrawal of Federal assistance.   We will not attempt to enter upon the merits of this controversy.

[6] A few grants were made after Dec. 1, 1935.

The opposition to relief and preference for a works program was well expressed by the Conference of Mayors of cities with a total population of 25,000,000 persons. The report read in part:

"The mayors and executives of our cities are more intimately and responsibly concerned with unemployment and destitution than any other group of public officials in America. . . .

"As chief executives of these major cities, we are of the opinion that any honest and impartial analysis of the work being prosecuted in the important cities of the country will reveal that practically every project represents a useful and, in most cases, a permanent public improvement. Secondly, there remain a multitude of additional useful things to be done under future work programs. And finally, it is apparent that the city officials of America will never consent to the abandonment of the work principle in giving relief assistance. The dole, based upon idleness and groceries, has no place in our American scheme of society."[1]

Evaluation of Works Programs and Observations on Problems Involved.—Apart from the factor of market support and stimulation, the argument in favor of work projects as a method of supporting the unemployed can be stated quite briefly. It runs in terms of specific benefits which accrue both to the worker and to the community, and which, for the most part, are not realizable otherwise.

Chief among the values to the workers is the conservation of physique, dexterity, and skill, through the offering of employment fitting as nearly as possible into their previous training, aptitude, and experience. It is, of course, well known that protracted idleness leads to a loss of skill and work capacities, the undermining of confidence and initiative, and eventually to unemployability.[2] However, the argument for relief work

[1] Statement of H. L. Hopkins, Hearings on First Deficiency Appropriation Bill for 1936, p. 29.

[2] The National Industrial Conference Board, in 1935, emphasized that the deteriorative effects of unemployment of skilled workers was a factor in the then alleged shortage of skilled labor.

"The most tragic factor in the skilled labor shortage is that prolonged unemployment has caused mature workers to lose their skill and ability. Unemployed in some cases for two or more years, completely separated from the machine shop and its atmosphere of orderly precision and steady application, these workers, who, before the depression, apparently had ten or twenty years of useful employment ahead of them find, on their return to the shop, that they are not the craftsmen they once were. . . . Where they expected to pick up where they left off, they find that this is not so easy. In some cases, methods and machines have changed during their absence. New types and designs of machines sometimes call for a higher degree of mechanical skill. Special skills acquired in the pre-depression period may have become obsolete. The world of machinery has progressed; they have stood still.

"But most disastrous is the physical and mental deterioration which, unknown to them, has sapped their energy and vitality and broken their morale. Where they were confident in their ability, knew what was wanted and how to do it, they find they have

as a means of protecting skills is probably somewhat exaggerated, since the loss in skill may not be as great as alleged, while the regaining of dexterity may be more rapid than is generally supposed.[1]   Also, it should be noted that most of the unemployed are unskilled workers,[2] who would be injured not in skill but in physique, attitude, and will to work.   Given, however, an employment program sufficiently broad in scope to accommodate the professional, skilled, and other workers, the preservation of work habits is still dependent upon certain other requisites.   Among these conditioning factors are work projects of a high standard upon which efficiency and discipline are maintained.   Lacking these, it is certain that inefficient, unsatisfactory, and injurious work habits will frequently result.

It is also contended that a desirable consequence of work programs is their contribution to the maintenance of worker morale and normal family relationships, that regularity in work and income are essential for the preservation of normal outlooks, self-respect and self-reliance, initiative, independence, social stability, and a sense of responsibility to the community.   To the extent that work projects approach those providing normal employment, the morale of the worker and his family will be comparable to those of regularly employed workers.   This implies projects of a genuinely useful and purposeful character, under efficient management, with standards of accomplishment comparable as nearly as possible to those of private industry.

There can be no doubt that the morale value of work programs has been considerable, especially of those undertakings launched early in the depression, when uncertainty and destitution were extremely prevalent.   It would appear, however, that with the continued use of relief work, its value in maintaining morale tends to diminish, not only because its shortcomings and limitations become more evident to the workers, but also because it takes on the semblance of a social institution for dealing with unemployment permanently.   Such tendencies would, in part, be counteracted, and the value of work as a morale safeguard enhanced, in direct proportion to the degree that it were divorced from the obvious

---

slowed down, are bungling, and have lost their dexterity." *Wanted: Skilled Labor*, National Industrial Conference Board Studies, No. 216 (1935), p. 5.

[1] *Work Relief in the State of New York*, Governor's Commission on Unemployment Relief, 1936, p. 20.

[2] The labor inventory of workers on relief (March, 1935), showed that 11.2 per cent of the total were white-collar workers; 79.5 per cent were manual workers, of whom 14.7 per cent were skilled; while the remaining 9.3 per cent were farmers.   Nevertheless, the varied projects of the WPA have been such that four-fifths of the total relief labor supply possessed work experience which could be directly utilized on them.   The remaining one-fifth were placed in activities which matched their skills as closely as possible. *Report on the Works Program*, March 16, 1936, pp. 20–22.

manifestations of relief status, and to the degree that it discarded periodic investigations of the worker's economic condition and demonstrated destitution as a requirement for employment. Further, proper morale of worker and family can hardly be maintained in the face of any uncertainty, confusion, and change of work policies, emphasizing, alternately, jobs and relief, any prospect of lower relief-work earnings, and any threat of replacing cash relief with relief in kind. The latter brings with it the end of freedom or choice in buying habits, the loss of prestige in the eyes of vendors and neighbors, and attendant problems inherent in its administration.[1]

The value of relief work from the point of view of the community is represented not only in benefits accuring to the workers but also in the utilization of the surplus man power and its conversion into useful and necessary projects of lasting worth to the community.[2] These represent a valuable return for the relief outlays on projects and improvements which the community would not otherwise have.[3]

Furthermore, inasmuch as relief work costs more per capita than does cash relief or unemployment compensation, it has the effect of expanding public expenditures, and, other things equal, of increasing purchasing power and stimulating business. The stimulation is, however, most immediate and greatest in industries providing ordinary consumption goods, whereas stimulation is most needed in the durable- and capital-goods industries, where depression is generally deepest. For on relief work, the proportion of funds spent for materials and equipment is designedly least, that for labor greatest. Relief works are therefore in this respect inferior to ordinary public works. Moreover, other things

[1] A number of communities have demonstrated conclusively that cash relief is superior to commodity relief even on the basis of comparative costs. See a recent study made of relief costs in cash and kind in nine cities of the United States, by Joanna Colcord of the Russell Sage Foundation. *Cash Relief* (1936), pt. IV, pp. 201–218.

For a survey of public relief in twenty-four European countries, all but one of which employ cash grants rather than food orders, see Hertha Kraus, *Aiding the Unemployed*, Advisory Committee on Planning of the Temporary Emergency Relief Administration, New York, June, 1935.

[2] After an inspection of 599 projects in New York State, the Governor's Commission concluded that 95.5 per cent of them were worth while and desirable, 85.9 per cent had definite survival value, 96.8 per cent were in line with the development of the communities, 90.1 per cent were provided with competent plans and designs, only 4.8 per cent of the finished work was poor, while 23 per cent was very good. *Work Relief in the State of New York*, p. 35.

[3] In the Report of the Governor's Commission on Unemployment Relief for the State of New York, there is a unanimity of opinion that white-collar projects, such as music, art, drama, and others of this nature, sometimes termed "boondoggling," while not providing any great measure of employment, find their value in the cultural contributions which they have made to communities for which financing had never heretofore been provided on any comparable scale. *Work Relief in the State of New York*, pp. 36–41.

may not remain equal; funds must be secured through taxes levied or debt incurred. Fiscal effects must be considered along with any market stimulation accompanying additional public expenditures.

It would appear that relief and near-relief projects are accompanied by problems not found at all, or in considerably less degree, in true public works programs. Many of the relief projects are likely to have limited community value. With workers selected largely, when not entirely, from relief rolls, there is not a desirable selection and retention on the basis of fitness;[1] only with the greatest variety of projects and with much more care than is generally exercised can workers be assigned to suitable tasks. Discipline is likely to be more or less lax, with results indicated above. Incidentally, as our recent experience has shown, there is likely to be encroachment upon parts of a true works program, upon the normal functions of government, and even upon the area ordinarily occupied by private enterprise. Examples of this are found in the transfer of highway and other conservation and maintenance work from its usual place to relief-work payrolls. To the extent this is true there is no additional market support; workers on ordinary payrolls are displaced by workers on relief payrolls.

Unlike true public works for the prosecution of which standard or prevailing wages are paid, the question of the rate of pay (and whether work shall be for a shorter or longer number of hours per week) inevitably arises in connection with other work projects. What the rate of wages should be has been widely and long debated in European countries as well as in the United States. And with the subject debated, the policy of our government has wavered, and has finally been changed to call for the payment of prevailing hourly wages to WPA workers.

In this country and elsewhere, organized labor has generally been strongly of the view that prevailing wages should be paid in all cases. "Justice," it is said, calls for it. Moreover, paying a lesser wage tends to undermine wage standards in private employment. That is antisocial and uneconomic.

On the other hand, it is desirable to conserve funds and spread them rather widely so as to provide more workers with jobs. Moreover, if prevailing wages are paid and requirements are not as strict as in private employment, there is not only a tendency for workers to remain on public projects when they might obtain suitable employment in industry,[2] but

---

[1] The Governor's Commission on Unemployment Relief in New York State estimated that the average efficiency of operation on work-relief projects of the public-works type was 74.8 per cent of that on like projects "under average contract prosecution." *Ibid.*, p. 35. See, also, the Commission's study, *Work Relief Projects of the Public Works Type— an Estimate of Their Worth and of the Effectiveness of Their Management and Prosecution* (1935), pp. 75ff.

[2] This factor thus far has been inconsequential in view of the fact that earnings on public works have generally been less than those prevailing in private industry. It has also

also a likelihood that there will be objection to the curtailment of public work. Finally, it may be said that the efficiency, if not the application, of the unemployed considered as a group is such that to pay them prevailing wages is to pay them relatively higher wages than prevail in industry and thus add substantially to the cost of work done.

The arguments on both sides of the wage question have merit. Except upon public works manned and prosecuted on a business basis, it appears that the one or other set of difficulties is unavoidable.

Because of the problems found in relief work, it is to be regarded only as a necessary evil in the absence of a better program. In general, this has been fully appreciated by an administration accepting responsibility for far-flung CWA and WPA ventures. In a better program, true public-works projects, unemployment compensation, and a modernized relief system,[1] together with a system of labor exchanges and other things already discussed, find appropriate place.

A true public-works program, such as has been described in the beginning of this discussion, can be so planned and conducted that it can largely avoid problems such as those we have briefly mentioned. Whether the government does its own work or operates through contractors, the workers would be hired, retained, and paid or discharged on the basis of fitness and efficiency, and quite without reference to relief rolls or charitable list. Of course, prevailing wages and other fair standards would or should be accepted. Yet there are two questions or groups of questions which call for discussion. One of these relates to the volume of available work that might find place in a public-works program, with special reference to its power to "prime the pump," stimulate industry, and assist in absorbing the unemployed. The other concerns conditions which should be observed and special problems arising in connection with public works.

---

been frequently asserted that those on direct relief will not work while those on work relief will not take jobs when offered. This charge of "job refusals" and the unwillingness to accept private employment needs exploding. FERA studies made in Memphis, Baltimore, Buffalo, and Washington, D. C., completely disprove this. In Washington, D. C., for example, out of the 220, in a total of 16,000, reported as refusing jobs, it was found, upon inquiry, that the charges were supported by fact in only four cases. See H. B. Arthur, "Summary Study of Alleged Job Refusals," *Monthly Report*, FERA, November, 1935, pp. 6–10, and Roslyn Serota, "The Myth of Work Refusals," in *This Business of Relief* (American Association of Social Workers, 1936), pp. 33–40.

[1] It may well be contended that it was a mistake to follow CWA with WPA; perhaps it would have been preferable had a Public Works Program and the CCC been stressed more than they were, and to have made Federal grants to the states for the relief of all types of destitution, on the conditions that such grants were matched and that sound standards of relief administration were observed by the states. Certainly, with the transfer to the states of the problem of caring for the unemployable residue among the destitute, a sad state of affairs has developed in many areas in the actual administration of relief.

Attention may be called to the data already presented concerning the outlays on government construction of one kind or another. Though the volume has been small relative to man power unused during the acute depression of the 1930's, it has been large enough to be of no little importance as a source of employment. Moreover, the amount of public work to be done is no fixed thing; at certain points it can be expected to expand with changing ideals and the trend toward an increasing role to be played by government. In any event there are public buildings to be erected; rivers and harbors need to be improved; soil conservation and reforestation projects have come forward; there are many maintenance projects originating with, or known to, the Department of Agriculture, the Department of Interior, and other departments of the Federal Government. There is also a large amount of work that might be advantageously done by or in the general domain of the state and local governments, such as highway construction, the elimination of grade crossings, sanitary improvements, the development of recreation centers, low-cost housing, etc. While a considerable part of this work is of such character or so badly needed that its prosecution should not be postponed so as to fit into an unemployment program, much of it, whether neglected or postponed in prior years, is available at a given time, and much of it can be brought forward and put into operation in advance of the time it would usually be done. In other words, there is in the realm of appropriate government works the possibility of adding, as a result of postponement or of anticipation, a considerable volume to the average amount of public work and to the amount commonly prosecuted in depression.

The importance of the volume of public work undertaken must not be tested merely by the number of men directly employed upon the projects. Both primary and secondary indirect employment must also be considered. Primary indirect employment accrues to those engaged in the raw-material and preliminary processing, transportation, and final fabrication of the materials and equipment needed on public-works projects. Under the PWA this has been, on the average, about three times as great in volume as direct work at site of construction.[1] Nor should the secondary indirect employment, resulting from the increased spending power of those directly and indirectly employed, be ignored. As Mr. Ickes has stated:

"Only when the amount of primary and secondary indirect employment is added to the amount of direct employment resulting from the construction of the Public Works Administration projects, can the record of this Administration in its attack upon the unemployment problem be properly evaluated. On the basis of studies which have been made of typical classes of the Public Works Administration projects, it has been

[1] *The First Three Years*, Public Works Administration (1936), p. 27.

shown that on the average, for every person employed at the site of a Public Works Administration project, employment is given to five more persons."[1]

As a rule, therefore, where the amounts of both direct employment and wage expenditures are low, the ratio of indirect employment and expenditures for materials is likely to be high. This means, however, a higher per-man cost for those directly employed on public-works projects. Thus, a study of 825 audited PWA projects costing $74,042,317 shows that 27,496 man-years of direct employment were provided at a man-year cost to the Federal government, on a 30 per cent basis, of $741, or a total cost to all concerned of approximately $2,470.[2] As contrasted to this latter figure, the near-relief programs of the CWA show a total man-year cost of $900, and those of the CCC, $1,000.[3] However, the higher cost under the PWA is accounted for, and to a large extent justified by, the higher proportion of outlays going into materials and equipment serving, ultimately, to stimulate to a greater degree the heavy goods industries so adversely affected during a depression and which must be revived before substantial recovery and reemployment can be attained.

Studies made by the United States Bureau of Labor Statistics,[4] covering the operation of the PWA over the three-year period ending June, 1936, show that 40 per cent of all employment created by PWA orders was found in three industries: steel, cement, and lumber. Of total PWA expenditures for materials amounting to $1,288,755,000, more than $780,000,000, or 60 per cent, flowed into these three industries. Certainly to these PWA orders, and to those of CWA, CCC, WPA and other programs, must be attributed a considerable part of the substantial rise in the volume of production and employment of these benefited industries when, during the three-year interval from 1933 to 1936, the annual index of lumber production rose more than 32 per cent, cement, 75 per cent, and iron and steel and their products, 91 per cent. Employment also increased but not to such a degree, the increase in lumber being 31 per cent, cement, 32 per cent, and iron and steel and their products, 43 per cent.[5] It may be concluded that public-works orders have served as a market support and stimulant for large segments of the extractive, processing, and allied industries, and, to a considerable degree, orders for such materials have benefited virtually all manufactur-

[1] Statement of H. L. Ickes, *First Deficiency Appropriation Bill for 1936, Hearings before the Subcommittee of the Committee on Appropriations*, U. S. Senate, 74th Congress, 2d Session on H. R. 12624, p. 333.

[2] *The First Three Years*, Public Works Administration (1936), p. 28.

[3] J. M. Clark, *op. cit.*, p. 82.

[4] *Monthly Labor Review*, vol. 43 (1936), pp. 838–845.

[5] Computed from indexes of the Division of Economic Research, U. S. Bureau of Foreign and Domestic Commerce, *Survey of Current Business*.

ing industries, enabling them to maintain or increase their volume of production, employment, and profitability.[1]

Unfortunately, the secondary effects of these public-works spendings in terms of market stimulation throughout the entire economy, the increasing demand for consumer's goods and subsequent expansion of output of producer's goods are not susceptible of precise statistical measurement. There is, however, evidence that increased spending, within certain limits, multiplies its effects in cumulative form, in terms of successive receipts and spendings of income.[2] Allowing for leakages, time lag between spendings by successive recipients, and other factors, J. M. Clark calculates the multiplier, or the ratio between the original expenditure and its secondary effects, to be three. Thus, under these conditions, government spendings of a million dollars every two months may increase the national income by three million dollars each two months.[3] Similar estimates by Professor Douglas show the secondary effects in quantitative terms to be $2.80 for each dollar originally spent.[4]

However powerful these primary and secondary effects of public-works expenditures have been in supporting and stimulating the market, there are certain theoretical considerations and practical conditions to be observed in pursuing a program of public works in order that the best results may be obtained.

In addition to standards of performance and other such requisites of work programs as have already been mentioned, American experience indicates the need for anticipating the problems which arise in the use of public works in a stabilization program, and the necessity for developing procedures and techniques of advance planning both to minimize these difficulties and to maximize the possibilities of planned public works. Briefly, the scope of advance planning of public works must cover a threefold front, viz., the advance selection of suitable and sufficient projects, procedures for their prosecution and administration as between local, state and Federal governments, and adequate advance financial planning of the revenues and expenditures involved. As will be indicated presently, these elements which constitute proper advance planning are indispensable to the strategic timing of public-works expenditures upon which the effectiveness of a public-works program as a market stimulant may ultimately depend.

[1] See *Monthly Labor Review*, October, 1936, pp. 843–844, for an itemization of orders placed by PWA in approximately 100 manufacturing industries. For WPA, see *Report on the Works Program*, March 16, 1936, pp. 31–33.

[2] The leading exponents of this method of approach are R. F. Kahn and J. M. Keynes. See Kahn, "The Relation of Home Investment to Unemployment," *Economic Journal*, June, 1931, and "Public Works and Inflation," *Journal of American Statistical Association, Proceedings*, March 1933; J. M. Keynes, *The Means to Prosperity* (1933).

[3] J. M. Clark, *op. cit.*, p. 90.

[4] P. H. Douglas, *Controlling Depressions* (1935), p. 125.

The proper selection of public-works projects in advance will avoid the principal cause of delay which faced the PWA in 1933, and also the lack of a sufficient number of suitable projects available for immedate construction. An adequate list of projects should be carefully drawn up, these scheduled on a basis of priority and located as nearly as possible to centers of unemployment, particularly in those areas where needs are great and local facilities inadequate. Projects must be sufficiently broad in scope to accommodate not only the unskilled workers, who will predominate in number, and the skilled, but also to give employment to others in worth-while activities devoted to those research and cultural programs which have often and ignorantly been labeled "boondoggling." Attention should be given to time of completion of projects so as not to "run over" into prosperity periods and accentuate a boom; considerations of cost, the relative values of projects in respect to initial outlay, maintenance and future replacement, will be important; to be preferred, of course, are those noncompetitive public works which promote private spending, such as roads, schools, conservation, and others, rather than those which tend to displace or discourage private enterprise.[1]

A second aspect of advance planning is to avoid as far as possible administrative difficulties and legislative delays in the launching of public works when the time for their prosecution arrives. In the interrelationships of local, state, and Federal governments, many legislative and administrative obstacles can be greatly reduced by advance agreement on projects and construction sites, contractual terms, coordinated budget policies and provisions, the fulfillment of grant requirements made by the Federal Government, and other matters relative to state and local participation in such a program. How great is the need for planning administrative affairs well in advance is evident from a study of the time intervals involved in the expansion of public improvements in the city of Philadelphia, where the usual time required for completion of the necessary legal procedure varied from 190 to 257 days, depending upon the type of expenditure.[2] Difficulties and problems such as these indicate the necessity for coordinated administrative relationships between the governments concerned, the development of explicit policies and procedures, and the elimination of legislative and other delays if strategic timing of expenditures is to be accomplished.

In order that adequate funds for a public-works program may be available for timely expenditure and their maximum effectiveness realized, advance planning must necessarily cover a third element—that of financing. The haphazard and uncertain financing of recent work and

---

[1] It may well be, however, that government operations in power, housing, and other fields, in competition with private enterprise, would have salutary effects.

[2] William E. Loucks, *The Stabilization of Employment in Philadelphia through the Long Range Planning of Municipal Improvement Projects* (1931), pt. III, pp. 150–151.

relief programs, the helplessness of many of the state and local governments due to constitutional restrictions and cumbersome financial
procedures, the consequent uneconomic taxation policies which have
resulted, and which are inconsistent with the objectives of a stabilization program, emphasize the need for advance financial planning. Definite financial procedures should be outlined, flexible budgets established
and coordinated into a Federal-state-local expenditure policy, and the
way cleared for bond issues and such tax revision as may later be required
in order that debt repayment can be made. A prime necessity will be to
free many of the state governments from restrictive constitutional limitations upon their right to borrow and spend funds,[1] to loan to and assist
their own local governments, to vary the rates applicable to particular taxes and other things[2] which now make difficult an adequate and
timely participation[3] by subordinate governments in a public-works
program of emergency spending.

From experience both in this country and abroad it is obvious that
the volume of public-works spending, in order to be effective in any major
depression, cannot be limited to reserves built up in advance or to the
returns from current taxation. As has been noted, not only is it difficult
to accumulate reserves of sufficient size, but attendant problems arise,
such as investment of funds, their administration, and their effect upon
fiscal policy and the monetary system as a whole.[4] Further, it has been
demonstrated that even under the most favorable circumstances any
possible reserves which might be accumulated would be inadequate and
ineffective in smoothing out any but comparatively minor fluctuations of
the business cycle. Nor is the raising of funds by taxation during a
depression suitable for the expansion of work programs of any considerable magnitude. Politically, such a procedure during depression would
be hazardous, and economically the effects of increased taxation upon
prices, production, and the national money income would, for the most

---

[1] Limitations upon the borrowing powers are found in the constitutions of most of the
states. In twenty-three states the incurring of state debt is possible only by the long
process of constitutional amendment; in fifteen others the approval of a majority of those
voting must be obtained; in only ten states does the legislature possess power to borrow
without electoral sanction or constitutional amendment. The provision for emergency
relief funds by borrowing required a constitutional amendment in California, Pennsylvania,
and Texas, and electoral approval in four states. The state of Washington, constitutionally
prohibited from borrowing except for repelling invasion, insurrection, and war, evaded the
restriction by pleading the existence of incipient insurrection. L. Ecker-R, "State Relief
Borrowing," *Monthly Report*, FERA, August, 1935, pp. 8–10.

[2] See Simeon E. Leland, *op. cit.*, pp. 156–158.

[3] As has been indicated, state and local participation in financing relief and work programs was tardy and inadequate at a time when needs were greatest. Their total contributions were only $338,793,000 in 1933, $641,808,000 in 1934, $714,637,000 in 1935, and
$1,224,953,000 in 1936. WPA Release 4-1518, May 3, 1937.

[4] See A. D. Gayer, *op. cit.*, pp. 391–395.

part, be highly undesirable. Furthermore, a great part of such taxation may involve simply a transfer of purchasing power from one group to another rather than effect an increase in the national money income and total purchasing power. If, however, a progressive form of taxation reaches income which would not be spent by the individual or banked and invested, the effect of the public spending of funds thus derived would be largely beneficial. Yet, the great decline in net incomes during depressions greatly limits the amount of revenue from this source and higher tax rates are likely to produce detrimental psychological effects; on the whole, taxes during a depression should be lowered rather than raised if increased purchasing power is to result.

It may be suggested, therefore, that the great bulk of depression expenditures for market supporting programs should be financed by loans. The use of this method finds economic justification from the fact that times of decreased business activity are generally characterized by the presence of idle funds,[1] either in bank deposits or individual hoards; and through the mechanism of public borrowing these uninvested funds may be returned to the income stream through productive expenditures of the government. As has been demonstrated during the 1930–35 depression, the Federal Government may be in a position to borrow such funds at an extremely low interest cost. Under such conditions, the Federal Government might well make this credit available to the subordinate governments through loans. This would provide cheaper and more ample credit to subordinate governments at a time when banks are either unwilling or unable to meet their needs, and increase state and local participation in a public-works program.[2] Moreover, it would provide a basis for cooperative control and integration of interests and policies of the governments concerned.

Of course, the policy of deficit financing of public works ultimately faces the problem of budgetary unbalance and pressures for fiscal balancing of receipts and expenditures on a yearly basis. There are numerous objections to balancing the budget on a fiscal-year basis during periods of depression. For our purposes it is sufficient to note that when private industry is contracting expenditures, similar policies on the part of government only serve further to decrease monetary purchasing power and in effect amount to a "campaign for the intensification of unemployment."[3] For this and other reasons, many authorities on government finance who

---

[1] " . . . there is usually during depression periods a surplus of idle funds seeking secure investment at attractive returns, which private business is unable or unwilling to utilize in the face of uncertainty, declining prices and excess productive capacity, its use by public bodies need involve no transfer inasmuch as the capital would otherwise not have been employed at all." A. D. Gayer, "Public Works," *Encyclopaedia of the Social Sciences*, vol. 12, p. 697.

[2] S. E. Leland, *op. cit.*, pp. 156–157.

[3] J. M. Keynes, quoted in P. H. Douglas, *op. cit.*, p. 135.

hold the view that budget-balancing on a fiscal-year basis is purely arbitrary have advocated cyclical budgeting covering the whole period of the business cycle.[1]

In considering, finally, how the costs of public works should be allocated between the different levels of government, it may be noted that beginning with the emergency program of 1933 the cost has fallen largely on the Federal Government. The economic effect has not been undesirable since the Federal Government has access to the more fruitful and immediate sources of revenue and credit; moreover, its taxes being more progressive in character rest upon those better able to pay out of surplus income or savings without unduly restricting consumption. And to the extent that the responsibility for, and benefits from, stabilization through national public works are coterminous with the national area over which the causes of instability and unemployment operate, Federal financing would seem to be called for. State and local governments, moreover, at present have restricted and limited tax jurisdictions; their revenues, drawn largely from property taxes, fees, and consumption levies, are, of course, usually regressive. While these conditions may in part be corrected, and while more progression and greater revenue can be obtained through tax and financial planning, yet to a degree increased tax levies by state and local units must reckon with tax delinquencies[2] and movements pressing for legal tax and debt limitation; also, to the extent that such taxes enter into overhead costs, prices may be increased, consumption restricted, business recovery and stabilization retarded, in short—a partial neutralization of the intended effects of a public-works program. Yet, in the formulation of a long-run public-works policy, special benefits derived from projects, interests of state and local cooperation and control, considerations of adequate financial support, administrative efficiency, economy, responsibility, and matters of political expediency will argue for a division of costs among the levels of government coextensive with

---

[1] A modified concept of budget-balancing was that adopted by the Roosevelt administration, viz., dividing federal expenditures into two parts, one representing ordinary current expenses and the other representing extraordinary outlays on permanent assets (public works) and on temporary emergency needs (relief works and outright relief). The purpose of this budgetary classification was to make possible increased emergency expenditures and at the same time to allay fear by preserving a balance between current revenues and ordinary expenses of government so far as possible.

[2] In Detroit the accumulated tax delinquencies were equal to 91 per cent of the total levy for 1933–1934. The corresponding figure for Chicago was also 91, for Akron, 103. A number of other cities showed still greater delinquencies, as, for example, Jacksonville, Florida, where it was 148 per cent. U. S. Bureau of Census, *Realty Tax Delinquency*, vol. 2, *Urban Tax Delinquency*, 1934, p. 21.

A compilation as of June 30, 1933, showed the general property-tax delinquency of all state and local levies of 1932–1933 averaged 20.5 per cent, or $909,465,000 on levies of somewhat less than 4½ billion dollars. U. S. Bureau of Census, *Realty Tax Delinquency*, vol. 1, *Current Tax Delinquency by States and Counties*, 1934, p. 6.

the interests involved.[1] Moreover, in a long-run program where projects
and costs are jointly planned, and with initiative and leadership provided
by the Federal Government, coordinated action in the timing of public
works can then be obtained.

The problem of timing is essentially one of when and how far public
works should be expanded in times of depression. The original theory
of public works advocated by Bowley as well as that of the President's
Conference on Unemployment (1923) called for an expansion before
excessive deflation had occurred in order that any great amount of unemployment might thereby be prevented. It has been widely advocated
that public works should be placed in operation as soon as the index of
employment has fallen by, say, five or ten points. With the increasing
severity of fluctuation in business activity and unemployment, however,
the argument has been advanced that public works cannot stem the
downward swing, that only after deflation has run its course, and needed
readjustments in prices and costs have been made, should public works
be launched to stimulate recovery.[2] It seems reasonable, however, that
an intermediate timing policy[3] might be more advantageously used.
Instead of waiting until business has become virtually prostrate and an
uneven deflation has occurred, with its many crucial problems, it seems
probable that an expansion program of public works might, after the
most essential cost-price readjustments have been made, not only reduce
the seriousness of industrial depression, but also prevent the occurrence
of an emergency situation. In other words, any difficulties occasioned
by an intermediate timing of public works are to be preferred to the
ineffectiveness and undesirability of those launched before deflation and
likewise to those inaugurated only after the costly processes of deflation
have run their full course.

It should be noted that the entire rationale of timing assumes that
cycle theory with its techniques and indexes of measurement is sufficiently
advanced to reveal something of the advent of the cycle, its extent and
severity of fluctuation, and the time when counteracting and remedial
programs should be launched. Of course, such an assumption finds no
substantial approximation to reality. Our indexes of the volume of
employment, for example, are both limited in coverage and reveal little
of such factors as the shifting of hours worked and the partial unemploy-

---

[1] There is, of course, no doubt that some of the cost of public works can be borne by
state and local governments. During the five depression years from July 1, 1930, to
June 30, 1935, the states spent only $533,000,000 on relief or hardly 4 per cent of all their
total expenditures. This figure includes, moreover, substantial values in capital assets.
L. Ecker-R, "State Relief Borrowing," *Monthly Report*, FERA, August, 1935, p. 4.

[2] S. H. Slichter, *Towards Stability* (1934), "The Economics of Public Works," *American
Economic Review, Supplement* (March, 1934), and "The Adjustment to Instability,"
American Economic Review, Supplement (March, 1936).

[3] See J. M. Clark, *op. cit.*, pp. 65–66, and A. D. Gayer, *op. cit.*, pp. 397–399.

ment which may exist. Nor have we any measure of, or sufficient information on, the underlying situation and its contributing forces. Clearly, improved and more composite indexes need to be developed.[1]

A coordinated policy based on accurate forecasts is indispensable not only for effectively timing the expansion of public works but also for a proper contraction of such expenditures as business activity and employment increase. Credit must then be curtailed, governmental budgets adjusted, the productivity of the revenue system increased through heavier progressive taxation, and accumulated debt from public-works expenditures must be retired as promptly as possible so that public credit will be available for future emergencies.[2] Such measures as these, taken in conjunction with appropriate policies of government in other spheres, will tend to promote a maximum of industrial stability.

COOPERATIVE SELF-HELP

One outgrowth of the severe unemployment in 1931 and 1932 and the inadequate provision for relief was the development of various types of cooperative self-help projects among the unemployed. In scope and structure these cooperative organizations varied widely. Some stressed producers' self-help activities; others turned more to the barter and exchange of commodities which might, or might not, have been cooperatively produced. The great majority of cooperative projects were purely local in operation, although some were intended to be nation-wide in scope,[3] while still others sought a reorganization of the entire economy on a cooperative basis. An element common to all was the attempt to produce and exchange commodities without, or with a minimum of, the regular media of exchange by the substitution of scrip, certificates, vouchers, and the like. At the depth of the depression, more than 280 barter groups are known to have been in existence.

The initial success of certain of these "production-for-use" cooperatives[4] was widely heralded, and with the approval of the FERA in the summer of 1934, this type of project seemed destined to attain great

[1] Other types of indexes which have been suggested as indicators of cyclical fluctuations are a general business index and a construction index. For discussion, see J. M. Clark, op. cit., p. 79.

[2] Cf. A. C. Pigou, A Study in Public Finance, 2d ed., p. 233, and S. E. Leland, "Debt Retirement and the Budget," American Economic Review, Supplement, vol. 27, no. 1 (March, 1937), pp. 75–85.

[3] F. D. Graham, The Abolition of Unemployment (1932).

[4] One of the earliest and most successful self-help organizations was launched in Seattle, Washington, in 1931. See Arthur Hillman, The Unemployed Citizen's League of Seattle (1934). For an account of the self-help movement as a whole, see Monthly Labor Review, vol. 36 (March, April, May, and June, 1933).

importance.[1] However, essential weaknesses, limiting the development of self-help organizations, soon became evident. Since the activities were largely local in character, the number and variety of products available for the exchange system were strictly limited. Invariably, there was a dependence upon outside sources, either public or private, for funds to purchase such necessities as were required both by the workers and self-help enterprises.[2] Lack of sufficient cash funds was ever a major problem limiting the effectiveness and extension of productive activities. Moreover, cash incomes of self-help groups were rigidly limited, since, as a condition of FERA grants, cash sales by self-help organizations had to be restricted largely to products which would not overload the competitive market, arouse the hostility of business and labor interests,[3] or result in reductions in prices or wage rates. Production was therefore confined for the most part to the demand within the self-help organization itself. As between groups, barriers of distance, crudities of the barter process, and inadequate funds made exchange of products virtually impossible. Under such restricted conditions, many of the cooperators became disheartened, numerous groups regarded their activities merely as a temporary expedient to be abandoned with the advent of better times; in almost all cases efficient and stable management was difficult to secure and retain, and, for the most part, government guidance and supervision was found to be necessary.

Those self-help organizations which have survived have tended to be projects located in farm communities, and confined to relatively simple activities, such as growing foodstuffs, canning, obtaining fuel, and making clothing; those in the large cities, despite Federal grants, have not prospered. On the whole, the outstanding accomplishment of these self-help groups has probably been in maintaining the morale of the unemployed. As an alternative mode of economic organization operating outside the regular channels of trade and as a method of support and rehabilitation of the unemployed, it must be concluded that these barter organizations have been definitely unsuccessful. Yet, in the future, self-help cooperatives may, under more favorable conditions, find a more important place

---

[1] By December, 1934, more than 350,000 persons were employed on production-for-use projects under the FERA program. A wide variety and substantial volume of goods were produced. FERA *Monthly Report,* September, 1935, pp. 2–10.

[2] *Cf.* Clark Kerr and Paul S. Taylor, "The Self-help Cooperatives in California," in *Essays in Social Economics in Honor of Jessica Blanche Peixotto* (1935), pp. 191–225.

[3] In Ohio, for example, a portion of the relief funds was used to put the unemployed to work in idle factories. Some twelve production units were "either operating at a standard of efficiency comparable to private enterprise or were rapidly approaching such a standard," the products were distributed only to the state relief population, but in May, 1935, the project was liquidated because the products competed indirectly with those of private enterprisers. FERA, *Monthly Report,* September, 1935, p. 12.

in a well-rounded security program. With the aid of adequate Federal funds,[1] which were entirely discontinued with the inauguration of the works program, and with proper organization and supervision, it is reasonable to believe that self-help organizations might become moderately efficient in the production and exchange of certain commodities. Moreover, if a substantial residue of permanent unemployment persists, which today is largely outside the scope of current social-security legislation, cooperative self-help may be an economical and essential part of a program providing security for, and serving those more or less permanently displaced from, industry.

Sharing Work and the Shorter Workday

The wider distribution of available work has in recent years been increasingly practiced as a substitute for indefinite layoffs or discharges of those for whom there was no present need in the establishment because of seasonal slack or depression. Employers in increasing numbers have appreciated the importance of good will and good morale, and of retaining the services of efficient workmen who have become familiar with the requirements of the establishment. For the reasons indicated, employers have for some years been more inclined, or more easily persuaded,[2] to substitute part-time work for full-time work rather than to have a decidedly reduced number on the payroll. Nor has it by any means been purely a matter of "business." Many employers share the feeling of the outsider, and act upon it, that it is better that 100 per cent (or a large percentage) of the employees should work part time and have something to protect their standards of living, than that 65 per cent should work full time and the other 35 per cent become wholly unemployed. The unions in increasing number have also taken this view of the matter.[3] This is especially true of the needle-trades organizations and of others with a liberal outlook, for they see in "equal division of work" an expression of the feeling of brotherhood and something which makes for solidarity as well as a device for supporting the workers. Hence, those union agreements which provide for a division of work "as nearly equal as practicable" in the "slack season."

---

[1] From August, 1933, through October, 1935, Federal grants made to self-help groups in the various states totaled only $2,831,413. Records of the FERA show that for every grant dollar expended, more than $2.50 has been obtained in benefits. *Monthly Labor Review*, March, 1936, p. 611.

[2] Early in the depression of the 1930's, there was in this country an organized campaign to share work widely. The result was an extraordinary amount of work-sharing. More recently the attitude of management toward it has not been so favorable.

[3] Of course, those unions which emphasize seniority rights do not share work so readily. Nevertheless, the printers, among others, have in acute depressions generally required their members to surrender days to workers without regular "situations."

Such division of work, however, has its faults. It means that the less as well as the more efficient are retained; workers may be set at tasks with which they are not familiar or which they do not have "in hand"; it may be accompanied by efforts to stretch out the work in order to avoid layoffs; it involves more or less administrative difficulty. In trades especially depressed and in trades with a decreasing demand for labor as the years pass, sharing of work may result in the loss of the better workers who quit their jobs in search of employment elsewhere. Yet, at the same time, in contracting and decaying trades a premium may be placed on the retention of jobs with inadequate earnings, and prevent or retard a needed redistribution of labor as between employments.

The above observations apply particularly to those cases in which there is permanent tenure of jobs and sharing of work in the seasonal trades. Of general applicability is the very important fact that when sharing of work is employed in depression in order to lessen the amount of public relief or as a substitute for unemployment compensation, the cost is saddled upon the workers themselves; sharing work is in a real sense sharing earnings. Furthermore, if the volume of work becomes too small, the workers cannot earn enough to maintain themselves. Sharing work may involve slow starvation. Nevertheless, when not too rigorously applied, when due care is exercised to safeguard against too great a reduction in the earnings of those retained on the payroll, and when there is no system of unemployment compensation, there is a strong case for a wide distribution of work as against a drastic reduction in the number on the payroll.

Where technological change rapidly displaces workers and when depression is acute, unusual interest develops in a reduction of the standard number of hours per day and per week as a method of solving the problem of unemployment. The shorter-hours movement has become very strong among the miners, the railway workers, the needle workers, and other organized groups; since 1932 the American Federation of Labor has advocated the thirty-hour week. A week of thirty hours is now with the Federation a "paramount objective." Shorter hours, with the same wages per hour or the same piece rates, are merely a method of spreading work and much can be said for them in time of depression. The shorter hours generally advocated by organized labor are not, however, designed as a temporary work-spreading device, but rather an arrangement for the indefinite future, with advances in wage rates to offset, at least in large part, the loss which otherwise would occur in wages or earnings per day or week. An argument for such an arrangement is that it will absorb the unemployed into industry and will increase purchasing power, which is needed to prevent depression. The possibilities of avoiding or solving the problem of unemployment by the introduction of the shorter day or week are, however, much exaggerated by organized labor. Certainly the recurrence of general depression after the hours of labor have been reduced, as they so strikingly have been, is significant. There is, as we have seen,[1] no fixed amount of employment. The old labor doctrine, still widely current, that if the hours of labor are reduced 20 per cent, the number of workers who will be employed in industry will increase correspondingly, is an erroneous one. For the number who will be employed will vary with changes in the amount of work done per hour and with the wage that is paid. This has been adequately explained elsewhere.[2] Here it is necessary only to repeat that if by reason of changes in hours and wage rates, such as would be expected with a thirty-hour week, labor was made more expensive, there would be a tendency to economize on labor by the employment of more mechanical aids, and that if total costs were increased, the demand for all productive factors might be adversely affected. Any reduction in hours, combined with wage adjustments, that increases labor costs and overhead costs per unit, will tend to deepen rather than to cure unemployment—unless there is inflation resulting in price increases.

[1] See vol. I, Chap. IX.
[2] *Ibid.*, pp. 502–508.

CHAPTER III

THE PROBLEM OF UNEMPLOYMENT (*Concluded*): UNEMPLOYMENT INSURANCE

One of the interesting facts is that most, but not quite all, of the students of the subject of unemployment have become convinced of the need of unemployment insurance.[1] The proponents of this type of insurance are generally convinced that, even though the labor reserve be reduced and the volume of unemployment minimized by such methods as have been suggested in the immediately preceding chapter, the problem of unemployment would still remain a large one. They do not believe that public or private charitable relief is either an adequate or an altogether suitable means of maintaining the unemployed. They do believe that a cash benefit is needed by the unemployed worker to give him an income sufficient to tide him over and to protect his standard of living until he can find employment. They believe that the incidence of the burden of support is important; the burden of support should find the appropriate resting place. They are nearly all of the opinion that, if properly worked out, unemployment insurance will be distinctly helpful in arousing the interest necessary for the adoption of the parts of the program already discussed and in contributing toward the prevention of unemployment. The majority of them hold, also, that it will allay discontent, improve morale, and maintain efficiency on the job.[2]

Though the need for the application of the principle of insurance to this risk is now usually regarded as obvious, the application has been induced or required chiefly by public authority. Commercial insurance companies have long written insurance against accident, sickness, and death, but they have not written individual policies insuring against unemployment. The needed actuarial basis has not been present, and the fluctuations in employment make the matter of reserves both important and difficult. Very much more important, however, are the facts that the private insurance company would not be in position to protect itself against improper claims because it neither hires nor allocates labor, that the cost of acquisition would be very heavy, and that because of the inevitably high premiums, those who insured would, for the greater

---

[1] Unemployment compensation is a preferable term and is tending to come into use. In this discussion, however, the terms "unemployment insurance" and "unemployment compensation" are used interchangeably.

[2] *Cf.* Paul H. Douglas and Aaron Director, *op. cit.*, pp. 484–497.

number, be bad risks.[1]   Until recently, when some firms and when some industries through agreements between unions and employers introduced systems of unemployment insurance in this country, it was only labor unions that provided for the payment of unemployment benefits.   Such American unions have, however, been few in number and small in membership, and their experience with unemployment insurance has not been such as to commend it to others.[2]   In European countries generally, previous to government activity in this connection, the situation was very much the same save that the payment of out-of-work benefits by labor organizations was less exceptional than in the United States.   Hence unemployment insurance has been mainly government insurance of one kind or another.

UNEMPLOYMENT INSURANCE IN FOREIGN COUNTRIES

The governments of most of the European countries have adopted one or the other of two systems of unemployment insurance.   One of these is the "Ghent system," which has been in operation in Belgium for more than thirty-five years.[3]   With variations in detail, it has been adopted in several other countries: Czechoslovakia, Denmark, Finland, France, Greece, Holland, Norway, Spain, Sweden, and in certain cantons in Switzerland.   The system is characterized by the granting of national and local subsidies out of the general revenues to such voluntary organizations, almost exclusively trade unions, as provide out-of-work benefits for their members in accordance with minimum standards established by the government.   In most cases the subsidy approaches half of the total outlay; in some cases it is materially larger.[4]   The object of the subsidy system is to encourage provision on a voluntary basis and to shift part of the burden from labor.   It has succeeded in encouraging such provision, for the number and membership of subsidized societies

---

[1] This, of course, does not apply when a company provides group insurance for an employer.

[2] See below, pp. 137–140.

[3] Inaugurated in Ghent in 1901, with national subsidy paid since 1907.   France was the first of the several countries to grant (1905) a national subsidy.   For convenient accounts of the several arrangements, see Joseph L. Cohen, *Insurance Against Unemployment* (1921); Paul H. Douglas and Aaron Director, *op. cit.*, Chaps. 23 and 24; and Abraham Epstein, *Insecurity, A Challenge o America* (1936), Chap. 19.   For a more detailed statement of the Belgian experience, see Constance A. Kiehel, *Unemployment Insurance in Belgium* (1932).   For brief summaries of unemployment insurance in effect in 1933, 1934, see Mary Gilson, *Encyclopaedia of the Social Sciences*, vol. 15, pp. 162–163, and *Monthly Labor Review*, June, July, August, and September, 1934.   The four articles in the *Review* have been brought together in *Operation of Unemployment Insurance Systems in the United States and Foreign Countries*, U. S. Bureau of Labor Statistics, Serial No. R-166.

[4] During the depression of the 1930's, government contributions were substantially increased in most of the countries.

have materially increased, and more rapidly than of societies without subsidy. Nevertheless, the organizations now receiving subsidies in the several countries mentioned have a total of only a few million members. The coverage under these voluntary systems is given in Table 19.

TABLE 19.—SUBSIDIZED VOLUNTARY INSURANCE PLANS, 1935[1]

Country	Date of law	No. of insured
Belgium	1920	899,000
Czechoslovakia	1921	1,407,000
Denmark	1907	375,000
Finland	1917	15,000
France	1905	192,000
Greece	[a]	46,000
Netherlands	1916	564,000
Norway	1915	54,000
Spain	1931	62,000
Sweden	1934	240,000
Switzerland (12 cantons)[b]	1924	307,000
Total	....	4,161,000

[a] No information available on the date of the law.
[b] Nine of these cantons specify that communes may enforce compulsory insurance within their borders.
[1] Social Security Board, *Social Security in America* (1937), p. 7.

In all of these countries a majority of the wage earners are not insured, and the number of unskilled workers in the uninsured class is disproportionately large. The subsidy system has, therefore, not met the test of adequacy. A second deficiency as seen by most students of the subject lies in the fact that, except in Denmark, and, in some instances, in Spain and Switzerland, the entire cost is borne by the public and the insured, for the employers are not required to make a direct contribution to the insurance funds.[1]

Another group of European countries, Queensland, Canada, and all of the American Commonwealths, have adopted compulsory unemployment insurance rather than the Ghent system in order to make it more inclusive and to distribute the burden of support in a different manner. Compulsory insurance was experimented with first in Switzerland, where communal funds were established in Berne in 1893 and in St. Gall[2] in 1895. These experiments aroused widespread interest, but the plans were shortly discarded because of weaknesses in the particular schemes

[1] For an analysis and summary of Voluntary State Plans of Unemployment Insurance, see Metropolitan Life Insurance Company, *Unemployment Insurance*, Mon. I (1931), in a series on Social Insurance. With Spain and Finland not reported, the number insured in 1930 was 3,097,000. In Denmark and Belgium approaching one-half of the eligible wage earners are insured, but in most of the countries the percentage is very much smaller. See also, *International Labour Review*, vol. 23, pp. 48–66.

[2] T. G. Spates and G. S. Rabinovitch, *Unemployment Insurance in Switzerland* (1931).

TABLE 20.—COMPULSORY UNEMPLOYMENT INSURANCE PLANS, 1935[1]

Country	Year of original law	Contributions per week	Amount and duration of benefit	Approximate number insured[a] (in 1935)
Austria................	1920	Regular, ½ workers, ½ employers Emergency, State Emergency Subsidies	Varies with wages and family Regular, 20 weeks Emergency, 30 weeks	1,012,000
Bulgaria..............	1925	Workers, employers, state, each 1 leva	15 leva per day[b]; maximum: 12 weeks	280,000
Germany..............	1927	Regular, workers 3.25 per cent wages, employers same	Varies with wages, family, and cost of living Regular, 20 weeks	13,472,000[d]
Great Britain..........	1911	Regular, workers, employers, state, each 9d.[b] Transitional, all by state[c]	17s. per week[b] Regular, 26 weeks Transitional, as extended	14,003,000
Northern Ireland.......	1911	Same as Great Britain	Same as Great Britain	
Irish Free State........	1911–1920	Workers 6d., employers 7d.,[b] state 5½d.	15s. per week[b]; maximum: 26 weeks	380,000
Italy..................	1919	Workers 0.70 to 2.10 lira, employers same	1.25 to 3.75 lira per day, depending on wage scale Maximum: 90–120 days	4,500,000
Poland Manual workers.......	1924	Workers, 0.5 per cent; employers, 1.5 per cent; state, 1 per cent of wages	30–50 per cent of wages; maximum: 13 weeks	957,000
Salaried workers.......	1927	Workers and employers in variable ratio with joint contribution = 2.8 per cent of basic wage	30–100 per cent of wages; 6 months	
Queensland (Australia)...	1922	Workers, employers, state, each 6d.	14s.–17s. per week[b]; maximum: 15 weeks	175,000
Switzerland 13 cantons and Zurich..	1924	Varies in cantons	Up to 50 per cent of wages, 90 days	245,000
Canada[e]..............	1935	25¢[b] per week by insured; same by employers; government ⅓ as much	$6.00[b] per week for not to exceed 78 days of continuous unemployment, as the general rule	1,784,000[e]
Yugoslavia.............	1935	f	Amount varies with earnings. Maximum: 16 weeks. Extraordinary allowances also	f

[a] Social Security Board, Social Security in America (1937), p. 6.
[b] Rates for single adult male; rates slightly lower for females.
[c] See pp. 133–135.
[d] The recent sharp decline in members insured is due to the elimination of unemployed workers who have exhausted their rights to benefits and to new restrictions in coverage.
[e] Act declared invalid by the Supreme Court of Canada whose decision was sustained on appeal to the Privy Council. See Canadian Labour Gazette (February, 1937).
[f] Data not yet available.
[1] International Labour Office, Studies and Reports, series M, no. 13, vols. 1 and 2, International Survey of Social Services, 1933 (Geneva, 1936).

and in their administration. Of the countries now providing compulsory state-wide insurance, Great Britain was the first to adopt it—under the National Insurance Act (1911).[1] More recently compulsory insurance

[1] 1 and 2 Geo. V, Chap. 55.

has been adopted by the Irish Free State (1911–1920), Italy (1919), Austria (1920), Russia (1922),[1] Queensland (1922), Poland (1924), Bulgaria (1925), Germany (1927), Canada (1935), Yugoslavia (1935), some of the Swiss Cantons, and all of the American states.

No two of the systems of compulsory unemployment insurance are alike. Some of them are rather inclusive, others of more limited coverage. In some cases contributions are made by the government, the employers, and the insured workers, while in other cases contributions are made by the government or by the employers and the insured, or by employers alone. The rules of eligibility to benefit differ widely, as does the duration of benefit period. In some cases the benefits are based upon rates of wages, while in others flat rates are employed; extra allowances may or may not be made for dependent members of the insured's family; insurance may or may not be systematically supplemented by relief funds, etc. The more important features of the several foreign systems, as adopted or revised, have been summarized in Table 20.

Unemployment Insurance in Great Britain.—Of the several systems of compulsory insurance, that of Great Britain has been longest in effect and best lends itself to an exposition of some of the problems connected with this type of legislation. Therefore of the foreign systems it alone will be described, and this will be done in rather general terms.

The National Insurance Act (1911) made insurance against unemployment compulsory in seven of the more unstable industries; in 1916 it was applied to a number of others concerned directly or indirectly with munitions work; in 1920 it was so extended as to apply to all important wage-earning groups except agricultural laborers, domestic servants, and public employees; in 1936 it was extended to cover the first of these excepted groups. With agricultural laborers now insured, more than 13 million[2] workers, about 30 per cent of whom are women, are within the embrace of the law.

Under the British law each worker between the close of compulsory school attendance age (now fourteen) and sixty-five years of age, in an insurable trade, is insured against unemployment.[3] The cost is covered by equal contributions by employer, the insured, and the Exchequer. The contributions by employer and his insured employee are made through stamps purchased and affixed weekly by the employer to the insured's unemployment insurance card, which is surrendered to the worker when he is laid off or discharged or when he quits. As a condition of securing benefit, the worker deposits his card with a labor exchange and

---

[1] A compulsory law was passed in Russia in 1922, but benefit payments were suspended in 1930. See Social Security Board, *Social Security in America* (1937), pp. 6, 17–54.

[2] This is some 65 per cent of gainfully employed persons.

[3] A salary or wage limit of £5 per week, or £250 per year, for nonmanual workers excludes a large number of clerical and professional workers.

applies for a job.[1] If a suitable job does not present itself within three[2] working days, the worker begins to draw out-of-work benefit and continues to do so until he can be provided with suitable employment or until his insurance right expires, this provided that the idleness is due to lack of work rather than to disinclination to work, disability, discharge for cause, or strike or lockout.

The administration of benefits is connected with the labor exchange. Denial of claim to benefit is subject to appeal to a Court of Referees, consisting of a representative of employers and a representative of the workmen, and presided over by a chairman appointed by the Minister of Labour. Further appeal may be made to an umpire if the insurance officer and the Court of Referees disagree.

The administration of the British system has been fairly efficient. The costs of administration, including the expenses of the employment exchanges, have been comparatively light—at times less than 10 per cent and in only exceptional years in excess of 12.5 per cent of the total benefit expenditures. The several government investigations made have shown that cases of imposition and fraud have been comparatively few.[3] British, as well as other, experience shows that from the administrative point of view, unemployment insurance is practicable when accompanied by an efficient system of labor exchanges and a good civil service. Nevertheless, important problems developed in Britain's experience. For the most part, however, these were due, not to things inherent in unemployment insurance, but to the economic plight into which the country was plunged by the war and to stretching the fund to cover cases it was not designed to cover.

In a changing and trying economic situation, with political exigencies and with lessons taught by experience, the British system of unemployment insurance has undergone frequent revisions as regards contributions, scale of benefits, and eligibility requirements. Under the original act, placed in operation in July, 1912, the insured and the employer each contributed 2½d. (five cents) per week, while the Exchequer added one-third, or 1⅔d., making a total of 6⅔d. per insured man or woman. Benefits were 7s. per week for an insured man or woman over eighteen years of age and half as much for a boy or girl under eighteen. Benefits were not paid for the first six days of unemployment and were limited to fifteen weeks in the year. Moreover, benefits were limited to one week for each five contributions made by, and on account of, the unemployed person. Those who had been discharged for cause or had quit their employment without adequate cause, also those involved in strike or lockout, were ineligible for benefits; the right to insurance benefit ceased when suitable employment became available.

---

[1] In some cases the worker's trade union serves instead of a government labor exchange.

[2] Reduced from six days in April, 1937.

[3] See Mary B. Gilson, *Unemployment Insurance in Great Britain* (1931), pp. 272–282.

When, in 1920, the system was extended, rates of contribution, weekly benefits, and other details were changed. Because of the high cost of living and the generous bonus or dole (29s. for men and 25s. for women) made available out of Exchequer funds for returned soldiers and others whose care was a moral obligation accepted by the Government, the weekly benefit under the Act was fixed at 15s. for the insured man and 12s. for the insured woman.[1] Contributions were necessarily increased to 10d. per week—4d. from the insured, the same amount from the employer, and 2d. from the Exchequer. Between this time and 1936, both contributions and benefits were frequently changed. The main figures made effective at various dates are shown in Table 21.[2]

TABLE 21.—CONTRIBUTIONS AND BENEFITS UNDER THE BRITISH UNEMPLOYMENT INSURANCE SYSTEM, 1920 TO 1936[1]

| Date | Contributions per week, d. | | | | | | Benefits per week, s., d. | |
| | On account of insured man | | On account of insured woman | | Contribution from Exchequer | | Adult | |
	Worker	Employer	Worker	Employer	Males	Females	Male	Female
November, 1920.....	4	4	3	3½	2	1⅔	15	12
July, 1921..........	7	8	6	7	3¾	3¼	15	12
April, 1922..........	9	10	7	8	6¾	5¼	15	12
January, 1926.......	7	8	6	7	6	4½	18	15
April, 1929.........	7	8	6	7	7½	6½	17	15
October, 1931.......	10	10	9	9	10	9	15/3	13/6
June, 1934..........	10	10	9	9	10	9	17	15
July, 1936..........	9	9	8	8	9	8	17	15

[1] Great Britain Parliamentary Papers, *Accounts and Papers*, 1930–1931, vol. 32, "Abstract of Labour Statistics," pp. 62–67; *Ministry of Labour Gazette* (July, 1934), p. 230, and *Statesman's Yearbook* (1936), pp. 28a and b.
Royal Report, 1932, pp. 19–20, shows rate of benefit changes at different dates from changes in rate of contribution.

The weekly benefits paid were advanced or reduced from time to time in view of needs and changed cost of living, political exigencies, and the resources of the insurance fund. More important was the change in the nature of the system itself. In the beginning it had been formulated so as to conform to insurance principles. After 1920, however, various amendments were made which involved important departures from these

[1] In 1919, the weekly benefit had been increased from 7 to 11s.
[2] The smaller contributions made on account of, and the benefits paid to, unemployed young males and females are not shown in the table because not necessary for the purposes of this summary treatment. The present contributions for young men and women, eighteen to twenty-one, are 8d. and 7d.; for boys and girls of seventeen, 5d. and 4½d.; for boys and girls of sixteen, 5d. and 4½d.; for boys and girls of fourteen to sixteen, 2d. For these four subordinate groups, the weekly benefits are 14s. and 12s., 9s., and 7s., 6s. and 5s., and none.

principles. For one thing, allowances for dependents were introduced in order to fit benefits to needs in a better manner. The weekly allowance for dependent wife (or husband or housekeeper) was fixed at 5s. in 1921, increased to 7s. in 1928, again increased to 9s. in 1930, reduced to 8s. in 1931, and then restored to 9s.; while the allowance for each dependent child was fixed at 1s. in 1921, increased to 2s. in 1924, and then advanced to 3s. in 1935. More important was the provision for "uncovenanted" or "extended" benefits introduced in 1921, in order that those without the necessary contributions to their credit or with prolonged unemployment might be eligible. To begin with, such benefits were limited to a specified number of months in the year, but, after various changes had been made, the distinction between "ordinary" benefits and "extended" benefits was for practical purposes eliminated in 1927. Likewise the restriction involved in a ratio of benefits to contributions disappeared. The eventual outcome was that if a claimant was able to meet other statutory requirements, he was, at the discretion of the Ministry, entitled to benefit if he had paid eight contributions during the preceding two years or thirty contributions at any time. At times persons receiving "extended" benefits exceeded in number those receiving "ordinary" benefits. Thus, many of the early restrictions and safeguards were eliminated; contrary to the assumptions of insurance, little relation remained between contributions and benefit right. And in another respect were insurance principles departed from. The Act of 1920 permitted "insurance by industry," *i.e.*, through a separate fund. This would, of course, relate contribution and degree of risk in the industry. The plans submitted by only two industries (banking and insurance), both with little unemployment, were approved. The fewness of the exceptions permitted was due chiefly to the fact that it would have been the industries with the least risk of unemployment that would most likely have taken advantage of the provision of the law, and this was regarded as undesirable when depression was continuing and the insurance fund was inadequate to pay the benefits promised. The government therefore gave notice that no extension of the principle of insurance by industry would be approved as long as the emergency situation existed, and later (1927) abolished the right of an industry to establish a separate fund. Hence, as the system developed, the flat-rate contribution was exacted in all cases (except for distinctions between men and women and between adults and boys and girls), without regard to unemployment experience.

Through these various amendments voted in order to meet an emergency situation, when large numbers of people were unemployed and in distress and when the Poor Law Relief, resting upon local rates, was both inadequate and burdensome in its weight, the British insurance system was transformed into a combination of insurance and relief.

Relief (unearned benefits paid) was financed by a tax on industry's payroll and the worker's poll, not by taxes on property or on income, except in so far as the Exchequer's contributions and loans were made out of revenues drawn from taxes so levied.

The number of persons in receipt of benefits changed with employment conditions and increased with the withdrawal, partial or complete,

TABLE 22.—UNEMPLOYMENT INSURANCE IN GREAT BRITAIN, 1921 TO 1935[1]

Fiscal year[a]	No. of insured[b] (000 omitted)	No. of insured un-employed[b] (000 omitted)	Percentage unemployed	Receipts and payments of the unemployment fund, in pounds sterling (000 omitted)			
				Total receipts	Total benefit payments[c]	Total expenditures	Treasury advances outstanding[d]
1921	11,081	1,928	17.4	37,447	34,126	35,422	
1922	11,181	1,444	12.9	43,024	52,848	58,453	14,323
1923	11,232	1,282	11.4	46,673	41,881	47,880	15,315
1924	11,404	1,094	9.6	50,227	35,972	41,188	6,679
1925	11,623	1,261	10.8	50,179	44,573	51,551	8,106
1926	11,774	1,672	14.2	46,865	43,658	49,291	10,498
1927	11,876	1,083	9.1	28,562	38,689	42,753	24,710
1928	11,629	1,323	11.3	43,200	36,474	42,777	24,530
1929	11,834	1,141	9.6	42,309	46,730	53,693	35,960
1930	12,138	2,002	16.5	50,367	45,923	53,397	38,950
1931	12,500	2,732	21.8	64,902	92,245	101,332	75,390
1932	12,543	2,839	22.6	83,305	110,911	122,833	115,000
1933	12,620	2,438	19.3	117,808	104,571	117,808	115,000
1934	12,690	2,101	16.6	111,562	88,635	101,609	106,690
1935	12,780	1,919	15.1	108,928	86,004	98,786	105,660

[a] Until 1927 the fiscal year for the Insurance Fund began on July 1. In 1927 the date was moved forward to March 31. The figure for 1927 therefore covers only nine months. The data for Treasury advances outstanding are as of Dec. 31 of each year.

[b] Data for July of each year and covering insured persons, aged sixteen to sixty-four. Juveniles, fourteen and under sixteen years of age, became insurable as from September, 1934, but are here excluded. In 1935, approximately 928,000 were insured. It may be noted that the number of uninsured unemployed persons registered at the employment exchanges is small relative to the total number of insured unemployed. In December, 1932, a total of 2,723,267 persons were registered as unemployed. Of these, only 130,363 were uninsured and of this number 50,000 were boys and girls under sixteen years of age.

[c] Includes, in 1929–1930 and subsequent years, the following amounts for transitional benefits, payments, and unemployment allowances:

1930...	£ 3,690,000
1931...	19,247,000
1932...	30,742,000
1933...	50,400,000
1934...	48,442,000
1935...	42,199,000

[d] The apportioned shares of the debt attributable to Northern Ireland and the Irish Free State are excluded from these figures as from the respective dates of severance, viz., Dec. 31, 1921, and March 31, 1922.

[1] Great Britain Parliamentary Papers, *Accounts and Papers*, 1922, vol. 17, and 1923, vol. 19; *Twenty-First Abstract of Labour Statistics* (1934); *Ministry of Labour Gazette* (August, 1934 and 1935); and *Statistical Abstract for the United Kingdom* (1936).

of such safeguards and restrictions as have been mentioned. Table 22 shows the number of insured persons, the number of these registered as unemployed, the total expenditures, and the receipts from contributions and other sources, other than Exchequer loans, for the years 1921–1935.

The alleviation of distress through this modified system of insurance involved the collection and expenditure of large sums, especially in those years marked by the most unemployment. The expenditures also expanded with the liberalization of the law which has been touched upon above. With limited capacity on the part of the workers to pay when employment was irregular and contributions had to be made on account of sickness and other forms of social insurance, and with the taxation involved resting in large part directly on industry and entering into its costs, it is not surprising to find that in most years the outlays of the insurance fund exceeded its income. The balance in the fund when the system was greatly extended under the act of 1920 soon turned into a deficit. On numerous occasions it became necessary to obtain loans from the Exchequer, and little of the borrowings was repaid. The indebtedness of the insurance fund to the Treasury increased steadily from 1924 until 1932, when loans to the fund were discontinued. As shown in Table 22, the indebtedness of the fund at the time borrowings were discontinued was £115,000,000.

The departures from insurance principles were approved by nearly all of the immediately interested groups and by intelligent British men and women generally, because of the widespread distress due to prolonged unemployment following in the wake of the War, because of the effective safeguard of the standard of living and the protection against discontent afforded by unemployment benefits, and because of the generally recognized unfitness of ordinary Poor Law Relief to meet the needs of the unemployed. Among others, the experts contributing chapters to the *Third Winter of Unemployment* gave general approval to the earlier departures from the Insurance Act.[1] The criticisms of the Blanesburgh Committee were limited to details of the system; the important departures from insurance principles were accepted by it.[2] The Committee conceived the function of unemployment insurance to be one of providing benefits for "all insured persons who can fairly be described as genuinely unemployed."[3] As acute depression continued, however, the financial problem was aggravated, various criticisms of the effects of the system were voiced, and an increasingly strong demand was made by individuals and certain groups for a return to sound insurance principles. Unemployment insurance itself did not become a national issue, but the system

[1] *Third Winter of Unemployment* (1922). The contributors included W. T. Layton, J. J. Astor, Professor A. L. Bowley, and B. S. Rowntree.

[2] The Blanesburgh Committee, *Report* (1927).

[3] *Ibid.*, Par. 74.

as operated did; in 1930 a Royal Commission was appointed to investigate and report and far-reaching amendments were made in the law.[1]

Among the criticisms made by some British, and still more by casual and ill-informed observers from abroad, was that unworthy people were living on the "dole" and that willingness to work was being undermined by the payment of benefits. The numerous investigations made by Parliamentary commissions, however, have shown very much less of dishonest practice in the operation of the system than is commonly found in the administration of poor relief. Nor had there been much evidence of an undermining of a willingness to work—in fact, less than accompanies relief as ordinarily administered. Nevertheless, there were "anomalies" under the Insurance Act. Seasonal workers employed for a few months in the year at waterside resorts found it possible to get on without seriously looking for other employment. More serious was the fact that married women by working for wages irregularly could qualify for insurance and piece out the family income while most of the time engaging in the occupation of housewife.

Another criticism was that the insurance placed a tax upon mobility of labor as between areas and occupations. Without question benefits paid had made it possible for workers to remain in a "blighted" area when employment might possibly have been found elsewhere, but the experience of the Industrial Transference Board has shown the limited opportunity anyway for employment of those who desired to transfer out, with or without training. Until quite recently, in any event, mobility of labor has been limited chiefly by lack of opportunity for employment. Yet the necessity for making adjustments was in some cases removed. In the earlier postwar years claimants received benefits when they declined employment in an occupation, say, domestic service, in which they had once engaged but had left for more attractive work. This practice, however, had been largely corrected by redefinition of "suitable employment" in the administration of claims before criticisms became numerous. The evidence shows that the chief check on mobility fairly chargeable to unemployment insurance has been due to the unwillingness of insured persons to enter an uninsured occupation, such as domestic service.

The weightiest criticisms made of unemployment insurance were that it involved a burdensome tax on industry, unrelated to the degree of unemployment in plants and industries, and that it prevented a readjustment of wages and labor costs, with the result that it stood in the way of recovery and increased the amount of unemployment.[2]

[1] For an excellent review of the problems and recommendations, see Royal Commission on Unemployment Insurance, *Final Report*, Cmd. 4185 (1932).

[2] For significant discussions of these criticisms see Sir William Beveridge, *Unemployment, A Problem of Industry* (1930), Chap. 16; Henry Clay, *The Problem of Industrial*

It is true that the contributions by workers and employers to unemployment and other forms of insurance were not a light tax. The tax rested with all the greater burden because the full contribution per week was payable whether full or part time was worked. More important, the employer's part of it could not always be treated as a cost of production and added to the price of the product. This was especially true in the export trades, so important in the British economy, which have been in such sad plight in postwar years.

As a state of bad trade continued year after year, it was realized that costs of production were too high, especially in the export trades. No longer was there the former elasticity in wage rates. Previous to the very general organization of labor and the standardization of wages through collective bargaining, previous to the fairly general application of the legal minimum wage in the low paid unorganized industries, and previous to the protection of the standard of living by unemployment insurance, workers had soon been driven to accept work at greatly reduced wages when the state of trade became bad. Only about a quarter of the workers had been protected by the unions against drastic wage cuts. But in postwar years, wages were generally standardized and protected against reductions by collective agreement or wages-board order. Of course, wage rates were still readjusted but only slowly and tardily because of the procedures which had come to be employed. The standard of living was protected in so far as the workers had employment, but costs remained high relative to market prices. Moreover, both labor costs and overhead costs became higher by premature return to the gold standard in 1925. In this situation unemployment insurance, naturally enough, was blamed for wage maintenance because insured persons could not be driven by their poverty to accept whatever wages they could obtain. Low wages caused a vacancy to be termed "unsuitable." While destitution was alleviated and the standard of living protected by unemployment insurance, all of this was less appreciated by an increasing number of critics of this insurance; it was increasingly blamed for wages that were too high in the state of British trade.

The legislation of 1931 is explained by the increasing indebtedness of the Insurance Fund, the "anomalies," the burden of the tax on industry, and high production costs.

Most of the anomalies mentioned above were dealt with in the Unemployment Insurance Act (no. 3) of 1931. The Economy Act of the same year was characterized by its attempt to return to insurance principles

Relations (1929), pp. 103–120 (found also in Economic Journal, vol. 38, pp. 1–15); J. M. Keynes, Political Quarterly, vol. 1 (January, 1930), pp. 110–124; A. C. Pigou, Economic Journal, vol. 37, pp. 355–367; Jacques Rueff, Revue Politique et Parliamentaire, vol. 125 (1930), pp. 425–436; Arnold Tolles, Unemployment Insurance in Great Britain, 1911–1931 (1932), especially pp. 149–187 (unpublished dissertation, The University of Chicago).

and to meet the financial condition of the insurance fund, also by a decrease in the charge to be levied upon industry. To be entitled to benefit, the claimant, in addition to other statutory requirements, must have made a minimum of eight contributions during the preceding year or thirty contributions during the preceding two years. Moreover, he might no longer draw benefit extended beyond twenty-six weeks in twelve months. Provision was made for transitional payments for those who exhausted their regular claims, but only in case and to the extent of "need." This, however, did not mean recourse to ordinary Poor Law Relief upon which those in distress had relied. Each case was to be examined by local administrators or boards, and the amount of relief required, if any, was to be determined by them;[1] payments were to be made in cash through the employment exchanges. The Exchequer paid the bill. Thus, Britain legislated to give expression to the sound view generally adopted by continental countries that the unemployment insurance fund should have a limited liability, that benefits should not continue to be paid indefinitely in cases of prolonged unemployment, and that a system of unemployment insurance must be supplemented by a system of relief.[2]

In an effort to make the insurance fund actuarially sound, contributions were increased and the scale of benefits reduced under the Economy Act. On account of an insured man, the contributions by him, his employer, and the Exchequer, were increased to 10d.; on account of a woman, to 9d. per week, thus making the weekly contributions on account of the two, respectively, 30d. and 27d. The weekly benefit for a man was reduced from 17s. to 15s. 3d.; for a woman from 15s. to 13s. 6d. The Economy Act also repealed the statute authorizing the granting of loans from the Exchequer to the Insurance Fund. All deficiencies in the Fund were to be met by direct parliamentary grants and the debt earlier incurred was to be repaid in stipulated sums per year.

---

[1] Known as "the means test."

[2] As revised, the British system has become similar to that adopted in Germany in 1927. There the insurance fund was supplemented by a fund to provide relief for the unemployed upon the expiration of their claims to ordinary benefit. Underneath there were, of course, the communal poor-law funds. In Britain, during 1932, persons entitled to "transitional" grants were about as numerous as those entitled to benefits. During the last five weeks of that year, £4,931,000 was paid out for statutory benefits and £410,000 for administration. During the same weeks the Exchequer expended £5,260,000 in transitional payments. (Abraham Epstein, *op. cit.*, p. 362.) From Jan. 25, 1932, to Sept. 3, 1932, 18.3 per cent of the 936,757 applications for transitional benefits were not allowed (Royal Commission on Unemployment Insurance, *Final Report*, p. 62). On June 26, 1933, the number of persons on the registers of the employment exchanges was 2,438,-108. This number included 1,009,479 persons with claims for insurance benefits; 1,087,789 insured persons with applications for transitional payments; 225,789 insured persons not in receipt of insurance benefits or transitional payments; and 115,581 uninsured persons. *Ministry of Labour Gazette*, July, 1933, p. 247.

While the granting of allowances under a means test to those whose insurance rights had expired but who were in need had the desired effect of bringing the system into accord with insurance principles and reducing benefit expenditures greatly, the application of this test brought much complaint.   It involved inquiry into family income, property, and needs; not always were the inquiries made in a sympathetic or tactful manner. In fact, some of the relief authorities were niggardly; very different standards were employed in different localities.   The Unemployment Act of 1934[1] was designed to improve the administration of the test, but it also effected changes in the Insurance Act.   It extended insurance to workers between fourteen and sixteen years of age; benefits were restored to the level of 1929–1931.   Benefits normally continued to be limited to 156 days in the year, but in the case of a person insured for five years, the maximum benefit period could be extended by three days for each five contributions made, less one day for every five[2] days' benefits received by him during the last five years.   An Unemployed Assistance Board was established and given supervision over unemployment-assistance grants and over retraining.   Those whose insurance rights have been exhausted and those who have not been insured but who would normally be attached to insured trades are eligible for assistance, provided they are in need, are not in receipt of other benefits, are capable of and available for employment, are registered at an exchange, and are not idle because of industrial dispute.   Standards for grants in certain sums per week for the household and its variable number of dependents are established in regulations,[3] these approved, as a whole and without amendment, by Parliament. These standards conform fairly closely to those used in unemployment benefits.   The grants, however, take the household as an economic group, and income and other items are deducted[4] from the basic figures in determining the weekly assistance to be granted, whereas unemployment benefits are paid as a matter of right and without regard to needs, income, etc.

[1] 24 and 25, Geo. V, Chap. 29.

[2] Effective in January, 1937, *five* was changed to *eight*, the change liberalizing additional benefits somewhat.

[3] Regulations were issued in 1934 and again in 1936.   For a summary of those effective at the end of 1936, see G. Grant McKenzie (Secretary, Labour Party, Local Government Department), *Unemployment Assistance Guide* (1936–1937 ed.), p. 18 *et seq.*

[4] The regulations relating to deductions for wage incomes of members of the applicant's family group, for more or less fortuitous receipts, for casual earnings, for savings, for use of property owned, etc., are most detailed.   Not all receipts are counted and deducted from the basic allowance figures.   Moreover, room for discretion is provided.   The Act and the regulations have the effect of distinctly liberalizing the allowances, particularly in those areas where the relief authorities had been illiberal.   Yet, cases remain in which young wage earners live apart from their families in order to reduce the strain incidental to the system as now operated.   The regulations concerning deductions, etc., are well covered by G. Grant McKenzie, *op. cit.*, p. 21 *et seq.*

The detailed work—the investigations, determination of grants,[1] adjustments, and reinvestigations (usually monthly) with changing income and needs—is done by the staffs of some 240 offices located in areas within some twenty-eight districts into which the country is divided for administrative purposes. Though the means test remains, its administration has been liberalized, and the whole scheme is supervised by a central authority, and fairly uniform standards are observed. In the week ending June 26, 1936, 620,000 persons were receiving unemployment-assistance payments. The cost of providing these allowances rests in part upon the counties and boroughs; each council is to appropriate to the separate fund maintained, three-fifths of the savings realized by the county or borough by the granting of allowances. The remaining and the bulk of the costs are met by parliamentary grants.

Thus, after a tortuous course, the British system of unemployment insurance has again become one which does not greatly violate ordinary insurance principles. The rights of insured persons are definite but limited; the insured and their employers no longer pay contributions for charitable relief. At the same time, it is definitely recognized that insurance benefits must be supplemented by appropriate relief of insured persons whose benefit rights have expired, under a specially devised and appropriately supported system.[2] Ordinary Poor Law Relief lies on beyond for those destitute persons who are quite outside the insurance and assistance systems and for unemployables.

For several very lean years, the benefit payments, with administrative costs added, exceeded the contributions paid into the insurance fund. Changes in rates of contribution and of benefit were made. But the fund became still more heavily in debt to the Exchequer. However, with the changes recounted above made and with some economic recovery, the fund began to show annual surpluses. In view of these and the desirability of reducing the insurance tax, the contributions were by order reduced in 1936[3] to the figures set down in Table 23, which is designed to show rates of contribution and benefit in effect in 1936. The new (reduced)

---

[1] Determinations are subject to appeal and machinery is established for that purpose.

[2] Though revised regulations have removed some of the injustices experienced, there appears to be increasing opposition to the unemployed assistance under the Act of 1934. The administration is too centralized; the administration is criticized as being "mechanized" and as granting too little here and too much there because of variations in cases and in the cost of living. Another criticism is that there is not the desired coordination of assistance and the social services. Little use has been made of local boards. It has been suggested by R. C. Davison that the central authority should establish only a general policy and that this should be applied by committees with membership drawn in part from regions, in part from small areas. Clearly the provision for the insured who have exhausted their insurance rights has not as yet been placed upon a satisfactory basis.

[3] S.R. & O., 1936, no. 351.

rates were based upon the recommendations of the Unemployment Insurance Statutory Committee, which estimated that the percentage of unemployed during the next trade cycle would be 16.25 to 16.75 and that the lower rates should yield a surplus of more than three million pounds sterling per year.

TABLE 23.—RATES OF CONTRIBUTION AND BENEFIT OF BRITISH UNEMPLOYMENT INSURANCE, 1936[1]

Contributions (from July 6, 1936)

Class of Insured Person		Weekly Contribution (Pence) by Each Contributing Party (Worker, Employer, and Exchequer)
Men	(21 and under 65)	9
Women	(21 and under 65)	8
Young men	(18 and under 21)	8
Young women	(18 and under 21)	7
Boys	(under 18)	5
Girls	(under 18)	4½
Children	(under 16)	2

Benefits (under the Unemployment Insurance Act, 1935)

Class of Insured Person		Weekly Rates of Benefit
Men	(21 and under 65)	17s.
Women	(21 and under 65)	15s.
Young men	(18 and under 21)	14s.
Young women	(18 and under 21)	12s.
Boys	(17 and under 18)	9s.
Girls	(17 and under 18)	7s. 6d.
Boys	(under 17)	6s.
Girls	(under 17)	5s.

Allowances for dependents:	
Adult	9s.
Child	3s.

[1] The Statesman's Yearbook (1936), pp. 28a and b.

It remains to note that in 1936, after the proposal had been considered for years and recommended by a Statutory Committee[1] in 1935, the Unemployment Insurance (Agriculture) Act was passed, bringing approximately 750,000 farm laborers and workers in horticulture and forestry within the insurance system, but with special, lower rates of contribution and benefits considered appropriate in rural areas, and with limits on length of benefit period and other important details differing from those under the general system.   With relatively low rates of benefit and with 7.5 per cent as the estimate of expected unemployment (average), the contributions of worker, employer and Exchequer were fixed at 4½d. in the case of men and 4d. in the case of women twenty-one years of age or

[1] The Committee consisted of Sir William Beveridge, Chairman, A. L. Ayre, Arthur Besant, Arthur Shaw, Katherine I. Stephenson, and Mary Stacks.

over.[1] The corresponding sums for males and females, respectively, between eighteen and twenty-one, are 4d. and 3½d.; for boys and girls, age sixteen or seventeen, 2d. and 1½d.; for those under sixteen, 1½ and 1d. The weekly benefits are as follows: adult males, 14s.; adult females, 12s. 6d.; males and females between eighteen and twenty-one, 10s. 6d. and 9s. 6d., respectively; for boys and girls of seventeen, 6s. and 5s.; for boys and girls of sixteen, 4s. and 3s. 6d.[2] Allowances are added for dependents as follows: adult, 7s.; for each child, 3s. In no case, however, are benefit and allowances to exceed 30s. per week.

UNEMPLOYMENT INSURANCE IN THE UNITED STATES BEFORE THE SOCIAL SECURITY ACT

The United States has been in marked contrast to most of the European countries in the tardiness with which it has adopted social insurance laws. Workmen's compensation and widows' pensions are the only branches of social insurance which had made much headway up to a few years ago, although six states and one territory[3] had adopted optional or mandatory old-age pension laws previous to 1928. Bills had been introduced into the legislatures of many of the states, but Wisconsin alone had adopted an unemployment insurance law prior to the formulation of plans for federal legislation. There had, however, been a considerable amount of experimentation with union and employer-union insurance funds and with employers' reserve funds.[4]

Local and international unions experimented with out-of-work benefits, but without much success. The interest of organized workers in adding unemployment benefits to their other union plans had been dampened by the almost prohibitive cost if they alone contributed to the fund and by the feeling that a large share, if not all, of the cost should be met by industry or the public. Moreover, in the great majority of cases union plans placed in effect failed or were surrendered because of administrative difficulties or because of insufficient funds to meet obligations. Most locals were not equipped to administer benefits efficiently and the local group was too small to spread the risk of unemployment as widely

[1] The agricultural plan provides for the making of rebates to both employer and employee if there is a yearly or half-yearly employment contract. This amounts to a sort of merit rating. There is no similar provision under the general system though the original act allowed rebates to employers whose unemployment experience was favorable.

[2] No provision is made for benefits for those under sixteen.

[3] Alaska, Colorado, Kentucky, Maryland, Montana, Nevada, and Wisconsin.

[4] For a full and admirable account of these, see Bryce Stewart, *Unemployment Benefits in the United States* (1930). More recent summaries may be found in Paul H. Douglas and Aaron Director, *op. cit.*, pp. 464–480; in B. N. Armstrong, *Insuring the Essentials* (1932), pp. 531–546; in U. S. Bureau of Labor Statistics, *Bulletin 544* (1931); *Monthly Labor Review*, vol. 38 (1934), pp. 1288–1318; and in Constance A. Kiehel, "Security of Job Tenure and Trade-Union Out-of-Work Benefits, 1926–1929 and 1930–1933," *American Economic Review*, vol. 27 (1937), pp. 452–467.

as needed.   The internationals, on the other hand, were not in position to check adequately on claims presented.   In April, 1931, some thirty locals in the printing trades and some fifteen others were known to provide for the payment of out-of-work benefits.   The total membership of the forty-five locals was approximately 45,000.[1]   These plans were in part new ventures, in part the remaining few of the many plans inaugurated at various times since 1831.   During the depression of the 1930's, a number of locals established benefit plans, while a great many more inaugurated relief plans.   Both the out-of-work plans and the relief plans, however, operated under great strain; reduction in benefit rates occurred generally; many of the plans were discontinued.   It is reported that in 1934 only thirty-nine local unions were known to have had out-of-work benefit plans in effect.[2]   The membership covered was no doubt smaller than in 1931.

There were also three internationals[3] which in 1934 provided unemployment benefits, as against a considerably larger number, including the Cigar Makers and the Lithographers, which had once made such provision.   In 1934, perhaps approximately 42,000 workers were insured through their trade unions, local or national.   This was approximately 1 per cent of the union membership of the United States at that time. The plans, local and national, varied widely in their details; the benefits, sometimes not paid in full, ranged from $4.00 to $35.00 per week.

Beginning in 1920, there was a more hopeful development of insurance under joint agreements between unions and employers.   The greater part of this was found in the needle trades.   Of some 69,100 persons insured under such joint plans at the beginning of 1931, 55,000 were employed in the men's clothing industry, 7,000 in full-fashioned hosiery, 2,100 in cleaning and dyeing, 2,500 in the manufacture of hats and caps, 1,100 in women's clothing, 450 in the wall-paper industry, and 400 in the lace industry.   In some instances, benefits were paid for the weeks short of a number guaranteed; in others, along the more usual lines of unemployment insurance.   In some instances, the employers alone contributed, while in others the workers did so as well.   Waiting periods, amount of benefit, and other details varied widely from plan to plan.[4]

---

[1] Barbara N. Armstrong, op. cit., pp. 532–535.

[2] *Monthly Labor Review*, vol. 38 (1934), pp. 1288 ff.

[3] The three were Deutsche Amerikanische Typographia, Siderographers, and the Diamond Workers, whose memberships in 1934 were approximately 511, 80, and 300, respectively, a total of about 900.

[4] The best known of the guarantee plans was that in the Cleveland cloak and suit trade. It was introduced in 1920 as a result of an arbitration award.   After undergoing many revisions, the plan was discontinued in 1932.   The arrangement in the men's clothing industry in Chicago has been the best known of all the insurance plans and had an important influence in shaping the employer-union systems established after 1923.   Under the Chicago agreements, beginning in 1923, the manufacturer has deducted 1.5 per cent of the earnings of his union employees.   To this he added another 1.5 per cent till 1928, when his con-

Here, again, the mortality was heavy.   Some of the plans were discontinued because of the breakdown of bargaining arrangements, left-wing opposition, or maladministration.   The greatest mortality occurred, however, as the depression deepened.   In 1934, only five of the plans remained in operation.[1]

During the 1920's and the early depression years, employers' plans for paying unemployment benefits aroused most interest in the United States and received wide publicity.   Though in one or two instances plans were established by nonunion employers because of union provision in the trade or industry, by far the greater number were established as a part of the industrial relations programs of the more farsighted employers who, in addition to their desire to develop good will and to reduce the turnover of labor, were actuated by humanitarian motives.

The first company plan for unemployment benefits was introduced by the Dennison Manufacturing Company in 1916, and the first benefits were paid in 1920.   Between 1916 and 1929, fourteen such plans, covering twenty-nine establishments, were initiated.   The mortality of these plans was so high, however, that in 1929 only eight of the fourteen were still in existence and these covered only 5,500 employees.   More than two-thirds of this number of employees were covered by the Procter and Gamble Company plan, which guaranteed a minimum number (forty-eight) of weeks of employment per year, and therefore was an employment guarantee rather than an unemployment insurance plan.

In 1930 the General Electric Company announced two plans, one guaranteeing fifty weeks of employment annually to the 4,500 employees in the twelve lamp works; the other providing unemployment benefit for

---

tribution became 3 per cent.   In more recent years the first rate of contribution has again prevailed.   The combined contributions have been paid over to boards of trustees with a common chairman and executive officer, have been accredited to the given establishment (or group of establishments in the case of contractors), and have become available for paying benefits to the workers on the payroll of the establishment or the group of establishments when losing time because of lack of work.   The benefit provided under the plan was originally 40 per cent of the worker's wages, but not to exceed $20 per week, and was not to be paid for more than five weeks in the year.   The industry is seasonal and in Chicago was depressed even prior to 1930, so that the rate of benefit has been changed from time to time in order to protect the funds.   In 1936 it was 30 per cent of the worker's wage, but not to exceed $15 per week, and was not to be paid for more than seven and one-half weeks in the year.   During the depression benefits have been paid for only two or three weeks. At all times, practically all of the workers have drawn benefits for the full number of weeks, this because of the seasonal character of the industry.   In fact, the plan in Chicago has worked out, in essentials, as a subsidized compulsory savings plan, with the worker securing two payments per year.   The payment of benefits began May 1, 1924, and has continued to date (1938).   During the thirteen years ending May, 1937, the benefits paid to the workers totaled $8,559,325.

[1] In the men's clothing industry in Chicago, New York, and Rochester, the lace industry in Scranton, Pa., and in the cloth hat and cap industry in Philadelphia.

45,000 workers in the twelve apparatus plants. The announcement of these plans stimulated the hope that other industries would follow this example in protecting laid-off employees. Five companies in Fond du Lac, Wis., with about 300 employees, joined the movement in that year. In 1931, nineteen companies in Rochester, N. Y., including the Eastman Kodak Company, announced a joint plan covering 17,000 employees. In the same year, Hill Bros. Company and the J. I. Case Co. (Racine, Wis.), in 1932, the Minnesota Mining and Manufacturing Company, and in 1934 the Wrigley Company and one other established unemployment benefit or work guarantee plans.[1]

The severity of the depression prevented many more companies from initiating unemployment benefit plans and at the same time put a severe strain upon the plans already in operation. From 1920 to April 1, 1933, the benefits paid under these plans totaled $3,826,816, more than 80 per cent of which had been paid since the beginning of 1931. The predominant position of the General Electric plan is indicated by the fact that of the total, $3,111,816 had been disbursed by that company, and only $715,000 by all others.[2] By 1932 the heavy drain on the collected funds and the exhaustion of benefit rights by the employees of the General Electric Company forced that firm to change its program to provision of goods in kind for employees in need of assistance. Of the remaining plans, only thirteen were active in July, 1933. These thirteen plans covered thirty-five companies, of which nineteen were in the Rochester group. The coverage of eligible employees was then approximately 32,000, of whom 17,000 were in the Rochester group.[3] By 1934, however, the number of plans in effect had increased to eighteen.

While these plans helped to ease the burden of unemployment for the workers covered, only a fraction of 1 per cent of the wage earners in the country were covered by them, with little prospect that the system would be widely extended in the near future. Even in a favorable state of trade, some of the requirements, such as length of service, also tended to reduce the number eligible for benefits, while the standards set up were often inadequate as to amount of benefit and the number of weeks in a year during which such benefits would be paid.

It is evident that only a very small fraction of American workers were protected by voluntary unemployment insurance plans placed in effect and operated in "good times." Only the extension of compulsory insurance could be expected to change the situation in any important

[1] See *Monthly Labor Review*, vol. 38 (1934), pp. 1288–1318. These several plans are summarized, pp. 1292–1313.

[2] J. Douglas Brown, "Company Plans for Unemployment Compensation," *American Labor Legislation Review*, December, 1933, p. 179. The figures were compiled by the Industrial Relations Counselors, Inc.

[3] *Ibid.*

degree.[1] Such legislation received little consideration in the United
States until the great increase in unemployment after 1929, except in
Wisconsin, where the Huber "Unemployment Prevention Bill" received
more or less attention in committee during three sessions of the legislature, beginning in 1921. This measure in most of its details paralleled
the British law.[2] Yet the Wisconsin plan was in strong contrast to
the British at one point and also in its underlying thought and object.
While in Britain the funds have been drawn from employers, workers,
and the public treasury, the Huber Bill proposed that the employer, under
a reserve system, should bear the entire cost, including that of general
supervision by the State Industrial Commission. The chief object of the
British law was to substitute benefits for charity and to protect the
standard of living of the workers. This was also an object of the Huber
Bill, but it was secondary; the primary object was to prevent unemployment by making it expensive to the employer, who, it was claimed, has
power to stabilize business in a marked degree. A measure containing
most of the essentials of the Huber Bill was finally enacted in Wisconsin
in 1932.[3]

Except in Wisconsin, as has been stated, there was little active interest
in unemployment insurance legislation until the depression deepened.
Then an active interest developed and grew rapidly. In 1933, 105
unemployment insurance bills were introduced in state legislatures and
Congress; eight commissions investigated the subject and all reported
favorably.[4] The measure receiving most attention at the hands of
proponents of state insurance was one drafted by a committee set up
by the American Association for Labor Legislation.[5] Like the Huber
Bill and the Wisconsin law, it would exact contributions from employers
only, but workmen might voluntarily contribute to enlarge the benefit
fund. Opportunity would be provided for working out the requirements
through plant organization or otherwise. At every point, the control
to be exercised by the state would be reduced to the minimum.

[1] Mr. Henry Dennison has stated, "I do acknowledge, by force of all American experi-
ence beginning in 1915 and greatly intensified in the past three years, that compulsory
unemployment measures are necessary if we are to have more than 2 per cent coverage of
American employees. We have no grounds to believe voluntary efforts go beyond that."
(Quoted by Mary B. Gilson, in *Unemployment Insurance*, Public Policy Pamphlet 3,
University of Chicago Press, 1933, p. 17.)

[2] The essentials of the Huber Bill will be found conveniently in Allen B. Forsberg,
Unemployment Insurance (1926), pp. 124–153.

[3] Session Laws, Special Session of 1932. The law, together with an analysis of its
provisions, etc., may be found in R. S. Hoar, *Unemployment Insurance in Wisconsin* (1932).

[4] *Social Security*, vol. 7, no. 7, p. 1.

[5] For this measure, see *American Labor Legislation Review*, vol. 20 (December, 1930),
pp. 349–356. In 1932 a joint commission of the states of Connecticut, Massachusetts,
New Jersey, New York, Ohio, and Pennsylvania recommended that these six states adopt
what was practically the Wisconsin law.

The American movement for unemployment insurance had been held in check by a number of things—among them the strong opposition of the American Federation of Labor, although, it is true, that organization finally changed its position radically. At its Cincinnati convention (1932) it approved a report and suggestions for a compulsory unemployment insurance plan submitted by the Executive Council.[1] The Federation took the position that the employers alone should contribute, as in Wisconsin, but that there should be a centralized fund or pool; "We are unalterably opposed to company-controlled unemployment reserves and believe that without state administration plant reserves will prove but another 'company union' device."[2] Beyond these most of the Federation's suggestions were general except for some designed to protect union men and the strength of organized labor.[3]

From Ohio, Minnesota, and the American Association for Social Security, Inc., came detailed plans standing in sharp contrast to parts of the Wisconsin and the Industrial Commission plans, while the socialists evolved bills which would have provided liberal benefits to be paid out of public revenues derived from taxes.

The plan recommended by a majority of the Ohio Commission on Unemployment Insurance[4] provided for a general system of unemployment insurance, with a central state fund out of which benefits were to be paid to insured workers unable to find suitable employment, and with contributions by both employer and worker. These contributions were to be 2 and 1 per cent by employer and worker, respectively, until 1937, after which time the state administrative commission to be established might make adjustments and establish rates of contribution which would differentiate between industries with different amounts of unemployment. In no case, however, was the employer's contribution to be less than 1 or more than 3.5 per cent of the payroll; the employee's rate would remain fixed at 1 per cent. The rules relating to eligibility were, broadly speaking, those generally applied in Great Britain; to be entitled to benefit the applicant must have been employed in an insured trade for at least twenty-six weeks in the preceding twelve months or have been employed in an insured trade and have made forty contributions during the last two years. In order that the fund might be adequate to provide the needed benefit in cases of prolonged unemployment, the waiting period recommended was three weeks. For the same and other reasons, benefits paid to those engaged in seasonal industries were to exclude

---

[1] For the suggestions, see *Report of the Executive Council*, American Federation of Labor (1932), pp. 23–26.

[2] *Ibid.*, p. 24.

[3] *Ibid.*, p. 25.

[4] See the Unemployment Insurance Bill, in *Report of the Ohio Commission on Unemployment Insurance* (1932), pt. 1, pp. 67–80.

"the longest seasonal period or periods which the best practice of such industry or class of employment will reasonably permit." Benefits to be paid on account of total unemployment were to be 50 per cent of the worker's wage rate but not to exceed $15 per week. Short time was not to be compensated for except when the loss was in excess of 40 per cent of weekly wages; in such cases it was to be compensated through benefits varying between 10 and 40 per cent of weekly wages, according as the loss was between 40 and 55, or 85 per cent or more. Finally, the total of benefits paid in any case in the course of twelve months should not exceed the sum represented by sixteen weekly benefits on account of total unemployment.

The Minnesota plan[1] was likewise characterized by provision for contributions by both employer and worker, each contributing 2 per cent of wages. Instead of providing a common fund against which all benefits would be charged, and with variable contributions exacted from employers, as under the Ohio plan, this plan provided for separate funds for groups of industries, "such as retail, wholesale, and construction, and in manufacturing such divisions as food, printing and publishing, textile and the like."[2] "Although the proposed plan provides for a state reserves fund in which all funds are kept, industries or groups of industries would have separate credits or reserves in the fund, from which their own benefit liabilities would be paid. An industry with a small amount of unemployment would not, in consequence, be compelled to pay for the cost of excessive unemployment in another industry. Moreover, large companies that could give evidence of financial stability and a relatively favorable record of employment would be allowed to have separate credits or reserves in the fund; this would limit their responsibility to their former employees. The employers and employees of any company or industry which, because of steady employment, would be able to build up a reserve equal to 12 per cent of the average annual payroll of those covered by the act, might be allowed to reduce or even cease their contributions until their reserve had fallen below such limit in consequence of the payment of unemployment benefits."[3]

To be eligible for benefit under the Minnesota plan, the unemployed person must have been employed for a minimum of forty weeks during the preceding two years. The benefit proposed was 40 per cent of the worker's weekly wages; in case of short time, it was to be 40 per cent of the difference between what was actually earned and 80 per cent of what had been formerly earned. The most distinctive feature of the plan

---

[1] Alvin H. Hansen and Merrill G. Murray, *A New Plan for Unemployment Reserves* (1932).

[2] Quoted, with permission, from Alvin H. Hansen and Merrill G. Murray, *A New Plan for Unemployment Reserves* (University of Minnesota Press, 1932), p. 41.

[3] *Ibid.*

was the long waiting period provided for, *viz.*, a minimum of eight weeks. This was designed to provide adequate funds to pay benefits in cases of prolonged unemployment. The number of benefits was to be limited to one for each four contributions made during the preceding four years, and to forty in any twelve months.[1] Like the Ohio plan, this one made a distinction between seasonal and other unemployment, the provision here being an increase by the commission of not more than eight weeks in the waiting period.

The proposed bill presented[2] in revised form by the American Association for Social Security, Inc., differed from the American plans thus far noted in that the government as well as employers and workers would make contributions to the insurance fund to be established. The state would make a contribution of 1 per cent of the employer's payroll, the insured worker 1 per cent of his earnings. The employer would contribute 2 per cent of his payroll during the first three years, after which his premium would be fixed for his class in view of the hazard of unemployment, with a minimum of 1 and a maximum of 4 per cent of the payroll. In order to qualify for benefit, the insured worker must have been employed at least 104 days during the preceding twelve months or at least 160 days during the preceding twenty-four months, and meet the usual qualifications with regard to separation from job, unavailability of suitable employment, etc. The normal waiting period would be four weeks (of accumulated total or part-time unemployment); in seasonal industries the insurance would cover only the part of the year determined by best practice. The weekly benefit in case of total unemployment would be 40 per cent of the insured's full-time wage, but not to exceed $10; an allowance of 10 per cent of wages but not to exceed $2.50 would be made for the spouse, with an equal allowance for two or more dependent children under eighteen years of age and half as much for one such dependent child. In compensating for losses due to part-time employment, only that loss equal to or in excess of 20 per cent of the normal hours would be considered, and the compensation would be at the rate of 50 per cent of the rate of weekly wages. Benefit rights would expire with payments for twenty-six weeks in the year, but the Commission would have authority to provide extended benefits "in any period of general and extended unemployment."

Then there were the Lundeen Bill submitted to the Congress and socialist measures presented to state legislatures. The Lundeen Bill would have fully compensated all unemployed wage earners and even

---

[1] If the worker had made 208 contributions during the preceding four years, the remaining twelve (52 − 40) would be carried over into the next twelve-month period. It should be added that the state commission would be empowered to reduce the maximum from forty to not less than thirty benefits in order to conserve the fund.

[2] In *Social Security* vol. 7, no. 9 (November, 1933), Supplement.

self-employed persons out of tax revenues. Though an extraordinary measure in coverage, compensation, administrative problems which would inevitably be involved, and source of support, the plan found many adherents.

In spite of widespread interest, 1933 and 1934 passed without a state being added to the lone one (Wisconsin) which had adopted a plan of unemployment insurance. There was confusion and disagreement on the type of plan desirable; it was felt that deep depression was not the time to inaugurate such a plan; there was a question of constitutionality. A general and efficient system of public employment offices, so necessary in the administration of unemployment insurance, had not been developed; perhaps most important, each state felt that it would seriously injure its industry were it to adopt and place in effect a plan in advance of legislation in the other states.

Such was the situation in 1934, when the Federal Administration established the Committee on Economic Security and charged it with the task of reporting a comprehensive plan. The outcome was the enactment of the Social Security Act,[1] one part of which was intended to induce the adoption of unemployment insurance by the several states.[2]

The Social Security Act and Unemployment Compensation

The Committee on Economic Security and its research and advisory personnel were faced with thorny problems. The desirability of unemployment insurance being assumed, should the system be an outright national one, or a Federal-state system jointly financed, or a Federal-state system with the Federal Government making "block grants"—unmatched—to pay the bills, or a tax-offset system after the fashion of the Wagner-Lewis measure which had been before the Congress? And what, if any, contribution should insured workers make?

Not a few students of the subject found a truly national system attractive, for a number of reasons:[3] (a) It would make uniformity of rules, conditions, and benefits possible; (b) a federal administration would likely be more efficient than any other; (c) records would be centralized and needed research would thereby be furthered; (d) the problems incidental to worker migration across state lines would be obviated; (e) it would permit the National Government to levy a large part of the neces-

---

[1] Public no. 271, 74th Congress (H. R. 7260). Approved Aug. 15, 1935.

[2] The other parts of the Act, especially those relating to old-age benefits and old-age assistance, are discussed elsewhere in this volume. Wisely, the Committee devoted little attention to health insurance, and limited itself to reporting measures for improving the public-health service and related matters.

[3] An excellent discussion of the Committee's report, the debates in Senate and House, and of the many provisions of the Social Security Act is found in Paul H. Douglas, *Social Security in the United States* (1936). It has been extensively used in our discussion. See, also, Social Security Board, *Social Security in America* (1937), pp. 92–95.

sary expense upon persons in the upper income brackets and upon the excess profits of corporations, thus avoiding or minimizing payroll taxes and furthering "social justice." This last-mentioned (e), it may be remarked, has been weighted heavily by most of those students who have been interested in social insurance above other questions.

A national system would, however, raise constitutional questions.[1] Moreover, benefits would have to be administered through the public employment offices, and under the Wagner-Peyser Act (1935) a Federal-state system was being established. Again, there was the feeling against centralization and for states' rights. Very important, also, was the fact that supporters of the Wisconsin idea were well represented in the research and advisory group; they in particular desired state freedom in details rather than uniformity so that the Wisconsin plan could be fitted in.

There were those who favored and those who opposed the tax-offset plan. This plan carried with it financing the system by a payroll tax, uniform among the states. This would meet the convenience, if not the needs, of the Treasury, with its emergency expenditures and a large deficit and with heavy taxes already levied on those in the upper income and estates brackets. On the other hand, a payroll tax enters into the costs of production and affects prices or/and profits. Moreover, it was evident that the rate of unemployment differs rather widely among the several states;[2] the revenues drawn from a payroll tax, uniformly applied, would not serve needs equally well. However, the states would be left free to impose taxes as they deemed necessary and advisable and the Federal Government would not be pressed for ever-increasing aid. Finally, while a tax-offset plan would give opportunity for experimentation, it would tend to stand in the way of imposing desirable standards upon the states and to embarrass the authority who would attempt to enforce regulations.

As Professor Douglas points out,[3] the group opposed to the offset method proposed as a preferable substitute "block" or unmatched grants to the states equal to approximately the full cost of paying standard unemployment benefits. Under such an arrangement, the Government would secure its revenue as it willed—from payroll taxes alone, or in part, or not at all—and distribute it according to needs of the respective states. Among the advantages claimed for such a plan were: (a) the greater possibility of imposing needed standards, and (b) the better allocation of funds

---

[1] The American Federation of Labor, in 1932, had looked toward a national system, but was impressed by the constitutional question.

[2] It appears that in 1930–1933 the ratio of unemployment (to payroll) varied between 66 in Georgia and 133 in Michigan, while the Census had shown for April, 1930, percentages of unemployed varying between 3.9 and 13.9. See Paul H. Douglas, *op. cit.*, p. 41.

[3] *Ibid.*, p. 44.

relative to needs. However, in connection with the last-mentioned point, one must hold in mind the unfavorable reaction which inevitably develops against diversion of revenue derived from special direct taxes from one state to another for use there.

While a national system of old-age benefits and a Federal-state-matching system of old-age assistance were adopted by the Congress, the unemployment insurance provision of the Social Security Act is on the tax-offset basis, as recommended by Cabinet officers serving as members of the Committee on Economic Security.

The Social Security Act did not itself establish a system of unemployment insurance, but it was designed to induce the several states to establish such plans as they might elect within the choices made available, with few limitations incorporated in the Act. The payroll tax is levied and is to be collected quite independently of any action taken by a state. Thus, fear of injuring a state's industry if it adopted a system, because of the unequal competition of other states not adopting such a system, was almost, if not quite, removed. If a state adopted and operated an approved system, funds would be forthcoming from the Federal Government for the payment of benefits and also to cover the costs of administration. If, on the other hand, a state did not establish and operate an approved system, it would receive back from the Treasury no part of the taxes paid by its citizens.

Beginning in 1937, employers, unless excepted, became subject to a tax of 1 per cent on their payrolls (wages and salaries) for 1936, to a tax of 2 per cent for 1937, and to a tax of 3 per cent for 1938 and each year thereafter. Employers who employ fewer than eight persons on at least one day in each of twenty weeks in the year, are excepted,[1] as are all employers engaged in certain divisions of employment. In the language of the Act,

"The term 'employment' means any service, of whatever nature, performed within the United States by an employee for his employer, except

"(1) Agricultural labor;

"(2) Domestic service in a private home;

"(3) Service performed as an officer or member of the crew of a vessel on the navigable waters of the United States;

"(4) Service performed by an individual in the employ of his son, daughter or spouse, and service performed by a child under the age of twenty-one in the employ of his father or mother;

"(5) Service performed in the employ of the United States Government or by an instrumentality of the United States;

---

[1] Sec. 907(a). It was estimated that the exclusion of groups smaller than eight would reduce the number insured by about six million.

"(6) Service performed in the employ of a state, a political subdivision thereof, or an instrumentality of one or more states or political subdivisions;

"(7) Service performed in the employ of a corporation, community chest, fund or foundation, organized and operated exclusively for religious, charitable, scientific, literary or educational purposes, or for the prevention of cruelty to children or animals, no part of the net earnings of which inures to the benefit of any private share-holder or individual."

It is scarcely necessary to observe that self-employed persons are not within the embrace of the Act, but it is important to note that all persons employed by an employer liable to tax are within its embrace, regardless of whether they work for wages or for salary and that the taxes to be paid are on the entire payroll. There is, for example, no exemption of any part of a salary which exceeds $3,000 per year, as in the case of contributions for old-age benefits. The possible coverage of the Act, *i.e.*, when the laws of all states were approved and in operation, was estimated at some 25,500,000 persons, which would include a majority of all wage earners.[1]

A state may enact a law levying a (normal) payroll tax of more than 3 per cent, and it may levy a tax on the worker's wage also. Provided its plan is approved, and continues to be approved, by the Social Security Board, the employers of a state are entitled to use the taxes they pay to the state as an offset when paying the federal tax. This offset is, however, limited to 90 per cent of the Federal tax; each employer liable to tax must in any event pay to the Treasury taxes of 0.1, 0.2, and 0.3 per cent of his payrolls for the years 1936, 1937, and 1938 and thereafter, respectively. These minimum rates are designed to finance the cost of administration in the several states. Out of its revenues, the Federal Government is to make allotments to cover the costs of administration of approved plans, the allotments to be made on certification by the Social Security Board whose "determination shall be based on (1) the population of the state; (2) an estimate of the number of persons covered by the state law and of the cost of proper administration of such law; and (3) such other factors as the Board finds relevant."[2] The funds collected by each state, and earnings thereon, are to be used exclusively for the payment of benefits.

Additional credits may be given the employer under merit-rating provisions of state laws and under employer reserve funds and work-guarantee plans which, as well as nondiscriminating pooled-fund systems, may be adopted, in order to encourage stabilization of employment.[3]

---

[1] By July 1, 1937, approved unemployment compensation laws had been enacted in forty-eight states, Alaska, Hawaii, and the District of Columbia. The Social Security Board estimated the number of persons covered by these laws at 25,500,000.

[2] Section 302(a).

[3] Sections 909 and 910.

In order to provide safety and to provide the government with leverage which may be used for stabilization purposes, all monies collected by the state are to be deposited immediately with the Federal Treasury. These monies, together with the collections made by the federal agents, constitute an "Unemployment Trust Fund."[1] Except for such part as may not be needed for current withdrawals, they are to be invested by the Secretary of the Treasury in the obligations of the Federal Government or in obligations guaranteed as to both principal and interest by the United States. No payments are to be made to any state to finance benefits or to cover administrative costs except upon certification by the Social Security Board. Certification is to be made under Sec. 303 of the Act. Because of its importance, the section is quoted in full:

"Sec. 303. (a) The Board shall make no certification for payment to any State unless it finds that the law of such State, approved by the Board under Title IX, includes provisions for—

"(1) Such methods of administration (other than those relating to selection, tenure of office, and compensation of personnel) as are found by the Board to be reasonably calculated to insure full payment of unemployment compensation when due; and

"(2) Payment of unemployment compensation solely through public employment offices in the State or such other agencies as the Board may approve; and

"(3) Opportunity for a fair hearing, before an impartial tribunal, for all individuals whose claims for unemployment compensation are denied; and

"(4) The payment of all money received in the unemployment fund of such State, immediately upon such receipt, to the Secretary of the Treasury to the credit of the Unemployment Trust Fund established by Section 904; and

"(5) Expenditure of all money requisitioned by the State agency from the Unemployment Trust Fund, in the payment of unemployment compensation, exclusive of expenses of administration; and

"(6) The making of such reports, in such form and containing such information, as the Board may from time to time require, and compliance with such provisions as the Board may from time to time find necessary to assure the correctness and verification of such reports; and

"(7) Making available upon request to any agency of the United States charged with the administration of public works or assistance through public employment, the name, address, ordinary occupation and employment status of each recipient of unemployment compensation, and a statement of such recipient's rights to further compensation under such law.

"Sec. 303. (b) Whenever the Board, after reasonable notice and opportunity for hearing to the State agency charged with the admin-

---

[1] Each state is to have an account.

stration of the State law, finds that in the administration of the law there is—

"(1) a denial, in a substantial number of cases, of unemployment compensation to individuals entitled thereto under such law; or

"(2) a failure to comply substantially with any provision specified in subsection (a);

"the Board shall notify such State agency that further payments will not be made to the State until the Board is satisfied that there is no longer any such denial or failure to comply.   Until it is so satisfied it shall make no further certification to the Secretary of the Treasury with respect to such State."

Related to the provisions of Section 303, are those found in Section 903, which reads, in part, as follows:

"Sec. 903.   (a) The Social Security Board shall approve any State law submitted to it, within thirty days of such submission, which it finds provides that—

"(1) All compensation is to be paid through public employment offices in the State or such other agencies as the Board may approve;

"(2) No compensation shall be payable with respect to any day of unemployment occurring within two years after the first day of the first period with respect to which contributions are required;

"(3) All money received in the unemployment fund shall immediately upon such receipt be paid over to the Secretary of the Treasury to the credit of the Unemployment Trust Fund established by Section 904;

"(4) All money withdrawn from the Unemployment Trust Fund by the State agency shall be used solely in the payment of compensation, exclusive of expenses of administration;

"(5) Compensation shall not be denied in such State to any otherwise eligible individual for refusing to accept new work under any of the following conditions: (A) if the position offered is vacant due directly to a strike, lockout, or other labor dispute; (B) if the wages, hours, or other conditions of the work offered are substantially less favorable to the individual than those prevailing for similar work in the locality; (C) if as a condition of being employed the individual would be required to join a company union or to resign from or refrain from joining any bona fide labor organization."

Such are the essential provisions of the Social Security Act, positive and negative, in so far as the Act relates to unemployment benefits. Type of insurance system, if any, adopted, whether the workers as well as employers shall contribute, waiting period, rate of benefit, and other important details are left to the discretion of the states.   The Act gives wide latitude for experimentation.   What have state legislatures done? After this question is answered in summary fashion, we shall discuss issues and standards involved and then some of the economic implications of unemployment insurance.

As has been noted, Wisconsin alone had enacted unemployment compensation legislation prior to the development of a federal program of social security. Then, in view of pending federal legislation or subsequent to the adoption of the Social Security Act, approved laws had, by the end of July, 1937, been passed by all of the other states, by Alaska and Hawaii, and by Congress for the District of Columbia. It scarcely needs to be observed that the tax-offset method has been more persuasive or coercive than any subsidy plan could have been. The analytical table here presented (Table 24) is designed to show the more important details of the acts adopted, with such amendment as had been made by August, 1937.

The somewhat diverse plans revealed by the analytical summary, taken together with the unemployment legislation of other countries, raise a number of issues, the more important of which should receive consideration in a discussion of unemployment compensation standards and the problems, real or fancied, connected with this branch of social insurance.[1] What employees, by industry engaged in and by income groups, should be brought within the embrace of an unemployment insurance plan? What numerical groups, if any, should be excluded? What parties should be required to contribute to the fund or funds? Should there be a single fund or "central pool," or should insurance be by industry or through employer reserves and work-guarantee plans? If there is a single fund, should premiums or contributions be varied as between industries and firms experiencing substantially different degrees of risk? What is an appropriate waiting period? What should be done about partial unemployment when work is shared? What should the weekly benefit be and should it be varied in order to fit the needs of the dependent members of the insured person's family? What should be the relationship, if any, between number of contributions by, or on account of, the worker and number of his benefits? The more important details presented in Table 24 will be summarized incidental to the answers given to these and other questions of importance.

The coverage of the several laws has, of course, been rather narrowly controlled by the Social Security Act. Only slightly more than one-half of employed persons have been brought within the embrace of the unemployment insurance plans, partly because of the extensive exclusions set down in that measure. When compared with foreign legislation, the coverage is found to be greater than that under some but considerably narrower than that under other systems, as, for example, that of Great

---

[1] The constitutional issues raised by the Social Security Act and the state unemployment compensation acts are, as a matter of convenience, discussed along with the issues involved in old age benefits. See Chap. VIII, pp. 409–417.

TABLE 24.—ANALYSIS OF STATE UNEMPLOYMENT COMPENSATION LAWS IN EFFECT, AUGUST, 1937[1]

State and date of legislation	Size of firm covered (min. no. of employees)	Type of fund	Contributions [percentage of wages and merit rating (M.R.)]		Employment qualification	Benefits		
			Employer	Employee		Weekly benefits for total unemployment (*a*) percentage of wages; (*b*) min.; (*c*) max.	Waiting period (in weeks)	Ratio and maximum duration of benefit[a]
Alabama: 9/14/35 Amended: 4/21/36 3/1/37	8	Pooled fund, merit rating	0.9, 1936 to 2.7, 1938 M.R., 1941	1	Earned wages of 16 times weekly benefit in first 3 of last 4 quarters	(*a*) 50%; (*b*) no fixed minimum; (*c*) $15	3 in 52	⅙ of uncharged wage credits; maximum: 20 times weekly benefit amount
Arizona: 12/3/36 Amended: 3/23/37	3	Pooled fund, merit rating	0.9, 1936 to 2.7, 1938 M.R., 1941	None	Earned wages of 14 times weekly benefit in first 3 of last 4 quarters	(*a*) 50%; (*b*) $5 (or ¾ wages, whichever is less); (*c*) $15	2 in 13	⅙ of uncharged wage credits; maximum: 14 times weekly benefit amount
Arkansas: 2/26/37	1	Pooled fund, merit rating	1.8, 1937 to 2.7, 1938 M.R., 1942	None	Earned wages of 16 times weekly benefit in first 3 of last 4 quarters	(*a*) 50%; (*b*) $5 (or ¾ wages, whichever is less); (*c*) $15	2 in 13	⅙ of uncharged wage credits; maximum: 16 times weekly benefit amount
California: 6/25/35 Amended: 6/30/37 9/29/37	4	Pooled fund, merit rating; guaranteed plans exempted	0.9, 1936 to 2.7, 1938 M.R., 1941	0.45, 1936 to 1, 1938, but not to exceed 50% of employer's contribution	$156 in 2, 3, or 4 quarters or average of $39 per quarter for 5 or more quarters	(*a*) 50%; (*b*) $7; (*c*) $15	4 in 52 until 1940; 3 thereafter	Schedule of benefits; maximum: 20 times weekly benefit amount
Colorado: 11/20/36 Amended: 6/3/37	8	Pooled fund, merit rating	0.9, 1936 to 2.7, 1938 M.R., 1942	None	Earned wages of 16 times weekly benefit in first 3 of last 4 quarters	(*a*) 50%; (*b*) $5 (or ¾ wages, whichever is less); (*c*) $15	2 in 13	⅙ of uncharged wage credits; maximum: 16 times weekly benefit amount in 52 weeks
Connecticut: 11/30/36 Amended:	5	Pooled fund, merit rating	0.9, 1936 to 2.7, 1938 M.R., 1941	None	Earned wages of 24 times weekly benefit in first 4 of last 5	(*a*) 4% of highest quarterly earnings in 1 of last 4 quarters;	2 in 13	⅛ of wages in 8 quarters; maximum: 13 times weekly benefit

1/27/37
6/21, 22/37

State		Type of fund	Law dates		quarters	(b) $7.50 (but not more than 6% of highest wages in 1 of last 4 quarters); (c) $15		amount in 52 weeks
Delaware: 4/30/37	1	Pooled fund, merit rating	1.8, 1937 2.7, 1938 M.R. 1942	None	Earned wages of 13 times weekly benefit in first 3 of last 4 quarters	(a) 50%; (b) $5; (c) $15	2 in 13	1/6 of uncharged wage credits; maximum: 13 times weekly benefit amount
District of Columbia: 8/28/35	1	Pooled fund, merit rating	1, 1936, 3, 1938 M.R. 1941	None	13 weeks in 52	(a) 40% of wages plus allowances; (b) no fixed minimum; (c) $15	3 in 13	1:3 in 104 weeks; maximum: 16 times weekly benefit amount in 52 weeks; additional benefits
Florida: 6/9/37	8	Pooled fund, merit rating	1.8, 1937 to 2.7, 1938 M.R. 1943	None	Earned wages of 16 times weekly benefit in first 3 of last 4 quarters	(a) 50%; (b) $5 (or 3/4 wages, whichever is less); (c) $15	3 in 26	1/6 of uncharged wage credits; maximum: 16 times weekly benefit amount
Georgia: 3/29/37	8	Pooled fund, merit rating studied	1.8, 1937 to 2.7, 1938	None	Earned wages of 16 times weekly benefit in first 3 of last 4 quarters	(a) 50%; (b) $5 (or 3/4 wages, whichever is less); (c) $15	2 in 13	1/6 of uncharged wage credits; maximum: 16 times weekly benefit amount in 52 weeks
Idaho: 8/6/36 Amended: 3/17, 18/37	1	Pooled fund, merit rating; guaranteed plans exempted	0.9, 1936 to 2.7, 1938 M.R. 1941	None	Earned wages of 16 times weekly benefit in first 3 of last 4 quarters	(a) 50%; (b) $5 (or 3/4 wages, whichever is less); (c) $15	3 in 52	1/6 of uncharged wage credits; maximum: 20 times weekly benefit amount in 52 weeks
Illinois: 6/30/37	8	Pooled fund, merit rating	1.8, 1937 to 2.7, 1938 M.R. 1942	None	Earned wages of 16 times weekly benefit in first 3 of last 4 quarters	(a) 50%; (b) $5 (or 3/4 wages, whichever is less); (c) $15	3 in 13	1/6 of uncharged wage credits; maximum: 16 times weekly benefit amount in 52 weeks
Indiana: 3/18/36 Amended: 3/9/37	8	Employer reserve accounts with a pooled account	1.2, 1936 to 2.7, 1938 M.R. 1939	None	Earned wages of $50 per quarter in each of first 3 of last 4 quarters, or a total of $250	(a) 4% of wages in previous quarter; (b) $5; (c) $15	2 in 13	1/6 of uncharged wage credits; maximum: 15 times weekly benefit amount in 52 weeks

a In this column where the ratio sign is used, it indicates the relationship of number of weeks of benefit to number of weeks of contribution.
1 This analysis has been made by Robert K. Burns from the statutes, with the aid of Dan Goldy. In so far as possible, revisions of laws to August, 1937, have been used.

TABLE 24.—ANALYSIS OF STATE UNEMPLOYMENT COMPENSATION LAWS IN EFFECT, AUGUST, 1937.—(*Continued*)

State and date of legislation	Size of firm covered (min. no. of employees)	Type of fund	Contributions [percentage of wages and merit rating (M.R.)]		Employment qualification	Benefits		
			Employer	Employee		Weekly benefits for total unemployment (*a*) percentage of wages; (*b*) min.; (*c*) max.	Waiting period (in weeks)	Ratio and maximum duration of benefit[a]
Iowa: 12/24/36 Amended: 2/25/37 5/1/37	8	Pooled fund, merit rating	0.9, 1936 to 2.7, 1938 M.R., 1942	None	Earned wages of 15 times weekly benefit in first 4 of last 5 quarters	(*a*) 50%; (*b*) $5 (or weekly wage, whichever is less); (*c*) $15	2 in 13	⅙ of wages or $65 per quarter, whichever is less; maximum: 15 times weekly benefit amount in 52 weeks
Kansas: 3/26/37	8	Pooled fund, merit rating	1.8, 1937 to 2.7, 1938 M.R., 1942	None	Earned wages of 16 times weekly benefit in first 3 of last 4 quarters	(*a*) 4% of wages in previous quarter; (*b*) $5 (or 6% of wages in previous quarter); (*c*) $15	2 in 13	8% of wages in first 8 of last 9 quarters
Kentucky: 12/29/36	4	Employer reserve accounts with a pooled account	0.9, 1936 to 2.7, 1938 M.R., 1942	None, 1936, then 1, but not to exceed 50% of employer's contribution	20 weeks in 52	(*a*) 50%; (*b*) $5 (or ¾ wages, whichever is less); (*c*) $15	3 in 26	1:4 in 104 weeks; maximum: 15 times weekly benefit amount in 52 weeks
Louisiana: 6/29/36	8	Pooled fund, merit rating	0.9, 1936 to 2.7, 1938 M.R., 1942	None, 1936, then 0.5	13 weeks in 52	(*a*) 50%; (*b*) $5 (or ¾ wages, whichever is less); (*c*) $15	4 in 52	1:4 in 104 weeks; maximum: 15 times weekly benefit amount in 52 weeks; additional benefits
Maine: 12/18/36 Amended: 4/24/37	8	Pooled fund, merit rating studied	0.9, 1936 to 2.7, 1938	None	Earned wages of 16 times weekly benefit in first 4 of last 5 quarters	(*a*) 50%; (*b*) $5 (or ¾ wages, whichever is less); (*c*) $15	2 in 13	⅙ of wages or $65 per quarter, whichever is less; maximum: 16 times weekly benefit amount in 52 weeks
Maryland: 12/17/36	4	Pooled fund	0.9, 1936 to 2.7, 1938	None	Earned wages of 16 times weekly benefit	(*a*) 50%; (*b*) $5 (or ¾ wages, whichever is	2 in 13	⅙ of uncharged wage credits; maximum:

Amended: 6/1/37	4				in first 4 of last 5 quarters	less); (c) $15		16 times weekly benefit amount in 52 weeks
Massachusetts: 8/12/35 Amended: 4/30/36 5/29/37	4	Pooled fund, merit rating; exempted plans	1, 1936 to 2.7, 1938 M.R., 1941	None, 1936 to 1, 1937	Earned wages of $160 in 3 quarters or $240 in 8 quarters	(a) ½ of highest quarterly wage in first 8 of last 9 quarters; (b) $5; (c) $15	3 successive weeks in 52	⅙ of uncharged wage credits; maximum: 16 weeks in 52; additional and extended benefits provided
Michigan: 12/24/36 Amended: 8/5/37	8	Pooled fund, merit rating	0.9, 1936 to 3, 1938 M.R., 1942	None	Earned wages of $50 in each of 3 of last 5 quarters or a total of $250	(a) 4% of highest wages in 1 of first 8 of last 9 quarters; (b) $7 (not to exceed 6% of such wages); (c) $16	3 consecutive or 5 unaccumulated weeks in 52	⅙ of wages in first 8 of last 9 quarters; maximum: 16 times weekly benefit amount in 52 weeks
Minnesota: 12/24/36 Amended: 3/2/37 4/24, 26/37	1	Pooled fund, merit rating; optional employment accounts start 1/1/39	0.9, 1936 to 2.7, 1938 M.R., 1941	None	Earned wages of 16 times weekly benefit in first 4 of last 5 quarters	(a) 50%; (b) $6 (or ¾ wages, whichever is less); (c) $15	2 in 13	⅙ of uncharged wage credits; maximum: 16 times weekly benefit amount in 52 weeks
Mississippi: 3/23/36 Amended: 9/19/36	8	Pooled fund, merit rating studied	0.9, 1936 to 2.7, 1938	None	13 weeks in 52	(a) 50%; (b) no fixed minimum; (c) $15	2 in 13	1 : 4 in 104 weeks; maximum: 12 times weekly benefit amount in 52 weeks; additional benefits
Missouri: 6/17/37	8	Pooled fund, merit rating	1.8, 1937 to 2.7, 1938 M.R., 1942	None	Earned wages of 16 times weekly benefit in first 4 of last 5 quarters	(a) 4% of highest quarterly wages in base period; (b) $5 (or 6% of quarterly wages); (c) $15	3 in 13	⅙ of uncharged wage credits; maximum: 12 times weekly benefit amount in 52 weeks
Montana: 3/16/37	1	Pooled fund, merit rating	1.8, 1937 to 2.7, 1938 M.R., 1942	None	Earned wages of 16 times weekly benefit in first 3 of last 4 quarters	(a) 50%; (b) $7 (or ¾ wages, whichever is less); (c) $15	3 in 13	⅙ of uncharged wage credits; maximum: 16 times weekly benefit amount in 52 weeks
Nebraska: 4/30/37	8	Employer reserve, earnings from investment pooled	1.8, 1937 to 2.7, 1938 M.R., 1940	None	Earned wages of 16 times weekly benefit in first 3 of last 4 quarters	(a) 50%; (b) $5 (or ¾ wages, whichever is less); (c) $15	2 in 13	⅙ of uncharged wage credits; maximum: 16 times weekly benefit amount in 52 weeks

TABLE 24.—ANALYSIS OF STATE UNEMPLOYMENT COMPENSATION LAWS IN EFFECT, AUGUST, 1937.—(Continued)

State and date of legislation	Size of firm covered (min. no. of employees)	Type of fund	Contributions [percentage of wages and merit rating (M.R.)]		Employment qualification	Benefits		
			Employer	Employee		Weekly benefits for total unemployment (a) percentage of wages; (b) min.; (c) max.	Waiting period (in weeks)	Ratio and maximum duration of benefit[a]
Nevada: 3/24/37	1	Pooled fund, merit rating	1.8, 1937 to 2.7, 1938 M.R., 1942	None	Earned wages of 16 times weekly benefit in first 3 of last 4 quarters	(a) 50%; (b) $7 (or $\frac{3}{4}$ wages, whichever is less); (c) $15	2 in 13	$\frac{1}{6}$ of uncharged wage credits; maximum: 18 times weekly benefit amount in 52 weeks
New Hampshire: 5/29/35 Amended: 6/20/35 5/12/36 8/3/37	4	Pooled fund, merit rating	1, 1936 to 3, 1938 M.R., 1941	None	Earned wages of $175 in first 3 of last 4 quarters	(a) $1/26$ of highest quarterly wage; (b) $5 (or $\frac{3}{4}$ of $1/13$ of h.q.w., whichever is less); (c) $15	3 successive weeks, but further requirements in law	$\frac{1}{6}$ of uncharged wage credits; maximum: 16 times weekly benefit amount in 52 weeks
New Jersey: 12/22/36	8	Pooled fund, merit rating	0.9, 1936 to 2.7, 1938 M.R., 1942	None, 1936 and 1937; then 1	Earned wages of 16 times weekly benefit in first 4 of last 5 quarters	(a) 50%; (b) $5 (or $\frac{3}{4}$ wages, whichever is less); (c) $15	2 in 13	$\frac{1}{6}$ of wages in first 4 of last 5 quarters or maximum of 16 times weekly benefit amount in 52 weeks, whichever is less
New Mexico: 12/16/36 Amended: 3/15/37	4	Pooled fund, merit rating	0.9, 1936 to 2.7, 1938 M.R., 1942	None	Earned wages of 16 times weekly benefit in first 3 of last 4 quarters	(a) 50%; (b) $5 (or $\frac{3}{4}$ wages, whichever is less); (c) $15	2 in 13	$\frac{1}{6}$ of uncharged wage credits; maximum: 16 times weekly benefit amount in 52 weeks
New York: 4/25/35 Amended: 3/18/36 5/23/36 3/31/37	4	Pooled fund	1, 1936 to 2, 1937 to 3, 1938	None	Earned wages of 18 times weekly benefit amount in base year	(a) 50%; (b) $7; (c) $15	3 in 13	$\frac{1}{6}$ of wages in base period; maximum: 16 times weekly benefit amount in 52 weeks

North Carolina: 12/16/36 Amended: 3/13/37 3/22, 23/37	8	Pooled fund, merit rating studied	0.9, 1936 to 2.7, 1938	None	Earned wages of 16 times weekly benefit in first 4 of last 5 quarters	(*a*) 50%; (*b*) $5 (or ¾ wages, whichever is less); (*c*) $15	2 in 13	⅙ of wages or $65 per quarter, whichever is less; maximum: 16 times weekly benefit amount in 52 weeks
North Dakota: 3/16/37	8	Pooled fund, merit rating	1.8, 1937 to 2.7, 1938 M.R., 1942	None	Earned wages of 16 times weekly benefit in first 3 of last 4 quarters	(*a*) 50%; (*b*) $5 (or ¾ wages, whichever is less); (*c*) $15	2 in 13	⅙ of uncharged wage credits; maximum: 16 times weekly benefit amount
Ohio: 12/17/36 Amended: 5/7/37 5/12/37	3	Pooled fund, merit rating	90% Fed. tax, 1936 to 2.7 payroll, 1938 M.R., 1942	None	20 weeks in 52	(*a*) 50%; (*b*) no fixed minimum; (*c*) $15	3 in 52	⅙ of wages or $65 per quarter, whichever is less; maximum: 16 times weekly benefit amount in 52 weeks
Oklahoma: 12/12/36	8	Pooled fund, merit rating	0.9, 1936 to 2.7, 1938 M.R., 1941	None	Earned wages of 16 times weekly benefit in first 4 of last 5 quarters	(*a*) 50%; (*b*) $8 (or ¾ wages, whichever is less); (*c*) $15	2 in 13	⅙ of wages in first 4 of last 5 quarters or a maximum of 16 times weekly benefit amount in 52 weeks, whichever is less
Oregon: 11/15/35 Amended: 3/10, 11/37	4	Employer reserve accounts with a pooled account	0.9, 1936 to 2.7, 1938 M.R., 1941	None	Earned wages of 16 times weekly benefit amount in base year	(*a*) 50%; (*b*) $7 (or ¾ wages, whichever is less); (*c*) $15	3 in 13	⅙ of wages in base period; maximum: 16 times weekly benefit amount in 52 weeks
Pennsylvania: 12/5/36 Amended: 5/18/37	1	Pooled fund	0.9, 1936 to 2.7, 1938	None	Earned wages of 13 times weekly benefit in first 4 of last 5 quarters	(*a*) 50%; (*b*) $7.50; (*c*) $15	3 in 52	⅛ of wages in first 8 of last 9 quarters or 13 times weekly benefit amount in 52 weeks, whichever is less
Rhode Island: 5/5/36 Amended: 4/29/37	4	Pooled fund, merit rating studied	0.9, 1936 to 2.7, 1938	1, 1937 to 1.5, 1938 and after	Earned wages of 16 times weekly benefit in last 4 quarters	(*a*) 50%; (*b*) $7.50 (or ¾ of wages, whichever is less); (*c*) $15	2 in 13	⅙ of uncharged wage credits; maximum: 20 weeks in 52
South Carolina: 6/6/36	8	Pooled fund, merit rating	0.9, 1936 to 2.7, 1938 M.R., 1941	None	13 weeks in 52	(*a*) 50%; (*b*) $5 (or ¾ wages, whichever is less); (*c*) $15	2 in 13	1:4 in 104 weeks; maximum: 12 times weekly benefit amount in 52 weeks; also additional benefits

TABLE 24.—ANALYSIS OF STATE UNEMPLOYMENT COMPENSATION LAWS IN EFFECT, AUGUST, 1937.—(Continued)

State and date of legislation	Size of firm covered (min. no. of employees)	Type of fund	Contributions [percentage of wages and merit rating (M.R.)]		Employment qualification	Benefits		Ratio and maximum duration of benefit[a]
			Employer	Employee		Weekly benefits for total unemployment (a) percentage of wages; (b) min.; (c) max.	Waiting period (in weeks)	
South Dakota: 12/24/36 Amended: 3/9/37	8	Employer reserve accounts with pooled account	90% Fed. tax, 1936 to 2.7, payroll, 1938 M.R., 1940	None	Earned wages of 20 times weekly benefit in first 3 of last 4 quarters	(a) 50%; (b) $5 (or ¾ wages, whichever is less); (c) $15	3 in 13	⅙ of wages or $65 per quarter, whichever is less; maximum: 14 times weekly benefit amount in 52 weeks
Tennessee: 12/18/36 Amended: 3/5/37	8	Pooled fund, merit rating	0.9, 1936 to 2.7, 1938 M.R., 1941	None	Earned wages of 16 times weekly benefit in first 4 of last 5 quarters	(a) 50%; (b) $5 (or ¾ wages, whichever is less); (c) $15	3 in 13	⅙ of uncharged wage credits; maximum: 16 times weekly benefit amount in 52 weeks
Texas: 10/27/36 Amended: 3/24/37	8	Pooled fund, merit rating	0.9, 1936 to 2.7, 1938 M.R., 1941	None	Earned wages of 16 times weekly benefit in first 3 of last 4 quarters	(a) 50%; (b) $5 (or ¾ wages, whichever is less); (c) $15	2 in 13	⅙ of uncharged wage credits; maximum: 16 times weekly benefit amount in 52 weeks
Utah: 8/29/36 Amended: 3/11/37	4	Pooled fund, merit rating	0.9, 1936 to 2.7, 1938 M.R., 1941	None	Earned wages of 16 times weekly benefit in first 3 of last 4 quarters	(a) 50%; (b) $7 (or ¾ wages, whichever is less); (c) $15	2 in 26	⅙ of uncharged wage credits; maximum: 16 times weekly benefit amount in 52 weeks
Vermont: 12/22/36 Amended: 1/27/37 4/10/37	8	Pooled fund, merit rating or election of employer reserve accounts	0.9, 1936 to 2.7, 1938 M.R., 1941	None	Earned wages of 16 times weekly benefit in first 4 of last 5 quarters	(a) 50%; (b) $5 (or ¾ wages, whichever is less); (c) $15	3 in 26	⅙ of uncharged wage credits; maximum: 14 times weekly benefit amount
Virginia: 12/18/36	8	Pooled fund	0.9, 1936 to 2.7, 1938	None	Earned wages of 16 times weekly benefit in first 4 of last 5 quarters	(a) 50%; (b) $5 (or ¾ wages, whichever is less); (c) $15	2 in 13	⅙ of wages or $65 per quarter, whichever is less; maximum: 16 times weekly benefit amount in 52 weeks

TABLE 24.—ANALYSIS OF STATE UNEMPLOYMENT COMPENSATION LAWS IN EFFECT, AUGUST, 1937.—(*Continued*)

State and date of legislation	Size of firm covered (min. no. of employees)	Type of fund	Contributions [percentage of wages and merit rating (M.R.)]		Employment qualification	Benefits		
			Employer	Employee		Weekly benefits for total unemployment (a) percentage of wages; (b) min.; (c) max.	Waiting period (in weeks)	Ratio and maximum duration of benefits[a]
Washington: 3/16/37	8	Pooled fund, merit rating	1.8, 1937 to 2.7, 1938 M.R., 1942	None	Earned wages of 16 times weekly benefit in first 3 of last 4 quarters	(a) 50%; (b) $7 (or ¾ wages, whichever is less); (c) $15	2 in 13	½ of uncharged wage credits; maximum: 16 times weekly benefit amount
West Virginia: 12/17/36 Amended: 3/19/37	8	Pooled fund, merit rating	0.9, 1936 to 2.7, 1938 M.R., 1941	None	Earned wages of 12 times weekly benefit amount in first 3 of last 4 quarters	(a) 50%; (b) $5 (or ¾ wages, whichever is less); (c) $15	2 in 13	½ of uncharged wage credits; maximum: 12 times weekly benefit amount in 52 weeks
Wisconsin: 1/29/32 Amended: 1932, 1935 and 1937	6	Employer reserve accounts with separate guaranteed employment accounts. Exempted plans	2 through 1937 to 2.7, 1938 M.R. provided	None	4 weeks employment by given employer	(a) 50%; (b) $5 per week; (c) $15	3 per employer in 52	1:4 in 52 weeks; maximum: from 14 to 20 in 52 weeks
Wyoming: 2/25/37	1	Pooled fund, merit rating	1.8, 1937 to 2.7, 1938 M.R., 1942	None	Earned wages of 14 times weekly benefit in first 3 of last 4 quarters	(a) 60%; (b) $7 (or ¾ wages, whichever is less); (c) $18	2 in 13	½ of uncharged wage credits; maximum: 14 times weekly benefit amount

Britain.[1] The coverage should include industries which present any great problem, provided the administrative problems are not as a result multiplied and made too difficult. The American legislation meets this test fairly well, though when the great administrative problems involved in present legislation have been solved reasonably well, the inclusion of some of the (industry) groups now excluded should receive serious consideration. This is called for in order to solve the problem adequately. Moreover, with some trades insurable and others not, the migration of workers between them is interfered with in a measure.

Twenty-five of forty-nine laws analyzed in Table 24 and in effect July, 1937, exclude firms in insured trades employing fewer than eight employees on at least one day in each of twenty weeks,[2] thus conforming to the section of the Federal Act levying the payroll tax. This has the advantage of involving fewer accounts to be handled and of administrative convenience. On the other hand, it is less inclusive than most of our workmen's compensation legislation and the old-age benefit part of the Social Security Act; it leaves a considerable portion of those employed in industries within the embrace of the Act without right of benefit and will interfere somewhat with the migration of labor between the larger and the smaller plants. Much can be said for the smaller numerical exception of three, four, five, or six employees found in the laws of fourteen of the states,[3] if not for the absence of any numerical exclusion found in the law enacted by Congress for the District of Columbia, and in the laws of Arkansas, Delaware, Idaho, Minnesota, Montana, Nevada, Pennsylvania, and Wyoming.

Most of our legislation is in considerable contrast to that of foreign countries. Under foreign systems it is usual to except from the compulsory provisions of the law at least those nonmanual workers who earn more than stipulated amounts per month or year. The underlying assumption is that such persons can maintain their independence. The explanation of the provisions of a majority (forty-three) of our state laws and that of the District of Columbia is, of course, found in the Social Security Act, which levies the tax without regard to size of wage or salary. Kentucky, Massachusetts, Michigan, and Rhode Island exclude employer or employee contributions on that part of the salary

---

[1] In Great Britain, since the extension of insurance to agricultural workers and gardeners, 65 per cent of gainfully occupied persons are covered. In the United States, the coverage is approximately 25,500,000, the number of persons who would normally be gainfully occupied, in excess of 50,000,000.

[2] Iowa has the same requirement except that the employment need be for only fifteen instead of twenty weeks.

[3] In Arizona and Ohio, three; in California, Kentucky, Maryland, Massachusetts, New Hampshire, New Mexico, New York, Oregon, Rhode Island, and Utah, four; in Connecticut, five; in Wisconsin, six.

which exceeds a stipulated amount,[1] and New York exempts from coverage employees with earnings in excess of $3,000 per year. The inclusion of all employees, however, makes for the simplest arrangement in administration.

The Federal Act levies an excise on the employer's payroll and does not require the states to make any contribution out of general revenues. With precedent established by Wisconsin in 1932 and with the provisions of the Federal law as they are, forty-one of the state laws and that of the District of Columbia provide for the levy of a tax on the employer alone and usually at the rates levied under the Federal Act. On the other hand, in order to secure more revenue or as a "matter of principle," seven of the states exact contributions from the workers, after 1936 if not in the beginning, most frequently at the rate of 1 per cent of wages or one-half of the employer's contribution. In the case of the District of Columbia alone has any appropriation been made out of general revenues.[2]

The provisions relating to contributions stand in considerable contrast to foreign practice and to the proposals made by important groups in this country some years ago.[3] How should the burden be distributed, particularly as between employer and the insured? Should any part, or all, of the revenues be derived from taxes other than those on payrolls?

Such questions as these are properly answered only in terms of relative advantage and disadvantage and in the light of a country's institutional arrangements and economic and political conditions. Competent students of the subject are likely to arrive at different conclusions. The authors state their views and their reasons for holding them.

There should be joint contributions by employers and the insured workers. Few would contest the position that employers should contribute. To an extent unemployment is a responsibility of industry; it is difficult to secure the needed funds without a tax on industry; moreover, the employers collectively should benefit from the maintenance of the efficiency and morale of the workers, so likely to suffer in the absence of unemployment benefits; the employers collectively should benefit by the avoidance of discontent; the exaction of such a tax might strengthen somewhat existing motives for regularizing employment in so far as this lies within the employer's power; finally, the discharge of the responsibility should be effective in improving the attitude of this important group in the population toward the problem presented by unemployment.

---

[1] In Massachusetts the employee pays taxes on wages or salary up to $2,500 per year; in Kentucky, $2,600; employers in Michigan and employees in Rhode Island pay taxes on the first $3,000 only.

[2] The appropriations made in the District are $100,000, $125,000, and $175,000 for the years 1936, 1937, and 1938, respectively.

[3] Cf. pp. 141–145.

For a number of reasons the authors are, however, not of the view that the entire cost should be imposed upon employers through a payroll tax, though difficulties of one sort or another may have quite properly led to drafting the social security bill along the lines it took. The first of these reasons is found in the limited control employers can exercise over the volume of employment, a matter already discussed (*supra*, Chap. II). From the point of view of prevention, unemployment is, contrary to an assumption of stout proponents of the Wisconsin plan, a substantially different problem from that presented by work injuries. Much of the instability of employment is due to national and international forces over which an employer individually or employers collectively have little or no control. The causes of work injuries, on the other hand, looked at from the point of view of prevention, are found within the plant. In so far as work injuries can be prevented, the methods are at the command of the employer and his workmen. A second reason is found in the incidence and effects of payroll taxes, whether for financing unemployment compensation, old-age benefits, or sickness benefits. Though in the long run, much, and possibly all, of the employer's contribution will, under certain conditions, be shifted to consumers through higher prices or be offset through adjustments in wage rates, there are limitations upon any such shifting process, especially at times when prices and wage rates are not rapidly rising, and large contributions might under certain conditions work injury to industry and increase unemployment. Fortunately, in this country the taxes are being introduced gradually and at first prices and wage rates were rising. Moreover, the taxes are mainly national, not levied by isolated states. This protects the employer greatly. But, even so, the relation between size of payroll, total costs, and profit margins varies greatly between industry and industry. So do conditions affecting the market, such as the elasticity of the demand for the products or services. These and related matters will be discussed more fully later. In the third place, there are sound reasons why the workers should also contribute to the unemployment compensation fund.

Of course, the compensation received by the unemployed worker is only partial; there is a waiting period, the number of benefits is limited, and the rate of benefit is a smaller or larger percentage of the worker's rate of wages. Hence, the larger part of the loss in wages is, as a rule, still borne by the insured worker. But, as the British Royal Commission points out,[1] the worker's position under unemployment insurance is improved and he can therefore afford to contribute. Beyond this argument, contribution by the workers is helpful in preventing the benefit received from being tainted by any element of charity, and also to some degree in safeguarding the fund against unjust claims. Finally, and highly important, if the entire bill is charged against employers, what

[1] Royal Commission on Unemployment Insurance, *Report* (1932), pp. 215–216.

the size of that bill will become is perhaps as uncertain as the bill for government (noncontributory) pensions. Joint contributions, especially if equal contributions, tend to prevent unemployment insurance from becoming a "political football."

Whether the government itself should make a direct contribution is a more debatable question. It is our opinion that the government should pay the costs of operating the labor exchanges, so important in the administration of unemployment compensation, if not all of the administrative costs. But it seems best that the government should not make a direct, regular contribution to the insurance fund as it has in England. In emergencies insurance funds prove to be inadequate; unemployment insurance is no panacea; a second line of defense is needed in a relief fund to provide for those whose insurance becomes exhausted; this should be established and supported by the government. Indeed, experience has shown that a third line of defense is needed, especially for those who have not been within the embrace of the insurance plan or have not become eligible to benefit. Unemployment insurance must be supplemented by an adequate system of relief. This, experience has definitely shown.

The authors would charge the government with these supplementary provisions, but not with a direct contribution to the unemployment insurance fund. They recognize, of course, that the position taken is not acceptable to those who would charge the entire cost of caring for the unemployed to the government, to be met out of its usual revenues. While, as will be noted at a later point in our discussion, some would rely entirely upon relief of those in need and not provide benefits as a matter of insurance right, others would charge much, if not all, of the cost to government as a matter of "social justice." It would appear that the latter are especially interested in effecting a substantial change in the distribution of wealth by increasing the taxes upon the wealthy and using the revenues to finance social insurance. The authors are in complete accord with the use of highly progressive taxes in order to effect a distinctly less unequal distribution of income and property, but it appears that most of those interested in "social justice" do not appreciate the fact that the taxes already imposed in the United States upon incomes in the higher brackets and upon large estates are relatively heavy. Certainly few students of government finance would advocate the imposition of higher rates than are now levied in the upper brackets. Most of those who are greatly interested in a less unequal distribution of wealth are not advocates of lower exemptions and of substantially higher rates applied in the lower and middle brackets, though the one or the other or both of these would be required if a much larger revenue were to be gained from income and inheritance taxes. And, it may be added, there is no special reason why revenues obtained from still more onerous income and estate taxes should be allocated to social insurance funds rather than to the general revenues.

As has been stated,[1] there had been sharp division of opinion as to the type of unemployment compensation system which would be best, but the Social Security Act left the states comparatively free to introduce the type they preferred. An examination of Table 24 shows that all except six of the laws provide for the central or "pooled-fund" type, with or without provision for merit rating. Standing over against this type is the Wisconsin system, which provides for employer reserve accounts with guaranteed employment accounts as special plans. Nebraska has also enacted a law of this type.[2] In Indiana, Kentucky, Oregon, and South Dakota the pooling is limited and place is made for employer reserve accounts, while in Vermont the employer elects whether to maintain his own reserve or to make payment into the pooled fund. And, it is to be added, provision is made in California, Massachusetts, and some of the other states, whereby special employer plans may be substituted for the more general arrangement.

The pooled-fund system, with or without merit rating, is that generally found in foreign countries. Whatever the source or sources of income and however the given employer's rate of contribution is determined, all the revenues derived are paid into a single fund and benefits are paid from that fund, without regard to the industries, occupations, or plants in which the insured persons have been employed. In Wisconsin and Nebraska, on the other hand, each employer is liable only for the compensation due his employees; his employees have no recourse to any fund except their employer's reserve account. With the plan in normal operation in Wisconsin since January, 1938, the employer pays a payroll tax of 2.7 per cent. Hereafter 2.7 per cent will remain the "standard" contribution, but the employer's actual contribution will be based upon his employment experience. If it has been poor, he will be required to pay a higher rate but not more than 4 per cent; benefits to his employees may have to be "scaled down." If, on the other hand, his employment experience has been favorable, he will pay less than 2.7 per cent or nothing, provided he has met his benefit obligations during the preceding year, his reserve is five times the largest amount paid out in any of the preceding three years, and his reserve exceeds 7.5 per cent of his payroll.[3]

This, briefly, is the Wisconsin individual employer reserve system. There is also provision for such employment guarantee plans as are approved by the Industrial Commission. To be approved, a plan must guarantee a minimum of forty weeks of work and wages for at least two-thirds of full-time hours or for thirty hours per week, whichever is greater. If, however, the guaranteed employment is for more than forty

[1] *Supra*, pp. 145–147.

[2] The first Utah law was of the Wisconsin type, but this law was repealed before it became effective.

[3] Chap. 20, Laws special session 1931–1932, as amended by Chaps. 172 and 446, Laws of 1935.

weeks in the year, one hour is deducted from the number of hours per week, with twenty hours as the minimum in any event. Security, or assurance, satisfactory to the State agency, must be given for the fulfillment of such guarantees.[1] These provisions are in accord with the provisions of the Social Security Act.[2] So also are the provisions found in the other states where employer reserves or guaranteed employment plans are permitted.[3]

In passing, we note Professor Douglas' observations[4] on the provisions of the Social Security Act relating to guaranteed employment plans.

"This amendment,[5] therefore, not only permits the weaknesses of the plant reserves system with its inequality of benefits but also makes possible further inadequacies by permitting the guaranteed employment plans to operate on a rather low level of employment. Thus, a firm which in good times was accustomed to work fifty-one weeks of forty hours each and hence to afford a full-time worker 2,040 hours of employment, need offer only 1,200 hours of employment and indeed possibly only 1,000 hours in order to escape paying benefits. If a firm, therefore, employed these men for forty weeks at only thirty hours a week, it need not pay benefits either for (a) the ten hours of lost time in each of the forty weeks, or (b) the eleven weeks in which no work at all was offered. Under an ordinary unemployment insurance system a worker would at least receive benefits for the eleven weeks of lost employment subject to the deduction of a given waiting period."

Yet, in spite of what Douglas says concerning the possibilities, it may be said that, holding in mind the fact that not all weeks will ordinarily be short-time weeks and that not all short-time weeks will ordi-

---

[1] Wisconsin Laws, 1935, Chap. 446.

[2] Sections 909, 910.

[3] The California law relating to guaranteed employment plans (California Laws, 1935, Chap. 352, Sec. 47) is more liberal than the minimum requirements of the Social Security Act. The coverage must be of all employees with eight weeks of service; guarantees of employment according to the following schedule of weeks and hours in each week are required:

Minimum No. of Weeks in Year	Minimum No. of Hours in Each Such Week
42	36
43	34
44	32
45	30
46	28
47	26
48	24
49	22
50	20

[4] Quoted, with permission, from Paul H. Douglas, *Social Security in the United States* (McGraw-Hill Book Co., Inc., 1936), p. 139.

[5] The La Follette amendment which was adopted and became a part of the Social Security Act.

narily be equally short and at the minimum, and that with ratio of benefits to contributions and maximum weeks of benefit per year in the compensation laws, the guaranteed employment plans should usually not be more illiberal to the workers than the central pooled plans.   There will, however, be exceptional cases just as there will in all probability be cases in which pooled funds will prove to be inadequate.

Of course, the guaranteed employment plan is merely a variant from the employer's reserve plan.   The reserve plan might be that of a single employer or of a group of employers.   What of the issue raised by employers' reserves, as in Wisconsin?

The case for employers' reserves, group or individual, is (1) that taxing each group or firm for the maintenance of its own unemployed workers would make for the maximum of unemployment prevention; and (2) that, as has been shown (Chap. I), the amount of unemployment varies greatly as between industries and firms and that an industry or firm should not be taxed to support another's unemployed.   Both of these contentions have a measure of merit.   On the other hand, it must be pointed out that industries and firms have limited ability to stabilize business and employment, unless it be in seasonal industries and by one firm stabilizing its business at the expense of another.   Frequently the gain of one may involve loss by another.   For example, the extension of a clothing season by a cut in wholesale prices may be to a firm's advantage, but it is almost sure to reduce the business of competitors as its chief effect.   Or, as under the former guarantee plan in the ladies' garment industry in Cleveland, the manufacturer may limit inside manufacture so as to give regular employment and use contractors irregularly in order to meet above-the-average load.   It is to be pointed out next, and emphasized, that the chief problem is to make adequate provision for the unemployed.   Is it clear that all industries and all firms are so circumstanced that they can accept full responsibility for supporting their unplaced former or laid-off employees?   Certainly not unless the contributions are to be unlimited or in many cases so high as to be prohibitive.   Under the Social Security Act, it is true, the limitations upon employers' reserves (and guaranteed employment plans) are designed to protect the workers under them so that they will receive treatment substantially equal to that received under a pooling arrangement.   Yet, the Wisconsin reports are rather disconcerting; it is likely that in not a few cases employer reserves will be inadequate to pay standard benefits.[1]

Under the laws enacted, pooled funds are the general rule, reserve plans the exception.   Yet, as indicated above, the employer in some states may elect to establish his own reserve, with or without payment

[1] Though contributions had been made for two and a half years, the payment of benefits during the first six months greatly depleted the reserves of a number of employers.   Operation during a longer period of time will provide significant data.

into the pooled fund. Where special plans are allowed, the normal effect should be that those industries and firms experiencing the least unemployment and, other things equal, having the greatest ability to pay, will tend to devise their own reserve or guarantee plans. This would have the effect of increasing the difficulty of financing the benefits to be paid out of the central pool. A measure of protection is, of course, given against this in those states in which a fraction of the taxes paid by employers maintaining their own reserves is paid into the pooled fund. This compromise arrangement is an improvement on the Wisconsin plan, but it falls short of the straight pooled-fund arrangement in so far as meeting the needs of the unemployed is concerned. Special arrangements also present administrative problems connected with separate accounts and the migration of workmen from one employment to another. A mixture of pooled-fund and elective plans is open to serious objection.

The soundest policy would seem to be to create a system of unemployment compensation under which unemployed workers, other things being the same, would have equal and uniform treatment, and under which the employers providing the most stable employment would have preferential treatment in their contributions. This is the object of merit rating, which, while difficult, seems to be practicable; it finds place in commercial insurance. A majority (thirty-two) of the states and the District of Columbia which have legislated have provided for a central pool with merit rating. The spread between maximum and minimum rates varies widely.[1] The spread may be right or wrong; experience will tell. The degree of preference should be decided upon with due regard to the desire to further stabilization of employment on the one hand, and the safety of the fund and the desire to distribute the burden involved in carrying the cost with proper reference to ability to pay on the other. In one of its aspects, unemployment insurance is a system of taxation for a special purpose.

Yet experience may show that merit rating presents too many problems to warrant its use. If so, the choice would be among undiscriminating pooled funds, employer reserve funds, and employer reserve funds accompanied by payments into a central pool in order, within limits, to insure the adequacy of the individual reserves to meet the claims made upon them.

Under a provision of the Social Security Act, no benefits may be paid until a state law has been in effect for two years.[2] The object of this

---

[1] Five states, Georgia, Maine, Mississippi, North Carolina, and Rhode Island provide for a pooled fund and a study of merit rating looking toward its eventual adoption.

[2] Under this provision benefits became payable before Jan. 1, 1938, in Wisconsin only. In that state, beginning in July, 1936, by Feb. 28, 1937, 40,000 payments had been made to 18,000 beneficiaries, the total paid out being $276,000.00 (approximate figures). The total paid out, July, 1936, to June 30, 1937, was $963,793.94.

provision is, of course, to permit needed reserves to be built up. And, when benefits may be paid, the worker must qualify by having been employed in an insured trade for a specified length of time or have earned a given amount in wages in insured employment within a year or other period.

The laws of four states provide for qualifying weeks of employment, ranging from four weeks with one employer in Wisconsin up to twenty weeks of employment within fifty-two, as in Kentucky and Ohio. These provisions are patterned after those found in foreign legislation. The newer laws generally and many of the older ones, by amendment, however, provide for qualification upon the basis of earnings rather than weeks of employment. This is the most striking change made in unemployment compensation legislation as the movement has progressed. The substitution has been made to simplify record-keeping and administration and to bring these into greater harmony with those involved in old-age benefits. In a majority of the states, the unemployed worker must have earned in insured employment at least sixteen times his weekly benefit rate in the first three of the last four or in the first four of the last five quarters.

In determining the rate of benefit of a claimant under the laws enacted, the general rule is to take a percentage of his rate of pay, as in most European countries other than Great Britain, and as under our American workmen's compensation systems, with a few exceptions. The percentage of the wage rate in all but nine states is 50,[1] but, again, as under workmen's compensation, there are prescribed maximum, and, in most states, minimum sums per week. In every state except two,[2] the maximum is $15; the minimum in twenty-two states is $5 per week or three-fourths of wages, whichever is less; in twenty-one other states, the minimum varies from $5.00 per week in a majority up to $8.00 a week or three-fourths of wages, in Oklahoma. In Alabama, the District of Columbia, Mississippi, and Ohio, no minimum is provided.

Unemployment insurance laws may or may not make provision for benefits in case of partial employment. With few exceptions, the American states do. The general rule is to compensate for loss due to part-time work where it reduces earnings to a point less than the weekly benefit or within a dollar or so of that amount. The benefit payable is

---

[1] District of Columbia, Connecticut, Indiana, Massachusetts, Kansas, Michigan, Missouri, New Hampshire, and Wyoming are the nine exceptions. In the District of Columbia, the percentage is 40, with 10 per cent added for dependent spouse and 5 per cent for each dependent relative, the total not to exceed 65 per cent of wage or $15, whichever is less. In Connecticut, Kansas, and Missouri, the rule is 4 per cent of total wages during the quarter of highest earnings among the last four quarters. The same rule is found in Michigan except that the quarter taken is from the first eight of the last nine. In Wyoming, the rate is 60 per cent of average weekly wage.

[2] In Michigan it is $16 and in Wyoming, $18.

most frequently that which will bring the total of earnings and benefit up to the benefit for total unemployment or a dollar or so in excess of that sum.

These provisions relating to benefits raise some questions inviting consideration. One of these is whether it would not be better to provide flat-rate benefits as in Britain or various fixed sums applicable to as many classes of workers, these classes based upon earnings. Certainly either arrangement, and especially the former, reduces the difficulties in administration of benefits when many insured persons are involved. Over against this consideration, however, it can be said that basing benefits directly upon rates of wages is better calculated to protect the standards of living of the different types of insured persons—clerical, skilled, semi-skilled, and unskilled—who have different modes of living when in employment and who have different commitments. Unless benefits are based directly upon wage rates or vary as between classes based upon these, they must be very low as compared to the normal wage incomes of all workers except the unskilled. This is of particular significance in the United States, where wage differentials are unusually great. Finally, as already indicated, the general provision in our unemployment compensation laws is in harmony with American practice in awarding compensation for industrial injuries.

Allowances for dependents are provided for in the District of Columbia alone. Should benefits be varied with the number of dependents, as under the German law of 1927, or should specific allowances be made for spouse and dependent children, as in Great Britain, or should benefits be paid without regard to dependents? Certainly the case for allowances for dependents is stronger in European countries than it is in the United States because of the greater strain there on working-class incomes. But, even in the United States the advantage of allowances is obvious; they would protect the standards of living more effectively. Moreover, it may be noted that the system of allowances has made distinct progress in our workmen's compensation laws. Yet, other considerations are involved. The granting of allowances is out of harmony with insurance principles. Workers who contribute should expect equal treatment in respect to benefits. However, when the workers make no direct contribution, or only a small one, this consideration loses some of its force. in spite of the expected shifting of the tax burden.

Under the American laws, unemployment compensation will be less than 50 per cent of wages lost in nearly all cases, even while it is being paid. This is somewhat less liberal than the benefits paid under the more progressive of our workmen's compensation laws. Unemployment compensation, however, is not designed to provide a living independently, but to carry workers for comparatively short periods of time until they return to their jobs or succeed in finding new ones. In any event, indefinitely large revenues cannot be collected, year after year. The problem is so to fix the rate of weekly benefit, the length of waiting period and the maximum duration of benefit as to make the wisest use of the funds which can be appropriately[1] raised for, and devoted to, unemployment compensation.

Under most of the unemployment-insurance systems in effect abroad as well as under the laws relating to other forms of social insurance, benefits begin after the loss of six working days. So has it most frequently been under workmen's compensation in the United States. Reference to analytical Table 24 (pages 152–159) shows that in an exercise of their discretion, the states have provided a waiting period of three or four weeks in fifty-two or of two or three weeks in thirteen, with a limitation on the total number of waiting-period weeks in the year, usually five. The longer waiting periods are in accord with the thought of some of the best of the special commissions reporting on the subject.[2] Much is to be said for the tendency in the more recent legislation to provide for a waiting period of two weeks in the quarter but generally not to exceed three additional weeks in the year—a total of five.[3] As Professor Douglas has said, "A waiting period should be imposed in order to lessen administrative difficulties, permit investigation of the statements of claimants, and prevent the diffusion of funds upon cases where both the loss and the need are comparatively slight."[4] In other words, administrative problems, the ability of the unemployed workers to get on for a time without compensation, and the conservation of the insurance funds should receive due consideration in fixing the duration of the waiting period. A judgment as to whether some of the waiting periods are not too long must be rendered in view of the fact that payment of benefit will ordinarily be made about two weeks after the necessary waiting period has elapsed.

The maximum period of benefit must be fixed in view of the revenues to be collected, and the taxes imposed must be fixed in view of the waiting period, the rate of benefit, and the maximum period of duration desired. This must be done if the insurance principle is to be observed at all and revenue and other problems avoided, or, in any event, safeguarded against. While some of the states have levied heavier payroll taxes than are called for by the Social Security Act, most of them have not done so. Whether or not the revenues will be more or less than adequate to finance the benefits to be paid, only experience will tell. Moreover, it is to be

---

[1] The authors do not wish to imply that the taxes now being levied are as high as they might appropriately be.

[2] See, for example, the Ohio and Minnesota reports referred to on pp. 142–144.

[3] It is noteworthy that this provision for a waiting period of two weeks in the preceding thirteen is found in the laws of twenty-seven states. See analytical Table 24, pp. 152–159.

[4] Paul H. Douglas, *Standards of Unemployment Insurance* (1933), p. 64.

held in mind in this connection that the unemployment rate has differed greatly as between states as well as from year to year. The states, in view of estimates made and in an exercise of their discretion, have fixed the maximum of ordinary benefits in one year at from twelve to twenty times the weekly benefit amount, or have fixed the maximum duration at from twelve to twenty weeks.[1] Five of the states enacting laws have also provided for the payment of additional benefits under certain conditions. The duration of these additional benefit periods, when any, is generally for a period of 10 or 10.6 weeks, except in Massachusetts where extended and additional benefits are provided on the basis of long-time earnings. On the whole, the period of benefit right is shorter than is found under foreign legislation. It should be extended to a maximum of twenty-six weeks in the year. No doubt, this would call for an increase in the taxes generally levied, but the addition could well be placed upon the wages of the insured workers, as contended above.

If insurance principles are to be observed, there must be a relation between the benefit rights and the contributions by, or on the account of, each insured person. In the absence of this relation and of a limit upon the benefit period, a system of compensation would greatly favor those persons who, mainly because of the personal factor, are most frequently out of work, to the disadvantage of others in the insured group. With a few exceptions, the earlier laws adopted limited the number of weeks of ordinary benefit to one for every four weeks of employment during a two-year period. The ratio to be applied to claims for additional benefit, when such benefit may be paid, is very generally one benefit for each twenty uncharged weeks of employment during the preceding 260 weeks or, approximately, four years. As noted above, in connection with qualification for benefit, however, important changes are found in the laws more recently enacted. Many of these laws do not establish a direct relation between number of weeks of employment and number of benefit weeks, but relate the amount of benefits, at prescribed rates, to wages earned. In most of the states, benefits are limited to one-sixth of wages earned in the first three of the last four or the first four of the last five calendar quarters.

It remains to note that the insured person becomes disqualified, for a time at least, if he voluntarily leaves his job, is discharged for misconduct, goes on strike, or refuses to accept suitable employment.

The details relative to disqualification of an insured person for voluntarily leaving his job vary considerably from one law to another. The very general provision is, however, that an insured person, otherwise eligible, does not lose right to benefit completely, but that he shall be ineligible for benefit in the week he quits and for a number of weeks

[1] See analytical Table 24, pp. 152–159.

thereafter (this in addition to the waiting period).[1] In a number of
states the same measure of disqualification is provided for in cases of discharge for misconduct. In about half the states, however, the disqualification in such cases is longer than in cases involving leaving the
job voluntarily.[2]

Under all the state laws persons participating in strikes become
ineligible for benefit while the strike is in progress. In Indiana, however,
exception is made for a strike fomented by the employer, and to this
Utah adds strikes caused by the employer's failure to comply with laws
relating to wages, hours, or conditions of work. Another variation is
found in other states, for example, in Louisiana, Mississippi, and Idaho,
where the disqualification is limited by a clause equivalent to "unless he
[the claimant] and any member of his grade or class is not participating in,
financing, or directly interested in the dispute." And still another variation is found in New York, where instead of the disqualification being
for the period the strike is in progress, it takes the form of an extension
of the waiting period to ten weeks.[3]

A final ground for disqualification for benefit, found in the state as
well as in all other unemployment compensation legislation, is refusal to
accept suitable employment. The definition of "suitable," however, may
vary widely; important results hinge upon the definition adopted. The
discretion of the state has been limited, and properly, by the Social
Security Act. A claimant is not to be denied compensation because he
has (1) refused an offer of employment in a position vacant due directly
to strike, lockout, or other dispute, (2) or if the wages, hours, or other
conditions of the work offered are substantially less favorable than those
prevailing for similar work in the locality, or (3) if as a condition of
employment he would be required to join a company union or to resign
from, or refrain from joining, any bona fide labor organization.[4]

[1] In New York there is no waiting period; however, benefits cease completely if an offer
of suitable employment, including the job left, is refused.   The penalty in other states, in
addition to waiting period, is loss of benefit: Pennsylvania, one week; Connecticut, Oregon,
and Washington, two weeks; Alabama, California, District of Columbia, Indiana, Ohio,
New Hampshire, New Jersey, Rhode Island, Texas, and Vermont, three weeks; Massachusetts, Missouri, and Wisconsin, four weeks; Kentucky, two to nine weeks; Michigan,
three to nine weeks; in the other states (twenty-seven), except Florida, where it is one to
seven, it is from one to five weeks.   This analysis ignores minor details and variations.

[2] In New York the disqualification is for ten weeks; while in Rhode Island it is from one
to ten weeks.

[3] Other exceptions are found in Pennsylvania and Rhode Island, where in the case of a
strike, three weeks and eight weeks, respectively, are added to the waiting period.   Under
the Wisconsin Act, as interpreted, a worker in receipt of benefit when a strike develops,
continues, subject to the 1 to 4 ratio, to draw benefits while the strike is on.   This is true
in various other states also.

[4] Section 903(a) 5, quoted supra, p. 150.

These provisions are incorporated in the several state laws. The propriety of restriction (1) will not be questioned, for it is to avoid pressure being exercised to cause unemployed persons to become strikebreakers. Restriction (3) is a natural one, in view of the provisions of the National Labor Relations Act. Restriction (2) is less restrictive than provisions of the laws or the regulations generally found in foreign countries, for "suitable" is not limited to that particular occupation in which the claimant has been most recently or ordinarily engaged, or to an employment at a wage fully equal to that which has been earned or to that which prevails for similar work in the locality. The definition contained in the Alabama law is typical of the definitions found in other state laws. It defines suitable employment as "any employment for which the employee in question is reasonably fitted, which is located within a reasonable distance of his residence or last employment, and which is not detrimental to his health, safety, or morals." Of course, the word "reasonable" as well as the term "substantially less" in connection with wages will have to be defined in concrete cases and is capable of somewhat different definitions. But whatever the rulings may be, they may be expected to be less restrictive than the British rulings made in the earlier 1920's. The rulings should therefore be less restrictive of the mobility of labor than were those earlier rulings in Great Britain.

The claimant who refuses to accept suitable employment, however defined, is disqualified for benefit during the whole of his period of unemployment in California, Delaware, Missouri, New York, Ohio, Oklahoma, and Wisconsin. However, in more than four-fifths of the states, and not illogically, the limited disqualification is for about the number of weeks applied in cases of voluntary quitting. In slightly over half of the states, the disqualification is for the week in which refusal occurs plus one to five weeks following; in Massachusetts and Oregon for four weeks; in Alabama, the District of Columbia, Indiana, New Hampshire, New Jersey, Rhode Island, and Vermont, the loss is the week in which the refusal occurs, plus three weeks following; in Connecticut, the one week plus the two following; in Kentucky, the one week plus the two to nine following; in Pennsylvania, one week only.

It is obvious that a considerable variation in detail incorporated in the forty-nine laws under analysis has resulted from the freedom to experiment. It is clear, also, that the number of questionable rules involved is greater than would have occurred had an outright national system or a national-state system with carefully considered standards been adopted. But, as already stated, the hastily adopted legislation will be considerably revised and at many points departures from good standards will be corrected. Indeed, many revisions for the better have already been made.

Some of the deficiencies in the state laws have been pointed out. In addition to these, there are other deficiencies involved which could be avoided under a national system established by Federal act. Less efficient administration has been mentioned earlier in our discussion, as has the prospect that the revenues available from the not substantially different tax rates levied in the states will probably vary in adequacy because of the great differences in unemployment experienced by them. It is not unlikely that in the course of time a national pool or equalization fund will be required. Then, too, the system adopted has, for better or worse, tied compensation to a particular type of taxation. Again, perhaps the system will cause it to be more difficult to develop the system of relief which must complement unemployment compensation and be available when the right to benefit expires. Finally, a national system might readily avoid the problems presented by workers moving between states, a problem not adequately solved under state laws, though most of them contain provisions relating to the matter.

One of the problems foreseen under state laws, as over against a national system, relates to labor in interstate employment. This has given the Social Security Board much concern. To facilitate coverage of interstate workers and to further uniformity of treatment under the various state laws, a draft provision was drawn up covering interstate employment. The great majority of the states (thirty-nine) have legislated to incorporate this and have provided interstate coverage where (1) the service, though interstate, is localized in the state of the employee's residence; (2) employment is outside of the state of residence but incidental to service within it. Coverage under the latter provision only is found in the laws of four states (Kentucky, Louisiana, Mississippi, and Vermont). The remaining six laws (Alabama, District of Columbia, Connecticut, New Hampshire, New York, and Rhode Island) extend coverage if the greater part of the employment is in the state of residence.

It should be noted also that there is a growing recognition of the need for flexibility in meeting problems of this nature and for delegating increased discretionary power to the administrative agency. Under the laws of all the states save six,[1] the unemployment compensation administrator is given authority to make reciprocal arrangements with other states and the Federal Government to facilitate coverage of migratory and interstate workers as well as to deal with other problems. The willingness of many states to amend their laws in line with improved methods developed elsewhere and to provide a flexible and discretionary method of administration tends to remove the interstate difficulties involved in state systems of unemployment compensation.

---

[1] The six states which make no provision for reciprocal arrangements are Virginia, South Carolina, Oregon, Louisiana, Kentucky, and Idaho.

FURTHER CONSIDERATIONS ON UNEMPLOYMENT COMPENSATION

So much for a description of the main provisions of the present American legislation relating to unemployment compensation and for evaluations in terms of standards. It remains to discuss some important issues that arise in connection with unemployment insurance and to make some observations on how far reliance may be placed upon insurance in solving the problem of unemployment.

Many spokesmen for commercial insurance companies, with more or less dislike for anything in the nature of state, nonprofit insurance, and also some economists have contended that unemployment is an uninsurable risk. The insurance spokesman has asserted that there is no actuarial basis in experience, that the risk varies greatly from year to year, and that it varies greatly as between industry and industry as well as between the more and the less acceptable workers. The assertions are true, but are regarded as conclusive only by those who are limited in their thinking to the principles and procedures of the organized commercial insurance business, and to pooled funds without merit rating. In connection with the first assertion it may be observed that an actuarial basis may be provided, as it has been provided for various branches of insurance, by accumulative experience with such insurance. Of course, the second point is real; the volume of unemployment varies greatly from year to year and these variations present an important problem. The variations make it necessary to provide adequate reserves and to limit benefits carefully or to look to the government for additional funds in time of emergency. As has been learned in Britain and elsewhere, not all unemployment can be compensated for on an insurance basis; wisdom requires the provision of a second line of defense. In connection with the third point, attention has been called to the possibility of varying premiums as between industries and firms by means of merit rating. Most of our state systems look forward to such rating of premiums when there is an adequate experiential basis. Finally, it may be said that in providing social insurance, it is neither necessary nor desirable to observe fully the principles which have been applied by private insurance companies. If it is argued that workers are not a homogeneous group[1] and that unemployment insurance taxes the better workman heavily for the benefit of the less good workman,[2] this may be admitted but also

[1] See, for example, R. S. Meriam, "Unemployment Reserves: Some Questions of Principle," *Quarterly Journal of Economics*, vol. 47 (1933), pp. 326–327, also, "Some Theoretical Aspects of Unemployment Reserves," *American Economic Review, Supplement*, vol. 23 (1933), pp. 28–29.

[2] The British Royal Commission on Unemployment Insurance, in its final report, stated that 35.2 per cent of the persons continuously insured between 1923 and 1930 had received no benefits at all, and that another 38 per cent had received benefits for less than

defended within limits.   On the one hand, there are limitations upon the
duration of benefits; on the other hand, it must be held in mind that
unemployment insurance is a system of taxation for a special purpose, and
that, within limits, it is proper to tax according to ability to pay.   It
may be added, also, that most of the revenue to be collected under the
American laws will be derived from taxes on the employers, not, except
by shifting process, on the wages of employees.   This fact to a limited
extent meets the argument of inequitable treatment of the superior or
more fortunate workers.

It has been and is still asserted by some persons that the proper solution of the problem of unemployment is not found in insurance but in
prevention.   All will agree that full employment would be the ideal thing,
but no one with more than a very superficial knowledge of our economic
organization could regard it as possible of realization.   Maladjustments
are inevitable in a system of comparatively free enterprise.   Maladjustments as between industries, technological change, and business cycles,
not to mention the effects of changing tariff barriers and a host of other
things, are real and the unemployment which accompanies them cannot
be reduced to that volume where the maintenance of the unemployed is
no longer a problem.   Moreover, there is no serious inherent conflict
between prevention of unemployment and compensation of the workers.
Indeed, there are many persons who contend that unemployment insurance is more or less helpful in regularizing industry and in stabilizing
employment.

Though a compensation system might tend to cause employers to
lay off or discharge workmen because provision had been made for their
maintenance, rather than to permit them to share in the work available,
this tendency can be checked by merit rating under which there is reason
for each employer to put forth additional effort to regularize his business
and employment within it.   Nor is the motive to be found for so doing
entirely in a small saving in contributions to be paid into the compensation fund; the factor of prestige should be of moment.   The extent to
which regularization is within the hands of employers, singly or in association, has been discussed at an earlier point.

A contention put forward and emphasized by many proponents of
unemployment insurance is that it will assist in checking booms and
will add to purchasing power in depression.[1]   The argument runs somewhat as follows: The larger part of the contributions required to finance

---

10 per cent of the time.   In contrast to these there were, of course, others who received
benefits a good share of the time.

[1] Good discussions of this phase of the subject are found in Paul H. Douglas, *Controlling
Depressions* (1935), pp. 245–262; Sumner H. Slichter, *Towards Stability* (1934), pp. 149–154,
and Slichter's "The Economics of Public Works," *American Economic Review, Supplement,*
vol. 24 (1934), pp. 174–185.

unemployment compensation is collected in normal and boom times. Receipts then exceed expenditures, and as a result the expenditure on consumption and capital goods is reduced. This should serve as a check on expansion and booms. Then during the depression, expenditures under the compensation system exceed receipts, and the purchasing power of the unemployed is maintained at a higher rate than would otherwise be the case. And by steadying the consumer-goods industries, the capital-goods industries will be bolstered up somewhat. Consequently the volume of employment will be stabilized to some extent.

Though this line of argument has merit, it is easily possible to exaggerate it. In passing, it should be observed that the big swings in production and employment are in the capital-goods industries and industries producing durable consumption goods. The changes in the production and consumption of nondurable goods and services are not nearly so great. Yet, without question additional spending power in the pockets of the workers would assist somewhat in supporting the market for food, clothing, and the like, and even of more durable articles in times of bad trade. Looking at the other phase of the picture, however, one wonders whether a small difference in the purchases of consumer goods would have any particular effect upon expansion in the capital-goods market at other times.

On the contrary, it has frequently been contended, and for a number of reasons, that unemployment insurance has the effect, or tends to have the effect, of increasing the volume of unemployment. One contention has been that the collection of large funds in boom times and the availability of these for investment would act as a mild inflationary factor. Then, on the other hand, when it becomes necessary to pay large amounts in benefits in time of depression, and securities are sold, this has the discouraging effect of depressing values.[1] Certainly the problem presented by large reserves, unless they are sterilized in some way, is important in connection with unemployment compensation and still more so

---

[1] Professor Slichter has proposed a plan whereby the effect of unemployment reserves upon the money market may be controlled. He suggests that a part or all of the reserves be deposited with the Federal Reserve System, where the fund could be utilized to help stabilize credit and demand. Thus, during a depression, the excess of benefit payments over receipts from contributions would mean a flow of money from Reserve Banks to member banks, commercial-bank borrowings would be reduced, and the purchasing power of the unemployed increased without depressing the price of securities or disturbing savings. Similarly, in times of prosperity, an excess of receipts over expenditures would transfer funds from member banks to Reserve Banks, thereby tightening the money market and serving in part to check undue credit expansion. [See Sumner H. Slichter, "Making Booms Bear the Burden of Relief," *Harvard Business Review*, vol. 11 (1932), pp. 327–335, and *Towards Stability*, 1934, pp. 149–154.]

It should be noted, however, that under this plan, the government would obtain no interest on the unemployment reserve fund.

under the system of old-age benefits established under the Social Security Act.   Discussion of the problem may be postponed to a later point.[1]

Another argument sometimes advanced by critics of unemployment insurance is that were funds not used for paying benefits, they would be employed productively and would provide work.   This is mentioned in passing because it has occasionally been advanced by persons of economic training as well as by many persons without such qualification rather than because of any merit that might be imputed to it.   The contention will not be taken seriously by those who have observed that there is usually an abundance of idle funds when industry is depressed.   The problem, then, is not a lack of capital but a lack of acceptable collateral and of active business enterprise.

Will not unemployment compensation injure business?   This is the great fear when compensation legislation is under consideration or a system is being introduced.   The chief cause of the fear is that the employer will be under the necessity of contributing through a payroll tax.   Of course, there is substantial ground for such a fear when the tax is levied by, say, *one* state, and the industries of that state must compete in an interstate market on unequal terms.   Indeed, the fear is so great that it is almost idle to talk of state experimentation with social insurance,[2] whether it be unemployment compensation or something else, if a payroll tax on the employer is involved.   One of the merits of the Social Security Act is that it places a tax on employers in insured trades generally, which for the first time leaves the states free to experiment.   The particular question, therefore, becomes this: with employers in most trades taxed, will unemployment compensation injure business?   Another is, will it injure business because of the weight of the payroll tax?   A third question is, may business be injured in some other manner?

Beginning in January, 1937, employers in insured trades were required to pay taxes on their payrolls for the purpose of financing unemployment compensation and old-age benefits.   Combined, the two taxes for the first year were 2 per cent.   Of course, a tax on payrolls is not in constant relationship to total costs or the usual margins of profit.   The wages bill may be less than 5 per cent of the total cost in one industry and as high as 60 per cent in another.   A study made by H. P. Mulford for the Social Security Board[3] shows the following ratios of payrolls to "value of output of sales" for 1933:[4] wholesale trade, 5.3; retail trade, 11.6; electric light and power, 14.8; manufacturing, 21.1; service trades, 25.4; metal

[1] See Chap. VIII, pp. 401–402.

[2] This is written in view of the position taken by a political party in 1936, that the entire matter of unemployment should be left to the states, without Federal legislation on the subject.

[3] Summarized in part in *Selected Current Statistics*, Social Security Board, November, 1936, pp. 47–54.

[4] Of course, these ratios change with the phases of the business cycle and other factors.

mining, 28.7; construction, 38.9; street railways, 40.6; steam railroads, 47.4; telegraph, 52.9; bituminous coal, 55.4; anthracite coal, 59.5. Equally great variations are found in different branches of manufacture, the minimum being 5.0 (distilled liquor), the maximum 52.2 (aircraft and parts). Hence the 2 per cent payroll tax payable for 1937, would vary between 1.2 per cent of the value of anthracite coal and 0.1 per cent of the business in wholesale trade.

In view of such computations, it might be thought that many employers would elect to bear the tax, not seek to shift it through higher prices of product or service or through lower wages than they would otherwise pay. There is no doubt that some of them have so elected. Other employers, however, with payroll more important in total cost and with narrow margin for profit could scarcely do so. Moreover, it must be held in mind that the costs of things other than labor used in a business may be enhanced because of the tax levied on wages of workers employed in the production of materials and equipment. And, far more important, the taxes increase periodically until they become 6 per cent, not including the tax deducted from the pay envelopes of the insured persons. It is a payroll tax of this size whose shifting and incidence we have for consideration. Will it rest upon employers, be shifted to workers through adjusted wage rates, or be shifted through higher prices to consumers generally, these including insured and uninsured wage earners and others?

An accurate answer to this question of shifting and incidence cannot be made except in the light of conditions which have important bearing. And the same answer cannot be expected to be correct in all cases. Only the most careful research will yield valid conclusions with reference to the matter if one desires to go beyond generalities. It may be said, however, that when, as in 1937, business is improving, prices rising, and wage rates advancing as the tax levies become effective, in comparatively few instances would one expect employers to cut wages in order to shift the tax paid by them. Unions would protest, and successfully, any such attempt, and even nonunion workers would react strongly against it. But, with upward adjustments of wages being made, one would expect the added labor cost due to the taxes to be given full consideration by employers generally. Even arbitration boards would be expected to take social-insurance protection and costs into consideration when making wage awards. Whether set by employer, by collective bargaining, or by arbitration board, wage rates would generally not be advanced as much as they otherwise would be. It is to be added in this connection that it is unlikely that the workers would take the boon of old-age benefits and unemployment compensation lightly, and migrate to uninsured trades unless wage rates there were distinctly attractive. Hence the absence of the tax in many employments would not protect labor in insured trades against adjustments of wages to shift the taxes.

The discussion has thus far related to the readjustment of wages in time of rising prices and increasing wage rates. It would appear to be difficult to shift the tax in full measure in time of depression, for there are distinct limits upon wage reductions even when business losses are being sustained. Employers generally do not cut wages to that point where profit will be restored, but they curtail production and lay off men because wage rates remain high as compared to the value of the workers' product. This is even truer when unemployment compensation is in operation, for it undoubtedly tends to increase the rigidity of wage rates. This particular point will be discussed further presently.

Unless the employers are able to shift the tax to the workers when adjusting wage rates, they may ask and receive higher prices for their product and services, for their profit margins will usually not allow them to shoulder the tax without greater sacrifice than they are willing to bear. There are, however, important checks on a forward shifting of a payroll tax in the direction of, if not to, ultimate consumers. One of these is found in established and advertised prices which are decidedly sticky. Another check on increases in prices (or their maintenance when otherwise they would fall) is found in consumer resistance. This resistance, of course, varies with elasticity of demand for the product or service. In some cases this is great and an increase in price will have the effect of reducing the volume that will find a market, and will also reduce profits and employment. In other cases, the demand is relatively inelastic. In such cases any tax, like any other element in cost, is likely to be more or less accurately reflected in price changes.

Of course, some industries are more monopolistic than competitive. In these cases, it is not inevitable that the payroll tax burden will be shifted. To determine the likelihood of shifting or of absorption by the monopolist, however, it is necessary to distinguish between those situations in which the monopolist has been charging the price which produces largest net profit (a "true monopoly price") and those in which he has not yet succeeded in discovering and establishing such a price. Of course, the monopolist has as much desire as a competitive seller to pass a payroll tax charge on to someone else; and if upon reexamining conditions, as he is likely to do when confronted by the extra payroll outlay, he finds that he has not been charging all he advantageously could, he will raise prices. In this case, the payroll tax will thus lead to the imposition of the price that is theoretically most profitable, and consumers will bear the burden of the tax. On the other hand, there undoubtedly are cases in which the price actually obtained by the monopolist exceeds true monopoly price. This is, of course, merely to say that the price charged is higher than the one yielding maximum net profit in view of the cost situation and the elasticity of demand for the product. In the majority of such cases it is likely that it will be economic for the monopolist to assume part or all of the tax. If the price charged has been a "true monopoly price," the monopolist, finding his labor costs of production increased, will of course have occasion to reexamine costs per unit as they vary with the number of units produced, as well as the number of units consumers will buy at different prices. If he is operating under decreasing unit costs (*i.e.*, cost per unit decreases as output increases) and if demand for the product is extremely elastic (*i.e.*, if the total revenue area is less at a high price than at an intermediate or a low one), the monopolist will obviously be confronted by two circumstances deterring him from raising price: the curtailment of gross income that would result and the higher cost of producing each unit. Where demand for the product is inelastic and unit costs decline as output is curtailed, the monopolist is of course more likely to limit output and increase price. It may be noted, as still another possible situation, that the enterpriser may possess the attributes of monopoly but may be unable to exercise them because regulative bodies prohibit him from doing so. In this case, the question of whether a payroll tax will be shifted depends on the attitude of the regulatory authorities with respect to treatment of this tax (and perhaps ultimately on the courts). But as a general matter it can be said that, except where prices are regulated by public authority, the monopolist is only less likely than other business men to shift the payroll tax when it is large enough to affect cost in any considerable measure.

While different factors enter in to affect the shifting and incidence of a wage tax, it is generally true that in the course of time most of it will be shifted to the workers through lower wage rates than they would otherwise receive or to consumers through higher prices than would otherwise prevail. The shifting through wage adjustments appears to be more likely than the shifting through price changes. This is so because a payroll tax represents a direct addition to labor costs and the employer, finding his marginal labor costs out of line with the marginal productivity of the workers, will attempt to reduce wages or will reduce employment. Furthermore, if the shifting is made through price changes, the burden is carried by the workers in so far as they are the consumers of the product or service. The general conclusion is therefore that the larger part of a substantial wage tax will usually be borne by the workers.[1] Their gains

---

[1] A brief list of economists who hold, subject to qualifications, that employers' contributions to social insurance taking the form of a wage tax will rest in large part on the wage earners, includes: A. C. Pigou (*Industrial Fluctuations*, 1929, pp. 372–373); Alvin H Hansen *et al.* (*A Program for Unemployment Insurance and Relief*, 1934, p. 49); Alvin H. Hansen (*Economic Stabilization in an Unbalanced World*, 1932, Chap. 12); R. S. Meriam [articles in *American Economic Review*, Supplement, vol. 23 (1933), pp. 23–24, and in *Quarterly Journal of Economics*, vol. 47, (1932), p. 317]; Harry Gunnison Brown [in *Journal of Political Economy*, vol. 30 (1922), pp. 68–69]; and Dale Yoder [in *Quarterly Journal of Economics*, vol. 45 (1931), pp. 635–636].

from an insurance system are not a net addition to their wages or what these will purchase. This is, of course, not a conclusive argument against old-age benefits or unemployment compensation, the objective of which is to spread earnings and purchasing power of the individual workers more advantageously through a period of months or years.

It must be noted, however, that like many other taxes, a wage tax may be offset, in part or in whole; other things may not remain equal. Old-age benefits may be expected to improve the morale of the workers generally and to remove a financial burden from the shoulders of those among them who, in the absence of old-age benefits, must accept responsibility for the care of old persons. Such responsibility may impair efficiency because of poor housing, inadequate food, curtailment of schooling, and the like; in any event, the financial charge frequently involves financial harassment. Unemployment compensation should in a measure relieve insured workers of a sense of fear and uncertainty and assist in maintaining efficiency and morale. These are not small considerations. In so far as efficiency and morale are maintained and improved, the tax is offset and the tax burden to be borne is reduced because of lower labor costs per unit of output. It is easily conceivable that under certain conditions a wage tax levied for social insurance would quite pay for itself in increased product or service.

We now return to the question of a wage tax and injury to business. This question is answered largely by what has already been said. In so far as the wage tax imposed upon employers is shifted quickly and fully, injury is avoided except any that may result from adversely changed industrial relations or shrinkage in demand for product or service. In so far as it is not shifted at all, if we may assume such cases, it comes out of profit and may injure the business involved. Any injury to business is, of course, limited pretty much to the process of readjustment. And, here, it is to be held in mind that industries differ in the weight of the tax imposed because of differences in wages as an element in cost and of differences in the market phase of the matter. On beyond the period of adjustment there is, of course, the question of savings, capital formation, and industrial advance. A change in the distribution of income in favor of labor may adversely affect the amount of saving and investment. But over against this is the question of human well-being and efficiency which are not without important bearing upon economic progress.

Of economic considerations, we have left for discussion the subject of unemployment compensation and the amount of unemployment. This aspect of the matter has already been discussed in part. The contention that a system of unemployment insurance tends to stabilize industry and employment and the exact contrary have been noted. Injury to business while readjustments are in process of course reflects itself in the volume of employment. The chief matter for consideration is, however, the effect of unemployment compensation on the rigidity of wage rates and of rigidity of wage rates on the amount of unemployment.

As stated in our discussion of theories of wages,[1] in so far as employers know accurately the details involved and are motivated largely by economic considerations, they will not normally employ workers at a wage in excess of the value of their contribution to the value-product. There is, therefore, a tendency for wages to be determined by the worker's economic worth. Looked at from one angle, it can be said that the cause of many employable persons remaining unemployed is that wages are too high. At some lower scale of pay the unemployed would be absorbed and set at work. It has been noted,[2] also, that one effect of unemployment insurance in Great Britain has been to protect wage rates against the drastic reductions which had prevailed at an earlier time. In other words, the effect of unemployment benefits was to cause wages to be relatively inelastic in depression situations, when, otherwise, dire necessity of finding employment at some wage or going on discredited poor relief would have caused wages to fall. However, the extent to which it is true that unemployment compensation makes for rigidity of wage rates depends in considerable measure upon the rules applied in granting to or withholding benefits from those who decline jobs available. In the earlier 1920's the British definition of "suitable employment" ran very much in terms of the occupation last engaged in and prevailing or trade-union rates of pay. In so far as this definition of "suitable" is departed from and compensation is denied those who decline employment in related trades, or in trades they have once followed, or in occupations for which their training is reasonably adequate, and at wages not substantially or not unreasonably less than the rates prevailing, this tendency to cause wage rates to become rigid is lessened.[3] In concluding this phase of the subject it must be observed that one must weigh over against the increased volume of unemployment which may accompany unemployment compensation the problem presented by low levels of wages established during a state of bad trade. All too frequently these are not easily or quickly corrected when a normal state of trade returns.

A charge made, usually by the uninformed, is that unemployment benefits foster idleness. This has been discussed elsewhere and may be dismissed as relatively unimportant.[4] In another way, however, a

---

[1] Vol. I, Chap. IV.

[2] *Supra*, p. 132.

[3] It has been made clear that the American legislation makes such denial possible. *Supra*, p. 173.

[4] E. Wight Bakke has concluded: "The behavior of the unemployed in searching for new employment gives no evidence that the possibility of saving unemployment benefits has retarded the efforts of the unemployed to get back to work." (Quoted, with permission, from E. Wight Bakke, *The Unemployed Man*, E. P. Dutton & Company, 1933, p. 143.)

system of unemployment compensation may add to the volume of unemployment. We have reference to decreased mobility between industries.

An effect of insurance is to cause workers to become disinclined to leave employment in insured trades where they have "rights," to take employment in uninsured trades. This, as we have noted, has been experienced in Great Britain. With industrial progress and changes in consumer habits and demands, industries do not record the same history. Some expand rapidly, some moderately, some not at all, while others wane. A measure of mobility is therefore essential if needed shifts of production factors are to be made readily. Any delay in needed shifts means less employment. But in this connection, it is to be held in mind that unemployment compensation and old-age benefits are being applied for the most part to those general divisions of employment which have been and are absorbing an increasing proportion of the workers of this country. The interference with mobility would be greater if the contrary trend were operating in our economic growth. Moreover, as in the case of rigid wage rates, the problem of immobility is lessened somewhat by a more careful definition of "suitable employment."

UNEMPLOYMENT COMPENSATION AND RELIEF

It is evident from our discussion that unemployment compensation is not without its problems and that it is no panacea. Partly because of these problems, partly for other reasons, there are those who would rely entirely upon public relief for the maintenance of the unemployed.[1] Among them are to be found some social workers as well as the many whose fear of new institutional arrangements and whose lack of appreciation of the importance of human welfare cause them to oppose social insurance. Dismissing the many to whom reference is made, the question raised by the others is, why not attack the problem only through an acceptable system of relief?

The case may be stated somewhat as follows:

1. We now (January, 1938) have almost 12,000,000 unemployed persons and, assuming recovery to the level of 1929, for years there will be several millions of them.

2. Even under the most inclusive system of unemployment compensation, there will be many wage earners as well as self-employed persons outside of its embrace. Hence any system will not be coextensive with need due to causes over which those in need have no control.

3. Next, those who experience long periods of unemployment will exhaust their right to benefits and will have to be given relief.

4. Again, while unemployment compensation will be paid to many who could get on without it, others in need will receive benefits paid as a

[1] That is, in so far as private relief does not suffice.

matter of right which will frequently prove to be inadequate as tested by an acceptable budget. Hence, the larger funds collected and paid out under a system of compensation do not fit into human needs accurately and adequately.

5. The mass of wage earners are not able to bear the wage taxes assessed against them or shifted to them.

6. The needed funds should be collected from those whose large incomes or holdings of property give them ability to pay. Moreover, such an allocation of the burden would improve the distribution of income and wealth.

7. The administration of unemployment compensation is accompanied by serious problems and involves expense.

8. Finally, many of those who get benefits as a matter of right will not make wise use of the money received. The guidance of the trained and experienced social worker is needed.

As has been indicated in our discussion, much of this is true. If we may repeat what we have already said, from one point of view a system of unemployment compensation is a specialized system of taxation for a special purpose. It is designed to provide funds collected largely in times of good trade in order to have them available for use when unemployment becomes a serious problem. If reliance is placed upon public relief, this means that the government must borrow or increase tax rates in effect or introduce new taxes. In acute depression relief funds are secured in all three of these ways. Increasing taxes in a time of bad trade is undesirable in so far as it can be avoided. Bad taxes are as likely as good taxes to be introduced. If heavy taxes on large incomes and holdings of property are not already employed in the tax system, they should be so employed. There is no reason why they should be employed only in time of acute unemployment or why their proceeds should be used for relief rather than for other purposes. In any event, reliance upon public relief means that ready provision has not been made in advance of need. Perhaps constitutional limitations are to be reckoned with; legislative opposition and delay stand in the way of getting any large part of the revenue needed at the time it is needed. Time is required. Almost certainly important functions of government are seriously interfered with. Such has been the experience at home and abroad. This experience need not be related in its detail; suffice it to recall to the attention of the reader a matter of common knowledge.

In view of what has been said elsewhere in our discussion, the objection that the masses of the insured workers cannot bear the burden of the taxes imposed may be dismissed with two observations. Increasingly, the wage earners in many countries have shown a willingness to make necessary contributions. Ability to pay is more general among American wage earners than among those in nearly all other countries.

Relief must be administered with a means test, more or less inquisi-
torial in nature.   However well and considerately the test may be applied,
most persons do not like it and all too frequently will escape it by hiding
need.   And, however well relief may be administered, most people
desire funds to which they feel they have a right; they do not want
"charity."   At present, a stigma attaches to relief.

With reference to the unwise use of money, it may be said that there
is much less waste in the spending of benefit funds than in the use of
earnings in the more normal situation.   In addition, it may be said that
most families wish to be free from the advice of "outsiders" in regard to
those things entering into ordinary living.

When all is said, it is a fact that increasingly those who have discussed the matters involved and have profited from experience, have
come to the conclusion that both a well-devised system of unemployment
compensation and an enlightened and efficient system of public relief are
essential in caring for the unemployed.   It is not a question of the one
or the other.   Rather, it is a question of how far the one can be advantageously employed and how far reliance must be placed upon the other.
Unemployment compensation, because of administrative problems
involved, cannot have universal coverage; and it should not be permitted
to become a mere system of relief, defying the principles of insurance.
Where compensation cannot be appropriately provided, or when it is
inadequate or when it leaves off, there should be adequate provision
under a system of relief.   The two systems must be complementary.

It follows that the proponent of unemployment compensation (or of
old-age or sickness benefits) should also be interested in an enlightened,
planned, well-ordered, efficiently administered system of relief.   Political
disabilities sometimes resulting from the receipt of relief by the unemployed should be removed, government financial systems should be so
planned that funds, whether derived from loans or taxes, should be forthcoming in timely and adequate fashion, the work of the different branches
of government should be coordinated and responsibilities assigned, and
the administration of relief should be placed in the hands of those who by
training, interest, and experience can efficiently and humanely take care of
families who are in need because income has failed and other appropriate
provision has not been made.[1]

---

[1] It is not within the scope of this book to discuss the question of relief in detail.   An
excellent statement of the problem is found in a pamphlet prepared by Maxwell S. Stewart
in cooperation with the staff of the Committee on Social Security of the Social Science
Research Council.   The pamphlet bears the title *This Question of Relief* and is Public
Affairs Pamphlet 8 of the Public Affairs Committee (1936).   Selected references on the
subject may be found on p. 32 of this pamphlet.   *Cf.* footnote 1, Chap. II, p. 107.

CHAPTER IV

THE PROBLEM OF WORK INJURIES: INDUSTRIAL ACCIDENTS AND OCCUPATIONAL DISEASE

THE PROBLEM

A much smaller problem than that presented by unemployment is involved in industrial accidents and occupational disease. Nevertheless, it is an important problem, especially in the United States where the comparable data show that the accident rate has generally been higher than in England, Germany, and other European countries. The fact that work accidents have been of more frequent occurrence here than in most other countries is explained in part by the employment in large numbers of various races and of many who have not understood English, in part by less general care exercised to prevent accident, and in part by the greater speed in production processes. This last factor suggests another matter of importance, *viz.*, that the problem of industrial accident is to a large extent a result of the revolution in industry; it has loomed largest in transportation, the heavy industries, and in mining. To say that the problem is one of the "machine age" is merely an exaggeration.[1] There is certainly a tendency for the number of accidents to increase with the mechanization of industry, a tendency partially and sometimes completely overcome by the exercise of more care in accident prevention.

It is extremely hazardous to state the size of the problem of industrial accidents in terms of American data, for, though reporting has greatly improved in recent years, it is still incomplete and inadequately standardized. In some cases only fatal accidents are reported; in others, no distinction is made between those resulting in permanent and those resulting in temporary disability; and in reporting those resulting in temporary disability only, some are presumed to include all cases of disability of one day, others beyond five days, a week, or more. Consequently, only rough estimates can be made. It is probable, however, that the number of workers killed in the course of duty in this country each year, times of acute depression excepted, exceeds 20,000; that the number completely disabled for life approaches 2,000; that the number partially permanently disabled by the loss of an eye, an arm, a leg, or

[1] For comparative accident rates, see National Safety Council, *Accident Facts* (1936 ed.); John R. Commons and John B. Andrews, *Principles of Labor Legislation* (1936 ed.), p. 165; Barbara N. Armstrong, *Insuring the Essentials* (1932), pp. 171–223; and U. S. Bureau of Labor Statistics, *Bulletin 490*.

otherwise, is around 100,000; that the number temporarily disabled for a day or more is 2,500,000, for three days or more, 2,000,000, for a week or more, 1,500,000, for four weeks or more, in excess of 400,000.[1] The yearly loss of working time due to temporary disability has been estimated at almost 38,000,000 days, to permanent partial disability at approximately 79,000,000, to permanent total disability at almost 10,000,000, to fatal accidents at 120,000,000.[2] The annual wage loss due to industrial accidents in the United States is estimated at a billion or more dollars, the cost of medical care at a quarter of a billion. These concern labor directly. There are also losses in production due to interruptions when serious accidents occur and to the necessary shifts and substitutions in personnel. Perhaps the total cost mounts up to two billions a year.[3]

Though a large total figure, the economic loss of wage earners caused by industrial accidents is a comparatively small percentage (perhaps between 2 and 3) of the total wage income. The problem, however, lies mainly in the fact that the more serious accidents develop emergency situations for the victims and their dependents. As Downey has said, "The ugly fact is that American wage earners, with few exceptions, [and the exceptions among wage earners in most countries are much fewer] are always near the poverty line. To a man so situated, even if no one but himself is dependent upon his earnings, the loss of a few weeks' wages means privation, and permanent incapacity means beggary. But the wage worker without dependents is quite exceptional. Three-fifths of the victims of work accidents are heads of families and one-third of the remainder contribute to the support of others. Of 2,608 wage earners killed on the job in Pennsylvania, 1,588 left 4,723 dependents, of whom 3,198 were children under the age of sixteen; 303 were contributing to the support of parents or of younger brothers and sisters, and only 718, or 28 per cent of the total, were without known economic responsibilities.

[1] For various estimates, see Federated Engineering Societies, *Waste in Industry* (1921), pp. 22–23; C. H. Verrill, *American Economic Review*, vol. 12 (1922), p. 140; E. H. Downey, *Workmen's Compensation* (1924), Chap. 1; C. Hookstadt, *Monthly Labor Review*, vol. 17 (1923), pp. 991-999; J. R. Commons and J. B. Andrews, *op. cit.*, p. 361; R. M. Woodbury, *Workers' Health and Safety: A Statistical Program* (1927), p. 7. The latest presentation of American accident statistics will be found in U. S. Bureau of Labor Statistics, *Bulletin 541* (1931) and *582* (1933).

[2] See C. H. Verrill and R. M. Woodbury, cited above.

Dr. C. O. Sappington, director of the industrial health division of the National Safety Council, estimates that 7 per cent of all industrial absenteeism is caused by industrial accidents, 3 per cent by occupational diseases, and the remaining 90 per cent by sickness of nonindustrial origin, although decidedly industrial in effect. Cited by E. H. Briggs in *Safety Engineering*, March, 1935, p. 133.

[3] I. S. Falk, says, "the full cost of industrial accidents to employers and employees is not far from $5,000,000,000 annually." (Quoted, with permission, from I. S. Falk, *Security Against Sickness*, Doubleday, Doran & Company, 1936, p. 299.) The estimated total varies widely with the estimated loss due to premature death.

In the great majority of instances, therefore, a serious work accident deprives a necessitous family of its sole or chief support. The immediate result, in the absence of systematic accident relief, is poverty and the long train of evils that flow from poverty. When a skilled craftsman is killed or injured in the course of duty, the children are taken out of school, the family removes to less comfortable quarters in a more undesirable neighborhood, the mother takes in boarders or goes out to work, the boys sink to the rank of the unskilled and the girls marry beneath the economic class in which they were born. When a similar calamity befalls a common laborer, the widow and the older children eke out such scanty earnings as they can at casual labor or in the sweated trades; if the family are numerous or the children young, the hopeless struggle too often ends in pauperism."[1]

Such concrete data as may be found in Gilbert L. Campbell, *Industrial Accidents and Their Compensation*, and in Crystal Eastman's *Work-Accidents and the Law*, though old, give one a more realistic picture. Miss Eastman reports[2] that in Allegheny County (Pittsburgh) there were 526 fatal work accidents in 1906–1907. Of the victims, 258 were married; 206 of the married men left one or more children under sixteen years of age; all but eighty of the 467, whose economic responsibilities were learned, had others more or less dependent upon them, while 63 per cent were the sole or chief support of others so that death meant a sudden cutting off of most or all of the accustomed income.

This was in the days prior to the modern compensation laws. Of 235 Pittsburgh families studied in detail, fifty-nine received no compensation; sixty-five received less than $100; forty, from $100 to $500; forty, from $500 to $2,000; thirty-one, more than $2,000. Provision through insurance and other savings was comparatively meager. Of 214 cases of married men studied, only 7 per cent had more than $2,000; 10 per cent, $1,000 to $2,000; 12 per cent, $500 to $1,000; 18 per cent, $100 to $500; 10 per cent, not to exceed $100; the remaining 43 per cent, no insurance at all. Under the circumstances it is not surprising to find from investigation of 132 cases continued over a number of months that besides those who had recourse to charity to meet the situation presented, thirty-five widows got assistance from their families, thirteen went to live with their parents, fifty-five secured employment, as did twenty-two children, fifteen of whom were under sixteen years of age. Moving to cheaper quarters, taking in boarders and lodgers, and other details may be fitted into the picture by the reader.

Occupational diseases, such as lead poisoning, arsenical poisoning, anthrax, caisson disease, and the like, present similar costs and problems.

---

[1] Quoted, with permission, from E. H. Downey, *Workmen's Compensation* (The Macmillan Company, 1924), pp. 13–14.

[2] *Work-Accidents and the Law* (Russell Sage Foundation, 1916), pp. 119ff.

Work with harmful substances, work under insanitary conditions, bad lighting, bad ventilation, excessive heat or cold in the place of work, fatigue due to long hours, all record their effects upon wage earners and undermine health and efficiency.   Without question the industrial basis of incapacitating sickness is an important one.   Nevertheless, the number of compensable cases of occupational disease is very small as compared to the number of industrial accidents, owing partly to the difficulty involved in establishing a direct and immediate relation in the individual case between the specific disease and the nature of the work or the conditions under which it is done.   But the problem involved in the two forms of injury is essentially the same, and when occupational disease is established, it calls for the same treatment as industrial accident.

EMPLOYERS' LIABILITY

The concrete details presented above have been drawn from pre-compensation days when employers' liability was still the law in Pennsylvania as it was, in some form or other, in England and elsewhere as well as in the United States until replaced by workmen's compensation or a system of accident insurance.   To appreciate the full significance of modern workmen's compensation and accident insurance, one needs a background in the law of employers' liability—its assumptions, its provisions, and its actual operation.   Though the law differed from one country to another, it may be stated in terms of its application in the United States.   The statement must be in very general terms and must be taken with the understanding that the law as developed by courts and legislative bodies was not the same in any two of our states.   Some of the variations were, indeed, really important.

The underlying assumption of the law was simple.   Accidents in industry were the result of someone's fault.   The duty and responsibility of the court, therefore, were to ascertain who had been at fault.   If the employer had been remiss in meeting his responsibilities, and if the worker had not by some act or omission contributed to the occurrence of the accident, a wrong had been committed for which the latter should be compensated; if the worker were at fault, he had no legitimate claim upon the employer or upon society for financial recompense and necessary medical and surgical attention.   The loss should fall upon him who was at fault.   In other words, the employer was under no special liability because he was an employer.

Under the common law[1] the employer was charged with making reasonable provision for the safety of his employee as to place of work, tools, and fellow employees, and was liable for damages when he failed

[1] For a good statement of the law of employers' liability, see Lindley Clark, *The Law of the Employment of Labor* (1911), Chap. VII, and Walter F. Dodd, *Administration of Workmen's Compensation* (1936), pp. 3–16.

to meet this responsibility. The injured party, in the absence of a suitable settlement, might sue. But as the law developed in the equity courts, the employer had certain defenses. He might present the defense of contributory negligence when the victim was also at fault in any degree. He might offer the defense that the fault was not his or that of a recognized agent, but of a fellow worker—the doctrine of common employment or fellow service. A third possible defense was that the accident was really no one's fault, but due to an ordinary risk of the trade—the doctrine of assumption of ordinary trade risk. Finally, it is to be noted that in some jurisdictions this last doctrine was extended to cases where the employer was at fault because he made less than reasonable provision, but this fact was known to the employee who continued to work. In other words, a fourth defense might be found in the assumption of extraordinary risk. In a Massachusetts case, the court ruled, if a servant "assumes the dangers of the employment to which he voluntarily and intelligently consents, and, while ordinarily he is to be subjected only to the hazards necessarily incident to his employment, if he knows that proper precautions have been neglected and still knowingly consents to incur the risk to which he will be thereby exposed, his assent dispenses with the duty of the master to take such precautions."[1]

This common law, thus stated in general terms, was, with the passing of time, more or less modified by statute. In fact, by 1908 Congress and the legislatures of a majority of states had enacted laws bearing upon the matter, but for the most part the legislation did not result in extensive modifications. The most important modification perhaps was the elimination in some of the states of the fellow-service doctrine in the operation of trains, where it was far-fetched to treat a locomotive engineer and a negligent switchman as fellow servants. Less frequently this modification found place in other trades. Again, in some states, where the victim was somewhat but not chiefly at fault, the law was modified to reduce but not to eliminate the liability of the employer at fault. A good example of both of these types of modification is found in the Federal law of 1908 fixing the liability of interstate carriers.

During the first decade of this century the law of employers' liability was assailed more and more vigorously as a method of compensation in this country as it had been years before by Joseph Chamberlain and others in England. The counts in the indictment were numerous.[2] The more important ones to be mentioned were: (1) It was unjust; (2) it was uncertain and inadequate as a method of compensating for injuries; (3) it was uneconomical; (4) it was morally degrading; (5) it did not place a premium upon, or arouse interest in, accident prevention. Inasmuch as employers' liability still maintains its place in Arkansas and Mississippi, the inter-

---

[1] *Leavy v. Boston & A. R. Co.*, 139 Mass. 580 (1885).

[2] For a summary but realistic discussion of this, see W. F. Dodd, *op. cit.*, pp. 16–26.

state operation of trains, and in maritime work other than that of long-shoremen, and, moreover, still finds some place in every American jurisdiction with a compensation law, these criticisms may be briefly developed.

It was quite properly alleged that the doctrine of fellow service was unjust when, as a rule, the worker had no choice of his associates at work and it was too much to ask him to surrender his job to avoid risk. It was alleged with equal weight that it was unfair to leave the victim or his dependents without recourse in the majority of cases because, in the opinion of the courts, the accidents simply happened; no one was particularly at fault. It was asserted to be unjust to withhold compensation in cases of some contributory negligence, especially in view of the fact that negligence may be only apparent, and an act or failure to act may be due to fatigue from long hours of arduous labor.[1] Again, it was unfair to require the plaintiff to assume the burden of proof, especially in fatal cases where fellow employees were disinclined to jeopardize their jobs by appearing as witnesses. Finally, the system was regarded as unjust in that it imperiled the job of the victim when seeking compensation for loss due to temporary disability or permanent partial disability. Naturally the victim of an ordinary accident usually brought no suit; very generally he accepted the offer of settlement made by the employer or his insurance carrier or went without compensation.

That employers' liability was inadequate as a system of compensation has become clear from the preceding paragraph. In Wisconsin a special commission reported on 556 cases. In 33 there was a settlement, fair or unfair to the worker or dependents; in 53 suit was brought; in 470 no claim was pressed. Of the cases where suit was brought, nine were lost, dismissed, or dropped, twelve were dropped because of settlement effected pending suit, twelve suits were successful and not appealed, three cases were on appeal, and seventeen were pending in the lower courts. This is more or less typical of the operation of employers' liability laws.

Neither settlements nor awards under employers' liability observed any well-defined standards. Some awards were excessive as measured by the requirements of an acceptable compensation law, but usually the contrary was true. Thus, in one state (Minnesota) there was no compensation in twenty-seven of fifty-four fatal accident cases investigated. In thirteen of the twenty-seven where there was compensation, the amount was $1,000 or less; in eight, more than $1,000 but not to exceed $2,000; in two, $2,500 each; in four others, $4,000, $4,256.94, $5,000, and $6,352, respectively. When averaged over the fifty-four cases, the com-

---

[1] For discussion of the relation between fatigue and the accident rate, see a series of articles by Dr. Emory Bogardus, in *American Journal of Sociology*, vol. 17 (1911–1912); also H. M. Vernon, *Industrial Fatigue and Efficiency* (1921), and P. Sargant Florence, *Economics of Fatigue and Unrest* (1924).

pensation was $536 per case; under the first, rather substandard, compensation law in that state, the compensation would have averaged $1,981 per case, or more than three times as much as was received, without making any allowance for attorney's fees, which so frequently took a substantial share of damages awarded. There were also six cases of complete permanent disability. In three of these there was no compensation; in the others compensation was in the sums of $150, $175, and $4,500 each. Incidentally it may be mentioned that in the last case the hospital bill was $1,700, the lawyer's fee $3,000. To continue, in fourteen of fifty cases of permanent partial disability, there was no compensation. The awards varied widely in the other cases, as, for example, from $290 to $2,700 for loss of an eye, from $405 to $4,200 for the loss of a hand, from $50 to $3,000 for the loss of a foot. The record is completed by noting that of forty-three serious cases of temporary disability, six received no compensation whatever, four received medical treatment only, fifteen received less than their medical bills and lost wages by an average of $65.50 each, while eighteen received more than the total of medical bills and lost wages. Certainly, employers' liability was both inadequate and uncertain as a method in Minnesota as it has been everywhere.

The system was uneconomical in that only a fraction of what the employer paid out as insurance premiums or in direct settlements found its way into the pockets of the victims or their dependents. To cite one of the more conservative research results, 327 New York firms, according to the Special Commission reporting, paid out $192,538, of which $104,643, less attorneys' fees which might well absorb a third, went to victims and dependents.

The last two counts in the indictment may be dismissed with a word. Employers' liability has been accompanied by the ambulance chase, bogus cases, sharp practices, and similar evils. Employers' liability can claim little credit for developing interest in accident prevention; workmen's compensation and accident insurance systems have claimed much in this connection.

In view of the nature of the law and the abundant data bearing upon how it worked out in practice, Elihu Root's language was fully justified when he spoke of "the . . . foolish, wasteful, ineffective, and barbarous law of employers' liability."

The Workmen's Compensation and Accident Insurance Movement

Almost everywhere there has been a revolt against employers' liability, and workmen's compensation or a system of insurance has been wholly or partially substituted for it in accident cases, if not always in cases of occupational disease. Germany and several other countries have legislated in terms of insurance, while England and most English-speaking countries have adopted workmen's compensation.[1]

In this, as in other fields of social insurance legislation, the United States was tardy. The multiplicity of our political divisions, the traditional individualism of our people, the relative well-being of the working classes, and the uncertainty as to constitutionality all inhibited the development of this type of social insurance until the second decade of the twentieth century. There had, it is true, been some earlier legislation, but the compensation movement in the United States really did not get under way until 1910, when New York State enacted a law compulsory in its application to twelve specified dangerous occupations.[2]

That the courts should have regarded the new legislation as a radical departure is not surprising, nor is it to be wondered that for a time a considerable portion of the public—and some jurists—assumed that the abrogation of the common-law defenses and the making of the employer liable without fault on his part was tantamount to nullification of the rights guaranteed by the Fourteenth Amendment. The New York statute of 1910, when it came before the Court of Appeals of that state in 1911, was declared to be, "judged by our common-law standards, . . . plainly revolutionary. Its central and controlling feature is that every employer who is engaged in any of the classified industries shall be liable for any injury to a workman arising out of and in the course of the employment by 'a necessary risk or danger of the employment or one inherent in the nature thereof.'"[3] The story of the judicial vicissitudes of workmen's compensation legislation, and of the ultimate establishment of its constitutionality, should be traced briefly at this point.

There has never been a leading court decision in which the statutory modification of the fellow servant and contributory negligence rules have been held to be beyond legislative power. As the New York Court of Appeals phrased it in the case just alluded to, "These doctrines, for they are nothing more, may be regulated or even abolished." For a time, however, there appeared to be serious question as to whether making the employer liable without fault on his part did not constitute the taking of property without due process of law. To quote from the Ives decision: "[This statute] provides that they [employers] shall be liable to their employees for personal injury by accident to any workman arising out

---

[1] For an inclusive review of accident insurance and workmen's compensation systems, see International Labour Office, *Studies and Reports*, Series E and M. See, also, B. N. Armstrong, *op. cit.*, pp. 223–281.

[2] Laws of 1910, Chap. 674. As has been said, the law applied to twelve dangerous occupations. The employer was made liable to pay compensation, at rates set in the law, in case of (a) a necessary risk or danger of the employment or one inherent in the nature thereof, and (b) his own failure, or that of his officers, agents, or employees, to exercise due care, or to comply with any law affecting the employment.

[3] *Ives v. South Buffalo Railway Co.*, 201 N.Y. 271 (1911).

of and in the course of employment which is caused in whole or in part, or is contributed to, by a necessary risk or danger of the employment. . . . It is conceded that this is a liability unknown to the common law and we think it plainly constitutes a deprivation of liberty and property under the Federal and State Constitutions. . . . The right of property rests not upon philosophical or scientific speculations nor upon the commendable impulses of benevolence or charity, nor yet upon the dictates of natural justice. The right has its foundation in the fundamental law. That can be changed by the people but not by legislatures. . . . If the legislature can say to an employer, 'you must compensate your employee for an injury not caused by you or by your fault,' why can it not go further and say to the man of wealth, 'you have more property than you need and your neighbor is so poor that he can barely subsist; in the interest of natural justice you must divide with your neighbor so that he and his dependents shall not become a charge upon the State'?" While the argument that the risk of an employee should be borne by the employer because it is inherent in the employment "may be economically sound . . . it is at war with the legal principle that no employer can be compelled to assume a risk which is inseparable from the work of the employee, and which may exist in spite of a degree of care by the employer far greater than may be exacted by the most drastic law. . . . In its final and simple analysis that is taking the property of A and giving it to B, and that cannot be done under our Constitutions." Nor could the Court find anything in the police power to justify such "taking of the employer's property without his consent and without his fault. . . . It [the workmen's compensation law] does nothing to conserve the health, safety or morals of the employees, and it imposes upon the employer no new or affirmative duties or responsibilities in the conduct of his business. Its sole purpose is to make him liable for injuries which may be sustained wholly without his fault, and solely through the fault of the employee . . . it attempts to reverse the very provisions of the Constitution."

The New York legislature acted upon the intimation of the state's highest court that the right of property, having its foundation "in fundamental law," could be changed only by the people, and in 1913 a constitutional amendment was submitted to popular referendum and adopted, thus removing the Ives disability;[1] and in 1913 a new law was

[1] "Nothing contained in this Constitution shall be construed to limit the power of the legislature to enact laws for the protection of the lives, health, or safety of employees; or for the payment, either by employers, or by employers and employees or otherwise, either directly or through a state or other system of insurance or otherwise, of compensation for injuries to employees or for the death of employees resulting from such injuries without regard to fault as to the cause thereof, except where the injury is occasioned by the willful intention of the injured employee to bring about the injury or death of himself or of another, or where the injury results solely from the intoxication of the injured employee while on duty; or for the adjustment, determination, and settlement, with or without trial by

enacted.   The shadow of constitutional doubt hovered over the legislation after the 1911 New York decision, however, and it was to this fact that the elective rather than compulsory character of a considerable number of laws was due.

In 1917, however, the Supreme Court of the United States proved that the action of New York State in amending its constitution had been unnecessary; the public interest in legislation of this type is sufficiently great to make such "taking of the employer's property without his consent" as may be involved a proper exercise of the police power.   When the New York law of 1913 came before the highest court of the land,[1] it was urged against the statute: (a) that the employer's property would by its provisions be taken without due process of law, because he was subjected to a liability for compensation without regard to any neglect or default on his part or the part of any other person for whom he was responsible, and in spite of the fact that the injury might be solely attributable to the fault of the employee; (b) that the employee's rights were interfered with in that he was prevented from having compensation for injuries arising from the employer's fault commensurate with the damages actually sustained, and was limited to the measure of compensation prescribed by the act; and (c) that both employer and employee were deprived of their liberty to acquire property by being prevented from making such agreement as they chose respecting the terms of employment.   The reasoning whereby the Court reached the conclusion that none of these contentions was valid may be presented, for the most part, in its own language.

The common-law rules—most of them, in fact, of comparatively recent origin, are "subject to modification or abrogation by a State upon proper occasion. . . . The statute sets aside one body of rules only to establish another system in its place.   If the employee is no longer able to recover as much as before in case of being injured through the employer's negligence, he is entitled to moderate compensation in all cases of injury, and has a certain and speedy remedy without the difficulty and expense of establishing negligence or proving the amount of the damages. . . . On the other hand, if the employer is left without defense respecting the question of fault, he at the same time is assured that the recovery is limited and that it goes directly to the relief of the designated beneficiary. . . . The act . . . is intended as a just settlement of a difficult prob-

---

jury, of issues which may arise under such legislation, or to provide that the right of such compensation, and the remedy therefor, shall be exclusive of all other rights and remedies for injuries to employees or for death resulting from such injuries; or to provide that the amount of such compensation for death shall not exceed a fixed or determinable sum; provided that all moneys paid by an employer to his employees, or their legal representatives, by reason of the enactment of any of the laws herein authorized, shall be held to be a proper charge in the cost of operating the business of the employer."

[1] N.Y. Central R.R. Co. v. White, 243 U. S. 188 (1917).

lem. . . . In such an adjustment, the particular rules of the common law affecting the subject matter are not placed by the Fourteenth Amendment beyond the reach of the law-making power of the State. . . . The loss of earning power [consequent upon industrial accidents] . . . is a loss arising out of the business, and, however it may be charged up, is an expense of the operation, as truly as the cost of repairing broken machinery' or any other expense that ordinarily is paid by the employer. . . . It is not unreasonable for the State, while relieving the employer from responsibility for damages measured by common-law standards and payable in cases where he or those for whose conduct he is answerable are found to be at fault, to require him to contribute a reasonable amount, and according to a reasonable and definite scale, by way of compensation for the loss of earning power incurred in the common enterprise, irrespective of the question of negligence. . . . Liability without fault is not a novelty in the law. . . . In excluding the question of fault as a cause of the injury, the act in effect disregards the proximate cause and looks to one more remote—the primary cause, as it may be deemed—and that is the employment itself. . . . Viewing the entire matter, it cannot be pronounced arbitrary and unreasonable for the State to impose upon the employer the absolute duty of making a moderate and definite compensation." In another decision rendered during the same term,[1] the right of a state to establish an exclusive state fund and to classify industries, for purposes of payment, according to their respective hazards, was upheld.

Meanwhile, more states had been enacting workmen's compensation laws. Twenty placed such legislation on their statute books by 1913,[2] two in 1914,[3] and eight in 1915.[4] In 1916 a law was adopted in Kentucky and one by Congress, this Federal act relating to civilian employees only. By 1920, workmen's compensation had found place in the statutes of all except seven of the southern states and the District of Columbia (in case of private employees). More recently, compensation laws have been adopted in Georgia (1921), Missouri (1926), District of Columbia (1927), North Carolina (1929), Florida (1935), and South Carolina (1935). At present, only in Arkansas and Mississippi has the law of employers' liability not given way, at least partially, before the compensation movement.[5]

---

[1] *Mountain Timber Co. v. Washington*, 243 U. S. 219 (1917).

[2] California, Illinois, Kansas, Massachusetts, New Hampshire, New Jersey, Nevada, Ohio, Washington, and Wisconsin in 1911; Arizona, Michigan and Rhode Island in 1912; Connecticut, Iowa, Minnesota, Nebraska, New York, Oregon, and Texas in 1913.

[3] Louisiana and Maryland.

[4] Colorado, Indiana, Maine, Montana, Oklahoma, Pennsylvania, Vermont, and Wyoming.

[5] F. Robertson Jones, in his *Digest of Workmen's Compensation Laws* (14th ed., 1935), gives estimates of the number of employees in forty-one of the forty-six states having compensation laws, the total coverage being approximately 23,725,000. If the ratio between

Workmen's compensation legislation differs from the old law of employers' liability in several respects. In the first place, the naive notion that someone was negligent or at fault whenever an accident occurred, and that justice demanded merely the ascertaining of who had been guilty of the negligence or at fault, has been abandoned. The presumption is in favor of assessing the cost upon the employer, not because he is personally responsible, but as a matter of social policy. In the second place, workmen's compensation legislation attempts to provide a fixed scale of benefits for each injury, the amount depending upon such factors as the nature of the disability incurred, the amount previously earned by the injured worker, and the existence or nonexistence of dependents. In the third place, annuities to compensate for the loss from death or disability, rather than payment of damages in a lump sum, characterize workmen's compensation. This feature is a logical concomitant of the difference in the underlying assumptions of the two types of legislation. Employers' liability laws contemplated payment for a specific wrong already committed; when the court had established that a wrong had been committed, the pecuniary award to the wronged person was due. With the abandonment under workmen's compensation legislation of this assumption, annuities have generally been substituted for lump-sum damages. Finally, workmen's compensation laws frequently recognize the desirability of requiring employers, by insurance, to protect their employees from the risk, in order that the purpose of compensation may not be defeated by bankruptcy or withdrawal from business.

Just as striking as the spread of the method of compensating for industrial injuries sustained have been the changes in the standards set and the scope of the law.[1] The earlier legislation, based in large part upon the British model of 1896, had as its main objective the settlement of claims rather automatically and quickly by the payment of standardized sums to victims or dependents. But more recently, as a result of experience and changing ideals, medical rights, rehabilitation, etc., have been stressed, while claims to, and the amount of, money benefit have undergone numerous changes. Yet, great gaps are still to be found between the standards accepted in law and the minimum standards the better students of the subject would incorporate in a model system. In other words, sound and adequate compensation has been only partially realized; great gaps remain to be filled in.

---

the number of employees covered and the number of employees gainfully occupied be applied to the remaining five states, we would have an estimated total of somewhat more than 25,500,000 employees covered by workmen's compensation in the forty-six states.

[1] For legislative tendencies in the scope of compensation laws, see W. F. Dodd, *op. cit.*, pp. 37–52.

It is rather generally agreed among industrial accident commissioners, experts, and students of the subject that the compensation law should provide the exclusive remedy and should cover employments generally, the so-called nonhazardous as well as the hazardous, and small groups of workers as well as the large. The matter was well put by Mr. Fitzgerald when, in reporting a measure for the District of Columbia, he said, "All employees except casual workers whose employment is not in the course of the trade, business, profession or occupation of the employer will be eligible to compensation benefits under this bill. . . . The Committee believes that to exclude any class of worker other than the 'casuals' would be fallacious, for the reason that there is no industry unattended by danger. . . . It is obvious that the hazard varies in different lines of work and therefore that the amount of insurance premium will vary. *In all cases the fact of occupational injury should be the test of the need for protection under an accident compensation law.*"[1] At most a reasonable case can be made for the exclusion from compensation laws of casual workers, farm laborers, and domestics whose employment is under somewhat exceptional circumstances and the inclusion of whom under workmen's compensation would involve administrative difficulty.

When the American legislation is examined, however, only hazardous industries are frequently found to be covered. Moreover, numerical limitations are frequently found and in some cases are so high that employment in exceptional cases is required to bring a case within the scope of the law.

In eleven of the forty-six compensation states the laws apply only to hazardous employments as defined, but the principal industrial employments are uniformly included. Employers of less than a stipulated number of employees are exempt from the operation of the laws of twenty-six states. The number fixed upon is as high as sixteen in Alabama, fifteen in South Carolina, eleven in Virginia, and ten in Georgia, Missouri, and Vermont. It scarcely needs to be pointed out that a large proportion of wage earners in these states are employed in smaller groups than ten, eleven, fifteen, or sixteen.[2]

With agriculture and domestic service excluded from the scope of the compensation acts of all but a few states, with some or all public employees now and then excluded, with nonhazardous employments not included in a fourth of the number, and with numerical limitations operative in more than half of the states, it is obvious that a considerable

---

[1] Quoted from *American Labor Legislation Review*, vol. 12 (1922), pp. 59–60.

[2] The limiting figures in other states are two in Oklahoma, three in Arizona, Florida, Kentucky, Ohio, Rhode Island, Texas, Utah, and Wisconsin, four in Colorado, New Mexico, and New York, five in Connecticut, Delaware, Kansas, Maine, New Hampshire, North Carolina and Tennessee, and six in Massachusetts. Association of Casualty and Surety Executives, *Digest of Workmen's Compensation Laws* (15th ed., 1937), p. xiii.

fraction of employment is not within the embrace of the laws. Coverage there is by the law of employers' liability. Furthermore, it is to be pointed out that only the Federal laws and those of fourteen of the states are compulsory upon employers within their embrace.[1] Elsewhere the law is elective, and though in nearly all cases election is presumed unless notice to the contrary is given,[2] and though the common-law defenses have been abrogated where election is adverse, by no means all employers eligible to do so actually come under the compensation laws. There is frequently also the right of election by the employee, but this is infrequently exercised. Here, in the elective character of most of the legislation, is another deficiency. Compensation legislation should be fairly inclusive in its embrace and compulsory upon both employer and employee. As matters stand, a combination of compensation and employers' liability is found, with the latter occupying a really important place in a number of states. And, it will be remembered, two states have adopted no compensation law at all.

As stated above, occupational disease presents essentially the same problem as industrial accident. Both types of injury should be covered by the compensation law. None of the early laws enacted, however, made specific provision for compensating occupational diseases. The dominant idea of accident has given way by degrees, however, until at the present time compensation, either for occupational diseases generally or for designated diseases of this class, is allowed under the Federal law[3] and those of about three-sevenths of the states.[4]

The usual methods of covering occupational diseases in the workmen's compensation acts are of three types, viz., (1) by blanket coverage of all occupational diseases; (2) by employing the word "injury" instead of "accident" in the law; and (3) by listing the specific occupational diseases which are compensable.

---

[1] Arizona, California, Idaho, Illinois, Maryland, Minnesota, New York, North Dakota, Ohio, Oklahoma, Utah, Washington, Wisconsin, and Wyoming. Compensation is compulsory in Indiana and Iowa for coal mining; in Texas, for motor-bus companies.

[2] In twenty-two of the elective states—Alabama, Colorado, Connecticut, Delaware, Florida, Georgia, Iowa, Kansas, Kentucky, Louisiana, Missouri, Nebraska, New Jersey, New Mexico, North Carolina, Oregon, Pennsylvania, South Dakota, Tennessee, Vermont, Virginia and Wisconsin. In Kentucky, Maine, Michigan, Montana, Nevada, New Hampshire, and Rhode Island, positive acceptances must be filed with designated state authorities, while in Massachusetts, Texas, and West Virginia, insuring in accordance with the law signifies election.

[3] The Federal Employees' Compensation Act and the Longshoremen's and Harbor Workers' Act.

[4] In twenty-two states: California, Connecticut, Delaware, Illinois, Indiana, Kentucky, Massachusetts, Michigan, Minnesota, Missouri, Nebraska, New Jersey, New York, North Carolina, North Dakota, Ohio, Pennsylvania, Rhode Island, Washington, West Virginia, Wisconsin, and in the District of Columbia, Hawaii, Puerto Rico, and the Philippine Islands.

The first of these—that of blanket or complete coverage of all occupational diseases—is found in the laws of six states[1] as well as in the Federal legislation. Examples of this broad and more liberal type of coverage are found in the legislation of Connecticut which defines occupational disease as "a disease peculiar to the occupation in which the employee was engaged and due to causes in excess of the ordinary hazards of employment as such," and in Illinois where blanket provision for compensation is allowed for disability, injury or death from occupational diseases with the further stipulation that the occupational-disease act shall be administered separately from that of workmen's compensation due to injury.

Three states (California, Massachusetts, and Wisconsin) employ a somewhat similar method, which is the equivalent of blanket coverage, whereby the term "injury" instead of "accident" is used in the law. The California and Wisconsin laws have definitely specified that the word "injury" is to include occupational disease, while the Massachusetts law employing the word "injury" in lieu of "accident" has been interpreted by the courts to include "any injury or disease which arises out of and in the course of employment, which causes incapacity for work and therefore impairs the ability of the employe for earning wages."[2]

The third method, whereby specific diseases are scheduled as compensable, is used extensively in the compensation systems in a number of European countries, particularly England, Germany, and Switzerland.[3] In the United States, the compensation laws of nine states[4] cover certain listed occupational diseases for which compensation is paid. Of these, New Jersey lists ten occupational diseases; Delaware, twelve; Pennsylvania, fifteen; Washington, twenty-one; Ohio, twenty-two; Minnesota, twenty-three; North Carolina, twenty-five; Rhode Island and Michigan, thirty-one; while the New York schedule covers certain specified diseases, and, in addition, under an amendment adopted in 1935, provides general coverage for "any and all occupational diseases" in "any and all employments enumerated."[5] Under the laws of certain other states, such as

---

[1] Connecticut, Illinois, Indiana, Missouri, New York, North Dakota, and also the District of Columbia, Hawaii, and the Philippine Islands.

[2] *Johnson v. London Guarantee & Accident Co.*, 104 N.E. 736 (1914); *H. P. Hood & Sons v. Maryland Casualty Co.*, 92 N.E. 329 (1910).

[3] U. S. Bureau of Labor Statistics, "Occupational-Disease Legislation in the United States, 1936," *Bulletin 625* (1937), pp. 3–5.

[4] Delaware, Michigan, Minnesota, New Jersey, North Carolina, Ohio, Pennsylvania, Rhode Island, Washington, and also Puerto Rico.

[5] *New York Laws*, 1935, Chap. 254, Sec. 1.   Early in 1933, the New York State Industrial Commissioner, Frances Perkins, urged that the law be extended to cover all occupational diseases and declared that the increased cost to industry would not exceed 0.2 per cent and that no increase in premium rates would be needed to meet the additional cost. See M. N. Newquist, *Medical Service in Industry and Workmen's Compensation Laws* (The American College of Surgeons, 1934), p. 38.

those of Kentucky, Nebraska, and West Virginia, compensation is limited to silicosis and/or diseases peculiar to smelting or metal refining.

The compensation laws of twelve states[1] expressly exclude all diseases except those which result from occupational accidents. The remaining laws cover only "accidental injuries" or "injuries by accident," although in several states these terms have been interpreted by the courts to include some diseases of gradual contraction.[2] Thus it can be said that one of the important deficiencies in the laws of most of our states is that they do not cover occupational diseases at all or only inadequately.

With respect to such provisions as do exist, it should be noted that the great majority of compensation administrators and experts are in favor of complete coverage rather than "schedule" coverage of occupational diseases. The successive National Conferences on Labor Legislation have consistently advocated such provision,[3] and from the experience of the states providing complete coverage, such as California, New York, and Wisconsin, it appears that the cost of including all occupational injuries and disabilities is relatively insignificant and would add not more than 3 per cent to the present insurance cost of accident disabilities.[4] In the state of Wisconsin, for example, during the ten-year period from 1925 through 1934, the number of cases of occupational disease averaged 415 per year, compensation and medical cost averaged $326 per case, with total costs approximating but $135,000 yearly.[5]

As has been indicated, insurance charges for full coverage of occupational disease, when spread uniformly over the industrial and mercantile establishments throughout a state, are negligible.   Under such conditions "it appears possible that an adequate occupational-disease fund appli-

---

For an excellent discussion of the development of occupational disease legislation in New York and its administration, see Charity M. Tinker, "Compensation of Occupational Disease in New York," *Social Service Review*, vol. 11, no. 1 (March, 1937), pp. 78–100.

[1] Alabama, Arizona, Georgia, Idaho, Louisiana, Montana, South Carolina, South Dakota, Utah, Vermont, Virginia, and Wyoming. In addition, the law of Texas, somewhat ambiguous in terms, has been construed to cover only accidents.

[2] For an index of leading judicial decisions in regard to occupational disease under the law, see Association of Casualty and Surety Executives, *Digest of Workmen's Compensation Laws* (15th ed., 1937), Sec. 9 of the digest for each state.

[3] *Monthly Labor Review*, April, 1934, p. 781; November, 1935, p. 1261; and December, 1936, p. 1438.

[4] See summary section of the Committee on Costs in the *Report of the Pennsylvania Commission on Compensation for Occupational Diseases* (1933).

[5] In contrast to these data for occupational disease, the average yearly number of compensable accidental-injury cases, during this same period, amounted to 18,904; compensation and medical cost averaged $240 per case with total yearly payments approximating $4,532,000. Thus, in Wisconsin, the cost of complete coverage for occupational disease has involved expenditures of only 2.9 per cent of those for compensable accidents. See *Report of the Industrial Commission of Wisconsin* (1935).

For a summary table of the Wisconsin experience, see *Industrial Medicine*, vol. 5, no. 3 (March, 1936), p. 140.

cable to all characteristic occupational diseases may be provided through a premium of not more than 3¢ per $100 of employer's payroll."[1] However, if the prime principle of compensation is to be observed whereby each industry bears its own burden and charges the costs to production, as in Wisconsin, for example, protests against the rather heavy expense of full occupational disease coverage are certain to arise. These, of course, emanate not from the great majority of industries whose frequency of claims and compensation costs are low, but from the relatively few hazard-hit industries, such as the foundry, smelting, and granite industries, where the loss costs are high and where, consequently, full coverage may mean a 10 per cent increase in premium cost over and above that for occupational accidents.[2]

Here, however, as in the case of occupational accidents, prevention points the way to low costs.[3] It will suffice to say that competent students of the problem have concluded that "it is a practical possibility to prevent essentially all occupational disease. At once it may be asserted that at least three-fourths of all occupational diseases need not arise."[4]

From these matters pertaining to the embrace of compensation laws, we pass to a consideration of the minimum of compensation or service which should be provided and that which is now actually provided.

A compensation law, first of all, should provide for the industrially injured adequate medical and surgical treatment, and hospital and nursing care. These are called for not only on humane grounds, but also in order to protect against permanently impaired efficiency, to shorten the period of disability, to save loss of wages, and to reduce the amount

[1] Dr. Carey P. McCord of the Industrial Health Conservancy Laboratories (Cincinnati, Ohio) and Sue Eyster, "The Monetary Cost of Occupational Disease Liability Insurance," *Industrial Medicine*, vol. 5, no. 3 (March, 1936), p. 143.

In Ohio, where the entire insurance fund represents a state monopoly, the premiums for coverage of accidental injuries vary from industry to industry but the premium for occupational disease insurance (covering 21 diseases) is uniformly spread over all the insurers in the state. The trivial charge of 1 cent per $100 of payroll (*i.e.*, $5.00 for a payroll of $50,000) was sufficient to build up a surplus in the Occupational Disease Fund (a subdivision of the Ohio State Insurance Fund) which amounted to $735,483.13 at the beginning of 1935.

[2] *Ibid.*

[3] *Cf.* Harry A. Nelson, Director of Workmen's Compensation, Wisconsin Industrial Commission, "Silicosis Problem Solved in Wisconsin," *American Labor Legislation Review*, vol. 26, no. 2 (June, 1936), pp. 53–60; Dr. C. O. Sappington, "The Integrated Control of Occupational Diseases," *American Journal of Public Health*, vol. 26 (1936), pp. 781–785; "Occupational Diseases—The Situation in Illinois," *Industrial Medicine*, vol. 5, no. 2 (February, 1936), pp. 71–73; and "The Control of Occupational Diseases by Laboratory Methods," *Journal of Industrial Hygiene*, January, 1935. *Cf.* also, F. Robertson Jones, "Problems in Compensation for Occupational Diseases," Occupational Disease Conference of the Illinois Mfrs. Association, January 31, 1935.

[4] Carey P. McCord and Sue Eyster, *op. cit.*, p. 143.

paid out in cash benefits. In the second place, it (a) should provide for proper compensation for loss of wages due to total temporary or partial permanent disability; (b) should make proper provision throughout life for those completely and permanently disabled; and (c) in the fatal case, should provide a funeral allowance and pensions for surviving widow or widower until death or remarriage and for dependent children until eighteen years of age. All of this should be provided at the expense of the employer, with the expectation that it will place a premium on accident prevention and with the further expectation that the bill, like other costs, will generally be shifted to the consumer. And, to be mentioned here, though it will be discussed later in this chapter, adequate provision should be made for the rehabilitation of those who are handicapped as a result of industrial injury and whose efficiency and earning power can be restored completely or in substantial measure. All of this, in general terms, is almost unanimously agreed upon by the students of the problem as finding place among the minimum essentials of an adequate compensation law.[1]

Before discussing medical and cash benefits of the different kinds just mentioned, it will be well to explain why the entire cost involved in providing them should be charged to the employers rather than covered by premiums paid by employer and workers as under Germany's system of social insurance in so far as the first thirteen weeks of care is concerned.

The main reason for levying the entire charge upon the employers is that industrial injuries are incidents in the industrial process and the bills involved are almost as properly to be regarded as costs of production as the bills involved in repairing broken machinery and replacing spoiled raw materials. This is certainly true of that proportion of industrial injuries not to be avoided by the exercise of reasonable care on the part of employer and worker. And, of course, the employer should bear the cost involved in injuries sustained by workmen which might be prevented by a sound policy of accident prevention. So, a second reason for thus assessing the costs involved is that it will make for prevention. A further reason is found in the fact that the most liberal compensation administratively possible will be only partial compensation. Only a part of the loss in wages can be covered by benefits. Inevitably a considerable share of the money loss as well as the other sacrifice will be borne by injured workmen and their dependents.

For the most part, the costs entailed by workmen's compensation are assessed in their entirety against the employer. Some exceptions are, however, found in American practice. These occur in connection with medical and hospital service and are largely due to the provision made for such service under organizations set up in western states by railroad,

---

[1] Cf. American Association for Labor Legislation, *Standards for Workmen's Compensation Laws* (revised to Jan. 1, 1937); W. F. Dodd, *op. cit.*, and E. H. Downey, *op. cit.*

mining, and other companies in pre-compensation days. But be the explanation what it may, in Oregon the employer may make reasonable deductions from the workers' pay, but not to exceed ten cents per day, for medical, surgical, and hospital care.[1] In Arizona, Nevada, and Washington, one-half of the cost of maintaining the "medical fund" may be charged by employer to workmen, but in the first two states such charge may not exceed $1.00 per month.

COMPENSATION RIGHTS AND STANDARDS

It is interesting to note that a majority of the early compensation laws provided only the most perfunctory medical service for the injured workers despite the fact that the number requiring medical attention would be much larger than the number entitled to compensation. In the evolution of American compensation legislation, however, the medical and hospital benefit has been more and more emphasized. Great progress has been made, for those compensation commissions and persons who have studied the matter thoroughly "have come to recognize that the purposes of workmen's compensation are: first, prevention of industrial accidents and injuries; second, the provision of medical service; and third, cash compensation."[2]

Yet, largely owing to opposition of the insurance companies and even some of the state funds, liberal provision has been rather haltingly made and all sorts of compromises between adequate and inadequate provision have occurred.

Fifteen years ago, in only a few states did the law provide medical and hospital care without limitation in time or amount of money per case. By 1932, however, the Federal law and the laws of almost a third of the states "had no money or time limits on the medical care guaranteed . . . , and several other states had so amended their laws that in effect the medical provisions were without legal limit of either time or money." A compilation as of May 1, 1935, shows twenty-five states with unlimited medical provisions.[3] In some of the other states, however, the limitation is still illiberal.

With the increasing emphasis upon medical care, as one of the objectives of compensation legislation, it is estimated that approximately $70,000,000 per year is paid to physicians and hospitals in injury cases. The Bureau of Medical Economics of the American Medical Association, using data for the years 1929–1931, reported that $67,264,944 was paid for medical care and $159,552,024 in compensation.[4]

---

[1] Section 6644, Laws of 1920, as amended by Chap. 208, Acts of 1927.
[2] I. S. Falk, *op. cit.*, p. 297.
[3] *Ibid.*, p. 298.
[4] In *Judicial Relations Under Workmen's Compensation* (1933), pp. 98, 99, it also finds "that in the compensation business handled by stock companies, each premium dollar is

Much more of a problem is involved in medical service under workmen's compensation than is found in such undue limitations as remain on the number of weeks it shall be available or the cost it may entail. Indeed, the matter bristles with problems which are much discussed by administrators, students, doctors, and insurance companies. Under the compensation acts, the employer or the insurer is charged with supplying medical care, but who shall select the doctor? Who may practice and what shall the fee schedule be? What sort of evidence shall be available in contested compensation cases involving medical questions?

The general rule has been to permit the one who pays the bill to decide upon the doctor and the hospital. This means the employer, or, likely, the insurance company, or the state fund. This arrangement is contended for not only on the ground that he who pays should make the arrangements, but also on the ground that better treatment and earlier restoration to work will result than if the choice is made by the injured worker. Moreover, the employer or company is, under such an arrangement, protected against improper claims for cash compensation. The workman, however, usually wishes to have his own physician, if he has one, because he has confidence in him and because it will stand him in good stead in contested cases. Compensation doctors serve as witnesses when claims are contested as well as provide medical care. In the worker's interest, a few states have provided for free choice by the injured.[1]

Much more could be said for the employer's selecting the doctors did this not all too frequently mean that his insurance company makes the selection and all too frequently with an eye to saving money. The stock company has a heavy, relatively fixed, acquisition cost; the rate of cash compensation is controlled by law; the amount of profit depends upon the remuneration of the doctor and the hospital and upon how soon the injured is returned to work and compensation ended. And in this connection it must be held in mind that the provisions for cash and medical benefits have become more liberal or less illiberal year after year; this has tended to cut the margin of profit. While not a few companies have followed a liberal policy, others have not. Advantage has frequently been taken of the competitive situation to force down the doctor's remuneration. And considerable group practice, much of it not maintaining good standards, has developed. From the point of view of complete restoration of the injured, much of the medical service is deficient. And in deciding contested cases the administrator is confronted by much biased testimony.

---

divided about as follows: the company receives 42 cents, the injured worker receives 38 cents in cash, and 20 cents goes for medical care."

[1] In Massachusetts, Rhode Island, New York, North Dakota, and (as to state-insurance cases only) Ohio.

Professor Dodd, in his recent volume, has set forth splendidly the problem of medical service as well as the other aspects of workmen's compensation administration.[1] After a detailed exposition of findings in different states, his conclusions with reference to the point under discussion are, in part, as follows:[2]

"The compensation statutes, with a very few exceptions, make the employer, which means the insurer, responsible for paying medical benefits, thus giving these parties a financial interest in keeping medical costs as low as possible. This they succeed in doing in most cases through control of the employee's attending physician since the laws in most states give the employer or insurer the power to select such doctor. Thus a bargaining power is delivered into the hands of a few, and this has encouraged group practice of medicine with its hospital association, contract hospital, industrial or insurance clinic, as the case may be, whose chief appeal lies in its claim to cheapness.

"The worst feature of this commercialization of medical practice has been the exploitation of the health of the employee. Whether it be under the contract hospital in West Virginia, the hospital association in Washington, the industrial or commercial clinic in New York, or the insurance clinic or doctor in any state, there is always the danger that the quality of medical treatment will be sacrificed to the desire for profit. The material in this chapter collected from official and other responsible sources has shown not only the danger but the reality of this exploitation. The forms of contract or commercialized medical practice vary, but the results to the employee are much the same no matter what shape it assumes. The hospital or hospital association rendering treatment under contract receives a fixed amount of income during the term of the agreement; this means that the shorter the period of medical care given injured workmen and the less costly the methods of treatment used the greater will be the amount of money left over for profits. Thus it is to the financial interest of such an organization to rush the employee back to work at the earliest possible date and to give him the least expensive types of medical and surgical service."

He continues,[3] "If contract hospitals and the like have been guilty of unsavory practices, the doctors and specialists in the service of some of the insurance companies do not present a much more favorable picture. Here again the desire to reap a profit or to lighten a loss lies at the root of the trouble. Doctors are hired by the insurance companies on either a salary or a case basis. The qualifications and abilities of physicians who will serve an insurance company for a fixed salary,

---

[1] Walter F. Dodd, *Administration of Workmen's Compensation* (Commonwealth Fund, 1936). His discussion of the medical problem is found in Chap. 10, pp. 408–505.

[2] *Ibid.*, pp. 489–490 (quoted with permission of the Commonwealth Fund).

[3] *Ibid.*, pp. 490–491.

usually not a princely one, are apt to be meager and the retention of their jobs is likely to depend more upon their success in minimizing the disabilities or defeating the claims of injured workmen than on their professional merits. The quality of medical care which such physicians give is therefore likely to be inferior and their attitude hostile to the patient. The specialists to whom an insurance company sends its claimants may be able in their field and capable of rendering a high type of professional service, but if too great a proportion of their findings are favorable to the claimants these specialists will no longer receive the patronage of the insurance companies. To withstand this economic pressure requires either the loftiest ethical and professional standards on the part of the physician or so large an income from other sources that insurance company practice is not needed. The reports of official investigations summarized in the preceding pages, the scrutiny of hundreds of records in each of several states by investigators engaged in this study, and their steady attendance for consecutive periods at compensation hearings in these states, afford convincing proof that insurance company practice in the chief industrial centers of each jurisdiction studied is, on the whole, restricted to a relatively small group of doctors whose written reports and findings and verbal testimony favor their employers, the insurance companies, with monotonous regularity. The conclusion is inescapable that most of these doctors are selected or retained for their legal ability in defeating employees' claims rather than for their medical skill in healing their injuries. From the standpoint of the employer or insurance carrier, the value of a physician's services must be largely measured by his competence as a witness rather than by his skill in medical treatment. A few of the larger insurance companies take a more intelligent view of medical problems arising in compensation and regard it as not only good ethics but also good business to supply the best of medical attention for the period it is needed, but the number of these companies is unfortunately small."

Professor Dodd also finds an unsatisfactory condition where the worker has free choice of physician. His proposed solution of the urgent problem is as follows:[1]

"An ideal solution of all the medical problems in compensation would give protection to the legitimate interests of the three parties most directly concerned, namely, the employee, the insurance company, and the doctor. The employee should be guaranteed adequate and proper medical care during the period of disability and he should be given some voice in choosing the doctor who treats him so that he may feel confidence in the physician and so that the relationship between them is not purely impersonal. The insurer should be protected against the danger of padded bills and excessive charges by the doctors rendering treatment.

[1] *Ibid.*, pp. 494–495.

Compensation practice should be open to all physicians qualified to give it and they should not have to resort to fee splitting with lay solicitors or business managers in order to secure cases of industrial injury. Nor should the physician rendering medical service have a primary pecuniary interest in whether the compensation claim of his patient is granted or denied. While it is recognized that no program can be devised which will prevent all the evils in the medical field of compensation, it is believed that the plan outlined below will go a considerable distance toward improving conditions.

"All insurance clinics and all commercial clinics and hospital associations or other organizations which are operated to treat industrial injury cases for private profit should, by law, be abolished and the treatment of all compensation cases except those requiring first aid should be confined exclusively to the members of a panel of physicians, surgeons, and specialists nominated by the officers or a committee of the medical society in the county or area concerned. A selection based primarily upon action by representatives of the medical profession should offer at least some guarantee of the professional qualifications and capacities of the doctors designated, for the medical societies are presumably in a better position than any other body to know of the training and judge of the capabilities of the members of the profession. The employee, in his turn, should be given a considerable voice in the selection of his own doctor, thus encouraging the confidence in the physician which is so essential an element in recovery.

"While the power of nominating the panel should be entrusted to the medical profession, it would be advisable to give to the compensation administrators authority to remove from this panel any physician, surgeon, or specialist, upon proof of malpractice, fee splitting or other unprofessional conduct."

Of course, the question of fee schedules is involved in such an arrangement for medical service very much as it is under compulsory health insurance. In fact, the problem of the doctor and the hospital is in large part the same under workmen's compensation as under health insurance—a subject discussed in Chaps. VI and VII.

Turning from medical and hospital care, we shall now discuss briefly cash benefits in cases of temporary disability, permanent partial disability, loss of life, and permanent total disability, in this order.[1]

In compensation for temporary disability the length of waiting period and the scale of compensation are both important—the former determining the number of the industrially injured to be compensated, the latter how much cash shall be received to protect the standard of living.

---

[1] For a concise analysis and discussion of the scale of compensation provided under the various state laws, see American Association for Labor Legislation, *Standards for Workmen's Compensation Laws* (revised to Jan. 1, 1937).

If only those are compensated who are disabled for more than three days, the number is reduced by almost a third, for more than a week, by half, for more than two weeks, by two-thirds.   The ideal would be to compensate in all cases for serious loss, but not in those involving relatively small amounts because of the administrative problem that would arise.   Almost all students of the subject agree with the standard advocated by the American Association for Labor Legislation, viz., a waiting period of not less than three days and not more than a week at the beginning of disability.   Fifteen years ago, there were many states in which the waiting period was unduly long, but with revision of many of the statutes such states have come to be comparatively few.   At present there is no waiting period at all in Oregon and South Dakota; in forty-one states and under the three Federal laws, the waiting period, as recommended above, is not less than three nor more than seven days; in Colorado the waiting period is ten days, in Alabama and Iowa, two weeks.

If the object of a compensation law is to protect the standard of living and to promote safety in the work place rather than to cover the absolute necessities of life, it should be the largest percentage of the victims' wages[1] possible without begetting simulation or creating an inducement to incur minor injury or placing a premium upon remaining away from work after the disability has ended.   Many of the experts advocate benefits in terms of 75 per cent of the rate of wages; few persons would not go as far as the American Association for Labor Legislation, which maintains that, as a minimum, the "disabled workman should receive during disability, 66⅔ per cent of wages."   Most of the early compensation laws, however, fixed the percentage at 50.   Because of the unfairness and inadequacy of such a standard, a number of the older laws have been liberalized and most of the newly adopted systems have provided for compensation in excess of 50 per cent of wages.   Yet, because of illiberal percentages still remaining and low maximum sums, commented on presently, the great majority of the standards are illiberal and inadequate. The Bureau of Labor Statistics, in its 1929 analysis, stated:

"Using as a basis the rates for temporary total disability, it appears that 50 per cent of the employees' wages is allowed in compensation in 15 States [Alabama (60 per cent if two or more children), Colorado, Connecticut, Delaware, Georgia, Illinois (65 per cent if three or more children), Montana, New Hampshire, New Mexico, Oregon (40 to 66⅔ per cent, according to number of dependents), Porto Rico, Rhode Island, Tennessee, Vermont, and Virginia]; 55 per cent in three States [Idaho (increased 5 per cent for each child, total payments not over $16 weekly), Indiana and South Dakota]; 60 per cent in seven States (Hawaii, Iowa, Kansas, Nevada, Philippine Islands, Texas and Utah); 65 per cent in seven States (Alaska, Arizona, California, Kentucky, Louisiana,

---

[1] In all of the states except Washington and Wyoming disability compensation is based on a percentage of wages, rather than on a flat rate regardless of wages.

Pennsylvania and Wisconsin); and 66⅔ per cent in sixteen States (District of Columbia, Maine, Maryland, Massachusetts, Michigan, Minnesota, Missouri, Nebraska, New Jersey, New York, North Dakota, Ohio, Oklahoma, West Virginia and the Federal statutes for civil employees and for longshoremen)."[1]

It is obvious from this summary that the standards set have been influenced by the idea of maintenance. The granting of additional compensation for dependents is thus explained. So are the maxima and minima, in terms of so many dollars per week, rather than by the desire to maintain the standard of living, be it high or low, in the given case. All but two states, Arizona and Wisconsin, set a maximum sum per week which the compensation is not to exceed. One state has a maximum of $12, two of $14, eight of $15, three of $16, one of $16.50, one of $17, eleven of $18, while some fourteen have maxima varying from $18.75 in Ohio up to $25 in California, New York and South Carolina. A few states fix maxima in terms of so many dollars per month. Over against the maximum, a minimum of so many dollars per week or of full wages not to exceed a specified sum is ordinarily set. Hence it may be said that, generally speaking, it is the American practice to provide compensation in a percentage of the wage, within limits of minimum and maximum sums.

In the early days perhaps these fixed sums had narrow application. During the period of inflation and of high wages (1919–1921), however, the maxima came to have great effect. Indeed, in some states a majority of cases were compensated in terms of the maxima then in effect. For a time perhaps compensation did not average more than 25 per cent of wages. More recently, however, most of the maxima have been increased somewhat, but they are still low for skilled men disabled in the building and other trades.

Taking waiting period, percentages of wages, and maximum and minimum sums into consideration, it is found that about 50 per cent of the burden is placed upon the workers in states with the most and from 65 to 80 per cent in states with the less liberal legislation.[2] This statement,

---

[1] Quoted from U. S. Bureau of Labor Statistics, *Bulletin 496* (1929), p. 16. The analysis is as of Jan. 1, 1929, and therefore does not include the Florida and North and South Carolina laws.

By Jan. 1, 1938, a number of states, such as Alabama, Iowa, Montana, Virginia, and Wisconsin, had liberalized their provisions. At present, one state, Wisconsin, provides for disability compensation on a basis of 70 per cent of wages, thirteen states on a basis of 66⅔ per cent, six states on 65 per cent, nine on 60 per cent, four on 55 per cent, while the remaining states make provision either at a lower percentage of wages or at flat rates. Seven states provide additional allowances when there are dependents. If such allowances are included, three more states are brought into the group above 50 per cent, while four, whose basic allowances are above 50 per cent, have still higher percentages if there are dependents. Three of the seven states allow higher maximum sums in such cases.

[2] U. S. Bureau of Labor Statistics, *Bulletin 496*, p. 18.

however, applies to compensation in general, not to compensation for temporary disabilities alone.

A not small percentage of compensable industrial injuries involve permanent partial disability. In principle, these call for an application of the rule used in cases of temporary disability, but with the benefit fixed in proportion to the loss of earning power. Thus, if earning power were reduced a third, the worker would be entitled to one-third of the weekly benefit he would receive in case of complete temporary disability. The compensation laws have frequently been drafted in such terms. But what is the degree of disability from the loss of a finger, a hand, a leg, or an eye? Frequently decisions must be more or less arbitrary. Hence, to serve administrative convenience and also to have the matter disposed of definitely and not let it stand in the way of attempt at rehabilitation of earning power, definite allowances for loss, or loss of use, of different parts have rather generally been established in the compensation law or the rules for its administration. These allowances run in terms of number of weeks of full compensation payment, inclusive of, or in addition to, any period of total disability.[1] Thus the number of weeks' payment in case of loss of, or loss of use of, a hand may be 170, a thumb, 70, an index finger, 40, a leg, 190, a foot, 135, one eye, 120. It is obvious that to make allowances for loss of hand or foot or eye without regard to occupation would be very unfair, for the impairment of the earning power of one worker might be great, of that of another comparatively slight. Justice calls, therefore, for consideration of occupation in connection with specific losses. Perhaps most attention has been given to this difficult problem in California and there a schedule has been developed to show probable degree of impairment of earning power caused by each specific injury to a worker according to age and occupation. In most of the states, however, it cannot be said that partial-disability cases are being compensated with substantial justice to all.

There should be an appropriate burial allowance, say $150, in all cases of fatal injuries, whether there are surviving dependents or not. The compensation for surviving widow (or dependent widower) and dependent children, parents, brothers and sisters, etc., should be designed to fit their needs or to protect their standard of living which will be adversely affected by the death of a breadwinner. Of course, this means in the case of a widow that suitable compensation should continue through life, or until remarriage, when an allowance, say, of two years' payments, is not inappropriate; in the case of dependent children, until they reach age eighteen. The widow's compensation should be about 35 per cent of the husband's wage; 15 per cent (of that wage) should be added for each child, but the total of allowances for widow and children should not exceed 66⅔ per cent of wages. In the event there is no surviving widow, the allowance

[1] For an analysis of the schedules employed, see U. S. Bureau of Labor Statistics, *Bulletin 496*, pp. 18–20.

for the first dependent child should be 25 per cent. Other dependents than widow and children should receive similar allowances, in so far as there is a balance left in the total available (the 66⅔ per cent) after benefits have been provided for widow and dependent children.[1]

These, briefly stated, are the desirable standards for workmen's compensation in fatal cases. In all but about ten states, there is a burial allowance whether or not there are dependents. The maximum allowed is usually $150 or $200.

Except in a very few states, the earlier compensation laws left much to be desired in fatal cases. Influenced by the concept of damages and the desire to close the matter definitely, most of the laws provided compensation for so many weeks, but within a total sum. Moreover, the number of weeks was generally limited to the total in a period of three, four, or five years, and the total allowances were correspondingly limited. The more recent legislation has, however, generally been more liberal. Compensation has been allowed for a larger number of weeks and the maximum amounts per case increased. More important, there has been a tendency to remove at least the first of these limitations and to provide benefits in terms called for by the standards suggested above. At present the legislation varies greatly. Under the Federal laws and those of seven states,[2] the widow's compensation, unlimited in time or aggregate amount, continues until death or remarriage, the children's compensation until a specified age is attained. Compensation in other states runs in terms of so many weeks' payments, or within a limit of three or four years' earnings,[3] and, with exceptions, within specified sums.[4]

Total permanent disability involves greater economic loss than does death, for the disabled workman must be provided for through life. Compensation in such cases should be for life and should not be less than 75 per cent of wages. Indeed, a good case can be made for larger compensation, approaching full wages, for there is no problem of malingery to be avoided. Where unusual outlay is involved because of necessary personal attendance or appliances, supplementary compensation should be provided. The earlier legislation, however, tended strongly to treat total permanent disability in the same manner as death, and to grant so many weeks' wages, within specified maxima. More recently, there has

[1] Much can be said for the payment of a specified sum to the state when there are no dependents. Otherwise there may be discrimination in employment between those with and those without families.

[2] Arizona, Nevada, New York, Oregon, Pennsylvania, Washington, and West Virginia; also District of Columbia. Delaware, Massachusetts, and New Jersey set only an age limit for compensation to the children, but limit the duration or sum of the benefits paid to the widow.

[3] Three years in California, Kansas, New Hampshire; four years in Illinois, South Dakota, Wisconsin.

[4] In twenty states the sums vary, from $3,000 in South Dakota to $15,000 in North Dakota.

been a strong tendency to recognize the greater loss involved in, and the greater need presented by, complete disability. This has found expression in an increasing number of laws which provide for compensation for life. Such is the provision in the laws of seventeen states[1] and under the Federal law for Government employees where compensation for total disability is payable during the continuance of the disability.

It is evident from this review that most of our compensation laws fall considerably short of desirable standards and that an unduly large part of the economic loss involved in industrial injuries rests upon the victims and their dependents.

INSURANCE OF THE RISK

Inasmuch as the risk of industrial injury is inherent in employment, it calls for insurance for the protection of both employer and employee and his dependents. Even in the old days, employers in increasing number insured in casualty companies against the settlements they might have to make under employers' liability laws. Under workmen's compensation this became more necessary because of the larger amount likely to be involved. While more and more generally the risk was insured against voluntarily, the practice of insurance did not become universal. In fact, many employers did not insure, with the result that frequently the compensation provided for was not forthcoming because of the employer's inability to pay. To meet the problem thus presented, most of the laws now require insurance in some form or other—through private insurance (stock or mutual) companies, self-insurance (proof of solvency, with or without the giving of a bond or other security), or by insurance in state funds. Indeed, with improvements in the legislation at this point, only Alabama and Louisiana[2] do not now have this essential feature of a good compensation system.

The requirement of insurance has been accompanied by problems calling for legislative action. Perhaps the carrier needed to be examined to insure solvency. Perhaps there was need for the direct or indirect control of insurance charges as they were increased as workmen's compensation was substituted for employers' liability. At any rate, a considerable amount of direct control of charges has been introduced, while a number of states have established "state funds" to guarantee

---

[1] In Arizona, California, Colorado, Idaho, Illinois, Massachusetts, Missouri, Nebraska, Nevada, New York, Ohio, Oregon, Pennsylvania, Utah, Washington, West Virginia and Wisconsin.

[2] Section 22 of the Louisiana Act provided that a district court might order that a bond be furnished if there was reasonable room for uncertainty as to the financial responsibility of an employer against whom liability for compensation had accrued. This was declared unconstitutional by the Supreme Court of Louisiana as being an executive rather than a judicial function and therefore outside the determination of the court. *In re Southern Cotton Oil Co.*, 86 So. 656 (1920); *Zehner v. Mader*, 97 So. 34 (1923).

fair rates, to improve the administration of benefits, and to reduce the cost to industry.[1]

Seven[2] of the forty-six compensation states have established "exclusive" state funds (i.e., insurance of the risk must be made in them), while eleven[3] others have established "competitive" funds in which the employers may insure as an alternative to insurance in a private company or self-insurance. The greatest struggle connected with American compensation legislation some years ago was over the questions as to whether there should be a state fund, and if so, whether it should be exclusive or competitive. Argument was met by counterargument and charge by countercharge.

On the one side, it has been argued that if the government compels insurance, it should provide a carrier available to all and the insurance at cost of service. It has been pointed out that some firms, with poor experience records, cannot secure insurance from private companies or only at very high premium rates. It has been claimed that under an exclusive fund, with a large business and only nominal acquisition costs, waste is eliminated and the cost very much reduced.[4] Moreover, a public authority then administers the entire system; there is, presumably, a guarantee of fairness, while, with profit-making companies, the injured workman may be granted less than the compensation to which he is entitled. In addition to some of these arguments, it has been said in behalf of a competitive state fund that it gives the needed competition to guarantee fair rates and good service at the hands of the private companies.

The insurance companies, with an interest to protect, and other organizations without such an interest, have opposed state funds on the following grounds, among others: (1) that government should not engage in business to the injury of private concerns; (2) that state funds have not been, and cannot be, well administered; (3) that they "get into politics"; (4) that the private company could and does give better service. As between the exclusive and the competitive fund, they would favor the latter, asserting that competition should be looked to for improvement in service and cost and to show in the long run what type of carrier is best fitted to serve.

---

[1] For a full discussion of security for payment of compensation, see W. F. Dodd, op. cit., pp. 506–616.

[2] Nevada, North Dakota, Ohio, Oregon, Washington, West Virginia, and Wyoming. In some of these states, e.g., Washington, the original concept was that of accident insurance rather than compensation. In other cases the fund was created after compensation had been in effect.

[3] Arizona, California, Colorado, Idaho, Maryland, Michigan, Montana, New York, Oklahoma, Pennsylvania, Utah.

[4] See David McCahan, State Insurance in the United States (1929), for an analysis of the expenses of both competitive and exclusive state funds.

As a theoretical matter, there is a sound case for the state fund, especially of the exclusive type, for it can provide greater security and be more economical. Experience shows, however, that in practice the outcome depends to a great extent on the efficiency and integrity of management. In point of economy, of dispatch, and other matters of moment, the Ohio State fund, efficiently administered, had, for some years, an enviable record.[1] Competitive funds have also served well in California and certain other states. On the other hand, some of the state funds have not been efficiently or economically managed, or intent on giving the best service. The best and also some of the poorest administration of workmen's compensation has been experienced at the hands of state-fund officials and their aids.[2]

ADMINISTRATION OF WORKMEN'S COMPENSATION[3]

However good the standards incorporated in a law, the actual service and compensation depend to a large extent upon the character of the administration. This is true of most laws, and compensation laws are

[1] See the *Actuarial Survey*, Ohio State Insurance Fund, Report to the Governor's Investigating Committee, Workmen's Compensation Law, Nov. 26, 1934, Woodward and Fondiller, Inc., New York; see, also, Ohio Government Survey Committee, *Booklet R7* (1935), The Industrial Commission, Columbus, Ohio.

Among other things, the Commission recommended an increased legislative appropriation in order to enlarge personnel to the point where current problems could be efficiently administered. The Commission reported, "that both the examination and settlement of claims are delayed"; that there were 9,300 claims of various kinds pending, "whereas 1,700 would represent a satisfactory working condition"; that "auditing of payrolls, necessary to enforce compliance with the law, is seriously neglected," the number of unaudited payrolls being 146,000; that an estimated increase in income of $1,500,000 should be realized from employers not complying with the law. (Ohio Government Survey Committee, *op. cit.*, p. 4.)

See, also, the legal and procedural, medical, and insurance recommendations of the Governor's Committee on Workmen's Compensation of Pennsylvania and the three studies made of the Pennsylvania system as contained in the Workmen's Compensation Supplement of the quarterly bulletin of the Department of Labor and Industry, *Labor and Industry*, vol. 21, no. 4 (November, 1934).

[2] See, in addition to W. F. Dodd, *op. cit.*, pp. 533–573, U. S. Bureau of Labor Statistics, *Bulletin 301* (1922), for report of the results of an investigation made in 1920 by the late Carl Hookstadt of state funds and insurance through stock and mutual companies. Hookstadt investigated all seven exclusive and nine competitive funds. He also investigated the administration of compensation in five states in which there were no state funds. The tests applied by him were cost, promptness, adequacy and liberality, and security of the compensation. With the assumption "that each type of insurance has furnished the same kind of service," he found that, "using one figure only, the average expense ratios are as follows: Stock companies, 38 per cent; mutual companies, 20 per cent; competitive State funds, 10.6 per cent; and exclusive State funds, 4 per cent," p. 10. For an excellent discussion of compensation insurance, see E. H. Downey, *Workmen's Compensation* (1924), Chap. 5. This book also contains a good bibliography.

[3] An excellent, detailed discussion of the several phases of this subject is found in W. F. Dodd, *op. cit.*

no exception to the rule. Unless there is an adequate check on settlements made directly by employers or their agents, substandard settlements will frequently occur because most workers and their dependents are ignorant of their rights in such matters. Unless they know that there is readily available opportunity, at the hands of an impartial authority, to secure a settlement in accord with the law, the victims of accidents may take what they can get, or, perhaps worse, employ attorneys as they did under employers' liability and pay in fees a considerable part of what is intended to be theirs without cost. In the absence of good machinery in New Jersey in the early days of compensation, there was frequent and wide departure from legal standards.[1] New Jersey's experience was not exceptional.

Primarily to secure proper administration of their compensation laws, most states have established industrial accident boards or the functions of such a board have been assigned to an industrial commission or other state authority. At present, in contrast to early beginnings, the desirability of an administrative agency charged specifically with the supervision of the compensation laws is recognized by all but six states[2] having such laws. The best of these commissions check on private settlements; all, with the aid of arbitrators, decide disputed cases; they receive, compile, analyze, and report on the statistics of accidents sent in to them. A few of them have shown a real interest in accident prevention. But if the state authority is inefficient or worse—and this is sometimes the case—the objectives of the law are inadequately realized. In recent years in Illinois, for example, there have been many settlements not in accord with law, "adjusters" have been extremely busy, and the whole result has borne as much resemblance to the employers' liability of the past as to what workmen's compensation is presumed to be.

Perhaps better than any other type of case evidencing the importance of careful and efficient administration is that involving partial or full lump-sum settlements.[3] As Professor Dodd has said, "The general theory of compensation laws in the United States has been that the economic interests of the injured employee or of his dependents in case of death are best served by regular payment of compensation over a period of years, in substantially the manner in which wages would have been paid." In a considerable number of cases that do not involve compensation for temporary disability only, it may, however, be in the interest

---

[1] See *American Labor Legislation Review,* vol. 5 (1915), pp. 33–102, for results of investigation of the operation of compensation in New Jersey.

[2] These are Alabama, Louisiana, New Hampshire, New Mexico, Tennessee, and Wyoming. The law in these states is administered by the courts, but the operations of the law or some of its provisions are to a certain extent supervised by the labor or compensation commissioner or other designated officials.

[3] For an excellent summary discussion of lump-sum settlements, see W. F. Dodd, *op. cit.,* pp. 719–736.

of the beneficiary to have a settlement once for all in order to meet obligations or to make a new start as a shopkeeper or in some other way. Moreover, it is not infrequently true that full settlements must be made before the psychology of an injured worker can become such that rehabilitation can be effected. Then, too, there are instances in which, without such settlement, compensation will be jeopardized by the employer leaving the jurisdiction of the state or otherwise. And it may be to the interest of the employer to get his obligations "cleared up." Hence, the workmen's compensation laws make certain provisions for lump settlements, but only with the approval of the industrial commission or accident board or of the court. And, unfortunately, the law has not been well drafted in many of the states. Yet, the problem in connection with lump-sum settlements has been, and is, largely one of too lax and inefficient administration, not the weakness of the law. It has been all too common, as, for example, in New York years ago and in Illinois, especially prior to 1933, for the central authority to approve without investigation or much consideration settlements agreed upon by the beneficiary and the employer or his insurance carrier. When such is the case, a premium is placed upon lawyers, insurance companies, real estate agents, and others with things to sell to become active in arranging settlements and to see to it that necessary requests are brought to the authority whose approval of lump-sum settlements is required. Thus, a memorandum prepared by the Director of the New York Rehabilitation Division said with reference to the experience in the Buffalo district some years ago:

"They had an interesting time because from the enactment of the workmen's compensation law the power of the Industrial Board to commute periodical payments to one or more lump sum payments 'provided the same shall be in the interests of justice' had been a wide open door through which claimants made requests and received their compensation in a lump sum payment, usually without any investigation and upon a superficial knowledge of the character, intelligence and competency of the claimants. Lawyers, runners, pseudo friends and leeches attached themselves to injured workers who were drawing compensation and persuaded them by the thousands to request their money as a lump sum in order that they might get a part of it."[1]

Fortunately, this lax administration in New York ended some years ago. Now requests for lump-sum settlements involving $500 or more are investigated by the Rehabilitation Division—a proper arrangement for rehabilitation is in some sense involved in most such cases. Even this, however, has by no means established the efficacy of payment in terms of lump-sum settlements. In fact, a three-year investigation recently made by the Rehabilitation Division of New York State of some

[1] Quoted, with permission of the publisher, from W. F. Dodd, op. cit., p. 732.

322 cases where recipients received cash settlements of $1,000 or more has revealed serious weaknesses in the lump-sum method of payment.[1]

While improvement in health was claimed to be one of the benefits obtainable under the lump-sum settlement system, the "investigation showed that a year or more after the settlement, two-thirds of the men had not made recoveries . . . slightly less than one-third of the entire group were found to be in better health than at the time of the settlement,"[2] and many of these would have improved regardless of the type of settlement while others improved because of re-employment. Further, it was demonstrated that lump-sum settlement did not serve as a strong incentive to find employment. In fact, in 62 per cent of the cases studied the persons were not employed and many of those who were at work had not sought employment until after their compensation had been spent. In respect to how the cash settlement was spent, it was found that the sums paid seldom lasted for as long a duration as was assumed. In 207, or 65 per cent of the cases, part or all of the money was used to pay debts. In fifty-one cases, the settlements were largely dissipated in injudicious investments, the total losses being $45,000. And the contention that lump-sum payment enables the claimant to rehabilitate himself by using such funds to establish a business, operate a farm, truck garden, or set up other means of support, was largely disproved. "The facts gathered show that only 4 per cent of the entire group of men were successful in rehabilitating themselves by going into business with the use of their compensation money. Three-quarters of the men starting business ventures either were quick failures or were in the process of a lingering business death."[3]

As a consequence of these and other factors, Norcross concluded that "lump-sum settlements do not accomplish the purpose for which they are made. Except for isolated instances, they fall far short of the intended results. Lump sums often result in harm rather than in benefit to the injured workers."[4]

In the great majority of nonscheduled cases, therefore, it appears that installment compensation rather than lump-sum settlement is preferable. The duration of the award in terms of weeks of compensation should be fixed in the aggregate by the referee, acting upon the advice of compensation physicians, rather than follow the present rather general method of leaving the actual bargaining to the insurance company and the claimant or his lawyer. Prompt and early settlements should be effected. Lastly,

[1] Carl Norcross, *Vocational Rehabilitation and Workmen's Compensation* (1936), Rehabilitation Clinic, 28 East 21st Street, New York City. For a summary, see the same author's "Lump-Sum Settlements in Workmen's Compensation in New York," *Monthly Labor Review*, vol. 43, no. 6 (December, 1936), pp. 1364–1369.

[2] Carl Norcross in *Monthly Labor Review*, vol. 43, pp. 1365–1366.

[3] *Ibid.*, p. 1367.

[4] *Ibid.*, p. 1365.

it should be made clear to the claimant that once the award is made, he stands to receive the full amount spread on an installment basis through time "regardless of his health and employment status and that he will not have to remain sick or unemployed to get his money."[1] By procedures such as these, compensation settlements can be more effectively conserved and utilized, and a greater incentive will be provided for the claimant to return to employment as rapidly as possible.

A further matter which calls for comment is the manner in which administrative expenses are met. There are two methods of financing workmen's compensation administration, viz., by legislative appropriation and by self-support either through an assessment on the insurance or by making use of part of the insurance revenue for meeting administrative costs.[2] Reliance upon fluctuating legislative appropriations almost invariably results in deficient administration, as recent studies in Ohio and elsewhere have shown.[3] Administrative planning in respect to an adequate personnel and program becomes a matter dependent largely upon the amount of the appropriation made. As Marshall Dawson of the United States Bureau of Labor Statistics has stated:[4] "There is but one way of assuring progress from deficient to adequate administration, i.e., by changing the method of financing from legislative support to self-support. Such a change at one stroke removes a tax item from the general appropriation list, makes the commission financially autonomous, and helps to remove workmen's compensation administration from the recurring political struggle for the means of survival." Owing to the variations in the various state acts and the different practices and procedures followed, the method of supporting workmen's compensation administration varies considerably. Nevertheless, the experience of those state administrations dependent upon legislative support has been such as to cause the Second National Conference on Labor Legislation

[1] Ibid., p. 1368.

[2] Between 1914 and 1928, the province of Ontario experimented with both methods of support but since then has gone over to a standard of complete self-support. Section 95 of the Workmen's Compensation Act of Ontario reads:

"The board shall in every year assess and levy upon the employer in each of the classes such percentage of pay roll . . . . as it shall deem sufficient to pay the compensation during the current year in respect of injuries to workmen . . . . and to provide and pay the expenses of the board in the administration."

[3] See infra, p. 230.

[4] "Methods of Financing Workmen's Compensation Administrations and Funds," Monthly Labor Review, vol. 42, no. 3 (March, 1936), p. 599. In respect to the effect of the depression in impairing workmen's compensation service, the Bureau reported: "In the year 1935 the outstanding feature of workmen's compensation administration was the impairment of service by deficient support of the administrative agencies. There are other causes of impaired service, but in 23 States visited only one State was found where the support was considered adequate by those responsible for the administration." Ibid., p. 595.

(1935) to recommend that the "cost of administration . . . be defrayed not by legislative appropriation, but by an assessment on insurance [companies] and self-insurers. Administrative cost of State funds to be taken directly out of insurance premiums or income."[1]

ACCIDENT PREVENTION[2]

Obviously it is more important to prevent industrial injuries in so far as the costs of doing so permit than to alleviate their consequences, which is the primary object of compensation and insurance. Economic as well as humane considerations call for prevention above all else. Compensation can be only partial; the injured workers are inevitably sacrificed. Work injuries have costs to industry, also, for accidents increase overhead costs because machinery remains idle while the injured workmen go to the plant dispensary or doctor for medical relief; they necessitate the hiring of new employees, and therefore involve the costs of selection, induction and training, and the lower output of inexperienced workers; they result in a slower pace by workers who have been injured or know of the accidents occurring to their fellow employees; the lowered efficiency of workers and interrupted production increase the amount of spoilage and wastage of materials; work injuries involve the direct cost of treatment and the compensation bill or the insurance premium. And, society in general is interested, because it frequently must share the costs where work injuries reduce or destroy the usual means of support, and because it gains from enlarged production and the elimination of waste.

Beginning in Massachusetts in 1877, much legislation has been enacted in the different states to safeguard against accident in factory, mine, and elsewhere. It may be said, however, that until thirty years ago, the United States was quite backward in accident prevention, especially as compared with countries like Germany where great steps forward had been taken. The "safety-first" movement in this country may be said to have begun in the steel industry about 1907. More recently, especially with the advent of workmen's compensation with more of the loss charged to industry, and with a growing appreciation of the costs to industry other than those taking the form of insurance premiums, the movement has become a strong and effective one. While there is still widespread neglect of, and lack of interest in, the problem, the United States has rapidly come

---

[1] See the Report of the Committee on Workmen's Compensation, National Conference on Labor Legislation, Asheville, N.C., Oct. 4–5, 1935, *Monthly Labor Review*, vol. 41, no. 5 (November, 1935), pp. 1261–1263.

[2] For an excellent treatment of this problem, see H. M. Vernon, *Accidents and Their Prevention* (1937); H. W. Heinrich, *Industrial Accident Prevention* (1931); American Engineering Council, *Safety and Production* (1928); and M. S. Viteles, *Industrial Psychology* (1932), Chaps. 16 to 18.

to the fore in accident prevention.   The National Safety Council, organized in 1912, now has several thousand members, most of them very large employers of labor, and stimulates and guides safety work; other associations, largely on an industry basis, have taken great interest in the subject; the insurance companies, desirous of profiting from reduced compensation outlays, have been very active—stressing "merit rating," and providing engineering service to their clients; management, in more and more instances and in an increasingly large number of industries, has stressed prevention; a number, but, unfortunately, as yet only a minority, of the compensation states have been functioning well through their Industrial or Compensation Commissions, while Federal agencies, such as the Bureau of Mines, have been active in stimulating "safety first."

The causes of industrial injuries are commonly classified into *objective* and *personal*.   Employers' organizations have frequently contended that between 70 and 80 per cent of all industrial accidents are personal and attributable to carelessness of the workers rather than to objective conditions for which the employer is immediately responsible.   Some substantiation has been given this conclusion by experience in plants where the most advanced safety devices have been introduced and "model" conditions established, but the accident rate was reduced by only 14 or 15 per cent.   Labor spokesmen, on the other hand, may assert that an overwhelming share of work injuries is due to management.   The conflicting statements are explained in part by the fact that the classification into objective and personal is not altogether satisfactory.   As has been pointed out earlier in this chapter, seeming carelessness on the part of workmen may be due to long hours, ill-adapted speed at work, and the like.   In any event, it is not very important to try to assess fault.   It is important to recognize the problem presented by work injuries, to face forward, and to try to find ways and means of preventing their recurrence. Prevention involves safeguards of many kinds—railings, closed elevator shafts, covered belts and gears, and all sorts of physical appliances, adequate lighting, proper washing facilities, proper selection of help, proper speed in processes, and the education of the workers in the exercise of care in all matters.

The safety engineer well knows that the establishment of safeguards against accident and industrial disease and the education of the workers in the exercise of care are responsibilities of management, and that the success of the latter is largely dependent upon the intelligence and good faith underlying the former.   Unless the employer does all in his power to make the conditions of employment safe, the workers cannot be expected to give a very sympathetic hearing to safety-first propaganda.   Also, the two phases of prevention are closely interrelated, for frequently the establishment of safeguards is futile unless the workers are instructed regarding their nature and use.

The problem of providing physical and mechanical safeguards is largely a technological and engineering one, the details of which vary from plant to plant and from industry to industry. Each industry has its own hazards, such as the point of operation in machine industries, the falling of materials and scaffolding in building construction, and the falling of coal and roof in coal mining. Safety features should be established as an intrinsic part of the physical layout and operation of the plant in view of what the special hazards may be. Experience has demonstrated, for example, that the great majority of accidents in machine industries occur during ordinary operation as distinguished from such duties as adjusting tools or throwing belts, and that provision for automatic feeding may make many machines practically accident-proof. The exhaust system for machines which emit flying particles is another effective device, now required by law in a number of states.

The channels through which workers may be educated as to the importance and means of avoiding accidents are many. Some firms issue "safety books," giving instruction in nontechnical terms, which all workers are required to carry with them constantly; and the device of unannounced examinations of employees as to the specific rules used in their departments has been an effective means of forcing employees to learn the rules. Safety publicity work may be carried on through the shop committee, mutual-benefit association, or other organization of the employees; and reliance is also placed by many firms upon lectures, motion pictures, posters, bulletin boards, and articles in the plant magazine. The development of a "safety organization" of employees and the stimulation of interdepartmental or individual contests have been still other devices. Of especial importance in the safety movement is the foreman, because of his constant contact with the men on the job, his knowledge of the peculiar characteristics of each workman, and his knowledge of the machines and the peculiar hazards in the type of work carried on in his department. Education of foremen is, therefore, even more important than education of the rank and file of the workers.

The administrative organization for handling safety work varies among plants, and it must be said that some plans have not realized their maximum possibilities simply because insufficient attention has been given to the problem of organization. The drafting and enforcement of safety codes by executives and workers' committees has the advantage of inducing the cooperation of the workers, but some sort of administrative supervision of these committees is necessary.[1] In some plants a

---

[1] For example, Professor Gordon S. Watkins suggests that the following committees may well be set up: an inspection committee, whose duties include the making of periodical inspection of the plant and the studying of accident hazards, lighting, items of maintenance, etc.; a fire committee to make inspection of fire hazards and all fire equipment; a first-aid and sanitation committee, having charge of first-aid work, hospitals, and medical sup-

special office, called that of the "safety supervisor" or "safety engineer," has been created, the official in charge having general oversight of all departmental or plant safety work.

Prevention of industrial injury is a primary responsibility of management, but if management is to accept this responsibility, it must rather generally be stimulated or coerced, and if it is to function efficiently, it must have organized assistance. Hence, the large amount of activity elsewhere than in the plant, where prevention is actually effected.

The insurance companies play a large role in the prevention of accidents. They participate in meetings where the subject is considered; some of them have carried on an educational campaign with lectures and slides; they make surveys and provide their clients with expert engineering service. Of most importance, perhaps, has been the introduction and spread of "merit rating" in fixing premiums for the insurance provided. Merit rating varies the premium from that established by "manual" rating, in which the industries are classified according to risk involved and rates made for each industry accordingly. Merit rating may take the form of (a) schedule or (b) experience rating. Under schedule rating, the individual firms in an industry are given credits or debits according as their physical, mechanical, and other conditions are favorable or unfavorable. Experience rating is based upon the actual accident experience of the plant. Under both schedule and experience rating the better firms secure lower premiums than do their competitors and thus save something on the cost of compensation.

If there is to be really effective prevention, there must be investigation and constructive work. These call for organized effort at the hands of associations of employers and at the hands of government bureaus and commissions. For an intelligent attack, good accident statistics must be collected, showing numbers involved, causes, and result. In a sense, here is the beginning of the attack upon the problem. Unfortunately, requirements for reporting accidents are not uniform among the states, frequently undesirable forms for recording and reporting accidents are used, and very frequently no adequate provision is made for carefully analyzing and measuring the special problems which call for attack. Good uniform accident reporting is an essential in accident prevention.

When the special problems have been located and analyzed by industry, trade, appliance, and condition, ways and means are to be devised. Then these are to be reduced to codes and "sold" to employers or their adoption made mandatory upon them.

There has been a great deal of code-making by industrial associations and under the National Safety Council. The American Engineering

plies; a publicity committee, which has charge of the bulletin boards, instructs men about the plant, and plans the monthly meeting on safety; and an accident investigation committee, which makes an investigation of all serious accidents and reports on the causes and on methods of prevention. *Labor Management* (1928), pp. 501–502.

Standards Committee has for some years been working out national codes through widely representative committees, with much success. In 1926, it was reported that "intensive work on a group of some forty national safety codes has been actively under way for the last six years. Of these, fourteen have been completed and issued and are now in use by industry and by state regulatory bodies."[1]

After all, voluntary effort, guidance, and stimulation of prevention, while tremendously helpful, are not sufficient. Government authority must find place.

Passing reference has been made to legislation relating to safeguarding against accident in factory, mine, and railway operation. Legislation was necessary, but it came tardily and spasmodically. Some of it was good, but, in the absence of investigation and accurate knowledge on the part of legislators of the problem or of ways and means, most of it was poorly conceived. Moreover, in a changing situation, the best of it likely soon become ill-adapted. In any event, effective inspection and enforcement were not usually provided for. This once general condition with reference to legislation, inspection, and enforcement still obtains in a great majority of the states, but a few of them, including some of those industrially most important, have done things of the greatest merit. The accident-prevention work under the Industrial and Compensation Commissions or Labor Departments of Massachusetts, New York, New Jersey, Pennsylvania, Ohio, Wisconsin, and California merits high praise.

An account of the methods and accomplishments of these seven leading states may be easily found elsewhere;[2] hence a general summary statement of the matter will suffice. Accident reports received are statistically analyzed and the problems thus located are carefully studied. Ways and means are tentatively devised. Conferences are then called for one trade or industry, with representation of management, workers, and experts. A code is evolved. Public hearings are then held at which suggestions or objections may be made. If required, revision of the proposed code or rule is made and a mandatory order issued under the authority conferred to formulate and promulgate such orders as are deemed necessary for the protection of the life, health, and safety of employees. When an order is placed in effect, investigation continues, and revisions of the code are made as they become necessary. Thus the regulation is made practicable and kept reasonably well up to date.[3]

---

[1] Quoted, with permission, from *Annals of the American Academy of Political and Social Science*, vol. 123 (1926), p. 51, where P. G. Agner, Secretary of the American Engineering Standards Committee, describes his organization and its work and lists the codes completed.

[2] Most conveniently in a series of papers published in *Annals of the American Academy of Political and Social Science*, vol. 123 (1926), pp. 55–85.

[3] For a description and appreciation of this method, see John R. Commons, *Labor and Administration* (1913), Chap. 22. The method was really one of Professor Commons' many inventions, made when a member of the Wisconsin Industrial Commission.

The enforcement of codes promulgated in such states as Wisconsin is rendered much easier because the employers and workers have had a hand in their formulation and because the codes are practicable. Moreover, steps are taken to educate all parties concerned. In Wisconsin a safety magazine has been distributed monthly; in California lecturers have been sent out with slides, and a safety museum, showing how accidents may be prevented, has been maintained.

All of this is helpful in arousing interest, begetting the right attitude, and in encouraging steps in advance of the law to be taken. The inspection service is also a marked improvement over the old. Still speaking generally rather than in the precise terms called for by the method pursued in any one state, qualified inspectors are employed. When nonobservance is found, helpful suggestions are made and time is given for necessary changes to be introduced. It is only when a firm does not cooperate by making needed changes that the power to prosecute is applied in order to secure observance. And, it may be noted in conclusion, in Wisconsin the compensation act was amended in 1925 to increase the cash benefit 10 per cent where an injury is sustained because of nonobservance of law or order by the employer, and to reduce it by the same percentage where injury is sustained by nonobservance by the worker.

When the attack is made scientifically, cooperatively, and earnestly, experience shows that prevention can avoid at least half of the loss due to industrial injuries. Astounding results have been realized in many plants and in a large number of industries. The frequency rate (per million hours' exposure) for engineers, firemen, conductors, brakemen, and baggagemen in yard, freight, and passenger service on Class I railroads fell from 48.94 in 1916 to 25.30 twelve years later.[1] The record of steel has perhaps been most striking. The frequency rates (per million hours' exposure), as reported for 1910 and 1924, were, by divisions, as follows: blast furnace, 622.5 and 142.5; Bessemer converters, 837.0 and 121.5; open-hearth furnaces, 630.0 and 214.2; foundries, 737.0 and 484.8; heavy rolling mills, 471.0 and 158.6; plate mills, 726.0 and 163.2; sheet mills, 341.0 and 117.1; tube mills, 762.0 and 79.1. The severity rates[2] were only less strikingly reduced: blast furnace, 68.2 and 47.07; Bessemer converters, 103.0 and 14.27; open-hearth furnaces, 50.0 and 33.12; foundries, 12.0 and 11.32; heavy rolling mills, 43.0 and 19.79; plate mills,

[1] U. S. Bureau of Labor Statistics, *Bulletin 490* (1929), "Statistics of Industrial Accidents in the United States to the End of 1927," pp. 174–176. For a good collection of data drawn from different employments, see pp. 158–187 of that bulletin.

[2] *Ibid.*, pp. 147–152. The "frequency rate" is derived by dividing the number of accidents by the number of man-hours. It makes no distinction between the more and the less severe accidents. The "severity rate" does this. It is determined by dividing the number of days lost by the number of man-hours' exposure and expressing the result in terms of 10,000 hours' exposure.

61.0 and 17.63; sheet mills, 47.0 and 11.72; tube mills, 28.0 and 11.04. Corresponding results may be taken from the records of hundreds of firms intent upon preventing accidents. They are not to be found elsewhere. Indeed, as already stated, the waste of life and limb and working time tends to increase with the increasing mechanization of industry and with machinery driven at higher speed.

That accident prevention with even large outlays pays the workmen and society there can, of course, be no question. That industrial injuries give rise to a variety of costs has been indicated. Though many employers have not been converted to the doctrine that safety pays, the savings effected may yield a handsome profit on the outlays involved in a safety program. The American Car and Foundry Company spent $1,000,000 for prevention over a period of fourteen years, and saved $2,700,000. In ten years, United States Steel spent $9,763,063 and made $14,609,920.[1]

But, of course, it is not to be concluded that prevention to the point of elimination would pay. Elimination would come only with suspension of industry due to prohibitive cost. But experience shows that in a country with a higher accident rate than commonly found elsewhere, there is much room for the reduction of this form of waste, with profit.[2] And, there is sound reason for reduction beyond the point where it is a source of profit to employers.

REHABILITATION OF CIVILIANS

The first object of workmen's compensation has been to pay for damage done, rather than to restore the worker to self-supporting independence. However, if adequate provision is to be made for those who are industrially handicapped, restoration to self-supporting independence must be made readily possible. That is the object of "rehabilitation,"

[1] See series of papers on safety in specific industries in *Annals of the American Academy of Political and Social Science*, vol. 123, pp. 86–147. The above examples are taken from the article, "Does Accident Prevention Pay?" by G. A. Orth, in that volume, p. 21.

[2] The Third National Conference on Labor Legislation on November 9, 10, and 11, 1936, made the following recommendations with respect to industrial accidents and safety: (1) That special studies of health hazards be made by the state labor departments assisted by the U. S. Department of Labor; (2) That state laws and procedure be strengthened with respect to safety and other codes for the protection of wage earners; (3) That a safety laboratory be established by the U. S. Department of Labor and made available to the states through travelling exhibits; (4) That state labor departments develop adequate safety education programmes in cooperation with employers and employees; (5) That there be obligatory reporting of industrial injuries and diseases to the state agency charged with the enforcement of labor laws; (6) That casualty companies be required to file with the labor department copies of inspection reports as to health and safety hazards, including elevators, boilers, and factory equipment conditions.

For the complete list of recommendations and other information, see Ethel M. Johnson, "Industrial Accident Prevention Work in the United States," *Industrial Safety Survey*, vol. 12, no. 6 (November-December, 1936), International Labour Office, pp. 153–162.

which began to find place in American thinking about the beginning of the Great War but did not result in legislation until a few years later.

It has been pointed out that each year tens of thousands of American wage earners sustain injuries in employment which permanently handicap them. The toll of nonindustrial or "public" accident is even larger. Moreover, there are other persons handicapped (cripples, etc.) as a result of disease or congenital defect. Some are beyond repair, but it is probable that each year accident and disease add between 50,000 and 60,000 persons of working age who need assistance to restore or fit themselves for earning the living which most of them formerly earned.[1]

A real interest in rehabilitation came with the War; the supply of man power became short, new ideals found place, and the physical restoration and re-training of men under the colors pointed the way to what could be done in the case of the undermined and handicapped civilian. In 1920, following upon the enactment of a Federal law relating to the rehabilitation of veterans passed in 1918, a measure was enacted providing for the rehabilitation of civilians.[2] Meanwhile, however, no fewer than ten of the states had legislated on the subject, and before the Federal Act became effective more or less active work had begun in eight of these.

The Federal Act provided for "the promotion of vocational rehabilitation of persons disabled in industry or otherwise and their return to civil employment." As stated by the Board of Vocational Education,[3] charged with supervision of operations under the law, "any person is eligible to receive the benefits of vocational rehabilitation under the Act, who, by reason of a physical defect or infirmity, whether congenital or acquired by accident, injury, or disease, is or may be expected to be

[1] *The 13th Annual Report* (1929), Federal Board for Vocational Education, contains these estimates for the year 1928 (p. 47):

Permanently disabled by industrial accident	135,000
Permanently disabled by public accident	144,000
Permanently disabled by disease	36,000
Disability due to congenital causes	8,000
Total	323,000

It was estimated that one in every five or six of the above calls for rehabilitation. Earlier studies (before 1934) found the *number of disabled* persons in selected cities, communities, or states to be about *six per thousand population*. Surveys conducted during the fiscal year 1934, however, show the number to be much greater. "In the State of Mississippi, for example, which was completely covered by a house to house canvass, a recent survey found the number to be *30 per thousand population*. On the basis of these more recent surveys the number of the permanently disabled persons may be conservatively estimated to range from 15 to 20 per thousand population." *Annual Report of the Secretary of the Interior* (fiscal year 1934), pp. 292–293.

[2] Public no. 236, 66th Congress, Second Session, Chap. 219, June 2, 1920.

[3] Until 1933, this Board was under the chairmanship of the Secretary of Labor. It was then transferred to the Department of the Interior and a few months later its functions were assigned to the Commissioner of Education.

totally or partially incapacitated for remunerative employment in industry, or in a legitimate occupation, and who may reasonably be expected to be fitted to engage in a remunerative occupation after completing a rehabilitation course." Money appropriated for use in this connection was to be allotted to the states in proportion to population, with a minimum of $5,000 in any case, an allotment being conditional upon acceptance by the legislature of the state, a matching of the money dollar for dollar, and the presentation each year of a program of work approved by the Federal Board. Continuation of an allotment was made conditional upon acceptable work being done; any money spent out of the matched sum for purposes other than those within the scope of the Act (*e.g.*, equipment, buildings, and maintenance of persons being rehabilitated) was to be charged to and deducted from the next allotment. Except for the initial year, the annual Federal appropriation for rehabilitation under the Act was $1,000,000. Under the Act of 1924,[1] effective to June, 1930, the appropriations were in the same sum. Through further legislation enacted in 1930 and 1932, the same amount was made available to 1937. When matched and additional funds provided for items outside of the Federal Act, the total in recent years has been between two and three millions annually.[2] It is important to note that the appropriations have now been made permanent under the Social Security Act.[3]

An increasing number of the states have qualified for this Federal aid. By 1921 the number was thirty; by 1923, thirty-six; by 1928, forty-one. By 1930, the District of Columbia, Connecticut, Maryland, and Texas had also qualified and the necessary appropriations had been made. At the beginning of 1934, the state of Washington initiated its rehabilitation program, bringing the number of cooperating states under the national program to forty-five.[4] However, the cooperation on the part of many

[1] Public no. 200, 68th Congress, First Session, Chap. 265, June 5, 1924.

[2] The total available in 1936 was $3,213,538.07, of which $1,442,219.32 was of Federal funds, $1,771,318.75 of local funds. The Federal funds included the $841,000 provided for that year under the Social Security Act. Amounts expended in this year were less than the total available by over $600,000, since the Social Security Act was not passed early enough in the year to allow for sufficiently increased numbers to be put into training. Total expenditures were $2,602,676.70, of which $1,244,576.24 was from Federal funds and $1,358,100.46 was from state and local funds. Over half the excess of state over Federal expenditures is accounted for by New York's expenditures for maintenance during rehabilitation, coming from the funds made available for that purpose. Most of the states have appropriated little in excess of Federal funds allotted, a number the same amount, and some even less. See Tables 24 and 25 in *Digest of Annual Reports of State Boards for Vocational Guidance to the Office of Education*, 1936, United States Department of the Interior.

[3] Section 531.

[4] During 1936–1937, Kansas and Vermont passed legislation providing for cooperation. The Vermont program is to start July 1, 1938, the Kansas program when its legislature appropriates funds for it. This leaves only Delaware not cooperating.

of the states has been limited by their failure to provide sufficient appropriations as contemplated by the national program.   At the close of 1935, of the forty-five states cooperating in rehabilitation, seventeen had more than matched the available Federal aid,[1] seven had fully matched it,[2] while twenty-one states had only partially matched such Federal grants.[3] It seems evident that these states only partially matching the Federal appropriations have failed to avail themselves fully of the advantages under the plan of Federal-state cooperation in meeting the admitted rehabilitation needs.   Insufficient appropriations may have the following effects:[4] (1) the personnel of the rehabilitation agency may be undermanned and the facilities for rehabilitation inadequate; (2) a limitation on the effectiveness of the rehabilitation agency in taking care of cases referred to it by the workmen's compensation commission, such as investigation and study of those listed for lump-sum settlements, etc.; (3) the rehabilitation agency is prevented from dealing properly with those industrial injury cases where difficulties of vocational restoration are involved whether due to the nature of the injury, old age, lack of education of the worker, or in those cases where the worker has a family dependent upon him and the meagerness of his compensation makes him loath to accept the offer of rehabilitation if he has to go elsewhere for it; (4) a limitation of the scope of the program.   Not all of the candidates for rehabilitation by the workmen's compensation commission can be accommodated and preference will probably be given to the younger and more easily rehabilitated cases, while the more pressing but expensive cases, particularly of older workers, may be slighted.   The inadequacy of the funds tends to make impossible a satisfactory study of job opportunities and placements for the rehabilitated.   In fact, during 1935 the three Federal surveys and studies of state rehabilitation programs made for the purpose of rendering more effective service to the handicapped were in Iowa, Georgia, and Illinois, states whose appropriations more than exceeded the Federal grants.[5]

Though the opportunities for rehabilitation have been open to those crippled by disease or nonindustrial accidents, as well as to those injured in employment, a majority of those actually selected for rehabilitation in

[1] California, Georgia, Illinois, Indiana, Iowa, Kentucky, Maine, Michigan, Minnesota, Mississippi, Nebraska, New Jersey, North Carolina, Oklahoma, Tennessee, Virginia, and Wisconsin.

[2] Florida, Idaho, Louisiana, Ohio, North Dakota, West Virginia, and New York.

[3] Alabama, Arizona, Arkansas, Colorado, Connecticut, Maryland, Massachusetts, Missouri, Montana, Nevada, New Hampshire, New Mexico, Oregon, Pennsylvania, Rhode Island, South Carolina, South Dakota, Texas, Utah, Washington, and Wyoming.

[4] See Marshall Dawson, "Cooperation of Workmen's Compensation Administrations with Rehabilitation Agencies," *Monthly Labor Review*, vol. 42, no. 2 (February, 1936), pp. 300–311.

[5] *Annual Report of the Secretary of the Interior*, 1935, p. 318.

THE PROBLEM OF WORK INJURIES 231

the earlier years were industrial cripples, and it is only very recently that such persons have become a slight minority.[1] This is explained largely as a result of the close cooperation of the state vocational boards and the compensation commissions and of the fact that the cost of maintenance has been met in the main out of the compensation benefits and supplements thereto. A disproportionate number of the registrants are still industrial cripples. Many who are suitable subjects for rehabilitation do not avail themselves of the service, partly because the program has not been fully enough developed[2] and made known in many localities, partly because of the delay in reaching the injured cases—either through failure or reluctance of injured workers to come forward for aid,[3] partly also because of inability to finance themselves. No part of the sum resulting from matching Federal allotments may be used for maintenance, and only a minority of the states provide allowances for this purpose.[4] Naturally, the number of registrants has been a fraction of those who would profit from rehabilitation and the number rehabilitated, of course, still smaller. The total number rehabilitated during the period 1921–1936 was 87,411. As shown by the reports of the forty-five states, 10,338 had been vocationally rehabilitated and 44,625 were in the process of rehabilitation during 1936 (see Table 25).

As the term "rehabilitation" is employed, it includes placement in a job (alone or in conjunction with other things); physical restoration;

---

[1] The number injured outside of industry has been increasing. By 1935–1936, slightly less than one-half of those rehabilitated were recipients of workmen's compensation. See "Vocational Rehabilitation of the Physically Handicapped," U. S. Office of Education, *Vocational Education Bulletin 190*, Rehabilitation Series, no. 25 (1936), pp. 23–24.

[2] For a discussion of how the Social Security Act provides for the extension and strengthening of programs for the vocational rehabilitation of the physically disabled, see *infra*, pp. 233–234.

[3] This can be corrected through a more prompt reporting and coordination with the compensation commission as well as through a publicizing among the workers of the functions and benefits obtainable from the rehabilitation service. See "Organization and Administration of a State Program of Vocational Rehabilitation," U. S. Office of Education, *Vocational Education Bulletin 161*, Rehabilitation Series, no. 21 (revised, 1935), pp. 5–19.

[4] The total amount expended from Federal and state funds for vocational rehabilitation for the year ended June 30, 1929, was $1,490,122.37. The amount spent on maintenance was $100,868.04 by 14 states. The states expending more than $5,000 for maintenance were:

New York	$52,135.98
Oregon	13,939.41
North Carolina	12,873.38
Montana	6,998.50
Wisconsin	5,303.98

13th Annual Report (1929), Federal Board for Vocational Education, pp. 92, 95–96. During the year ending June 30, 1932, of the 5,550 persons rehabilitated outside of the District of Columbia, only 524, or less than 10 per cent, were provided with maintenance. See *16th Annual Report* (1932), Federal Board for Vocational Education, p. 106.

TABLE 25.—NUMBER REHABILITATED AND AMOUNTS EXPENDED FOR VOCATIONAL
REHABILITATION, 1921 TO 1936[1]

Year	No. of rehabilitated	No. in process of rehabilitation	Total expenditures	Federal funds	State funds
1921	457	1,682			
1922	1,890	8,147	$ 736,268	$ 312,463	$ 423,804
1923	4,530	11,267	1,188,081	525,281	662,800
1924	5,594	13,044	1,242,588	551,096	691,463
1925	5,852	12,542	1,187,219	519,553	667,666
1926	5,604	13,604	1,273,572	578,940	694,631
1927	5,092	16,148	1,406,757	631,376	775,381
1928	5,012	16,393	1,541,121	653,858	887,263
1929	4,645	16,787	1,490,180	664,739	825,441
1930	4,612	20,298	1,690,344	734,690	955,654
1931	5,138	23,714	2,042,710	932,718	1,109,992
1932	5,550	27,403	2,189,140	997,811	1,191,329
1933	5,613	30,619	2,176,126	999,549	1,176,577
1934	8,062	37,681	2,079,905	915,659	1,164,246
1935	9.422	40,941	2,247,948	1,031,818	1,216,129
1936	10,338	44,625	2,602,677	1,244,576	1,358,100

[1] *Digest of Annual Reports of State Boards for Vocational Education*, Office of Education, Vocational Division, 1935, pp. 9 *et seq.; ibid.*, 1936, Table 25; and *Annual Report of the Secretary of the Interior*, 1937, p. 293.

provision of artificial parts and other mechanical appliances; and training, which may be in employment, in an educational institution, by correspondence course, or by tutor. In some cases, rehabilitation, though a statistical fact, means little; in others, a very great deal. To refer an undermined man to an employment office or to provide an artificial leg is one thing—a little guidance or a little money suffices; to educate a crippled man with good ability but limited previous education to be a bookkeeper, a milk inspector, or a layout man in a factory means much more. At all times, and especially in certain states, a very large percentage of the rehabilitations have involved placement only, as against training or physical restoration. In 1935–1936, for example, out of a total of 10,338, 4,151 were rehabilitated through institutional training, 1,288 through employment training, and 494 through other training.[1]

The trends in rehabilitation work have been in the right direction. It remains to extend the system, to make more extensive provision for maintenance through revision of the compensation laws or otherwise, and to bring the standard of performance of many of the states, where it is still poor, up to the standards realized where the work is done best. When cases are well selected and efficient work done, rehabilitation pays. In 1927 the Federal Board made a survey of work accomplished. The 6,391 cases studied had been rehabilitated, with the result that all except

[1] See Table 22 in *Digest of Annual Reports of State Boards for Vocational Education to the Office of Education*, 1936.

a small minority were earning as high wages as they had earned before disability was incurred, and in a considerable number of cases they had been able to advance occupationally and were earning much more. The restoration and increase of earnings greatly exceeded the costs, which in 76 per cent of the cases were reported as having been less than $150.[1] Bowers has estimated, on the basis of 350 rehabilitated cases in Ohio, that "the cost of rehabilitation to the governments concerned was only a little more than 2 per cent of the probable increased earning power during the life of the rehabilitant."[2] It is probable that the average cost of rehabilitating a disabled person, including the expenditures from both Federal and state funds, does not exceed $300.[3] From an economic point of view the significance of such a program of vocational rehabilitation is evident when it is realized that this comparatively small and nonrecurrent investment enables a disabled person to become self-supporting, whereas the cost to society of maintaining such a person is a recurrent burden amounting perhaps to $300 to $500 per year throughout life.[4]

The further development of the rehabilitation service is fostered by the Social Security Act in two important respects, viz., by extension of cooperative relations between this service and other agencies dealing with the disabled and functioning in allied fields, and by additional Federal appropriations for the expansion of rehabilitation.

Under the operation of the Social Security Act the need for cooperation and reciprocal relations with those agencies handling unemployment insurance, pensions, service to crippled children and the blind, and public-health activities, will be considerably increased.   Moreover, Federal aid will become increasingly important in the rehabilitation program.   During the past few emergency years, the increased needs falling upon the rehabilitation service have in part been met through emergency appropriations, the additional amount available under the Federal Emergency Relief Administration during 1935 being approximately $840,000 for aiding the enlarged state rehabilitation programs. The vocational rehabilitation section[5] of the Social Security Act made this additional amount available for 1936 and 1937; the total annual appropriation thereafter was to be $1,938,000. These funds, when apportioned to the states on a matched basis, may, however, serve to restrict the effectiveness and development of state rehabilitation programs to those states willing and financially able to provide such funds and to leave those

[1] For details, see "A Study of Rehabilitated Persons," Federal Board for Vocational Education, Bulletin 132 (1928). For results of a later survey of this particular group, see Vocational Education Bulletin 190, pp. 27–30.

[2] Quoted with the permission of Houghton Mifflin Company from E. L. Bowers, Is It Safe to Work? (1930), p. 124.

[3] For average costs, 1922–1934, see Vocational Education Bulletin 190, p. 27.

[4] 16th Annual Report (1932), Federal Board for Vocational Education, p. 54.

[5] Public no. 271, 74th Congress, pt. 4, Sec. 531a.

communities whose appropriations are deficient without sufficient funds despite the fact that the need for rehabilitation may there be greatest. It is, however, encouraging to note that in states whose legislatures met during the fiscal year 1935, no state appropriations for rehabilitation were reduced, a few were maintained at their previous level, while in the majority of states increased funds were provided. At that time the states were in a position to absorb approximately $1,500,000 of Federal aid for vocational rehabilitation. With the passage by the states of social-security legislation, it was estimated that the cooperating states would be able to absorb an additional million dollars in Federal appropriations by 1938.[1] It seems clear, therefore, that with the needs of rehabilitation by no means adequately met today, the future development of the rehabilitation service will be increasingly a Federal responsibility.

With the provision of old-age and unemployment insurance under the Social Security Act, there may be danger that workmen's compensation will be slighted by neglecting needed improvements in content and administration which ought to be made. As Dodd points out, it is desirable that compensation plans and other forms of social insurance be kept separate both as to administration and basis of actuarial cost. "The charge to industry of the cost of workmen's compensation should not be united with other types of social insurance. Workmen's compensation should be an obligation of industry; other types of social insurance, if undertaken, should be an obligation of society, of which industry is but a part."[2]

[1] *Annual Report of the Secretary of the Interior*, 1935, pp. 328-329.
[2] W. F. Dodd, *op. cit.*, p. 829.

CHAPTER V

THE PROBLEM OF SICKNESS AND NONINDUSTRIAL ACCIDENT AMONG WAGE EARNERS

THE PROBLEM

Sickness and nonindustrial accidents constitute a problem extending beyond the field of "labor problems," as this term ordinarily is used, but their industrial and labor implications are so important that due emphasis must be placed upon them in a general labor treatise. The welfare of the workers is tremendously affected by these risks; in the aggregate, indeed, the problem presented by sicknesss and by disability and premature death due to natural causes or to nonindustrial accident is much larger than the one occasioned by work accidents and occupational diseases, as discussed in the preceding chapter. A larger number of workers are affected each year; more poverty and want are engendered; to a greater extent the standard of living and the development and efficiency of dependents are undermined. The various institutions, including compulsory sickness insurance, that have been established for dealing with the problem are in themselves evidence of its importance as a determinant of the worker's welfare.

Though morbidity statistics in the United States are even less satisfactory than our accident statistics, several surveys have been made by official and unofficial organizations which give us fairly reliable samples with which to work. One of the more recent of these, that of the Committee on the Costs of Medical Care,[1] resulted in an estimate that on any average day in the year 2 per cent of the working population are disabled

---

[1] Alden B. Mills, *Extent of Illness and of Physical and Mental Defects Prevailing in the United States.* (Publications of the Committee on the Costs of Medical Care, no. 2, 1929.)

While proof for this volume was being read, the reports of The National Health Survey, 1935–1936 were appearing in mimeographed form. The Survey was conducted by the United States Public Health Service. Covering some 800,000 families, with 2,800,000 persons, living in 84 cities and 23 rural areas in nineteen states, it was the most extensive survey of sickness thus far made. The canvass appears to have been made with care. While the results do not check at every point with those set forth in the text, they strongly confirm our statement of the problems presented by sickness. Had the canvass of families not been made between October and March or at a time of depression, perhaps there would have been a closer correspondence between the results obtained from it and from the canvasses and records used by us in preparing the text. As a matter of convenience we present, as they are in point, some of the more important results of the Survey in footnotes,

by illness of some type.[1]   On the average, seven to nine days per year are lost by male workers, and between eight and twelve by females.   The Committee estimated that in the prosperous years 1928–1930 the annual wage loss approached $1,000,000,000 a year.[2]   Partially disabling sickness, accident, physical defect, and premature death, the losses from which are exceedingly difficult to estimate, would add greatly to this total.[3]

Then, too, the medical bills, not only of the wage earner himself, but of his dependents, add to the strain imposed upon the budget.   In 1929 the Metropolitan Life Insurance Company found from a sample of 3,281 families among their industrial policy holders that the average annual medical bill per wage-earning family was $140.   One must conclude from other evidence, however, that this finding exaggerated the outlays for all families, and for wage-earning families in particular.   The sample used was predominantly of families in large urban communities and the data were for the six months from January to June, when there is more morbidity than during the summer and autumn months.   In any event, a survey of 8,199 families of the field employees of the Metropolitan, covering a full year ending in October, 1931, showed an average outlay of $104.20 per family.[4]   Moreover, the Committee on the Costs of Medical Care, in a survey of 8,581 families living in many communities and representing the several economic groups, found the average outlay to be approximately $30 per person and $108 per family.[5]   Without question the outlays of wage-earning families would be somewhat less, for, as a group, they have less ability to pay than other economic groups and more frequently forego needed medical care.[6]

[1] The National Health Survey found that 4.5 per cent of more than 2,300,000 persons, wage earners and others, canvassed in urban areas were disabled by illness or accident at the time of the visit at the house.   The percentages were largest for those age sixty-five and over, and relatively large for those under age fifteen.   The percentage for those between fifteen and twenty-four was 2.5, for those between twenty-five and sixty-four, 4.4.   (*The National Health Survey: 1935–1936*.   Preliminary Reports, Sickness and Medical Care Series, Bulletin 1, J-1305, p. 2.)

[2] Michael Davis, "The American Approach to Health Insurance," *The Milbank Memorial Fund Quarterly*, vol. 12, no. 3 (July, 1934).

[3] The cost of tuberculosis alone in the United States has been estimated at $1,500,000,000 a year.

[4] D. B. Armstrong, L. I. Dublin, and E. J. Steele, *The Cost of Medical Care* (1934), p. 11.

[5] I. S. Falk, M. C. Klem, and N. Sinai, *The Incidence of Illness and the Receipt and Costs of Medical Care Among Representative Families* (Publications of the Committee on the Costs of Medical Care, no. 26, 1933), pp. 209–210.

[6] The larger the income the greater is the amount spent on medical care, and not merely because of the application of the sliding scale more or less observed by physicians. It has been found that families with incomes of $10,000 or more spend four times as much for medical care as those having incomes of $1,200 to $2,000, although the percentage of annual income spent for medical care is smaller for the high income group than for the

The Committee on the Costs of Medical Care has estimated the total of medical outlays in the United States at approximately $3,600,000,000 per year.[1] This is about 4 per cent of the normal national income. A part (about 14 per cent) of this enormous sum represents public expenditures out of government revenues. While philanthropy and industry, respectively, absorbed 5 and 2 per cent of the total, the major share (79 per cent) was paid by the "patients." What fraction of the total represents medical bills paid by wage-earning families is difficult to say, but rough approximations may be made. The Committee on Economic Security accepted a figure of $900,000,000 lost income by persons with

latter. Moreover, the strain and medical neglect, or medical charity, among families with relatively small incomes per person is shown by the findings of Metropolitan studies. "Both surveys have disclosed a little known fact, namely, that size of family does not affect the average expenditure per family for medical care. This, of course, means simply that as the number of members in most families increases the expenditure per person decreases. For all incomes combined the average per capita expenditure for families with no children was $47.01, as compared with $13.44 in families of six or more children" (see D. B. Armstrong, L. I. Dublin, and E. J. Steele, *op. cit.*, p. 12).

[1] According to I. S. Falk, formerly associate director of study of the Committee, the expenditures were distributed as follows ["Fundamental Facts on the Costs of Medical Care," reprinted from the *Milbank Memorial Fund Quarterly Bulletin*, vol. 11, no. 2 (April, 1933)]:

TOTAL EXPENDITURES[a] FOR MEDICAL CARE IN THE UNITED STATES[b]

Service	Total	Sources of funds				Per capita (1929)
		Patients	Governments	Philanthropy	Industry	
Total..................................	$3,656	$2,886	$510	$182	$79	$30.08
Physicians in private practice[c]..................	1,090[d]	1,040[d]	....	....	50	8.97
Dentists in private practice[c]....................	445[d]	445[d]	....	....	....	3.66
Secondary and sectarian practitioners............	193	193	....	....	....	1.59
Graduate nurses, private duty....................	142	142	....	....	....	1.17
Practical nurses, private duty....................	70	60	....	....	....	0.49
Hospitals:						
Operating expenses........................	656	278	300	54	24	5.40
New construction.........................	200	......	100	100	....	1.64
Public health..................................	121	......	94	28	....	1.00
Private laboratories[e]...........................	3	3	....	....	....	0.02
Orthopedic and other supplies[e].................	2	2	....	....	....	0.02
Glasses[e]......................................	50	50	....	....	....	0.41
Drugs[e].......................................	665	665	....	....	....	5.47
Organized medical services[f]....................	29	8	16	[g]	5	0.24

[a] All figures in millions of dollars. Discrepancies which appear in this table are due to the use of round numbers.

[b] With a few minor and unimportant exceptions, the data apply to the year 1929. They are probably representative of any normal year in recent times.

[c] Physicians and dentists holding part-time salaried positions are included with private practitioners. Expenditures for the services of those employed in hospitals, clinics, public-health departments, and organized medical services are included under total expenditures for the respective agencies.

[d] These totals include payments by government and philanthropic agencies to private practitioners for services to indigent persons.

[e] Not included in other items.

[f] University, industrial, and Army and Navy medical services, exclusive of hospital care.

[g] $210,000.

incomes less than $2,500. The medical bills were estimated at $1,500,-000,000, a total of $2,400,000,000. Inasmuch as the great mass of receivers of incomes under $2,500 are wage earners, the total for lost wages and medical bills may be estimated roughly at $2,000,000,000 per year.[1]

Not only does illness involve this large direct cost to the wage earner in loss of income and in medical expenses, but it also adds to the employers' costs through unbalanced sections which require substitutions of men on the job, and through increased labor turnover.[2] The reduction of output becomes more severe in highly integrated industries, where, for example, the absence of a key man may disrupt a whole assembly line.

One of the most valuable studies of the extent of sickness is that made by the Illinois State Health Insurance Commission in 1919.[3] An examination of the experience of mutual benefit associations with 663,163 wage-earning members showed that 19.9 per cent of them were compensated in the course of a year for disabilities lasting a week or more, with an average of 27.4 days of disability per case.[4] In terms of loss of wages, the data indicated that of the entire group 8.8 per cent lost 10 per cent or more, and that 4.8 per cent lost 20 per cent or more of what their earnings would have been in the absence of disabling sickness.[5]

In an effort to get an accurate and representative sample of the working population, the Illinois Commission investigated 3,048 families with 12,450 members living in forty-one blocks in Chicago. These blocks were occupied chiefly by wage earners and were selected to give a typical cross section of the city. The number of wage-earning families was 2,708. It was found that during the immediately preceding twelve months, 66.5 per cent of these families had had one or more cases of serious illness. Serious illness was defined as sickness or nonindustrial accident which was severe enough to cause disability for work or school attendance for a week or more. This included chronic cases. Of wage earners, 27.3 per cent had been ill. The average loss of wages per worker was $24.95, or 3.33 per cent of the year's earnings. If medical bills paid are included, the loss amounted to 5.8 per cent of the average family income from all sources.

---

[1] *Hearings before Committee on Ways and Means*, House of Representatives, 74th Congress, 1st Session, on the Economic Security Act, H. R. 4120, p. 50.

[2] Sumner H. Slichter regards sickness as the primary cause of labor turnover. See *The Turnover of Factory Labor* (1919), pp. 403–405.

[3] See *Report of the Health Insurance Commission of the State of Illinois*, May 1, 1919.

[4] The National Health Survey found the severity rate (days of disability per case) for males and females between fifteen and sixty-four years of age to be 63. Those suffering from chronic disease were of course included (Preliminary Reports, J-1305, p. 4).

[5] See *Report of the Health Insurance Commission of the State of Illinois*, May 1, 1919, pp. 151–152.

The Illinois Commission examined the loss of wages of the 20 per cent of the workers covered by its investigation who had been disabled a week or more with the results shown in Table 26.

TABLE 26.—NUMBER AND PERCENTAGE OF WAGE EARNERS SICK AND OF WAGES LOST, 1917–1919[1]

No. of workers	Percentage of workers	Percentage of annual wages lost
286	31.7	Less than 5
221	24.4	5 but less than 10
82	9.1	10 but less than 15
99	11.0	15 but less than 20
83	9.2	20 but less than 30
46	5.1	30 but less than 40
17	1.9	40 but less than 50
52	5.8	50 but less than 75
15	1.7	More than 75

[1] Report of the Health Insurance Commission of the State of Illinois, May 1, 1919, p. 15.

These results would be fairly typical of wage losses due to disabling sickness and nonindustrial accidents sustained by workers. The loss due to cost of medical bills would be only less unequally spread, and, taken as a group, those workers who lost the largest percentage of wages would also have the largest bills to pay. Lee K. Frankel found, in the study previously cited, that while 6 per cent of the families with Metropolitan policies had no medical expenditures, 20 per cent bore 64 per cent of the total, and 1 per cent, or thirty-eight families, bore 10.9 per cent, with

TABLE 27.—AMOUNTS EXPENDED BY FAMILIES FOR MEDICAL CARE, COST OF SICKNESS SURVEY, JANUARY TO JUNE, 1929, METROPOLITAN LIFE INSURANCE COMPANY[1]

Amount of total expenditure of family[a]	No. of families reporting	Percentage of all families	Total expenditure of group	Percentage of total expended by all groups	Average expenditure per family
No expenditure	198	6			
Less than $25	1,113	34	$ 12,535	5.4	$ 11
$ 25 to $ 49.99	654	20	23,678	10.3	36
50 to 99.99	655	20	46,282	20.0	71
100 to 199.99	397	12	55,625	24.1	140
200 to 299.99	135	4	32,758	14.2	243
300 to 399.99	55	2	18,982	8.2	345
400 to 499.99	36	1	15,907	6.9	442
500 and over	38	1	25,140	10.9	662
Total	3,281	100	$230,907	100.0	$ 70

[a] The more important items in the total outlay were as follows: physician, 42.7 per cent; medicines, 12.9 per cent; hospital, 12.5 per cent; extra household, 10.7 per cent; dentist, 7.9 per cent; operations, 6.9 per cent; nurse, 3.8 per cent.

[1] Lee K. Frankel, Cost of Medical Care, Metropolitan Life Insurance Company, for the Committee on the Costs of Medical Care (1929), pp. 6–8.

an average expenditure of $662. The table (27) is given in full and deserves careful examination.

The Committee on the Costs of Medical Care found that 57.8 per cent of the 8,581 families covered by its survey had medical bills less than $60 per year and paid 17.9 per cent of the total outlay; that 31.9 per cent had bills of $60 or more but less than $250 and paid 40.9 per cent of the total; while an unfortunate 10.3 per cent had bills in excess of $250 and paid 41.2 per cent of the total costs of medical service. Or as one writer, using a different grouping, has stated, "An unlucky sixth of our people . . . pays in one year half the total sickness bills paid by everybody in that year." He adds that, "No one can tell in advance whether his family, during the next year, will be in the lucky half, the moderately lucky third, or the unlucky sixth."[1] It is these extreme variations which make sickness a nonbudgetable emergency as long as individual families must deal with it out of their own resources.[2]

Not only is the burden unevenly spread; it falls with greatest weight upon those who are the less well off. Thus, an investigation in seven cotton-mill villages in South Carolina disclosed the rates of disabling sickness shown in Table 28.

TABLE 28.—DISABLING SICKNESS PER 1,000 IN RELATION TO INCOME OF ADULT MALE[1]

Half-month income per adult male unit	Disabling sickness per 1,000		
	All persons	Wage earners	Non-wage earners
Less than $6.00	70.1	80.0	65.0
$6.00 to $7.99	48.2	51.6	45.8
8.00 to 9.99	34.4	18.8	53.1
10.00 and over	18.5	14.9	22.5
Average	45.2	40.2	49.1

[1] U. S. Public Health Reports, vol. 33 (1918), pp. 2044–2045.

The correlation between low wages and sickness indicated is due in part to the fact that those workers who were ill suffered a reduction of income, but that is not the whole explanation. This is shown by the sickness experience of non-wage earners as recorded in the last column in Table 28.

The Illinois Commission also found an increase in the sickness rates in the groups with lower incomes. In tabulating the data obtained by its agents, the Commission grouped the families on the basis of need of income in view of family composition and on actual income plus wages

[1] Michael Davis, Health Security and the American Public (1936), p. 3.
[2] See Michael Davis, Paying Your Sickness Bills (1931), and I. S. Falk, Security Against Sickness (1936), Chaps. 1 and 2. Both books contain valuable studies of sickness and how the costs are and should be met.

lost by reason of sickness.   The method indicated was used in order to obtain uninterrupted or normal income.   The families were divided into three groups: Class C, those who could not meet a conservative charity budget used in granting relief; Class B, those who had a margin of less than 41 per cent above this charity budget; and Class A, those whose incomes afforded a larger margin.[1]

TABLE 29.—DISABLING SICKNESS AND COSTS, BY FAMILY STATUS[1]

Class	Percentage of families with disabling sickness	Sickness costs (wages and medical bills) expressed as per cent of earnings
C	76.0	14.9
B	73.0	8.5
A	63.4	7.7

[1] *Report of the Health Insurance Commission of the State of Illinois*, May 1, 1919, pp. 17–18.

This statement of the problem has run in terms of disabling illness or accident.   From the point of view of what might be done to restore health, to increase efficiency and prolong life, the problem is much more extensive.   Many defects, injuries, and diseases which do not completely disable, but do lower efficiency and frequently handicap workers in securing employment, call for medical care.   The losses from nondisabling defects and diseases are particularly difficult to estimate, but they are nevertheless real.   Very few studies of a complete cross section of working-class families have been made in the United States, but some indication of the extent of nondisabling defects and diseases can be gained from the following figures: In Framingham, Mass., intensive

[1] See *Report of the Health Insurance Commission of the State of Illinois*, May 1, 1919, pp. 17–18.   In general, corresponding results were obtained from another canvass made under different circumstances.   G. St. J. Perrott and Selwyn D. Collins, in a study of the relation of sickness to income and income change, have shown that the families in the lowest income group had the highest rate of disabling sickness, the excess found in such families over families in a "comfortable" group being 23 per cent on the basis of income per person and 30 per cent on the basis of income per family.   "Particularly significant are the facts that the highest illness rates were observed among those who had suffered the greatest *change* in standard of living and that the excess in illness existed among children as well as adults."   The survey covered almost 12,000 white families in ten communities.   *U. S. Public Health Reports*, vol. 50 (1935), pp. 595–622.   Quotation from p. 622.

The National Health Survey showed frequency rates (disabling illnesses per 1,000 persons—12-month period) for families as follows: Relief families, 234; non-relief families, with income under $1,000, 174; same, with income $1,000 to $2,000, 155; same, with income $2,000 to $3,000, 150; same, with income $3,000 and over, 149.   Divided between acute and chronic cases, the rates for these five groups were, in order: 163 and 71; 119 and 54; 117 and 38; 113 and 37; 111 and 38.   (Preliminary Reports, Sickness and Medical Care Series, Bulletin 2, J-1310, p. 10.)

examinations of the general population made during the World War disclosed that of 4,473 persons, 1,017 were normal, while 2,343 were suffering from "minor" and 1,113 from "serious" affections.[1] Of over two and one-half million men between the ages of eighteen and thirty drafted during the World War, it was found that forty-seven out of every 100 had some defect or disease. Twenty-one per cent were so defective as to be rejected, and these men were in the prime of life.[2] An examination of Detroit grade-school children revealed that 64.0 per cent had one or more defects. In Gary, Indiana, 95.2 per cent of the preschool children were found to have one or more defects. Defective tonsils and decayed teeth were the most common.[3] Although these data are not as satisfactory as might be desired, they do indicate the vast amount of human suffering and economic loss occasioned by defects, injuries, and illness. The continuance of this loss, some of which is preventable, indicates the need of widespread and organized use of preventive and curative measures now known.

Sickness is a disrupting factor in family life if no organized provision is made to meet it. It is, in fact, one of the chief reasons why people seek charity. More than twenty-five years ago the United States Immigration Commission found that sickness was present in 38.4 per cent of the applications and in 40.4 per cent of the cases in which assistance was granted by the many charitable organizations whose records were examined. A study made of the records of a number of charity organizations in Illinois, including three in Chicago, showed that sickness had been a cause or an accompanying condition of dependency in from a third to a half of the cases.[4] Moreover, the standard of living is undermined by sickness in many cases in which families are not reduced to dependency. Thus sickness caused 343 of the 2,708 wage-earning families investigated by the Illinois Commission to be shifted from a higher to a lower class—i.e., from A to B or from B to C.[5]

The problem as thus far analyzed may be stated in summary form as follows:[6]

(1) Rather more than 2 per cent of the population are disabled by sickness or nonindustrial accident at a given time; (2) the percentage not disabled but who have serious affections which may need medical care is distinctly larger; (3) approximately two-thirds of the wage-earning families will have one or more cases of serious illness in the course of a year and in more than half of these two-thirds the illness will include

[1] *Framingham Monograph 4*, pp. 17–18.

[2] Committee on the Costs of Medical Care, Publication 2, pp. 38–39.

[3] *Ibid.*, pp. 43–47.

[4] Illinois Health Insurance Commission, *Report*, p. 153.

[5] *Ibid.*, p. 19.

[6] *Cf. ibid.*, p. 153.

that of a wage earner; (4) something more than a quarter of the workers will be sick or sustain nonindustrial accident in the course of the year and a fifth of the entire number will lose a week or more of employment because of the disability caused thereby; (5) the average loss of working time due to sickness or nonindustrial accident is perhaps more than seven days per worker each year; (6) the wage loss alone is approximately $900,000,000 a year; (7) well over 90 per cent of wage-earning families have medical bills in the course of the year which exceed by about 50 per cent the loss in wages caused by sickness; (8) the wage loss and medical outlays amount to some 6 per cent of workers' incomes; (9) the burden of sickness and nonindustrial accident is very unevenly distributed and, in the absence of cooperation in carrying it, frequently undermines the standard of living and often reduces families to poverty; (10) sickness and nonindustrial accident present a problem to industry as well as to the worker and to society as a whole.

THE CAUSES OF SICKNESS

The larger elements in our problem have been noted. Lesser ones, some of them accompanying the institutional setup for dealing with the problem, must also be noted but this may be done incidentally. Before turning to a discussion of the methods of attack upon the problem, a brief statement needs to be made relative to the causes of and responsibility for sickness.

Much illness is due to infection and the more or less inevitable wearing-out process.[1] Next to be noted is that the personal factor in sickness is not a small one. Overeating, overdrinking, neglect, and a great variety of things which connect with personal hygiene, taken together, are an important cause of sickness. A third cause, or set of causes, is found in what may be called the general social, nonwork environment. Here one could mention deficient disease control, bad water, bad milk, bad housing, poor public sanitation, and scores of other factors. Finally, a whole set of causes is found in industry—in the work situation. First to be mentioned is inadequate wages, which mean undernourishment, inadequate clothing, poor housing, inadequate medical and nursing care, and worry and nervous strain. In view of the discussion earlier in this treatise,[2] nothing need be added here concerning inadequate wages as a cause of sickness. Nor need we do more than call attention to the

[1] Edgar Sydenstricker and Rollo H. Britten have studied the results of physical examinations of 100,924 white males made by the Life Extension Institute. Physical impairments were correlated with age. Both the prevalence of specific impairments at different ages and the wearing-out process are shown. See Edgar Sydenstricker and Rollo H. Britten, "The Physical Impairments of Adult Life," in *American Journal of Hygiene*, vol. 11 (1930), pp. 95–135.

[2] Vol. I, Chap. V.

responsibility of bad hours of work—night work, the twelve-hour shift, the seven-day week, excessive overtime, and no vacations. Fortunately bad hours of work are very much more exceptional than they were a generation or two generations ago. Also to be mentioned is monotony of work, which produces strain and fatigue; speed, which has the same result; unnatural pace of the machine; heavy work, with its hernias; standing, with its varicose veins; bad ventilation; exposure; improper heating; dust; noise; and other things the reader will readily think of. And finally, poisonous substances may be mentioned—sulphur, white lead, and others, which may produce not only occupational disease in the form of "phossy jaw," lead poisoning, and the like, but also a much larger number of cases of illness not definitely to be established as cases of occupational disease.

If this brief statement is correct, it at once shows two things: (a) a divided causal responsibility for sickness, resting upon the individual, society at large, and to no small degree, upon industry; (b) the numerous points at which the problem may be attacked, especially in its preventive aspects.

METHODS OF ATTACK UPON THE PROBLEM

In so far as there is a solution for the sickness problem, three things are obviously called for: (a) prevention, in so far as it can be reasonably accomplished—and it can be in considerable measure; (b) adequate medical, surgical, hospital, nursing, and dental care; (c) compensation through a money benefit when earnings are interrupted. Many of the students of the subject are of the opinion that if prevention is to be realized in desirable degree; if medical, surgical, hospital, and nursing care are to be effectively organized and made generally available to persons of small means; if financial support is to be given when earnings are interrupted; and if the bill is to be apportioned somewhat according to responsibility for the problem or according to ability to pay, a system of compulsory health insurance is necessary. This is merely one way of stating the case for such a system. What compulsory health insurance is and the case for and against it will be considered presently. Consideration will also be given to the plan proposed by the Committee on the Costs of Medical Care. First, however, we must get a more accurate idea of what is being done and with what result in the absence of such a system, for compulsory health insurance always has been, and inevitably would be, built largely upon existing institutional arrangements. In a way, it is a coerced reorganization of them. Moreover, insurance is no cure-all. Other attacks must find place in connection with the problem of sickness just as other methods must find place along with insurance in the attack upon the problem of unemployment.

The Prevention of Sickness

To what extent can physical defects be remedied? To what extent can disabling sickness be prevented? To what extent can death be postponed by preventing disease or by more successful treatment of illness when it occurs?

It would carry us too far afield to attempt to answer fully these questions. It would mean entering a field which requires the knowledge and judgment of specialists because of the nature and variety of things involved, and in which inevitably there would be great diversity of opinion. Because of this and because of space limitations, a few observations must suffice. Nothing will be added to what has been said concerning rehabilitation in the immediately preceding chapter. The prevention of disabling sickness alone will be commented on, and in this connection the observations will be limited to the public-health service and health service in industry.

An efficient public-health service and efficient health service in industry are only two of several important agencies for preventing sickness. Federal, state, and local governments and numerous voluntary nonofficial agencies in the United States carry on a wide variety of activities usually classed under the term "public health."[1] It is impossible here to describe and evaluate all these activities, but some of the most important should be mentioned. These usually include an attempt to prevent and control communicable disease and tuberculosis, food inspection, housing and sanitation, child hygiene, and public-school health work, as well as laboratory work and hospitalization in cases of communicable disease. In 1927, Federal, state, municipal, and county hospitals provided 70 per cent of all hospital service in the United States. This of course, included the service of mental, tuberculosis, and other special institutions, as well as general hospitals.[2] Since 1929 the proportion of hospital and medical service provided by the government has increased because of increasing reliance upon Federal, state, and local revenues. The public expenditures for hospital care, mental diseases, and public-health work have been about $600,000,000 per year. This sum does not include material relief granted to families because of the illness of wage earners.[3]

The important gains which have come through public-health activities in reducing morbidity and mortality rates are well known to the medical

[1] Description of the activities of the public-health department in the United States and Canada may be found in U. S. Public Health Service, *Bulletin 184* (1929). Other bulletins of the Public Health Service report special studies of disease and of hazards of industries, such as *Bulletin 210*, "Mortality of Coal Miners" (1933).

[2] Allon Peebles, *A Survey of Medical Facilities in the United States* (Committee on the Costs of Medical Care, Publication 3, 1929), p. 47.

[3] Michael Davis, *Milbank Memorial Fund Quarterly*, vol. 12 (October, 1934), p. 290.

world, yet it is not commonly realized that the cost of these services is usually less than for any other item of medical care.   In Shelby County, Ind., the total expenditure for public health was found to be only $0.28 per capita, or 1.3 per cent of the cost of all medical care.[1] In Philadelphia the combined expenditures by Federal, state, and local agencies were only $1.10 per capita, or 2.1 per cent of the total medical cost.[2] For the United States as a whole the expenditure for prevention is only one-thirtieth of the amount spent on cure.[3] The presence of preventable diseases, such as smallpox, diphtheria, typhoid fever, and tuberculosis, indicated, in the Shelby and San Joaquin County reports, that public-health work might be profitably expanded.[4] That a greater emphasis on preventive medicine would result in a reduction or practical elimination of these and certain other diseases is indicated by American experience[5] as well as by that of other countries.[6] It is the opinion of leading public-health authorities that the effective annual expenditure for public health in the United States should be at least two and one-half times the present rate, or $250,000,000 a year instead of $100,000,000.[7] But in addition to the more liberal financial support required, the public-health service in most places needs to be taken out of politics and adequately trained men employed and given security of tenure in their positions.

It is obvious from what has been said concerning the causes of sickness that good personal hygiene might do much to prevent disease.   The problem here is one of knowledge and its application toward right living. The sickness rate also depends upon the character of medical service and

[1] Committee on the Costs of Medical Care, Publication 2, pp. 149–151.

[2] Nathan Sinai and Alden B. Mills, *A Survey of the Medical Facilities of the City of Philadelphia: 1929* (Committee on the Costs of Medical Care, Publication 9, 1931), pp. 254–255.

[3] Michael Davis, *Paying Your Sickness Bills* (1931), p. 244.

[4] Committee on the Costs of Medical Care, Publication 2, pp. 122, 125; and Publication 12, *A Survey of the Medical Facilities of San Joaquin County, California: 1929*, by Nathan Sinai (1931), p. 174.

[5] The Committee on Community Dental Service of the New York Tuberculosis and Health Association, *Health Dentistry for the Community* (1935).   This study stresses the importance of regular periodic dental care, especially for children, and the relation of dentistry to an integrated health program.   The extent of dental defects and the present methods of meeting the problem are discussed.

[6] Ralph A. Reynolds, "How Necessary Is Illness?" *Atlantic Monthly*, June 1930.

[7] Michael Davis, *The Milbank Memorial Fund Quarterly*, vol. 12 (October, 1934), p. 296. Dr. Thomas Parran, Jr., then Commissioner of the New York State Department of Health, has said, "In public health we stand today where we were in public education in the middle of last century." Quoted from an address before a joint meeting of the Illinois Department of Health and the Chicago Board of Health, March 2, 1936.   For a review of public-health work and outlays for the United States and for each of the states, see *Health Departments of States and Provinces of the United States and Canada* (U. S. Public Health Service, *Bulletin 184*, revised, 1932).

its availability. These depend upon research, training, organization of the service, and other things upon which our later discussion will have more or less bearing. Finally, the whole work environment is of great importance in this connection. Some aspects of this have already been touched upon. At this point only those aspects with which health service in industry has to do will receive consideration.

Health service has taken organic shape in only a minority of American establishments. An investigation by the National Safety Council showed that only 191 of 3,580 selected industrial establishments, or 5.3 per cent, had some form of health supervision of their employees.[1] Yet, the importance of the then health service in industry was much greater than these figures would indicate, for it found place chiefly in the programs of the larger firms engaged in manufacturing, trade, transportation, and mining.[2]

In part, institutionalized health service is a direct outgrowth of steps taken in connection with workmen's compensation and accident prevention. Why, it has been asked, not apply the idea to the larger field? In part it came independently from a realization that there is a causal relation between the work environment and the rate of sickness, and, in turn, between the rate of sickness and output and cost. For sickness impairs quality, diminishes output, and enhances cost because of its adverse effect upon attendance, nervous energy, skill, morale, and turnover. With a health program introduced, the employer has generally been convinced that it was a good investment. Others have adopted the pattern provided, and, of course, a humanitarian motive has been not unimportant.

Health service in industry is largely preventive rather than curative, and the National Industrial Conference Board has found that within the last few years the emphasis upon prevention has increased. Much more attention than years ago is now devoted to medical examinations,

[1] See quotation in Pierce Williams, *The Purchase of Medical Care Through Fixed Periodic Payments* (1932), p. 16, from the National Safety Council Health Practices, Pamphlet 12, *Prevailing Practices in Industrial Health and Medical Service* (Chicago, 1930).

[2] It is probable that great advance has been made since 1930. In any event, the National Industrial Conference Board, reporting on 2,452 replies to a questionnaire circulated by it, states: "Medical service of some kind is provided for employees by 1,598 companies or 65.2 per cent of the total number covered. . . . The most frequently reported form of medical work, and also the most elementary, is organized first aid work. However, 1,154 companies have a company dispensary or hospital, 867 have a plant nurse, and 722 have either a full-time or part-time physician, or both. Nearly half of the companies give physical examinations to new employees and 471 provide periodic examinations to enable employees to discover and arrest incipient physical troubles. Special services, such as dental and optical clinics, are provided in a few cases." (Quoted from *What Employers Are Doing for Employees*, National Industrial Conference Board Studies, 221, 1936, pp. 17–18.)

health education, and other preventive work.[1] Of 303 companies submitting data on health service to employees, only twenty-seven, with 130,934 employees, reported that they gave treatment for disease, and in these cases the employees contributed to the funds. In thirteen of the twenty-seven cases the employee's family also received medical care.[2]

The type and extent of the services vary widely from plant to plant. In some there is simply a first-aid kit and corresponding service. Other plants are fully equipped to dispense medicines and not only give ordinary physician's and nursing care, but also employ dentists, oculists, surgeons, and other specialists full or part time.[3]

The various parts of industrial health service, taken in its broader reaches, are indicated by Professor Watkins' summary.[4] He says:

"In the promotion of health and safety among industrial wage earners four general lines of procedure are possible:

"(a) The provision of a satisfactory working environment.

"(b) Intelligent employment policies and methods.

"(c) A constructive program of betterment activities.

"(d) A well-organized and efficient medical and safety service."

Rarely is such a program fully attained. Indeed, the parts of it employed are all too frequently expected to render the other services unnecessary. However, the importance of the health program as an aspect of efficient personnel management has come to be recognized and accepted by a great majority of the large employers.

INSURANCE AGAINST LOSS OF TIME

The problem presented by loss of income due to disabling sickness and by burial costs and the end of personal earnings incident to death has caused a variety of mutual associations to provide their members with sickness and/or life insurance. More important from the point of view of numbers insured is the fact that commercial carriers have entered and extensively exploited the field. How extensive is such insurance and how adequate is it to meet the problem?

Mutual Benefit Associations.—Since 1870 mutual benefit associations have become increasingly important in the provision of health and disability insurance. They now number about 1,000 and have from 1,500,-000 to 2,000,000 members.[5] These associations are of a bewildering

---

[1] National Industrial Conference Board, *Medical Supervision and Service in Industry* (1931), p. 2.

[2] Pierce Williams, *op. cit.*, p. 16.

[3] National Industrial Conference Board, *Medical Supervision and Service in Industry*, Chaps. 1 and 2.

[4] Gordon S. Watkins, *Labor Management* (1928), pp. 465–479.

[5] Space limitations prevent more than a summary statement of the insurance provided by mutual benefit associations and other carriers. Students interested in more detail may consult the sources cited. One of the most comprehensive studies, of 430

variety of types and membership rules. They are sometimes initiated by employees, but more often by employers in the hope of increasing morale and loyalty and reducing labor turnover, and sometimes as a part of an "open-shop" device to defeat unionism. The contributions to the fund are in some cases made exclusively by the employees or by the employers, but the tendency has been toward contributions by both employers and employees, with the employees bearing the bulk of the costs.[1]

The primary function of mutual benefit associations is to pay cash benefits to members disabled otherwise than by compensable work injuries, but in many cases they also pay death benefits varying from $50 to $5,000, and more rarely, but to an increasing extent, provide medical benefits.[2] The disability benefits paid were found by the National Industrial Conference Board to vary from $2.50 to $40 per week, the predominant rates being $5 and $6. The length of time during which disability benefit might be received varied widely, but it was usually limited to thirteen weeks for a single disability and to twenty-six weeks in a year. Provision for permanent disability is very rarely made.[3] In view of the importance of cases of extended and permanent disability, the limitation on number of weeks during which benefit may be received seriously reduces the usefulness of many of the plans. The employee also usually loses his benefit rights when he leaves the employ of the firm.

Trade Unions.—Trade unions in the United States have centered their attention upon increasing wages, improving working conditions, and reducing hours of work, and, in so far as they have succeeded in these aims, they have indirectly contributed to the health of their members.[4]

---

associations, was made in 1926 by the U. S. Bureau of Labor Statistics (see *Bulletin 458*). Of 177 associations reporting membership, 76 per cent (758,000) of the employees of the firms involved were members (p. 59).

The National Industrial Conference Board reported in 1936 (Study 221, pp. 11, 26) that 692 of 2,452 companies replying to its questionnaire had mutual benefit associations. As against 17.6 per cent in 1927, 25.6 per cent of the companies in 1936 had mutual benefit associations providing sickness and accident benefits. Inasmuch as the 692 companies with mutual benefit associations employed 2,444,795 workers, the 528 with associations providing sickness and accident benefits perhaps employed more than 2,000,000. See also Eleanor Davis, *Company Sickness Benefit Plans for Wage Earners*, Princeton University, Industrial Relations Section (1936).

[1] Illinois Health Insurance Commission, *Report*, p. 544.

[2] The provision for medical benefit on an insurance basis will be discussed briefly later in this chapter, p. 262.

[3] *Experience with Mutual Benefit Associations in the United States*, National Industrial Conference Board, *Research Report 65* (1923), pp. 106, 110. See also the analysis of plans made by Eleanor Davis (Eleanor Davis, *op. cit.*, p. 68), where the conclusion was reached that the cash benefits paid the sick were less liberal than under health insurance systems.

[4] The contention of the unions that short hours are a necessary health measure was strengthened by the publication of Miss Josephine C. Goldmark's *Fatigue and Efficiency* in 1912, and the brief, *The Case for the Shorter Work Day*, by Felix Frankfurter, assisted by Miss Goldmark, in 1915.

Some unions, notably the International Ladies' Garment Workers,[1] have done excellent work in improving unsanitary and unhealthful shop conditions. The interest of the unions in health problems has been largely of a preventive nature, and the provision for sick and disability benefits has not been typical. However, some unions, especially the railway unions, which had their origin as benefit associations, do pay sick or disability benefits to their members as well as the more common death benefit.

In a comprehensive study of American trade unions in 1927–1928, the United States Bureau of Labor Statistics found sixty-three international unions paying death benefits, but only fourteen paying benefit for disability and eleven for sickness.[2] Of course, some local or district organizations also provide sickness benefits, but these are exceptional. The American Federation of Labor reported that in 1934 thirty-one national and international unions (including unaffiliated railroad unions) and an unknown number of their local unions paid sick benefits totaling $1,908,779, and eighteen internationals paid disability benefits totaling $2,280,618.[3] However, many of these unions paid negligible amounts; ten unions paid nearly 90 per cent of the total of sickness benefits. One union, the Brotherhood of Railroad Trainmen, accounted for more than one-half of all expenditures for disability benefits. The amount of sick benefit varied from $4 to $10 per week, $5 being the most common amount. The benefit period was commonly thirteen weeks, but varied from seven to sixteen weeks. The maximum disability benefits allowed by trade unions showed less uniformity than did sickness benefits. The disability payment usually was a lump-sum payment varying in amount from $50 to $800. As an exceptional arrangement, the Locomotive Firemen and Enginemen pay $50 per month during disability.

Obviously union benefits are so restricted in time and amount as to cover only a small part of the losses involved, especially in cases of prolonged illness or disability. That the amounts are not more adequate is explained chiefly by the difficulty in getting members to finance more liberal benefits. Connected with this, and accounting in part for the limited number of unions paying sickness benefits, is the difficulty in securing efficient administration of the funds through the local unions.

Fraternal Orders.—On the eve of the adoption of sickness insurance in Great Britain, friendly societies were the greatest providers of sickness and disability insurance for workmen. In the United States such societies have not been as extensively developed, and the insurance

---

[1] See Louis Levine, *The Women's Garment Workers* (1924).

[2] "Beneficial Activities of American Trade Unions," *Bulletin 465* (1928).

[3] American Federation of Labor, *Report of the Proceedings of the Fifty-fifth Annual Convention* (1935), pp. 100–104.

provided by them has been chiefly life insurance,[1] although about one-fourth[2] of the orders provide sickness and accident benefit either through their grand or through their local lodges. On Jan. 1, 1934, there were a total of 6,414,000 adult benefit members in fraternal societies in the United States.[3] About one-half of these were industrial workers.[4]

The disability benefit provided by fraternal organizations varies widely between orders, from $2 to $120 per month, with the most frequent amount being $3 to $7 per week. The maximum benefit period ranges from six to twenty-six weeks, thirteen weeks being the most frequent. Usually the most powerful orders draw the bulk of their membership from non-wage-earning classes and protect themselves by refusing to accept "bad risks." The fraternal orders are, of course, democratic nonprofit associations. On the average the cost of administering the insurance funds is relatively low. The chief difficulties are that the funds are frequently actuarially unsound, that the amount and length of benefit are often inadequate, and that a large number of societies are abandoned.[5]

Insurance Companies.—Insurance written by private stock and mutual insurance companies against sickness and disability is more extensive than that written by any other type of carrier. In 1933 the net total accident- and health-insurance premiums written by insurance companies were $158,575,000, and the total of losses and expenses paid was $103,000,000.[6] With an estimated average annual premium of

[1] The amount of life insurance, the number of policies, and the number of societies reporting at the end of the year are given in the following table:[a]

Year	No. of orders	No. of certificates	Amount of life insurance in force at end of year
1903	509	5,644,619	$6,606,608,321
1909	645	7,909,626	8,920,716,227
1914	498	7,868,554	9,171,284,722
1920	336	8,578,039	9,159,041,634
1924	228	12,514,499	9,805,447,751
1929	269	8,974,914	9,155,358,213
1933	206	6,118,114	6,394,564,616
1935	266	6,462,293	6,182,537,610

[a] *Insurance Year Book, 1936,* Life Insurance Volume, p. 896.

[2] This is a rough estimate based on the figures of the Illinois Health Insurance Commission, *Report,* pp. 119–120.

[3] *The Fraternal Monitor,* "Statistics of Fraternal Societies," 1934.

[4] Estimate of H. R. Gordon, Executive Secretary of the Health and Underwriters' Conference, Aug. 7, 1934.

[5] See footnote 1, above. The table shows the steady decline in the number of societies since 1909 and in the number of certificates since 1924.

[6] *Argus Chart,* "Casualty and Surety" (National Underwriter Co., 1934), p. 152. The totals are composed of $127,777,000 premiums written and $81,392,000 losses sustained by stock companies, a ratio of 63.7 per cent, and $30,797,000 premiums written and $21,934,000 losses sustained by mutual companies, a ratio of 71.2 per cent.

$18.00, the number insured was approximately 8,800,000.   If the number insured through accident policies offered by newspapers is included, the total reaches 10,000,000.[1]

The companies, under pressure of competition, have shown considerable ingenuity in the adaptation of methods and policies to the desires and needs of their customers.   The tendency to expand health insurance in connection with commercial life insurance was, however, given a definite check with the announcement by the insurance companies in 1931 that they would no longer write life insurance containing the total-disability and permanent-disability clause.[2]   More accident and health insurance has been dropped during the depression than any other form of insurance.   Between 1929 and 1935 nearly $50,000,000, or between 40 and 50 per cent of all accident and health insurance, was dropped.[3]

The individual health-insurance policies of the commercial companies are usually written for the period of one year, although a small percentage of them are of the noncancelable type.   The companies have naturally sought business chiefly among higher income groups and in those communities which have a low sickness risk.[4]   Often workers in certain occupations and, sometimes, entire communities are excluded because they have had an unfavorable experience.[5]

The early health-insurance policies insured against only specified causes of disability, but the tendency has been to broaden them to

[1] Estimate of Harold R. Gordon, executive secretary of the Health and Accident Underwriters' Conference, Aug. 7, 1934.

[2] Pierce Williams, op. cit., p. 271.   At that time over 250 companies had written accident and health policies in conjunction with $30,000,000,000 of life insurance.

[3] National Underwriter, June 13, 1935.

[4] The insurance companies have a standard classification of occupations according to expected risk.   For example, accountants, bank tellers, and school teachers have an AA rating; automobile salesmen and physicians a B rating; bookbinders a D rating; lumber workers an H rating; and underground miners an I rating.   Nearly all the health- and accident-insurance business is written for workers in the safer occupations.   In 1933 the distribution of volume of accident and health premiums by classes was as follows (H. R. Gordon, executive secretary of the Health and Accident Underwriters' Conference, 1934):

Class	Monthly premium, per cent	Annual premium, per cent
AA	27	66
A	21	15
B	15	7
C	13	7
D	21	2.5
E	3	
F	1	
G	Less than 1	1.5
H	Less than 1	

[5] Pierce Williams, op. cit., pp. 262-266.

include nearly all diseases and nonindustrial accidents. The benefit payments usually extend for six to eight months and are also larger in the amount of benefit per week than those ordinarily paid by fraternal societies and trade unions. The companies protect themselves from overinsurance and malingering by limiting benefits to a percentage (50 to 75 per cent) of income when the insured is at work.

The type of insurance most extensively written for wage earners is industrial (life) insurance, paid for on a weekly basis. Industrial insurance is written both for adults and children and is, of course, written in much smaller policies than ordinary life. In 1935 the average policy was approximately $218.[1] The number of policies held increased phenomenally in the years prior to 1929 and reached the enormous total of 88,664,000 policies in force in that year.[2] The number of policy holders is variously estimated at between 40 and 60 million.[3] In connection with industrial life insurance, the large life insurance and casualty companies offer disability insurance of several types. One type pays a cash benefit of a certain percentage (perhaps one-half) of the face value of the policy in case of total disability. A more usual type is that offered by the casualty companies of a flat rate of 5 cents for each dollar of weekly benefit.[4] Industrial policies are a highly unsatisfactory form of insurance, for the costs are high for the benefits paid, the lapse ratios are extremely high, and, despite the inadequate protection offered, the cost to the workers in 1932 averaged 5.9 per cent of their income[5]—a cost approaching that of the broad protection obtained under a system of compulsory health insurance.

A more promising development than individual health insurance through commercial companies is that of group life and disability insurance. Group insurance is essentially a plan of selling insurance wholesale to cover risks of the members of a group. Originally it was sold to employers who wanted to insure the lives of their workers, but more recently it has been applied to sickness and accident as well.[6] Table 30 gives combined group-insurance statistics as reported by the eight companies which wrote more than 90 per cent of all the group-insurance policies in force at the end of 1934.[7]

---

[1] *Insurance Year Book, 1936*, Life, p. 791.

[2] *Ibid.* In 1935 the number of policies in force had declined to 83,971,000 and the amount of insurance in force was $18,298,000,000.

[3] Maurice Taylor, *The Social Cost of Industrial Insurance* (1933), p. 54. This book contains an excellent discussion of the value and limitations of industrial life insurance.

[4] Pierce Williams, *op. cit.*, p. 269.

[5] Maurice Taylor, *op. cit.*, p. 193.

[6] A more complete description of group insurance as well as employers' motives in providing it can be found in the study by the National Industrial Conference Board, *Recent Developments in Industrial Group Insurance* (1934).

[7] *Ibid.*, pp. 5 and 25.

TABLE 30.—COMBINED GROUP-INSURANCE STATISTICS OF EIGHT LEADING INSURANCE CARRIERS, DECEMBER 31, 1933[1]

Kind of group insurance	No. of policies in force	No. of employees insured	Average number of employees per policy	Amount of insurance		Average age benefit per employee	Percentage of 1933 sales of total in force
				Sold in 1933 (in thousands)	Total in force (in thousands)		
Group life.............	15,125	4,487,377	297	$343,747	$8,206,775	$1,828	4.2
Group accidental death and dismemberment....	1,764	505,278	286	96,784	744,129	1,473	13.0
Group accident and health	4,475	1,228,918	252	1,884[a]	15,974[a]	13.00[a]	11.8
Group annuities and pensions.................	226	193,796	4,150	1,651[b]	8,435[b]	43.53[b]	19.6

[a] Weekly benefits.
[b] Monthly income.
[1] Recent Developments in Industrial Group Insurance, National Industrial Conference Board (1934), p. 25.

Prior to the depression, which forced many employers to cancel their policies, the amount of group insurance sold expanded rapidly. In smaller volume new policies continued to be written even during 1932 and 1933, and with industrial recovery a further extension of group insurance may be expected. By far the greater part has been purchased by the larger employers as a part of their program of "welfare capitalism." Usually the policy covers all employees in the firm and is issued after the insurance company examines the age, health, and other qualifications of the employees covered. The employer is responsible for payment of the premium, but it has become more common in recent years to require employee contributions. Since 1924 two-thirds of the new plans have been contributory; the insurance written by the larger companies is now almost entirely of that type. In a few cases the employees make contributions covering the entire cost of their insurance, but in most cases the employers bear some part of the cost, most frequently 25 per cent. Although employees under the newer plans are bearing an increasing share of the cost of group insurance, the majority of the plans in effect are still of the noncontributory type and the employers bear the larger share of the life insurance. Since group disability insurance is a more recent development than group life insurance, the cost is much more likely to be borne largely or entirely by the workers. One of the chief causes of the shift from noncontributory to contributory group insurance is the belief that employee contributions tend to reduce turnover.

The cost of acquisition and administration of group insurance is comparatively low (from 7 to 10 per cent of the premium), and the policies frequently cover employees who would not be eligible for other kinds of insurance. The benefit is also more nearly adequate than that provided by most trade unions or mutual benefit associations, and even by most fraternal orders. The chief criticism of group insurance is that it has been used as a means of reducing the mobility of labor and "tying the worker to the employer." Experience has shown, however, that if other conditions are unsatisfactory, group insurance has little effect in reducing labor turnover.

A Summary View of the Extent of Insurance.—The multiplicity of carriers of insurance against death and disability indicates the widespread recognition of the need for such insurance, and at the same time makes it possible for the majority of workers to get insurance if they will. In fact, the majority of male heads of wage-earning families do carry life insurance, and in many cases the amount is more than sufficient to cover funeral expenses. Yet well-informed insurance men estimate that 40 per cent of wage earners in the United States die without any insurance. It is significant also that the largest number of families without insurance and the largest number with small policies are among those with lowest incomes in relation to needs.[1]

Insurance against sickness is much less common than insurance against death, and usually that carried defrays only the smaller part of the loss due to sickness or disability.

Perhaps no one can estimate at all accurately the percentage of American wage earners now insured against sickness and accident, but, with a large margin of error, the Illinois Commission, as a result of its survey in 1918, concluded that perhaps 30 per cent of the wage earners in that state had such insurance. Though substantial progress was made during the next ten years or so, especially with an increasing number of benefit associations and the spread of group insurance, it is not likely that more than one-fourth of American wage earners are now insured through the numerous institutions available. Voluntary sickness insurance remains the exception, noninsurance the rule. And most of it is substandard and inadequate. Moreover, those wage earners most in need of sickness insurance partially to compensate for wage losses when disabled are least likely to have it. Not only are there rejections of the bad or the less good risks, but it is also chiefly those earning good wages who can pay the premiums usually necessary. But, whatever the explanation, the Illinois Commission found that the wage earners in Class *C*, least able to bear the financial loss incident to disabling sickness, least frequently drew sickness benefits when disabled for a week or more. The percentage of such persons drawing benefits was 7.4; the percentages

---

[1] For example, the Illinois Commission found in its study of wage-earning families that as against 60.8 per cent of those in the best-off and 60.1 per cent of those in the second-best-off classes, only 50.7 per cent of those in the least-well-off class (Class *C*) had insurance. Other studies have yielded similar results. (*Report*, p. 143.)

for those in meager circumstances (Class *B*) and those relatively well off
(Class *A*) were 12.1 and 15.8, respectively.

Briefly summarized, these are the essential facts concerning one phase
of the matter—insurance against loss of wages caused by disabling sickness or death.   The other phase concerns medical care.

MEDICAL CARE AND MEDICAL BENEFITS

There were in the United States in 1932 more than 1,000,000 persons
who devoted all or part of their time to providing medical service and
from it derived their livelihood.   About one-half of these were engaged in
private practice; the other half were employed in medical institutions
or in the sale of commodities.   There were nearly 7,000 hospitals, with
slightly less than 1,000,000 beds, about 66 per cent of which were in
Government institutions.   From the point of view of the number and
training of persons rendering medical service and the medical facilities
available, the people in the United States were the best equipped in the
world.   They spend on medical care more than $3,500,000,000 annually,
and yet many persons do not receive adequate care either in quantity or
in quality and the costs are inequitably distributed.[1]   "The result is a
tremendous amount of preventable physical pain and mental anguish,
needless deaths, economic inefficiency, and social waste.   Furthermore,
these conditions are largely unnecessary.   The United States has the
economic resources, the organizing ability, and the technical experience to
solve this problem."[2]

[1] See further the admirable *Medical Care for the American People: Final Report of the
Committee on the Costs of Medical Care* (1932), pp. 1–37.

[2] *Ibid.*, p. 2.

Of the three and one-half billion dollars spent annually for medical service, 125 million
dollars is spent for services of osteopaths, chiropractors, naturopaths and allied groups,
and faith healers, and 360 million dollars is spent for "patent medicines."   Much of the
former sum and practically all of the latter are wasted.   (*Medical Care for the American
People*, p. 15.)   It is undoubtedly true that a good many people resort to patent medicines
and self-medication because they cannot afford regular medical service, and that if medical
service were made more regularly and cheaply available, the use of patent medicines would
decline.   The use of quack remedies cannot be attributed entirely to the high cost of more
scientific care, however, since ignorance and misleading advertising lead many people to
have a preference for patent medicines.

The United States has some 36,000 sectarian medical practitioners—about 7,650
osteopaths, at least 18,500 chiropractors, naturopaths, and the like, and some 10,000
Christian Science and New Thought religious healers.   In the aggregate they are almost
one-fourth as numerous as practicing doctors of medicine.   (Louis S. Reed, *The Healing
Cults*, Publication 16 of the Committee on the Costs of Medical Care, 1932, p. 106.)
Although these sects seem to be a peculiar American phenomenon, the existence of sects is
not new.   [With the exception of Christian Science, all of these sects are peculiar to America.
Some 1,800 Christian Science healers are in practice throughout the rest of the world as
compared with approximately 9,000 who practice in the United States.   Approximately
100 osteopaths and probably even fewer chiropractors practice abroad.   (*Ibid.*, pp.

The Committee on the Costs of Medical Care found, in a study of 9,000 families living widely scattered in many communities in the United States, that families in the lowest income groups received far less of nearly every type of medical care than those in the highest income groups. Those in the lowest income group received only 50 per cent as many days' hospitalization and 41 per cent as many calls from physicians as those in the highest income group. Only one-fifth as many persons received any dental attention in the lowest income group as in the highest.[1]

The distribution of facilities for medical care and the amount of medical care rendered, in so far as private practice is concerned, depend primarily upon supposed or real ability of patients to pay and not upon need. This largely explains the fact that the lowest income groups receive less medical service than the highest, and it also is the chief factor explaining the uneven distribution of practitioners and medical facilities throughout the country. It is only natural that a physician or dentist should attempt to establish a practice in the locality in which he thinks there is the best chance of making a living. The result, however, has been that in California in 1929 there was one physician to every 571 persons, while in South Carolina there was one to every 1,431 persons. In 1928 there were 19 dentists per 100,000 population in Mississippi, and

---

106–107.)] Previous to modern medicine, the whole field of medical practice, in a sense, was occupied by disputing sects, each with its own theory of health and disease. But in becoming scientific, medicine eschewed sectarianism. Logically, present-day medicine has no place for sects. Usually, however, the existence of a sect indicates a deficiency in regular medical practice. Christian Science, for example, is in part the fruit of the medical profession's inattention to the ills of the mind and to the neglect of psychotherapy. Yet, much can be said against the sects; it is a serious matter when persons not properly trained in the medical sciences are permitted to practice. (*Ibid.*, pp. 3–4.)

[1] *Medical Care for the American People*, p. 7. To quote a summary statement by Michael Davis (see Michael Davis, "Problems and Issues of Medical Service," in *Socialized Medicine: The Ninth Annual Debate Handbook, 1935–1936*, vol. 1, edited by Bower Aly, pp. 50–51): "The investigations of the Committee on the Costs of Medical Care and the more recent studies of the Metropolitan Life Insurance Company, the California and the Michigan State Medical Societies, all demonstrated that the amount of medical care received is much less among those of small means than among those in more comfortable circumstances. A series of sickness surveys made in a number of cities and towns during the ten years beginning in 1917 and covering some 25,000 persons, showed that 25 to 30 per cent of those with disabling sickness went through their whole period of sickness without any attention from a physician. The studies of the Committee on the Costs of Medical Care in 1929–1931, including almost 9,000 families of all income groups and in all sizes of communities throughout the United States, showed that nearly 50 per cent of the persons in the lower income brackets went through a year without any medical attention. This proportion decreased steadily as income rose, being less than 15 per cent among families with $10,000 a year or more. Several studies of the United States Public Health Service and of the Milbank Fund have shown the need for care among the lower economic groups to be somewhat greater than among the higher. The disparity between care needed and care actually received is still greater in dentistry and in private nursing."

101 in Oregon.[1]   The rural communities, on the whole, have less adequate facilities than have the cities.

The typical method in the United States of meeting the costs of
medical care is still through cash payment by the person in need of it.
Doctors commonly adjust their fees on a "sliding scale" according to
their estimate of the patient's income.[2]   As a counterpart of the sliding
scale there is the charity work done by doctors, either through low fees or
through city hospitals and free dispensaries.   Then, of course, there has
been the "poor" doctor for public charges.   The depression greatly
decreased collections from fees[3] and at the same time increased the number of persons requiring free medical care.   Within the last decade some
county medical societies have attempted to reduce the burden of providing medical care for the indigent by contracting with their local governments to provide it for the recipients of charity in return for a fixed
annual payment.[4]   The burden of charity work has also been considerably relieved by the payment of fees for medical and dental care by the
Federal Emergency Relief Administration.

An important modification of the traditional American policy of fees
based on a sliding scale supplemented by charity work has been the
development of clinics at which patients are treated at uniform and
modest fees, with a proportion of charity work.   The aim of these clinics
is to provide an efficient low-cost service which will make available the
services of specialists to those who could not otherwise afford such treatment, and at the same time in some cases to insure a more steady income
to the practitioner.   With only 150 in 1890 and 3,944 in 1921, "in 1931
it was estimated that there were over 2,000 clinics as the out-patient
departments of hospitals, and about 5,700 unattached to hospitals,
receiving in 1931 at least 35,000,000 visits from patients and in 1934 (on
account of the depression) about 50,000,000."[5]   The number of different
individuals who, as charity patients or in return for a modest fee, received

---

[1] *Medical Care for the American People*, pp. 3–5.

[2] An excellent description of American medical practice is given in *Medical Care for the
American People: The Final Report of the Committee on the Costs of Medical Care* (1932),
especially the statement of Walton Hamilton, p. 191.

[3] By far the largest proportion of practitioners are on a fee basis.   Of 6,328 physicians
replying to questionnaires sent out by the American Medical Association in 1928, 853 were
on a salary basis.   (R. G. Leland, "Income from Medical Practice," *Journal of the American Medical Association*, vol. 96, May 16, 1931, pp. 1683–1691.)

[4] In Marion County, Iowa, the county medical society was paid $2,430 for such service
in 1932.   At least ten other counties in a few other states made similar provision.   (*Medical Care for the American People*, p. 74.)

[5] Michael Davis, in *Socialized Medicine*, pp. 36–37.   A considerable number of the
older "unattached" or "independent" clinics (those not hospital outpatient departments)
provide curative treatment, but the primary function of these institutions is preventive.
They function in an important way in child welfare, venereal disease, tuberculosis, etc.
More than half of them are governmental in origin and control.   They scarcely compete
with but generally supplement the outpatient department.

some care in clinics is estimated at between 10,000,000 and 15,000,000. These clinics vary a great deal in type of service offered, size and kind of staff and equipment, how they are administered, and how financed.

In addition there are an increasing number of "private group clinics." The number now is considerably larger than the 150 or so in 1931.[1] These private group clinics, rapidly increasing in number, are largely a postwar development. "The distinguishing features of a private group clinic are: (1) its physicians are engaged in the cooperative practice of medicine and use many facilities in common; (2) all or most of the physicians are engaged full-time in clinic work; (3) two or more of the major specialties are represented on the clinic's staff, and an attempt is made to give complete service to all patients who are accepted; (4) the patients, although frequently under the charge of a single physician, are the responsibility of the whole group; (5) the financial responsibility rests with an employed business manager; (6) the income is 'pooled' and the remuneration of practitioners is determined by agreement among the practitioners, rather than according to the services rendered."[2] This type of clinic represents a profound modification of the traditional method of rendering medical service, yet it should be noted that as long as the clinics charge patients a set fee for each service rendered, the incidence of medical costs upon the individual still depends upon the amount of sickness experienced. The private group clinic coordinates medical service and reduces its cost, but does not necessarily put medical care on an insurance or group-payment basis.

A further stage in the evolution from individual to "organized medicine" appears when the private group clinic offers a complete medical service on the basis of fixed periodic payments. The medical cost to the patient in this case is determined in advance and does not vary with the amount of service rendered. Of such clinics there are as yet only a few, but their appearance is significant in the development of organized medicine.

One such clinic is that started by Doctors Ross and Loos in Los Angeles County in 1929.[3] This clinic offers a complete medical service to groups of subscribers on the basis of $2 per month per family. The clinic grew steadily throughout the depression and in 1934 occupied a large five-story building elaborately equipped for clinical purposes,

[1] In many cities groups of three to twenty physicians or dentists have reduced their overhead costs through joint utilization of office space, waiting rooms, equipment, and technical and clerical personnel. Customarily the participants in such a plan maintain separate financial relations with patients and complete professional independence. Such arrangements may be considered as a temporary phase in the transition from individual to private group practice.

[2] *Medical Care for the American People*, pp. 76–77.

[3] For a more complete description of this clinic see the publication of the Committee on the Costs of Medical Care, Alden B. Mills and C. St. C. Guild, *The Ross-Loos Medical Group: A Description of a Voluntary Health Insurance Plan*.

employed fifty-five physicians and 110 other attachés, operated an ambulance service, maintained doctors in twenty suburban towns, and, including families and dependents of subscribers, was responsible for the medical and surgical care of approximately 50,000 persons.[1] The service is said to be equal in quality and far to exceed in amount that which similar economic groups are able to purchase from private practitioners. There is no question as to the professional competence or responsibility of the staff.[2] Unquestionably the clinic has given the individual practitioners the severest kind of competition, and these practitioners are fighting the clinic with all of their resources. If the clinic wins, the days of many private practitioners are limited, for they cannot furnish comparable service for $24 per year per family.

Stimulated by the depression and the activities of group clinics, there has been most recently on the Pacific Coast, and especially in Washington and Oregon, an important development of medical service bureaus which apply the principle of insurance to medical care provided under the auspices of the local medical societies.

The most significant development in medical care is found, however, in group hospital plans. While some of these date back to 1912, the great majority have been organized during the depression, which has had the effect of decreasing ability to pay and of reducing the income of the general hospitals operated on a fee basis. The growth has been most rapid since the American Hospital Association in 1933 and the American College of Surgeons in 1934 officially indorsed group hospitalization as a means of budgeting hospital expenses and laid down certain principles for guidance.[3] In 1937 (March) hospital care was being purchased from

[1] Among the larger groups subscribing to the service were the (Los Angeles) Department of Water and Power, 2,250; public-school teachers, 2,900; county employees, 1,375; firemen, 1,075; policemen, 1,750; and city employees, 1,200 (*New York Times*, April 29, 1934).

[2] Yet Doctors Loos and Ross have been severely criticized for "unethical" practices, and were expelled from the county medical association. The expulsion was, however, not sustained by the Judicial Council of the American Medical Association, on the ground that the county society had not followed proper procedure.

[3] The rapid growth in membership of six typical hospital service associations may be seen from the following table from "Six Typical Hospital Service Associations," *Hospitals*, April, 1937:

Name of association	Date of origin	Present membership[a]	No. of affiliated hospitals
1. Associated Hospital Service (New York City)	May, 1935	Mar. 1, 1937—256,704	252
2. Minnesota Hospital Service (Minneapolis and St. Paul)	July, 1935	Mar. 1, 1937— 75,000	16
3. Cleveland Hospital Service (Cleveland, Ohio)	Sept., 1934	Jan. 1, 1937— 43,585	16
4. Rochester Hospital Service (Rochester, N. Y)	June, 1935	Feb. 15, 1937— 57,195	6
5. Hospital Saving Association of North Carolina, Inc.	May, 1935	Feb. 15, 1937— 21,862	76[b]
6. Hospital Service Plan of the Holston Valley Community Hospital (Kingsport, Tenn.)	July, 1935	Feb. 15, 1937— 6,594	1

[a] Including dependents. Associated Hospital Service, New York, membership rose to 657,631 by April, 1938.

[b] Theoretically, all hospitals in North Carolina are participants in the plan and some seventy-six have signed contracts—the great majority of which are community general hospitals of the nonprofit type.

hundreds of hospitals in upwards of sixty communities in which the directors had succeeded in enrolling more than 1,600,000 members;[1] more than 500 business organizations, more or less national in character, had subscribed to hospital-service plans through the payroll-deduction method.[2]   At present (1937) a plan for the entire state of North Carolina is in operation under the sponsorship of the North Carolina Hospital Association, the North Carolina Medical Society, and lay groups.   Under these group hospital plans the subscribers pay in advance a fee, ranging from 40 to 85 cents per month, depending upon the scope of services and types of illnesses covered.[3]   Ordinarily the patient may receive as much as twenty-one days' care in the hospital, including the use of a semiprivate room, meals, nursing service, and the services of the operating room and the laboratory.   Beyond this, provision may be made for further care at some percentage, say 75 per cent, of the usual charges.   Ordinarily the patient must pay his own physician's fee.[4]   The noninclusion of the medical service is explained primarily by the position taken by the organized medical profession.[5]

While this recent development of clinics, group purchase of medical care, and group hospitalization is the most promising and important in voluntary health insurance, a number of carriers have for some time provided medical benefits on an insurance or group basis.   In some cases

[1] See *New Plans of Medical Service* (Julius Rosenwald Fund, 1936); also, *Hospitals*, April, 1937.   The Bureau of Medical Economics of the American Medical Association, however, reports smaller figures as of January, 1937.   See *Group Hospitalization: A Report of Experiences* (1937), p. 87.

[2] *Report* (mimeographed), Committee on Hospital Service, American Hospital Association (March, 1937).

[3] C. Rufus Rorem, "Group Hospitalization," *American Journal of Nursing*, vol. 37, no. 2 (February, 1937), p. 1.

[4] These statements are designed merely to give a general idea of the nature of group hospital plans.   The plans differ widely in the services provided as well as in the payments required.   They also differ considerably in the location of control.   In some cases the plans are more or less commercialized.   The whole institutional arrangement is very well summarized and examined in *Group Hospitalization or Periodic Payment Plan for the Purchase of Hospital Care* (prepared by the Committee on Group Hospitalization of the Canadian Medical Association, 1935), p. 51.   Valuable data may be found in the issues of the *Modern Hospital* and *Hospitals*.

The plan of the Associated Hospital Service of New York City is of interest and during the last three years has served as a pattern.   Organized in May, 1935, it had 129,716 members in September, 1936, 256,704 by March 1, 1937, and 657,631 by April 1, 1938.   For $10 per year, or 3 cents per day per person, it provides, for not to exceed 30 days, semiprivate hospital service, x-ray and laboratory examinations, anesthesia, insulin, serums, ordinary drugs and dressings, and routine medical examinations.   Beyond 30 days, the patient pays at the rate of 67 per cent of the usual charges.   There is a ten months' waiting period for obstetrical cases.   Under regulations recently adopted, the charge for a person and spouse is $18 per year; for these and children under nineteen years of age, $24 per year.   There is an age limit of sixty-five years at time of enrollment, but there is no physical examination, occupational or salary limitation.   The doctor's fee is not covered by the plan.

[5] For the position taken by the medical profession see below, p. 333.

the carriers which provide cash benefits in case of accident or sickness also provide for medical benefits or hospital and medical care in kind. However, insurance against medical costs is very much less common than insurance against loss of income.

Of 189 mutual benefit associations surveyed by the United States Public Health Service, forty-three either paid for or provided some kind of medical service.[1] In some cases treatment did not extend beyond first aid, while in exceptional cases full medical and nursing service was provided and in rare cases provision for hospital care was made. Occasionally free dental service or dental service at cost was found.[2] In most cases the benefit payable for medical expenses was limited to a fixed amount of money. The limits might be set as low as $30 and as high as $375. It is not possible to estimate the number of industrial employees entitled to some kind of medical, surgical, or hospital care as the result of their membership in mutual benefit associations, but the conclusion seems to be justified that such associations play a relatively unimportant role in providing medical care for the people of the United States on an insurance basis.[3] Certainly the associations function in a still more limited way in medical care than in providing financial benefits.

Very few trade unions in the United States provide medical or hospital benefits for their members. Pierce Williams, in a careful canvass of trade unions, could discover only six locals which undertook to provide actual medical or hospital care for members disabled by sickness or nonindustrial injury.[4] However, a number of important unions carry on general health work; and some operate homes for their disabled members. In the men's clothing industry the Amalgamated Clothing Workers have since 1926 had an arrangement whereby union members may receive a careful medical examination and advice on health matters. In Chicago the union's new building contains a dental clinic with x-ray laboratory. The emphasis of the union has been on preventive medical service.[5] The Brotherhood of Locomotive Engineers found that, in death claims presented to their insurance department, 47 per cent of the cases were due to preventable diseases which could have been discovered by periodic examinations. The Brotherhood then established a voluntary system of examinations on a fee basis, and a health department in their *Journal* to which members could write for information.[6]

---

[1] *U. S. Public Health Reports*, Sept. 4, 1931. The sample may have been too small to be typical.

[2] National Industrial Conference Board, *Research Report 65*, p. 17.

[3] Pierce Williams, *op. cit.*, p. 290.

[4] *Ibid.*, p. 291.

[5] U. S. Bureau of Labor Statistics, *Bulletin 465*, p. 82.

[6] *Ibid.*, p. 83.

In the printing trades tuberculosis and lead poisoning were so prevalent that the International Typographical Union, which originally had jurisdiction over all the printing trades, undertook to provide care for its afflicted members. When the various printing trades broke away from the parent organization, they continued the practice. Now the Printers' Union and the Printing Pressmen's International Union each has a tuberculosis sanatorium, and the locals of the Stereotypers' and Electrotypers' Union support a small home where tubercular members may receive treatment. The Photo-Engravers' Union provides for medical examinations.[1]

In cooperation with the United States Public Health Service, the International Ladies' Garment Workers in New York in 1914 created a joint board with medical and dental divisions. In 1919 this became the Union Health Center which is operated on a cooperative but noninsurance basis.[2] The Center in 1927 was under the joint management of nine locals of the International with a membership of approximately 45,000. The Center gives (1) information on health matters, (2) examinations of members claiming sick benefits, and of applicants for union membership, (3) such treatment as may be necessary. A part of the income of the Center comes from those unions whose members have access to its facilities, but of late its great source of support has been the fees of the patients themselves. The rapid increase in union membership since 1933 has enabled the Center to become practically self-supporting through the nominal fees paid by union members for treatment received. Following a large growth in membership, the International Ladies' Garment Workers' Union, with more than 100,000 members in New York City alone, assumed sole financial responsibility for the Health Center in 1934. At that time the dental department was closed and plans were made for enlarging the medical facilities and equipment in order to provide more adequate health service. During the first six months of 1935, 17,370 patients were served.[3]

The fraternal societies usually make no provision for medical benefits. Some societies, however, do maintain hospitals in which members may obtain free treatment. Many societies maintain tuberculosis sanatoria and some also provide free nursing service.[4]

In no instance are insurance companies known to provide direct medical service other than the nursing care now provided by a few large ones engaged in industrial insurance. Medical benefits usually take the form of cash payments to cover certain medical expenses, hospital and

---

[1] Ibid., p. 84.
[2] Ibid., p. 81.
[3] New Plans of Medical Service, The Julius Rosenwald Fund (1936), p. 24.
[4] Pierce Williams, op. cit., p. 270.

doctor bills. Such benefits are, however, a relatively unimportant part of commercial health and disability insurance, constituting only 10 per cent of total benefits paid in health insurance and 3 per cent in accident insurance.[1]

A considerable amount of medical care is now provided in industry. One of the most noteworthy and completely developed plans for health service is that of the Endicott-Johnson Corporation of New York State.[2] The company employs about 19,000 workers and offers comprehensive medical service to all of them and their immediate dependents. The service was inaugurated in 1918 as an outgrowth of workmen's compensation requirements. In 1928 the company spent $896,800 for medical care, only $23,000 of which was for treatment of cases of industrial accident. The service includes not only ordinary care by physicians, but also hospital care, both general and maternity, nursing service, dental care, and x-ray or any form of special treatment. About 94 per cent of those eligible, or 38,500 persons, used the service in 1928. In that year, the average cost per person was $25.49. The service has emphasized the treatment of illness rather than preventive medicine or research.[3] During the depression the company announced to the workers that it was impossible for it to continue to furnish medical service and the workers agreed to meet the costs from wage deductions. In 1934, when the company again was making profits, these contributions for medical service were repaid.[4]

Employee group medical service has been long established in the lumber, mining, and steam-railroad industries in the United States. In these industries fixed payment for medical service developed partly as the result of the isolation of the communities in which the workers live, but in all cases the development of provision for nonindustrial injury and illness is now closely related to the provision of medical care under workmen's compensation laws. In some instances these plans were already of

[1] *Ibid.*, pp. 258–259.

[2] For a description of the Endicott-Johnson medical service, as of 1928, see Niles Carpenter, *Medical Care for 15,000 Workers and Their Families* (Committee on the Costs of Medical Care, Publication 5, 1930).

[3] The Company in 1936 employed a full-time staff of more than 100 persons, consisting of approximately forty physicians, five dentists, and a staff of five dental hygienists, four physical therapists, twenty-six trained nurses, five bacteriologists, five pharmacists, technicians, office clerks, and assistants. The local hospitals are used for the care of patients through a contractual arrangement whereby the workers' medical service pays standard rates for services rendered to subscribers by the nonprofit hospitals in the community. In 1934 the corporation paid a total of $364,438 to outside hospitals and private nurses. In addition, approximately $10,577 was paid to specialists and consultants among the private practitioners in Binghamton and neighboring towns. In that year the Endicott-Johnson physicians made 133,580 house and hospital calls, and received 183,160 calls at the clinic. (*New Plans of Medical Service*, Julius Rosenwald Fund, 1936, pp. 16–18.)

[4] *New York Times*, June 3, 1934, pt. 4, p. 6.

long standing when state compensation laws were enacted.[1] Usually the state requires strict segregation of the payments into the workmen's compensation and nonindustrial medical funds and often that treatment must be rendered in separate hospitals, but employers who are self-insurers may in some states provide both types of service with the same staff and hospital facilities. Medical care for nonindustrial injury and disease is made available to the employee by the company in consideration of a fixed, periodic payment deducted from his wages. In many concerns the payroll deduction entitles dependent members of the employee's family also to medical service. The number of mining and lumber employees covered by payroll-deduction medical-service plans in April, 1930, was estimated as 540,000.[2]

Pierce Williams found that in twenty-seven of the important trunk-line railroad systems in the United States, a fixed regular payment in the form of a deduction in wages entitled employees to complete care in hospitals, operated by the employee hospital association. Treatment was provided for both "duty" and "nonduty" injury and sickness. The total number of employees on railroads with hospital associations was estimated at 530,000, or 34 per cent of the employees of Class I steam railways in April, 1930. Dependent members of employees' families were not entitled to free service, but were offered special rates.[3]

We conclude from this summary review of the costs of sickness and accidents that the problem presented ranks next to unemployment in importance, and, in spite of all preventive work that can reasonably be done, will remain a major social problem. The loss of wage income and the costs of medical care total nearly $4,500,000,000 in a normal year, and this huge burden is distributed very unevenly among the population. Compensation for loss of time and wages, and provision for meeting the costs of medical care are called for. To an increasing extent the costs of medical care are being met on an insurance basis or by fixed periodic payments, but such voluntary insurance is usually limited to special groups in the population and there is little likelihood that wage earners generally will be brought within the present system. A variety of institutions, mutual benefit associations, trade unions, and fraternal societies, as well as commercial insurance companies, now provide insurance against loss of income due to illness or accident, yet only a minority of wage earners are protected in this way. The proportion so protected is probably smaller than in England on the eve of the enactment of compulsory health insurance.

Significant, also, is the fact that there has been, even before as well as during the depression, an increasing amount of tax-supported medical

[1] Pierce Williams, *op. cit.*, p. 8.
[2] *Ibid.*, p. 3.
[3] *Ibid.*, p. 4.

care. Public hospitals, providing much care without charge, have become increasingly important. And here and there in recent years, as in the state of New York, "indigent" has become much more liberally defined for the practice of the "poor doctor" and for hospitalization.

It has been recently estimated that tax-supported medical service and voluntary health insurance now provide perhaps one-quarter of the total costs of medical care among families with incomes under $2,500 per year. The largest share of this is provided by government through taxation, the amount of tax revenues so used for medical service for all income groups being estimated at $510,000,000 per year.[1]

Doctors, Dentists, Nurses, and Hospitals

This statement of the sickness problem has been in terms of the people to be served. In order to give a truer picture of the entire problem, a few words should be added concerning the doctor's income and the position of the nurse, the hospital, and other persons or agencies finding place in the institutional setup.

Though the physician's bill may be high relative to the ability of a large part of the sick to pay, the average income of the doctors, when allowance is made for overhead and incidental expenses and for uncollected bills, is certainly not a large one, considering the type of man entering the profession and the training required. In 1929 (one of the best years for physicians' incomes) the average professional net income of physicians in private practice was $5,467. The range of net incomes was from more than $30,000 to a deficit. One-third of all private physicians had incomes of less than $2,500, while more than one-seventh, these largely specialists, had net incomes of more than $10,000.[2] The average gross income of all physicians in 1929 was $9,000, approximately 40 per cent of which was required for professional expenses, such as office rent. In "good times" collections average about 10 to 20 per cent below the amount charged,[3] but in periods of depression the proportion of uncollectable bills greatly increases. From 1929 to 1933 the average net income of physicians in private practice declined 40 per cent.[4] A survey of the income of dentists revealed similar results.

According to the United States Census of 1930, there were 294,189 graduate nurses and nurses in training, and within the next four years

---

[1] I. S. Falk, *Security against Sickness*, p. 48.

[2] Maurice Leven, *The Incomes of Physicians* (Committee on the Costs of Medical Care, Publication 24, 1932), pp. 20, 85, 117. According to the study of physicians' incomes made by the Committee on the Costs of Medical Care, specialists had an average net of $10,000 in 1929, partial specialists $6,100, general practitioners $3,900 (*Ibid.*, p. 117).

[3] *Ibid.*, pp. 24, 95.

[4] U. S. Department of Commerce, Bureau of Foreign and Domestic Commerce, *National Income in the United States, 1929–1935*, p. 213.

this number had increased by 100,000.[1] The usual charges for trained-nursing service are from $5 to $8 per day, which places the service beyond the reach of the average family income, yet unemployment and underemployment is so common among trained nurses that their annual incomes are often inadequate.[2] As a result of its study of the income of physicians, dentists, and nurses, the Committee on the Costs of Medical Care concluded that, "Certainly no solution to the problem of medical costs can be reached through a reduction in the average of professional incomes."[3]

With the development of scientific medicine, the specialization and elaborations of medical techniques and equipment, the hospital has

TABLE 31.—CAPITAL INVESTMENT AS OF DECEMBER 31, 1928, IN 6,852 HOSPITALS REGISTERED BY THE AMERICAN MEDICAL ASSOCIATION[1]

(in Thousands)

Control	General	Nervous and mental	Tuberculosis	Special	Institutional	Totals
Federal..................	$ 122,841	$ 38,595	$ 28,034	$ 1,530	$ 8,715	$ 199,715
State...................	51,664	660,401	49,012	7,056	25,335	793,468
County.................	86,915	44,270	43,890	5,260	6,925	187,260
City....................	136,774	23,486	20,517	28,430	1,882	211,089
City and county..........	17,441	182	4,726	1,149	1,510	25,008
Total governments.......	$ 415,635	$766,934	$146,179	$ 43,425	$44,367	$1,416,540
Independent.............	$ 585,019	$ 20,934	$ 20,457	$ 72,656	$ 7,668	$ 706,734
Church.................	627,498	12,301	9,275	23,951	4,112	677,137
Fraternal...............	11,821	....	1,967	3,411	3,345	20,544
Total nonprofit associations................	$1,224,338	$ 33,235	$ 31,699	$100,018	$15,125	$1,404,415
Individual and partnership.	$ 81,642	$ 12,192	$ 7,647	$ 14,336	....	$ 115,817
Incorporated.............	102,027	7,650	8,850	9,700	....	128,227
Industrial...............	25,124	....	....	....	....	25,124
Total proprietary.......	$ 208,793	$ 19,842	$ 16,497	$ 24,036	....	$ 269,168
Total registered hospitals.	$1,848,766	$ 820,011	$194,375	$167,479	$59,492	$ 3,090,123

[1] C. Rufus Rorem, *The Public's Investment in Hospitals* (1930), p. 27. The distribution of investment according to types of control and type of institution was substantially the same in 1935 as in 1928. The data for number of beds under different types of control, however, indicate a continued increase in the proportion of beds under governmental supervision, and a further decline in the proportion of beds in proprietary hospitals. The trend in investment would probably indicate a similar shift.

[1] Elizabeth Burgess, *Survey Graphic* (December, 1934), p. 600. In addition there were in 1930 about 153,000 untrained nurses.

[2] Data as to the income of nurses are not satisfactory, but a survey in 1927 indicated that the incomes of private-duty nurses averaged around $1,300 and showed no tendency to increase with years of service. The income of institutional and public-health nurses was somewhat higher (*Medical Care for the American People*, p. 68).

[3] *Ibid.*, p. 22.

assumed an increasingly important role as a social institution. In the United States more than $3,000,000,000 has been invested in hospitals, less than 10 per cent of which sum was invested with the hope of profitable return. The distribution of this investment according to type of hospital and type of organization sponsoring and controlling the hospital is shown in Table 31.

It will be noted that nearly one-half (46 per cent) of the investment in hospitals has been made by governmental bodies—Federal, state, county, and city—but that the proportion of investment by the government varies widely among the different types of hospitals. Thus less than one-fourth of the investment in general hospitals as against more than 90 per cent of that in mental and approximately three-fourths of that in tuberculosis hospitals is governmental. The relatively small investment in proprietary hospitals is concentrated in general hospitals; church and independent hospitals dominate in this field.

One of the most striking phenomena regarding hospitals has been the decline in small hospitals and the corresponding increase in large ones. During the decade ending with 1934 the number of hospitals with less than ten beds declined from 665 to 191, while hospitals with 300 or more beds increased in number from 451 to 580.[1]

The increase in size of hospitals explains the fact that, while the number of registered[2] hospitals declined from 7,320 to 6,189 during the period 1924–1936, the number of beds increased from 755,722 in 1923 to 1,096,721 in 1936. In fact, the number of beds increased at an almost uniform rate of 25,000 per year during the twenty-seven years from 1909 to 1936, with comparatively little difference made by war, depression, or other conditions.[3] Table 32 sets forth the number of hospitals, the number of hospital beds, the percentage of beds occupied, the number of patients admitted, the average census, patient days, and average length of stay, according to control.

Governmental general hospitals care for a larger proportion of chronic cases than do the general hospitals under voluntary auspices, so that the average length of stay in governmental general hospitals is 18 to 20 days,

---

[1] "Hospital Service in the United States," *The Journal of the American Medical Association* (March 30, 1935), pp. 1075–1090. This fourteenth annual presentation of hospital data by the Council on Medical Education and Hospitals of the American Medical Association was characterized as the "most complete, accurate and up to date ever assembled in any publication in this country." (*Ibid.*, p. 1175.)

[2] Registered with the American Medical Association. In 1936, 581 institutions were refused recognition because of "unethical or questionable practices." Usually these hospitals were not offering a high quality of medical service, but some were refused admission because their service was on an insurance basis.

[3] "Hospital Service in the United States," *The Journal of the American Medical Association*, vol. 108 (Mar. 27, 1937), p. 1036. During this period the average increase has been approximately 25,024 beds per year.

TABLE 32.—STATISTICS OF ALL REGISTERED HOSPITALS, ACCORDING TO CONTROL, 1936[1]

Type	Hospitals	Beds	Percentage of beds occupied	Bassinets	Patients admitted	Average census	Patient days	Average length of stay (days)
Federal......................	323	84,234	81.6	675	426,570	68,752	25,163,232	59
State.......................	524	503,306	95.1	1,136	534,652	478,778	175,232,748	328
County......................	484	87,541	87.1	2,388	497,706	76,277	27,917,382	56
City........................	332	78,950	82.9	3,947	885,058	65,508	23,975,928	27
City-County.................	61	9,809	76.6	496	108,873	7,520	2,752,320	25
Total governmental..........	1,724	763,840	91.2	8,642	2,452,859	696,835	255,041,610	104
Church......................	969	113,288	65.3	16,360	2,286,064	74,037	27,097,542	12
Fraternal...................	64	4,938	67.6	116	33,057	3,341	1,222,806	37
Associations and restricted corporations....................	1,678	157,650	66.0	21,122	2,939,651	104,169	38,125,854	13
Total nonprofit..............	2,711	275,874	65.8	37,598	5,258,772	181,547	66,446,202	13
Individual and partnership.......	1,204	28,496	47.9	4,356	437,797	13,672	5,003,952	11
Corporations (unrestricted as to profit)....................	550	28,511	57.7	3,629	497,457	16,462	6,025,092	12
Total proprietary.............	1,754	57,007	52.8	7,985	935,254	30,134	11,029,044	12
All hospitals.................	6,189	1,096,721	82.8	54,225	8,646,885	908,516	332,516,856	39

[1] "Hospital Service in the United States," *Journal of the American Medical Association*, vol. 108 (Mar. 27, 1937), pp. 1036–1041.

as compared with less than 14 days in voluntary general hospitals. The governmental hospitals include nearly half a million beds in institutions for mental diseases. These are mostly state hospitals, whose patients have a long period of hospitalization (328 days).

The number of hospitals and the number of beds in hospitals under the control of individuals and partnerships have declined since 1927, presumably because such investments have not been profitable. One factor in this situation is that the percentage of occupancy of beds is low. In 1929 the percentage of beds occupied in such hospitals was 54.2, but by 1934 the percentage had declined to 40.9. During the same period the percentage of beds occupied in government hospitals increased from 88.9 to 89.8. The seriousness of the problem of unused bed-capacity, from the financial point of view, becomes more apparent when it is realized that the average investment per bed in all American hospitals is approximately $3,500, ranging from about $2,000 for state nervous and mental hospitals to more than $6,000 for general hospitals conducted by independent associations.[1] It should be added that the tendency is for the investment per bed to increase. The high overhead costs of hospital

[1] C. Rufus Rorem, *op. cit.*, p. 32.

service have, in general, made investment in hospitals unprofitable and, as we have noted, more than nine-tenths of the investment in hospitals has actually been made without expectation of profit. The majority of hospitals are supported by taxes or receive a large share of their incomes from voluntary contributions, endowments, or subscriptions from persons who are not direct beneficiaries of the hospital.[1] Often hospitals in their charges to patients do not attempt to include costs due to fixed charges, and therefore many of the regular pay patients are in effect receiving part-pay or charity medical service. In addition, of course, much of the service of hospitals is on a direct and recognized charity basis. Funds for such services are commonly obtained through community-chest drives, but with the increasing need for charity service during the depression, a shift to tax-supported medical service was necessary.

The other parts of the picture may be left to be filled in by those interested. Enough has been said concerning the problem of sickness in a country with a limited amount of sickness insurance and still less of organized medicine. Except for relatively fewer persons without ability to pay the costs individually, and the financing of hospitals, the problem in most respects is not essentially different from the problem in European countries years ago, which led them to adopt subsidized or compulsory sickness insurance. The one really important difference is that in Europe hospital care was generally, except for the well-to-do, tax-supported and did not find a place in working-class budgets. In the United States, on the other hand, approximately 40 per cent of the total expenditures for medical care by people with small and moderate incomes is for hospital care and the accompanying professional services given patients while in the hospital.[2]

[1] Dr. Falk says: "Of the $656,000,000 spent by hospitals annually for operating costs in a normal year, approximately $302,000,000 is paid by patients through fees, $54,000,000 represents contributions and endowments, and about $300,000,000 is derived from taxation. Most of the $302,000,000 from fees is paid not by the 125 million potential patients but by the 5 million 'pay' patients admitted to the nongovernment institutions for acute medical and surgical conditions. Most of the $300,000,000 spent by governments is used to support hospitals for nervous and mental and for tuberculosis cases, or for the treatment of 'indigent' patients requiring general medical or surgical care. Voluntary contributions have greatly declined. The income from endowments, which reached a maximum of $20,000,000 in 1929, has declined greatly since then, and shows little prospect of growth in the near future." (Quoted with permission from I. S. Falk, *Security Against Sickness*, Doubleday, Doran and Company, 1936, p. 28.)

[2] Michael Davis, *The American Approach to Health Insurance* (reprinted from the *Milbank Memorial Fund Quarterly*, vol. 12, July, 1934, p. 211).

CHAPTER VI

COMPULSORY HEALTH INSURANCE ABROAD

A GENERAL REVIEW OF COMPULSORY HEALTH INSURANCE[1]

Most of the European countries and a few others now provide for partial compensation for loss of earnings and for medical care through compulsory health-insurance systems. First developed into a general system in Germany in 1883,[2] twelve European countries had before the War adopted general compulsory insurance systems. A number of other European countries "inherited" such a system from the countries of which they were a part in prewar years or have adopted it in postwar years, in part because of the adverse conditions in which the masses of their populations were placed. Health insurance has also in postwar years been adopted by Japan, Chile, Ecuador, Peru, Brazil, and two Canadian provinces. The several countries which have adopted compulsory insurance measures, with date and approximate number insured, are shown in Table 33.

Thus compulsory health insurance has been adopted by twenty-nine countries with a combined population of over 500,000,000. Over against these countries which have adopted compulsory insurance are a number which grant government subsidies to voluntary organizations insuring their members in an acceptable manner. Important among these countries are New Zealand, Belgium, Sweden, Denmark, and Spain. Formerly the list of such countries was much longer than at present, for several of them have changed from subsidized voluntary to compulsory insurance. Indeed, it is not too much to say that there has been a strong tendency to substitute compulsory for voluntary insurance once a government has become actively interested in the sickness problem from the insurance point of view. One important reason for the change from the one type of law to the other is found in the fact that generally subsidies have not been sufficient to induce most of those in need of it to insure. The experience of Denmark, where in 1934 some 65 per cent of the wage earners were insured through voluntary organizations, assisted by sub-

---

[1] Instead of "sickness insurance" the authors prefer to use the expression "health insurance," because it is in general usage in the United States. Of course, a government does not insure health. It insures against losses from disabling sickness and provides medical care.

[2] Health insurance had years before been made compulsory for certain limited groups in Germany, France, and perhaps other continental European countries.

271

TABLE 33.—COMPULSORY HEALTH-INSURANCE SYSTEMS, 1937[1]

Country	Date of original law[a]	Approximate number insured in 1933-1934
Germany	1883	16,800,000
Austria	1888	1,262,000
Czechoslovakia	1888, 1924	2,900,000
Yugoslavia	1888, 1922	680,000
Italy	1888, 1928	1,796,027[b]
Poland	1889, 1920	1,600,000
Luxemburg	1901, 1925	48,000
Hungary	1907, 1927	870,000
Norway	1911, 1930	568,209
Great Britain	1911	17,010,300[c]
Northern Ireland	1911[d]	
Irish Free State	1911[d]	474,000
Switzerland (several cantons)	1911, 1926	
Estonia	1912	40,173
Latvia	1912, 1930	165,000
Rumania	1912, 1933	600,000
Netherlands	1913, 1929	
U.S.S.R.	1922	23,513,600
Japan	1922	2,667,000
Bulgaria	1924	251,268
Chile	1924	500,000
Lithuania	1926	42,096
France	1928	7,509,819
Portugal	1933	
Greece	1934	
Canada		
Alberta	1935	
British Columbia	1936, 1937	
Ecuador	1935	
Peru	1936	
Brazil	1936	

[a] Two dates for Czechoslovakia, Yugoslavia, Italy, and Poland mean that new legislation was adopted usually after the country was made independent of another which had legislated on health insurance earlier. Italy, for instance, did not pass its legislative decree for health insurance until May 6, 1928, although many of her former Austrian provinces had insurance acts as early as 1888. Health insurance in Italy is strictly compulsory only for seamen and airmen and in the new provinces; but the above decree (legislative decree of May 6, 1928) concerning collective agreements stipulates that "such agreements may not be approved or published unless they contain definite provision for the protection of the workers in case of sickness." International Labour Office, Studies and Reports, Series M, no. 13, vol. 1, p. 447. In the cases of the other countries, two dates signify that the original law was either extended to a more general application or delayed in its operation.

[b] Includes figures for compulsory health and maternity insurance for those in industry and commerce in the former Austrian provinces, compulsory insurance for seamen and airmen, and insurance on the basis of collective agreements for those employed in industry and commerce and for land and river transport workers. It does not include figures for the following: compulsory maternity insurance for women employed in industry and commerce (840,000), compulsory tuberculosis insurance for all employed persons (6,250,000), or insurance provided in collective agreements in agriculture.

[c] Annual Report of the Ministry of Health (England and Wales) and Department of Health (Scotland), 1934; see also p. 290 below.

[d] The "British" legislation.

[1] Source: International Labour Office, Studies and Reports, Series M, no. 12, The International Labour Organization and Social Insurance (1936), pp. 203–209, and no. 13, International Survey of Social Services, 1933 (1936), vols. 1 and 2. Also Monthly Labor Review, vol. 42, pp. 921, 1507; vol. 43, pp. 332–335; and vol. 44, pp. 559–563, 875–876.

sidies, is exceptional; more nearly typical is the experience of Sweden where roughly one in seven is insured. As Epstein says, the adoption of compulsory insurance was due "to the failure of voluntary insurance to meet the insistent need of security against sickness in spite of governmental subventions and great educational campaigns."[1] A second, less important, reason for the change from subsidies to compulsion has been the desire to place a part of the burden of support upon industry and perhaps to relieve the general revenues of the government. To explain: normally under the subsidy system the burden of support has rested upon the dues of the insured and the tax revenues, while under the compulsory systems the necessary contributions are almost always exacted from employers and the insured, perhaps with a smaller part of the needed revenues provided from public funds.

Compulsory insurance is as a rule confined to the working population; only in a few countries[2] does it cover all classes of persons with incomes below a certain figure. And, as Epstein says:[3]

"Even in the case of workers the various systems vary in scope. The International Labor Office finds the degree of coverage to vary all the way from 15 to 86 per cent of the employed population. The differences are explained by the variable importance of the wage-earning groups in each country, as well as by the inclusiveness of the laws. Increasingly, however, compulsory health insurance is being extended to wider and wider groups of wage-earners. Since the risk of sickness is universal, the tendency definitely is to extend the circle of persons insured. Twenty out of the twenty-five nations with compulsory insurance plans now cover the bulk of all workers in industry and commerce."[4]

The inclusion of wage earners other than those in industry and commerce is not so general, in some cases because of the difficulty involved in collecting premiums, in others because of less need or because of other provision made. Yet, it is interesting to note that of the systems established by the countries or groups of provinces noted above, approximately half include agricultural laborers, and also a half include domestic servants. On the other hand, public officials, civil servants, and

---

[1] Quoted by courtesy of Random House, Inc., from A. Epstein, *Insecurity; A Challenge to America* (1936), p. 471.

[2] The systems of Chile, Rumania, and the Swiss cantons are exceptional.

[3] A. Epstein, *op. cit.*, pp. 471–472.

[4] Mrs. B. N. Armstrong, in *Insuring the Essentials* (1932), p. 348, reports the following percentages of all employed persons and of the total population as insured under the compulsory systems in the countries specified: Austria, 75 and 34.3; Bulgaria, 67.46 and 4.74; Czechoslovakia, 65.54 and 19.25; Germany, 76.8 and 32; Great Britain, 86.4 and 35; Hungary, 44 and 11.65; Norway, 73.1 and 21.3; Poland, 44.4 and 7; Russia, 83 and 6. Of course, where dependents are entitled to medical care, or where maternity benefits are paid to the wife of the insured, or where funeral benefits are paid upon death of a dependent, benefit rights are given to persons not "insured" (against loss of time). Hence, the percentages given really understate the relative number with rights to medical care, etc.

school teachers, whose salaries continue during sickness, are in most countries excluded from insurance. Finally, it may be said that the right to insure voluntarily and to take advantage of the system is usually accorded to persons who do not come within the compulsory provisions of the law, provided their incomes do not exceed a certain amount. In other words, the compulsory system is usually accompanied by a less important subsidy system.

The funds required to finance sickness insurance, generally amounting to from 4 to 7 per cent of the wage-earner payroll, are obtained from contributions by the insured, the employers or the public treasury, or some combination of these.[1] The largest group of countries, about two-fifths of all,[2] exact contributions from all three sources. The proportions exacted differ widely but in a majority of cases the workers pay the same amount or twice as much as the employer, with the state paying various proportions up to a third of the total, as in Bulgaria. The next largest group of countries derive their revenues from contributions by the insured and employers, without direct help from the state.[3] The Swiss cantons exact contributions from the insured only, but these contributions are supplemented by government subsidies. In Russia the entire cost is placed upon industry, while in Rumania it is placed upon the insured. Finally, in Portugal all the resources of the corporative insurance funds come from contributions made by the employers and workers at rates fixed by collective agreement and approved by the National Labor and Provident Institution.[4]

Provision is made under these compulsory health-insurance systems for partial compensation for loss of income and for medical benefits in all, and for maternity and funeral benefits in a majority of cases. With a waiting period in most countries ranging from a few days to a week, financial benefits at flat rates or, with exceptions, at from two-fifths to two-thirds of wages are paid the eligible insured while disabled, for maxima of thirteen weeks to fifty-two weeks in a period of twelve months. In some cases financial benefits are paid in reduced sums for a second further period of disability. The benefits paid provide only partial compensation, because of the necessity of conserving the funds available and the need for discouraging malingering. The partial compensation is, however, designed in so far as practicable to provide the insured and his

---

[1] For details concerning contributions, see B. N. Armstrong, *op. cit.*, Chart VI, pp. 602–607; also see International Labour Office, Studies and Reports, Series *M*, no. 12 and no. 13.

[2] Including Bulgaria, Chile, France, Great Britain, Northern Ireland, Irish Free State, Japan, Latvia, Lithuania, Luxemburg, Norway, and Peru.

[3] Including Austria, Hungary, Czechoslovakia, Estonia, Greece, Germany, Italy, Netherlands, and Yugoslavia.

[4] International Labour Office, *International Survey of Social Services 1933*, Series *M*, no. 13 (Geneva, 1936), vol. 2, p. 368.

dependents with the essentials for maintenance without becoming charges upon others.

The second main benefit provided is that of medical care. In Great Britain,[1] except for the supplementary provision made out of excess funds, this is limited to the ministrations of the general medical practitioner and a minimum of medicines and appliances. In most countries, as in Germany,[2] the medical benefit includes also the services of specialists, hospitalization, nursing care, dental care, and a liberal allowance for medicines and appliances of one kind or another. Indeed, in approximately half of the several countries, his dependents have the same, or substantially the same, rights to medical care as are given to the insured. In such of these countries as have large wage-earning populations most of the medical care is provided under the compulsory health-insurance systems. Independent medical practice has become rather the exception than the general rule. But it is to be noted that for the most part insurance is a method of paying bills; except for standardization most of the service is given by doctors, hospitals, etc., as before insurance was introduced; of state medicine in the sense of salaried government doctors or government hospitals, little has been added under the insurance regime.[3]

Another cash benefit is the burial benefit. This is provided under the health-insurance systems of the several countries, except in Great Britain, the Irish Free State, France, Northern Ireland, Netherlands, Portugal, and a few others. Sometimes this is a fixed sum, but, under the influence of German law, the usual rule is to make an allowance equal to from twenty to thirty times the basic (daily) wage. In five countries the right to burial benefit, sometimes in reduced amount, is extended to dependents of the insured also, while in a number of other countries such provision has been optional under the statutes.

Omitting reference to incidental benefits provided in exceptional cases, the final one to be noted is the maternity benefit. Under practically all of the systems of health insurance a cash benefit is paid in a specified sum or in terms of the disability allowance for a period of from four to sixteen weeks, the more usual period being eight weeks. This is in the cases of insured women. The laws in half of the countries require or permit similar provision to be made for the wives or other dependents of the insured, but perhaps in reduced amount. Except in Great Britain,

---

[1] See below, pp. 296 ff.

[2] See below, pp. 279–281, 282–288.

[3] For the most part the general medical service is provided by panel doctors remunerated on a per capita basis. While in some countries a minority of the insurance carriers own and operate hospitals, for the greater part the needed facilities and attendant services are secured under contract from government or provident hospitals. And frequently the payment made to government hospitals covers only a part of the cost; hence the service is in part tax-supported.

nearly all of the countries also provide obstetrical and possibly nursing care as a part of the medical right.

The insurance is usually organized through acceptable nonprofit-making, voluntary associations, supplemented by local funds or organizations established by the government to serve those who do not qualify for membership in mutual associations and the like or do not care to join them. Profit-making organizations find little place as insurance carriers except in Great Britain where the industrial companies have been permitted to qualify "on the insurance side." Steps are taken to see that the carriers are democratically governed,[1] and representation in the administrative organization is related to the contributions exacted for the support of the insurance system.

These paragraphs have been designed to give a rough general picture of the extent and nature of compulsory health insurance now in effect. In order to give a more accurate conception of what such compulsory insurance is, its accomplishments, and its problems, the systems of three leading countries will be briefly reviewed. The three are those of Germany, Great Britain, and France. The French system was the last important one to be adopted in Europe and presents novel and suggestive features. That of Britain is very important for the lessons to be drawn from experience under it. The German system has provided the pattern for the legislation enacted by many other countries.

Compulsory Health Insurance in Germany[2]

Though its roots reached far back in institutions designed to cope with the sickness problem of special groups,[3] the German system may be said to date from Bismarck's time and a statute adopted June 15, 1883. Its objectives were to check the trend toward Marxian socialism and to build up a national feeling of gratitude to a generous state, as well as to solve some of the more pressing problems connected with sickness and the system of poor relief.

---

[1] A change was made in Fascist Germany in 1934. See below, p. 281.

[2] The authors are greatly indebted to Dr. Gertrud Kroeger for obtaining and checking statistics and for suggestions used in this section.

[3] The idea of mutual help can be traced back to the guilds of the Middle Ages. Some years prior to 1883, insurance had been made compulsory for miners and certain other working groups. The Prussian Code of 1845 had empowered local authorities to require journeymen in the handicrafts and other workmen to join mutual benefit organizations for protection against sickness, need, and death. Four years later, another law had authorized the local governing bodies to require factory owners and master craftsmen to insure their workmen against sickness, the necessary contributions to be made by employers and the insured in equal amounts. In other German states there had been similar developments. Hence, at the beginning of the 1880's, there were some thousands of mutual associations providing sickness benefits for perhaps 2,000,000 persons. For details see W. H. Dawson, *Social Insurance* (1912).

The Act of 1883 made membership in a health-insurance organization obligatory upon wage earners employed in mines, salt works, metallurgical establishments, quarries, building operations, factories and all other manufacturing establishments, in miscellaneous trades, and on railroads, river steamships, and wharves. Salaried employees were also included, provided their incomes did not exceed M. 2,000 per year. Other persons of small means might come under the plan voluntarily. At the end of the year 1885, the number of insured persons was in excess of four millions. With this as a beginning, the coverage of the mandatory provisions was extended by laws enacted in 1892, 1900, and 1903 to commercial employees, to miscellaneous clerical workers, and to various public employees with the same income limit as that prescribed for salaried employees, by then M. 2,500. The Insurance Council was authorized at its discretion to include homeworkers also. The Code of 1911 contained many revisions of the law. For the first time, all agricultural workers, seamen, domestic servants, and homeworkers were required to become insured. In 1923 certain professional groups, such as persons employed in education, welfare work, and nursing, were brought under the system. Finally, it may be noted that from time to time the income figure for determining whether or not certain classes were required to insure was changed, and usually in the upward direction. In October, 1927, it was fixed at M. 3,600 for persons in industry and M. 2,700 for nonmanual employees. The net result by the end of the 1920's was that more than 20,000,000, or approximately two-thirds of all gainfully occupied persons, found membership in the system. If dependents with rights to medical care are also considered, it is estimated that in 1932 some 44,000,000 in a total population of 65,000,000 had at least certain rights to medical care under health insurance.

The number of insured persons as of certain years is shown in Table 34. The proportion of those compulsorily insured and the proportion volun-tarily insured has changed from year to year. In some recent years the ratio between the two classes has been about 10 to 1.[1]

The plan was to require membership in democratically governed organizations which would serve as insurance carriers and provide or arrange for medical care. If they met certain standards, miners' funds, mutual aid societies, guilds, building-trades funds, and establishment funds were accepted as insurance organizations. Commercial insur-ance companies were not accepted because they were profit-making institutions. But to the pre-existing types of organization accepted as carriers, two types were added in order to provide carriers for those

[1] Those who fall out of insurance because of prolonged unemployment, as well as certain other classes of persons, may voluntarily insure. The number of persons thus insured greatly increases when employment conditions are bad, as in 1932, when the number rose to 3,438,000 (I. S. Falk, *Security Against Sickness*, p. 80).

TABLE 34.—NUMBER OF PERSONS INSURED IN GERMANY, 1885 TO 1934[1]
(In Thousands)

Year	Male	Female	Total
1885	3,882	789	4,671
1900	7,942	2,217	10,159
1914	10,744	5,782	16,526
1920	11,637	6,730	18,367
1925	12,091	6,962	19,053
1930	12,813	7,531	20,344
1934	11,740	6,331	18,071

[1] As reported in *Statistik des Deutschen Reichs*, vol. 484, *Die Krankenversicherung*, 1934, (Berlin, 1936), p. 46. The figures presented in this chapter do not check with those given by Dr. Isador S. Falk, *Security Against Sickness* (1936), a copy of which became available as this material was undergoing revision. The difference is explained by the fact that membership in "substitute funds" is not included in the above table.

persons who could not qualify for membership in, or who did not wish to join, any organization of the older types.

From time to time, in the interest of economy, administrative convenience, and quality of service, changes have been made in the standards applied to organizations desiring to be accepted as carriers, and, even more interesting and important, the legislation has given to the government-created funds a more important position in the system. The greatest changes were made by the Code of 1911. The minimum number of members required in order to be accepted was increased, higher standards were imposed, and some of the old types of carriers were eliminated. Since the Code of 1911 came into effect, seven types of organizations have served as carriers, viz., general locals (Ortskrankenkassen); rural locals (Landkrankenkassen); works or establishment funds (Betriebskrankenkassen); guilds (Innungskrankenkassen); miners' funds (Bezirksknappschaften); the Seamen's fund; and the Ersatzkassen, or substitute mutual funds. The general nature of most of these organizations is obvious. The difference between the general local and rural funds, it may be explained, is not merely one of urban or rural source of members. Agricultural workers, traveling vendors, and, within certain limits, domestic employees provide the membership of the rural funds. Other insured persons, unless, of course, they belong to another type of fund, have membership in the Ortskrankenkassen.

The total number of carriers had increased from 18,942 in 1885 to 20,568 in 1890, to 22,508 in 1900, and to 23,188 in 1910. With the new standards relative to minimum number of members and other matters required under the legislation of 1911 and more recent years, the number of carriers has decreased to 6,191,[1] though the number of insured persons had by 1934 increased by more than one-half. At the same time increasing percentages of the insured persons have had membership in the

[1] The total for 1914 was 10,011; 1930, 7,237; 1934, 6,191.

general and rural funds. The combined percentage for the two had increased from 49.4 in 1885 to 59.5 in 1913. In 1925 it was 71.3; in 1934, only slightly less. With the Seamen's Fund omitted, the number of each type of carrier or fund in 1934 and the distribution of membership among the several types are shown in Table 35.

TABLE 35.—GERMAN FUNDS, THEIR NUMBER AND MEMBERSHIP, 1934[1]

Funds or carriers	Number	No. of members (000 omitted)
Local.	1,857	12,124
Rural.	408	1,802
Establishment.	3,135	3,002
Guild.	710	529
Miners' funds.	33	564
Substitute.	47	1,878

[1] *Statistik des Deutschen Reichs*, vol. 484, pp. 11, 13.

Each of these carriers or funds must provide, as minimum requirements, certain cash benefits and medical services and must collect revenues sufficient to cover its operating expenses and to provide the necessary small reserve. Though there have been some exceptions to this rule, the contributions are usually exacted in the proportions of two-thirds from the insured and one-third from the employer.[1] For fixing the amount of the periodical contributions and also for determining the sums to be paid as cash benefits, a basic wage is fixed for each of several groups. The contribution and likewise the benefit are given percentages of the basic wage for the class in which the insured person falls. The employer is legally responsible for the insurance and for the contributions of those of his employees within the embrace of the compulsory provisions of the law. In other words, the contributions are collected at the source. The maximum of contributions has varied under the different laws, but is now fixed, generally, at 6 per cent of wages.[2] Of course, the funds have some incidental revenues also, but these are of slight importance. The benefits provided are of two types, cash and medical care, broadly defined.

Medical care, as it has developed under the German health-insurance system, is a relatively inclusive service. The minimum embraces the services of a physician, and, when needed, a specialist, certain limited dental services, drugs and medical appliances (within prescribed limits), and maternity care. At the discretion of the attending physician, and with the consent of the patient and the approval of the executive board

[1] Under a decree issued in July, 1934, the contributions by worker and employer are to become equal.

[2] Reduced by presidential decree from 7.5 per cent, in 1930. In 1934, the actual rate varied between 3 and more than 8, and averaged approximately 5 per cent.

of the carrier, hospital treatment may be given. In this case, the usual cash benefit, described later, is diminished or disallowed, but a domestic benefit (Hausgeld) may be paid to the dependents of the insured for their sustenance as well as pocket money to the patient. To begin with, the medical care in a given case was to be provided for thirteen weeks in the year but in 1903 this was changed to twenty-six weeks. The institutional arrangements for this medical care will be described at a later point.

The most important cash benefit is for loss of time[1] caused by disability for work in the insured's occupation.[2] It must be paid from the fourth day of disability and has all the while been 50 per cent of the appropriate basic wage, with a prescribed maximum daily figure.[3] Originally the cash benefit, like the medical benefit, was limited to thirteen weeks in the year, but in 1903 the prescribed maximum was raised to twenty-six weeks. If disability extends beyond twenty-six weeks, further benefits are provided under invalidity and old-age insurance.[4]

The funeral benefit is another but minor cash benefit. The minimum is twenty times the basic wage of the insured. In the event other health-insurance rights have been exhausted, this claim is to be paid provided death occurs within a year, the insured was continuously incapacitated, and the cause of death was a sickness which caused the exhaustion of insurance rights.

The maternity benefits have become extended and somewhat complicated in their details. Originally the benefit ran in terms of cash benefit for disability. At first granted for a period of three weeks, this was extended to four weeks in 1892, to six weeks in 1903, and to eight weeks in 1911. During the War, and again during the period of inflation, numerous changes were made in the law. At present the ordinary cash benefit is paid an insured woman for four weeks prior to and six weeks following confinement and at three-fourths of the wage rate before confinement, provided she does not engage in gainful employment. Moreover, there is a lump sum payment of Rm. 10. The services of a trained midwife and a physician are provided in addition to these cash benefits. Provision is also made for nursing care, and, in lieu of a part of the cash benefit, care in a maternity home is provided. Since 1930, medical care, on somewhat different terms, must also be provided for the wife and such dependent daughters as share the roof of the insured man. The extent

---

[1] Payment is made for Sundays as well as for week days.

[2] That the insured might be able to work at something else makes no difference in the right to benefit.

[3] In 1903 the maximum wage to be used in determining the benefit was increased from 71 to 95 cents. It is now fixed at $2.38 per day.

[4] Some funds, however, pay benefits beyond the twenty-six weeks. The invalidity and old-age insurance is responsible for the care of disabled persons when the sickness benefits terminate.

of health insurance maternity service (extended also to noninsured dependents of insured workers) is shown by the fact that in 1929, 834,000 out of a total of 1,200,000 births came within its embrace.

These are the four minimum benefits which must be provided or arranged for by each carrier. These may be liberalized or extended.[1] Indeed, in 1930, after medical care had been voluntarily extended by most carriers to the dependents of the insured, such provision was made mandatory for a period of thirteen weeks but with various limitations and with only half of the cost of medicines and appliances provided by the fund. The medical care for insured persons may include convalescent care, home nursing, physiotherapy, etc., and it may be extended to fifty-two weeks in the year. In 1914 medical care had been provided for more than twenty-six weeks by 5.7 per cent of the carriers, these including a disproportionately large number of the more important ones. The corresponding percentage in 1924 was eleven. Similar liberality has been shown in maternity and funeral benefits, the latter sometimes being increased to the maximum of forty days' wages. Funeral benefit may also be extended to dependent wife and child. More than minimum cash benefits were paid by 20 per cent of the carriers in 1914.[2] In 1924, 36.2 per cent of the organizations paid cash benefits in excess of half but not exceeding two-thirds of basic wages, while 9.1 per cent more paid in excess of two-thirds but not exceeding three-fourths of basic wages.

At this point brief mention should be made of the administrative machinery established to supervise the operations of the funds and to decide contested claims.

Until 1934 each insurance carrier had for these purposes an executive board and a committee, representing the insured and the contributing employers. Under the revisions then made, the principle of "democratic" government gave way to that of "leadership," the leader being appointed by a superior officer. Each organization is now, however, to have an advisory council in which the insured and the employers are represented in equal numbers. Moreover, under the reorganization made in 1934, a physician is given membership on each council. The operations of each carrier and the application made of the law and regulations have been supervised by district, superior, and the central insurance offices. Appeals from decisions on claims made by committees or administrators have been settled authoritatively through a system of insurance courts.

---

[1] Provided the tax levied does not exceed 5 per cent of the basic wage. In 1934, two-fifths of the general local funds, more than half of the rural funds, four-fifths of the guild funds, nine-tenths of the miners' funds, and practically all of the establishment funds were allowed to grant additional benefits.

[2] Appelius and Ashenheim, "Die socialhygienische Bedeutung der deutschen Social-versicherung," in *Handbuch der Social-Hygiene,* p. 369.

With the extension and enrichment of the German health-insurance system, and the growth in claims upon it, the budget has become a larger and larger one.[1] The total expenditures on benefits are shown for the years specified in Table 36.

TABLE 36.—BENEFIT EXPENDITURES OF THE GERMAN HEALTH-INSURANCE SYSTEM, 1885 TO 1934[1]

Year	M. or Rm. (000 omitted)
1885	52,759
1900	174,012
1914	487,996
1925	1,169,744
1930	1,649,946
1934	1,020,902

[1] Statistik des Deutschen Reichs, vol. 484, p. 48.

Table 37 shows the per member cost of each of the branches of service under the system, also the administrative costs.

TABLE 37.—ANNUAL COST PER MEMBER OF HEALTH INSURANCE, 1885 TO 1934[1]
(In Marks or Reichsmarks)

Year	Physicians, dentists, and other medical personnel	Drugs, appliances, etc.	Hospital care	Cash benefits	Domestic and other allowances	Maternity benefits	Funeral benefits	Total[b] benefits	Administration	Grand total
1885	2.14	1.74	1.10	5.62	0.05	0.14	0.51	11.62	0.78	12.40
1900	3.59	2.80	2.16	7.60	0.16	0.25	0.57	17.56	1.00	18.56
1914	7.44	3.80	4.46	11.85	0.54	0.76	0.68	30.17	2.99	33.16
1925	15.46	7.30	8.67	24.09	1.73	3.11	0.78	62.16	4.48	66.64
1930[a]	23.46	10.15	13.78	25.04	2.47	4.69	1.01	81.64	6.82	88.46
1934[a]	19.62	7.39	11.18	11.75	0.92	4.83	0.53	57.16	5.98	63.14

[a] Includes seamen's insurance.
[b] Figures include costs of benefits unaccounted for in previous columns.
[1] Compiled from Statistik des Deutschen Reichs, vol. 484, p. 49. The following table shows the outlays of German health insurance in 1930, by object. (From ibid., vol. 420, Die Krankenversicherung im Jahre 1930, pp. 86–87.)

Object	Rm.	Object	Rm.
Physicians' services	311,397,714	Physiotherapy (baths)	14,352,264
Dentistry	79,655,814	Hospital care	238,660,171
Medical care by persons other than physicians or dentists	3,131,674	Home nursing	235,304
		Convalescent care	9,974,302
Drugs and minor appliances	185,605,653	Cash benefits	540,912,585
Major appliances	10,706,229	Hausgeld (benefits for dependents of persons hospitalized)	37,123,751

It will be noted that the per member cost in 1930 was more than two and a half times as high and in 1934 was almost twice as high as it had

[1] Until economies were effected in the 1930's. See Tables 36 and 37.

been in 1914, when it was two and a half times what it had been in 1885. It will be noted, also, that the increase is found more or less strikingly in every item except funeral benefits. It will be noted, in the third place, that the preponderance of the outlays shifted from cash benefits paid to the disabled to the several items involved in medical service. In 1885, the system was, more than anything else, one for providing maintenance for workers disabled by sickness; 45 per cent of the outlays represented cash benefits. Doctors, drugs, appliances, and hospital service accounted for 40 per cent. Administrative costs, which until the lean years of the 1930's varied between a little less than 6 and 9 per cent of the total, amounted to 6.3 per cent. In 1930, the cash benefit was 28 per cent; in 1934, less than 20 per cent of the total. The corresponding percentages for physicians, dentists, drugs, and hospital care were 54 and 60, and if maternity benefits are included, were 59 and 68. The German system has become more and more one for providing medical service.

The cost of cash benefits has mounted with increases in money wages— and these have not been small since 1885 or 1900—with payments for longer periods under more liberal laws, and with payments in excess of the statutory minima and the increasing tendency to disregard the waiting period.   And, of course, the cash benefits as well as the volume of medical work have varied with the amount of illness and resulting claims.   The costs of medical care have been affected by any higher remuneration of doctors and dentists, the prices of drugs and appliances, and the like, by the extension of medical rights for much longer periods, by the extension of medical care to dependents, and by the enrichment of the service at many points.   The medical service of the late 1920's was not the limited service it had been at the turn of the century or in 1885.[1]

In explaining these increased costs much has been said concerning malingery and a recorded but questionable increased volume of illness. At all times there has been malingery by some persons who were, or had become, able to work but who preferred sickness benefits.   There has been more or less of it under the German system just as there has been more or less of it under commercial insurance.   Not all doctors certify and re-certify disabling sickness with a sufficient degree of strictness because they are also giving treatment.   Yet malingery and imposition have not constituted an important problem in German experience in normal times.   Prior to the adoption of unemployment insurance in 1927, however, the number of claimants and the volume of recorded illness increased strikingly in times of depression and widespread unemployment.   An example is found in lean years during the 1920's.   The explanation was twofold.   Workers desired maintenance.   On the other

[1] For further development of this and significant detail, see I. S. Falk, *Security Against Sickness*, Chaps. V and VI.

hand, workers in unknown number came forward for treatment of defects and diseases neglected until a convenient time to suspend work occurred. As the authors of *The Way of Health Insurance* have said, "The greatest cause of the growth in expenditures is the remarkably steady increase in the amount of sickness for which medical service must be supplied and compensation paid."[1] The increase in recorded sickness of insured persons is shown in Table 38.

TABLE 38.—NUMBER OF DAYS OF SICKNESS PER INSURED MEMBER, 1885 TO 1934[1]

Year	Male	Female	Both sexes
1885	6.02	5.68	5.97
1900	6.96	6.71	6.91
1913	8.53	9.14	8.70
1920	b	b	b
1925	12.91	12.89	12.90
1930[a]	11.73	11.45	11.63
1934	8.36	9.53	8.77

a Salaried employees of Ruhr Mining Fund not included.
b No data given.
1 *Statistik des Deutschen Reichs*, vol. 484, p. 46.

The recorded sickness is frequently presented in terms of duration of cases of disabling illness. When thus presented, the average number of days for males was 14.1 in 1885, 19.1 in 1913, 22.5 in 1925, 26.5 in 1930, 28.6 in 1932, and 24.2 in 1933. The corresponding averages for females for the same years were 14.1, 24.4, 28.0, 28.9, 30.2, and 28.0. It will be noted that the averages for women have been rather consistently larger than for men. When the data are combined for the two sexes, the percentages for the years cited have been 14.1, 20.6, 24.4, 27.3, 29.3, and 25.6.[2]

Were these data combined with the number of cases of sickness, they would, of course, yield the number of days of sickness per member (or

TABLE 39.—NUMBER OF CASES OF SICKNESS PER 100 MEMBERS, 1885 TO 1934[1]

Year	Males	Females	Both sexes
1885	42.2	40.4	41.9
1900	41.3	33.4	39.6
1913	45.4	37.5	43.1
1925	56.0	46.0	52.4
1930[a]	44.3	39.6	42.6
1934	36.0	34.9	35.6

a Salaried employees of Ruhr Mining Fund not included.
1 *Statistik des Deutschen Reichs*, vol. 484, p. 46.

1 A. M. Simons and Nathan Sinai, *The Way of Health Insurance* (1932), p. 56.

2 These averages are taken from a table on p. 110 of I. S. Falk, *op. cit.* Compare data presented by B. N. Armstrong, *op. cit.*, pp. 286–287.

100 members). Inasmuch as the number of cases of sickness per 100 members is of value as a check on one's thinking, the figures are presented in Table 39.

These data relating to sickness and the duration of disability have been as frequently as not interpreted in an erroneous manner. Not infrequently the increase in the average of the days of illness has been cited as evidence of imposition, malingery, and failure of the system to improve health and to reduce morbidity. A common mistake has been to overlook the fact that the data are for recorded days of disabling illness, not true morbidity figures. The average duration in terms of days means nothing unless the changing system—in respect to duration of medical rights and other things—is given due consideration. Of course, with the liberalization of the law an increasing number of cases have had long duration and have increased the average. The number of cases of sickness per 100 members has more significance than the duration of cases or the number of days of illness per 100 members. And, the number of cases per 100 members yields no evidence for an indictment. It is true that it ran high in the 1920's, but this is explained, in part at least, by the effects of the War and the tendency for claims to be made in large numbers in times of acute unemployment. If the number of cases through all the years appears high, it must be said that the number of cases of medical care per 100 would be expected to be larger with the care paid for under a system of insurance rather than on a fee-for-service basis. Without question there are cases without merit which stand over against cases of medical neglect before the system was introduced and outside of it since its introduction. It is true, also, that cases of a newer type have become more common, but that would be expected with medical advance and an improved standard of living. It is found in the United States where "private medicine" prevails as well as in Germany. It may well be, however, that a psychology of sickness tended to develop with all the care exercised and the publicity incidental to it. The American student in Germany prior to 1933 was likely to conclude that such was the case.[1]

Naturally enough, there have been numerous criticisms of the German system, among them the limited amount of malingering just touched upon, the increased cost with medical progress and the enrichment of the benefits provided, the troubles of the doctors, the druggists, etc. But it is admitted that medical care for the masses of the people has been greatly improved and the principle of health insurance and the main parts of the system have been very generally approved. After considering the substitution of other plans, the National Socialist government in 1934 made only a limited, though important, revision of the insurance system as it

[1] At present great emphasis is being placed upon health rather than sickness, also upon personal hygiene. The recent morbidity statistics may reflect this.

had developed in a half century.   Passing over minor matters, only a few larger issues will be noted and briefly discussed.

The doctors have had grievances.   The problems of the relationship of the physician to the health-insurance carrier have centered around the following points: the contractual relationship between physician and carrier; the organization of the service; remuneration; choice of physician; control and supervision of medical work; disputes and their settlement.

For many years the carriers secured the necessary service under individual contracts with the doctors.   The absence of standards for the service to be rendered, the lack of supervision of the medical work done, in the earlier years, and an increasing number of doctors seeking insurance practice resulted in a price war among the physicians.   Out of this situation, among other things, developed the *Verband der Aerzte Deutschlands*,[1] so active until 1934, when it was dissolved by the government.   Since the organization of the *Hartmannbund*, the doctors have generally made their views and wants known in an organized way.   At times they have gone on strike in various localities, *i.e.*, while ministering to the needs of sick persons as individuals and privately, they suspended working relations with the carriers.   Making headway under the Berlin agreement (1913), the doctors obtained the right to enter insurance practice by registration, but provided there was an opening under the standards set in terms of one physician to a given number of insured persons in the area.   Recognition of the right of free choice of doctor was increasingly secured.   For years remuneration has been disposed of by collective bargaining, but because of such incidents as the general strike in Berlin in 1923, the government developed machinery for handling authoritatively issues involving an emergency.[2]

The remuneration of the physicians under health insurance has become increasingly important, for more and more of the medical care has been provided under that system.   Eighty per cent of the doctors

---

[1] Commonly called *Hartmannbund* because founded by Dr. Hartmann.

[2] In the reorganization effected under the decrees issued in 1933 and 1934, an association of health-insurance physicians (Krankenkassenaerztliche Vereinigung Deutschlands) has been established as the only representative of the insurance doctors.   Membership in it is compulsory.   It is a public corporation and has the right to issue rules and regulations. It is a party to all contracts for the doctors' services.   It assumes responsibility for the necessary supply of doctors, has to do with admissions to practice, and is responsible for supervising medical work.   Arrangements are made for supplying more doctors where there is a deficiency and for reducing the number where there is an excess.   The rate of remuneration is scaled, the rate decreasing with the number to be served; family allowances for the doctors' dependents may be made out of an equalization fund created by the physicians' organization.   While the individual doctor is placed under a greater degree of control than heretofore, the organized doctors through their association have been recognized and given power not previously possessed.   One principle underlying the revisions is to give the doctors complete control over professional matters.

engage in insurance practice,[1] and with the extension of the system and the impoverishment of the middle class in postwar years, insurance work became the principal source of their professional incomes. This as well as what they have at times regarded as underpayment for work done resulted in discussions which at times became rather heated. Some years ago the issue over ambulatories or clinics established by health-insurance organizations became acute and developed into an emergency situation.

With the progress of medicine, diagnostic facilities and the like became increasingly important and steps were taken by the funds to make them accessible. Partly in this way, partly because of a feeling that economies could be effected, and also as a result of strikes, an interest developed in the organization of clinics to provide medical care. Such clinics were organized in Berlin at the time of the doctors' strike in 1923, and they continued to operate after the strike had been settled. In 1927 there were some forty of these, large and small, general and special, located in working-class-residence districts in Berlin. The staffs consisted of full-time doctors working on salaries. The great general insurance fund operating these ambulatories provided medical care for the dependents of its members only at the clinics or, if they were bedfast, at the hands of the clinical doctors who then made home calls. A part of the medical care of the insured was provided in the same manner. A few clinics developed in a similar way in other localities than Berlin. While in some respects the ambulatories marked an advanced step in medical provision, the diversion of work from the general practitioners on the panels became a great threat to which the doctors reacted strongly. The organized opposition was successful in removing the threat caused by the ambulatories and clinics in 1927.

As has been noted, medical care includes, in addition to the services of physicians and dentists, the provision of hospital care, nursing service, drugs, and medical appliances. A few of the funds maintain their own hospitals but most of the hospital service is arranged for under contract, at special rates, and most of the time the fund is the stronger bargainer. In some cases the payments made cover scarcely more than half of the full cost.[2]

The original practice, one that continued to be the more prevalent, was for the carrier to purchase drugs and appliances from private com-

---

[1] B. N. Armstrong, *op. cit.*, p. 355. Three-quarters of the dentists have an insurance practice.

[2] In this connection one must hold in mind that any person in Germany, regardless of his income, may enter a hospital as a "third-class patient," *i.e.*, paying the lowest rate per day, a rate which by no means covers the operating cost. In other words, the community feels responsible for providing a minimum of hospital care for any person regardless of his income.

mercial sources. In the interest of economy, however, even before the War some of the carriers established their own distributing centers, and after the War many of them did so. Not only did distributing centers greatly increase in number and importance, but the field of open retailing was entered also, the extent of the retail business varying among the different sections of the country. Moreover, a wholesale purchasing company was established. Finally, some of the carriers began to produce needed appliances, such as bandages and eyeglasses. For obvious reasons, the apothecaries, the opticians, the bandage makers, and other groups protested against these activities. A government decree (Oct. 19, 1933) directed at this "new competition" advised the closing of all such distributing centers.

The German system has also been criticized on the ground that prevention of sickness has not been properly emphasized. The criticism is perhaps aimed at direct attacks not being made upon situations responsible for disease and at inadequate coordination with the public-health service. Of course, good medical care, without delay or worry, is preventive; the mass of German people have had that. It is admitted that the maternity benefits have been of great value. Moreover, some of the carriers have made direct attacks from the point of view of prevention. Examples are found in the provision made for undernourished children, the health bulletins published and distributed, and even such things as medical advice given those who wish to participate in athletics. Then, too, in certain ways at least, health insurance has stimulated a more general interest in prevention and provided data of importance in developing positive programs. For example, the published reports of such organizations as the large general fund in Berlin have been of great value in showing the relation between such a disease as tuberculosis and housing, family income, etc. The records of the large carriers provided data needed in the field of public health by the late Dr. Alfred Grotjahn and others carrying on research. Yet it may be true that preoccupation with insurance has tended somewhat to sap interest in another attack upon the problem or that the cost of insurance has made it more difficult to secure funds for public-health work. Certainly, from the point of view of prevention, there were deficiencies in organization, objectives, and control of the health-insurance system. Some of the recent revisions have been directed at these deficiencies. Under the last reorganization, the health and the invalidity insurances are brought into cooperation for attack upon special diseases. Moreover, the carriers are now specifically authorized to devote funds to preventive work, and the administrative officers of the district organizations, etc., have responsibilities for prevention placed upon them. In part, this has been in an effort to place a check upon the increasing cost of health insurance and to limit the outlays to what the contributors can afford to pay. There has been much uneasiness over the increasing claims and increasing bills at a time of decreased ability to pay.

HEALTH INSURANCE IN GREAT BRITAIN

In 1911, perhaps 4,500,000 wage earners in the United Kingdom were insured against loss of wages through friendly societies, trade unions, sick clubs, and employers' provident funds, and a substantial number of these were being provided with some measure of medical care and attendance as well.   In 1912 these 4,500,000, and approximately twice as many others, were swept into compulsory insurance under the National Insurance Act, for the total number of insured persons in October, 1912, was reported as 13,709,047.   The insured embraced the overwhelming majority of manual workers and a no small fraction of the nonmanual workers, those earning less than £160 per year.   Certain classes of persons were exempted, but these were relatively few, for the number of insurable persons granted certificates of exemption may be placed at 111,500. Some 300,000 others were in "excepted" classes because they were engaged in "excepted employments," such as teachers, civil servants, and the like.   These were permitted to remain out of insurance because they were being provided with benefits at least as favorable to them as those provided under the Act.   Hence, the embrace of the compulsory provisions of the Act was very inclusive.

Provision was made for voluntary insurance, or "voluntary contributors," also.   The actuaries had estimated the number who might enter the system as voluntary contributors at 829,000.   The fact is that the number of such contributors in England, Wales, and Scotland at the end of 1912 was only 21,930, and a year later it was less than 20,000.   It was not until 1926, when health and old-age insurance were linked together under the legislation of 1925,[1] that voluntary insurance became attractive.   Since that date the number of voluntary contributors has been about 500,000.[2]   This, however, is a small percentage of the total, and no further reference to voluntary subsidized insurance needs to be made.[3]

---

[1] *Stat.* 1925, 15 and 16 Geo. V, Chap. 70.

[2] At the end of 1934 it was 565,000.

[3] The voluntary contributor has had a savings account derived from his own periodic payments and the usual government subvention.   His benefits and also a sinking-fund requirement have been charged against this.   This sinking-fund requirement has absorbed most of the subvention, hence the arrangement did not prove to be attractive except as a temporary device.   Moreover, in 1918, the privilege of becoming a voluntary contributor was limited to those who had been in insurance, because it had not been attractive to non-wage earners of small means, and because most of the accounts were short-lived and therefore generally inadequate to pay cash benefits of any considerable amount.   It has been the attraction of pensions which accounts for the several-fold increase in the number of voluntary contributors since 1925.

Various changes have been made in the law from time to time, in the light of experience and problems. One of these changes was to substitute £250 for £160 in fixing the dividing line between those nonmanual workers who must and those who need not become insured. This was done in 1919, when prices and wages had greatly increased owing to the War situation. During the 1920's various amendments were made to prolong the insurance rights of unemployed persons. Again, as already noted, there was the linking of health insurance and old-age insurance under the legislation of 1925. But basically the system now in operation is that introduced in 1912. Under it the great mass of wage earners, and approximately a third of the population, have been insured against sickness.[1] The approximate number of insured persons in Great Britain, by sex and carrier, is shown for the years 1912–1934, in Table 40.

There are great contrasts between the British system and the systems of Germany and of other continental countries whose legislation was

TABLE 40.—APPROXIMATE NUMBER OF PERSONS INSURED THROUGH APPROVED SOCIETIES OR AS DEPOSIT CONTRIBUTORS, IN ENGLAND, WALES, AND SCOTLAND, 1912 TO 1934[1]

Year	Approved societies			Deposit contributors			Grand total
	Men	Women	Total	Men	Women	Total	
1912–13	8,937,849	3,831,904	12,769,953	232,700	103,700	346,400	13,116,153
1914	9,151,176	3,900,237	13,051,413	225,800	96,800	322,600	13,374,013
1915	9,265,700	4,036,900	13,306,600	224,850	98,600	323,450	13,630,050
1916	9,486,600	4,390,900	13,877,500	216,800	130,000	346,800	14,224,300
1917	9,481,100	4,685,200	14,166,300	230,700	155,600	386,300	14,552,600
1918	9,589,100	4,998,700	14,597,800	223,090	170,590	393,680	14,991,480
1919	9,663,200	4,957,600	14,590,800	290,930	171,010	461,940	15,052,790
1920	9,670,100	4,926,500	14,596,600	259,070	133,960	393,280	14,989,880
1921	9,691,100	4,860,000	14,551,100	185,010	101,770	287,440	14,838,540
1922	9,745,200	4,867,500	14,612,700	185,700	91,880	277,890	14,890,590
1923	9,878,700	4,814,400	14,493,100	178,000	90,800	268,800	14,761,900
1924	10,057,500	4,942,900	15,000,400	175,200	101,700	266,900	15,266,900
1925	10,191,700	5,034,100	15,225,800	174,900	96,600	271,500	15,497,300
1926	10,422,500	5,085,500	15,508,000	179,700	102,700	282,400	15,790,400
1927	10,044,000	5,250,000	15,294,000	162,100	97,900	260,000	15,554,000
1928	9,967,000	5,382,000	15,349,000	151,000	97,000	248,000	15,597,000
1929	10,095,000	5,466,000	15,561,000	147,800	102,500	250,300	15,811,300
1930	10,306,000	5,538,000	15,844,000	145,300	109,100	254,400	16,098,400
1931	10,406,000	5,557,000	15,963,000	143,400	110,400	253,800	16,216,800
1932	10,491,000	5,556,000	16,047,000	138,200	114,800	253,000	16,300,000
1933	10,513,000	5,561,000	16,074,000	131,700	119,800	251,500	16,325,500
1934	11,052,500	5,697,400	16,749,900	130,300	130,100	260,400	17,010,300

[1] Annual Reports of the Ministry of Health (England and Wales) and Department of Health (Scotland).

[1] The percentage of the population insured in England and Wales increased from thirty-two in 1912 to 35.5 in 1921. This increase is explained in part by the change in age distribution, in part by the large number of persons drawn into industrial employment during the War.

based upon the German. The more important of these differences will become evident in the summary of the British system.

All persons between sixteen and sixty-five[1] engaged in manual labor under a contract of service are required to become insured. The same is true of all persons likewise engaged in nonmanual labor whose rate of wages is not in excess of £250 per year. Workers engaged on contract work, subcontractors, and share fishermen are likewise within the embrace of the compulsory provisions of the Act. The general exceptions are persons employed without money wages. Persons in the employment of the Crown, those in the employment of local and other public authorities, and clerks or salaried officials in the service of a railway or other statutory company, who are entitled to rights in a superannuation fund established by Parliament, are special exemptions.

It is the legal obligation of the employer to see that his eligible employees are insured. Government inspectors each year inspect from 15 to 20 per cent of the establishments, including those most likely to breach the law, to see that this obligation is observed and the proper contributions made.

Insurance is through friendly societies, trade unions, and other mutual societies of the type providing benefits for their members before the compulsory system was introduced, plus the industrial insurance companies. These companies were made eligible to serve as carriers provided they organized for the purpose on a mutual nonprofit basis. The opposition of the existing societies was such that no additional funds, like the General, Local, and Rural Funds in Germany, have been created. There is, however, a minor exception to be noted. Each approved society has had unrestricted right to exclude any person from membership except upon the ground of age. In order that excluded persons and such others as did not care to join an approved society should not be without insurance, provision was made for them as "deposit contributors." This meant that they had individual or savings accounts, similar to those of the "voluntary contributors." As might have been foreseen, this presented a distinct problem in the cases of those unfortunate enough to become seriously ill or to be in general bad health. To meet this problem the legislation of 1928[2] constituted such persons a special group and gave them the status of a society, in order that they might have the same status as the members of an approved society.[3]

---

[1] Previous to 1925, persons between sixteen and seventy, for then the age for qualifying for the noncontributory pension was seventy.

[2] *Stat.* 1928, 18 and 19, Geo. V., Chap. 14, Sec. 11.

[3] As Percy Cohen, in his *Social Insurance* (1932), pp. 8–9, puts it, " 'Deposit contributors' unable to become members of approved societies because of the state of their health, now [under the legislation of 1928] became eligible for the ordinary benefits of the Act and were grouped into a specially constituted section. Hitherto, they were only entitled to medical benefit and cash benefits up to the limit of the contributions paid into their accounts (after a deduction for cost of administration)." Thus was met the "plight of the handi-

Some 3,000,000 of the 8,000,000 or 9,000,000 not in insurance at the time the National Insurance Act became effective secured the necessary insurance through friendly societies, trade unions, and other organizations of the type which had been providing benefits for their members all the while. The largest share of the new insurance was, however, secured through the industrial insurance and collecting societies which had limited their profit-making business pretty much to burial insurance. Fearing loss of such insurance to other carriers if these served as carriers of insurance against sickness, and knowing that their burial insurance would expand if health insurance were provided by them, the "assurance" companies had insisted upon being accepted as approved societies. Then, with their house-to-house agents already in the field, they entered upon a campaign to secure as much of the new business as they could. As the years have gone by, these companies, on the "sickness-insurance side," have gained relatively to the other approved societies for a number of reasons. Not only have company agents been active; the companies have not been so concerned with the quality of membership as have some of the friendly societies, nor have they been under the limitations of the trade unions whose membership rises and falls with changes in the state of trade. Moreover, the agents, collecting weekly premiums on burial insurance, have had personal knowledge of young persons entering employment and required to come into insurance. Again, the agents see to it, as many approved societies do not, that insurance is made easy. They answer questions, they provide and, at the end of the half year, collect and turn in the stamped books,[1] and they pay sickness, disablement, and maternity benefits at the house. Where agents are not employed by an approved society, there is not the same closeness of touch; the insured must secure his book and return it to an office, and perhaps go there to collect his cash benefits. And, finally, there has been a tremendous decrease in the number of small approved societies because of their inability to give good service or to carry on within the limits placed upon administrative charges. Whatever the explanation may be, the friendly societies of different types had 46.5 per cent of the approved-society membership in 1912; the trade unions, 11.5 per cent[2]; employers' provident funds, 0.5 per cent[2]; the industrial and collecting societies, 41.5 per cent.[2] In the valuation of funds in 1928, the friendly societies, had 43.5 per cent of the approved-society membership, the trade unions' share had decreased to 9.1 per cent, the employers' prov-

---

capped deposit contributors," which had been recognized from the inception of the system in 1912, and increasingly complained of all the while.

[1] The employer's and the insured person's contributions take the form of stamps which are pasted in a booklet.

[2] Royal Commission on National Health Insurance, *Appendix to Minutes of Evidence*, pt. I (1924), p. 57.

ident funds remained approximately as before, at 0.6 per cent, while the industrial and collecting societies' share had increased to 46.8 per cent.[1] Thus, approved societies are, with minor exceptions, the carriers of the insurance. Though their number has strikingly decreased by amalgamation and otherwise,[2] they, with their administrative units, still number in the thousands. The number of societies and branches, with membership, 1912 and 1922, is presented in Table 41.

TABLE 41.—BRITISH APPROVED SOCIETIES AND MEMBERSHIP[1]

Year	No. of societies	No. of branches	No. of administrative units	Membership in societies	Membership in branches	Total membership
1912	2,481	14,388	16,869	9,458,698	2,936,920	12,395,168
1922	1,161	7,266	8,427	11,331,800	3,280,900	14,612,000

[1] Adapted from Royal Commission on National Health Insurance, *Appendix to Minutes of Evidence*, pt. I, pp. 59–60.

Since 1922 there have been further reductions in number, both of societies and branches. Of approved societies there are now in the United Kingdom approximately 900, and of branches some 6,000, a total of something less than 7,000 insurance units.[3]

Health insurance is financed by contributions by employer and the insured, and by the Exchequer through subsidy and Parliamentary Grants. The employer is responsible for his own and his workers' contributions. Unlike contributions in Germany, the weekly taxes are "flat rates" for men and women. The rates of contribution were increased in 1920, and again altered in 1925.[4] The employer's and the insured person's normal[5] contributions are now as follows:

Normal weekly rates payable by	Men, d.	Women, d.
Employer...............................	$4\frac{1}{2}$	$4\frac{1}{2}$
Employee...............................	$4\frac{1}{2}$	4
Total..................................	9	$8\frac{1}{2}$

[1] Percentages computed from data in W. J. Foster and F. G. Taylor, *National Health Insurance* (1935), p. 263.

[2] See pp. 308–309 for a discussion of the problem presented by the approved-society system.

[3] Approximate figures taken from Estelle M. Stewart, "British Health Insurance," U. S. Bureau of Labor Statistics, *Monthly Labor Review*, vol. 39 (1934), p. 835.

[4] The original contributions totaled 7d. and 6d. for males and females, respectively. In 1920 the corresponding figures became 10 and 9. The present, somewhat lower, figures were introduced when old-age and health insurance were linked, in 1925.

[5] From the beginning the employer has been required to assume a part or all of the contributions of the low paid, *i.e.*, sweated female workers, but the requirement has scarcely altered the distribution of the tax between employer and employee.

The insured person's stamped card is turned in to his approved society at the end of the half year, and each society, in turn, makes a return of its collections to the Government. It is then charged with the cost of medical care and other items. The balance is available to the society for cash and such "additional benefits" as it may provide otherwise than in cash. The contributions made by employer and the insured person are partially matched by the Government; at present it adds to contributions made on account of men and women, respectively, one-seventh and one-fifth.[1] In addition, the Government bears the entire cost of the central administrative machinery. Moreover, while further financial aid by the Government has not been important for a decade or more, it found itself in the earlier years required to assume additional obligations. Thus, in 1921 its contributions amounted to more than 28 per cent of

TABLE 42.—RECEIPTS OF THE BRITISH NATIONAL HEALTH-INSURANCE SYSTEM, 1912 TO 1934[1]

(In Thousands of Pounds)

Year	Contributions	Interest and other receipts	Parliamentary votes and grants	Total	Accumulated funds at end of year
1912–1913	£26,572	£ 452	£ 6,395	£33,419	} £ 22,983
1914	16,797	618	5,737	23,152	
1915	18,284	899	6,457	25,640	32,749
1916	17,784	1,199	5,159	24,142	41,224
1917	18,166	1,628	5,765	25,559	51,446
1918	18,245	2,265	7,455	27,965	62,118
1919	18,205	2,721	8,634	29,560	71,880
1920	22,688	3,271	10,206	36,165	81,441
1921	25,190	3,695	11,759	40,644	92,228
1922	25,019	4,118	8,420	37,557	100,434
1923	26,204	4,754	6,947	37,905	109,469
1924	27,379	5,323	7,046	39,748	116,617
1925	27,721	5,644	8,073	41,438	126,627
1926	24,456	5,967	6,995	37,418	126,652
1927	26,382	5,571	7,573	39,526	125,178
1928	25,979	5,660	7,135	38,774	126,429
1929	26,005	5,535	7,631	40,171	125,696
1930	26,039	5,930	7,335	39,304	126,426
1931	25,769	6,202	7,074	39,045	127,936
1932	25,030	6,075	6,184	37,289	127,568
1933	25,750	6,005	6,009	37,764	129,561
1934	26,466	6,084	6,176	38,726	129,760

[1] Compiled from:

a. *Statistical Abstract for the United Kingdom for 1927*, p. 58; *ibid., 1933*, p. 74.

b. *Fifteenth Annual Report of the Ministry of Health, 1933–1934* (England and Wales), pp. 360–363 and 384–387; *Sixteenth Annual Report, 1934–1935*, pp. 328 and 348.

c. *Fifth Annual Report of the Department of Health for Scotland, 1933*, pp. 139–140 and 146; *Sixth Annual Report, 1934*, p. 182.

[1] The original additions were two-ninths and one-fourth.

the receipts, less interest. This fell, however, to 19 per cent in 1927, and has since tended to remain at about this figure. The receipts into the Health Insurance Fund are shown in Table 42.

The British system is rather exceptional in the kinds of benefits and also in the limited medical care it provides. Moreover, the administrative machinery differs rather radically from that in Germany and most other health-insurance countries.

Largely because of the opposition of the industrial assurance companies and the friendly societies, Britain departed from the German model and did not provide for a burial benefit. On the other hand, with no provision for payments on account of invalidity in her old-age pension system, and with some of the societies providing benefits for a second or extended period, she incorporated a disablement benefit. Hence, the benefits required by law have been these four: (1) sickness, (2) disablement, (3) maternity, and (4) medical.[1] Beyond these there are the "additional benefits" provided out of disposable balances by most of the approved societies. The first three of the statutory benefits are administered by the societies under a degree of supervision; the medical benefit is arranged for and supervised by local insurance committes and panel committees.

The sickness benefit is paid for any illness, except a compensable disease or disability due to industrial injury which results in incapacity for work for more than three days. Payment begins with the fourth day and continues for the period of total incapacity, up to a maximum of twenty-six weeks in any twelve months. To qualify for the receipt of sickness benefit, an insured person must have been in insured employment and have made payments for a period of twenty-six weeks, and, for full benefit, for a period of 104 weeks. The weekly benefit, like the contribution, is a fixed sum, viz., 15s. for a man, 12s. for an unmarried woman, and 10s. for a married woman.[2] If, however, contributions have been made for twenty-six but less than 104 weeks, the rate of benefit is reduced by one-half. Also, in the event that the insured is in arrears, less than the full benefit is paid.

Sickness benefit is paid upon notification of the carrier and a physician's "certificate of incapacity for work." Such certificates are required as long as incapacity continues. Upon recovery the doctor certifies that the patient is able to return to work. The administration of this and related benefits will be described more fully presently.[3]

---

[1] From 1912 to 1920 there was also the sanatorium benefit. It was discontinued when a different attack was made upon the problem of tuberculosis. See below, pp. 304–305.

[2] The original rates were 10s. and 7s. 6d., respectively, for men and women. These were increased to 15s. and 12s. in 1920. The rate for married women was later reduced to 10s., partly because of the special problems connected with that group of insured persons.

[3] See pp. 296–299.

The disablement benefit is really a continuation of sickness benefit, but at one-half the full rates, *i.e.*, at 7s. 6d., 6s., and 5s. for men, unmarried women, and married women, respectively. It commences after the twenty-six weeks of sickness benefit have been exhausted, and continues as long as the member remains incapable of work, or until age sixty-five is reached, when he qualifies for a pension. Disablement benefit may therefore be regarded as a continuation of sickness benefit in a case of prolonged illness but at a rate more appropriate for the carrier to pay, or as a bridge leading over to pensionable age. It may not be claimed until contributions have been made for 104 weeks. Otherwise, it is subject to the same conditions and regulations as those governing sickness benefit and is paid in the same manner.

As succinctly stated by Miss Stewart,[1] the maternity benefit conferred upon all employed contributors, male and female, is a lump sum of 40s.,[2] "which becomes payable after 42 weeks in insurable employment and after the payment of 42 contributions. In the case of a male employed contributor this benefit takes the form of outright payment to his wife upon the birth of a child . . . the money is regarded as the property of the mother. . . . If the wife is an employed contributor she receives the 40s. due her in her own right and that due her husband as well, or £4 in all. An insured married woman whose husband is not insured also receives the double benefit, the second sum being met by her society."

The British maternity benefit stands in contrast to the German in that there is usually no insurance claim to medical, nursing, or other treatment or care. This matter will also be discussed at a later place in this chapter.[3]

The right to medical benefit begins as soon as a worker becomes an employed contributor and is retained as long as he remains in insured employment, not limited to any given number of weeks; it is not affected by arrears, and, unlike the cash benefits, continues after the insured worker becomes a pensioner at the age of sixty-five.

The medical benefit provided under the National Insurance Act made the least possible departure from the contract arrangement found among the friendly societies, sick clubs, doctors' clubs, and provident dispensaries, also from private, individual practice. In contrast to the very extensive provision made in Germany, hospital, nursing, and specialists' services have had no place in the system except as additional benefits, nor has the right to medical care been extended to the dependents of the insured. It has embraced only treatment of the insured by the panel doctor and the customary drugs and appliances;[4] it has not included care of eyes or teeth.

[1] *Monthly Labor Review*, vol. 39 (1934), 828–829.
[2] Previous to 1920, 30s.
[3] See pp. 303–304.
[4] By 1924 the list of "appliances" included adhesive plaster, nine kinds of rolled band-

In each area there is a large insurance committee which is presumed to arrange for necessary medical and drug service and to give necessary supervision. As constituted, it gives representation, among others, to the insurance and other doctors, the health authorities, the insured, and the public. In fact, the major arrangements have always been made by the central authorities; the remuneration of the doctors, the kinds and qualities of drugs, and the general regulations have been decided or agreed upon by them in conference with the other parties. In any event, the doctors are comparatively free from control and supervision by the insurance carriers. In this respect their position is in contrast to that of the insurance doctors in Germany and most continental countries other than France, Norway, and Russia.

Unless he has been removed for cause by the Minister of Health, any registered physician has a right to be placed on the panel of insurance practitioners. As shown by the fact that there are approximately 16,000 panel doctors, most (some 70 per cent) of the physicians engaging in general practice have become members of the panel.[1] The insured person has choice of panel doctors in his area, subject to acceptance by the doctor. He also has the right to change doctors with brief notice. The general allowance made for the doctor's services is 9s. per insured person per year. Though there were for a time a few exceptions, each doctor is remunerated on this per capita basis, which is most acceptable to the medical fraternity. Mileage and other allowances are made in exceptional circumstances. In the interest of adequate care, no panel doctor may carry an active list of more than 2,500 insured workers unless he employs a permanent assistant, when he may add such additional names not to exceed 1,500, as the committee of his district may approve. The panel doctor also engages in private practice.

Naturally, complaints arise concerning the service given by the doctor. These are handled by a subcommittee established by the Insurance Committee, which has the power of review. It usually consists of a lawyer and two doctors. Review of an insurance practitioner's work is also possible through the regional medical staff attached to the Ministry of Health. This staff is organized into several regional divisions which have regional medical officers and a somewhat larger number

---

ages, two kinds of castrators, three kinds of absorbent cotton, eight kinds of gauze, gauze and cotton-wool tissue, ice bags, lints, oiled silk and other kinds of protectives, splints, cotton suspensory bandages, carbolized and unmedicated tow, and wood wool (*Medical Benefit Consolidated Regulations*, 1924, Second Schedule, p. 55). To these were added in 1925, ring pessaries, eye droppers, eye baths, triangular bandages, and (for self-administration of insulin) hypodermic syringes and needles (*Medical Benefit Amendment Regulations*, no. 2, 1925, p. 3). Crutches, trusses (these because not needed while not at work), and many other things have been held not to be necessary appliances. They are, however, being provided by many approved societies under "additional benefit" (*ibid.*, no. 16).

[1] One reason why the doctor has engaged in panel practice is to safeguard or to extend his practice among the dependents of the insured.

of deputies under the direction of a divisional medical officer for each division.[1] These are full-time salaried officials, whose chief duty is to examine insured persons referred to them by the approved societies or by the insurance doctors.

What has been said concerning the arrangements for medical service applies generally to those for drugs and appliances.

Thus far we have noted only the minimum or "statutory" benefits to be provided under the British health-insurance system. These have been added to through the "additional benefits" provided by approved societies with disposable surpluses—and more extensively than expected by Lloyd George and other leaders of the movement at its inception.

Under the British system periodic examinations of the assets of the societies are made by the Government Actuary to ascertain what funds beyond those required to pay the minimum benefits and for reserve purposes are disposable or distributable. These are then made available for "additional benefits," these to be selected by the society from a list approved by the central authority. The selections are made with the approval of the Ministry of Health, arrangements perfected, and the funds usually expended by each society with a declared disposable surplus.

As a result of each of the valuations made, a great majority of societies, with more than 90 per cent of the members, have had disposable surpluses. The amount made available for distribution has, as would be expected because of differences in sickness experience, cost of administration, etc., varied greatly among the societies. Some have been able to add as little as a fraction of one unit, others several "units,"[2] of benefits or service. The richness of total benefits or service for members has therefore varied greatly as between one group of the insured and another. Of course, an insured person may transfer from one society to another in an effort to secure the best service, but such transfers are limited by the requirements of membership for three and five years to be eligible for additional medical and cash benefits, respectively.

Disposable surpluses have been used increasingly to provide additional non-cash benefits. Under the first distribution, effective in 1921, £6,750,000 in a total of slightly less than £8,000,000 was allocated for increases in cash benefits. Under the next distribution, effective in 1925

---

[1] England and Wales are divided into five divisions, to which there are attached 34 regional medical officers. (*Report of the Chief Medical Officer of the Ministry of Health for the Year, 1933*, p. 114; *1936*, pp. 253–254.)

[2] "Unit" is a technical term. A unit of cash benefit comprises 1s. per week of additional sickness benefit, 6d. per week additional maternity benefit. When the segregation was made in 1918, societies with 2 per cent of the insured were involved in deficits, societies with 9.6 per cent had no disposable surplus, while, at the one extreme, those with 17.4 per cent had disposable surpluses of less than one "unit," and, at the other, societies with 3.9 per cent had disposable surpluses of five units or more.

or 1926, £13,240,000 was made available for additional cash benefits, and approximately £13,750,000 for non-cash or treatment benefits. Under the distribution effective from 1930 or 1931 to 1935 or 1936, the sums allocated for the two types of benefits were £8,300,000 and £11,500,000, respectively.[1] This changing distribution is explained in part by the fear on the part of societies that substantial increases in pecuniary benefits would lead to malingery, or, more likely, would interfere with their business of providing voluntary insurance, in part by increasing appreciation of the need for treatment in addition to that to be provided by the panel doctor.

A considerable number of treatment benefits have been approved for the elections to be made by societies with disposable surpluses.[2] According to the Ministry of Health in 1926–1927,[3] societies with approximately 95 per cent of the insured provided dental treatment; with 90 per cent, ophthalmic treatment (eye examinations, etc.); with 80 per cent, additional medical and surgical appliances; with 65 per cent, hospital treatment; with 20 per cent, nursing care; with 75 per cent, convalescent home treatment. The other non-cash benefits were of less importance and less frequently provided.

The great popularity and generality of dental treatment and certain other benefits will be noted. On the other hand, societies with only approximately three-fifths of the insured memberships have assisted in providing the much needed hospital aid. And it is not to be inferred from the details cited that the additional benefits necessarily or generally make full or adequate service available in all cases. The fact is that the aid is usually more or less limited; only a comparatively small number of the societies have been able to provide benefits equal to the minimum non-cash benefits provided by every fund in Germany.[4] But even so, some 30 per cent of the medical service provided under the British system is provided by the societies as "additional benefits," not through the Insurance Committees. As would be expected, there is not the desired degree of coordination.

The expenditures, by class of benefit and cost of administration, of the British Health Insurance system, 1912 to 1934, are shown in Table 43.

[1] These sums are totals for the five-year period.

[2] The list of additional benefits approved by 1930 may be conveniently found in Percy Cohen's *Social Insurance* (1932), pp. 31–35.

[3] See the *Eighth Annual Report of the Ministry of Health, 1926–1927*, pp. 164 and 187, and the *Eighth Annual Report of the Scottish Board of Health, 1926*, p. 257.

[4] The most important additional benefit is the dental. The insured person obtains a "dental letter," goes to the dentist of his choice, and his society pays a part of the bill on terms arranged between it and the dentists. The fraction paid in dental care averages about 60 per cent. The ophthalmic, hospital, and other benefits are commonly provided, in part, in the same manner.

LABOR'S RISKS AND SOCIAL INSURANCE

TABLE 43.—EXPENDITURES ON BENEFITS AND ADMINISTRATION, BRITISH NATIONAL
HEALTH-INSURANCE SYSTEM, 1912 TO 1934[1]

(In Thousands of Pounds)

Year	Benefits						Administration costs			
	Sickness	Disablement	Maternity	Medical	Sanatorium and others	Total	Approved societies	Central departments	Total	Grand total
1912–1913	£ 6,038	......	£1,223	£ 3,755	£ 711	£11,727	£3,157	£ 918	£4,075	£15,802
1914	6,458	£ 184	1,368	5,620	817	14,447	2,316	686	3,002	17,449
1915	5,119	832	1,270	4,571	771	12,563	2,475	702	3,177	15,740
1916	4,370	1,108	1,221	5,010	692	12,401	2,442	693	3,135	15,536
1917	4,102	1,232	1,045	4,728	790	11,897	2,391	765	3,156	15,053
1918	4,887	1,309	1,009	5,561	859	13,625	2,515	852	3,367	16,992
1919	5,081	1,396	1,188	6,507	1,233	15,405	2,946	1,116	4,062	19,467
1920	6,163	2,002	1,924	10,017	1,084	21,190	3,666	1,313	4,979	26,169
1921	8,096	3,063	1,194	10,710	605	24,468	3,900	1,489	5,389	29,857
1922	9,199	3,784	1,845	9,614	388	24,830	3,748	1,131	4,879	29,709
1923	8,623	4,276	1,748	9,198	661	24,506	3,802	1,057	4,859	29,365
1924	9,840	4,684	1,702	9,174	709	26,109	3,788	1,028	4,816	30,925
1925	10,339	5,103	1,704	9,428	937	27,511	3,867	1,041	4,908	32,419
1926	12,543	6,182	1,757	9,555	1,961	31,998	4,043	1,010	5,053	37,051
1927	13,034	7,175	1,738	9,784	3,980	35,711	4,171	1,018	5,189	40,900
1928	11,276	.6,146	1,750	10,093	3,045	32,310	4,277	986	5,263	37,573
1929	13,215	6,432	1,735	10,338	2,783	34,503	4,342	1,053	5,395	39,898
1930	11,173	6,333	1,802	10,282	3,351	32,941	4,592	1,066	5,658	38,599
1931	11,087	6,072	1,762	10,683	3,310	32,914	4,646	1,047	5,693	38,607
1932	11,048	6,280	1,707	9,970	2,876	31,881	4,582	1,010	5,592	37,473
1933	11,337	6,106	1,575	10,164	2,603	31,785	4,655	1,016	5,671	37,456
1934	9,822	6,353	1,589	10,068	2,579	30,411	4,518	1,079	4,597	35,008

[1] Compiled from:

a. *Statistical Abstract for the United Kingdom for 1927*, p. 59; ibid., *1933*, p. 75.

b. *Fifteenth Annual Report of the Ministry of Health, 1933–1934* (England and Wales), pp. 362–363 and 386–387. *Sixteenth Annual Report, 1934–1935*, pp. 328–329, 348–349.

c. *Fifth Annual Report of the Department of Health for Scotland, 1933*, pp. 146–147. *Sixth Annual Report 1934*, pp. 181–182.

Between 1912 and 1936, the expenditures on benefits and administration totaled £632,451,000. The annual administration costs increased from an average of £4,000,000 during 1912–1923 to £4,597,000 in 1936. The total outlays increased more rapidly than the number of insured persons, the per capita figure increasing from $6.00, more or less, down to the War period, to $9.78 in 1921, $10.18 in 1925, $11.64 in 1930, $11.14 in 1933, and $10.02 in 1934. Little of this increase is found in administrative costs, which fell from 19.1 per cent of the total outlays for 1912–1923 to 14.5 per cent for the years 1930–1934. The explanation of increased per capita costs is found largely in the increased rates of the cash benefits made in 1920, the increased cost of supplies, the better remuneration of the doctors, the increased morbidity rate to which reference has been made earlier in this chapter, and the provision of "additional benefits."

It will be noted that for the period 1930–1934 sickness benefits accounted roughly for a third, the disablement benefits roughly a fifth, the maternity benefit about 5 per cent, and the medical benefit approximately 32 per cent of the total outlay for benefits. In passing from a description to an appraisal of the British system some observations may be made on these several benefits. Incidental to or following that, a number of problems will be briefly discussed.

The ordinary weekly sickness and disablement benefits are low as compared to the earnings of wage earners when in health, and also as compared to the benefits paid workers when unemployed. It will be recalled that under health insurance, disabled men receive (since 1920) 15s., disabled women 12s. or 10s., and that the corresponding disablement benefits are fixed at one-half of these sums. The unemployment benefit, on the other hand, is 17s. for adult males, and 15s. for adult females. There are also under unemployment insurance the added allowances of 9s. for dependent spouse, and 3s. for each dependent minor.

Primarily for administrative reasons, and in a desire for simplicity, the Government decided that contributions and benefits should be in fixed sums, or flat rates, rather than percentages of the wages of the insured. That inevitably meant that the statutory cash benefits in the majority of cases would be small as compared to the rates of pay of the disabled, for they could not be fixed at more than an appropriate fraction of the wage of low paid labor. Then, too, the benefits had to be limited to the resources of the less-well-off approved societies. Again, some of the approved societies desired that the benefits should be low, lest there be interference with the taking of voluntary insurance the carriers also provided. Such voluntary insurance was expected to help out substantially in the case of skilled workers. It has done so in part, for four or five millions of the insured have also had voluntary insurance.[1] This additional insurance, additional cash benefits of 2s. or more (averaging about 4s.) paid after 1920 by societies in which a substantial majority of the insured have had membership, individual savings, and credit have combined with the low statutory benefits under the Act to tide most disabled persons over and to keep them "off the Poor Law," except in cases of prolonged illness, and especially when so prolonged that disablement benefit is paid. In other words, it appears that destitution due to disabling sickness is generally prevented. Nevertheless, it is generally recognized that the statutory sickness and disablement benefits are not based upon good standards and that it is illogical to maintain them at lower levels than the benefits paid the unemployed or than observed by

[1] Evidence of Sir Walter Kinnear before the Royal Commission on Health Insurance, in 1924. *Minutes of Evidence*, vol. 1, p. 25.

the poor-law authorities in administering relief. In recognition of these facts, the Royal Commission on Health Insurance, in its report submitted in 1926, recommended that when funds could be made available, but after the scope of medical benefit had been extended, allowances should be provided for dependents of insured persons in receipt of sickness or disablement benefit.[1]

In this connection reference may be made to excessive claims to sickness and disablement benefits. In the earlier years, there was much, and widely publicized, criticism of the insurance system on this score. Investigation by a sympathetic Fabian Committee[2] and by the official Schuster Departmental Committee[3] found that there was considerable abuse. In a certain proportion of cases too much was being made of comparatively slight ailments; in a much larger number of cases abstention from work was unreasonably prolonged. Not a few of the insured, with a combination of voluntary and compulsory insurance, were entitled to benefits approaching or equal to the wages they might earn; some of the certifying doctors were lenient in giving and renewing certificates of incapacity for work; the approved societies were themselves sometimes lenient because of the competition for members, and, more important, many of them were not in position to send out an adequate number of visitors to check on the condition of the claimants and the certifications made by the doctors incidental to treatment; at many points the law and benefit rights remained unclear. In more recent years, however, with the law bearing upon claims made clear, with less competition among the societies for members, with the supervising medical officers checking on more individual cases and particularly on those certified by doctors in unusual proportion to the numbers on their lists or recertifying for long periods, there has been very much less abuse than in the earlier years under the Act. Nevertheless, it is notable that when unemployed persons have fallen out of insurance in unusual numbers or when important strikes have occurred, the proportion of the insured claiming sickness benefit has substantially increased. At times during the 1920's, for example, increases in the amount of illness alone could not well have explained the increase in claims. With relief carefully administered, the number of claimants to sickness benefit greatly increased during the Miners' Strike in 1926. In Scotland during the last seven months of that year, 31,422 cases of doubtful incapacity were submitted to the medical referees as against 10,590 during the first five months of the year. Of the men examined during January to May, 28 per cent were found to

---

[1] *Report of the Royal Commission on National Health Insurance*, Cmd. 2596 (1926), p. 280.

[2] See *Appendix to the Report of the Departmental Committee on Sickness Benefit Claims*, vol 2, Cd. 7689 (1914), p. 382.

[3] See *ibid.*, Cd. 7688, 7689, and 7690 (1914) and *Report*, Cd. 7687 (1914).

be no longer incapacitated, while of those examined after the strike set in, 44 per cent were found to be capable of work.[1] In 1927–1928, sickness and disablement claims became excessively heavy in the "necessitous areas" where unemployment was working havoc. And it must be added that at all times married women have presented a problem, for the value of their time at home may easily outweigh the difference between the benefit and the wages lost. The problem of certification has not been adequately solved. In England in 1924, 468,476 cases (out of a grand total many times as large) were referred to the medical officers. Of those actually examined, incapacity for work was confirmed in 179,010 cases; absence of incapacity was reported in 67,078. The most conscientious certification cannot be had by all doctors so long as they combine treatment with certification for sick benefit, for the fear of loss of the insured and his dependents as patients is too frequently present.[2]

In conclusion, it should be said that it is easily possible to exaggerate the problem of excessive claims allowed. After the first few years particularly, all the evidence is to the effect that the greatest number of certifications have been carefully and efficiently made. Any well-grounded complaint could be directed at only a small fraction of the certifying doctors. And there is reason to think that any abuse under the British compulsory insurance system may be less extensive than under voluntary insurance with commercial carriers or under insurance with sick clubs and other carriers before the National Insurance Act became effective. Yet it must be admitted that a problem remains. The checking on claims in recent years has shown that at times as many as 12 per cent of those in benefit were not incapacitated for work.[3]

The British maternity benefit, as we have noted, stands in strong contrast to the provision made in Germany and nearly all other health-insurance countries. The provision usually made there is to pay cash benefits to insured women for time lost due to child bearing and to give them, and perhaps the noninsured wives of insured men, the needed medical attention. The provision in Britain, on the other hand, takes the form of a fixed sum paid in cash, this designed to provide nourishment and other needed things in all cases and to compensate insured women for loss of work. Perhaps this benefit has been the most popular of all of those provided under the British system, but it has been severely criticized as inadequate by persons and institutions especially interested in the welfare of mothers and infants. No provision is made under the

---

[1] *Scottish Board of Health, Report, 1926*, pp. 254–255. In passing judgment on such data, one must, of course, keep in mind that there was more or less delay in checking on certifications made, also that during unemployment health conditions are impaired.

[2] *Cf.* I. S. Falk, *op. cit.*, pp. 186–187.

[3] See summary statements in each of the annual reports of the Ministry of Health.

Act for medical care in maternity cases; this is left to private doctors and to the public-health authorities and voluntary organizations. The fact is that the fees of the doctors and midwives were advanced and absorbed most, and sometimes all, of the cash benefit provided under the original Act. Because of the neglect of medical care under the Act, Mr. Broadbent, who had devoted most of his life to the furtherance of public-health work, especially in its bearing on the welfare of mothers and children, in his evidence before the Royal Commission,[1] regarded the maternity benefit as "a great opportunity missed." "The real purpose which Parliament had in view," he said, "was undoubtedly to make childbirth safer alike to mother and child. This purpose cannot be fulfilled merely by a grant of money." The British Medical Association, among its recommendations, said:[2] "Maternity benefit, whether in its present, or in an extended form, should cease to be administered by Approved Societies and be administered both in money and in kind by local authorities; which, in their turn, should be made definitely responsible for providing medical attention."[3]

Before evaluating the medical benefits under the British system, brief reference should be made to the sanatorium benefit provided in the original Act but discontinued in 1921. It was designed to provide insured persons disabled by tuberculosis with institutional care. This, however, was found not to meet the needs of the situation. Tuberculosis presents cases requiring prolonged as well as specialized treatment. Moreover, the larger number of the tuberculous were not in insurance, but dependents of the insured or quite outside the division of the population with which health insurance had to do. Finally, an effect of the War was greatly to increase the number who were not in insurance but in need of care. In view of these facts, and because tuberculosis presents a special problem and one which must be approached from the public-health point of view, the sanatorium benefit administered by the approved societies was eliminated and the solution of the problem entrusted to the

---

[1] Cmd. 2596 (1926), pp. 51–52 and references to evidence there cited.

[2] *Ibid.*, p. 51.

[3] In 1932 there appeared the *Final Report of the Departmental Committee on Maternal Mortality and Morbidity*. The Committee noted that since 1900 the general death rate in Britain had decreased by one-third, mortality from tuberculosis likewise by one-third, and infant mortality by more than one-half, but, in contrast to Germany, maternal mortality had not decreased at all. The Committee was convinced that maternal mortality could be reduced by half. The chief avoidable causes were four:

   a. Lack of prenatal care, found in 32 per cent of the cases studied.

   b. Errors in judgment on the part of the doctor or midwife, found chiefly in cases with domiciliary care and in 42 per cent of all cases studied.

   c. Negligence on the part of patient or friends, found in 17 per cent of the cases.

   d. Lack of necessary facilities, found in 8 per cent of the cases. These facts revealed by study of fatal cases are significant in connection with medical benefit and the fact that domiciliary care obtained in roughly three-quarters of the maternity cases.

public-health authorities. Under them the institutional provision has been greatly developed and made available for the whole community. The decision made was a very significant one for an attack upon the problem presented by this type of sickness.[1]

Under health insurance medical attention given the poor about doubled. To some extent, this was explained by unnecessary calls made upon the doctor but to a much larger extent by the giving of medical care in cases in which there had been none, chiefly because it could not be afforded on a noninsurance basis.[2] Moreover, it is generally agreed that the care given by the panel doctors compares favorably with the care given in private practice and is very much better than that given by contract doctors to members of "sick clubs" and other organizations previous to 1911. Few doctors have been found to be derelict in performing their duties. The ethical sense of the members of the profession in Britain is strong; the doctors have a selfish reason in efficient treatment of the insured because they desire to treat the members of their families; the medical organizations are cooperative.

To this summary statement may be added the findings of the British Medical Association. The evidence available, when properly interpreted, supports the findings. The Association, in its evidence before the Royal Commission, said:

"(a) Large numbers, indeed whole classes of persons, are now receiving a real medical attention which they formerly did not receive at all.

"(b) The number of practitioners in proportion to the population in densely populated areas has increased.

"(c) The amount and character of the medical attention given is superior to that formerly given in the best of the old clubs, and immensely superior to that given in the great majority of the clubs which were far from the best.

"(d) Illness is now coming under skilled observation and treatment at an earlier stage than was formerly the case.

"(e) Speaking generally, the work of practitioners has been given a bias towards prevention which was formerly not so marked.

"(f) Clinical records have been or are being provided which may be made of great service in relation to medical research and public health.

"(g) Co-operation among practitioners is being encouraged to an increasing degree.

"(h) There is now a more marked recognition than formerly of the collective responsibility of the profession to the community in respect to all matters of health."[3]

---

[1] See below, p. 343.

[2] About one-half of the insured receive treatment in the course of a year, and the number of attendances at offices and of domiciliary visits is about three and a half per insured person, or upward of 50,000,000.

[3] Quoted in *Report of the Royal Commission on National Health Insurance* (1926), p. 34.

The main criticism made by the spokesman for the Medical Association, by the representatives of other organizations and the insured, and by expert witnesses generally is that while the medical benefit has served well, it has been very inadequate because of its limited scope.

Brief reference may be made to suggestions made to the Royal Commission by a few representative groups.   The British Medical Association would "extend the [statutory benefit] provision so as to include complete consultant and specialist advice and treatment, full laboratory facilities for clinical purposes, residential institutional treatment so far as possible with limited accommodation, dental advice and treatment, such ancillary help as can be given by nurses and masseurs, and an ambulance service. . . . All these benefits," it stated, "should be equally available to all insured persons alike, regardless of their membership in any particular Society."   Moreover, it was of the opinion that the enriched medical benefit should be extended to dependents—giving a total of some 38,750,-000 persons, or roughly two and a half times the number then insured.[1] The National Medical Practitioners' Union, with between 3,000 and 4,000 members, recognized "that the State will presently be obliged to extend medical assistance to a much larger section of the community than at present," for "there can be little doubt that a very large proportion . . . is in need of the advantages which those now insured enjoy."[2] The Society of the Medical Officers of Health were of the opinion that "a commencement should be made to give medical benefit its true meaning by including (a) facilities to the medical profession for laboratory diagnosis, (b) specialist advice and treatment, (c) dental treatment, (d) treatment in general hospitals and other like institutions, (e) further accommodation for the treatment of tuberculosis, especially surgical tuberculosis, (f) treatment in convalescent homes, (g) home nursing when required, (h) all other necessary medical advice and treatment."   Moreover, all this, it was said, should be extended to dependents, for their "need for medical treatment . . . is, from a national and health point of view, even greater than that for the medical treatment of the insured person himself."[3]

Such are bits from the evidence given before the Royal Commission by important and representative groups.   In subsequent years there has been little, if any, change in opinion on these matters.   The Commission members themselves were impressed with the need for an extended and materially improved medical benefit.   "Medical benefit," they stated, "is at present a general practitioner service; but it cannot seriously be claimed that this is a satisfactory state of affairs.   It means that the medical service given in respect of the insurance contribution stops short

[1] *Royal Commission, Appendix to Minutes of Evidence*, pt. III, pp. 446–447.
[2] *Ibid.*, pp. 462–463.
[3] *Ibid.*, pp. 495–496.

just where the need is greatest."[1] But largely for financial reasons the solution was necessarily far off. The Commission, with four members dissenting, was at the time impressed with the necessity of keeping within the limits set by the existing insurance revenues taken as a whole. It therefore recommended that one-half of the surpluses of the approved societies should be taken and distributed on a per capita basis among all the societies. The revenues thus distributed should be used for instituting a general specialist service and laboratories for diagnostic purposes.[2] It was also of the opinion that the statutory benefit should include dental care.

Minor problems have appeared in connection with medical treatment, such as that leading to the regulations limiting the number of insured persons a doctor may have on his list. Space limitations preclude discussion of them. Something must, however, be said concerning the system and the panel doctor.

Any qualified doctor has a right to a place on the panel. At all times, from 1913, a majority of doctors have enrolled for panel practice.[3] There is free choice of doctor by the insured person—the doctor, however, having the right not to admit unsatisfactory persons to his list. With minor exceptions, the doctor's remuneration is so many shillings per person on his list, with mileage allowance, etc., in certain areas. In theory, the arrangements with the doctors are made by the local Insurance Committee, but at all times the per capita fee and other important details have been arranged between the Government and the Medical Association, representing the doctors. The average annual income of the panel doctor is in excess of $2,000,[4] his income from private patients not included, which is a very much larger and much more stable and dependable income than had been derived from general practice in pre-health-insurance days. Nevertheless, the per capita fee has been the doctor's chief grievance. At the outset there was a threatened general strike because the doctors regarded the allowance proposed as inadequate. A compromise fee was agreed upon and the doctors, rather reluctantly but of necessity, sought places on the panels. More than once in subsequent years there have been strong differences of opinion over the doctor's rate of pay but these differences have been composed without unsatisfactory results. The friction has been less great than in Germany, for the doctors have dealt with the Government—not with the insurance carriers. On the whole, the doctors have been well satisfied. Though they may complain half-seriously at keeping the necessary records and at the checking

---

[1] Cmd. 2596 (1926), p. 123.

[2] *Ibid.*, pp. 73, 120–121.

[3] In 1930, 52 per cent of registered physicians, including specialists and those who had retired, engaged in insurance practice.

[4] In 1930, it was approximately $2,300.

of their certificates of incapacity to work, and on occasion have reacted strongly in connection with their remuneration, they very generally subscribe to the value, if not the necessity, of the health-insurance system. Long since has the organization set up by those opposed to compulsory insurance ceased to have any significance or to receive a hearing.

The part played by the approved societies in the organization and administration of health insurance in Britain has been made clear. The societies were accepted and protected, for the purposes of the Act of 1911, save for the provision of medical and sanatorium benefits, because of the large number of persons already insured through certain of them, because of the desire and expectation that many persons would add voluntarily to their statutory insurance, because of appreciation of the work they had done in the past, because of the fraternal spirit which had obtained in many of them and the possibility of having democratic control of insurance through them, because of the value of their experience in the administration of benefits, because of the English habit of not displacing any institution unless it stands definitely in the way of things to be accomplished, and because of political considerations and necessity. And it was found necessary to permit the assurance companies also to qualify as carriers.

There has been considerable complaint that an effect of compulsory insurance, caused by the admission of many members under the necessity of finding a carrier and otherwise, has been to undermine the fraternal societies.[1] The complaint, to say the least, has been greatly exaggerated; for many years before 1911 there had been complaint of loss of the fraternal spirit and of the decay of the fraternal societies. On the other hand, there has been strong complaint against the approved-society system. The grounds have been many—a multitude of societies to supervise and have their funds evaluated; the unsuitability of many of the societies to serve because of size or character of membership or staffs; unreasonable rules; excessive cost of administration; unsuitability for providing non-cash benefits; grossly unequal benefits provided for the insured. On these, and perhaps on still other grounds, many critics have expressed the view that it was a mistake to have accepted the societies at all, or they have held that after experience with them, they should be displaced by territorial funds.

There are more or less valid reasons for the complaints noted. It must be said, however, that with the elimination of many of the small and of unfit or inefficient societies and the limitations placed upon their administrative costs and upon their operations, many of the complaints are less valid or less important than they were twenty years ago. The savings realizable by the substitution of new carriers organized on a territorial basis would not be considerable. Moreover, it is doubtful

[1] See Frederick L. Hoffman, *National Health Insurance and the Friendly Societies* (1920).

whether, on the whole, the administration of cash benefits would be much improved. The administration is, after all, by salaried persons working for an approved society or for a different type of fund. The valid and most significant complaints, careful consideration will show, are that the approved-society system stands in the way of a unified system of medical benefits so long as they administer the additional benefits; does not yield morbidity records of a character to serve as the best basis for public-health work; and is accompanied by grossly unequal benefits to the insured, a condition which cannot be more than alleviated by any practicable pooling of funds.   There is in British as well as in German experience, therefore, reason for avoiding an approved-society system of carriers. The problem is to substitute other carriers, for this would be a sad blow to existing health-insurance institutions.

One point remains for comment.   Compulsory health insurance has become a definitely established institution in Britain.   Though adopted as an experiment, it was almost certain to become an established institution, for that is true of most ventures rendering a new service to the masses of the people.   But in this instance it is generally conceded that the system, with all its defects and shortcomings, has earned its place.   The Royal Commission said, "We are convinced that National Health Insurance has now become a permanent feature of the social system of this country"; it "has fully justified itself and has, on the whole, been successful in operation."[1]   Any one who advocated its uprooting would have no following.

Yet, there have been those who expressed the view that it would have been better had a different attack been made upon the problem of sickness.   Dr. Brend, in his book *Health and the State* (1917), expressed the view that while "the weekly payments of sickness benefits have undoubtedly helped many poor people through a period of distress," and while "maternity benefit has been a substantial benefit to mothers and disablement benefit has constituted a small pension for incapacitated persons,"[2] it would have been much better had the money been spent in a different manner, in an effort to improve the public health.   It is noteworthy, however, that in more recent years few prominent medical men in Britain have expressed such views.   On the contrary, it appears that there has been increasing appreciation of efficient and adequate medical care as an essential part of a program of public health.[3]

---

[1] Cmd. 2596 (1926), p. 16.

[2] William A. Brend, *Health and the State* (1917), p. 263.

[3] Consult, among others, George F. McCleary, *National Health Insurance;* Sir Arthur Newsholme, *Ministry of Health, Public Health and Insurance,* and *Medicine and the State;* and the Annual Reports of the Ministry of Health.   For an excellent summary statement to the effect that sickness insurance is an aid to and part of a public-health program, see Sir George Newman, in *Ministry of Health, Report* (1931), pp. 218–220.

It is generally recognized that it is impossible in a country like Great Britain to secure good medical care of the mass of sick persons without recourse to the group-payment or insurance principle. Moreover, it may be emphasized that the state has more than one interest to serve in connection with sickness; it is interested in the prevention of destitution as well as in sickness prevention. In so far as possible, neither of these interests should be sacrificed for the other, as perhaps has all too frequently been done under health insurance. But in this immediate connection, it must be borne in mind that the same funds cannot be made readily available for sickness insurance or for public health. Revenues for distinctly public health work would not be readily secured in the manner they are for insurance. Though the revenues for the two are necessarily derived from the national income, they must be sought in somewhat different ways and have a somewhat different incidence.

HEALTH INSURANCE IN FRANCE

Voluntary insurance had long been practiced through mutual organization, miners' mutual insurance had been recognized since 1894, and general systems of social insurance had existed in a few provinces influenced by the German institution,[1] but it was not until 1928, after discussion extending over several years, that a general national system of insurance was adopted in France. It became effective in 1930, and in 1935 approximately 10,000,000 workers in industry, commerce, and other urban occupations, and some 1,150,000 workers in agriculture and forestry were within its embrace.[2]

In 1935 and 1936, some important amendments of the law and decrees were made.[3] The system as then reshaped merits consideration along with systems earlier established in Germany and Great Britain, for it is

[1] Ineffectual laws providing both old-age pensions and old-age insurance had been enacted in 1905 and 1910, and special provision had been made for seamen as early as 1693.

[2] Owing to depression, the number actually making contributions was substantially less—approximately 6,400,000 in commerce and industry and 700,000 in agriculture, in 1935. See "Rapport du Ministère du Travail sur l'application de la loi des Assurances Sociales" (January, 1934, to December, 1935), *Journal Officiel, Annexe* (Paris, Apr. 17, 1937), pp. 139–254.

[3] See *Journal Officiel* (Paris, Oct. 31, 1935) for the two Legislative Decree laws of Oct. 28 and Oct. 30, 1935, applying to workers in commerce and industry as well as to workers in agriculture. The general wage increases in 1936, resulting from the legislation establishing the 40-hour week and collective bargaining, necessitated adjustment of wage limits of persons in industry and commerce who are subject to compulsory insurance. For provisions of the law of Aug. 26, 1936, see *Journal Officiel* (Paris, Aug. 30, 1936). For a chronological account of legislative decrees and regulation prior to these, consult *Le Manuel Pratique des Assurances Sociales*, Repertoire Alphabetique, Comité Central des Assurances Sociales, Paris, 1935. The account is brought to 1936 by I. S. Falk, *op. cit.*, Chap. 11.

unique and suggestive in some of its aspects, especially in the arrangements made for medical care. Mrs. Armstrong appropriately observes of the Act of 1928,[1] "This legislation stands out as the most significant social insurance move since the World War."

The French system makes provision for (a) "distributional risks," i.e., illness, death, maternity, and medical care for both illness and invalidity, and (b) the "capitalization risks" of old age and invalidity. The two branches are separated in administration and the contributions are divided between them. Again, the insurance provided for the main body of wage earners differs somewhat from that provided for agricultural workers. Hence, our summary discussion of insurance against sickness and associated risks is divided into two parts, the one concerned with the general system for industrial and commercial workers and miscellaneous trades, the other with the special provision made for persons employed in agricultural and related pursuits. A discussion of the provision made for old age and invalidity ("capitalization risks") is not in point here.[2]

Insurance in Industry, Commerce, and Miscellaneous Trades.—The French system is a rather inclusive one. Except for groups specially exempted, all wage earners between thirteen and sixty years of age, whether manual or nonmanual, who earn not more than a stipulated sum ranging from 21,000 to 25,000 francs per year according to location and the worker's family responsibilities, were brought within its embrace. In 1935, coverage was extended to include homeworkers, certain traveling salesmen working for more than one employer, taxi drivers who do not own their vehicles, baggage porters in railway stations, female cinema and theater attendants, and hotel, cafe, and restaurant employees. Miners, seamen, railway and public utility employees, and civil servants are exempted because provision had been made for them before the general system was introduced.[3]

[1] Quoted, with permission, from Barbara N. Armstrong, *Insuring the Essentials* (The Macmillan Company, 1932), p. 341.

[2] The best and most accessible account of the entire system as introduced in 1930 will be found in Paul H. Douglas, "The French Social Insurance Act," in *Annals of the American Academy of Political and Social Science*, Publication 2549 (November, 1932). The revisions made in 1935 have been summarized in the U. S. *Monthly Labor Review*, vol. 42, no. 2 (February, 1936), pp. 328–333. A very good summary of the official report on the system to 1933 inclusive, may be found in the *Monthly Labor Review*, vol. 41, no. 4 (November, 1935), pp. 1185–1187, and vol. 45 (1937), pp. 106–110. An excellent discussion is found in I. S. Falk, *op. cit.*, Chap. 11.

[3] The legislation when adopted permitted persons not within the mandatory provisions of the law, provided their incomes were not in excess of those for wage earners required to insure, to secure voluntarily one or all types of insurance and pay the full contribution. Their contribution, however, might not exceed 10 per cent of earnings or be less than 270 francs per year. The finances for voluntary insurance were to be kept separate. This privilege was, however, withdrawn by decree law of October 28, 1935.

The insurance carriers are (*a*) "primary funds," including mutual benefit societies or their federations, trade unions, works funds, and voluntary associations of the insured; and (*b*) territorial funds created by the government. In 1935, the number of funds was 744, but the insurance of 57 per cent of those covered was through territorial (department) funds.

The cost of social insurance is covered by equal contributions by the insured and his employer, with subsidies by the government[1] and miscellaneous revenues. The payroll tax was, to begin with, 8 per cent and was to advance to 9 and, by 1940, to 10 per cent. However, owing to the reduced tax-paying ability in depression and to the fact that receipts had greatly exceeded outlays, the contribution was reduced to 7 per cent[2] for the year 1936.[3]   To begin with, as under the German system, the

[1] The Act provided for a subsidy equal to that paid under the earlier Pensions Act (540 million francs per year) plus a sum equal to the amount saved by the state and half the amount saved by the departments and communes in poor-relief expenditures by reason of the operation of the social-insurance system.   For detail, see Paul H. Douglas, *op. cit.*, p. 224.   However, by 1935, the State contribution to the General Guarantee Fund had been reduced from 540 to 140 million francs.   *Industrial and Labour Information*, vol. 56, no. 4 (Geneva, Oct. 28, 1935), p. 137.

[2] It is interesting to note that the 23d Congress of the General Confederation of Labor of France, Sept. 25 to 27, 1935, passed a resolution condemning the campaigns for the reduction of insurance contributions.   The Congress declared that such reduction would lead either to a heavy decrease in benefits or the bankruptcy of the insurance system.   A reduction in benefits was held to be even more serious in view of the reduction in the State contribution to the General Guarantee Fund.   Moreover, the Congress pointed out that the reduction of contributions would have an insignificant effect on the costs of production, and that social charges under the French insurance system were lower than those in other countries.   *Industrial and Labour Information*, vol. 56, no. 4 (Geneva, Oct. 28, 1935), p.137.

[3] The contributions and outlays to 1933, inclusive, were as follows:

Year	Contributions (francs)	Expenditures (francs)
1930 (6 months)	1,496,736,174	
1931	3,562,401,338	878,104,183
1932	3,261,798,160	1,086,429,127
1933	3,271,276,895	1,141,288,142
1934	3,175,994,197	1,196,607,018
1935	3,085,908,635	1,279,945,588
Totals	17,854,115,399	5,582,374,058

(Franc at par—3.92 cents; average exchange rate in 1933, 5.03 cents; in 1935, 6.60 cents.)

To the total of contributions should be added:

a. About 68 million francs received direct by agricultural social insurance institutions (up to Dec. 31, 1933).

b. Approximately 362 million francs representing employers' contributions for employed persons who either (1) receive more than the basic remuneration limit but less than 25,000 francs a year, (2) are on retired pay, or (3) are over sixty-five years of age.   For further detail, see Ministère du Travail, "Rapport sur l'application de la loi des Assurances Sociales," January, 1932, to December, 1933, *Journal Officiel*, Annexe (Mar. 12, 1935), pp. 195–332.

insured were divided on the basis of wage rates into five classes and the contributions were in fixed sum according to class. In order to avoid the administrative problems connected with variable employment and fluctuating wage rates, this classification was, however, abolished in 1935. Under the revised law, contributions are calculated on the actual salary or wage of the insured person. However, for persons earning in excess of 15,000 francs per year, family allowances excluded, no contribution is now required for the excess of earnings over that amount.[1]

The insurance system, in addition to old-age and other benefits provided under the capitalization branch, provides sickness, medical, death, and maternity benefits.[2]

Cash benefits are provided from the sixth[3] day of disability for insured persons who are ill or who are suffering from nonindustrial accident if the necessary contributions have been made under the revised law. The minimum contribution is thirty francs during the two quarters preceding the disabling illness or accident. With a minimum of three and a maximum of eighteen francs per day, the benefit is 50 per cent of the insured person's wage. Moreover, the benefit is increased by one franc per day for each dependent child. When hospitalization is paid for by the fund, however, the cash benefit is reduced by one-third if the

---

[1] This affects the contributions of the best remunerated class only. The returns for 1930–1931 give the following percentages of industrial and commercial workers in different wage classes, on the basis of leaflets and cards held:

Wage class	Percentage holding	
	Leaflets	Cards
Under 2,400 francs per year (8 francs per day)	6.12	5.80
2,400 to 4,499 francs per year (8 to 14.99 francs per day)	12.08	11.42
4,500 to 4,999 francs per year (15 to 19.99 francs per day)	12.33	11.75
6,000 to 9,599 francs per year (20 to 31.99 francs per day)	33.52	33.72
9,600 to 15,000 or 18,000 francs per year, according to location, etc. (32 to 50 or 60 francs per day)	35.95	37.31

See, *Monthly Labor Review*, vol. 41 (1935), p. 1187 and vol. 45 (1937), p. 106.

[2] The Act contained no provision for insurance against unemployment. Limited but rather liberal provision was made, however, for keeping the wage earners in insurance while unemployed. In order to obtain the benefit of the unemployment guarantee which, within certain limits, takes care of the contributions necessary for maintaining the right to benefit, the Act provided that the insured person must have had a minimum of sixty francs deducted from wages during the four quarters preceding unemployment. Moreover, any insured person of French nationality involuntarily unemployed and registered at a public employment exchange is entitled to thirty francs paid into his account for each quarter during which he can prove a minimum of fifty days unemployment. However, such a payment may not be made for more than two consecutive quarters yearly. *Industrial and Labour Information*, vol. 56, no. 8 (Geneva, Nov. 25, 1935), p. 296.

[3] From the fourth day in the case of a person with three or more dependent children,

insured has one or more children under sixteen years of age, by one-half if he is married but has no dependent children, and by three-quarters in the absence of wife and/or dependent children.

In France, limited invalidity insurance is combined with health insurance, as it is in Great Britain. The sickness benefit may be drawn for a period of twenty-six weeks if the disability has not ended. If, beyond the twenty-six weeks, the insured person's working capacity is reduced by two-thirds or more, an invalidity pension is paid provided he has been registered for at least two years prior to the disability and a minimum of sixty francs has been deducted from his wages in respect to each of these two years. Combined with this right is a right to medical attention for not longer than five years. If, after five years, his working capacity is still less than 50 per cent, the pension is placed on a permanent basis. The invalidity pension is based upon the rate of wages of the insured but varies with age at the time of entering insurance and the number of years in insurance. In one group are those who enroll in the system before the age of thirty. Their pensions are 40 per cent of wages, with an addition of 1 per cent for each year beyond thirty years of age for which contributions have been paid. On the other hand, in the case of those enrolling when past thirty, the pension is reduced one-thirtieth for each year or fraction thereof by which the actual age at entrance exceeded thirty. If they have paid contributions for as long as six years, however, the annual pension is to be not less than 1,000 francs.

The wife and dependent children under sixteen years of age as well as the insured man have a right to medical care. This care, without waiting period and for a maximum of twenty-six weeks for a given illness, embraces the services of the general practitioner, the specialist, the midwife, the surgeon, the dentist, and the hospital. In addition, the patient has a right, upon prescription by a physician, to pharmaceutical requisites and appliances. Thus, medical care resembles the more inclusive German system rather than the narrow type found in Britain.

The arrangements for medical care in France are unique and suggestive. They resulted from the stout position taken by the strongly organized doctors who demanded the fewest restrictions upon and interference with the existing practice of medicine.

As Professor Douglas states,[1] "the patient has a completely free choice in all of these services [mentioned above]. He can select any doctor who, whether or not he is a member of the medical association, merely signifies his willingness to abide by the rules of the law. The funds agree not to suggest to their members that they patronize some doctors rather than others.

---

[1] Quoted with permission from P. H. Douglas, "The French Social Insurance Act," in *Annals of the American Academy of Political and Social Science*, Publication 2549 (November, 1932), p. 226,

"The patient is not compelled to keep the practitioner . . . . for any length of time, but is free to change to another at any moment. The medical consultations take place, whenever possible, at the doctor's office. If the doctor is compelled to visit the patient in his own home he is authorized to charge an extra fee, and if he must make a journey to do so, an added travel allowance is given."

Thus, there are no panels or fund hospitals; there is free choice of practitioners and institutions, as in the absence of health insurance. The patient makes his choices, and his right to medical care is realized through the recovery of a part of his bill from his insurance carrier or through the advancement of this part to him. In extreme cases, the bills allowed under the law are paid in full, but in most cases recovery is limited to 80 per cent of the scale officially agreed upon by associations and the carriers.[1] As Professor Douglas states, "the rates which serve as a basis for reimbursement by the funds to the patient are fixed by the funds in agreement with the recognized branches of the medical, dental, and pharmaceutical associations. In fixing these rates, due regard is supposed to be paid to the lowest scale of fees of the medical associations in the district. . . .

"If it is impossible for the funds to come to an agreement with the medical and other associations, they may undertake the liability for a flat proportion of a schedule of fees drawn up by them, or they may pay a flat rate of so much a day to persons not receiving surgical or hospital treatment. If they do the latter, they cannot fix this sum at more than 20 per cent of the basic wage of the worker in question if they are to obtain reinsurance for this amount from the General Guarantee Fund, which is to be described later. If they pay more, therefore, they must bear the burden themselves."[2]

It should be added, as Professor Douglas notes, that "except in cases where special treatment is required, the total amounts paid by the funds for medical and pharmaceutical expenses shall not exceed 50 per cent of

[1] The insured person's share of pharmaceutical expenses is, as a rule, fixed at 20 per cent, but it is increased to 40 per cent in respect to the amount by which the cost of the pharmaceutical supplies exceeds 25 francs for each prescription. The 1935 Congress of the General Confederation of Labor of France, in a resolution relating to the Social Insurance Act, recognized that the establishment of the tariff rates of repayment of medical expenses incurred by insured persons represented an advance and urged that further efforts in this direction be made. Specifically, the Congress resolution held that the insured person should not be required to meet the often excessive difference between the rates of repayment of the funds and the scales of doctors' fees. It was further suggested that better use of resources and avoidance of waste and abuses could be effected, especially in connection with pharmaceutical specialties, by empowering the funds to possess their own pharmacies. *Industrial and Labour Information*, vol. 61, no. 4 (Geneva, Oct. 28, 1935), pp. 136–137.

[2] P. H. Douglas, *op. cit.*, pp. 226–227. In 1930, the Ministry issued a series of rates for medical services, dentistry, pharmaceutical supplies, and hospital supplies (*ibid.*, p. 227). There are decentralized revisions of these rates.

the basic wage of the insured workers."[1] This is a further limitation upon recovery by the insured and distinctly limits the amount of service which can be rendered to the more poorly paid workers.

The French system was shaped to meet the demands of the doctors, to conserve freedom in medical practice, and to safeguard against certain problems which had arisen elsewhere in connection with medical care under compulsory health insurance.[2] But what problems have arisen or may arise here? One might reasonably, at the time the Act was passed, have asked these questions: (a) Will fees be advanced and overcharging be resorted to? (b) Will overtreatment and unnecessary treatment occur? (c) With the greatest freedom of choice of physician, will loose certification of disability be encouraged and malingery be inadequately safeguarded against?

This French departure is highly suggestive as to how certain problems experienced elsewhere can be avoided. Whether Professor Douglas was right in saying,[3] "Perhaps the best thing that can be said for the whole system of medical provision under the Act is that it is the type which least arouses the opposition of the doctors"; or whether control will be so exercised that important problems of cost, overtreatment, and malingery will be avoided, only further experience will reveal. The system has been in operation too short a time and under such abnormal circumstances that experience has not afforded definite answers to the questions here raised. Certain observations may, however, be made. The limitations upon the amounts to be paid out of the fund for medical care in a given case will perhaps safeguard adequately against overtreatment. Indeed, the real question is whether or not the system can be expected to provide adequate medical care for those most in need of protection through a system of health insurance. In some localities, rightly or wrongly, the doctors increased their charges after the law went into effect, because the traffic would bear more owing to the greater capacity of the insured to pay medical bills. Great disparities appeared between the doctors' scales and the fund scales adopted for the purpose of reimbursement for medical bills paid. Though in some cases the professional scales have been reduced and in others the reimbursement scales have been raised, Dr. Falk states that there are cases in which the reimbursements are only 50 per cent, or even 33⅓ per cent, of the bills paid by the insured.[4] In

[1] *Ibid.*

[2] As I. S. Falk in *Security Against Sickness*, p. 230, says, "The profession took its stand for: (1) freedom of every licensed doctor to undertake the treatment of insured persons and their dependents, (2) free choice of the doctor by the insured, (3) freedom in the prescription of medicines, (4) payment of the doctor by the insured, (5) payment according to the medical act, (6) preservation of privileged communication, and (7) discipline of doctors by the profession." (Quoted by courtesy of Doubleday, Doran and Company.)

[3] P. H. Douglas, *op. cit.*, p. 228.

[4] I. S. Falk, *op. cit.*, pp. 233–234.

some cases, as Douglas says, "the system operated to increase the income of the doctors from each patient rather than to reduce the burden upon patients by the full amount of the subventions."[1]

In accordance with the doctors' demands, the French system requires only that the physician make a memorandum showing his medical acts in the given case and certifying incapacity of an insured person where that is involved. The nature of the disease is a privileged matter and is not reported. Incidentally, of course this means that valuable data for the development of ways and means of sickness prevention are not being secured. Moreover, it has made necessary the development of supervisory agencies for investigating many of the cases treated and of the certifications of incapacity, investigation being followed by complaint where required. The freedom demanded has not been, and obviously cannot be, fully realized.

Dr. Falk may be quoted at some length in this connection:[2]

"The method of remuneration adopted in France was what the professions wanted. But now that they have it, they are beginning to be less certain it is what they want. Each *caisse* must guard its treasury and balance its budgets. If it does not take appropriate measures, it finds itself exposed to serving as a large financial reservoir into which any unscrupulous physician, in collusion with an unscrupulous insured person,

<hr/>

[1] P. H. Douglas, *op. cit.*, p. 228.

The Annual Congress of the French Federation of Mutual Aid Funds, known as the *Mutual Aid Parliament*, was held in Paris from Sept. 20 to 22, 1935. This meeting was of great importance, in view of the wide scope which the Social Insurance Act leaves to insurance by mutual aid associations. In a resolution, the Congress protested against the steadily rising cost of medical and pharmaceutical aid, charging that there was not only considerable abuse in the prescription of medical specialties but also that a wide disparity existed between the prices charged by chemists and the cost of production of the medicines. The Congress further declared that the social insurance funds and mutual aid societies should not only discuss the rates for pharmaceutical benefits but should, if necessary, notwithstanding the opposition of the organizations of chemists, make use of their right under the Act of 1898 to establish and operate their own pharmacies.

The Congress further declared against threatened strikes put forward by medical associations at a recent Congress in defense of privileges and prerogatives which the Congress considered incompatible with the organization and operation of social insurance on a modern and scientific basis. Nevertheless, while deploring the antisocial attitude of a section of the medical profession, the Congress stated that it would continue the right of the members of the mutual aid societies to choose freely their own doctor, this right to be restricted to those doctors only who accepted medical practice on the basis of a moderate and uniform tariff of fees and charges.

Lastly, in order that the mutual aid societies might undertake a policy of health equipment and preventive medicine which would supplement the inadequate efforts of the Ministry of Public Health, the Congress decided to attempt the establishment of centers for diagnosis and treatment suitable to national and local needs. *Industrial and Labour Information*, vol. 56, no. 4 (Geneva, Oct. 28, 1935), pp. 134–135.

[2] Quoted, with permission, from I. S. Falk, *Security Against Sickness* (Doubleday, Doran and Company, 1936), pp. 234–236.

can dip his net.   It is therefore not surprising that the *caisse* has developed protective devices.   When the insured patient presents a certificate to show that he has paid for medical service and is entitled to reimbursement, usually no question is raised and no complex check-up is invoked if the amount is small and the illness of short duration.   But when the bill is large or incapacity for work is certified or the prognosis is for a long-continued illness, or the certification of incapacity is repeated once, twice, three times, the record is examined.   What is the history of the case? What was the nature of the illness?   What did the doctor say about it? What kinds of services were rendered and how many?

"In some cases a few inquiries are sufficient to settle all doubts, to justify the *caisse* in accepting the certificates, and to pay reimbursement for medical benefit and—when the patient is gainfully occupied but incapacitated—to pay cash sickness benefit on account of lost wages. In many cases, however, this is far from sufficient.   And with hundreds of thousands of such experiences occurring during the year, the problem before the *caisses* becomes of enormous magnitude.   The outcome has been the development by the large *caisses* of medical staffs and elaborately equipped facilities for the examination of patients—partial and complete physical examinations; independent diagnoses and prognoses; X-ray and laboratory examinations; special urological, dermatological, dental and other examinations, and consultations, etc.   Thus, the *caisses* find themselves engaged on a large scale in checking the work of the individual private practitioners.   While it is probably true that in France more than in any other large compulsory insurance country the plan of sickness insurance has operated to entrench the individual private practice of medicine, it also is true that there, more than elsewhere, it has led to the most extensive system of supervision over such practice of medicine.

"In Paris—and perhaps in the large cities generally—about 50 per cent of the cases are investigated, and in about 60 per cent of these the patient is examined by the physicians of the *caisse* to check on the record. Medical supervision, investigation, hearings, etc., 'bureaucracy,' conflicts of opinion on medical issues, conflicts of judgment on costs—these and other difficulties have not been avoided by the French system of remunerating the doctor.   On the contrary, by the victory of dictating the system of remuneration and of assuring all patients completely free choice of doctor, the French doctors achieved stringent limitation of fees, a complex and cumbersome fee schedule, necessity for close administrative supervision, conflicts with insurance authorities, and a considerable loss in public esteem.   The confusion which has followed upon this Pyrrhic victory seems to have exceeded what occurred in Germany with salaries, per-capita payments, and fee schedules, and is certainly vastly in excess of what has been customary in Great Britain under per-capita payments."

Maternity benefits are provided for both insured women and the wives of insured men, provided payment of contributions in a minimum of sixty francs has been made by the insured person during the four quarters preceding confinement and a minimum of fifteen francs was paid during the first of these quarters. Full medical care is provided for both insured women and the wives of insured men.[1] This includes the services of doctor or midwife at the time of confinement and also prenatal care during the entire period of pregnancy and postnatal care for six months following birth of the child. Cash benefits and allowances are also provided for insured women but not for uninsured wives. There are the usual sickness benefits of 50 per cent of basic wages which are paid for six weeks preceding and for an equal period following confinement provided gainful work is abstained from. There is also a nursing benefit for the insured mother who nurses her child. This is 150 francs per month for the first four months, 100 francs for the fifth and sixth months, and 50 francs for each month from the seventh to the ninth. If an insured woman is certified by her doctor as being unable to nurse her child, she may, if she rears the child at home, receive milk tickets equal to two-thirds of the value of these bonuses.

Death and related benefits are provided for the heirs of deceased insured persons. The most important is one of 20 per cent of the average annual wage of the deceased, with a minimum benefit of 1,000 francs.[2] Generally speaking, this is adequate for a modest funeral, but, as elsewhere, for little more. Added to this main benefit, however, is an allowance of 100 francs for each dependent child. In the event there are three or more dependent children, this allowance is increased to 120 francs for each child in excess of two.

Finally, attention must be called to specific provisions for the protection of wives. "The non-wage-earning wives of insured persons are admitted to certain insurance benefits. They are considered as compulsorily insured at an annual wage arbitrarily fixed at 1,500 francs. Their contribution is fixed at 8 per cent of this amount, or thirty francs per quarter. They are not entitled to the cash sickness benefits and are entitled to an invalidity pension only in case of total incapacity to attend to household duties. Half of the contribution is applied towards the old-age pension, which during a transitory period is fixed at 250 francs

[1] The new legislative decree, which deals in part with maternity insurance, relieves the insured person of any share in medical and pharmaceutical expenses. The French legislation in this respect now complies with the Childbirth Convention of 1919.

[2] In order for his dependents to establish a claim to survivor insurance, the insured person must have been on the register for at least one year and have had an amount of at least sixty francs deducted from his wages during the four quarters immediately preceding death. This benefit may not exceed two-thirds of the actual wages of the insured person.

per year.   Non-wage-earning married women can contract for this insurance without regard to the husband, in their full juridical capacity."[1]

Briefly presented, save for the pensions for the old, this is the French social-insurance system as it applies to nonagricultural workers.   For the five and one-half years ending with December, 1935, sickness benefits paid amounted to 4,597,520,544 francs, maternity benefits to 844,318,770 francs, and death benefits to 140,278,463 francs.[2]

Insurance of Agricultural Workers.—Because of differences in circumstances, cost, and tax-paying ability, the provision made for those engaged in agricultural pursuits is separated from that made for those engaged in industrial, commercial, and miscellaneous trades.

Wage earners in agriculture and forestry are required to insure and self-employed peasants may voluntarily do so, with liberal subsidies granted by the government.   The carriers are mutual aid societies and the like, whose membership is exclusively in agricultural funds or in the agricultural sections of the departmental funds, but approximately half of the insured employ the mutual aid societies as the carrier.   For those compulsorily insured the necessary annual contributions of 240 francs for men, 192 francs for women, and 144 francs for children under sixteen are shared equally by employer and the insured.   To these contributions the government adds 120 francs per year.   The carriers, in so far as those dealt with here are concerned, are permitted to determine the benefits.   Thus, there is much elasticity and opportunity for variation from one carrier to another and from time to time.

---

[1] Quoted from summary, U. S. *Monthly Labor Review*, vol. 42, no. 2 (February, 1936), p. 332.

[2] Including other benefits of 6,556,281 francs during this period, total disbursements from 1930 to 1935, for these various types of insurance, amounted to 5,582,374,058 francs. Rapport du Ministère du Travail sur l'application de la loi des Assurances Sociales, *Journal Officiel* (Paris, Apr. 18, 1937), pp. 139–254.   For a brief summary of this report, see *Monthly Labor Review*, vol. 45 (1937), pp. 107–110.

CHAPTER VII

THE COMPULSORY HEALTH-INSURANCE MOVEMENT IN THE UNITED STATES AND A SUGGESTED PLAN

During two fairly distinct periods compulsory health insurance has been under active discussion in the United States. The first of these began about 1915 and lasted for four or five years. The second period covers the last several years, during which the movement has again become somewhat active. It is certain that compulsory health insurance will soon become a real issue in this country, especially since existing legislation relating to old-age and unemployment insurance has been declared constitutional and since no great advance has yet been made in solving the problem of medical care upon an acceptable basis.

AN EARLIER MOVEMENT AND ITS MISCARRIAGE

In December, 1912, the American Association for Labor Legislation created a National Committee on Social Insurance which organized the First National Conference on the subject. This conference was held in 1913 and a statement was issued describing the general outline which the Committee would follow in drafting a bill for health insurance. In 1915, with the help of a committee of the American Medical Association, a tentative draft for a health insurance act was prepared which came to be known as the "Standard Bill." By 1918, second and third drafts had been made, and then the related Nicol (N.Y.) bill was accepted. Health-insurance measures were introduced in three states in 1915 and in twelve states in 1917. No bill was passed by any legislature, but several commissions were created to investigate and report. The peak of legislative interest was reached in 1917, when investigating commissions were established in eight states.[1] Some of these commissions reported favorably, others unfavorably, on the subject. However, before the more important of the reports were made, the movement had all but succumbed to the organized opposition aroused.

The American movement was due in considerable part to the adoption of the British Insurance Act of 1911, but the Standard Bill was based largely upon the German model. Except casuals and homeworkers, all

---

[1] California, Massachusetts, New Jersey, Ohio, Illinois, Connecticut, Pennsylvania, and Wisconsin. Provision was made for a commission in New Hampshire also, but it was not appointed for no appropriation was made.

321

manual laborers earning not to exceed $100 per month were to be insured through fraternal orders, trade unions, mutual benefit associations or other mutual, nonprofit-making organizations, or through local territorial funds to be established. The medical benefits to be provided corresponded rather closely to those then provided in Germany, and were to be extended to the wife and dependent children of the insured. The sickness benefit was to be two-thirds of the insured person's wage for not to exceed twenty-six weeks in any twelve months. There was also to be a burial benefit in a sum not to exceed fifty dollars. The cost of the scheme was to be divided among the employer, the insured, and the state treasury, the employer and the insured each being responsible for 40,[1] the treasury for 20, per cent.[2]

By the end of 1918, the health-insurance movement was badly crippled by the organized opposition and from that time on lost ground all the while. After a year or so it was regarded as a lost hope, except in New York, where it was given further, serious consideration. The strongest opponent was, of course, the organized insurance business, operating through the Insurance Economics Society and other agencies; the industrial insurance companies objected particularly because of the proposed funeral benefit,[3] the casualty companies because of the sickness benefit. Many of the fraternal orders were fearful of the effect of a system of health insurance upon them. While the official opposition of the American Medical Association dates from 1920 and while among the state and local medical organizations some went on record as approving some such system as that proposed,[4] the stronger local societies, as for instance those in Chicago and New York, were both bitter and active in their opposition. The druggists and patent-medicine manufacturers were just as actively opposed. For obvious reasons, the Christian Scientists added their opposition. Though many individual employers favored the proposed legislation, strong employers' organizations opposed it, among other reasons because of the charge which would be placed upon industry and the effect of increased costs where interstate competition was involved.

[1] This was proposed as the normal arrangement. If, however, earnings were less than nine dollars per week, the worker's contribution was to be reduced and the employer's increased according to a scale under which the employer would assume the entire charge when earnings were less than five dollars per week.

[2] A bill introduced in the New York legislature early in 1918 was accepted as the last version of the Standard Bill. Under it all manual workers would have been insured regardless of wage rate, and the cost would have been shared equally by employers and insured.

[3] A vice-president of one of the industrial insurance companies resigned from the Committee because of the inclusion of a funeral benefit in the Standard Bill.

[4] Mentioning only the stronger organizations, compulsory health insurance was endorsed by the State Medical Association of Wisconsin, the American Association of Industrial Physicians and Surgeons, the National Organization for Public Health Nursing, and the American Hospital Association.

And the American Federation of Labor was opposed in so far as President Gompers and the Executive Council were concerned.[1]   Their opposition was far more effective than the endorsements given by several internationals, a number of state federations of labor,[2] and a large number of city central bodies.   In the State of New York alone was there a strong labor movement actively interested in the enactment of compulsory health-insurance legislation.   Perhaps nowhere else was there a large, coherent organization of any of the parties directly concerned lending substantial support to the cause.

The success of the opposition to the proposed legislation was due more to self-interest on the part of many organizations, to fear, to misunderstanding, to wilful misrepresentation, to the charge that it was German, and to the fact that the country had not been prepared by investigation and discussion for a system of health insurance than to any of the weaknesses in what was proposed.   Instead of such a system being seen as effecting little more than an assembling of existing costs, it was generally regarded as something that would add an enormous and unsupportable burden.   It was denounced as unnecessary, socialistic, un-American, a wrong method of attack—sickness prevention was what was needed.   It would beget simulation and malingering; it would involve contract medicine, reduce the income of the doctors, destroy the close personal relationship between doctor and patient, and discourage and undermine medical research.   It was not working well in Europe.   Such were the more important sources of opposition and the most frequently voiced objections which, in the absence of a strong, coherent, actively interested group, brought to an early end the first period in an American health-insurance movement.

THE COMMITTEE ON THE COSTS OF MEDICAL CARE, ITS FINDINGS, AND RECOMMENDATIONS

But in the light of the analysis presented in Chap. V of this volume, there was a by no means small problem, and one that in the absence of constructive solution would in time again become an issue.   The question has recurred.   The current movement received a great impetus from the work of the Committee on the Costs of Medical Care, which was established to investigate and to find a solution for the problem of furnishing good medical care to all the people at prices which they could afford to pay.[3]   And, of course, the movement has received added support

---

[1] The American Federation did not take any position officially on the subject. A committee was set up in 1918 but disagreed, with the result that health insurance did not come up for discussion in the annual conventions.

[2] Up to 1924, three state federations had resolved against while eleven or more had endorsed compulsory health insurance.

[3] The Committee was established in 1927, after some preliminary conferences of

because of the enlarged medical problem experienced during the long depression.

With few exceptions, the research work done for the Committee and by the cooperating organizations was excellent. That in no other country have the data necessary for an analysis and statement of the problem been so well provided is not disputed. There has been general acceptance and little but praise of the fact-finding done. It has been freely used in our statement of the problem. But, as would be expected of a committee representing doctors, public-health men, dentists, hospitals, druggists, scientists, and the public, there were at certain points sharp clashes of opinion as to what should be recommended. A majority report, a minority report number one, a minority report number two, and individual statements by two members resulted. Twenty-five of the forty-eight members involved were physicians and, of these, seventeen signed the majority report. Minority report number one, it is interesting to note, was signed by eight physicians and had the support of one other. The second minority report was made by two dentists. It should be added, also, that there were dissents from some of the positions taken in the majority report, the most important one being on whether or not insurance should be compulsory. On that point nine of the members dissented from the position taken and recorded their approval of a compulsory system.[1]

Though there was sharp division of opinion on certain important matters, such as the form the coordination and organization of medical service should take and more decisively on the question of insurance,

---

physicians, health officers, social scientists, and representatives of the public, and developed a five-year program of research and study. For the greater part of this period, it consisted of fifty members, with Dr. Wilbur, then Secretary of the Interior, as Chairman. Its excellent research staff collected and exploited available data and made field studies. No fewer than twenty-six reports on fact-finding studies were published, together with the *Final Report*, which bore the title, *Medical Care for the American People* (hereafter referred to as *Final Report*).

The complete list of the twenty-eight major publications and fourteen miscellaneous publications of the Committee, as well as the lists of publications by cooperating persons and institutions, may be found at the end of the *Final Report*. The incidental expenses and the costs of research and publication were met by eight foundations: the Carnegie Corporation, the Josiah Macy, Jr., Foundation, the Milbank Memorial Fund, the New York Foundation, the Rockefeller Foundation, the Julius Rosenwald Fund, the Russell Sage Foundation, and the Twentieth Century Fund. The total expenditure was approximately $900,000. Most of this was incurred in making investigations and publishing the results.

[1] See the *Final Report* of the Committee, p. 130. Contrary to the position of the majority against compulsory health insurance *at this time*, nine members of the Committee believed that the industrial states at least should immediately begin to plan for the adoption of a system which would require all persons in certain income groups, certain occupations, or certain areas to subscribe for health insurance.

there was general agreement on a number of significant points, seven of which should be noted here. First to be mentioned is the emphasis placed upon the need for a medical service of the best quality as well as its general availability. Second, the doctors and other professional personnel and the several agencies should be adequately remunerated.[1] Otherwise a medical service of increasingly good quality cannot be had. Third, in any coordinated and organized plan of medical service—and the need for coordination was conceded by all—the doctors and other personnel concerned must be adequately represented on control and policy Boards, and must have control of technical professional questions. Fourth, the public-health service must be strengthened, enriched and better supported, and more carefully safeguarded. All reasonable efforts must be made to prevent sickness and to promote health.[2] Fifth, the government, out of tax revenues, should provide the needed medical care not only for veterans, soldiers, sailors, the indigent, and the inmates of certain institutions, but also for those afflicted with certain diseases, such as tuberculosis, and for the mentally diseased.[3] Sixth, it was generally agreed that grants-in-aid should be made to provide needed doctors, hospitals,

---

[1] The Committee stated (*Final Report*, p. 106), among other things, "The interests of the 1,100,000 persons in the United States who furnish medical service and the 123,000,000 who receive it are closely interwoven. The professional standards of physicians, dentists, nurses, pharmacists, hospitals, and other practitioners and agencies which furnish medical care must be carefully guarded in behalf of the people served, as well as in behalf of those who provide service."

[2] The Committee said (*ibid.*, p. 118), "The United States spends only $1.00 per capita for [its very deficient] public health services." It "recommends the extension of all basic public health services—whether provided by governmental or non-governmental agencies—so that they will be available to the entire population according to its needs. Primarily this extension requires increased financial support for official health departments and full-time trained health officers and members of their staffs whose tenure is dependent only upon professional and administrative competence." It was realized that some reconstitution of public health areas would be necessary and that the public health service must be coordinated with the general medical service. The definition of public health work was, very properly, a broad one. The Committee said (p. 119), "There is nearly universal agreement that the following are 'proper public health functions': (*a*) the collection and analysis of vital statistics; (*b*) the control of water, milk, and food supplies; (*c*) the control of sanitation; (*d*) the control, through quarantine and supervision, of communicable diseases; and (*e*) the provision of laboratory service. In addition . . . the Committee believes that the following activities are also proper public health activities: (*f*) the promotion of maternal, infant, and child hygiene, including medical and dental inspection and supervision of school children; (*g*) popular health instruction; (*h*) the provision of preventive dental care for children; and (*i*) the provision of special services for the prevention, diagnosis, and treatment of patients with tuberculosis, venereal diseases, malaria, hookworm, or any other disease which constitutes a special health problem in the community that cannot be solved adequately and effectively by the other available medical and health agencies."

[3] *Ibid.*, p. 122.

and nurses in thinly populated and remote areas with limited financial capacity.[1] And finally, under any insurance plan, medical care and the certification of insured persons for sickness benefit should be completely divorced.[2]

Consideration of the need of incapacitated persons for cash benefits in partial compensation for loss of income was no part of the task of the Committee. On this subject it therefore limited itself pretty much to the position just indicated.

Coming to the main issues on which the Committee divided, there were, as has been stated, two. The one concerned the medical plan, the other the distribution of the cost of medical care. The majority of the Committee were of the opinion that facilities for medical care must be coordinated and organized and that the insurance principle must be employed to pay the costs.[3] To the latter a number of doctors (those signing minority report number one) objected, whether the insurance was voluntary or compulsory. They opposed also the community-center, group-practice plan recommended in the majority report.

The majority held that in these days of specialized personnel, extensive investment, and specialized institutions, and with the lack of knowledge on the part of many people of where and to whom it is best to go for needed treatment, arrangements for the group practice of medicine are necessary if the quality of medical service desired is to be realized. It is true that the general practitioner has come to play a more limited role than he should, but he should find his place in the group organization as the rule. Community centers, developed around the hospital, with clinics, laboratories, and all else needed, were recommended as the form of organization.[4] The facilities of such centers would be coordinated and control of "specialism" and a variety of things would be exercised.[5]

Not only would medical care be improved under such a plan, but the costs would be little greater than the present outlay, for much waste would or could be eliminated, such as inadequately used hospital facilities, overhead of individual offices, expenditures for patent medicines, and the charges levied by quacks and practitioners of an unacceptable type.[6]

The majority of the Committee were driven by the facts as they interpreted them to the conclusion that the costs of medical care "should be distributed over groups of people and over periods of time." The problem lies not so much in the average cost of medical care as in its very

---

[1] See, particularly, *ibid.*, p. 52.

[2] *Ibid.*, p. 129. (Recommendation repeated a number of times.)

[3] *Ibid.*, p. 151 and elsewhere.

[4] See *ibid.*, Chaps. II and V.

[5] *Ibid.*, pp. 135–137.

[6] "A substantial part of the increased cost of supporting a satisfactory medical service could be met by the elimination of wastes in present expenditures. The net increase in cost would not necessarily be large." *Final Report*, p. 59.

uneven distribution—so uneven that many cannot pay the bills on a fee-for-service basis, even with an installment arrangement.[1] Moreover, a family cannot budget against medical bills. One paragraph of the *Final Report*, from among several, may be quoted, as follows:[2]

"The costs of medical care are felt as a burden more because they are unevenly distributed among the people than because of their total amount . . . that some families of moderate means spend substantial sums on 'luxuries,' yet are not able in times of sickness to meet the costs of medical care, is beside the point so long as the medical costs are met on an individual fee-for-service basis. The costs of luxuries can be planned in advance or met in installments; the cost of illness for the individual family cannot. On a group basis, however, both the incidence of illness and the probable cost of its care can now be predicted with reasonable accuracy."

The Committee recommended that the cost of medical care be placed on a group-payment basis, through the use of insurance, through the use of taxation, or through the use of both these methods. But this was "not meant to preclude the continuation of medical service provided on an individual fee basis for those who prefer the present method."[3] The majority, in spite of the shortcomings and inadequacy of voluntary insurance, did not advocate compulsory insurance for adoption at this time. Its position may be stated in the language of the *Final Report:*

"It [voluntary insurance] can reach only a certain fraction of the population. . . .

"Families with low or irregular incomes, even if they are self-supporting while employed, cannot usually be covered by any form of voluntary insurance."[4]

These quotations concern the inadequacy of voluntary insurance. It is important, however, to permit institutions to grow, to build upon existing arrangements and to be guided by experience:

"The majority of the Committee, although aware of the limitations of coverage and the possible difficulties of voluntary health insurance, nevertheless believe that the ultimate results will be far better if experience with actuarial and administrative details, and above all the evolu-

---

[1] Within ten years or so loan companies have increasingly made possible the use of installment payments. The rates of interest are high—12 to 43 per cent or more per year. The Committee deplored this. Moreover, it noted (*Final Report*, p. 95) that while the burden of payment is thus spread over a period of time, it is not so distributed that the public helps to lighten the burden when it threatens to destroy the solvency of the patient. The Committee opposed medical corporations operated for profit and all plans where the doctors and other personnel do not have an adequate degree of control and necessary independence.

[2] *Final Report*, p. 48.

[3] *Ibid.*, p. 120.

[4] *Ibid.*, p. 127.

tion of group practice units capable of rendering rounded medical service of high quality, precede the adoption of any compulsory plan by a state as a whole."[1]

"Unless there has been ample previous experience in a state with group practice as a basis of furnishing medical service, any law for required health insurance would make individual practice and not group practice the legal foundation of the whole system. Such has been one of the chief disadvantages which European countries have faced under compulsory insurance."[2]

The Committee went on to say:[3]

"There are also weighty administrative considerations against making health insurance compulsory as a general program for the United States. Compulsory insurance abroad has depended for its administration largely upon organized groups of employees, such as unions or cooperative societies. Their part in the administration has in some countries proved disadvantageous to quality and economy of service, partly because of the wide geographical dispersion of the membership, and partly because health insurance is likely to be a secondary interest of these organizations. Be this as it may, such industrial and cooperative associations are not sufficiently developed in most localities in the United States to include more than a small fraction of the population. It would be impossible, therefore, to use such organizations as the basis for administering compulsory health insurance. Usually it would be necessary to form new, local organizations. This would require a large amount of direct governmental administration, because the government would be the only available or recognized agency, capable of administering a compulsory insurance plan for the diverse and unorganized elements that make up the population of most American cities. . . .

"Finally, it is probable that no legislature would pass a compulsory health insurance law unless it included, from the start, a combination of medical care insurance with cash benefits for income protection; but these two forms of insurance should not be combined."

It has been noted that it was on this matter of compulsory insurance that several members of the Committee, chiefly several scientists and social workers, dissented. Their position was so admirably summarized in the *Final Report*, that we quote the summary in full.

"They take this position for the following reasons: 1. Most European countries, one after another, have gone from a voluntary to a required system of insurance, but many of the evils of the voluntary system are carried over to the compulsory plan. Vested interests are built up under voluntary insurance which are very difficult to dislodge, even though

---

[1] *Ibid.*, p. 127.
[2] *Ibid.*, p. 129.
[3] *Ibid.*, pp. 129–130.

they seriously hamper effective work. While it is true that the United States has few cooperative societies which could administer compulsory health insurance, this is a fortunate rather than an unfortunate circumstance. In European countries, such societies have almost completely outgrown their usefulness, so far as health insurance is concerned; but they still remain to clutter and confuse administration, and to prevent insurance statistics from being useful for public health purposes.

"2. Voluntary insurance will never cover those who most need its protection. No legerdemain can bring into a voluntary system the unorganized, low-paid working group who are not indigent but live on a minimum subsistence income. Yet any plan that helps those with less serious needs and does not reach those whose needs are sorest does not solve the fundamental problems of providing satisfactory medical service to all.

"3. There is no innate antagonism between required health insurance and the development of organized medical service. On the contrary, such health insurance might be a powerful stimulus to the formation of organized groups. If health insurance covers all major types of medical service, and if local communities are free to obtain medical service from organized groups, when such groups are available, the obvious benefits, economic and professional, of organized service will act as the most effective possible stimulant to the formation of such groups. The dangers of giving local communities this authority can be guarded against if all contracts are subject to approval by a state board that insists on fair treatment to the practitioners and the maintenance of good standards.

"4. Required insurance will undoubtedly be simpler and more direct to administer and, in the long run, more economical. There will be less tendency to create over-lapping agencies and to duplicate capital investment. Because a large proportion of the people will be included, it will be more stable.

"5. Governmental participation and regulation will undoubtedly be almost as necessary for voluntary as for compulsory insurance, if the worst abuses are to be avoided. Such participation will be more effective if it is started in the beginning."[1]

The dissenting doctors making minority report number one, while agreeing with the majority on many things, objected to the particular plan proposed for coordinating and organizing medical service and to sickness insurance as a method of distributing the costs.[2]

---

[1] *Ibid.*, pp. 131–132.

[2] In *Final Report*, p. 153, they stated: "with regard to the majority Recommendations 1 and 3, dealing with 'Organization of Medical Services' and 'Group Payment for Medical Services,' the convictions of this minority are so divergent from those of the majority that they must be discussed in detail."

Starting with the conservative principle, "the plan must safeguard the quality of medical service and preserve the essential personal relation between patient and physician," the minority viewed the proposed plan for organizing medical service as subversive and as one for "mass production." They regarded individual practice as superior to group practice and were of the opinion that in 85 per cent of the cases the general practitioner is wholly competent to give all the medical service required. With specific reference to the community-center suggestion, they said:[1]

"Among the many objections to the medical center plan which must occur to anyone familiar with the requirements of medical practice are the following: (1) It would establish a medical hierarchy in every community to dictate who might practice medicine. This is inherent in the plan since any new member of the center must be chosen either by the chief or by a small staff. (2) It would be impossible to prevent competition among the many such centers necessary for large cities; cost would inevitably be increased by the organization necessary to assign patients to the various centers. This would add to the evils of medical dictatorship those of a new bureau in the local government with its attendant cost. (3) Continuous personal relationship of physician and patient would be difficult if not impossible under such conditions.

"We look upon this plan as far-fetched and visionary. It has no practical relationship to the question the Committee has set itself to solve. Placed as it is at the very beginning of the Committee's recommendations it must create a doubt of the Committee's grasp of the problem to which it has addressed itself. It seems to us an illustration of what is almost an obsession with many people, namely, that 'organization' can cure most, if not all, human ills."

This minority was quite obviously much less impressed with the urgency of any existing problem of medical care than were their fellow members. They stressed as important the close personal relation between doctor and patient, which, it may be remarked, has largely disappeared in large urban and in important industrial communities because of the mobility of doctors and people and the turnover of labor. Moreover, the minority were obviously concerned with matters from the point of view of the general practitioner; the majority saw as a part of the general problem the special problems of the hospital, the laboratory, the nurses, and much else that with medical advance has become important and widely used by those who can pay.

The minority opposed much of the existing group practice as involving contract medicine and as subversive of good medical service.[2] Without opposing the principle of group payment, they were of the opinion that "there are great dangers and evils in insurance practice which must be set

[1] *Ibid.*, pp. 155, 169, 174.
[2] *Ibid.*, pp. 155–163. Definition of contract practice is given on p. 156.

over against the advantages of distributing the costs of medical care by this method and which . . . the majority report has minimized." It was asserted that "voluntary health insurance schemes have everywhere failed," and that "in Europe they have been replaced by compulsory systems which are now under trial."[1] The minority, not illogically, stated:

"It seems clear, then, that if we must adopt in this country either of the methods tried out in Europe, the sensible and logical plan would be to adopt the method to which European countries have come through experience, that is, a compulsory plan under governmental control."[2]

But "the objections to compulsory health insurance [were] almost as compelling to this minority group as [were] those to voluntary insurance." The objections were: (1) "The operation of every form of insurance practice up to the present time has resulted in a vast amount of competitive effort on the part of practitioner groups, hospitals, and lay controlled organizations. Such competition tends to lower the standards of medical care, degrade the medical personnel, and make medical care a business rather than a profession." Experience with medical care under workman's compensation was cited as American evidence.[3] (2) "The total cost of medical care is usually increased when it is paid for through insurance," because "the cost of operation of the insurance plan must be added to the cost of medical care," and because the number of persons sick and the number of days sickness per capita always increase under any system of insurance.[4] (3) "Compulsory insurance will necessarily be subject to political control and that such control will inevitably destroy professional morale and ideals in medicine."[5] (4) "The medical profession is now in many parts of the country extending and perfecting plans through which it can offer to the people in a more systematic way the services of all the physicians of each community at prices which all the people can afford."[6]

NEW DEVELOPMENTS AND ATTITUDES; EVALUATION OF INSTITUTIONAL DEVELOPMENTS AND EXPERIMENTS

Owing to factors present all the while, to the findings and recommendations of the Committee on the Costs of Medical Care, to the greatly enlarged problem in time of depression, and, in the Northwest particularly, to the health-insurance movement in the western provinces of Canada, important developments have occurred in recent years in the

[1] *Ibid.*, pp. 163, 166–167.
[2] *Ibid.*, p. 164.
[3] *Ibid.*, p. 165.
[4] *Ibid.*, pp. 165–166.
[5] *Ibid.*, p. 167.
[6] *Ibid.*

institutional arrangements for medical care. Moreover, a compulsory health-insurance movement has reappeared, exciting as much interest as it did some twenty years ago.

A summary statement of institutional developments has been presented incidental to our analysis of the problem in Chap. V of this volume.[1] At this point we need only to make a few observations by way of an evaluation of the developments which have been described. These may be limited to private group arrangements, organized medicine under the auspices of local medical societies, and group-hospital plans. All of these contain much that is good from a social point of view. However, they have deficiencies and some of them contain or have been accompanied by objectionable things.

While, as has been remarked, private group arrangements on an individual fee-for-service basis offer distinct advantages over the individual practice of medicine, they cannot solve the problem of providing adequate care for all of the people because they do not distribute the costs through a group-payment plan. Private group arrangements that do distribute the burden by providing care in return for a fixed periodic payment have much more merit. Yet, unless some part of the burden is charged elsewhere than to the persons actually served, the periodic payment may be more than many in the lower-income groups can easily bear. However, should an employed group subscribe, as it sometimes does, with the employer sharing the cost, as he might, this difficulty would be avoided. But without an element of compulsion present in group enrollment, the plan is confronted by the problems of voluntary insurance. Because of lack of interest or because of lack of ability to pay, only a minority of those in the lower-income groups can be expected to subscribe. Moreover, in the absence of strict regulation there is opportunity for much evil to develop. There is no guarantee that the commercial spirit will not enter in. In fact, it has, particularly in the Far West. Not without some reason, physicians have complained of unethical practice and unfair competition in specific cases. And scores of ventures in the West appear to border upon rackets. Plans have been announced, enrollments secured, and cash taken, without the promised service being rendered. It would appear that strict regulation must be resorted to or the necessary control found in a general organized system of medical care.

Most of the local medical societies that have been constructively active have introduced lower fees, possibly to meet a competitive situation, or have, as in the Detroit area, established machinery to ascertain what each patient can really afford to pay. The advantages and limitations of such arrangements are obvious. Here and there, however, and chiefly in the Pacific Northwest, medical societies have launched plans

[1] See pp. 258–266.

for the group payment of medical bills.   This is a recognition of a principle of distributing the costs that must be widely applied.   These plans, however, do not give the assurance of permanency, for they are largely a product of the depression.   Nor can they provide medical care for the people of the community generally unless much of it is on a charitable or semicharitable basis.   This is unfair to the physicians, who are entitled to fair remuneration for service rendered.

As has been said,[1] the most important single development during the last three or four years is found in the group-hospital plans placed in effect.   Nearly all of them merit approval so far as they go.   Nevertheless, three critical observations are warranted.   The service provided under many, if not most, of the plans is not liberal enough.   The reason for this is found, of course, in the costs involved.   The more liberal the provision for care, the higher the cost, and the higher the cost, the greater the difficulty in securing subscribers.

In the second place, the plans do not ordinarily cover the doctor's bill, which is a large item in hospitalized cases.   No doubt one reason for the exclusion of the doctor's bill is found in the position taken by the American Medical Association and most of the state and local medical societies.   Through its *Journal*,[2] the Association has poured cold water on group-hospital plans.   It regards hospital affairs and the physicians' affairs as something to be kept apart.   The sixth of its principles, adopted in 1934, read, "However the cost of medical service may be distributed, the immediate cost should be borne by the patient if able to pay at the time the service is rendered."[3]   Much criticized, this principle was reformulated in 1935 to read, "In whatever way the cost of medical service may be distributed, it should be paid for by the patient in accordance with his income status and in a manner that is mutually satisfactory."[4]   Though this reformulation would permit the method of group payment, without question the Association prefers fees for service rendered by the doctor on an individual basis.[5]

[1] Chap. V, pp. 260-261.

[2] *Journal of the American Medical Association.*

[3] The ten principles adopted in 1934 and modified slightly more recently, may be found in the *Journal of the American Medical Association* (June 30, 1934), p. 2200.

[4] *Ibid.* (June 29, 1935), p. 2364.

[5] The House of Delegates of the American Medical Association in June, 1937, laid down ten principles for group hospitals.   Of these, No. 4 is significant in this general connection. It reads, "The subscriber's contract should exclude all medical services—contract provisions should be limited exclusively to hospital facilities.   If hospital service is limited to include only hospital room accommodations such as bed, board, operating room, medicines, surgical dressings and general nursing care, the distinction between hospital service and medical service will be clear."   Organized medicine objects to the inclusion, under the contract, of "anesthesia, all radiologic services, every service that is rendered in the pathology department and any other service that can be construed as professional." Quoted from *Group Hospitalization* (American Medical Association, 1937), pp. 247, 243.

The third critical observation is related to the first. While approximately 1,600,000 persons have become subscribers for group-hospital service, the membership without question is more or less selective because of the inability of large numbers to pay, unaided, the necessary cost. No doubt an investigation would reveal that a great majority of the 1,600,000 subscribers are in the "moderate" and higher income groups. The problem bulks largest at a lower income level.[1] This inability on the part of many to pay, together with the mobility of population, ignorance, lack of interest and carelessness, inexperience in cooperative relationships, the problem involved in reaching possible subscribers, and also the possibility of medical charity, precludes all hope that these voluntary plans will in the course of time cover a larger percentage of the people than have the subsidized plans in the different European countries.

More progress in providing medical care has been made in the United States in the last five years than during the preceding twenty in so far as institutional arrangements are concerned. Yet, the problem remains only slightly reduced in magnitude. Moreover, as already indicated, new problems, incidental to free experimentation and to the profit motive, have appeared and call for attention unless they are cured by the introduction of a general, authoritative plan. What of compulsory insurance as a program?

MODEL BILLS FOR HEALTH INSURANCE AND OTHER SUGGESTIONS

The ventures we have been dealing with have in recent years absorbed most of the time and attention of those interested in the problem of medical care. Moreover, the report of the Committee on the Costs of Medical Care had as one of its immediate effects the discouragement of interest in plans based upon European programs. Nevertheless, there has been a renewal of interest in and discussion of compulsory health insurance.

In a sense, the "model bill" for health insurance prepared by Dr. Abraham Epstein and other members of the American Association for Social Security now occupies the place occupied twenty years ago by the Standard Bill. It is being brought to the attention of legislative bodies, and the thought of many persons interested in medical care, especially social workers and intellectuals, is being focused upon it.

This measure, with few exceptions, calls for the compulsory insurance of all manual wage earners, and also of other workers provided their

---

[1] As Dr. J. A. Kingsbury, recently of the Milbank Fund, has said, "The people in the lower-income brackets, who most urgently need an insurance plan, show the greatest inertia in coming into a voluntary plan. The poor, the mass of the workers, can be only partly, if at all, covered by voluntary insurance." Quoted from "Mutualizing Medical Costs," *Survey-Graphic*, June, 1934, p. 285. It may be added that only very exceptionally has membership in the plans been limited to persons in the low-income group.

wages do not exceed sixty dollars per week.   The exceptions are agricultural laborers and other workers employed in groups of fewer than three. It is estimated that under the measure 95 per cent of the wage earners would be compulsorily insured.   Moreover, it would provide for the voluntary insurance of any person whose income does not exceed sixty dollars per week.

The provisions for benefits and distribution of the costs resemble closely those found in leading foreign countries.   Though it contains some variations, the measure does not present a new and essentially different pattern.   Provision is made for both cash and medical benefits.

No burial benefit would be provided, but there would be a sickness benefit amounting to 50 per cent of the insured person's wage (or income), with a maximum of fifteen dollars per week and with allowances for spouse and dependent children.[1]   This sickness benefit would be paid if an insured person had normally made 104 contributions and was incapacitated for work for more than five days.   Normally, the benefit would not be paid for more than twenty-six weeks in the year.   There would also be a cash benefit of fifteen dollars in maternity cases, accompanying the medical services provided.

The medical benefits called for are comparatively inclusive in kind and would be provided not only for the insured but also for the members of his family.   They would become available after contributions had been made for three months and would continue while the person was in insurance except that they would be discontinued after six months in the case of continuous incapacitating illness, on the assumption that the case then becomes one of invalidity.[2]

The benefits, for the insured and the members of his family, would include: the physician's services; the specialist's services; surgical treatment; hospital care with necessary nursing, etc.; laboratory and clinical services; liberal dental care; drugs, appliances, etc., as needed—all without charge to the insured except as regards drugs, etc., where the Central Commission would be empowered to make regulations requiring some part of the cost to be borne by him.   Moreover, under certain conditions, nursing service outside the hospital, convalescent care, additional dental work, etc., might be provided.   Maternity care, including prenatal care, would be provided for insured women who had been insured for 205 days.   In addition to this care and the cash allowance of fifteen dollars already mentioned, the insured woman would be entitled to sickness benefit for six months before and six weeks after

[1] The allowances would be as follows: Spouse, 10 per cent of wages but not to exceed $3 per week; one child, 5 per cent but not to exceed $1.50 per week; two children, 10 per cent but not to exceed $3 per week; three or more children, 15 per cent but not to exceed $4.50 per week.

[2] There would, however, be limitations upon some of the minor services.

confinement, provided she did not engage in gainful employment. Insurance practice would be open to any licensed physician or dentist; the insured person would have free choice of doctor and hospital. The council in each local area would be empowered to make agreements for the remuneration of the doctors and others rendering service, but whether the doctor's payment would be on a salary, a per capita, or a visitation basis, or a combination of these, would be determined by majority vote of the insurance doctors.

To cover the costs of these benefits contributions would be required, under the mandatory provisions of the measure, by employer, the insured employee, and the government. The total would be 6 per cent of the wages of the insured employee, 1.5 per cent being for cash benefits and 4.5 per cent for medical benefits.[1] Of the 6 per cent the government would contribute 1.5. The remaining 4.5 per cent would be contributed by the employee and his employer under a sliding-scale arrangement. If wages did not exceed twenty dollars per week, the employee would pay 1 and the employer 3.5 per cent; if they were in excess of twenty dollars but not in excess of forty dollars, the employee would contribute 2, the employer 2.5 per cent; if, finally, they were in excess of forty dollars, the employee would contribute 3, the employer 1.5 per cent. Funds of local organizations, serving as carriers, would be pooled in order to insure adequacy and safety.

For the purposes of control and administration there would be a Central Health Insurance Commission of three, appointed by the governor and representing employers, the insured, and the health professions, respectively. Similarly, in each district the council established for administrative purposes would be representative of all interested parties.

Here and there medical organizations have shown interest in a general insurance plan. This has been most strikingly true of the California Medical Association. With an Interim Committee of the Senate of the California Legislature charged with the study of the problem of medical care and faced with the problems of acute depression, the House of Delegates of the California Medical Association, in special session at Los Angeles, March 3, 1935, adopted a resolution, recommending that legislation be proposed seeking to establish a health-insurance system, mandatory as to certain population groups and voluntary as to others. The proposed legislation should incorporate certain principles set out in the resolution. Full aid and cooperation were to be given the Interim Committee.[2]

---

[1] The provision for two funds would make it possible to separate sickness benefits from medical care. The bill provides, also, for certification for sickness benefit by a government physician, not by the physician giving medical care.

[2] See the Health Service Insurance Act prepared by the Committee of Six of the California Medical Association. Four guiding principles were as follows: (1) The patient should

An Association committee of six, with an advisory committee of sixteen physicians, and with the aid of economists and other advisers, drafted the only health-insurance bill prepared by a medical association in the United States. In its more detailed provisions, unusual care was exercised to protect the interests and privileges of the individual physician rendering service, but the most outstanding difference between this and other bills is found in the fact that it looked to the provision of medical care only. No cash benefits were to be provided. With minor exceptions, all employees who earned, or whose incomes from all sources were less than $3,000 were brought within its mandatory provisions; within the income limitation, persons other than employees might insure voluntarily. However, an exemption was to be made where railroad, industrial, or other private companies furnished their employees the same service as called for by the Act or a service equivalent to it, provided it was furnished for "no less than the same compensation, dues or payments by whomsoever paid, as would be required with respect to like groups of such employees if the contributions were paid into the health insurance fund." The primary benefits were to be seven in number: (1) services of the physician, for the insured and his dependents, at the home, the office, or hospital, for not to exceed twenty-six weeks; (2) such laboratory service as was prescribed by the attending physician; (3) dental service for extractions and such other dental care as might be authorized by the State Commission; (4) prenatal and maternity care; (5) hospital care and maintenance, with nursing care as might be prescribed by the attending physician; this without charge for twenty-one days, after which the charge would be 15 per cent of the daily maintenance cost; (6) medical care of and health work for infants and children under fourteen; (7) drugs and medicines as prescribed by the attending physician. In addition to these, funds permitting, the State Commission might arrange for nursing care outside of the hospital, convalescent care, and additional drugs and medicines. The contribution on account of employees was set at 5 per cent of wages and charged to the employer, who, however, might deduct from wages paid not to exceed 3.5 of the 5 per cent. Voluntary insurers were to be required to pay 5 per cent of the family income, from all sources. These premium rates, however, were to be subject to change and adjustment by the State Commission. This Health Service Insurance Commission was to consist of five members appointed by the Governor, but two of the five must have had at least ten years' experience in the licensed practice of medicine. A Health

have absolutely free choice of physician and hospital; (2) the medical profession should determine the scope, extent, standards, quality, compensation paid for, and all other matters and things related to the medical and auxiliary services rendered under the system; (3) there should be no provision for cash benefits; (4) the patient should receive adequate treatment and his physician should receive adequate compensation.

Insurance Advisory Council was also to be established to consider and advise the Commission on financial matters and medical administration. The Commission was to be empowered to arrange for and supervise the necessary medical service and to administer the Act. All practicing doctors and dentists, so long as they complied with the rules and regulations, might engage in insurance practice. All practice was to be individual practice. Freedom of election of doctor and hospital was to be limited in no way.

This Association bill was given serious consideration by the State Legislature. However, division of opinion developed within the Association over details in the proposed measure. Moreover, there were those among the doctors who opposed compulsory insurance—in many cases, no doubt, because of the opposition of outside medical organizations. The Association withdrew its support of the bill but did not disavow the principle of insurance. No measure was enacted into law, but the subject remains under consideration in California, where the people as well as the doctors are more favorable toward applying the principle of insurance in medical care than are the people and the doctors of any other state.

Standing over against those who favor insurance plans are others who favor group payment through taxation. For example, the Surgeon General, when Director of the Department of Health of the State of New York, took the position that "indigent" must be given a very liberal interpretation in providing medical care for the poor at public expense;[1] he has also more recently proposed that all persons participating in the old-age annuity and unemployment compensation under the Social Security Act and all others having annual incomes of less than $2,500, should be given "public care for costly illness."[2] Of the same general nature but more far-reaching is the program proposed by The Medical League for Socialized Medicine, which was organized as an independent medical organization by a group of New York doctors in 1933 and which by 1936 had a membership in excess of 1,200.[3] The program adopted by the League, in 1933, reads as follows:[4]

[1] This is provided for in the New York Public Welfare Law of 1930 (Chap. 629, Sec. 83), which reads: "Responsibility for providing medical care: The public welfare district shall be responsible for providing necessary medical care for all persons under its care, and for such persons otherwise able to maintain themselves, who are unable to secure necessary medical care, except in so far as, in cases of communicable disease, that duty may be imposed upon the health officer by law or the state sanitary code. Such care may be given in dispensaries, hospitals, the person's home or other suitable place."

[2] Edgar Sydenstricker, *The Changing Concept of Public Health* (1935), p. 309.

[3] Since January, 1936, this organization has published *The American Journal of Socialized Medicine*. This is one agency employed for furthering the League's program and provides a good source of information concerning that program.

[4] *The American Journal of Socialized Medicine*, vol. 1, no. 1 (January, 1936), pp. 12–13.

"(1) Adequate medical care of the sick and injured as a social function, right and duty, and not as a private or public charity.   Curative as well as preventive means, measures, and agencies to be included.

"(2) A socialized system of medical care in health, illness and injury, free of fees.

"(a) Under the auspices and with the subsidy of the state.
"(b) Financed by taxation, similar to the public educational system or other governmental functions,
"(c) Operated and regulated by the organized medical and allied professions, the medical and dental colleges and the officials of existing public health agencies.
"(d) This system to include all dental, pharmaceutical, nursing and allied services and personnel.

"(3) All hospitals, clinics, laboratories, pharmacies, etc., to be publicly owned and operated institutions, accessible to the sick and free of charge.   The hospitals, and the clinics to be the medical centers for ward and ambulatory cases, and to be properly organized, coordinated and geographically distributed.   House sick calls to be received at these centers and to be assigned to local or neighborhood physicians designated to cover specific local territories.

"(4) All equipment, supplies, laboratory and other facilities of a medical, surgical, dental, pharmaceutical, nursing or other nature, to be furnished free by the state.

"(5) All medical, dental, pharmaceutical, nursing and allied education to be furnished free by the state.

"(6) All duly licensed or registered physicians, dentists, druggists, nurses, etc., to be legally entitled to practice under the system as full time practitioners or workers.

"(a) Subject to established rules and regulations of admission and practice.
"(b) Proper safeguards of their rights and privileges under the system and the law.
"(c) With representation and a voice in the operation of the system.

"(7) Compensation to be adequate.

"(a) Graded according to time of graduation, length of service in the system, rank held, and type of work.
"(b) Salary increases and promotion to higher rank to be based on similar considerations and to be automatically enforced.
"(c) Pensions, sickness, old age and other disability and social insurance to be included and applied.

"(8) Hours of work to be assigned and regulated and scheduled so as to provide:

"(a) Adequate medical care for the sick and injured at all times.
"(b) Adequate time and opportunity for the physicians and allied workers for rest, recreation, vacations, and further professional study—with pay.

"(9) Organized cooperative groups and group methods to be employed under the system wherever possible. Special provisions to be made for rural and other territories inaccessible to regularly organized medical centers.

"(10) Individual private medical practice permissible under the same conditions and regulations as in private education, plus existing licenses and requirements by the state."

POSITIONS OF THE AMERICAN FEDERATION OF LABOR AND THE AMERICAN MEDICAL ASSOCIATION

With two exceptions, the attitudes of different groups and organizations toward state action in connection with the sickness problem are, in general, the same as they were during and soon after the War, when compulsory sickness insurance was under investigation and active discussion.[1] One of the significant changes is found in the position taken by the American Federation of Labor. Until recently, because of the position taken by Mr. Gompers, President of and spokesman for the Federation, it was commonly said that organized labor was opposed to compulsory health insurance. In 1935, however, after the Social Security Act had been passed, the Federation, upon favorable committee report, unanimously adopted the following resolution:[2]

"WHEREAS, Even in normal times sickness is one of the greatest hazards confronting wage-earners, constituting the chief cause of dependency; and

"WHEREAS, Outside of unemployment, it is today the outstanding fear confronting American workers; and

"WHEREAS, The American worker during times of illness is not only confronted with a loss of wages but is forced to pay exorbitant medical and hospital bills which frequently force him into debt and poverty; and

"WHEREAS, Although health insurance has been in successful operation in all industrial nations for more than a generation, the American social security act completely ignores this major problem; therefore, be it

"RESOLVED, That the Fifty-fifth Annual Convention of the A. F. of L., assembled at Atlantic City, hereby goes on record urging the enactment

[1] For a summary statement of those attitudes, see pp. 322–323.
[2] See *Report of Proceedings of the Fifty-fifth Annual Convention of the American Federation of Labor* (1935), p. 593.

of socially constructive health insurance legislation through Congress and the individual States."

On the other hand, the opposition of the American Medical Association, with its 100,000 members, has become official and, since publication of the report of the Committee on the Costs of Medical Care, more pronounced.[1] It takes a conservative position on the whole matter, and was extremely critical of the finding of the Committee on the Costs of Medical Care that there is any substantial problem. It maintains that the test is the quality of medical care which it finds to be satisfactory. It supports the individual practice of medicine, and sees danger in any departure from it. While the principles[2] adopted by the Association do not conflict with a distribution of the costs of medical care on the basis

[1] As Dr. Morris Fishbein, Editor of the *Journal of the American Medical Association*, has said, "The medical profession seems to have become more definitely opposed to nation-wide social insurance and state medicine than it was [in 1917]." In *The Medical Profession and the Public* (American Academy of Political and Social Science, 1934), p. 93.

[2] The principles adopted through the House of Delegates read as follows:

"First. All features of medical service in any method of medical practice should be under the control of the medical profession. No other body is legally or educationally equipped to exercise such control.

"Second. No third party must be permitted to come between the patient and his physician in any medical relation. All responsibility for the character of medical service must be borne by the profession.

"Third. Patients must have absolute freedom to choose a duly qualified doctor of medicine who will serve them from among all those qualified to practice and who are willing to give service.

"Fourth. The method of giving the service must retain a permanent, confidential relation between the patient and a 'family physician.' This relation must be the fundamental and dominating feature of any system.

"Fifth. All medical phases of all institutions involved in the medical service should be under professional control, it being understood that hospital service and medical service should be considered separately. These institutions are but expansions of the equipment of the physician. He is the only one whom the laws of all nations recognize as competent to use them in the delivery of service. The medical profession alone can determine the adequacy and character of such institutions. Their value depends on their operation according to medical standards.

"Sixth. However the cost of medical service may be distributed, the immediate cost should be borne by the patient if able to pay at the time the service is rendered. [As noted in the text, the sixth principle was reformulated in 1935 to read, "In whatever way the cost of medical service may be distributed, it should be paid for by the patient in accordance with his income status and in a manner that is mutually satisfactory."]

"Seventh. Medical service must have no connection with any cash benefits.

"Eighth. Any form of medical service should include within its scope all qualified physicians of the locality covered by its operation who wish to give service under the conditions established.

"Ninth. Systems for the relief of low income classes should be limited strictly to those below the 'comfort level' standard of incomes.

"Tenth. There should be no restrictions on treatment or prescribing not formulated and enforced by the organized medical profession."

Published in the *Journal of the American Medical Association*, June 30, 1934, pp. 2200 f.

of insurance or taxation, it contends that such a distribution is unnecessary and emphasizes the problems which it alleges are found in connection with the group systems established in many countries. Not one of the systems has been a success. There is real danger of political manipulation. Advance payment encourages frequent visits to the doctor, tends to develop a psychology of illness, and prolongs illness. There is no evidence that systems of "socialized medicine" reduce mortality or morbidity rates. Such systems inevitably add to the expense. Freedom and rights are at stake: "There is, moreover, a far greater concern than the rights of the physician to practice as his knowledge and training indicate is desirable. There is the question of Americanism versus sovietism for the American people. There is the question of the right of the American citizen to pick his own doctor and his own hospital, to pay his own bills with his own money, to be responsible to a doctor who is responsible to him."[1]

In most of this, no doubt, the Association reflects the current thought of a majority of the doctors, and especially of the older men among them.[2]

OBSERVATIONS AND CONCLUSIONS; A SUGGESTED PLAN

If laymen may be permitted, in the light of research in the United States and in Europe, to make observations on such a complicated subject as that under discussion, the following are believed to be in point.

Except with regard to compulsory insurance, the authors are in general agreement with the majority of the Committee on the Costs of Medical Care. There is a serious medical-care problem as well as one of loss of wages. The emphasis placed by the Committee upon a vigorous, extensive public-health-service program is proper and essential —just as essential as safety first and the stabilization of industry and of employment within it in the solution of the work injury and the unemployment problems.[3] Grants-in-aid are needed to develop adequate

---

[1] From an editorial in the *Journal of the American Medical Association*, Dec. 10, 1932, p. 2035. This general summary statement is based largely upon such editorial comments and observations. The position taken by the Association is found, among other places, in a paper by its editor and leading spokesman in *The Medical Profession and the Public* (1934), pp. 88–112.

[2] There has recently appeared a two-volume publication bearing the title *American Medicine: Expert Testimony Out of Court* (The American Foundation, 1937). The volumes contain a wealth of views of doctors thinking out loud on various aspects of medical care. Chapter 10 (vol. 2, pp. 976–1100) sets out the variety of views expressed on health insurance. There was no unanimity of opinion on the subject, but it is evident that the American Medical Association reflects the opinion generally prevailing among the doctors or that the doctors most frequently reflect the opinion of the Association. The views expressed are summarized on p. 1100.

[3] An important feature of the Social Security Act (1935), and one to be strongly commended, is that designed to promote the public health. It granted $10,000,000 to the U. S. Public Health Service. Of this, $2,000,000 was for research in methods of disease

medical services in financially weak and thinly populated areas, remote from well-to-do urban communities. Government should provide adequate medical care for soldiers, sailors, the indigent, the tuberculous, and those afflicted with venereal disease, the necessary costs to be met by tax revenues. Tuberculosis and venereal disease are special problems; they require specialized treatment. They are part of the public-health problem, and they do not fit properly into any arrangement designed to provide medical care for the sick in general. Moreover, a question not raised by the Committee on the Costs of Medical Care may be raised at this point. Is not the maternity and infant-welfare problem one of such nature and importance that it deserves special treatment at the public expense? Should there not be free public provision for prenatal and postnatal care and lying-in? One of the larger special medical problems is found in childbearing, and it becomes a more pressing problem with apartment-house shelter, the disinclination of general practitioners to take care of lying-in cases, and the need for careful nursing and feeding.

The authors agree with the view of the Committee on the Costs of Medical Care that any system adopted in this country should depart from European patterns in certain respects. There has been too great a tendency in certain quarters to draft American bills by copying the legislation of foreign countries, with a mixture of the good and the bad. Unsuitable organizations as insurance carriers should be avoided; those persons and institutions giving medical care should have an adequate but not a dominating share in control; and cash benefits should be divorced from medical care.

With reference to the general failure to divorce cash and medical benefits, it may be said that this failure has been an important source of difficulty in Germany and elsewhere. If the doctor is to certify incapacity for work as well as to treat the sick, he is placed in a difficult position, and, especially with free choice of doctor, is too likely to re-certify when the patient is able to return to work. For the treatment of the insured and also the members of his family may be lost. In any

control. The remaining $8,000,000 was to be allotted to the states for public-health work, the allotments to be made on the basis of population, special health problems, and the financial needs of the states. The Act also granted nearly $7,000,000 to the U. S. Children's Bureau for the health of mothers and children and for the care of crippled children. Grants from these funds were to be made on the basis of the number of live births, the number of crippled children, the health, needs, and the financial status of the state, preference to be given to the needs of rural areas. It is contemplated that state and local appropriations will match Federal funds and that proper standards of service will be required for a cooperative attack upon conditions undermining the health of the people and contributing to insecurity. Though this effort and assistance must be regarded as little more than a good beginning, the program is expected to advance health in this country to new and higher levels.

event, the certifying doctor is too generally placed under suspicion. Moreover, to protect against simulation, malingery, and poor judgment, as well as in the interest of economy, it has been regarded as necessary to have certifications extensively checked by independent doctors and otherwise. Of course, certification of incapacity must be made by a doctor, but the certifying doctor should be an independent one.[1]

There is an additional, important reason for separating cash from medical benefits. It is found in the fact that the classes covered need not be the same. Cash benefits can be paid in partial compensation of losses by wage earners and salaried persons only. All persons in the lower-income groups, whether wage earners or not, should be given consideration in connection with any plan for medical care.

It may be pointed out that the divorce of cash from medical benefits can be realized without great difficulty now that the Social Security Act has been adopted. It is suggested that this Act be amended so that the insured who become eligible for cash benefits when they cannot secure suitable employment may also become eligible for those benefits when disabled by noncompensable sickness or accident.[2] Of course, the contributions required to finance cash benefits would have to be increased, but in view of what is said later concerning the financing of medical care, the increased revenues required might be obtained from a light tax levied on the employer. Many employers have already charged themselves with financial responsibility in this connection. Moreover, in a country-wide system of insurance it does not greatly matter in the longer run where such a tax is placed because it will tend to find the same final resting place.

But is there a case for compulsory insurance to provide compensation for loss of income due to incapacitating illness? The answer must be in the affirmative if there is need for workmen's compensation in order to protect against need, for the two cases parallel.[3] From the point of view of need, the case for sickness benefits is perhaps stronger than it is for unemployment benefits, for on the expenditure side the

---

[1] Cf. I. S. Falk, Security Against Sickness, pp. 80–81.

[2] This suggestion has been made by other persons, also, among them Michael Davis (The Medical Profession and the Public, p. 29), Edgar Sydenstricker (Health Insurance and the Public Health, pp. 17–18), and I. S. Falk (Security Against Sickness, p. 280).

[3] While this material was in press, the Technical Committee on Medical Care of the Interdepartmental Committee to Coordinate Health and Welfare Activities issued a report on The Need for a National Health Program (Washington, D.C., 1938). Bearing upon the point under discussion, the Technical Committee states (p. 29): "Disability wage-loss amounts, in the aggregate, to something like 2.5 per cent of income. But it occurs among families variously in small and in large amounts. Disabling sickness hangs as an ever-present threat over the wage earner. He cannot budget individually against this risk. Provision through social insurance, or through systematic public assistance, or through both devices, is urgently needed to bring security of income against this common risk which threatens people of small and precarious earnings."

family budget is likely to be more disturbed during a period of incapacity than during an equal period of unemployment.

In many countries, but not in Great Britain, health-insurance systems provide funeral as well as sickness benefits. The need for such a benefit in the United States is however not very urgent, for some 60 per cent of American wage earners have industrial, if not ordinary, life insurance in substantial amount. Again, if the minimum of industrial insurance is carried, it may directly lead many to increase the amount. The carrying of a substantial amount of life insurance should be encouraged. Moreover, to propose a funeral benefit under health insurance is to invite strong opposition from the industrial-insurance companies and many nonprofit organizations and associations, including some trade unions. It was a mistake, years ago, to incorporate a provision for burial benefit in the Standard Bill.

As regards the medical services, the case made by the Committee on the Costs of Medical Care is a strong one. The medical services need to be effectively coordinated, and, because of the uneven distribution of the costs and because these costs cannot be successfully budgeted by the family, the principle of group payment must be applied. But should this principle be left to voluntary acceptance or be applied in compulsory fashion to groups of persons with small incomes, say, less than $2,500 per year?

If reliance is placed upon voluntary action, the growth of insurance is certain to be slow. The appeal will be successfully made largely to those with a fairly good standard of living under normal conditions, while those with small means will usually remain without benefit except where compulsion or subsidy is used by employing groups; and, unless protective legislation is enacted and effectively administered, the good is certain to be accompanied by much that is unacceptable or bad.[1]

---

[1] As Dr. Falk summarizes one of the arguments for compulsory insurance (*Security Against Sickness*, p. 327), "Many undesirable practices develop in medical service under voluntary insurance, and these are evils of a sort which only governmental control in compulsory insurance can prevent or cure because they arise principally from competitive practice. Experience with large numbers of voluntary insurance plans in the United States shows that, in many of them, groups of practitioners facing competition with other groups and in order to attract patients from their competitors have reduced their fees to the point of impairing service; proprietary clinics with contracts of service for voluntary insurance organizations have taken advantage of the economic difficulties in which individual physicians find themselves, have employed them at inadequate salaries, and have loaded them with more work than they could possibly do well. Other proprietary groups have utilized for profit purposes excessive fractions of the income from premiums, leaving small reserves (or none at all) for emergency needs, have restricted the scope of service to the minimum, or have added undesirably restricting clauses to their contracts, and have accumulated no reserves for improvement or expansion of facilities or service. Commercial 'racketeering' by voluntary insurance groups recently became a public scandal in California and required drastic action by law enforcement agencies. Compulsion and

This was recognized by the Committee on the Costs of Medical Care. The majority, in their report, however, were of the opinion that the United States should first experiment with and encourage voluntary insurance and thus profit from experience, elasticity in arrangements, and variety. With reference to this, we are in entire accord with Dr. Falk's excellent weighing of the arguments for and against compulsory insurance.[1] We quote from him at length:

"In following the Majority of the Committee, the ideal would be to recommend voluntary systems of group payment and utilize all possible means of *encouraging*—but not *requiring*—desirable forms of organized, efficient, group practice of the highest quality. Then, when the organization of medical service has progressed to the point where it is possible to guarantee the quality and sufficiency of service, the voluntary system should be made compulsory. But this is frankly a counsel of perfection. What is to encourage the rapid and effective organization of medical facilities? Certainly there is no ground in recent experience to warrant the view that the desired objective will be reached by waiting upon the experiments now in progress. There is as much likelihood that the swirling current of events will lead to the predominance of exploited contract practice as that it will intrench desirable forms of voluntary insurance. Commitment to a voluntary program holds no promise that *it* will bring us to that threshold which would warrant the establishment of a compulsory scheme. There is little evidence in experience, at home or abroad, to indicate that compulsory insurance may be expected to evolve out of the *successes* of voluntary insurance. History is on the other side of the argument.

"The reorganization of medical practice which is badly needed will not come of itself, the product of *laissez faire*. It will come—if at all —only as the fruit of strong and directed labors, the product of compelling forces. Of all the forces which society can muster in a program of medical reformation, the strongest is 'the power of the purse.' Thus, the case is inverted. *Instead of organizing for the payment of medical costs after having achieved improvement of service, society must organize for payment in order to achieve improvement of service.* In our opinion, this conclusion—when taken in conjunction with the strictly economic arguments and with the need for the compulsory principle to give an effective implementation to social insurance—tips the beam of the balance in favor of compulsory, as against voluntary, group payment. It compels us to recognize, however, that a compulsory scheme must be planned

government regulation are necessary to restrict sickness insurance to non-profit associations and to protect the public and the professions against commercial exploitation or undesirable competition among insurance practitioners." (Quoted by courtesy of Doubleday, Doran and Company.)

[1] *Ibid.*, Chap. 15, pp. 333-334.

in such a way that it calls for contributions and expenditures proportional to the availability of qualified medical facilities. Beyond certain minimum requirements, compulsion should be used in different degrees, calling for larger contributions in one place and for smaller in another, according to local circumstances with respect to the capacity to pay the costs and to furnish good medical care."

One more point in the Committee's argument for voluntary insurance calls for comment. The Committee noted that there are relatively few nonprofit organizations, such as arrange for medical services in many European countries, upon which to build; new organizations would have to be formed. This is true, but it should be pointed out that the use of such organizations in connection with medical service as over against cash benefits has been a chief source of difficulty and weakness.[1] Moreover, it is important to note that in Germany an increasing majority of insured persons have had membership in the local and rural funds established by the government, as over against the mutual associations which had grown up and were accepted; that the arrangements for medical care in Britain, except for the "additional benefits," are made with the doctors by local medical committees and the Ministry; and that in Alberta the whole amtter is to be cared for by mere registration at the offices of the "medical districts."

After all, health insurance is a much more complicated thing than unemployment insurance and old-age pensions. In its operation, much depends upon organization, the lodgment of control, and the efficiency of control. A discussion of these in detail is, however, beyond the scope of this book.

A word may be said about costs. While, from a financial point of view, compulsory insurance assembles existing costs, borne largely in its absence by the persons concerned and by the doctors and others engaged in rendering medical services, it would probably be accompanied by some increase in outlay on medical care. As the Committee on the Costs of Medical Care observed, however, "Good service to the sick is worth what it costs." And as the Committee further observed, the American people can afford to devote a somewhat larger percentage of the national income to the promotion of health and the care of the sick, for these are of first importance. Were sick benefits financed like unemployment benefits, perhaps the cost of medical care should be charged to the insured, with a sufficient contribution from the public treasury to develop and sustain public interest and to lighten the load.

In concluding this discussion, it may be said, in the language of the Committee on the Costs of Medical Care, that "thousands of persons are sick and dying in this country because the knowledge and facilities that we have are inadequately applied. We must promptly put this

[1] See summary of the *Final Report*, quoted on pp. 328–329.

knowledge and these facilities to work."[1]   One way of doing so would be to coordinate the service and to distribute the cost through compulsory health insurance. Most of the things the Committee on the Costs of Medical Care insisted upon are found in the permissive legislation adopted in the Province of Alberta in 1935.[2] There is no sick benefit provided for; only medical care is to be furnished. Medical districts may be established by vote of the electors of the area. A medical district is created where, with minor exceptions, all wage earners, salaried persons and other residents with incomes are required to register and to pay a tax. If the person is a wage earner or salaried person, the tax is $2.01 per month and the employer is collector. The employer also pays $0.99 on account of each such person. Other persons with incomes pay $33.83 per year or $2.82 per month. The municipality contributes $11.28 per year per registrant, less seven-ninths in the event of income from other sources. Similarly, the Province makes a contribution of $3.22 per registrant, with an offset of two-ninths. Financed in this way, a health district is to provide medical benefits to its residents as follows: (a) necessary hospitalization in a public ward; (b) necessary nursing service; (c) necessary medical and surgical attention, advice, and treatment; (d) necessary dental attention, advice, and treatment; (e) the benefit of laboratory services, such as x-ray and biochemical services; (f) all such drugs, medical and surgical supplies and appliances as may be prescribed by the medical practitioner under whose care the patient is for the time being. The patient has free choice of resident medical practitioners and dentists; the bills are paid according to tariffs adopted. Moreover, the medical district is authorized to maintain a broad public-health service. This may include, in addition to the usual subjects, prenatal clinics, "well-baby" clinics, clinics for children of preschool age, clinics for children of school age, periodic health examinations of all children, and "all services pertaining to the maintenance of community health and disease prevention."[3]

[1] *Final Report*, p. 150.

[2] *Statutes of Alberta*, Canada, 25 Geo. V, Chap. 45.

[3] More important from the point of view of result accomplished is the second Canadian law in this field—that adopted by British Columbia, March 31, 1936 (Statutes of British Columbia, 1936, Chap. 23)—for the Alberta Act becomes effective only as voted by the electors in a medical district, whereas that of British Columbia is mandatory. The plan adopted is of the more usual type, except that it provides for medical care only. There are no cash benefits. The Act covers workers in the lower income groups (earning less than $1,800 per year) and their dependents. It is estimated that the number of employees to be covered will be about 110,000 and the number of dependents 165,000—making a group of 275,000 insured persons in all, in a total population approximating 750,000. The original plan had covered all employees except in agriculture, and, possibly, domestic service and the like, but this coverage was objected to by the doctors and others. The coverage under the Act is not greatly in excess of half of that contemplated when the original bill was drafted. Another feature of the Act is that employees

The Alberta Act, with the approval of the community, is designed to promote the public health, to make needed medical services available to the people generally, and to distribute the costs among the people served, the employers, and the taxpayers.

---

already provided with equally good service are excepted if, at an election held under supervision, a majority so vote by secret ballot.

The plan is to be financed by contributions from employees and employers, without a contribution from the government. The government, however, has appropriated funds to cover the organization expenses of the Health Insurance Commission. The employee, under a check-off system, is to pay 2 per cent of his wages and the employer 1 per cent of his payroll for insured persons, with minimum and maximum contributions fixed for each (thirty-five and seventy cents per week for employees, and twenty and thirty-five cents for employers). There is the usual provision for voluntary insurance, and, of course, voluntarily insured persons pay the entire cost of their benefits and the administrative cost, under regulations to be established by the Health Insurance Commission.

The mandatory benefits are: (a) the services of physician, surgeon, or specialist, with freedom of choice—medical care including prenatal and maternity treatment; (b) necessary drugs, medicines, and dressings, with prescriptions to be filled by any qualified pharmacist, but the Commission may require the insured to pay not to exceed half of the cost; (c) hospital service for not to exceed ten weeks in any one illness, this in a public ward or with the excess of cost charged to the insured if the service is in semiprivate or private ward; (d) full laboratory service and diagnostic aids, including x-ray, biochemical, and other services. Other medical and also dental benefits may be provided, under the powers conferred upon the Commission, provided there are available funds.

The Commission makes its own financial arrangements with doctors, druggists, hospitals, laboratories, and other persons or agencies providing services. In the case of doctors, any one of three methods of payment may be used, a salary system, a per capita system, or a fee system with an allotted pool of money. If the per capita or the fee and pool system is used, it is provided that there shall be set aside for the payment of doctors not less than $4.50 per insured person per year. This sum is about one-sixth larger than had been figured on by the government when the original draft was reported. (See *A Plan of Health Insurance for British Columbia*. Department of the Provincial Secretary, 1935.)

Insured persons are registered; there is no requirement of membership in voluntary organizations or in government funds.

Such are the more important features of the first outright compulsory health-insurance system established on the North American continent. This legislation, passed March 31, 1936, was to come into effect upon proclamation; nevertheless, on Feb. 19, 1937, the Premier of the Province announced a postponement of its operation and a review of its provisions. A referendum of all the electors at the general provincial election was taken; at the plebiscite the proposal for "a comprehensive health insurance plan progressively applied" was endorsed by a majority of 30,000, although approximately 100,000 who went to the polls failed to mark their decision, perhaps because of confusion on the issues involved. Although the government has a clear mandate to put the health-insurance plan in operation, it is faced with at least noncooperation and perhaps revolt on the part of the medical practitioners who were not consulted and who strongly objected to what the Health Insurance Commission proposed to pay them for their services. (See, *Labour Gazette*, Department of Labour, Canada, vol. 37, March, 1937, p. 264, and *New York Times*, July 4, 1937, sec. 2–3, p. 8.) In October (1937) the plan was inoperative because of the refusal of the doctors to accept the schedule offered by the government.

Much is to be said for the scope and coverage of the Alberta plan. Yet, the coverage might well be limited to families in the lower-income groups. With reference to the scope of benefits an important observation needs to be made. As Dr. Fishbein has said, "without the cooperation of the medical profession no system of practice can succeed."[1] Most American physicians, organized and led as they are, would not be cooperative under an inclusive system of organized medicine at this time. It would break too sharply with what they are accustomed to and arouse fear. Any system established must, as the minimum, receive reluctant acceptance by the doctors. Moreover, upon analysis the real problem is found to bulk largest in cases of major or "high-cost" illness. In 80 or 85 per cent of the cases of illness only the care of the family physician and some drugs are needed. There is a large element of truth in a frequently made statement "that more than 80 per cent of all the ailments for which people seek medical aid can be treated most cheaply and most satisfactorily by a family physician with what he can carry in a handbag." Home or office treatment suffices. This, however, is not true of major illnesses or cases in need of hospitalization, specialist and laboratory services, and so on. The attitude of the doctors and the fact that the problem lies largely in cases needing hospitalization and related services, leads us to suggest, as Dr. Parran has suggested,[2] that any plan adopted should be limited in its scope to major illnesses. There is urgent need for distributing the costs in such cases, which constitute a relatively small percentage of the total but which account for approximately half of the outlays for medical care.

Such a plan would be the British plan turned upside down. By this is meant that the statutory medical care now provided by the British insurance doctor would here be left to private practice. Hospital service with its incidental nursing and laboratory service, the doctor's and surgeon's bills incurred in connection with hospitalization, and physical examinations would be provided for under a group hospital plan. Dental cases should be disposed of like other cases, though the drawing of lines here is more difficult than it is in illness.

The advantages of such a plan are obvious. It would tie in with the group-hospital-plan movement, substituting compulsion for voluntary subscription, substituting a stable for a more or less variable and uncertain group, and covering medical bills in serious cases as well as the hospital bills. It would distribute the costs of that medical care which seriously needs to be distributed for the lower-income groups. It would leave the major work of the general doctor only slightly altered. The patient would normally pass through his hands and be hospitalized, when necessary, on his reference. Finally, it would stabilize the situation

[1] Quoted from The Medical Profession and the Public, p. 90.
[2] Supra, p. 338.

and would safeguard against evils connected with some of the newer developments in the field of medical care.

Should such service be tax-supported or should the cost rest upon those who are to receive the benefits? The answer we would give is that the cost should rest in large part upon those who receive the benefits, but that there should be a government contribution. A number of considerations lead to this answer. Those who benefit should make a contribution because most of them are paying now. Hospital bills and the like are now met by the family purse to an extent. The need is not to relieve the beneficiaries as a whole of the entire burden but to distribute it so that it can be borne. A second reason why the beneficiaries, as a group, should pay is that such payment is needed as a check on unwarranted demands for a more and more expensive service. A third reason is that special taxation is needed, if the government spends tax revenues for a better public-health service and for adequate treatment of mental, venereal, tuberculous, and other cases requiring specialized care. But, on the other hand, there are reasons why an appropriate part of the cost should be covered by general tax revenues. One of these is that such a plan would result in some saving in relief costs. Another is that if the government made no contribution, the burden of support would perhaps be in excess of the ability of many of the beneficiaries to pay, unless, at the public expense, "indigent" was most liberally defined. Finally, it seems natural that a government exercising compulsion and a measure of control should pay a part of the cost out of its general funds.

Such, in general and with its several parts, is a suggested plan to meet in considerable measure the problem of sickness in the United States and to distribute the costs. It includes (1) an extended and improved public-health service; (2) a Social Security Act amended so as to provide cash benefits for wage earners when disabled by sickness as well as when unemployed because of lack of work; (3) appropriate tax-supported medical care for special groups; and (4) organized medical care of persons in the lower-income groups when involved in high-cost illness, with the costs met by compulsory insurance contributions and taxation.

As regards (4), of course, the suggested plan is presented only in a general and incomplete way. A plan involves a multitude of details and these call for careful consideration and decision at the hands of experts and representatives of the parties immediately concerned, around the conference table. Here, and by these persons, the dividing line must be drawn between major and minor, between high-cost and low-cost, illnesses. Here, and by these persons, the details concerning referrals for hospital and specialist treatment must be worked out. Here, and by these persons, devices must be found for preventing cases from being wrongfully referred for special treatment because the bills would be cared for out of funds in hand. Here, and by these persons, similar questions must be answered in so far as practical problems can be foreseen. Only in this manner can the most appropriate answers be made to practical problems. The objective should be to apply the insurance principle and government aid in the most practical way in solving the problem presented by high-cost illness.

CHAPTER VIII

THE PROBLEM OF THE INDUSTRIALLY OLD WORKER

THE PROBLEM

With the passing of time the problem presented by the industrially old worker has become more pressing, for a number of reasons. Perhaps the most frequently noted and emphasized of these reasons is the marked increase in both the absolute and the relative number who live, say, to sixty-five or seventy years of age. In the United States, for example, there were in 1920, 4,933,213 persons aged sixty-five or over; the corresponding number in 1930 was 6,639,000. In 1870 those aged sixty-five or over constituted 3.0 per cent of the population of the United States; in 1890, 3.7 per cent; in 1920, 4.7 per cent; and in 1930, 5.4 per cent.[1] It has been estimated that by 1975 those over sixty-five years of age will be 13 per cent of the total population.[2] This changing composition of our population is due chiefly to the declining birth rate. The fact that the birth rate fifty or seventy years ago was high, and since 1900 has steadily declined, has automatically increased the proportion of the old. The increased expectation of life (at birth) from around forty years in 1850 to about fifty-nine years at present is commonly cited as a cause of the increased proportion of elders. As a matter of fact, most of the gain has been in the decline of infant mortality through control of infant diseases. This would even partially offset the decline in birth rate. Little progress has been made in the control of "degenerative" diseases, and accordingly the most reliable life tables do not indicate much, if any,

---

[1] U. S. Census, 1930, *Population*, vol. 2, p. 576.

[2] P. K. Whelpton, "The Increase and Distribution of Elders in Our Population," *Journal of American Statistical Association, Supplement*, vol. 27 (March, 1932), p. 93. The estimate is based on the assumptions that immigration will continue at 200,000 annually, that the expectation of life will rise to seventy years, and that the birth rate will fall to 80 per cent of its present level.

The estimates of the actuarial staff of the Committee on Economic Security are slightly lower, 10.1 per cent of the population over sixty-five years of age in 1970, 11.3 per cent in 1980 and 12.7 per cent in the year 2000. Upon reasonable assumptions we must expect that for a number of decades the proportion over sixty-five years of age will increase steadily and that within the significant future it will be double the 1930 proportion. A table giving the actual and estimated number and proportion of the population sixty-five years of age and over, by decades from 1860 to 2000, may be found in the *Supplement to Report to the President of the Committee on Economic Security* (1935), p. 12.

increase in the expectation of life at the ages of sixty to seventy.[1] The reason for the marked increase in percentage of the aged is not, therefore, due to changed expectancy of life, but, as Whelpton has pointed out, is primarily due to changes in the birth rate.

But whatever the cause, the effect has been to increase the proportion of persons who are "too old to work and too young to die," and the burden of caring for our elders will increase unless with the passing of time the occupational distribution, work requirements, and employment policies become less unfavorable to the older workers. But precisely the opposite is commonly asserted to have been the case—that these, taken together, have become more unfavorable to the older worker.

The shifting occupational distribution has been discussed earlier in this treatise.[2] The general trend has been away from agriculture, where the aging man can ordinarily find a place, to industry of some type or other. This shifting occupational distribution means that a growing proportion of workers are wage earners or white-collar workers who are dependent upon the hiring and firing policies of others. The employers in industry must protect their own interests by having efficient workers; and if younger workers are stronger, speedier, and more adaptable, they will tend to crowd out the older men and women.

The percentage of people over sixty-five years of age who have been gainfully employed is shown in Table 44.

TABLE 44.—PER CENT OF GAINFULLY OCCUPIED PERSONS IN THE UNITED STATES WHO WERE SIXTY-FIVE YEARS OF AGE AND OVER, BY OCCUPATIONAL DIVISION AND SEX, 1920 AND 1930[1]

Occupational division	1920			1930		
	Male	Female	Both	Male	Female	Both
Agriculture	6.7	5.0	6.5	8.1	6.0	7.9
Extraction of minerals	2.1	2.3	2.1	2.5	2.5	2.5
Manufacture and mechanical	3.5	1.4	3.2	4.0	1.9	3.7
Transportation and communication	2.7	0.3	2.5	2.8	0.5	2.6
Trade	4.0	1.1	3.6	4.5	1.6	4.1
Public service (not elsewhere classified)	6.3	2.2	6.2	8.2	5.1	8.1
Professional service	5.2	1.1	3.2	5.2	1.5	3.5
Domestic and personal service	5.5	4.3	4.7	5.9	4.1	4.7
Clerical	2.1	0.2	1.5	2.5	0.3	1.4
Average	4.5	2.3	4.1	5.1	2.5	4.5

[1] U. S. Census, 1920, *Population*, vol. 4, p. 376; 1930, *Population*, vol. 5, p. 116.

In 1920 those over sixty-five years of age constituted 4.1 per cent of the gainfully occupied in all occupations and in 1930, 4.5 per cent. This

[1] Metropolitan Life Insurance Company, *Statistical Bulletin*, vol. 9 (March, 1928), pp. 5–8.

[2] Vol. I, Chap. I.

increase was almost as large as the increase in proportion of the total population of those over sixty-five years of age which was from 4.7 to 5.4 per cent during the same period. In interpreting these figures it must be remembered that they are affected by the migration of the younger workers into the expanding trades and that the small number of the aged employed in some of these occupations is therefore in part due to the dynamic situation. Some of these occupational groups, such as professional service, may eventually employ an even larger percentage of elderly persons than will be employed in agriculture. Again, the small number of old women in industry is due in large part to the tendency of young women to marry and drop out of gainful occupations and to the recency of the entrance of women into many lines of business.

The effects on the older worker of the introduction of machine methods into industry have been almost as varied as the machines introduced, but the very rapidity of the change, the introduction of new methods and new types of machines, make it difficult for the older worker, with more fixed habits of thinking and ways of working, to adjust himself to the new techniques. A new machine may make useless his carefully acquired skill and require the speed and endurance of a younger worker.

The effect of the introduction of machinery is not always, however, to eliminate the older men from the job. In some cases the new machine does away with so much of the physical strain involved in the work that older men are able to retain or even to regain their positions. In one case, for example, a number of old glass-bottle blowers were rehired after the introduction of machinery.[1] Usually, however, it is cheaper to train younger and faster workers than to try to "teach old dogs new tricks."

In other occupations heavy manual work rather than the speed of the machine causes older men to lose their jobs. The Ohio Commission[2] in 1919 found that of those engaged in such exacting occupations as brass working, boiler making, glass making, and pottery, very few were over fifty-five years of age. Only from 0.8 to 1.5 per cent of the workers in these trades were sixty-five or over—much below the average (4.1 per cent) shown in Table 44 for 1920. The average age of 40,000 men employed in twelve metal-working establishments was only thirty-one.[3] In six foundries employing over 500 moulders only three men over fifty were engaged in heavy floor moulding, with ten men over sixty engaged in light bench moulding.[4] The New York Commission in 1930 found

[1] Ohio Health and Old Age Commission, *Health, Health Insurance, Old Age Pensions: Report, Recommendations, Dissenting Opinions* (1919), p. 210 (hereafter referred to as Ohio report).

[2] *Ibid.*, pp. 208–209.

[3] W. B. Catlin, *The Labor Problem in the United States and Great Britain* (1926), p. 82.

[4] Ohio report, p. 210.

that the heavy work in mining, transportation and trade, and the steel industry "burned men up," while in contrast 14 per cent of the farmers were over sixty-five.[1]

The authors of *Middletown* show more vividly than do statistics what the heavy manual labor, the machines, and speed-up of modern industry have meant to the older worker:[2]

"The manager of [a] large plant in which 75 per cent of the men are under forty-five: 'We have a good many routine jobs a man can do if he is still strong. We try to find a place for these older men *even when they are as old as fifty-five* if there is no danger in their working near machinery.' . . .

"[The wife of] a molder, age fifty-one, said: 'He often wonders what he'll do when he gets a little older. He hopes and prays they'll get the State old-age pension through pretty soon.' . . .

"[The wife of] a pattern maker, age forty:'He is forty and in about ten years now will be on the shelf. A pattern maker really isn't much wanted after forty-five. They always put in the young men. What will we do? Well, that is just what I don't know. We are not saving a penny, but we are saving our boys.' (Both boys attend the small local college.)' "

In other trades where sheer physical strength and endurance are not so necessary, skill and directive ability may enable men to keep on after sixty-five. In Hamilton, Ohio, the skilled and semiskilled trades employed a large quota of old men. As a rule, the skilled men over fifty were not required to do hard work. The machinists, safe workers, patternmakers, and coremakers, because of their superior skill, seem to have been able to hold their own.[3]

There are also some occupations open to old men which require comparatively little skill. There is a striking preponderance of old men employed as janitors, city laborers, watchmen, and boarding-house keepers. In these occupations from 50 to 65 per cent of the men were past fifty years of age in 1910.[4] That this tendency has continued is indicated by the findings of the New York Commission in 1930, which show a high percentage of old workers in such occupations.[5] A good many of the men are, however, given these jobs as a substitute for a pension or poor relief and, where this motive is not involved, younger men are usually preferred.

---

[1] *Report of the New York State Commission on Old Age Security*, Legislative Document (1930), no. 67, p. 45 (hereafter referred to as New York report).

[2] Quoted, with permission, from R. S. and H. M. Lynd, *Middletown* (Harcourt, Brace and Company, 1929), pp. 33–35. (Italics are ours.) *Cf.*, also, their more recent volume, *Middletown in Transition* (1937).

[3] Ohio report, p. 222.

[4] U. S. Census, 1910, *Occupational Statistics*, p. 430.

[5] New York report, p. 45.

The age at which a worker is forced to retire from his trade or occupation depends not only on the type of work, the amount of speed, energy and skill required, but also on sickness and accident. Occupational sickness and in some cases accidents take an increasing toll with advancing age. Table 45 shows in the later age groups an increase in the annual number of days lost due to sickness, and this increase is particularly noticeable in the case of men.

TABLE 45.—DAYS LOST DUE TO SICKNESS, BY AGE GROUPS, 1930[1]

Age group	Days lost per year per person	
	Males	Females
15–24	5.3	12.8
25–34	5.6	14.1
35–44	7.0	11.5
45–54	7.1	13.2
55 and over	11.4	16.3
Average	6.5	13.1

[1] Taken from R. M. Olzendam, "Address before the National Association of Manufacturers" (1930), by A. M. Weimer in *The Older Worker in Industry* (Dissertation, University of Chicago, 1931), p. 8.

These figures correspond very closely to those obtained by A. F. Stevens, who found a very high correlation between advancing age and the amount of time lost due to accidents. Older workers required more time, on the average, to recover from accidents than younger workers, and the amount of time lost increased with each advance in age group.[1]

In addition to greater liability to sickness and accident, advancing age brings with it a general decline in physical efficiency. Eyesight may become less keen, muscles lose their elasticity and strength, and a general decline in physical vigor takes place. As efficiency declines, many employers shift workers to lighter or "pension" jobs, usually with a reduction in pay. In fact, this is probably the most common method of providing for employees who have grown old in the service of a company. A few companies, as a part of their programs of scientific management, make job analyses to determine which positions are best fitted to older workers. Here and there a company will make some attempt to retrain workers for new jobs. No doubt there is a good case for more of this than has as yet been practiced.[2]

Many companies, however, simply discharge their employees when they begin to decline in efficiency. When there is a large labor turnover, or seasonal fluctuation in employment, or shutdowns due to cyclical

[1] "Accidents of Older Workers; Relation of Age to Extent of Disability," *Personnel Journal*, August, 1929, pp. 138–145.

[2] For a recent study of possible methods of meeting the problem of the older worker, see Metropolitan Life Insurance Company, *The Older Employee in Industry* (1933).

depressions, it is comparatively easy for employers to weed out the older workers by "laying them off" and not reengaging them. Usually this is an entirely informal policy, but not infrequently a discharge age has been introduced and systematically applied. In Illinois only 12 of 431 firms reported the use of discharge ages, but 87 firms indicated that they released older workers when they began to decline in efficiency.[1] While many workers are in one way or another retained in employment after they have ceased to earn full wages, many older persons are separated from their jobs. It is generally much easier for an aged worker to retain his old job than to find a new one. Hiring-age limits are much more common than dismissal ages, and many firms with a policy of retaining old workers will not hire them.

About one-third (33.8 per cent) of the 431 firms in Illinois replying to a questionnaire stated that they had formal hiring-age limits ranging from thirty to fifty-five years, with the most common limit at forty-five.[2] The significance of these figures is increased by the fact that in general the large firms are more likely to adopt hiring-age limits than are the smaller ones. In Chicago, the average number of employees in firms using hiring-age limits was 345, while the average number in firms without such policies was 154.[3]

These figures apply only to those firms with fixed hiring-age limits. A much larger number have no formal limit, but give preference to younger workers. In actual practice a firm with no set rule, but with a policy of training young men in the business and of promoting from within, may effectively bar older workers from positions. The New York State Commission on Old Age Security in a survey of 350,000 wage earners in manufacturing industries in New York "found that some 72 per cent of the reporting concerns, employing 90 per cent of the employees, maintained some type of discriminatory age hiring policy."[4]

Hiring-age limits are adopted not only because younger workers may be more efficient, but also to protect the company from the burden of caring for employees who have not been in the service of the company for a long period of time. Companies with industrial pension plans have commonly adopted fixed hiring-age limits to prevent the hiring of workers who will be superannuated before they are eligible to a pension.[5] Even

[1] A. M. Weimer, *The Older Worker in Industry*, pp. 46–47.

[2] *Ibid.*, p. 38.

[3] *Ibid.*, p. 44.

[4] Quoted from a summary statement of findings and conclusions prepared by Solomon Barkin, in *Social Security*, July-August, 1933, p. 3.

[5] Elmer Spahr, *Report of the Second National Conference on Old Age Security* (New York, 1929), p. 29.

Moreover, additional factors are found in the higher premium rates charged and the limitations sometimes imposed by companies providing group insurance policies and the insurance required under workmen's compensation laws.

small companies without pension plans have felt the increasing social pressure against discharging superannuated workers and as a defense have hired fewer old men.[1] Surveys indicate that unemployment has fallen more heavily upon the older than upon the younger workers. The New York State Commission on Old Age Security found that the older employee experiences a 34 per cent rehiring handicap as compared with the average employee, while even more difficulty is experienced in finding new employment. "In comparison with the chances of the average male, the employee forty to forty-four years old is 32 per cent handicapped, those fifty to fifty-four years 66 per cent, and those sixty-five years and over 92 per cent." As the severity of unemployment increased, the proportion of unemployment among older men grew most rapidly.[2] These findings are similar to those presented by Clague, Lubin, and Myers in the studies of technological unemployment referred to in Chap. I of this volume.

These facts seem to indicate that the aged are finding it increasingly difficult to find employment in the modern industrial world, at least in the mechanical and heavy industries. A further indication of this can be found in the census figures for the gainfully occupied over age sixty-five, as shown in Table 46.

TABLE 46.—PERSONS GAINFULLY OCCUPIED, 65 YEARS OF AGE AND OVER, 1890 TO 1930[1]

Year	Percentage of those over 65 gainfully occupied			Percentage of total population gainfully occupied
	Men	Women	Both	
1890	73.8	8.3	41.7	47.3
1900	68.4	9.1	39.1	50.5
1920	61.5	8.0	34.3	50.3
1930	58.3	8.0	33.2	49.5

[1] U. S. Census, 1930, *Population*, vol. 5, Chap. 4; 1900 special reports, *Occupations*, Chap. 3.

These figures show an unmistakable decline in the proportion of aged persons who are gainfully occupied. While about one-third of those over sixty-five years of age are reported by the Census as being "gainfully occupied," not all of these are able to work regularly and the percentage of disability increases sharply with advancing age groups. The proportion of those over sixty-five who were superannuated was about 38 per cent, while only about 20 per cent of those over seventy years of age *could* do light work of some kind.[3] Paul Douglas has pointed out, how-

[1] *Survey*, Aug. 15, 1929, p. 526.
[2] Solomon Barkin, *op. cit.*, p. 3.
[3] Solomon Barkin, *op. cit.*, p. 4, and "Employment of the Older Worker," *Journal of the American Statistical Association, Supplement*, vol. 27 (March, 1932), pp. 102–108.

ever, that the decline in the number of old people gainfully employed may in part be due to the fact that, with a rise in real wages, there is less need for old people to work. But despite this qualification, the preponderance of evidence points to the fact that in many industries it has become increasingly difficult for an aged worker to retain his job, and even more so to get a new one. Even the most optimistic would hesitate to contend that in general employment opportunities for elderly people have been increasing at a rate which would insure employment to the increasing number of persons over sixty-five years of age who could work and were in need of employment.

Why do not people foresee the hard times ahead and save during the years when they are employed? Would not individual thrift and savings meet the problem of old-age dependency?[1] If a person does not expect to receive a pension or be dependent on others, and is to be faced with unemployment or irregular employment in his old age, he must save enough during his working years to live on if he is superannuated. A man at the age of sixty-five may normally expect to live eleven years and, according to some writers, would need a total of from $1,500 to $3,000 in order to maintain a subsistence minimum.[2] This is obviously a conservative estimate and probably a more accurate one is $8,000 for a couple at the age of sixty-five.[3] If a worker were superannuated at fifty-five or even sixty, he would need proportionately more.

There are no general data available as to the amount of workers' savings, but the figures for selected groups are available. In 1929 the average amount to the credit of each depositor in mutual savings banks in the United States was $756.79, in stock savings banks, $534.53.[4] Of 34,000 accounts in the Bowery Savings Bank, the average initial deposit was $813, but the median deposit was only $192.[5] This indicates that the average saving is as high as it is largely because the averages are heavily weighted by the larger deposits.

In the 1920's, the Massachusetts Commission and the National Civic Federation made studies of the savings of sample groups of nondependents over sixty-five, and the New York Commission made a study of all persons over sixty-five in four rural towns in Otsego County. Table 47 summarizes their findings.

The Otsego census has the advantage of including all persons over sixty-five, whether recipients of charity or not. While the data are not all that might be desired, they indicate that between one-half and three-

---

[1] Such questions may seem pedantic to those whose savings for old age have been wiped out by the decline in value of securities since 1929, or by unemployment. Not everyone has thus learned by experience, hence a discussion of the points is hazarded.

[2] Ohio report, p. 202.

[3] F. A. Miller, *Report of Second National Conference on Old Age Security* (1929), p. 26.

[4] *Annual Report of the Comptroller of the Currency for 1935* (1936), p. 133. The average amount due each depositor in 1935 was $749.41 and $525.89, respectively.

[5] New York report, p. 219.

fourths of the aged population have not saved enough to provide for their old age.

It is sometimes argued that it is now easier for workers to save than it was for those who have become old. As proof of this it is pointed out that within the last generation the amount of general money savings has increased threefold, and that since the War the amount of life insurance has increased tremendously. However, the general gain does not necessarily mean a gain to the working class. The total amount of savings

TABLE 47.—PERCENTAGES OF THOSE AGE SIXTY-FIVE AND OVER IN VARIOUS ECONOMIC GROUPS IN THE OTSEGO CENSUS COMPARED WITH THE MASSACHUSETTS AND NATIONAL CIVIC FEDERATION STUDIES[1]

	Otsego census[a]	Massachusetts study[a]	National Civic Federation study[a]
Owning property of $5,000 or over...........	21.9	40.8	47.6
Owning less than $5,000...................	78.1	59.2	52.4
Income of those owning less than $5,000:			
$1,000 and over.........................	2.3	14.6	15.3
500 to $1,000........................	10.3	10.7	11.3
400 to 500........................	6.7	1.5	1.5
300 to 400........................	8.6	2.0	1.5
200 to 300........................	11.2	2.9	1.3
100 to 200........................	11.2	4.3	3.2
0 to 100........................	11.9	6.4	5.8
None................................	15.9	16.8	12.4

a Both members of a married couple if sixty-five years of age or over are counted and placed in the same financial group in each study.

[1] New York report, p. 53.

must first be corrected for the decline in value of the dollar, and for the fact that most of the increase in savings has been made by corporations or by the salaried and higher-wage classes. Although the general level of wages has risen and although corporate paper has been made increasingly available to small investors, saving and investment are not so much easier as might be supposed. Higher standards of living, high-pressure salesmanship, and "help prosperity" campaigns generally play havoc with any intention to put by a sum for old age. Furthermore, carefully made savings and insurance intended for old age may be entirely dissipated by long periods of unemployment such as many workers suffered after 1929.

Even if it were possible for each worker to save enough individually for his own needs, this would be a wasteful method of providing such funds. As in the case of accidents and sickness, the needs of the individual are not predictable and the most economical method of meeting the risk is through a pooling of liabilities and resources in some form of old-age insurance.

The number of dependent aged in the United States is not known, but several estimates are available. Squier estimated in 1912 that there were 1,250,000 persons over sixty-five years of age dependent upon public or private charity.[1]	More recent estimates are larger.	Murray Latimer estimates that in 1930 at least 1,500,000 over sixty-five were unable to provide for themselves.[2]	On the basis of a survey of four eastern cities made in 1927 by the National Civic Federation, I. M. Rubinow estimated that of the 6,500,000 persons in the United States over sixty-five years of age in 1930, some 1,900,000 had no property and over 2,400,000 no earnings, while nearly 1,200,000 had neither, so that the problem of destitution was acute for nearly one-third of the entire group.[3]

The Committee on Economic Security in 1935 estimated that at least one-half of the approximately seven and one-half million persons over sixty-five years of age in the United States were dependent upon others for support.	The major burden of supporting these dependents was borne by children, friends, and relatives, but approximately 1,000,000 were dependent upon public support.	Approximately 850,000 were on Federal and local relief rolls, while an additional 180,000 were in receipt of pensions under the state old-age-pension laws.[4]

[1] L. W. Squier, *Old Age Dependency in the United States* (1912), p. 3.

[2] *Business Week*, Apr. 16, 1930, p. 38.

[3] *Encyclopaedia of the Social Sciences*, "Old Age," vol. 11, p. 456.

[4] Hearings before the Committee on Finance, United States Senate, 74th Congress, First Session, on S. 1130, *Economic Security Act* (1935), pp. 60–61.

While no detailed study of dependency in the United States as a whole is available, the Massachusetts Commission on Old Age Pensions in 1925 made a study of the composition of the aged population in that state [Massachusetts Commission on Pensions, *Report on Old-Age Pensions*, Senate, no. 5, 1925 (hereafter referred to as Massachusetts report)]. The findings are summarized in the following table (*ibid.*, p. 37):

Class	Persons 65 years of age and over		Persons 70 years of age and over	
	Number	Percentage distribution	Number	Percentage distribution
Estimated population, total	225,000	100.0	133,000	100.0
Public pensioners:				
U. S. military pensioners[a]	15,000	6.7	13,500	10.2
Federal, State, county, city and town civil pensioners[a]	3,000	1.3	2,100	1.6
Persons aided by organized charity:				
Almshouse inmates	4,123	1.8	2,740	2.1
Aided by public charity in outdoor relief	3,791	1.7	2,655	2.0
Residents of private homes for the aged	2,921	1.3	2,492	1.9
Aided by private organized charity in outdoor relief (cases reported)	1,471	0.7	1,119	0.8
Other recipients of relief	1,800	0.8	1,250	0.9
Persons under custodial care:				
In prisons, jails, etc.	250	0.1	90	0.1
In state institutions for insane	2,750	1.2	1,660	1.2
Persons not supported by public funds or by private organized charity (nondependent aged)	189,894	84.4	105,394	79.2

[a] Including only those with pensions of $360 or over.

While conditions in other parts of the United States might be found to differ substantially from those in Massachusetts, these figures bring out important points.	In the first

How much truth is there in the common feeling that personal depravity or negligence is largely responsible for old-age dependency? One poorhouse steward expressed the opinion that "rum and laziness" was the reason 90 per cent of the men were there.[1] However, the majority of careful students strongly disagree with this opinion. Old-age dependency is usually the result of social and economic factors beyond the control of the individual. In Pennsylvania a study of the applications for pensions showed this to be the case.[2] The discrepancy between the cost of living and the average worker's income, the changing industrial situation and employment policies, unemployment, strikes, sickness, accidents, and number of children, rather than personal virtues, are determining. It is these factors which have led to the widespread recognition of the fact that old-age security is a problem which cannot be met adequately by individual action.

Various Methods of Supporting the Aged

The different approaches to the problem of providing for the old include individual savings, care by children, fraternal organizations, public and private charity, private pensions, voluntary and compulsory insurance, and noncontributory public pensions. The extent and adequacy of each of these methods will be briefly considered.

Why should not the care of the aged be left to their children? Is it not the duty of children to care for and protect their parents? The states generally have laws requiring children (or near relatives) to support aged parents. In Massachusetts the passage of such a law in 1915 helped to check the increase in the number of almshouse inmates. From 1901 to 1915 the number of almshouse inmates in that state increased from 4,561 to 5,007. From 1915 to 1923 the number declined to 3,882, despite the increase in general population.[3] However, it is often difficult to find offspring who are able to support their parents and to induce them to assume the burden. In Otsego County, New York, 27.9 per cent of the single individuals and 16.4 per cent of married couples over sixty-five

place, there is a marked increase in dependency after sixty-five. The total number aided by organized charity is surprisingly low; at sixty-five years of age, 3.4 per cent of the total population in New York were in this class, or less than the number of military pensioners. However, the situation is not as satisfactory as would seem at first glance, for the fact that an aged person does not receive aid from organized charity does not mean that he is independent. Of the "nondependents" in Massachusetts over sixty-five, only 40.8 per cent had over $5,000 in property (including for married persons property of spouse). Only 35 per cent of the nondependents with less than $5,000 were self-supporting at the age of sixty-five. (Massachusetts report, p. 55, Table 8, and p. 56, Table 9.)

[1] Ibid., p. 80. In fairness to the steward it must be pointed out that this was a predepression estimate.

[2] Report of the Pennsylvania Commission on Old Age Pensions, 1927, p. 20 (hereafter referred to as Pennsylvania report, 1927).

[3] Massachusetts report, p. 77, Table 1.

years of age had no children and less than $3,000 in property or $400 in income.[1] In Massachusetts 55 per cent of those over sixty-five years, not receiving public pensions or organized charity, but owning less than $5,000 of property and receiving yearly incomes under $1,000, were aided by their children, but 70.6 per cent of the almshouse inmates had no children.[2]

In other cases, children support aged parents at a great sacrifice of their own and their offspring's standard of living. From the social standpoint, it is desirable that they be relieved of this burden. Care of the aged by children is, therefore, not possible in a large percentage of the cases and is not desirable in many more.

Outdoor relief, or aid given the poor in their homes, is rarely in the form of money, but usually consists of contributions of fuel, food, clothing, and other necessities. In the United States the common practice has been to aid in their homes all those whose mental or physical condition permitted them to be cared for outside of institutions. While in its very nature it is difficult to estimate the total amount of outdoor relief given, or to segregate the amount given to those over sixty-five, the tendency has been toward an increase in both public and private expenditures.

The same officials who are in charge of almshouses are often in charge of public outdoor relief. Of this system of administration a recent state commission report concludes, "the present day administration of public relief is, on the whole, characterized by inadequate investigation, poor case supervision, and almost no real case work looking to rehabilitation, social adjustment or other aid than material relief."[3] The amount of relief given has varied with need and ranged in value from three to ten dollars per week. While this has made the aid definitely a form of charity and carried with it a stigma and a feeling of shame on the part of the recipients, the relief has often been sufficient to keep the beneficiaries from going to the almshouse and therefore has been encouraged as the lesser of two evils.

Private outdoor relief is also objectionable. The disbursements have all too frequently been haphazard and wasteful, the amounts uncertain and insufficient, and the provision degrading. The common excuse for outdoor relief is that it meets a temporary situation. It is true that the amount of relief has varied with the business cycle and seasonable conditions of need and employment, but the amount of relief to the aged has not been as much affected by these factors as has the amount given

[1] New York report, p. 54.

[2] Massachusetts report, pp. 56, 84. In the same state, 23.2 per cent of the former group had no children (*ibid.*, p. 73).

[3] From New York report, p. 372. Of course, Federal participation in relief has greatly improved poor-relief administration throughout the United States, but how much of this gain will survive after the Federal government withdraws from participation remains to be seen. It would indeed appear that much of it has already been lost.

to the ordinary family. Of 5,262 persons in Massachusetts over sixty-five known to have received outdoor relief, 4,033 were permanent cases, 432 periodic and only 705 temporary.[1] Most of those over sixty-five who have received outdoor relief would be eligible to pensions under state laws. Since pensions carry with them less of the stigma of pauperism, and are much preferred by the aged themselves, advocates of state pensions have contended that pensions should be substituted for outdoor relief so far as possible, and to an increasing extent this is being done.

Of the several forms of public and private indoor relief, care in almshouses has been one of the most important[2] and certainly the most condemned. In 1923 and 1924, there were approximately 85,889 inmates of almshouses in the United States. These were maintained in 2,348 almshouses representing an investment of $1,752 per inmate. The annual disbursement amounted to $28,740,535, or $334.64 per inmate.[3] These expenditures varied widely between states, from $187 per year per inmate in Alabama to $865 in Nevada.[4] The administration is usually in the hands of counties and the lack of central supervision is one reason for the variations in condition of the almshouses within the states. Some of these institutions have been found to be in good order, while in others the conditions have been appalling. Dangerous firetraps, extreme filth, and grossest neglect have been discovered.[5] The Ohio Commission found thirteen of the almshouses in very bad condition, and nineteen below any decent standard, while only thirteen were fairly good.[6]

The cost of administration has consumed a large part of the total amount spent on almshouses. In Pennsylvania, for example, of $6,200,-000 spent on almshouses, at least $3,000,000 was spent on administration, and 1,000 employees were required to look after 8,000 inmates.[7]

Advocates of pension plans point out that it usually costs about one-tenth as much as this to administer pension funds (3 to 5 per cent of the fund), but the comparison is not entirely fair. Almshouses used to contain the old and the young, the sick and the able-bodied, without much attempt at segregation. In some states, especially in New England, there has been a progressive tendency to eliminate from the almshouses the young and the able-bodied, the insane and those with incurable communicable diseases, and to admit to them only those aged who need

---

[1] Massachusetts report, p. 107, Table 5.

[2] In 1935 there were about 100,000 old people in almshouses. (Hearings on S. 1130 cited previously, p. 58.)

[3] "Care of Aged Persons in the United States," U. S. Bureau of Labor Statistics, *Bulletin 489* (1929), p. 6.

[4] *Ibid.*, p. 7.

[5] *Ibid.*, p. 6.

[6] Ohio report, p. 244.

[7] Pennsylvania report, 1927, p. 21.

institutional care.[1]   In Massachusetts it was estimated that only 31 per cent of those over sixty-five in almshouses would be eligible for pensions and not in need of institutional care.[2]   But the policy of admitting to almshouses only those aged who are friendless and whose physical condition requires institutional care is more rigid there than in most states. The New York Commission, for example, found that 64.8 per cent of the almshouse inmates over sixty-five did not need institutional care.[3]   This is probably a more typical figure.

Recent data on the operation of pension plans seem to bear out the contention that in a large number of cases pensions can be substituted for almshouse care.   Even prior to 1929 the number of inmates in poorhouses was increasing rapidly.   In New York in the five years from 1924 to 1929 the increase was 20 per cent, in California 48 per cent, in Wisconsin 40 per cent, in Connecticut 32 per cent, and in Indiana 26 per cent. After 1929 the increase in total number of almshouse inmates was much more rapid.   For example, in the two years 1931–1932 the increase in almshouse population in Connecticut was 32.2 per cent, in Michigan 31.4 per cent, and in Indiana 23.5 per cent.   In New York and Massachusetts the total poorhouse population also increased during these two years but by smaller percentages (14.9 and 15.8, respectively) than in states without pension systems, but the increase in these states was in persons too young to be eligible for pensions.   In the first two years of operation of the pension system in New York, 1930 and 1931, the number of inmates over seventy years of age declined by 7.5 per cent.[4]

The fact that a large percentage of almshouse inmates need institutional care means that some such institution must exist even under a comprehensive system of social insurance and pensions.   This does not mean, however, that the present type of institution should be continued, but rather that the largest and best almshouses should be turned into combination homes and hospitals for the aged.   If the counties are too poor to maintain decent almshouses independently, they should combine into districts.

In addition to those in almshouses, there were in 1927 about 68,661 aged persons in homes of various types in the United States.   Of this number, over 16,500 were in fifty-one Federal and state military homes and the remainder in homes maintained by private organizations.

Of the private homes, 90 per cent had waiting lists of applicants for admission.   Usually the applicants are admitted on probation and if their character is not satisfactory, they cannot become permanent residents.   About 35 per cent of the homes require no admission fee,

[1] U. S. Bureau of Labor Statistics, *Bulletin 489*, p. 6.

[2] Massachusetts report, pp. 96–97.

[3] New York report, p. 434.

[4] *Social Security* (September–October, 1933), pp. 3–4.

but the usual fee has been about $500 and may be several times that sum.[1]

The condition of most of these homes is much better than that of almshouses generally.   A real attempt is made to make the residents comfortable in homelike surroundings.   Usually incurables are excluded, but the care of those needing hospital facilities is one of the biggest burdens on the homes.[2]

TABLE 48.—NUMBER OF BENEFICIARIES AND AMOUNTS DISBURSED UNDER PENSION PLANS, 1929[1]

Type of pension or annuity	No. in system	Number of beneficiaries	Amount spent in allowances in one year	Average per beneficiary
Federal:				
Military service....................	a	453,088	$228,965,672	$ 466
Civil service......................	a	15,383	10,990,454	734
State:				
Private citizens[b]..................	a	1,003	208,624	208
State employees[c]..................	31,572	1,458	968,984	550
Teachers[d]........................	371,835	13,094	5,977,675	457
Municipalities:				
Teachers[e]........................	54,776	3,949	3,829,989	970
Police and firemen[f]..............	67,765	20,327	14,768,605	726
Other municipal employees[g].......	93,374	4,619	3,373,644	730
Carnegie teachers' retirement fund........	7,600[h]	922	1,372,866	1,489
Labor organizations..................	a	11,306	3,350,995	296
Ministers' retirement[i]...............	a	14,806	5,594,862	373
Fraternal organizations..............	a	152	21,890	144
Private industrial pension plans[j].......	951,801	10,644	6,674,044	627
Insurance annuities..................	59,075[k]	a	a	a
Totals (incomplete)...............	....	550,751	286,098,304	519

[a] No data.
[b] Six states having old-age pension laws.
[c] Five state systems.
[d] Sixteen state systems.
[e] Seven city systems.
[f] Seventeen cities.
[g] Nine cities.
[h] Under annuity plan.
[i] Eleven national organizations.
[j] One hundred forty plans.   It has been estimated that more than 4,000,000 are covered by industrial pension plans.   In the Social Security Bulletin (March, 1938, p. 10) the number of beneficiaries has been estimated at 150,000.
[k] Written by eight large insurance companies and by the Massachusetts savings banks.
[1] "Care of Aged Persons in the United States" U. S. Bureau of Labor Statistics, Bulletin 489 (1929), p. 3.

The method now most commonly advocated of providing old-age security is through some form of pension or annuity, but until recently it found very limited application in the United States.   Table 48 gives some idea of the relative importance in 1929 of different types of annuity and pension plans, in the United States, the amounts disbursed and the number of beneficiaries of each.

[1] U. S. Bureau of Labor Statistics, Bulletin 489, p. 15.
[2] Ibid., p. 204.

It will be noted that military pensions were by far the most important; as a guess, all the other types combined had less than 150,000 beneficiaries in 1929.

Trade unions have devoted more and more attention to the problem of the care of those of their members who by reason of disability or age are unable to continue at work. The American Federation of Labor traditionally favored trade-union action exclusively, but it has changed its attitude and some years ago endorsed a model pension plan for state adoption. In addition to pressing for state legislation, twelve international unions had pension plans of their own, under which 11,306 members or their widows received $3,350,995 in 1928.[1] The amounts of these pensions varied between $60 and $70 a month and were available only to members of long standing who had attained a certain age and were unable to find work sufficient to support themselves. The period of membership required was usually twenty years, but in the case of the carpenters it was thirty years. The age of eligibility to retirement was commonly sixty or sixty-five.[2] The emphasis on the continuous period of membership shows that the unions have provided these benefits not only for benevolent purposes, but also to give their members added reason to remain in the union and to pay dues. The more dependent the worker is on the union, the larger his financial interest, the more he will fight for its program.

The funds for these pensions have been raised from membership dues, occasionally supplemented by special assessments. The majority of these old-age pension plans have been conducted on the cash disbursement basis and most of them sooner or later have drifted into a precarious financial condition. Several existing plans would fail if one-tenth of the membership survived to claim pensions and present financial arrangements were continued.[3] The tendency has been for the cost of pension systems to grow and to necessitate an increase in the per capita dues. The Bricklayers, Masons and Plasterers' Union has several times been forced to increase its levy, but its officers believe that these increases have placed the fund on a sound basis.[4]

Pension plans can be successfully adopted by only the larger and more prosperous of the unions. Actuaries advised the Union of Amalgamated Lithographers of America, with 5,700 members, that it was too small to maintain a pension plan except at prohibitive cost.[5] The secretary of the United Mine Workers of America has also testified that

---

[1] U. S. Bureau of Labor Statistics, *Bulletin 489* (1929), p. 89. In 1934, of A. F. of L. affiliates, fifteen national and local unions spent a total of $3,912,939.89 on old-age pensions. A. F. of L., *Proceedings* (1935), pp. 100–104.

[2] *Ibid.*, p. 87.

[3] Old Age Security Conference, *Report* (New York, 1929), p. 21.

[4] *Ibid.*, p. 29.

[5] U. S. Bureau of Labor Statistics, *Bulletin 489*, p. 95.

the organization could not finance a pension plan.[1] Trade-union pension plans at best, therefore, can cover only a small part of the workers in a limited number of unions, in that part of industry which is unionized.[2]

Industrial pension plans have varied from informal, noncontributory, discretional plans on a cash-disbursement basis to contractual, compulsory, contributory plans on an actuarial basis. Of the formal pension plans the majority have been of the discretionary type in which the employer has had exclusive control. There has, however, been a tendency toward a greater mutuality of obligations as is indicated by the spread of contributory, limited contractual plans.[3]

A worker to be eligible to a pension must have attained a certain age and have had a stipulated number of years of *continuous* service with the company. The most common requirement of continuous service has been twenty or twenty-five years, and if the worker resigned or quit work on strike, he lost all accumulated service credit. This is the pivotal point in industrial pension plans. Usually employers have adopted formal plans because they expected them to pay in reduced labor turnover, increased efficiency and loyalty of workers, and freedom from strikes.

The first industrial pension system in the United States was established in 1884, and the movement reached its peak rate between 1910 and 1916, when sixty-nine plans were established. After that time the movement slackened, but the number of plans never entirely ceased to grow[4] until the Security Act was passed. The United States Bureau of Labor Statistics, in 1925, estimated that there were well over 200 formal plans in existence, but "that it was impossible even to guess the number of employees covered."[5] In 1927, however, the Pennsylvania Commission on Old Age Pensions estimated that 4,000,000 workers were then covered by industrial pension plans.[6] This was probably somewhat in excess of the actual number, for in 1929 Murray Latimer found 364 concerns with pension plans and estimated the maximum coverage at 3,750,000 workers.[7]

As a rule, industrial pensions have been adopted only by the larger firms; 72 per cent of all concerns with formal plans employ over 1,000 workers and two-thirds of all persons covered by such plans are employed

---

[1] Old Age Security Conference, *Report*, p. 69.

[2] For a detailed discussion of trade-union pension systems, see Murray W. Latimer, *Trade Union Pension Systems* (1932).

[3] National Industrial Conference Board, *Industrial Pensions in the United States* (1925), p. 14.

[4] U. S. Bureau of Labor Statistics, *Bulletin 489*, p. 287.

[5] *Ibid.*, p. 287.

[6] Pennsylvania report, 1927, p. 7.

[7] Murray Latimer, *Industrial Pension Systems in the United States and Canada* (1932), vol. 1, p. 55.

by public-service corporations.[1]   About one-half of the pensioners, some 50,000, have been employed on the railroads alone.[2]   The financial condition of an appreciable number of the schemes at the end of 1932 was extremely precarious, and it has become reasonably certain that the movement would never have embraced more than a substantial fraction of the workers.[3]

The fact that industrial pension plans have covered only a small part of the workers in industry was only one of their limitations.   Another very serious limitation has been the effect of labor turnover on the number of workers eligible to pensions.   Murray Latimer estimated that, though pension plans covered 16 per cent of all workers engaged in industrial and clerical occupations in 1930, only from 1 to 5 per cent would remain with the same employers until they reached pensionable age.[4]   Only about 3.4 per cent of male workers and 2.4 per cent of female workers stay with the same concern for twenty years or more.[5]   The general figures for labor turnover, however, are not entirely satisfactory because they cover up variations in turnover between industries, individual plants, age and sex of the workers.   Much of this turnover is among the younger workers and as they grow older, many of them settle down to one job in time to become eligible to a pension.   Also the most progressive firms have been trying to cut down their labor turnover, in part through these pension plans.   The reductions effected would raise the percentage of those who would receive pensions somewhat above the figures indicated by general turnover.

The features which make industrial pensions advantageous to the employers may make them unacceptable to the workers.   The continuance of such a plan has been uncertain, for the company might fail, merge, or change hands, or the pension plan might be terminated by the employer, as a considerable number have been.   There has been no legal guarantee of a pension.[6]   Usually the plans have imposed many minor restrictions on the worker's conduct, and even then the loyal worker with accumulated service credit might be discharged.   A far more important objection has been that such plans undermine the worker's bargaining power by restricting his mobility.   If he has gone on strike or quit after several years of service, he has jeopardized his pension right.[7]

---

[1] A. Epstein, *Challenge of the Aged* (1928), pp. 161–162.

[2] G. S. Watkins, *Labor Problems* (1929), p. 395.

[3] Murray Latimer, *Industrial Pension Systems in the United States and Canada*, vol. 2, p. 945.

[4] *Business Week*, April 16, 1930, p. 40.

[5] Pennsylvania report, 1927, p. 7.

[6] Even in cases where the employee has contributed to the pension fund he may have no enforceable legal claim in case the company changes hands, or decides for financial reasons to discontinue the pension.   *Cowles v. Morris and Company*, 330 Ill. 11 (1928).

[7] Of course, the terms of settlement of a strike may preserve the pension rights of the employees returned to their jobs.

This has been particularly important to the older workers and has frequently caused them to accept wages and to tolerate working conditions which they otherwise would not.

Noncontributory Pensions and Compulsory Insurance in Foreign Countries.—Up to this point the discussion has been concerned with methods of providing for the industrially old worker other than by noncontributory ("straight") pensions, or by compulsory insurance. In most industrial countries other than the United States, straight pensions or compulsory insurance years ago came to be the most important methods of providing an income in old age. The legislation is to be explained in terms of a quickened social conscience, a desire to avoid the problems connected with relief so far as possible, and political objectives, as well as in terms of a problem tending to become greater with the extension of industry as against agricultural pursuits and the accompanying urbanization of population. A brief discussion of the situation in these countries, which made legislation necessary, and a summary of the development of such legislation in Germany and England will give a background for the study of the development of old-age-pension legislation in the United States and throw a great deal of light on the question of the comparative advantages of straight pensions and compulsory insurance.

In many respects the situation in foreign countries has been very different from that in the United States. The normal level of real wages in the United States has been much higher than in any other country[1] and this perhaps has made the need of state provision for old age somewhat less imperative here than elsewhere. With a higher level of real wages in the United States, it has been less of a hardship on children to provide for their aged parents and at the same time it has been less difficult to save for the future on a higher level of income than on a lower one. Yet, it must be admitted that this higher income accustoms people to higher standards and hence greater need in old age.

While the worker has been relatively better off here than in foreign countries in the matter of real income, the facts previously cited in this chapter show that it has been practically impossible for the majority of wage workers in the United States to save enough to provide security against the risks of old age and invalidity. There has been need of more adequate and efficient means of meeting these risks, perhaps by borrowing from the experience of other countries.

In most foreign countries the problem of providing for old age is treated as an integral part of a comprehensive national system of social insurance covering sickness, accident, disability, old-age retirement, and unemployment.[2]

[1] "Comparison of Real Wages in Different Countries," *International Labour Review*, vol. 20 (1929), p. 584.

[2] New York report, 1930, p. 276.

Thirty-six foreign countries, including all important industrial nations, had by 1934 adopted some kind of state or national provision for old-age security. Of these, twenty-five had compulsory contributory insurance and eleven provided straight pensions.[1] In Canada, Italy, and the Netherlands the governments contribute to voluntary insurance funds of groups not coming under the compulsory insurance or pension system.

The details of the foreign systems differ widely as to scope, financing, and methods of administration. In Sweden, for example, compulsory, contributory insurance is almost universal in scope. All citizens between eighteen and sixty-five years of age must make annual contributions to the insurance fund. The contributions vary from a minimum of six crowns to twenty crowns, according to the person's assessed income under the general income tax.[2] All persons sixty-seven years of age or over are entitled to pensions which vary with the amount of contributions made, or receive disability benefits at any age in case of permanent disability.[3] In the Netherlands the act of June 5, 1913, applies to wage earners over fourteen years of age whose incomes are under 2,000 florins ($804 par exchange).[4] The cost is borne (nominally at least) by the employer and the government. The contributions vary from ten to twenty-four cents a week, according to the age and sex of the worker. In Brazil the compulsory insurance system applies only to workers on public utilities.[5]

Of more importance than these differences is the distinction between contributory insurance and straight-pension systems. The great majority of countries now have contributory systems, and where the straight-pension system has been in force for some time, the governments have either changed over largely to a compulsory, contributory system or are contemplating such a change.[6] The reasons for this change and the essential differences in the two systems can perhaps best be brought out by a summary of the experiences of Germany with compulsory social insurance and of Great Britain with old-age pensions.

Germany was the pioneer in the field of national compulsory social insurance. The first law providing for compulsory old-age and invalidity

[1] Supplement to Report of the Committee on Economic Security (1935), pp. 13–14, Table 16.

[2] The Riksdag Act of June 6, 1935, permits contributions to cease at age sixty-five, but does not change the pensionable age from sixty-seven. However, the insurance system has been modified by the provision that all insured persons will receive a minimum basic pension of seventy crowns plus 10 per cent of the aggregate amount of contributions paid, provided that if the insured person has been insured for less than seven years, the basic pension is reduced by ten crowns for each year short of seven. I. L. O., Industrial and Labour Information, vol. 55 (1935), pp. 160–162.

[3] U. S. Bureau of Labor Statistics, Bulletin 561 (1932), pt. II, Table II, and pp. 337–341.

[4] Ibid., Table II and pp. 283–302.

[5] Ibid., p. 143.

[6] New York report, p. 275.

insurance was passed in 1889 and covered practically all workers over sixteen years of age who were employed in German agriculture, industry, and commerce, with the exception of specially exempted groups, such as those with salaries over 2,000 Marks, teachers, and public officials.[1] In 1911 the invalidity and old-age-insurance plans were consolidated under a single code of federal insurance against accidents, sickness, death, invalidity, and old age. The act extended the system of compulsory insurance to include salaried employees whose salaries did not exceed 6,000 Marks.[2] In 1923 the miners' insurance plans were changed from a state to a federal basis under the Miners' Insurance Association.[3]

The period of postwar inflation of the Mark in Germany wiped out the insurance reserves which had been built up[4] and necessitated a thoroughgoing revision of the system in the Federal Insurance Code of Dec. 15, 1924. With the stabilization of the Mark, the reserves began to be built up once more. The economic depression and the policy of rationalization led to an extensive fall in the number of employed insured persons and in wages and therefore in the amount of contributions. In 1929 the annual income from contributions was 1,092 million Rm., but by 1933 the income from contributions had fallen to 660 million Rm. In 1932 the deficit was 182 million Rm., and in 1933 it was 95 million Rm.[5] By the end of 1934, however, an increase in employment resulted in a surplus of 184.6 million Rm.[6] The soundness of the workers' pension fund in Germany thus depends in a large measure upon the general economic condition, the level of wages, and the volume of employment.

The administration of the German invalidity and old-age insurance has been through territorial and special "institutes" in each confederated state. These institutes have been under the general supervision of the central insurance office and have been run by highly trained experts. A board of arbitration assists in settling disputes concerning claims.

The contributions to the insurance funds are made by the insured persons, the employer, and the Federal Government. The contributions of the government are the costs of administration and a fixed sum for each worker pensioned (seventy-two Marks a year in 1929).[7] The

[1] "Workmen's Insurance Systems in Europe," U. S. Bureau of Labor, *24th Annual Report* (1909), vol. 1, p. 1362.

[2] *Monthly Labor Review* (1930), p. 722, paster no. 3.

[3] A. Epstein, *Challenge of the Aged*, pp. 359–360.

[4] The loss to the workers' pension scheme is estimated at 4,000 million Marks. "The Reform of Workers' Compulsory Pension Insurance in Germany, I" *International Labour Review*, vol. 31 (1935), p. 399.

[5] *Ibid.*, pp. 399–400.

[6] International Labour Office, *Industrial and Labour Information*, vol. 55 (1935), pp. 246–247.

[7] U. S. Bureau of Labor Statistics, *Bulletin 561* (1932), p. 212.

contributions of the insured person and the employer are equal and vary according to the wage received by the individual. For this purpose the workers are divided into six classes and the combined contributions vary from 0.30 to 2.00 Marks per week.[1]

The amounts of the invalidity and old-age benefits are based on a fixed grant from the state and a variable amount from the Insurance Institute, the latter depending upon the number of payments made by the worker and employer and the size of such payments. If the worker moves from one income group to another, his payments are averaged.

In 1930 there were about 22,000,000 persons insured under the social-insurance code. The twenty-nine territorial institutes were in that year paying 51,000 old-age and 1,998,000 invalidity allowances.[2] The average old-age benefit in 1929 was 33.54 Marks per month. The institutes in 1930 paid 1,178,000 survivors' (widows, orphans, etc.) allowances. In addition, 226,366 salaried employees[3] and their survivors, and 373,352 miners received benefits.[4]

When social insurance was first introduced in Germany, it met with strong protest. The agitation was directed especially against the system of making and recording contributions by buying insurance stamps. However, the workers and employers soon became accustomed to the system and within a few years serious opposition gave way to proposals for extending and improving the system.[5]

In Germany, before the adoption of compulsory insurance, the alternative of straight state pensions had been discussed and rejected in favor of national compulsory insurance. From that time there has been no movement to change the fundamental basis of the system. In England the development has been quite different and offers some very instructive comparisons.

The first attempt to provide old-age security in England was through individual savings and voluntary insurance organizations. Friendly societies or mutual self-help and savings associations are known to have existed in England as early as the sixteenth century. In 1793 Parliament passed an act to encourage "Societies for raising, by voluntary subscriptions of members, separate funds for their mutual relief and maintenance in sickness, old age, and infirmity."[6] Most of these societies, however, provided only a burial allowance and many others resembled mutual savings banks more than friendly societies. One of the chief difficulties of many of the friendly societies was that, as they became older and the proportion of old people receiving benefits increased, it became

[1] *Ibid.*, p. 212.

[2] *Ibid.*, p. 216.

[3] *Ibid.*, p. 224.

[4] *Ibid.*, p. 233.

[5] U. S. Bureau of Labor, *24th Annual Report* (1909), vol. 1, p. 978.

[6] *Ibid.*, vol. 2, p. 1551.

increasingly difficult to get young people to join, and the societies died out. Despite this difficulty a large variety of societies, some of them with large memberships in both Scotland and England, survived and are in existence today. Trade unions, in addition to strike, unemployment, sickness, accident, and funeral benefits, sometimes provided superannuation benefits.[1] The English government also experimented with voluntary old-age and invalidity insurance through postal savings banks, but the scheme did not have any great popularity.[2]

Persistent agitation by such men as Charles Booth and Cannon Blackley led Parliament in 1893 to appoint a Royal Commission to investigate the condition of the aged and the advisability of alterations in the system of poor relief. This commission and another in 1896 recognized the wretched condition of the aged poor, but both were unable to propose any method for improving the existing poor-relief system. However, a committee in 1899 took up the idea of old-age pensions and their conclusions provided the basis of the pension plan as finally adopted in 1908.[3] In that year, after rejecting all proposals for a contributory plan, all the parties united in passing the first Old Age Pension Act. The act required the following qualifications for receiving a pension: (1) attainment of age seventy; (2) British citizenship for at least twenty years; (3) the receipt of less than £31, 10s. ($153) income per year. Criminals, habitual tramps, asylum and workhouse inmates, and those in receipt of poor relief were ineligible. The maximum pension was five shillings ($1.22) per week, but this rate was reduced one shilling for each £2 12s. 6d. by which the annual income exceeded £21. To ascertain a person's eligibility the local pension officer had to calculate his means, or net income from wages, property, and other sources.

The Ministry of Health in England and the Boards of Health of Wales and Scotland became the central pension authorities. The local pension officer was an official of the Department of Excise and Customs and made his reports to a pension committee in charge of local administration. The local postmaster was in charge of issuing the forms for claims, assisted in filling them out, and acted as the local pay agent. The total costs were defrayed by the national treasury from tax funds.

The act of 1908 was amended in 1911, 1919, and 1924 to extend and liberalize the old-age-pension system. Among the most important of the changes were: (1) an increase in the amount of pension in 1924 to a maximum of ten shillings a week; (2) provision that receipt of outdoor relief no longer disqualified a person for a pension; and (3) raising the means limit, in 1910, to £49 17s. 6d. A departmental committee in 1919 recommended that the means qualification be set aside because it involved

[1] *Ibid.*, p. 1616.
[2] *Ibid.*, p. 1672.
[3] *Ibid.*, p. 1687.

irritating inquisitions into private affairs, injuriously affected thrift, and tainted the pension with charity.[1] However, the Treasury was not in position to meet the additional expense which universal pensions would involve and the means qualification was retained.

In 1925 the Baldwin (Conservative) government introduced and passed the Widows', Orphans', and Old Age Contributory Insurance Bill.[2] This act provided for compulsory contributory insurance which would supplement and gradually replace the straight-pension system. The advantages of the insurance basis were that it would make possible universal provision for old age without the severe drain on the treasury of a universal pension and at the same time it would eliminate the troublesome and objectionable means qualification. The system had the further advantage that its administration could be unified with the National Health Insurance Act. The employer now makes the combined health-insurance and old-age-pension contribution by affixing a stamp each week to the employee's insurance card. The contributions are collected and the pension payments made through the post office.

The contributions are not, as in Germany, graded according to income, but are a flat weekly rate of 9d. per man and 4½d. per woman, one-half of which is paid by the employer and one-half by the employee. To provide pensions for those who entered the system at ages higher than sixteen, the exchequer was to contribute four millions sterling a year for ten years beginning in 1926–1927. All persons who are members of the working population, except specially exempted groups and those nonmanual workers whose incomes exceed £250 a year, are required to become contributors.[3]

The contributory pension plan makes it possible for an insured person who has made 104 weeks' contributions, who has been insured at least five years, and who has lived in Great Britain for at least two years, to retire on an annuity at the age of sixty-five, and at the age of seventy to receive the maximum pension regardless of means. As indicated in the title of the Act, widows and orphans of insured persons receive benefits. The Act of 1929 further liberalized the provision for dependents by including widows between fifty-five and seventy years of age whose husbands were in the insurable class, but had died before the insurance act became effective. Other modifications made in 1929 permit pensioners to migrate to the dominions and continue to receive pensions, and do not reduce pensions of children and orphans because workmen's compensation has been received.[4] Table 49 gives the distribution of persons receiving old-age benefits and the total expenditures in each class for the fiscal year ended March 31, 1934.

[1] New York report, p. 287.

[2] 15 and 16 Geo. V. Bill no. 164; as amended, no. 219.

[3] U. S. Bureau of Labor Statistics, *Bulletin 561* (1932), pp. 236–245.

[4] "New English Act for Widows, Orphans, and Old Age Contributory Pensions," *Monthly Labor Review*, vol. 30 (1930), pp. 46–47.

TABLE 49.—OLD-AGE PENSIONS IN THE UNITED KINGDOM, 1933–1934[1]
(Year Ended Mar. 31, 1934)

Type of pension	Beneficiaries		Amount spent
	Class	Number	
Noncontributory, restricted old-age-pension acts, 1908–1924	Persons over 70 with less than £50 a year	775,281	£20,558,000
Contributory, unrestricted old-age pensions. Amendments to 1908–1924 acts in 1925 and 1929	Persons over 70 who have made contributions	861,624	21,145,000
Contributory pensions acts of 1925–1931, National Health Insurance	Workers (and wives) between 65 and 70 years of age	714,044[a]	18,289,000

[a] Number as of Dec. 31, 1933.
There has been a gradual shift of pensioners from the noncontributory class to the provisions of the act of 1925. In 1927 a total of 1,112,869 persons received pensions under the noncontributory act, while 171,102 received pensions under the contributory act of 1925. Eventually the noncontributory, restricted pensions will apply mostly to small shopkeepers and others who are not "employed" and not insured under the National Health and Contributory Pension schemes. At the end of 1931, of about 19,000,000 gainfully occupied persons, 16,232,000 received protection against old age and invalidity under the National Health Insurance Act. On Dec. 31, 1933, about 18,792,000 were insured under the contributory pensions acts.
[1] *Statistical Abstract of the United Kingdom*, no. 78 (1935), pp. 76, 77, 79, and 81.

Pension Legislation for Government Employees in the United States.

In the United States legislation to provide old-age security lagged behind that in almost all other industrial countries. Straight-pension or compulsory-insurance legislation had, however, beginning years ago, been adopted by some municipalities to provide for the retirement of certain classes of their employees. As indicated in Table 48, on page 367, the most common provision of this type was a retirement fund for firemen and policemen. The tendency here was toward a contributory system, but many of the funds have been on a precarious cash-disbursement basis. In 1927, twenty-one states, the District of Columbia, and six large cities had teachers' retirement funds,[1] and 17,043 teachers were receiving pensions (see Table 48). Many of these funds were defective; the allowances were low and the period of service, usually twenty-five years, was too long to benefit most of the contributors.

Besides these pension plans for special groups, six states after 1911 adopted retirement systems for their employees; 1,458 persons were receiving pensions under them in 1926.[2]

[1] U. S. Bureau of Labor Statistics, *Bulletin 489* (1929), p. 223   In May, 1937, twenty-three state and fifty-nine local funds covered 64 per cent of teachers. Beneficiaries of state funds numbered about 32,000 (*Social Security Bulletin*, March, 1938, pp. 8–9).

[2] U. S. Bureau of Labor Statistics, *Bulletin 489* (1929), p. 233.   Eleven states and about 6,000 beneficiaries in 1937 (*Social Security Bulletin*, March, 1938, p. 8).

The Federal employees in all classified branches in the civil service and certain other specific Federal employees are now protected in their old age by a compulsory, contributory insurance system enacted in 1920 and amended in 1926. The employees regularly contribute 3.5 per cent of their salaries, which is sufficient to meet all but the costs of administration and part of the original accrued liability which the Federal Government makes up.[1] At least fifteen years' service and the attainment of a specified age, usually seventy years, are necessary to qualify an employee for retirement. Disability retirement is sometimes permitted after fifteen years of service. The amount of the annuity depends upon the employee's salary for the last ten years and the length of service, with a maximum of $1,000 a year. As in the case of most contributory systems, if the employee withdraws from service, his contributions are refunded. This legislation of various kinds has applied only to special groups of government employees, and only within the last fifteen or twenty years has the movement for legislation covering the general population made any real progress.

Early Old-Age-Assistance Legislation by the States.—In 1915 an old-age pension law for Alaska was enacted which, in amended form, is still in effect. In the same year Arizona enacted an old-age-pension measure and abolished the almshouses, but the act was declared unconstitutional.[2] It was not until 1923 that Montana passed the first state pension law remaining effective. Despite adverse court decisions the number of states with general old-age-pension laws slowly increased until in 1929 there were ten states and Alaska with such laws. The depression after 1929 increased the number of dependent aged and clearly revealed the need for effective social legislation. As has often been the case in times of economic depression, there was a revival of political and social reform measures. In the field of old-age security this movement resulted in the enactment of pension legislation in a rapidly increasing number of states, and culminated in 1935 in the Social Security Act, Titles I and II of which relate to old-age security. This Federal legislation will be discussed presently, following a summary of the development and operation of the state legislation preceding it.

All of the state acts provided for noncontributory pensions limited to those citizens who could meet certain age and residence requirements, who had no children able to support them, and who were unable to maintain themselves. The pensions were therefore a substitute for poor relief for those persons who could qualify for them. A feature of most of the laws, which caused them to resemble poor relief even more closely,

---

[1] U. S. Bureau of Labor Statistics, *Bulletin 489* (1929), pp. 219–220.

[2] *Board of Control of the State of Arizona and Charles P. Osburn, Appellants v. L. H. Buckstegge*, 18 Ariz. 277, 158 Pac. 837 (1916).

was that the amount of the pension, within a maximum figure, was left indefinite and was determined by need. In many states, *e.g.*, California, New York, and Massachusetts, the pensions were administered by the regular poor-relief officials (with state supervision), but some states in an endeavor to avoid the appearance of relief, followed Wisconsin's example of separate administration of pensions and regular poor relief.[1] Whatever the administration, the pensions were admittedly not general pensions, but a means of more adequately and humanely giving poor relief.[2] In some states, *e.g.*, New York, some applications for pensions were denied because the persons were members of family groups in receipt of relief and it was thought advisable not to have two separate grants in the same family.[3] In Michigan in the first year of the pension law roughly two-thirds of the applicants had been receiving relief from the Emergency Relief authorities.[4] Under such circumstances the provision for old-age security through the grant of pensions to the dependent aged and that of regular poor relief were closely interwoven.

By the end of 1934, old-age assistance or pension laws had been enacted in twenty-eight states, including all industrial states and all northern states except South Dakota and Kansas, and also in Alaska and Hawaii. The number of states enacting this type of legislation is rather surprising even when it is considered that the laws were primarily relief measures. The gradual increase in effectiveness of the laws was also noteworthy.

The early (until 1929) acts threw the whole burden of administration and all of the costs on the counties and gave them the option of rejection or adoption of the pension system. The result was that few counties adopted a pension plan, but instead continued to support poorhouses and to provide outdoor relief. This was in spite of the fact that in every state except Kentucky the average pension paid was less than the cost of maintaining an almshouse inmate. Some progress was made, however, especially in Montana and Wisconsin, which by 1929 were paying pensions to 666 and 264 persons, respectively. In that year the other four states with optional pension plans paid pensions to only seventy-three persons. The depression greatly increased the financial pressure on the counties. Few of them were inclined to incur new types of obligations, and some of them stopped payment of pensions altogether. At the end of 1932, after ten years of operation, forty-four out of fifty-six counties in Montana, with 81 per cent of the state's population, were paying pensions. The other states with optional plans lagged far behind

---

[1] In many cases the laws enacted during the depression were frankly passed as, and called, relief measures.

[2] New York report, p. 222.

[3] American Association for Social Security, *Record of the Seventh National Conference on Social Security* (1934), p. 34.

[4] *Ibid.*, p. 67.

this record. In Wisconsin, nine out of seventy-one counties, in Minnesota five out of eighty-seven counties, in Colorado four out of sixty-three counties, were operating under their state pension plans. In Maryland only one county in twenty-four had made pension appropriations, but that county included Baltimore with 49.3 per cent of the population of the state. In Kentucky three counties out of 120 were paying pensions in 1928, but none paid pensions by 1933. In Nevada and West Virginia less than 3 per cent of the population was covered. At the end of 1932, in the seven states whose laws were then optional, only 28 per cent of the population was covered in contrast to 91 per cent in the states with mandatory laws.[1]

The optional laws were clearly ineffective as a means of providing old-age security. After 1929, however, all of the state laws enacted except in Florida and West Virginia were mandatory upon the counties.[2] But the states could not require the counties to pay old-age assistance when they were financially unable to do so, and to an increasing extent the states assumed the burden of payment. In Massachusetts the state paid one-third, the county two-thirds. California and New York required the counties to pay only one-half of the total. The New Jersey law of 1931 placed the state's share at three-fourths, while Delaware (1931) was the first state to assume the entire cost of its pension plan.

The increase in effectiveness of the state-wide plans was apparent almost immediately. As compared with 1931, the year 1932 showed an increase of nearly 35 per cent in the number of pensioners and 40 per cent in the amount disbursed. New York State, however, with 54,185 of the 102,537 pensioners and $15,454,308 of the $22,616,004 disbursed, accounted for the preponderant part of this increase.[3]

By the end of 1934, pension plans were in operation in twenty-five states[4] and two territories—with 56 per cent of the population of the United States. In states with optional laws, counties having the laws in effect included only 48.2 per cent of the population, while in states with mandatory laws the coverage was 93.5 per cent. The optional acts in Kentucky and West Virginia remained without effect in 1934, as they had in 1933, while the Maine act of 1933 was rendered inoperative through the failure of the legislature to provide funds. In many of the states the financial provision made for pensions proved to be inadequate. Special taxes failed to yield expected revenues,[5] or appropriations from general

---

[1] *Monthly Labor Review*, vol. 37 (1933), p. 257.

[2] The Hawaiian Act of 1933 was also optional.

[3] Statistics of the operation of old-age-assistance plans for the year 1932 may be found in the *Monthly Labor Review*, vol. 37 (1933), pp. 253–262.

[4] The laws of Kentucky, Maine, and West Virginia were not operative.

[5] These special taxes included per capita taxes in Nebraska, Iowa, and Michigan. In Colorado and Pennsylvania several special fees and levies were used, while in New Jersey

funds were too small to meet the needs of an increased number of persons eligible for assistance. The extreme case was presented by North Dakota, where the average monthly pension paid to the 3,914 pensioners in 1934 was only sixty-nine cents. The pensions in a number of other states, including Nebraska with a monthly average of $1.22 and Indiana with a monthly average of $4.50, were only less inadequate.

TABLE 50.—OPERATION UNDER STATE OLD-AGE-PENSION ACTS DURING 1934[1]

State	Law enacted in	Funds supplied by	No. of eligible age	No. of pensioners (end of 1934)	Amount disbursed	Monthly pension	
						Maximum payable	Average paid in 1934
Arizona	1933	State and county	9,118	1,820	$ 427,527	$30.00	$19.57
California	1929	State and county	210,379	19,619	4,288,508	30.00	20.21
Colorado	1927	State and county	61,787	10,098	1,256,190	30.00	9.74
Delaware	1931	State	16,678	1,583	193,231	25.00	9.91
Idaho	1931	County	22,310	1,712	138,440	25.00	6.74
Indiana	1933	State and county	138,426	23,533	1,134,250	15.00	4.50
Iowa	1934	State	184,239	8,300	220,000	25.00	13.25
Kentucky	1926	County	84,252	......	....	20.83	
Maine	1933	State and city	69,010	......	....	30.00	
Maryland	1927	County	92,972	267	65,228	30.00	24.43
Massachusetts	1930	State and city	156,590	21,473	5,628,492	a	26.08
Michigan	1933	State	148,853	3,557	103,180	30.00	9.99
Minnesota	1929	County	94,401	4,425	577,635	30.00	10.97
Montana	1923	County	14,377	2,780	177,426	25.00	5.32
Nebraska	1933	County	86,194	926	13,577	20.00	1.22
Nevada	1925	County	4,814	7	1,552	30.00	18.48
New Hampshire	1931	County	25,714	1,483	311,829	32.50	17.51
New Jersey	1931	State and county	112,594	11,401	1,773,320	30.00	14.87
New York	1930	State and county	373,878	51,834	12,650,828	a	20.65
North Dakota	1933	State	30,280	3,914	24,259	12.50	0.69
Ohio	1933	State	414,836	36,543	1,434,416	25.00	6.54
Oregon	1933	County	39,133	6,525	639,296	30.00	8.16
Pennsylvania	1933	State	289,706	18,261	386,717	30.00	21.18
Utah	1929	County	22,665	902	86,416	25.00	7.98
Washington	1933	County	101,503	1,588	103,408	30.00	5.43
West Virginia	1931	County	73,043	......	....	30.00	
Wisconsin	1925	State and county	112,112	2,127	459,146	30.00	19.95
Wyoming	1929	County	8,707	719	82,732	30.00	9.59
All states	......	....	2,998,570	235,397	$32,177,603	......	$14.68
Alaska	1915	Territory	2,935	454	108,485	$35.00	25.00
Hawaii	1933	County	7,638	354	27,427	15.00	7.06
All	......	....	3,009,143	236,205	$32,313,515	......	$14.69

a No limit.

[1] Data drawn from Report of Committee on Economic Security; *Monthly Labor Review*, vol. 41 (1935), pp. 304–313; and statutes. *Cf.* Marie Stevenson in *Law and Contemporary Problems*, vol. 3 (1936), p. 240.

the funds came from an inheritance tax. The most common and relatively more successful method was an appropriation from the general fund.

[1] The Social Security Act, Public no. 271, 74th Congress, 1st Session, approved Aug. 14, 1935.

Despite these difficulties, which are at least in part explained by the terrific pressure of the depression upon the state and local revenue systems, the progress made during 1933 and 1934 was far from negligible. In the latter year the number of persons who received old-age assistance increased to 236,205 and the amount paid to $32,313,515. True, the average monthly pension paid in 1934 was only $14.69 as compared with $19.33 in 1933, but this is explained more by the low averages in the states with newly effective laws than by a decline in average in the states paying pensions in 1933. Pensions paid in the southern and poorer agricultural states would be expected to be smaller than those paid in the northern and industrial states.

Table 50 is introduced on page 381 to show the states having pension laws in 1934, the year legislation was enacted, whether funds were supplied by state or local government or both, and the operation of the pension systems in 1934.

The Social Security Act and Old-Age Assistance.—Although there had been an encouraging increase in the number of states adopting old-age-assistance legislation, there was little prospect of the adoption of effective legislation in some of the states, and undesirable differences persisted in the laws in effect. Advocates of more uniform and effective legislation succeeded, in 1935, in securing the adoption by the Federal Congress of the Social Security Act,[1] Title I of which provides "Grants to States for Old Age Assistance." Section 3(a) of that act reads:

"From the sums appropriated therefor, the Secretary of the Treasury shall pay to each State which has an approved plan for old-age assistance, for each quarter, beginning with the quarter commencing July 1, 1935, (1) an amount which shall be used exclusively as old-age assistance, equal to one-half of the total of the sums expended during such quarter as old-age assistance under the State plan with respect to each individual who at the time of such expenditure is sixty-five years of age or older and is not an inmate of a public institution, not counting so much of such expenditure with respect to any individual for any month as exceeds $30, and (2) 5 per centum of such amount, which shall be used for paying the costs of administering the State plan or for old-age assistance or both, and for no other purpose: *Provided*, That the State plan, in order to be approved by the Board, need not provide for financial participation before July 1, 1937, by the State, in the case of any State which the Board, upon application by the State and after reasonable notice and opportunity for hearing to the State, finds is prevented by its constitution from providing such financial participation."

In order to be approved, the state act must, under Section 2a:

"(1) provide that it shall be in effect in all political subdivisions of the State, and, if administered by them, be mandatory upon them; (2) provide for financial participation by the State; (3) either provide for the establishment or designation of a single State agency to administer the plan, or provide for the establishment or designation of a single State agency to supervise the administration of the plan; (4) provide for granting to any individual, whose claim for old-age assistance is denied, an opportunity for a fair hearing before such State agency; (5) provide such methods of administration (other than those relating to selection, tenure of office, and compensation of personnel) as are found by the Board to be necessary for the efficient operation of the plan; (6) provide that the State agency will make such reports, in such form and containing such information, as the Board may from time to time require, and comply with such provisions as the Board may from time to time find necessary to assure the correctness and verification of such reports; and (7) provide that, if the State or any of its political subdivisions collects from the estate of any recipient of old-age assistance any amount with respect to old-age assistance furnished him under the plan, one-half of the net amount so collected shall be promptly paid to the United States. Any payment so made shall be deposited in the Treasury to the credit of the appropriation for the purposes of this title.

"2(b) The Board shall approve any plan which fulfills the conditions specified in subsection (a), except that it shall not approve any plan which imposes, as a condition of eligibility for old-age assistance under the plan—

"(1) An age requirement of more than sixty-five years except that the plan may impose, effective until January 1, 1940, an age requirement of as much as seventy years; or

"(2) Any residence requirement which excludes any resident of the State who has resided therein five years during the nine years immediately preceding the application for old-age assistance and has resided therein continuously for one year immediately preceding the application; or

"(3) Any citizenship requirement which excludes any citizen of the United States."

These standards and limitations imposed fall considerably short of those provided for in the original bill recommended by the Committee on Economic Security and the President. Among the amendments made was one to the effect that the Social Security Board established shall have nothing to say about the selection, tenure of office, and compensation of personnel concerned with the administration of old-age assistance in the states. Another, except for the limitations relating to age, residence, and citizenship imposed by the Act, leaves the states free to make such further restrictions as they choose, whereas the original bill had forbidden further restrictions than those specified in it. Still another, and very important, change made was by striking from the original bill the requirement that the old-age assistance grants must be sufficient, with other income, to provide "a reasonable subsistence, compatible with decency and health," thus setting no standard whatever to be observed. As Professor Witte says,[1] "As the act stands, the Social Security Board can neither review the old age assistance grants in individual cases nor object to the administration in any state because its average grants are ridiculously low."

These amendments greatly weakened the part of the Act relating to old-age assistance. Yet, in a very real sense, the requirements of the Act represent an attempt to eliminate defects which experience had shown to be of importance under state laws. Although there had been a distinct tendency for the states to liberalize their laws in respect to requirements for eligibility, none of those which had adopted legislation up to the time of the proposed Federal legislation was able to meet all the requirements for Federal approval.

The state laws had usually required long periods of residence in the state as a condition of eligibility. Only Delaware had a residence requirement as short as five years; in most states fifteen years of residence was required; the extreme in this respect was the Arizona law, which required a residence of thirty-five years. The purpose of such a requirement, of course, was to protect the state against the migrations of elderly people from states which did not grant pensions. While these residence requirements did not greatly reduce the number eligible for pensions,[2] they were much longer than necessary when the legislation became more general. Ten states, however, had before the end of 1935 changed their residence requirements to conform to the provisions of the Social Security Act. Indeed, a number of states replaced their old laws with new ones[3] and several which had not theretofore adopted pension plans enacted laws because of the inducement given by the Act. By April 1, 1937, approved old-age statutes were in operation in forty states, in the District of Columbia, and in Hawaii. Three months later, in July, 1937, approved plans were found in forty-six states and three territories.[4] By the first part of 1938, South Carolina's law had been passed and approved and Virginia had enacted a law.

Because of the absence of direct or indirect control of standards to be observed in the granting of assistance, it is important to make some observations on the more important characteristics of the laws, the amount of assistance which may be granted, and the operations under the legislation in effect in the early part of 1937.

---

[1] Edwin E. Witte, "Old Age Security in the Social Security Act," *Journal of Political Economy*, vol. 45 (1937), p. 5.

[2] In Massachusetts, for example, it was found that 92.3 per cent of the nondependents sixty-five years of age and over had lived in that state twenty-five years or more. Massachusetts report, p. 72.

[3] For example, Maryland, Minnesota, Montana, Oregon, Washington, and Wyoming.

[4] *Social Security Board Release*, July 13, 1937.

The maximum pension is most frequently fixed at $30 per month, or $1 per day. Such a limitation prevails in thirty-one states with approved plans.[1] In Delaware and Iowa, the maximum is $25, in Kentucky and Mississippi, $15 per month. One state, California, has a maximum of $35; another, Colorado, by referendum vote in 1936, established a maximum of $45. The remaining states (Arkansas, Louisiana, Massachusetts, Montana, New York, and also the District of Columbia) have no statutory limit; assistance is to be given according to need, provided, of course, funds are available. In all the laws except those of four states, no minimum pension is fixed. Of the latter, Delaware and Nebraska stipulate a minimum of $5 per month, while the California and Massachusetts laws provide that old-age assistance and other income shall not be less than $20 and $30, respectively. Property and income limitations, found in most of the laws, vary widely; a majority provide that a person must not have disposed of property in order to qualify for assistance.

The objective of assistance, and that only, remains in the law. Yet assistance has been liberalized in the more recent legislation and no doubt frequently in the administration of unchanged legislation. It is presumably granted with an application of a means test; the difference between the means one possesses and his needs, or the maximum fixed by law, is granted, funds being available. Yet it would appear that in some jurisdictions assistance is administered much as though it was a pension in stipulated sum. Liberalization is found in a measure also in changes in the obligations of offspring and other relatives of the aged person in need. It is still true, however, that the restrictions in this connection are greater than those found in effect under foreign pension systems. It is very questionable whether any income or property save that of the applicant or spouse should be considered in an application of the means test.[2]

It was expected that the Social Security Act would cause the assistance granted to be more nearly adequate than it had been without Federal aid. Yet there was the possibility that the Federal aid extended would be used merely or largely to relieve state and local treasuries of a part of the burdens they had assumed. Table 51 shows, by states, for April, 1937, the number of individuals receiving old-age assistance, the number of recipients per 1,000 estimated population sixty-five and over, the total of payments made, and the average per recipient.

[1] These and other details may be found in a tabular analysis prepared by the Social Security Board, Publication 16, *Characteristics of State Plans for Old-Age Assistance*, as of Apr. 1, 1937.

[2] See Twentieth Century Fund, *More Security for Old Age* (1937), pp. 111–113, where "The Committee recommends . . . that in determining eligibility for old-age assistance the states be required to take into account only the income of the applicant and spouse, if any, irrespective of the capacity of other relatives to support him. . . . "

Unfortunately, the comparisons to be properly made between data presented in this table are limited in number for, in several states, such

TABLE 51.—OLD-AGE ASSISTANCE DURING APRIL, 1937[1]

States with approved plans	No. of individuals receiving assistance	Total payments to individuals during the month	Average per recipient	No. of recipients per 1,000 estimated population 65 and over[a]
All states....................	1,297,321	$24,272,824	$18.71	186
1. Alabama.....................	10,553	120,103	11.38	87
2. Arkansas.....................	14,808	133,930	9.04	159
3. California....................	73,691	2,311,704	31.37	167
4. Colorado.....................	28,614	791,166	27.65	400
5. Connecticut..................	13,101	332,860	25.41	115
6. Delaware....................	3,000	32,099	10.70	146
7. District of Columbia...........	2,160	54,454	25.21	55
8. Florida......................	9,949	112,544	11.31	110
9. Hawaii......................	596	8,488	14.24	57
10. Idaho.......................	8,302	192,707	23.21	302
11. Illinois.....................	120,317	1,982,754	16.48	247
12. Indiana.....................	37,855	578,725	15.29	135
13. Iowa.......................	33,175	492,072	14.83	156
14. Kentucky...................	24,887	248,465	9.98	140
15. Louisiana...................	18,256	210,699	11.54	212
16. Maine......................	3,732	74,720	20.02	45
17. Maryland...................	12,988	223,008	17.17	121
18. Massachusetts...............	56,705	1,520,037	26.81	177
19. Michigan...................	34,463	577,467	16.76	123
20. Minnesota..................	60,568	1,164,557	19.23	321
21. Mississippi..................	17,780	72,598	4.08	205
22. Missouri....................	53,582	611,866	11.42	178
23. Montana....................	9,575	198,566	20.74	324
24. Nebraska...................	26,465	483,771	18.28	277
25. New Hampshire..............	3,348	72,922	21.78	65
26. New Jersey.................	23,507	391,930	16.67	97
27. New Mexico.................	3,268	31,987	9.79	174
28. New York..................	91,662	2,016,629	22.17	119
29. North Dakota...............	6,845	110,995	16.22	194
30. Ohio.......................	103,969	2,361,829	22.72	221
31. Oklahoma..................	59,619	881,658	14.79	517
32. Oregon....................	12,493	266,359	21.32	154
33. Pennsylvania...............	81,097	1,768,491	21.81	134
34. Rhode Island...............	4,093	72,052	17.60	92
35. South Dakota...............	9,400	176,581	18.78	227
36. Texas......................	127,772	1,784,005	13.96	464
37. Utah.......................	6,283	142,230	22.64	243
38. Vermont....................	3,900	46,492	11.92	105
39. Washington.................	30,694	631,086	20.56	262
40. West Virginia...............	15,718	240,909	15.33	180
41. Wisconsin..................	35,815	690,477	19.28	168
42. Wyoming...................	2,716	56,832	20.92	268

[a] Based on population estimates of the U. S. Bureau of the Census as of January 1, 1937.
[1] Social Security Board, *Public Assistance Monthly Statistics for the United States*, vol. 2, no. 4 (April, 1937).

as Illinois, the eligibility of many applicants had not been passed on. The ratios per 1,000, therefore, have limited meaning, and the same is true of the total paid out state by state. The table does show, however, a total of 1,297,321 individuals in these forty states, the District of Columbia, and Hawaii receiving assistance as against 236,205 in the several states and territories at the end of 1934. Taking states with assistance granted both in 1934 and in April, 1937, the totals are found to have increased from 233,924 to 828,763. It will be noted that the average monthly allowance, which had been $14.69 in 1934, was $18.71 in April, 1937. A comparison of data in Table 51 with those for 1934 (Table 50) shows that in a few states, such as New York and Massachusetts, which had had acceptable standards all the while, the average allowance changed little. The Federal aid was used to care for more aged persons or to reduce the burden on state funds. A great majority of the states, however, were enabled to spend more of their own funds and to increase the average monthly grant by from 50 to more than several hundred per cent. It is evident that in numerous instances low standards were replaced by much better if not adequate standards.[1] Yet a glance at Table 51 suffices to show that there are not a few states which, with every allowance made for the possession of some income by needy persons and for the cost of living, are maintaining low standards while receiving Federal aid. In a considerable number of areas old-age assistance is not on the level contemplated by the Committee on Economic Security. On the other hand, evidence is accumulating showing that as the laws are being liberalized and politics and inefficiency enter into the administration of them, old-age assistance is accompanied by much waste, encroaching upon funds needed for relief and other purposes and tending to provoke protest against plans for social security.[2] Partly because of the influence of Federal matching of funds, partly because of the influence of Townsendism, partly because of political aspirations, and partly because of the American trait of going too far when once an idea has been accepted, much questionable legislation has received and is receiving serious consideration in a number of the states. Even more important, the administration is more frequently lax than otherwise and, in not a few cases, controlled by political considerations. Hence, we find in such states as Oklahoma, Texas, and Colorado surprisingly large percentages

---

[1] Note the averages in these states: California, $20.21 and $31.37; Colorado, $9.74 and $27.65; Idaho, $6.74 and $23.21; Indiana, $4.50 and $15.29; Michigan, $9.99 and $16.76; Minnesota, $10.97 and $19.23; Montana, $5.32 and $20.74; Nebraska, $1.22 and $18.28, Ohio, $6.54 and $22.72; Oregon, $8.16 and $21.32; Utah, $7.98 and $22.64; Washington, $5.43 and $20.56; Wyoming, $9.59 and $20.92. (See Tables 50 and 51.)

[2] See A. Epstein, "Killing Old Age Security with Kindness," *Harper's Magazine*, July, 1937, pp. 182-192. Note, also, the requirements made by the Social Security Board as a condition of continuing the extension of Federal aid to Illinois and Oklahoma, where the laws were laxly administered. In December, 1937, in the latter state, 60 per cent of the residents over 65 years of age were receiving pensions, the average monthly pension being $39.61.

of those past sixty-five on the pension lists.[1] We find, also, in many places the means of eligibles not adequately investigated and the advances granted larger than contemplated by law.

Railway Employees Retirement Acts.—All of the state legislation has provided for "noncontributory pensions" or assistance. Except in making provision for superannuated public employees, the one departure from this type of legislation previous to the enactment of the Social Security Act is found in the Railroad Employees Retirement Acts. This legislation will be discussed briefly before attention is directed to the system of Federal Old-Age Benefits provided for in the Social Security Act.

In 1934 Congress legislated to establish a compulsory pension and retirement system for all railway, express, and Pullman employees. The situation to be met was more acute than that found among wage earners in general, because, with the number of persons engaged in railway work decreasing for years and with seniority rules generally applied, a very disproportionate number of those employed were old men. Because of the many younger men on furlough and because of the fear that the large number of older persons among those at work had been or would be a tax on safety and efficiency, it was desired to hasten retirements. But if retirements were to be hastened, pension legislation was necessary, for the private pension plans which were in effect on railways employing 86 per cent of the workers had been adversely affected by the depression and many of them were in danger of being abandoned or abridged.

The Act[2] provided for the compulsory retirement of employees at age sixty-five unless, by agreement, year by year, but not to exceed five, they were continued in employment. Retirement before sixty-five remained, of course, voluntary. The pension provided was based upon years of service and rate of pay, any excess over $300 per month not to be considered in computing "annuities." The monthly annuity in each case was to be equal to the number of years of service (but not to exceed thirty) multiplied by 2 per cent of the first $50 of the average monthly wage, 1.5 per cent of the next $100, and 1 per cent of the next $150.[3] In no case was the monthly grant to exceed $120. Such pensions were to be made available at once to employees retiring, including persons

---

[1] See Table 51, p. 386. More recently a maximum pension of $45 per month has become effective in Colorado. It is currently reported (December, 1937) that the state is paying out almost $1,500,000 per month for old-age pensions while some forty state departments and ten educational institutions are in a precarious financial condition.

[2] Public no. 485, 73d Congress, 2nd Session, Chap. 868 (S. 3231), June 27, 1934.

[3] Thus a superannuated worker, who had been in service thirty years and whose average basic wage had been $175 per month, would be entitled to a monthly annuity of $97.50. If, however, he had been employed only ten years, his annuity would be only one-third as much, or $32.50 per month.

not on the payroll but employed within the year preceding the enactment of the law.   The cost of these pensions the first year was estimated at $90,000,000.

The system established was contributory, self-sustaining, and of the pay-as-you-go type.   To explain, the employee's contribution was to be 2 per cent of wages, the employer's contribution twice as much.   If, however, the revenues became inadequate, these taxes could be increased by the Railway Retirement Board, which was established to administer the system, for it was empowered to alter rates of contribution in order to maintain solvency of the fund.   No government contribution or subsidy was added; no large reserve was required.[1]   Finally, it may be noted that all contributions were to be paid into a central, pooled fund. This was designed to give stability and to guarantee annuitants equal treatment.   Without this pooling arrangement neither stability nor equal treatment could be realized, for the positions of the carriers and their employees differed widely.

This railway pension act was contested in the courts, and, upon appeal by the Government from an adverse lower-court decision, the law was declared invalid by the Supreme Court of the United States.[2]   The Court, however, divided five to four.   The majority were of the opinion that there was no such relation between pensions and contented employees on the one hand and interstate transportation on the other as would give Congress the necessary power.   Speaking of the purposes of the legislation, the majority asked, and answered, this question: "Is it not apparent that they [pensions] are really and essentially related solely to the social welfare of the worker, and therefore remote from any regulation of commerce as such?   We think the answer is plain.   These matters obviously lie outside the orbit of Congressional power."[3]   But Chief Justice Hughes in his dissenting opinion, among other things, challenged this view and called attention to the responsibilities of the service and also to the Court's ruling in workmen's compensation cases.[4]   He asked:

"What sound distinction, from a constitutional standpoint, is there between compelling reasonable compensation for those injured without any fault of the employer and requiring a fair allowance for those who practically give their lives to the service and are incapacitated by the wear and tear of time, the attrition of the years?   I perceive no constitutional ground upon which the one can be upheld and the other condemned.

[1] With pensions made immediately available and with such a high proportion of old persons among employees, there was no occasion for a large reserve.

[2] *Railroad Retirement Board et al. v. Alton Railroad Co. et al.*, 295 U. S. 330 (1935). The dissenting members of the Court were Hughes, Brandeis, Stone, and Cardozo.   The Chief Justice presented the dissenting opinion of the four.

[3] *Ibid.*, at p. 368.

[4] *Supra*, Chap. IV, pp. 194–197.

"The fundamental consideration which supports this type of legislation is that industry should take care of its human wastage, whether that is due to accident or age. That view cannot be dismissed as arbitrary or capricious. It is a reasoned conviction based upon abundant experience. The expression of that conviction in law is regulation. When expressed in the government of interstate carriers, with respect to their employees likewise engaged in interstate commerce, it is a regulation of that commerce. As such, so far as the subject matter is concerned, the commerce clause should be held applicable."[1]

A very important ruling of the Court was that the pooling arrangement was unconstitutional because it denied due process of law to carriers discriminated against. The discrimination was found in treating all carriers as a single employer regardless of their individual obligations and the varying conditions found in their respective enterprises.

The Chief Justice, however, found in Supreme Court decisions precedents adequate to support such a pooling arrangement. The accident-insurance law of the state of Washington had been sustained.[2] The Court described that law as so operating (because a class of employment was treated as a whole, and not by firm) that "the enforced contributions of the employer are to be made whether injuries have befallen his own employees or not, so that however prudently one may manage his business, even to the point of immunity to his employees from accidental injury or death, he nevertheless is required to make periodical contributions to a fund for making compensation to the injured employees of his perhaps negligent competitors."[3] The Chief Justice also called attention to the facts that legislation levying assessments on banks for guarantee of deposits,[4] and that the recapture clause of the Transportation Act[5] had been sustained. He concluded:[6]

"This object of adequately maintaining the whole transportation system may be served in more than these two ways. The underlying principle is that Congress has the power to treat the transportation system of the country as a unit for the purpose of regulation in the public interest, so long as particular railroad properties are not subjected to confiscation. In the light of that principle, and of applications which have been held valid, I am unable to see that the establishment of a unitary system of retirement allowances for employees is beyond constitutional authority. Congress was entitled to weigh the advantages of such a system, as against inequalities which it would inevitably produce,

---

[1] 295 U. S., at p. 384.

[2] In *Mountain Timber Co. v. Washington*, 243 U. S. 219 (1917).

[3] 295 U. S., at p. 385.

[4] *Noble State Bank v. Haskell*, 219 U. S. 104 (1910).

[5] *Dayton-Goose Creek Railway Co. v. United States Interstate Commerce Commission et al.*, 263 U. S. 456 (1923).

[6] 295 U. S., at p. 387.

and reach a conclusion as to the policy best suited to the needs of the country."

Those commented on were the main points involved in the decision. It may be added, however, that the Court, with reason, called attention to and criticized the requirements that pensions were to be paid to persons no longer employed—some of whom had been discharged and were perhaps now elsewhere employed—to those who might be discharged for cause, and to those on the eve of retirement who had made no contribution.

In view of the position of the Court that such legislation could not be regarded as a proper exercise of the power to regulate commerce, the Congress in 1935 enacted new legislation: the Railroad Retirement Act,[1] which created a retirement pension system, based upon the power to appropriate funds, and the Carriers Taxing Act[2] for raising the necessary pension revenues, based upon the power to levy excise taxes. Two changes in the substantive provisions of the law may be noted. In the Retirement Act, former employees were excluded from those eligible for pensions. In the latter Act, of more interest, was an excise tax of 3.5 per cent on the payrolls of employers and an equal amount on the wages of employees, as under the Social Security Act. The strategy was to separate the two phases of the matter in the hope that the collection of the taxes would not be forbidden because not directly connected with the payment of annuities. However, on June 26, 1936, the United States District Court for the District of Columbia declared the tax act unconstitutional[3] on the same grounds as in the Alton case; viz., as transcending the powers of Congress, and ordered that until the case was finally determined the funds collected should be held in a special account. The Court, in an oral clarification of the original decision,[4] subsequently explained that its decision did not apply to the Retirement Act nor was the government prevented from paying pensions from general government funds since that Act had authorized appropriation from the Treasury to carry the Act into operation. Consequently, in July, 1936, the Railroad Retirement Board, acting upon the oral statement of the Court, began paying pensions to eligible employees.

In order to remedy the situation and work out a substitute pension system, the representatives of the twenty-one standard railroad labor unions and the railway managements, acting upon the suggestion of the President, met and in March, 1937, agreed upon a new retirement plan.[5] With some adjustments, the plan agreed upon was accepted by Con-

---

[1] Public no. 399, 74th Congress, 1st Session, approved Aug. 29, 1935.

[2] Public no. 400, 74th Congress, 1st Session, approved Aug. 29, 1935.

[3] *Alton Railroad Co. et al. v. Railroad Retirement Board et al.*, 16 Fed. Sup. 955.

[4] *Monthly Labor Review*, vol. 43, no. 2 (August, 1936), p. 329.

[5] For provisions of the new plan, see *Monthly Labor Review*, vol. 44, no. 5 (May, 1937), pp. 1126–1127.

gress.[1]   The provisions relating to contributions by carrier and employee are 2.75 per cent of payroll or wage for the first three years from 1937 to 1939, 3, 3.25, and 3.5 per cent, respectively, for the succeeding three-year periods, and 3.75 per cent beginning in 1949.   Annuity privileges for employee representatives of employee organizations are provided through a tax, ranging from 5.5 per cent in 1937 to 7.5 per cent in 1949, levied on the incomes of those representatives whose monthly salaries are not in excess of $300.   Voluntary retirement for pensioners is set at age sixty-five, or at age sixty after thirty years' service, the annuity, in the latter case, to be reduced by one-fifteenth for each year under sixty-five.   No credit is given for service after age sixty-five, though taxes continue during the additional years.   In case of total physical or mental disability, provision is made for retirement, after thirty years' service, with full annuity privileges.   In addition, there is provision for an optional joint and survivor annuity and also for death benefits amounting to 4 per cent of aggregate earned compensation less annuities received, payable to the heirs or estate of the deceased employee.   The maximum monthly annuity remains, as before, at $120, while a minimum annuity is provided for employees with at least twenty years' service, based on a graduated scale of percentages of the monthly compensation, with the stipulation that it shall not be less than would be payable under the Social Security Act.   However, no annuity will be paid to any employee who retires and then engages in regular gainful employment in some other line of work.   The new plan covers approximately 1,500,000 employees of railroads, express companies, sleeping-car companies, and their subsidiaries, and also includes employees of railroad associations and of railroad labor organizations who, under the Railroad Retirement Act of 1935, are excluded from the provisions for old-age benefits under the Social Security Act.

Social Security Act and Old-Age Benefits.—The Social Security Act extends this type of old-age security to some 37,000,000[2] workers, or approximately three-fifths of those normally gainfully occupied.   With stated exceptions, it covers all persons who are employed in the United States subsequent to Dec. 1, 1936.   The most important exceptions are self-employed persons, owners, and operators; agricultural labor; domestic servants; casual workers; employees of Federal, state, or local governments; also those employed on any vessel or by any nonprofit-making religious, charitable, or educational institution.   It may be noted that in this part of the Act there are no numerical limitations (number of

---

[1] The Railroad Retirement Act of 1935 was amended by the Railroad Retirement Act of 1937 (Public no. 162, 75th Congress, 1st Session, approved June 24, 1937).   The Carriers Taxing Act of 1937 (Public no 174, 75th Congress, 1st Session, approved June 29, 1937) repealed the previous Taxing Act.

[2] The approximate number of insured persons to whom numbers had been assigned by February, 1938.

employees per plant) such as are found in the provision for unemployment compensation or such as are found in workmen's compensation acts.

The major benefit to eligible persons provided for in Title I of the Act is a monthly retirement allowance. Professor Witte's excellent summary may be quoted:[1]

"To be eligible to this monthly benefit the applicant must have worked for wages for at least five years subsequent to December 31, 1936, and have earned after this date a minimum total of $2,000 in employments other than those specifically excluded. He must also be at least 65 years of age and have retired from his usual occupation. . . .

"The amount of . . . old age benefits is based upon the wages earned subsequent to December 31, 1936, and before attainment of age 65, in employments not specifically excluded. . . . If the total wages earned are between $2,000 and $3,000, the monthly benefit rate is one-half of one per cent of the total wages. If the total wages exceed $3,000, the monthly rate is a sum arrived at by adding together one-half of one per cent of the first $3,000, one-twelfth of one per cent of the excess above $3,000 up to $45,000, and one-twenty-fourth of one per cent of the excess above $45,000. The minimum monthly retirement allowance is $10, the maximum $85. . . .[2]

"If eligible persons die prior to becoming 65 years of age, a lump sum benefit is paid to their estates equal to 3.5 per cent of their total wages subsequent to December 31, 1936. The same benefit is paid to employees who on attaining age 65 cannot establish that they earned at least $2,000 subsequent to December 31, 1936, or were not employed for at least five days in each of five years after this date. If employees die after retirement, but before they have drawn at least 3.5 per cent of their total wages in monthly benefit payments, their estate is entitled to the difference between this amount and the payments they received during their lifetime."

Because of the position taken in the Railway Pensions case, Title VIII of the Social Security Act, providing for an excise tax on payrolls in employments falling within the Act, was made separable from, and from a legal point of view was expected to be quite independent of the parts of, the measure relating to benefits. The Act provides that the Congress shall make periodic appropriations to cover benefits and cost of administration. These may be made out of any funds available, but they are presumed to be financed from the proceeds of the payroll tax. The old-age benefit system, therefore, unlike the old-age assistance, is contributory. And, it may be added, the benefits are to be administered

---

[1] E. E. Witte, *op. cit.*, pp. 12–14.

[2] Thus, if one has in forty years earned a total of $50,000 in employments covered by the Act, his monthly benefit will be $15 (0.5 per cent of $3,000), plus $35 ($\frac{1}{12}$ of 1 per cent of $45,000 minus $3,000 or $42,000), plus $2.09 ($\frac{1}{24}$ of 1 per cent of $50,000 minus $45,000 or $5,000), a total of $52.09 per month.

entirely by the Social Security Board. The states have nothing whatever to do with it.

An employer in the branches of employment within the embrace of the Act is required to pay a tax on the entire wage earnings of his employees, except on the excess over $3,000 per year paid any person. The rate is 1 per cent per year for the calendar years 1937, 1938, and 1939; by three-year periods this rate is increased by 0.5 per cent until the full rate of 3 per cent is reached in 1949. These payments are to be charged against wages. On his own account, the employer pays the same sums. Hence, the old-age benefits are to be financed by equal contributions by the employee and his employer. Any reserve funds created by appropriation are to be invested in the obligations of the Federal Government or in other obligations guaranteed by the Government and are to bear interest at the rate of 3 per cent.

As enacted, the law will involve the expenditure of increasing sums because both the number of eligible persons and the average monthly benefit will increase more or less rapidly until about 1980. If the government (except to pay interest on reserve funds) makes no appropriations out of general revenues, it was estimated that it would be necessary to have a reserve fund of approximately 47 billion dollars by 1980[1] and the excise taxes were set at 6 per cent in order that this would be possible. There had been stout discussion of the wisdom of such a policy as over against one of the pay-as-you-go type. The Act itself, however, as Professor Witte points out,[2] left future Congresses practically unrestricted in financing the Federal old-age benefits as they might deem advisable. There is no contractual relation between the Government and the individual who pays taxes and on account of whom the employer pays equal sums. Congress is free to spend the revenues derived from the excise tax as it chooses and to find revenues to appropriate where and as it will. It can follow the policy of financing benefits with or without reserves. It was, however, expected that payroll tax revenues not currently needed would constitute a reserve and that the building up of a reserve out of the proceeds of a 6 per cent tax would cause the system to be self-sustaining without government aid from general revenues.[3]

---

[1] Forty-seven billions is only an estimate based upon certain assumptions such as that contribution and benefit rates remain unchanged for forty-three years, that average annual earnings will be $1,100 throughout the period, and that life expectancy remains unchanged. The actual reserve in 1980 might substantially differ from that figure were contribution and benefits left unchanged.

[2] E. E. Witte, op. cit., pp. 17–18.

[3] The Act provides [Sec. 201 (a)] that the Secretary of the Treasury shall submit each year to the Bureau of the Budget an estimate of the appropriations needed, the estimate to be "on a reserve basis in accordance with accepted actuarial principles." The Congress is authorized to appropriate each year for the Old-Age Reserve Account "an amount sufficient as an annual premium to provide for the payments required for old-age benefits."

Thus in the United States we now have a Federal-state system for extending assistance under a means test and a federal contributory system of old-age benefits. In fact, we have in military pensions a third system of considerable present and greater prospective importance—of greater prospective importance because of the inevitable tendency for military pensions to become service pensions, with more liberal payments. We now turn to a consideration of the issue of old-age assistance as against old-age insurance or benefits and to some of the questions raised in connection with the Social Security Act.

The chief disadvantages of a noncontributory system are that the general revenues must be increased to pay the bills, or new, special taxes introduced;[1] there may be doubt as to whether the needed funds will be appropriated year after year; in spite of any problems of finance, there is an inevitable tendency to lower the pensionable age, to increase the size of the pension, and to remove restrictions on eligibility. Moreover, "straight pensions," unless universal—and universal pensions would be enormously if not prohibitively costly—carry with them the taint of charity. A means test is applied. Inquiries must be made into property, income, family responsibility, and other details, and this is irritating. On the other hand, a system of noncontributory pensions can be made effective at once in meeting the problem of old age while a contributory system requires time. Moreover, it can be inclusive of all classes, while a contributory system cannot be because of administrative difficulties. Advocates of "straight pensions" claim for them greater "social justice"; the pensioners have by their service earned their pensions and these can be financed, not by taxes on the masses in the lower income groups, but by taxes levied according to ability to pay or by taxes needed to improve the distribution of wealth. Certainly, in spite of the difficulties involved in applying a means test, straight pensions are much simpler in administration than are benefits paid under a contributory plan. For, in the one case, the administrative authority needs to keep records only of applicants, pensioners, and payments made; in the other, the employer must keep records for each person employed and payments made on his account, and the government must keep corresponding records in great detail and for year after year. The work involved is enormously increased when, as in the United States and most other countries, contributions and benefits are based upon rates of wages and earnings, rather than taking, as in Great Britain, the form of flat rates. Though the problems presented are much greater than the uninitiated realize, it would be wrong to conclude that the cost of administration is great in comparison to the revenues collected and benefits paid

---

[1] A major political party, in its opposition to the Social Security Act in 1936, proposed to finance noncontributory pensions by a distinct direct tax widely applied. This perhaps meant a Federal sales tax.

or that the administrative problems are hopelessly large. So to conclude would be to ignore foreign experience.

If, for sake of emphasis, we may repeat in part what has just been said, a contributory system provides what is needed as a matter of "right" because partially paid for, not as a matter of charity. It insures against indefinitely increasing liberality because any increased outlay perhaps means increased contributions by those to receive benefits later. In other words, when successfully applied, it provides insurance, much needed in the United States, against such visionary schemes as that advocated by Dr. Townsend.[1] It can be made self-sustaining and avoid the burden otherwise imposed through increases in taxes already levied. On the other hand, a self-sustaining contributory system cannot readily make effective provision for those already old or for the self-employed and other groups commonly excepted. Ordinarily it does not come into full operation until those who at the beginning are entering industry reach pensionable age. Moreover, the contributions—special taxes—are new taxes and new taxes are likely to create problems. Certainly, until adjustments have been made in the course of years, payroll taxes cannot be expected to rest with the same effect upon employer-employee groups in the many industries. It may be added in this connection that contributions by employers have been questioned on the ground of equity. This position, however, cannot be accepted. As Professor Witte has said:[2]

"That employers should contribute something to the costs of retirement . . . is generally conceded. Such contributions are quite similar to the amounts which employers include in their costs to cover depreciation of machinery and equipment. A charge for the depreciation of the labor element in production is just as proper as is a charge for depreciation of capital. A retirement system under which employers can humanely replace old workers with younger men is of great value to them."

Certainly this position is supported by the private pension plans widely and voluntarily developed in the United States.

The choice between noncontributory and contributory pension systems is one not easily made. The real question is, however, whether a contributory system should be used at all, for when used it must be complemented by a system of noncontributory pensions if ordinary relief of aged persons is to be avoided. Not all persons can be brought within the embrace of an insurance system. But it is a significant fact that in providing for a contributory system as the larger fact in the Social Security Act Congress legislated in line with the trend in other countries.

---

[1] See University of Chicago Round Table, *The Economic Meaning of the Townsend Plan* (1936). Public Policy Pamphlet 20, Harry D. Gideonse, Editor.

[2] E. E. Witte, *op. cit.*, p. 27.

Because of financial and other reasons and because of a desire to deal with the problems of old age, unemployment, and sickness in the same general manner, there has been a distinct tendency to "insure" against old age rather than to pay straight pensions. In other words, the tendency has been for the different peoples to conclude that if wage earners should contribute funds to finance benefits to themselves when unemployed or sick, they should also contribute funds to finance old-age benefits.

Turning from a discussion of the different types of old-age systems, we must note that the old-age-benefit provisions of the Social Security Act have been criticized more or less seriously by experts in the field as well as by inadequately informed politicians and others. The more important of these criticisms require brief discussion in so far as they have not been touched upon already.

The first of the criticisms, one made chiefly by persons not well versed in social insurance legislation, has been with regard to coverage. Self-employed persons, owners, professional people, agricultural laborers, casual workers, domestic servants, and others, constituting some two-fifths of the gainfully occupied part of the population, are left without provision of old-age benefits.[1] The main reasons for the exceptions are the limited problem in the case of some groups and administrative inconvenience in the case of the others. The legislation of few countries includes owners, self-employed persons, and the like; that of most excludes those groups so circumstanced that the problems of administration would be very difficult. In workmen's compensation and unemployment-insurance legislation important groups are excepted and for the same reasons. No doubt, some of the classes now excepted might well be brought within the embrace of the contributory plan, but it seems wisest to do that after the administrative problems already involved have become clearer and have been adequately solved.[2] And, of course, it must not be over-

---

[1] In addition to self-employed persons, owners, and professional people, some 9.5 million salary and wage earners are excluded. The two largest groups among these are agricultural laborers and domestic servants, totalling more than 5 million. Those excluded because in the public service or employed by religious, educational, charitable, or other similar organizations total approximately 3.2 million.

[2] The inclusion of agricultural laborers would involve great administrative problems. It would be more feasible to extend coverage to domestic servants for they are for the most part employed in cities by persons who are accustomed to keeping records and paying taxes. Of course, lodging, board, etc., received would have to be allowed for and any system of reckoning would be more or less arbitrary. Except for the tax phase involved, there seems to be no good reason why coverage should not extend to the employees of charitable and other organizations, except of a public character. It would be only with appropriate action by the state and local governments, giving the Federal Government certain rights as agent, that coverage could be extended to their employees. (*Cf.* Twentieth Century Fund, *op. cit.*, pp. 114–120.) Much can be said for a general system like the Swedish (*supra*, p. 372), financed by a personal income tax, for many self-employed persons

looked that old-age assistance is available for those aged persons who are outside of the contributory plan and in need.[1] If adequate provision is to be made for the old, old-age benefits under an insurance plan must always be supplemented under a plan for old-age assistance.

Another criticism is that the relation between contributions and benefits is such that the younger workers pay more than the older for what they receive and are therefore unjustly treated. In the earlier years of the system there is considerable inequality. This cannot be denied. Considered apart from other factors it is objectionable. It should be held in mind, however, that under the Social Security Act those who contribute for many years will themselves receive in benefits or acquire for their estates more than they pay in taxes. Unless the employers' contribution is fully shifted to them, the workers are not involved in loss.

Still another criticism is that those within the embrace of the contributory system pay (in part) the cost of their benefits, while those not within its embrace will receive assistance out of the general revenues to which insured as well as uninsured persons will contribute. This is true. It must be held in mind, however, that those who make contributions have something approaching a guarantee of benefit when old and without means test or taint of charity, and that their monthly benefits will, in time, average much more than the grants of assistance contemplated by the Act. Yet it is also true that an insured person will make payments for years before his annuity will compare favorably with the "assistance" received by uninsured persons without means.[2] As the Twentieth Century Fund Committee has pointed out, there is need for adjustments so that there shall be a proper coordination of the public assistance and the old-age benefits.[3] Britain mitigated the problem in this way. But, of course, one must keep in mind in this connection that our old-age benefit system is also one of subsidized savings.[4]

---

need benefits in old age. The Committee of the Twentieth Century Fund would have urged consideration of such a plan had legislation not already been enacted.

[1] Contrary to what has been said by some critics, it is also available for those within the contributory system when their old-age benefits still leave them in need.

[2] Thus a worker earning $1,000 per year in insured employment will not be entitled to annuity of $30 per month until contributions have been made for twenty-one years. *Cf.* Twentieth Century Fund, *op. cit.*, on "Difficulties in Operating Two Systems," pp. 93–107.

[3] Twentieth Century Fund, *op. cit.*, pp. 123–137.

[4] No critic should complain of the exclusion of certain groups as unjust to them and at the same time complain that those included are taxed while others remain free of that burden.

It has not been generally recognized that after persons have been insured for several years the savings feature of the old-age benefit plan will provide larger sums at death than the individual insurance policies so generally carried by workingmen. The plan may be expected, in the course of years, to effect a great change in the industrial-life-insurance business. Possibly it is a realization of this that explains why some insurance men are

Another criticism is that the employers in the included employments pay a special tax to finance old-age benefits and also contribute equally with others to the revenues used to finance old-age assistance. The criticism contains truth but it is also true that the tax-paying employers should benefit from the improved morale of their employees and from the opportunity they will have to retire in a humane manner those who because of old age become underefficient. And there is a further fact of importance; *viz.*, that a considerable proportion of these employers have voluntarily financed, at least in part, private pension plans. While imposing taxes upon them, the Social Security Act will to an extent relieve them of any burden incidental to the contribution they have been making.

Still another criticism is that the special tax will injure business. Any new tax is, of course, likely to have effects and, as already noted, these may well differ in degree if not in kind. But in the present case, it is important to note that the levy is made at a time of improving industrial conditions and rising prices.[1] At such times the necessary readjustments are more easily made than under other conditions. Moreover, for a period of years the tax rate is a low one. Time is available for necessary readjustments.

Obviously the incidence of the payroll tax is of importance in connection with some of these criticisms noted. Were it not shifted at all, some of the results arrived at would be quite different from those which would be experienced were it shifted entirely through increases in prices or through readjustments made in wages. With reference to this matter of incidence one cannot be so dogmatic as those who state that the entire cost will be borne by the employees because of lower wages or that the entire cost will be reflected in increased prices of product or service. Of course, tax-paying employers will generally shift the tax in so far as they can by changes in price or changes in wages. Though in the longer run the more usual incidence will be on wages, wages will not be the one and invariable resting place. In the shorter run the matter of shifting will be different among industries and individual plants.[2]

Many persons, including most of the experts among the social scientists,[3] criticize the old-age-benefit provisions because the Government is not required to add a direct contribution to the contributions

---

ardent advocates of a pay-as-you-go policy and severe critics of the large reserve which may be built up under the present law.

[1] While this book was in press, a severe recession occurred. This has had the effect of increasing the weight of social security taxes.

[2] For a fuller discussion of shifting and incidence of payroll taxes, see Chap. III.

[3] See Eveline M. Burns, *Toward Social Security* (1936); Paul H. Douglas, *Social Security in the United States* (1936); and Abraham Epstein, *Insecurity: A Challenge to America* (1936).

made by employer and employee.   Most foreign contributory systems are supported in part by government contributions; the old-age-benefit part of our Social Security system is expected to be self-sustaining.   On this point Professor Witte's comments merit quotation.[1]

"This brings us to the question whether the federal government should pay part of the costs of old age benefits from general tax sources. This is a policy strongly advocated by many of the critics of the Social Security Act, but is at present a purely academic question.   No one proposes that the government should begin to make contributions from general tax sources at this time.   Not until 1965 or thereabout will there be any need of government contributions, as the receipts from the taxes under Title VIII will until then exceed the current disbursements under Title II.   Nor is there any way in which it could now be determined, as a matter of law, how the anticipated deficit in 1965 shall be financed when it arises.   In the budget procedure which prevails in this country, no appropriation could now be made to take effect in 1965 and an income or other tax levy to begin at that time would be ridiculous.

"Whether there should be contributions ultimately from general tax revenues toward the cost of old age benefits is debatable.   In opposition to such contributions it is to be pointed out that the entire costs of old age assistance—the first part of the present program for old age security—fall upon the general taxpayers.   To make them pay a part also of the costs of the second part of the program—the federal old age benefits—may well be argued to be burdening them excessively. . . . On the other hand, many good arguments can be made for ultimate government contributions."

Perhaps among these "many good arguments" Professor Witte had in mind are that Government contributions would make the taxes on the workers less onerous and those on employers less disturbing to business. In this connection, however, it may be said that the taxes are for some years to be imposed at low rates, that business will have time in which to make adjustments, and that the great majority of American workers have far greater tax-bearing capacity than have the workers of Continental Europe or of Great Britain.

Another argument which Professor Witte may have had in mind is that if the Government, to begin with, made contributions for the purpose, the pensions of older persons would be more nearly adequate and the burden imposed upon the younger workers to assist in financing the pensions of the older workers could be avoided, at least in part.   This is what Great Britain did when she turned from straight pensions to a contributory system.[2]

[1] E. E. Witte, *op. cit.*, pp. 27–28.
[2] *Supra*, p. 376.

And still another argument which Professor Witte may have had in mind is that government contributions would reduce the size of any reserve fund which may be employed under the Social Security Act.

There is much misunderstanding as to what might legally be done under the Social Security Act. In the next twenty years, Congress might spend the excess of excise revenues over current expenditures on annuities, and then after 1965, make appropriations out of general revenues to cover deficits. Or the annuities might be reduced or the excise tax rates increased. This would be an application of the pay-as-you-go principle.[1] But, on the other hand, it might in an effort to make the system self-sustaining make use of the reserve principle employed by insurance companies and, also, by many countries in their contributory pension systems. If the excise tax is to be continuously 6 per cent and the fund be self-sustaining, a large reserve must be built up in the earlier years, this reserve amounting to some 47 billions by 1980.

Among criticisms directed at the reserve system is that with the reserve funds invested, at least in large part, in Federal obligations[2] the reserve is only a paper thing, that it is merely a matter of bookkeeping. This is not altogether true. If the Government's obligations were not good, there would be little that was. Moreover, if there is a large debt, as there now is, the reserve will not be a matter of mere bookkeeping. For Federal obligations will be purchased and the interest which would otherwise be paid to banks and private investors will be paid to the fund and then invested. Nevertheless, the large reserve which would be required under the Act if the system is to be self-sustaining, may become a source of political and economic troubles. In the first place, its very existence is inviting demands for lower taxes and more liberal benefits. As Epstein observed,[3] "There is already talk in Congress of beginning benefit payments sooner and making them larger." Moreover, with a large reserve, will Federal obligations in necessary amount be available? Will the price of bonds not be "artificially" affected? Will a premium be placed upon debt creation? Will reserve-fund requirements freeze the public debt and cause it not to be retired when and as it should be? Will the purchase and holding of Government obligations for the reserve fund not withdraw from individuals and corporations, especially banks, a

---

[1] There is much loose thinking about "pay-as-you-go" and "reserve" systems. "Pay-as-you-go" might logically mean to secure sufficient revenue to meet all currently accruing obligations, but, as popularly used, it means to secure only sufficient revenue to meet obligations at the time or during the year. The reserve system is really one of pay-as-you-go, for it is designed to secure revenue sufficient to meet all currently accruing obligations.

[2] In so far as the reserve was invested in non-Government obligations, it would create no problem not involved in the reserves of private insurance companies. Of course, any losses sustained would have to be made good by the Government as guarantor.

[3] A. Epstein, *op. cit.*, p. 763. (Quoted by courtesy of Random House, Inc.)

desirable form of investment? The Congress will, in all probability, long before the reserve reaches 47 billions, find it advisable to amend the law and make any such large reserve unnecessary, by granting appropriations out of general revenues.[1]

A final word on this point is necessary. If the benefit system is to be self-sustaining, the choice is between reserves which will equalize the burden through a period of time and a pay-as-you-go policy which will involve increasing contributions or increasing government subventions with the passing of time. Upon the assumptions used in estimating the reserve at 47 billions in 1980, the contributions then required under a pay-as-you-go policy would be around 10 per cent of the payroll. A pay-as-you-go policy is not unlike the assessment system so widely used in the earlier history of life insurance and then discarded. Pension promises are much more likely to be realized under a reserve system.

Invalidity; Widows' and Orphans' Pensions.—In many countries, provision is made under social-insurance systems for the payment of benefits to those who, before they reach pensionable age, become seriously incapacitated and to widows and orphans of insured persons. In the United States, however, these problems have been attacked in other ways when not more or less neglected. At present, the advisability of amending the Social Security Act so as to provide for invalidity benefits and survivor's insurance along with old-age benefits is to be considered by the Advisory Council recently established.

The Social Security Act and accompanying state legislation make some provision for wage earners who are thrown out of employment;[2]

---

[1] No doubt, the Social Security Act will be amended in many respects. In May, 1937, the establishment of an Advisory Council on Social Security was announced by the Chairman of the Senate Committee on Finance and the Chairman of the Social Security Board. This Advisory Council consists of six representatives of employers, and twelve representatives of the public. It is to cooperate with the Senate Committee and the Board. While it may consider any pertinent matter, it is expected to consider the following specific subjects:

"1. The advisability of commencing payment of monthly benefits under Title II sooner than January 1, 1942;

"2. The advisability of increasing the monthly benefit payments under Title II for those retiring in the early years;

"3. The advisability of extending the benefits in Title II to persons who become incapacitated prior to age 65;

"4. The advisability of extending the benefits of Title II to survivors of individuals entitled to such benefits;

"5. The advisability of increasing the taxes less rapidly under Title VIII;

"6. The advisability of extending the benefits under Title II to include groups now excluded;

"7. The size, character, and disposition of reserves;

"8. Any other questions concerning the Social Security Act about which either the special Senate Committee or the Social Security Board may desire the advice of the Advisory Council."

See Social Security Board, *Selected Current Statistics*, June, 1937, pp. 13–16.

[2] See, *supra*, Chap. III.

aid has been provided for the care of dependent children under sixteen years of age who have been deprived of parental support through death, absence, or incapacity of a parent;[1] aid is extended to the blind;[2] lastly, a system of contributory old-age benefits and a noncontributory old-age-assistance program have been established to alleviate the problem of the aged. However, except for the invalidity protection provided under the Federal Civil Service Retirement Act[3] and the Railroad Retirement Act[4] no provision, other than outright relief, has yet been made for those under age sixty-five who are disabled for work through illness or other causes and who have suffered substantial loss in earning capacity, unless they happen to be blind, are covered under the disablement provisions of industrial-accident or occupational-disease legislation,[5] or are so disabled as to require institutional care.

A very large number of disabled persons who find no place in the above categories suffer substantial loss in earning capacity for which no compensation is forthcoming. Something of the incidence of invalidity was revealed in a study made some years ago by the Pennsylvania Commission on Old Age Pensions in which 5,000 persons were interviewed. Of the 658 who were partially impaired, more than 30 per cent had incurred a loss in earning power before reaching fifty years of age, 50 per cent before reaching fifty-five, and about 67 per cent before reaching age sixty. Of these, 490 had subsequently been forced by disability to stop work entirely; more than a quarter of them were found to have lost all their earning power before age fifty-five, two-fifths before sixty, and three-fifths before sixty-five.[6] It will suffice to note that these

[1] See below, pp. 407–408.

[2] The Social Security Act (Title X) provides for grants to states with approved plans for the care of the blind. The conditions to be observed and the limits upon grants correspond to those for old-age assistance. In October, 1937, the amount expended in thirty-three states and the District of Columbia was $1,045,205 [Social Security Board, *Public Assistance Statistics for the United States*, vol. 2, nos. 10–12 (October, 1937), p. 17 (bound with *Social Security Bulletin*, December, 1937)].

[3] Public no. 215, 66th Congress, 2nd Session, approved May 22, 1920.

On June 30, 1935, 407,200 civil-service employees were covered by the combined old-age and invalidity provisions of the Act. Benefits for old-age and invalidity were the same but varied in amount depending upon total contributions and length of service, the minimum qualifying period being fifteen years for old-age benefits. After five years' service, in the event of disability through sickness or injury, employees were eligible for invalidity benefits similar in amount to those for old age. Employee contributions were 3 per cent of salaries, while the normal annual Government contributions, under which the remaining cost of the scheme was met from Federal revenues, up to June 30, 1935, had averaged 2.71 per cent of payroll. *Cf. Fifteenth Annual Report of the Board of Actuaries of the Civil Service Retirement and Disability Fund*, 74th Congress, 2nd Session, Document 196 (1936), p. 8.

[4] Public no. 399, 74th Congress, Session I, approved Aug. 29, 1935, amended by Public no. 162, 75th Congress, 1st Session, approved June 24, 1937. For provisions of the Act, see, *supra*, pp. 388–392.

[5] See *supra*, Chap. IV, p. 212.

[6] *Report of the Pennsylvania Commission on Old Age Pensions* (1919), pp. 104–105.

disabled persons would not be covered under our present old-age-assistance laws, where the minimum age limit is sixty-five, nor would provision be made for most of them under workmen's compensation, since illness rather than accident has been found to be the leading cause of invalidity.[1]

Although more adequate relief grants might provide for all needy disabled persons without regard to age, it is highly questionable whether an extension of the relief program would be desirable because of the disadvantages inherent in that type of care.[2] Moreover, the administration of invalidity cases, at least under the present administration, would probably result in imperfect provision and in inadequate preventive measures being taken.

A better alternative provision for dependency resulting from invalidity, employed in many European countries,[3] is to insure against it. This is accomplished through membership in a health-insurance system as, for example, in England[4] and Denmark, or under a combined old-age-invalidity insurance program as in Germany.[5] Both types of plans require a certain minimum number of contributions as a condition of eligibility for benefits, the minimum being 104 weekly contributions in England and Denmark, and 200 in Germany. Under these and most other systems, provision is made for regular government contributions.[6] Invalidity is defined in terms of loss of normal earning capacity[7] and varies from a loss of one-tenth in Russia,[8] to one-third in Denmark, and two-thirds in France and Germany, while in England total disability must be established before benefits are paid.

[1] Sickness accounted for the destruction of earning power in 47 per cent of the cases; old age, 35 per cent; accident, 13.2 per cent; and various other causes, 4.8 per cent. *Ibid.*, p. 104. *Cf.* also *supra*, Chap. V, pp. 235 *ff*.

[2] For an evaluation of relief programs, see *supra*, Chap. II, pp. 94 *ff*.

[3] For details of systems in foreign countries, see International Labour Office Studies and Reports, Series *M*, no. 13, *International Survey of Social Services, 1933* (1936), vols. 1 and 2.

[4] See *supra*, Chap. VI, p. 296.

[5] See *supra*, Chap. VI, pp. 276 *ff*.

[6] Government contributions for old-age and invalidity in Germany, for example, have risen from 183,627,000 Marks in 1913 to 964,294,000 Marks in 1935. *Statistisches Jahrbuch für das Deutsche Reich* (1936), p. 429.

[7] While definitions of invalidity vary according to different plans such as "occupational incapacity" for specially insured groups and "general incapacity" for broad and more inclusive programs, the essence of every definition is that the disabled person, if covered by invalidity insurance, must be incapacitated for gainful employment which he could perform if he were not incapacitated. For an excellent discussion of this in light of European experience, see International Labour Conference, 16th Session (1932), *Invalidity, Old-Age and Widow's and Orphan's Insurance*, pp. 68–96.

[8] In Russia there is a classification of six disability groups, benefits are paid according to need with ability to earn and amount of invalidity expenses constituting the controlling factors. See, Sidney and Beatrice Webb, *Soviet Communism: A New Civilization?* (1935), vol. 2, p. 876.

The close relationship found in foreign countries between invalidity insurance and health insurance deserves emphasis, especially in a consideration of the invalidity problem in the United States. In general, benefits are paid only after the disabled person has exhausted the sickness benefits to which he is entitled, usually for a maximum period of twenty-six weeks. The theory is that a six months' period is sufficient to insure recovery of those not permanently incapacitated; those remaining disabled are then entitled to invalidity benefits which are paid until the disabled person either is again able to work or becomes eligible for an old-age pension. Hence, since sickness benefits, which begin almost immediately after work incapacity occurs and are continued until replaced by invalidity benefits which run until the insured reaches pensionable age, there is no time during which the insured disabled person is left without some provision for himself.[1] However, even with substantial government contributions, the amount of the benefit has been clearly inadequate[2] and the coverage limited; and the fact that state subsidies are now required would seem to indicate that contribution rates, especially from the low-wage groups, are already as high as can be reasonably borne and that further increases in benefits would necessitate additional government contributions in behalf of the lower-paid groups.

Invalidity is a large problem in the United States. In so far as it is not covered by workmen's compensation, it needs to be brought within the social security plan. Certification would present a difficult administrative problem and experience elsewhere shows that it is distinctly helpful to have invalidity insurance closely linked with health insurance. In the United States, however, a system of health insurance has not been adopted. Moreover, if sickness benefits were combined with unemployment compensation, as suggested at an earlier point in our discussion,[3] more than temporary invalidity cases could not be properly provided for because of the relation between earnings or weeks worked and benefits payable. Provision might, however, be made under the old-age-assistance laws and the old-age-benefit plan established under the Social Security Act. The Federal-state old-age-assistance plan might well be amended so as to provide assistance, with appropriate safeguards and certification, for those who have become incapacitated for work, are not eligible to compensation under the workmen's compensation laws, and are in need. Likewise, the old-age-benefit plan might well be amended so as to provide annuities for those of the insured who become

[1] Of the twenty-nine countries providing compulsory invalidity insurance, twenty-three make provision for survivor's insurance. See, International Labour Office, Studies and Reports, Series M, no. 12, *The International Labour Organization and Social Insurance* (1936), pp. 209–216.

[2] For the provisions of and amounts payable under the German, British, and French invalidity plans, see *supra*, Chap. VI.

[3] Chap. VII, pp. 344–345.

incapacitated before attaining age sixty-five.   Such provision might be limited to those who had been employed for a number of years.   Perhaps it would be appropriate for the Government to grant a subsidy to pay the cost of such annuities in order that the actuarial basis of the old-age-benefit plan should not be disturbed.

It cannot be denied that certification of invalidity involves a difficult problem.   And, of course, provision for invalids under an old-age-assistance or/and under an old-age-benefit plan would add substantially to the outlays under such plans.[1]   Nevertheless, invalidity presents an important problem, and in many cases government support in one form or another is inevitable.

There is also an extensive older workers' problem in the United States due not to invalidity before sixty-five years of age but to discrimination in employment against those past forty, forty-five, or fifty.[2]   In part this may be expected to disappear with the new social security legislation, for one cause of the discrimination practiced has been in pension plans on a private basis.   Another cause has been the higher premiums charged for group life insurance and workmen's compensation insurance where older workers, say past fifty, are employed.   There is no doubt, however, that the handicap under which the older workers have been placed is substantially larger than is warranted by any decrease in productivity or by any heavier insurance charges.   Much of the discrimination results from the automatic application of maximum hiring ages, which employers have been too prone to adopt without sufficient study of the factors involved and possibly merely because of patterns set by other employers in the industry or locality.   The results of research may prove to be helpful by dispelling unfounded beliefs which have received widespread acceptance.   Yet, in many occupations efficiency does noticeably decrease before normal pensionable age; and transfer to other occupations, with or without retraining, is required in the interest of efficiency.   The public employment offices should be as helpful as possible in finding suitable employment opportunity for those of declining efficiency, and adequate facilities for retraining should be stressed.   As long as persons are employable, employment is far better than financial aid, whether on an insurance basis or not.   An active interest in finding suitable work for those who

[1] In Australia the ratio of invalidity pensions to old-age pensions increased from 1 to 4.3 for the period 1910–1919 to 1 to 2.6 for 1936 (Commissioner of Pensions, Australia. *Invalid and Old-Age Pensions*, Statement for the twelve months ended June 30, 1936. Canberra, 1936.)   In Germany in 1922, 3.6 invalidity pensions were paid for every old-age pension.   This was under a liberal definition of invalidity and under conditions more or less peculiar to Germany.   Moreover, as the British experience shows, sickness and disablement increase during periods of unfavorable economic conditions, but invalidity is the more unstable and tends to mount more rapidly.   It is during such periods that the complex problems of administrative control of invalidity, medical certification, and rigid supervision of claims become evident.

[2] See pp. 354–360, where employment handicap is discussed.

lose in respect of efficiency but still remain employable can be effective in reducing substantially the size of this particular problem.

Though it had its beginnings earlier, provision of widows' and orphans' pensions is largely a product of postwar years.[1] By 1935, so-called survivors' insurance had been adopted by seventeen European countries, the Swiss Canton of Basle, and Uruguay.[2] The German and the British systems best repay study. In Germany the widow, provided she is sixty-five years of age or an invalid, and dependent children of an insured person who has died are entitled to pensions, the total of which is not to exceed 80 per cent of the pension to which the insured would have been entitled. In Britain, the widow of a man who has been insured against old age is entitled to ten shillings per week until death or remarriage; the first child is entitled to five shillings, each other child to three shillings per week until age fifteen, or age sixteen if in school. In the United States, some of the Canadian provinces, Denmark, and a few of the Australasian countries or states, on the other hand, the problem presented by widowhood and orphanage has resulted in the adoption of what we, in this country, commonly call funds-to-mothers acts.[3] Payments are made to mothers of dependent children under certain conditions and provided need is established. The first funds-to-mothers act was adopted in Illinois in 1911;[4] by 1919, thirty-nine states and two territories had adopted such measures; by the end of 1936, such legislation found place in all of the states except Georgia and South Carolina, also in the District of Columbia, Alaska, Puerto Rico, and Hawaii.

Partly because of the development of funds-to-mothers acts and partly because of the general type of old-age-benefit plan regarded as most acceptable, no direct[5] provision for survivors' insurance was made in the Social Security Act. In an effort to extend, standardize, and give badly needed financial support, provision was, however, made for grants to the states with approved plans for the care of dependent children. The conditions of approval correspond to those relating to the approval of old-age-assistance plans. The grant-in-aid is limited to one-third of the total, with maxima of $18.00 per month in the case of one child and of $12.00 for each child in excess of one in the family. It will be noted

[1] For a survey of widows' and orphans' pensions, see International Labour Conference, report on *Invalidity, Old-Age and Widows' and Orphans' Insurance* (1932).

[2] John R. Commons and John B. Andrews, *Principles of Labor Legislation* (4th rev. ed., 1936), p. 290.

[3] As the laws have been amended, they usually apply to deserted, and possibly to other, mothers as well as to widows.

[4] Ill. Stat., 1911, Chap. 28. This was the first state-wide law. It appears, however, that this had been preceded by a Missouri law applying to Jackson County only. *Cf.* B. N. Armstrong, *op. cit.*, p. 442.

[5] Of course, the widow and orphans of an insured man (his estate) are entitled to lump-sum payments if annuities paid do not equal 3.5 per cent of wages earned in insured employment.

that the Federal support extended is less liberal than in the case of old-age assistance and in the case of the blind. In March, 1937, approved plans were operating in twenty-seven of the forty-eight states and in the District of Columbia. The number of families receiving aid was 127,879; the obligations incurred for the month totalled $3,711,359.[1] The number of cases in which aid is given, the greater certainty and adequacy of the aid, and the improvement in administration all give evidence of the value of this part of the Social Security Act.

While it is true that the funds-to-mothers acts and the grants made under the Social Security Act make extensive provision where dependent children are involved, the problem presented by widows of insured persons is not now met except through the old-age-assistance laws in case they have attained age sixty-five and except through such balances as may be due them under the old-age-benefit plan. Moreover, the old-age-benefit plan does not differentiate between annuitants who have wives and those who do not. It has been suggested[2] that the Social Security Act should be amended so that $15.00 per month would be granted to wives of annuitants, provided they are over sixty years of age, and so that the annuities of deceased insured persons should be continued in the same amounts to their widows over sixty years of age as long as they remain unmarried. The seriousness of the problems and foreign precedent argue strongly for such amendment of the Act.

THE QUESTION OF CONSTITUTIONALITY OF SOCIAL SECURITY LEGISLATION

This discussion may be closed with brief comment upon the question of constitutionality of the two controversial parts of the Social Security Act, those relating to unemployment compensation and old-age benefits, respectively.[3] Inasmuch as the decision of the Supreme Court of the

[1] Social Security Board, *Selected Current Statistics*, June, 1937, p. 37. By October, 1937, approved plans were in operation in thirty-nine states, Hawaii, and the District of Columbia. Plans providing aid to dependent children, but not under the Social Security Act, were found in eight other states. During February, 1936, combined Federal-state payments of $602,926 were made to support dependent children in about 27,000 families. Comparable data for October, 1937, show combined expenditures of $6,203,699 for the care of 496,182 children in 199,667 families. Total Federal grants cumulative to October 31, 1937, had amounted to $26,120,834. Social Security Board, *Social Security Bulletin*, vol. 2, no. 6 (December, 1937), p. 48; and *Public Assistance Statistics for the United States*, vol. 2, no. 10–12 (October, 1937), pp. 9, 15, 16, 19 (bound with *Social Security Bulletin* just cited).

[2] Twentieth Century Fund, *op. cit.*, pp. 133 and 135.

[3] Among the valuable advance discussions of the constitutional issues are those by Paul H. Douglas, in *Social Security in the United States* (1936), Chap. 12; Barbara N. Armstrong, "The Federal Social Security Act," *American Bar Association Journal*, vol. 21 (1935), pp. 786–789, 792–797, and "The Federal Social Security Act and Its Constitutional Aspects," *California Law Review*, vol. 24 (1936), pp. 247–274; Harry Shulman, "The Case for the Constitutionality of the Social Security Act," *Law and Contemporary Problems*, vol. 3

United States on the latter phase followed immediately after its decision on the former, it will be most convenient to discuss first the constitutional issues involved in unemployment compensation.

Both state unemployment compensation laws and the Social Security Act have been attacked upon constitutional grounds, but their general validity is now definitely established. State laws have been upheld by the highest courts in a number of states[1] and the Alabama law and also the Social Security Act have been upheld by the Supreme Court of the United States. Because generally controlling, only the Carmichael and the Steward Machine Company cases decided by the Supreme Court on May, 24, 1937, need to be reviewed here.[2]

As our analysis of the state unemployment laws shows, the Alabama law was, except for the fact that it levied a tax upon employees as well as one upon the employer, very similar to most of the earlier laws adopted. Employers of fewer than eight were exempted and the exclusions provided for in the Social Security Act obtained. The Act provided for a central pooled fund as had the Railway Retirement Act which had been declared unconstitutional.[3] Provision. was also made for the introduction of merit rating.

In the Carmichael cases, the validity of the *tax qua tax* was questioned on various grounds but upheld as to each. One ground was that it was imposed only upon employers of eight or more workers. The Court pointed out that such classification and exemption are, however, not unusual and have been sustained. The exemption of employers of fewer than eight workers may be justified by administrative convenience and expense in the collection or measurement of the tax. "We cannot say that the expense and inconvenience of collecting the tax from small

---

(1936), pp. 298–314; and Charles Denby, Jr., "The Case Against the Constitutionality of the Social Security Act," *ibid.*, pp. 315–331.

The appropriations made for public health, the blind, crippled children, maternal and infant welfare, and old-age assistance were unquestionably constitutional. The discussion is, therefore, limited to the constitutional aspects of unemployment compensation and old-age benefits.

[1] *W. H. H. Chamberlin, Inc., v. Andrews, E. C. Stearns and Company v. Andrews,* and *Associated Industries of New York v. Dept. of Labor,* 271 N.Y.R. 1 (1936); *Howes Brothers Co. v. Massachusetts Unemployment Compensation Commission,* 5 N.E. (2d) 720 (Dec. 30, 1936); *Gillum v. Johnson* (California), 62 Pac. (2d) 1037 (Dec. 21 1936); *Beeland Wholesale Co. v. Kaufman* (Alabama), 174 So. 516 (March 18, 1937).

[2] *Carmichael v. Southern Coal & Coke Co.* and *Carmichael v. Gulf States Paper Corp.,* 301 U. S. 495 (May 24, 1937); *Chas. C. Steward Machine Co. v. Davis,* 301 U. S. 548 (May 24, 1937). The New York Act had been before the Supreme Court, after it had been upheld in toto by a majority (5 to 3) of the Court of Appeals of that state, but, with Justice Stone not participating, the Court divided 4 to 4 and the decision of the Court of Appeals prevailed. Though it was quite probable that a favorable decision would be rendered by the Supreme Court because Justice Stone is a liberal, such a decision would be in a new case.

[3] *Supra,* pp. 389–391.

employers would not be disproportionate to the revenue obtained. For it cannot be assumed that the legislature could not rightly have concluded that generally the number of employees bears a relationship to the size of the payroll and therefore to the amount of the tax, and that the large number of small employers and the paucity of their records of employment would entail greater inconvenience in the collection and verification of the tax than in the case of larger employers."[1]

A second ground was that employers of agricultural labor, domestics, and others were exempted from the tax. But, here again, such classification is not unusual and has been made, possibly for a number of reasons, such as to discourage this or to encourage that, or as a matter of administrative convenience and expense.[2]

A third ground of attack was that a tax is levied upon employees also, but the protesting employers could not object to a tax they were not asked to pay, at least if separable, "as we think it is, from the tax they must pay."[3]

The general position taken on the question of the validity of the *tax qua tax* was stated as follows:

"It is inherent in the exercise of the power to tax that a state be free to select the subjects of taxation and to grant exemptions. Neither due process nor equal protection imposes upon a state any rigid rule of equality of taxation. . . . A legislature is not bound to tax every member of a class or none. It may make distinctions of degree having a rational basis, and when subjected to judicial scrutiny they must be presumed to rest on that basis if there is any conceivable state of facts which would support it. . . . This restriction upon the judicial function, in passing on the constitutionality of statutes, is not artificial or irrational. A state legislature, in the enactment of laws, has the widest possible latitude within the limits of the Constitution. In the nature of the case it cannot record a complete catalogue of the considerations which move its members to enact laws. In the absence of such a record courts cannot assume that its action is capricious, or that, with its informed acquaintance with local conditions to which the legislation is to be applied, it was not aware of facts which afford reasonable basis for its action. Only by faithful adherence to this guiding principle of judicial review of legislation is it possible to preserve to the legislative branch its rightful independence and its ability to function."[4]

The validity of the Alabama statute was contested on the ground that its purpose was not a public one but the Court held that relief of unemployment is a public purpose. "The evils of the attendant social and

---

[1] 301 U. S. at p. 511.

[2] *Ibid.*, at pp. 512–513.

[3] *Ibid.*, at p. 513.

[4] *Ibid.*, at pp. 509–510.

economic wastage" involved in unemployment which has become a permanent incident of our industrial system "permeate the entire social structure. Apart from poverty, or a less extreme impairment of the savings which afford the chief protection to the working class against old age and the hazards of illness, a matter of inestimable consequence to society as a whole, and apart from the loss of purchasing power, the legislature could have concluded that unemployment brings in its wake increase in vagrancy and crimes against property, reduction in the number of marriages, deterioration of family life, decline in the birth rate, increase in illegitimate births, impairment of the health of the unemployed and their families and malnutrition of their children."[1] "The end being legitimate, the means is for the legislature to choose. When public evils ensue from individual misfortunes or needs, the legislature may strike at the evil at its source.   If the purpose is legitimate because public, it will not be defeated because the execution of it involves payments to individuals."[2]

Nor was the scheme of unemployment relief subject to any constitutional infirmity, such as had been argued, because of its not being limited to the indigent or because of extension to some less deserving than others. "Poverty is one, but not the only evil consequence of unemployment. Among the benefits sought by relief is the avoidance of destitution, and of the gathering cloud of evils which beset the worker, his family and the community after wages cease and before destitution begins. . . . Moreover, the state could rightfully decide not to discourage thrift.   And as the injurious effects of unemployment are not limited to the unemployed worker, there is scope for legislation to mitigate those effects, even though unemployment results from his discharge for cause."[3]

It was also contended that because benefits were limited to the employees of those who pay taxes, relief is withheld from many as deserving as those who receive benefits.   This, it was contended, was so arbitrary and discriminatory as to infringe the Fourteenth Amendment and deprive the statute of any public purpose.   The Court held, however, that "in establishing a system of unemployment benefits the legislature [was] not bound to occupy the whole field.   It [might] strike at the evil where it [was] most felt,"[4] that is, in industry.

As has been noted, the Alabama statute provides for a pooled fund. It was contended that this destroyed a necessary relationship between responsibility for and contribution to unemployment, taxes paid, and benefits received in return.   The dissenting Justices held that this was true and cited the decision in the Railway Retirement case.   Justice

[1] *Ibid.*, at pp. 515–517.
[2] *Ibid.*, at p. 518.
[3] *Ibid.*, at pp. 518–519.
[4] *Ibid.*, at pp. 519–520.

Sutherland, in his dissenting opinion,[1] said that because it firmly links discontinuance of employment at the hands of the employer and payment of benefit to the unemployed worker, "I entertain no doubt that the Wisconsin plan is so fair, reasonable and just as to make plain its constitutional validity; and that the Alabama statute . . . is so arbitrary as to result in a denial both of due process and equal protection of the laws."[2]

The prevailing majority were, however, of a different view. "Appellees' contention that the statute is arbitrary, in so far as it fails to distinguish between the employer with a low unemployment experience and the employer with a high unemployment experience, rests upon the misconception that there must be such a relationship between the subject of the tax (the exercise of the right to employ) and the evil to be met by the appropriation of the proceeds (unemployment). . . . Nothing is more familiar in taxation than the imposition of a tax upon a class or upon individuals who enjoy no direct benefit from its expenditure, and who are not responsible for the condition to be remedied. A tax is not an assessment of benefits. It is, as we have said, a means of distributing the burden of the cost of government. The only benefit to which the taxpayer is constitutionally entitled is that derived from his enjoyment of the privileges of living in an organized society, established and safeguarded by the devotion of taxes to public purposes."[3] Then, too, a legislature might conclude that it is impossible to apportion the burden among employers according to their unemployment experience. For, "unemployment in the plant of one employer may be due to competition with another, within or without the state, whose factory is running to capacity; or to tariffs, inventions, changes in fashions or in market or business conditions, for which no employer is responsible, but which may stimulate the business of one and impair or even destroy that of another. Many believe that the responsibility for the business cycle, the chief cause of unemployment, cannot be apportioned to individual employers in accordance with their employment experience; that a business may be least responsible for the depression from which it suffers the most.

"The Alabama legislature may have proceeded upon the view, for which there is abundant authority, that the causes of unemployment are too complex to admit of a meticulous appraisal of employer responsibility. It may have concluded that unemployment is an inseparable incident of modern industry, with its most serious manifestations in industrial production; that employees will be best protected, and that the cost of the remedy, at least until more accurate and complete data are available, may best be distributed, by imposing the tax evenly upon all industrial

[1] Concurred in by Justices Van Devanter and Butler.
[2] *Ibid.*, at p. 531.
[3] *Ibid.*, at pp. 521–522.

production; and in such form that it will be added to labor costs which are ultimately absorbed by the public in the prices which it pays for consumable goods."[1]

It is unnecessary to summarize this decision further, for the other significant points rested upon the decision which had just been rendered in the Steward Machine Co. case. In the Steward case the constitutional issues involved in the titles of the Social Security Act relating to unemployment compensation and the alleged coercion of the states resulting from its provisions and administration were ruled on.

The Steward Machine Co. filed a claim for a refund of the Federal payroll tax, which had been paid, on the ground that the sections of the Social Security Act relating to unemployment compensation were invalid. The claim was disallowed by the district court and this was affirmed by the Circuit Court of Appeals for the Fifth Circuit. The case then came to the Supreme Court.

Titles IX and III, the one relating to the levy of the tax, the other to the allocation of funds to the states to cover administrative expenses, were challenged on several grounds. Though the Federal Government had levied many special excise taxes and most of them had been declared to be valid,[2] the payroll tax here involved was challenged on the grounds (a) that it was not an excise tax; (b) that it was not uniform throughout the United States as excises are required to be; (c) that its exceptions were so numerous and arbitrary as to violate the Fifth Amendment; (d) that its purpose was not revenue but an unlawful invasion of the reserved powers of the states; and (e) that the states in submitting to this exercise of Federal power had yielded to coercion and had abandoned governmental functions which they were not permitted to do.

The first contention was that only taxes on commodities are excises; the payroll tax was one on employment which is a natural right, not a privilege. The Supreme Court found that taxes on various employments have been levied by states since colonial times and asserted that "the subject matter of taxation open to the power of Congress is as comprehensive as that open to the power of the states, though the method of apportionment may at times be different," as in the case of so-called "direct taxes." It found "no basis for a holding that the power in that regard which belongs by accepted practice to the legislatures of the states, has been denied by the Constitution to the Congress of the nation."[3]

The challenge of lack of uniformity was found to be without merit. In line with previous rulings, "uniformity" means geographical uniformity. Nor were the classifications and exceptions unwarranted: "The classifications and exemptions directed by the statute now in con-

---

[1] *Ibid.*, at pp. 524–525.
[2] Of course, the processing tax under AAA and certain others had been declared invalid.
[3] 301 U. S. at pp. 581, 583.

troversy have support in considerations of policy and practical convenience that cannot be condemned as arbitrary."[1]

The real issues within the Court which led to a division of five to four,[2] were whether the Act was an unlawful invasion of the reserved powers of the states and whether the states, by submitting to this exercise of Federal power, yielded to coercion and abandoned governmental functions, which they were not permitted to do.

The majority view was that "The excise is not void as involving the coercion of the States in contravention of the Tenth Amendment or of restrictions implicit in our federal form of government."[3] Rather, the Act created "a larger freedom, the states and the nation joining in a cooperative endeavor to avert a common evil."[4] Two facts were significant. The states had generally refrained from enacting compensation legislation because of fear that they would place their industries under a handicap; there had been a failure on the part of the states to contribute for relief according to the measure of their capacities, with the result that a disproportionate burden, and a mountainous one, had been laid upon the resources of the government of the nation. The purpose of the Federal Government had been "to safeguard its own treasury and as an incident to that protection to place the states upon a footing of equal opportunity. Drains upon its own resources [were] to be checked; obstructions to the freedom of the states [were] to be leveled."[5] Precedent was found for the tax-offset plan in the upholding as valid of Section 301 of the Revenue Act of 1926, under which 80 per cent of inheritance taxes imposed might be offset.[6] The Child Labor Tax Case[7] and the Processing Tax Case[8] were held to be easily distinguishable and not in point here.

The payroll tax is levied and collected from employers within the embrace of the Act without any reference to their conduct. This was not so in the Child Labor Case, where the tax was on incomes of employers who did not observe certain labor standards and whose business involved interstate commerce. Likewise, the tax is collected from the employers within its boundaries without any reference to whether a state has or does not have an approved unemployment compensation statute. "It is one thing to impose a tax dependent upon the conduct of the taxpayers, or of the state in which they live, where the conduct to be stimulated or dis-

[1] *Ibid.*, at p. 584.

[2] The majority opinion was read by Justice Cardozo and concurred in by Chief Justice Hughes and Justices Brandeis, Roberts, and Stone. Three dissenting opinions were rendered by Justice McReynolds, Justice Sutherland, and Justice Butler. That by Justice Sutherland was concurred in by Justice Van Devanter.

[3] 301 U. S. at p. 585.

[4] *Ibid.*, at p. 587.

[5] *Ibid.*, at p. 591.

[6] Upheld in *Florida v. Mellon*, 273 U. S. 12 (1927).

[7] *Bailey v. Drexel Furniture Company*, 259 U. S. 20 (1922).

[8] *United States v. Butler*, 297 U. S. 1 (1936).

couraged is unrelated to the fiscal need subserved by the tax in its normal operation, or to any other end legitimately national."[1]

The tax in the Processing Case was not a true one. The Act under which it was levied attempted to regulate production without the consent of the state in which production was affected, and the payments made to farmers were coupled with coercive contracts, unlawful in their aim and oppressive in their consequences. The payroll tax is different, for "the proceeds of the tax in controversy are not earmarked for a special group; the unemployment compensation law which is a condition of the credit has had the approval of the state and could not be a law without it; the condition is not linked to an irrevocable agreement, for the state at its pleasure may repeal its unemployment law . . . , terminate the credit, and place itself where it was before the credit was accepted; the condition is not directed to the attainment of an unlawful end, but to an end, the relief of unemployment, for which nation and state may lawfully cooperate; the statute does not call for a surrender by the states of powers essential to their quasi-sovereign existence."[2]

While a state is left free to enact or not to enact a compensation law, and while there is much freedom as to type of law, employee contributions, etc., when such a law is enacted conditions are, of course, laid down for using receipted state tax bills in payment of the Federal tax and for securing allocation of funds to cover administrative expenses. These conditions are, however, designed to serve as necessary safeguards and to protect the situation. They are not an invasion of the proper powers of the states. Nor, as was alleged, does the requirement that moneys collected by a state be deposited in the Federal Treasury involve "abdication." "All that the state has done is to say in effect through the enactment of a statute that her agents shall be authorized to deposit the unemployment tax receipts in the Treasury at Washington."[3] The funds are at its command; a state can repeal its statute and sever the relationship when it wishes to do so. "To find state destruction there is to find it almost anywhere. . . . The inference of abdication thus dissolves in thinnest air when the deposit is conceived of as dependent upon a statutory consent, and not upon a contract effective to create a duty."[4]

Though there were three dissenting opinions, the four Justices constituting a minority accepted a considerable part of the findings of the five constituting a majority of the Court. As Justice Sutherland said:

"I agree that the payroll tax levied is an excise within the power of Congress; that the devotion of not more than 90% of it to the credit of employers in states which require the payment of a similar tax under

[1] 301 U. S. at p. 591.
[2] *Ibid.*, at pp. 592–593.
[3] *Ibid.*, at p. 596.
[4] *Ibid.*, at pp. 596–597.

so-called unemployment-tax laws is not an unconstitutional use of the proceeds of the federal tax; that the provision making the adoption by the state of an unemployment law of a specified character a condition precedent to the credit of the tax does not render the law invalid.   I agree that the states are not coerced by the federal legislation into adopting unemployment legislation.   The provisions of the federal law may operate to induce the state to pass an employment law if it regards such action to be in its interest.   But this is not coercion.   If the act stopped here, I should accept the conclusion of the court that the legislation is not unconstitutional."[1]

The invalidity of the statute as seen by the dissenting members of the Court lay in the fact that it was not in accord with their views of the Federal-state form of government as established under the Constitution. There is, they held, a strict division and allocation of powers.   As phrased by Justice Sutherland, the precise question was whether "the congressional act contemplate[d] a surrender by the state to the federal government, in whole or in part, of any state governmental power to administer its own unemployment law or the state payroll-tax funds which it has collected for the purpose of that law."[2]   The answer is in the affirmative, for certain requirements are laid down; the Social Security Board acts as legislative counsel, bill drafter and censor; the funds collected by a state must be deposited with the Treasury at Washington; all monies drawn from the funds accumulated must be used exclusively for the payment of compensation; and the money is to be paid out in benefits by approved agencies.   To quote:

"The federal government . . . in the person of its agent, the board, sits not only as a perpetual overseer, interpreter and censor of state legislation on the subject, but, as lord paramount, to determine whether the state is faithfully executing its own law—as though the state were a dependency under pupilage and not to be trusted. . . .

"By these various provisions of the act, the federal agencies are authorized to supervise and hamper the administrative powers of the state to a degree which not only does not comport with the dignity of a quasi-sovereign state—a matter with which we are not judicially concerned—but which denies to it that supremacy and freedom from external interference in respect of its affairs which the Constitution contemplates— a matter of very definite judicial concern."[3]

Predicating his objections upon somewhat different grounds, Justice Butler said:

"The terms of the measure make it clear that the tax and credit device was intended to enable federal officers virtually to control the exertion of

---

[1] *Ibid.*, at pp. 609–610.
[2] Quoted from Sutherland opinion, *ibid.*, at p. 611.
[3] *Ibid.*, at pp. 613–614.

powers of the States in a field in which they alone have jurisdiction and from which the United States is by the Constitution excluded."[1]

The peril to our form of government, as seen by the minority, is great. As stated by Justice Sutherland in less emphatic language than that used by his associates:

"If we are to survive as the United States, the balance between the powers of the nation and those of the states must be maintained. There is grave danger in permitting it to dip in either direction, danger—if there were no other—in the precedent thereby set for further departures from the equipoise. The threat implicit in the present encroachment upon the administrative functions of the states is that greater encroachments, and encroachments upon other functions, will follow."[2]

Thus, the protest made by the dissenting justices was chiefly on the ground of a shift seen by them in the particular form of Federal-state government called for by the Constitution as interpreted by them. The prevailing opinion, on the other hand, was that under the Constitution the Federal and the state governments may cooperate in solving problems as provided for under the Social Security Act.

By a seven to two decision, following immediately upon that rendered in the Steward Machine Co. case, the Supreme Court sustained the constitutionality of the parts of the Social Security Act relating to old-age benefits.[3] Inasmuch as the system created is a Federal, not a Federal-state one, the constitutional issues involved were somewhat narrower than and differed in part from those involved in the unemployment compensation case just reviewed.

The history of the case was, briefly, as follows: A stockholder sought to stop payment by the Company of the excise tax and deduction by it of the income tax on the first $3,000 of each employee's wages. At the hand of a district court he sought an injunction and a declaration that the Social Security Act was void, but the injunction was denied and the case was dismissed. Appeal was taken to the Circuit Court of Appeals, First Circuit, which by a two to one decision, reversed the ruling of the district court.[4] The Company acquiesced in this decision, but the Commissioner of Internal Revenue and the Collector for the District of Massachusetts, who had intervened, appealed to the Supreme Court.

The constitutionality of both Titles VIII and II was challenged. The former, it will be recalled, levies an excise tax on the employer's payroll

---

[1] *Ibid.*, at p. 618. Justice McReynolds put it most emphatically: "By the sanction of this adventure, the door is open for progressive inauguration of others of like kind under which it can hardly be expected that the States will retain genuine independence of action. And without independent States a Federal Union as contemplated by the Constitution becomes impossible." *Ibid.*, at p. 609.

[2] *Ibid.*, at p. 616.

[3] *Helvering, Commissioner of Internal Revenue et al. v. Davis*, 301 U. S. 619 (1937).

[4] 89 F. (2d) 393.

and an equal income tax on the worker's wages, any excess of a worker's annual earnings over $3,000 not being levied upon in either case. Like internal-revenue taxes generally, the revenues are paid into the Treasury, and are not earmarked in any way. It is true that an Old-Age Revenue Account is established but funds are placed in it only by appropriations made by Congress from time to time. Title II provides for the payment of old-age benefits, the more important being monthly benefits, a less important one being lump-sum payments.[1]

The Circuit Court of Appeals had held that Title II was void because it was an invasion of the powers reserved by the Tenth Amendment to the states or to the people, and that Title II collapsing carried Title VIII along with it. As an additional reason for invalidating the excise tax upon employers,[2] the court held that it was not an excise as excises were understood when the Constitution was adopted. These findings were not sustained by the Supreme Court. The last-mentioned view had been found to be incorrect in the Steward Machine Co. case. The first-mentioned involved the main issue covered by the majority opinion in the case under review.

The majority decision on the main issue rested back upon the "welfare clause" of the Constitution, which reads that:

"The Congress shall have power to lay and collect Taxes, Duties, Imposts and Excises to pay the Debts and provide for the Common Defense and General Welfare of the United States. . . . "

From the beginning of the government, there was protracted debate as to the meaning and scope of this clause, with authorities dividing as to whether the view of Madison or that of Hamilton was the correct one. As Denby says, "The former asserted that the latter part of the clause conferred no independent power, but related to the specific powers enumerated in the subsequent clauses of the same section; whereas Hamilton maintained that the clause conferred a separate and distinct power to appropriate revenues raised through taxation for the general welfare of the United States, and not merely in order to carry out the powers elsewhere expressly enumerated."[3] In the AAA case of *U. S. v. Butler*, decided in 1936, the issue appears to have been authoritatively decided by the Supreme Court, and in line with Hamilton's view. As Denby says,[4] the Supreme Court interpreted the "welfare clause" as though it read:

"The Congress shall have power to lay and collect taxes, duties, imposts and excises, *in order to provide funds with which* to pay the debts

---

[1] See, *supra*, p. 393.

[2] The income tax on wages was not an issue, for it had been ruled below that neither the company nor a shareholder had an interest in the matter.

[3] Charles Denby, Jr., *op. cit.*, p. 326.

[4] *Ibid.*, pp. 326–327.

and to provide for the common defense and general welfare of the United States."

The Court said in the case under review that, "The conception of the spending power advocated by Hamilton and strongly reinforced by Story has prevailed over that of Madison, which has not been lacking in adherents." Congress may spend money in aid of the general welfare. Of course, a line must be drawn somewhere, but, in this, discretion rests with Congress, unless the choice made is clearly wrong. A significant observation was added: "Nor is the concept of the general welfare static. Needs that were narrow or parochial a century ago may be interwoven in our day with the well-being of the Nation. What is critical or urgent changes with the times."[1]

The Court in this instance took a realistic view of the problem the Social Security Act was designed to alleviate. The problem itself was stated in terms of the results of Federal and state investigations and studies. The Court observed that "Congress did not improvise a judgment when it found that the award of old age benefits would be conducive to the general welfare."[2] It observed, further, that "The problem is plainly national in area and dimensions. Moreover, laws of the separate states cannot deal with it effectively."[3] Congress, at least, had a basis for that belief, for the states are often lacking in financial resources, and are at times reluctant to increase so heavily the burden of taxation to be borne by their residents for fear of placing themselves in a position of economic disadvantage as compared with neighbors or competitors. Moreover, "A system of old age pensions has special dangers of its own, if put in force in one state and rejected in another. The existence of such a system is a bait to the needy and dependent elsewhere, encouraging them to migrate and seek a haven of repose. Only a power that is national can serve the interests of all."[4]

The Supreme Court, by a vote of seven to two, held that "The scheme of benefits created by the provisions of Title II is not in contravention of the limitations of the Tenth Amendment."[5] It held, also, that "Title II being valid, there [was] no occasion to inquire whether Title VIII would have to fall if Title II were set at naught."[6]

Two Justices dissented.[7] They presented no opinions, but it was announced that they were of the opinion that the provisions of the Act are repugnant to the Tenth Amendment.

[1] 301 U. S. at pp. 640, 641.
[2] *Ibid.*, at p. 641.
[3] *Ibid.*, at p. 644.
[4] *Ibid.*
[5] *Ibid.*, at p. 640.
[6] *Ibid.*, at p. 645.
[7] Justices McReynolds and Butler.

In the discussions of the constitutional issue presented by the Social Security Act much had been said concerning the separation of the tax provisions from the benefit provisions (in Title VIII and Title II). It was argued before the Court that the two titles were inseparable, but it found it unnecessary to pass on the specific issue.

The Act was attacked here, as it had been in the Steward Machine Co. case, on the ground that the excise levied upon the employer was invalid, but, as in that case, the Court held that "the tax upon employers is a valid excise or duty upon the relation of employment."[1] Here, also, as in the Steward case, the exemptions were an issue but the ruling was the same—"the tax is not invalid as a result of its exemptions."[2]

Thus, as the outcome of litigation, the central and most of the minor constitutional issues which might be raised in connection with the Social Security Act and state laws have been authoritatively decided by the highest court. Social security legislation, in so far as it relates to unemployment compensation and to old-age benefits, is not repugnant to the Constitution. Moreover, it is reasonably certain except where specific provisions of state constitutions stand in the way that taxes imposed upon those in low income groups to pay the costs of medical care will not be held invalid. The rulings have made it possible for the United States to proceed along paths of far-reaching importance in the solution of the problems of insecurity.

[1] 301 U. S. at p. 645.
[2] *Ibid.*, at p. 646.

INDEX

Unemployment insurance, compulsory, problems, 126–134, 145–147, 151, 164–167, 170–171, 174–184 (*See also* Payroll tax; Unemployment insurance, compulsory, coverage, effects on, evaluation of compensation systems, in foreign countries, Great Britain, and insurance principles, partial employment, and relief, suitable employment)

administrative, 126

insurability of risk, question of, 126, 175–176

Social Security Act, 145–147, 151, 164–167, 170–171, 174, 178–183

and relief, 128, 133, 135, 163, 174–175, 184–186 (*See also* Unemployment assistance)

Social Security Act, 145–175, 177–183, 409–417 (*See also* Unemployment insurance, compulsory, in U.S.)

standards (*See* Unemployment insurance, compulsory, benefits, contributions, coverage, type of system)

state laws, 141, 151–174

analysis of, 151–174

tabular, 152–159

benefits, 152–159, 164–165, 168–173

duration, 152–159, 170–171

eligibility for, 152–159, 168, 170–173

waiting period, 152–159, 168, 170, 172

changes, need of, 173

contributions, 152–161, 167

coverage, 151, 160, 174

partial unemployment benefits, 168–169

payroll tax plan evaluated, 161–163 (*See also* Payroll tax)

type of system, 152–160, 164–167

individual reserve, 152–155, 157–159, 164–167

and guarantee, 155, 159, 164–167

and limited pool, 153–154, 157–159, 164, 166–167

pooled fund, 152–159, 164, 166–167

with merit rating, 152–159, 164, 167

suitable employment, definition of, 131, 150, 172–173, 183

in Great Britain, 131, 173, 183

in U.S., 150, 172–173

type of system, 128, 141–148, 150–159, 164–167, 171, 173–176, 178, 414

federal-state relationships, 145–148, 151, 171, 173–174, 178, 414

block grants, 145–147

desirable, 145–147, 151, 171, 174, 178

national, 145–146, 173–174

pool, need of, 174

system, 145–146, 173–174

Social Security Act, 145–147, 151

Unemployment insurance, compulsory, type of system, federal-state relationships, state system, 145–146, 171, 174, 178

tax-offset system, 145–148, 151, 414

fund, 128, 141–144, 148, 150–155, 157–159, 164–167, 175–176

desirable, 151, 165–167

employer reserve plans, 128, 141–143, 148, 150–155, 157–159, 164–167

criticisms of, 142, 165–166

and guarantee, 155, 159, 164–167

and limited pool, 153–154, 157–159, 164, 166–167

Social Security Act, 148, 150–155, 157–159, 164–167

permitted under, 148, 150, 164

state plans, 152–155, 157–159, 164–167

guaranteed employment plans, 148, 151, 155, 159, 164–167 (*See also* Unemployment insurance, compulsory, type of system, fund, employer reserve plans)

criticism of, 165–166 (*See also* Unemployment insurance, compulsory, type of system, fund, employer reserve plans, criticisms of)

hybrid systems, 164, 167

criticism of, 167

individual employer reserves, 141–143, 148, 152–155, 157–159, 164–167

industry reserves, 128, 141, 143, 148, 166

in Great Britain, 128

merit rating, 142, 144, 148, 151–159, 164, 167, 175–176 (*See also* Unemployment insurance, compulsory, type of system, fund, employer reserve plans, guaranteed employment plans)

evaluation of, 167

practicability of, 167

and regularization of employment, 167, 176

pooled fund, 142, 148, 152–159, 164, 167

in U.S., 137, 141–175, 177–183, 409–420 (*See also* Unemployment benefits; Unemployment insurance, compulsory, state laws; specific subjects under unemployment insurance)

before Social Security Act, 137, 141–145

plans proposed, 141–145

American Association for Labor Legislation plan, 141